HARLEM: THE MAKING OF A GHETTO

Harlem: The Making of a Ghetto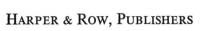

NEGRO NEW YORK, 1890–1930

By Gilbert Osofsky

HARPER & ROW, PUBLISHERS NEW YORK

TO MOM AND POP,
THE REAL SCHOLARS

Contents

51179

Illustrations

Preface

The following pages will explore the history of the Negro community of New York City in the late nineteenth and early twentieth centuries. As the major development of these years was the emergence of Harlem as a Negro ghetto, I have entitled this study *Harlem: The Making of a Ghetto.*

In order to fully understand the importance of the creation of this ghetto its history must be set against the background of pre-Harlem Negro life in New York City. This in turn must be related to the radical changes in patterns of race relations that were taking place throughout America in the late nineteenth and early twentieth centuries. The rapid growth of Negro New York in these years created social problems and racial tensions unequaled since slavery days. The poverty, violence and segregation of these years were typical of the difficulties Negroes confronted in every major northern urban area in the twentieth century. Part One will describe these developments and place them within the framework of our national history, Part Two will explain how and why a white upper-middle-class genteel community became the largest segregated neighborhood in America, and Part Three will show how the ghetto became the slum it remains today.

I have also attempted to re-examine some major themes of American Negro history and urban history. It has been customary, for example, to begin discussions of northern Negro life with the Great Migration of World War I. Although this was certainly dramatic and important, significant Negro migration to northern cities began in the 1890's. Harlem was an important area of Negro settlement *prior* to the war. The Negro ghettos of Philadelphia and Chicago were also founded before World War I.

Accompanying the increase in Negro population was an intensification of discrimination and racial hatred. Negroes never had full equality in northern life, but there were a few periods of relatively decent race relations in our history. One such period occurred between 1870 and 1890. What made the racial antagonisms of the years after 1890 especially tragic is that they followed a time which seemed to promise improvement in the position of the Negro in northern cities. The hopeful signs of the earlier years, however, were replaced by myriad examples of racial alienation. The most glaring symbol of the changed racial relationships of these years was the development, for the first time in American history, of the large Negro ghetto—the Harlem. "Cities within the city" was what contemporaries aptly called them.

The early twentieth century was also a period of significant reform in all areas of American life—one of the major periods of reform in our history. It has been customary for historians to argue that the Negro was the one blind spot of the Progressive movement. In fact, some have written, Progressivism contained significant overtones of racism. Whatever the truth of the statement for the rest of the country, it certainly was not true of New York City. The fourth chapter will describe the very significant positive and hopeful response of this generation of municipal reformers and social workers to the problems created by rapid Negro urbanization.

The book ends with the Great Depression. This is a natural historical breaking point. Not only had most Negroes and Negro institutions come to Harlem then, but the entire country was made aware of the existence of this ghetto. Slumming parties visited Harlem cabarets to share its supposedly gay life. Intellectuals gloried in the imagined exotic and erotic lives that Harlem Negroes lived. "White folks," a Negro writer said, "discovered black magic there." And, while intellectuals and bohemians created an image of a semimythical dreamland north of Central Park, Negro Harlem became the most appalling slum in the entire city; the slum that has not changed significantly since the 1920's.

Three outstanding teachers and scholars have helped ease my way into the complexities of historical scholarship: Robert D. Cross, John Higham and Eric L. McKitrick. Professor Higham opened my eyes to the subtleties and beauties of American history and Professor Mc-

Kitrick helped keep them open. My greatest debt is to Professor Cross, an amazingly warm, sympathetic and gifted person, who advised, cajoled and directed me throughout the writing of this book. I hope his demands for intellectual independence are somewhat met in the pages that follow.

Ernest Kaiser and Jean Blackwell Hutson introduced me to the treasures of the Schomburg Collection, and dozens of other librarians went out of their way and occasionally stretched regulations to assist me in my research. I would like to thank the staffs of Columbia University's Oral History Research Office, the New York City Municipal Archives, the Archives of the New York City Hall of Records, the New-York Historical Society, the New York Public Library, Yale University's James Weldon Johnson Memorial Collection and the Manuscript Division of the Library of Congress. Some of the chapters in this book have been published in different form in *American Quarterly, Journal of Negro Education, Freedomways* and *New York History;* they appear here with the permission of the editors of these journals. A University of Illinois Faculty Fellowship and grants from the University's Graduate Research Board permitted me to complete my research. Folkways Records made a generous gift of Negro folk songs, excerpts of which appear throughout the book. Whatever the value of this book, its style and content have been considerably enhanced by the interest and effort of Jeannette Hopkins of Harper & Row. Mrs. Ida Cullen Cooper, Langston Hughes, Mrs. Gerri Major of Johnson Publishing Company and Joan Meinhardt of Harper & Row aided in the securing of illustrations. Marcia, Lisa Kate and Judith Aileen, my swinging family, helped make the work enjoyable and worthwhile.

GILBERT OSOFSKY

University of Illinois
Chicago Circle

PART ONE

The Negro and the City

CHAPTER 1

"No Crystal Stair": Negro New York, the 1890's

"Life for me ain't been no crystal stair."
—LANGSTON HUGHES, *Mother to Son*

I

In the early twentieth century Booker T. Washington made a tour of eastern and western Europe to study working-class life. He wanted to find "The Man Farthest Down," he said, to gauge the relative position of American Negroes with poor people elsewhere. Washington doggedly avoided museums, art galleries, cathedrals and palaces to mingle with the peasantry, urban industrial workers and miners. When he completed his journey he believed that American Negroes were much like "men at the bottom" throughout the world, and that the future seemed promising for all. "To the man in the tower the world below is likely to look very small," wrote Washington characteristically. However, he concluded, he never found "things as bad as they were advertised." Had Washington made an intensive survey of Negro New York in the late nineteenth and early twentieth centuries, he most certainly would have judged the colored man "The Man Farthest Down" in America's largest metropolis.[1] To have concluded that the situation contained significant signs of improvement would have been utopian. Negro life in New York City was certainly "no crystal stair" in the 1890's; nor had it ever been.

The 60,666 Negroes of New York City at the turn of the century were widely scattered throughout the five boroughs, but most heavily concentrated in Manhattan. Some 5,000 were foreign-born, from many islands in the Caribbean, but primarily from the British West Indies. Although they represented an exceedingly small portion of the general population, there were more foreign-born Negroes in New York City than in any other city in America. Approximately two-thirds of all the Negroes in New York State lived in the city, and of these, more than half resided in Manhattan. There were considerably more Negro women in the population than men: "The excess of negro females," wrote Howard University professor Kelly Miller, "is a most striking feature of the Negro population in most of the large cities." In 1890 there were 810 Negro men for every thousand Negro women in New York City; in 1900, 809 for each thousand; in 1910, 850.[2]

This disproportionate number of women in the general Negro population, a reflection of the greater economic opportunities for Negro women in cities, created social problems of importance. Most Negro women in New York City were young and of marriageable age, but there were simply not enough men to go around: "In their hours of leisure," social worker Mary White Ovington recorded, "the surplus women are known to play havoc with their neighbors' sons, even with their neighbors' husbands, for since lack of men makes marriage impossible for about a fifth of New York's colored girls, social disorder results."[3] Nor did the typical married man earn enough money to support a family without the assistance of his wife. These conditions largely account for the fact that more than twice as many Negro women (59 per cent) in the city had to work to support themselves than did foreign-born (27.2 per cent) and native-born (24.6 per cent) white women. There was also, as W. E. B. DuBois noted in 1901, a high rate of illegitimacy among them.[4]

The greater financial stability of Negro women created serious social and psychological difficulties for Negro men. Forced reliance on female economic power minimized the sense of control and responsibility that Negro men had for their families, and often (more often than for other ethnic groups) led to disrupted or broken homes. This economic situation deprived Negro males of an essential symbol of full manhood. Family instability became a dominant characteristic of Negro urban life in the twentieth century.

Most of the Negro population in the 1890's worked at varieties of unskilled and low-paid jobs. The Negro middle class was quite small. The largest number, some 450, were clerks, followed, in descending order, by actors and actresses, musicians and music teachers, and small businessmen. A population of about 60,000 was serviced by only forty-two Negro physicians and twenty-six Negro lawyers. More than 90 per cent of the community, male and female, were employed as menials or laborers: servants, porters, waiters, waitresses, teamsters, dressmakers, laundresses, janitors and "laborers not specified" (as the census-takers termed it).[5]

Many members of the Negro community in the late nineteenth century believed that economic conditions had deteriorated since the Civil War. Samuel R. Scottron, an aged Brooklynite in the 1890's, a well-known inventor of household appliances, and a member of Brooklyn's Board of Education, spent a good part of his old age writing about the displacement of Negroes from occupations they supposedly dominated previously. "The ancient colored New Yorker didn't wait for some one to hire him," wrote Scottron, "he went at it alone and made a place for himself." "Think of our city's most famous caterers of forty or fifty years ago," he continued. "They were Downings, Watsons, Van Dykes, Ten Eycks, Drys, Greens and others, all colored. Their names were . . . representative of high class work. . . ." "In fact," Scottron concluded, "it would be quite difficult to name a livelihood in which [Negroes] had no representation." This, he and others bemoaned, was all gone now—"superseded by foreign white help"; "gone out of fashion."[6]

There was some truth in Scottron's observations. One of the key sources of wealth among New York Negroes in the nineteenth century was the catering business. Some caterers began as janitors in banking and business houses. At first they sold sandwiches and snacks to employees and eventually expanded their services to full-scale businesses. William H. Smith, for example, began as a janitor in the Bank of New York and died a comparatively wealthy owner of New York real estate. There were a handful of others with similar careers: Peter Van Dyke, Thomas Downing, Charles G. Bowser, David Roselle. Many of these people, and other members of the Negro middle class—small merchants, clergymen, journalists—lived in comfortable homes in Brooklyn, owned summer houses, and left substantial estates at their deaths. Their children often became lawyers, teachers, physicians, businessmen. "Had they been white," wrote Mary White Ovington, "they would have slipped into the population and been lost. . . ."[7]

These careers were far from typical of the general Negro population, however. They were the elite of the race, lived apart from the masses, and objected to being lumped together in the public image with lower-class Negroes. The small Negro middle class continually bemoaned the fact that white America refused to distinguish between

different Negro social classes, and equated them with the "worst class
[of the] great stream of rural immigrants from the South simply
because they happen to be of the same race." "All Negroes are not
alike," said one wealthy Negro in 1895. "There are various grades of
colored people. . . . We are not to be judged by the street loungers
and drunkards of our race."[8]

Scottron's memories, blurred by the passing of time, tended to
overlook the poverty of the race as a whole in the nineteenth century.
Many of the jobs he and others remembered as part of the glories of
the past ("occupied almost exclusively by Negroes") were in domestic service: coachmen, chambermaids, waiters, chefs, footmen,
valets. To employ Negro servants was a mark of stature among upper-
class white families in the city in the nineteenth century. This was
clearly a heritage of slavery when ownership of Negro slaves was a
sign of social distinction. "The Nineties," records one New York
historian, "saw about the last of the old family servants that were
part of every well regulated menage among the elite of the city . . .
as much fixtures to a house as the very walls themselves."[9] The
passing of this slave tradition was then not an unmixed blessing. Nor,
given the relatively small numbers of Negroes in New York City in
the early nineteenth century, is it conceivable that they dominated
even the service positions then: "Did the colored man have all this
fifty years ago when they were only one and a half per cent of the
population?" wrote a student of Negro life in the early twentieth
century. "If so, there were giants in those days. . . ."[10] It was historically true that a disproportionate number of Negroes were employed
as domestics in the city in the mid-nineteenth century but, in numbers, they ranked a far third behind Irish and German servants.[11]

Complaints of limited economic opportunities for Negroes, similar
to Scottron's, were often made in the age he characterized as a period
of prosperity. There was very little upward mobility among the
majority of Negro New Yorkers in the nineteenth century: "The
Negro American found it extremely difficult to rise above manual
labor and domestic service," concludes one historian of New York
City in the early nineteenth century.[12] When J. W. C. Pennington
escaped slavery in Maryland and arrived in New York City in 1829,
he was so shocked with the "misery, ignorance, and wretchedness of
the free colored people" that he, the slave, devoted his life to "*their*

elevation. . . ." (Pennington became a leading Negro clergyman and militant abolitionist.)[13] A teacher at a Negro school in 1830, Charles C. Andrews, wrote that the Negro student graduated "with every avenue closed against him which is open to the white boy . . . [he is] doomed to encounter prejudice and contempt because he is black."[14] Negro newspapers published articles on the low-paid jobs that racial prejudice forced Negroes to accept in Jacksonian America; complained that "colored youths" were barred from "workshops and offices" in the 1830's.[15] Negroes "are sunken much lower than they were a few years ago and are compelled to pursue none but the meanest avocations," concluded an observer in 1846.[16] In the 1850's the perceptive Frederick Douglass complained that Negroes "were shut from all lucrative employments and compelled to be merely barbers, waiters, workmen and the like at wages so low that they could lay up little or nothing."[17] Charles L. Reason, a prominent nineteenth-century Negro educator, echoed Douglass's views in 1854. As the Civil War began, abolitionist Henry Ward Beecher commented that the "only chance for a colored man North nowadays is to wait and shave and they are being driven from these as fast as possible."[18] Only a very small number of New York City Negroes could meet the qualification of a $250 freehold for voting established by the state constitution of 1821. In 1865, for example, 44 Negroes in a population of 9,943 owned enough property to vote.[19] "The Black man goes to the wall," was the *New York Tribune*'s summary of the economic status of Negro New Yorkers in the nineteenth century.[20]

II

And similar generalizations can be made about practically every other aspect of Negro life in the metropolis. The Negro population of New York City remained relatively stable and small throughout most of the nineteenth century, for example, primarily because of an exceedingly high death rate. Between 1800 and 1865 the numbers of Negroes living in Manhattan wavered between 9,000 and 15,000— about one per cent of the city's population on the eve of the "Rebellion." In each of the three decades preceding the Civil War the Negro population actually declined. By 1865, in fact, there were fewer Negroes in Manhattan (9,943) than there had been in 1820 (10,368).

It was not until southern and West Indian migrants came to New York City (in small numbers between 1865 and 1890, and in much larger numbers after that) that the Negro population actually expanded. By 1900, for the first time in New York history, more than half the Negro population (53 per cent) was born outside the state.[21]

An exceptionally high death rate had been a major fact of Negro life in slavery; it continued to be so after emancipation: "And Death heard the summons/And he leaped on his fastest horse," wrote poet James Weldon Johnson. Of all the peoples in New York City, foreign-born as well as native, Negroes had, proportionally, the highest mortality rates. In 1890, for example, 37.5 Negroes in every thousand died, contrasted with 28.5 deaths in the white population. Between 1895 and 1915, in fact, the Negro death rate in New York State exceeded the birth rate by some 400 annually. And what was true of the state was also true for the city.[22]

Death took a tragic toll of very young Negro children either through stillbirths or other causes in the first year of life. Consumption (the "Plague of the Cities"), and pneumonia, however, were the great adult killers. From 1884 to 1890 the Bureau of the Census conducted an intensive study of New York City and found that more Negroes died of these illnesses than of all others. Almost one-fourth of Negro deaths then were caused by tuberculosis, and the general rate of death among Negroes from this disease was twice that of the white population. "Tuberculosis in all its forms is met with everywhere," wrote a social worker active in the Negro districts.[23] Ironically, the Great White Plague took, and would continue to take, its highest toll among black New Yorkers.[24]

This "frightful mortality rate from lung and bronchial diseases" offered great opportunities to local quacks whose private and ingenious home remedies were reputed to cure everything from a broken heart and overly curly hair to the most lethal ailments. They exploited a real need of the Negro community—the desire for answers to medical problems which science itself had not yet found. ("If you want to prevent the contraction of tuberculosis," preached one Negro clergyman, "you must lead moral lives.")[25] One man who regularly advertised in the Negro press sold "Hale's Honey of Horehound and Tar" guaranteed to purge the recipient of every imaginable ailment.[26] Another, Dr. T. A. Slocum, was so sure that his formula cured tuberculosis that he gave free samples away.[27]

CONSUMPTION
<hr>

I have a positive remedy for the above
disease. . . . Indeed, so strong is
my faith in its efficacy, that I will
send TWO BOTTLES FREE. . . .

The continual presence of sickness and death in the Negro community permitted other bogus healers, Negro and white, to enrich themselves in similar fashion for generations. Reliance on quackery and medical superstition played a more harmful role in Negro social life than it did for any other minority group.

III

Throughout the nineteenth century most Negroes lived in the poorest working-class sections of the city. Negro neighborhoods were traditionally located in the less attractive residential areas on the outskirts of Manhattan Island, or along the east and west sides near the waterfronts—the sections doomed to become slums by the unimaginative grid pattern of urban planning instituted in 1811. Here Negroes lived apart in generally rundown quarters because of their poverty and were further separated from other working-class families in these neighborhoods on the basis of color. Within this pattern, however, was a built-in source of instability. New York was a rapidly expanding city throughout the nineteenth century and, as its population grew, new neighborhoods came into existence. What was the periphery of town or a slum for one generation was not necessarily the same for the next. As the city moved northward, so did the principal places of Negro residence.[28]

In the early nineteenth century New York Negroes generally lived in the Five Points district, on the site of the present City Hall and in the blocks surrounding it, which were then considered "well uptown." The Sixth Ward, which encompassed most of Five Points, was a heavily populated working-class neighborhood; the Negro section within it was popularly called "Stagg Town" or "Negro Plantations." This was the first place of major settlement of New York's freed slaves. The gradual abolition of slavery in New York began in 1799 and was finally completed on July 4, 1827. The Five Points, parts of which were grazing land, housed the freedmen.[29]

Descriptions of life in this section repeatedly emphasized its dire poverty, its squalor, its vice. It was known as a "notorious center of crime." Charles Dickens visited some of the local Negro homes in 1842 and described them as places where "dogs would howl to lie." Here, he wrote, "women and men . . . slink off to sleep, forcing the dislodged rats to move away. . . ."[30] A teacher in the area found that Negro children failed to come to school because they lacked proper clothing. "A large number of our colored people are very poor," he observed, "and [are] unable to provide for their children suitable clothing to attend school. . . ."[31] When a missionary came to comfort a dying "Poor Black Man," he found him lying on a homemade bed of straw surrounded by a ragged family.[32] Negroes lived in the rickety frame houses of this shantytown, and in unpaved cellars known as the "Dens of Death."[33] Others were housed in the "Old Brewery," an early-nineteenth-century beer factory turned into a tenement. Drunkenness and prostitution were commonly found in the neighborhood.[34] In response to these conditions of poverty and degradation, the Association for the Improvement of the Condition of the Poor built the Workingmen's Home in 1855. This first model tenement for the city's poor was constructed for Negroes at Elizabeth and Mott Streets.[35]

But poverty alone did not fully define Negro life in the Five Points. What the occasional visitor like Dickens failed to see were the solid institutions of the neighborhood and the more hopeful side of life there. The African Society of Mutual Relief, a Negro beneficial organization, was founded in 1808 and continued its existence into the twentieth century. There was a Negro theater, the African Grove, on Mercer Street in the 1820's.[36] Abyssinian Baptist Church, founded in 1808, was on present-day Worth Street. St. Philip's Protestant Episcopal Church (1809) was located on what is now Centre Street; Bethel African Methodist Episcopal Church (1819) was on Mott Street; and there were a few other churches as well spread across the Lower East and West sides.[37] At Leonard and Church Streets stood the queen of Negro religious institutions, "Mother Zion" Church (African Methodist Episcopal Zion), founded in 1796. In 1800 a frame building replaced the stable in which its founders worshiped; in 1820 a stone structure replaced the frame; in 1840 a solid brick building took the place of the stone.[38]

The outstanding nonreligious institution of the neighborhood was African Free School Number 2, founded by the New York Manumission Society on Mulberry near Grand Street in 1820.[39] Many of the most prominent Negroes of the city and the North in the nineteenth century were educated there. Charles L. Reason, teacher; Patrick Reason, engraver; J. McCune Smith, physician; Ira Aldridge, actor; Samuel Ringgold Ward, abolitionist; Henry Highland Garnet and Alexander Crummell, clergymen; and Thomas Downing, caterer, to mention a few of the outstanding, were all students at the school.[40] The "Old Mulberry Street School" was remembered with pride by its graduates. The Reverend Dr. Crummell delivered eulogies on John Peterson, a Negro teacher there for half a century.[41] Former students of "Number 2" gathered together in the John Peterson Association in the 1880's to preserve its memory and keep bright some outstanding aspects of Negro life in New York City in the nineteenth century.[42]

IV

By the 1830's the Negro population of Five Points began to decline. Some Negroes continued to live there until the end of the century, but it essentially became a backwash community as the majority of people moved north and west into Greenwich Village. A survey made of Five Points in 1860 found it to be an overwhelmingly Irish district. There were only a few hundred Negroes left there.[43] By the 1880's only a handful of Negroes remained: "In a few years there will not be a family living on the East Side of our city, that part known as Stagg Town, where the colored people lived years ago," an editorial in a Negro journal said in 1887.[44]

"Little Africa" replaced "Stagg Town"—Bleecker, Sullivan, Thompson, MacDougal and Carmine Streets took the place of their counterparts to the south and east. The public reputation of the Negro community in Greenwich Village was simply an adaptation of the previous general impressions of Five Points. By those who were attracted vicariously or directly to fast living, it was called "the notorious district,"[45] "Coontown,"[46] "Nigger Alley."[47] In it were "black and tan saloons" where all kinds of underworld and salacious activities could supposedly be bought for the right price.[48]

The general Negro population of the Village, those who worked regularly at hundreds of different menial jobs and were members of the many Negro fraternal orders, were unnoticed by the creators of such stereotypes. These Negroes, whose contributions built the fine churches which followed them into the new neighborhood, constituted the majority of the population. Between 1880 and 1890, however, their numbers began to decline. At the turn of the century they had dwindled to 1,900. In 1920, the few hundred Negroes of Greenwich Village were janitors living in basements of tenements that housed whites, or tenants in the very few houses still occupied by colored people.[49] "Look at West Broadway . . . Thompson Street, Sullivan Street, Bleecker Street and think of those streets . . . years ago," wrote Samuel R. Scottron in 1905. "Think of our people . . . and look upon the present occupants, all [Italians]."[50] The "Old Africa," Jacob Riis observed in 1890, "is now becoming a modern Italy."[51] As "Little Africa" had replaced "Stagg Town" a generation or so before, now the Tenderloin and San Juan Hill continued the "steady procession passing up the West Side."[52]

V

At the turn of the century most Negroes lived in what would be the present-day midtown area, on a wide range of blocks between Twentieth and Sixty-third Streets. Although there were sections of Negro concentration within this area, no single large neighborhood was an all-Negro community. Handfuls of small and densely populated ghettos, usually a block or two in length, were found throughout Manhattan Island, on the east and west sides, from Greenwich Village to Harlem and even further north. Thirty-seventh and Fifty-eighth Streets, between Eighth and Ninth Avenues, for example, were Negro blocks. They were surrounded by white people, the majority of whom were first- and second-generation Irish and German immigrants. There were six wards in Manhattan in 1890, the twelfth, fifteenth, sixteenth, nineteenth, twentieth and twenty-second, in which 2,000 to 4,000 Negroes lived.[53]

Of these sections the Tenderloin and San Juan Hill were the most heavily populated in the 1890's. They were areas "thickly studded with black and colored faces," recalled Negro journalist John Edward Bruce.[54] As the "Tenderloin" was a folk designation, its boundaries are nowhere clearly defined. Contemporaries sometimes spoke of an "Old Tenderloin" which perhaps ended near Forty-second Street, and a "New Tenderloin" which extended north from there through the upper Fifties.[55] The Negro sections scattered within this general area began at approximately Twentieth Street and ended at Fifty-third. The boundaries of San Juan Hill, on the other hand, are easily delineated. They stretched from Sixtieth to Sixty-fourth Streets, Tenth and

Eleventh Avenues. San Juan Hill was one of the most congested areas in America's most populated city—3,580 people, more than a town in itself, lived on just one of its streets.[56] The western boundary of this Negro neighborhood was the open railroad tracks that ran along Eleventh Avenue. (Because of the number of accidents involving children who played along the tracks, contemporaries called this street "Death Avenue.") San Juan Hill received its name after the Spanish-American War as a parody on the neighborhood interracial battles that took place on the steep upgrade leading to Sixtieth Street.[57]

Between 1890 and 1900 the Negro population of the city expanded by 25,000 people and both these new neighborhoods were a response to the demand for more Negro living space. As Negroes moved in whites moved to more desirable residences in upper Manhattan. When New York City built its elevated lines on the West Side in the late nineteenth century another stimulant for movement was created. The clatter and noise of the new trains made for less than pleasant living, and those who could afford it moved out. Apartments were taken over by Negroes ("The Choicest Apartments in the City for Select Colored Families"), many recent southern migrants, who were forced to accept second-class accommodations at first-class prices. Of the twenty-seven ethnic groups in the neighborhood, Negroes paid the highest rents—generally two to five dollars per month more than others. "A colored man in this city . . . pays higher rental and gets far less for his money than does the white man," a group of housing reformers recorded at the turn of the century. "The colored people of New York City suffer more injustice in the matter of rental than any other class of citizens," agreed the Negro journal, *New York Freeman,* in 1885. "The present housing conditions of the vast majority of colored families in New York," another man wrote, "can only be characterized as disgraceful."[58]

· New institutions as well as new neighborhoods were called for to meet the needs of an expanding population. For the first time in decades new Negro churches were founded in the city. In the last thirty years of the nineteenth century six new Negro churches were opened in the Tenderloin and San Juan alone.[59] Some, like Union Baptist Church, were housed in storefronts and catered to the needs of recently arrived southern migrants. The Reverend Dr. George H. Sims, pastor of Union Baptist and a Virginian himself, gathered the "very recent residents of this new, disturbing city" and made Christianity come "alive Sunday morning," a contemporary remembered. Union Baptist was known as a "shouting church."[60] Others, like St. Cyprian's Episcopal Church, offered somewhat more reserved services. By 1900 the majority of religious institutions formerly established in Greenwich Village had moved to the Tenderloin and San Juan Hill.

The reputation of the new sections was as unsavory as that of any former Negro neighborhood. The Tenderloin, for example, housed New York's red-light district and was generally known as the roost of underworld characters. Preachers called it "The Terrible Tenderloin." The Reverend Dr. Charles H. Parkhurst, always in the forefront of some antivice crusade, attempted to clean up the area in 1892–1895, but business was being carried on as usual in 1900.[61] Negroes and whites owned saloons, cafés and gambling houses that were scattered throughout the neighborhood.[62] "These dens of infamy . . . are little less than a corner of hell," warned a Negro clergyman. "Fathers and mothers, away down south, or far off in the West Indies, little know of the shame and degradation that have overtaken many of their sons and daughters who have come to the city. . . ."[63] The Reverend Dr. Adam Clayton Powell, Sr., of Abyssinian Baptist Church lived in a coldwater flat "with prostitutes living over me and all around me." He preached what he called "gospel bombardments" to the "pimps, prostitutes, keepers of dives and gambling dens," who sometimes attended his prayer meetings. They seemed to shout the loudest for the Lord's forgiveness. Others never came to church. Some "harlots would stand across the street on Sunday evenings in unbuttoned Mother Hubbards soliciting men as they left our service," Powell recalled.[64] The Tenderloin was also a plum for corrupt and grafting municipal officials. Policemen preferred to work there, it was said, to get their share of underworld graft. A means of reprimanding a disobedient officer was to move his beat from the vice areas. "Anyone who was captain of that district a year," said one man, "could live on tenderloin steaks the rest of his life."[65] Local police inspectors were known as "Czars of the Tenderloin."[66]

There was also a vital and hopeful aspect about life in this Negro community. It centered around West Fifty-third Street between Sixth and Seventh Avenues—the Main Street for respectable folk of Negro Tenderloin. "West Fifty-third Street," the pastor of Bethel African

Methodist Episcopal Church remembered, "was the principal place of resort for *our* group."[67] On this street could be found, in 1900 or shortly thereafter, many of the major institutions of Negro New York: Negro political clubs, Mount Olivet Baptist Church, St. Mark's Methodist Episcopal Church, St. Benedict the Moor Roman Catholic Church,[68] offices of the major Negro fraternal societies, two Negro hotels, varieties of small businesses and the Negro YMCA.

The YMCA was the center of intellectual and social life of New York Negroes in the first decade of the twentieth century. Lectures were given, plays and music performed, classes in liberal arts as well as industrial skills were offered to the public. The Y was originally founded in 1899 at Mount Olivet Baptist Church by its pastor, the Reverend Dr. Charles T. Walker. Walker, a clergyman of national reputation, appealed to his church members and to the Negro community for financial assistance. He wanted to establish a home in the metropolis for southern migrants: "So much trouble is made by the poor fellows having no place to go when they come here. What we need is a place that shall be known to every young man in the South as a home where he can come and find friends. . . ."[69] Walker raised enough money to lease a building on West Fifty-third Street for one year and applied to the general New York YMCA for membership in 1900. His appeal was accepted and the "Colored Men's YMCA" became one of the first of many all-Negro Y's established in northern cities in the early twentieth century.[70]

The Tenderloin was also known as the gathering place of "Negro Bohemia." New York City was the center of Negro vaudeville at the turn of the century and James Weldon Johnson has described the active and productive lives of Negro show people in these years. Bert Williams, George Walker, Aida Overton Walker, Will Marion Cook, Theodore Drury, Rosamond Johnson, Bob Cole, Harry T. Burleigh, Johnson himself—outstanding artists, actors, vaudevillians, song-writers—lived on West Fifty-third Street and met at Jimmie Marshall's Hotel to trade stories and discuss race problems: "Our room, particularly of nights, was the scene of many discussions; the main question talked about and wrangled over being always the status of the Negro as a writer, composer and performer in the New York theater and world of music," Johnson recalled. "It was an alluring world, a tempting world."[71]

Most of the performers earned money that would have staggered the imaginations of the majority of Negroes of San Juan Hill and the Tenderloin. The royalties that Johnson earned for a few songs were equal to twice his annual salary as principal of a Negro secondary school in Florida. The typical Negro of the neighborhood, and of the city as a whole, was employed as a laborer or servant and earned four to six dollars a week at the turn of the century. The average combined incomes of all the working members of a Negro family was twelve to fifteen dollars a week.[72] A greater proportion of this income than that of any other ethnic group in the area had to be expended for the necessities of life. Houses in which Negroes lived were reputed to be the worst of the district, often ill-ventilated and located in the rear portions of dumbbell-shaped tenements so that they could be reached only by passing through a long and often dingy alleyway: "from 61st Street to 62nd Street [Negroes] occupy 400 rooms that have no access to the outer air," concluded a study of a group of church reformers in the 1890's. To make ends meet more Negro women had to be employed ("the laundress is the economic supplement of the porter"), more lodgers taken in, and more children kept out of school than in any other minority group. The average Negro wage earner, male or female, had to work more hours to earn less money than anyone else.[73]

"Now I started at the bottom, and I stays right there, don't seem like I'm gonna get nowhere," runs a line from the Blues. "The rise of a nation, the pressing forward of a social class," wrote W. E. B. DuBois, "means a bitter struggle, a hard and soul-sickening battle with the world such as few of the more favored classes know or appreciate."[74]

CHAPTER 2

"Come Out from Among Them": Negro Migration and Settlement, 1890 – 1914

"There can be no doubt of the drift of
the black South northward."
—W. E. B. DuBois, 1901

"The Afro-American population of the large
cities of the North and West is being
constantly fed by a steady stream of new
people from the Southern States."
—*The New York Age*, 1907

I

The most important factor underlying the establishment of Harlem as a Negro community was the substantial increase of Negro population in New York City in the years 1890–1914. That Harlem became the specific center of Negro settlement was the result of circumstance; that *some* section of the city was destined to become a Negro ghetto was the inevitable consequence of the Negro's migration from the South. This pre-World War I population movement, the advance guard of the Great Migration (as the movement of Negroes during the First World War is generally called), laid the foundations for present-day Negro communities in Chicago and Philadelphia as well. These were the formative years for the development of Negro communities throughout the North.

In spite of the high Negro death rate, the colored population increased by "leaps and bounds"[1] in New York City in the early twentieth century. By 1910 there were 91,709 Negroes in the metropolis,[2] the majority southern-born: "A Census of the Negroes in any city of the North," said a speaker at the first organizational meeting of the NAACP in 1909, "would show that the majority

17

of . . . them . . . were more or less recent arrivals from the South."³ Mary White Ovington, in her excellent study *Half A Man: The Status of the Negro in New York,* found that most of the Negro neighborhoods were populated by southerners.⁴ Only 14,309 of the 60,534 Negroes in Manhattan in 1910 were born in New York State. The majority of the others (61 per cent) came from other states, practically all in the South. Virginia, North Carolina, South Carolina, Georgia and Florida, in perfect geographical order, were the major southern sources of New York's migrant population.⁵

Contemporaries in both the North and South, Negro and white, were aware of this movement. Unable to foresee that the First World War would bring even larger numbers of Negroes northward, they were staggered by the myriad problems this migration created for them: "There are more Southern Negroes in the North and West than original Northern ones, and they are coming all . . . the time," wrote a Negro journalist in 1913. "What to do with the needy and those who fall by the wayside is becoming a problem of the greatest magnitude. . . ."⁶ Historians, impressed by the enormity of changes that occurred at the time of the "Great War," have tended to overlook or underestimate the significance of the pre-World War I migration of Negroes to northern cities.

II

Since the end of the Civil War there was a steady but small movement of Negroes northward. It averaged 41,378 persons for each decade between 1870 and 1890. In the following ten years, however, the migration more than doubled as at least 107,796 southern Negroes moved north and west. The Negro populations of the states of New Jersey, Pennsylvania and Illinois increased some two and a half times between 1890 and 1910 and that of New York almost tripled.⁷ In 1910, New York City was the second largest Negro urban center in America (just behind Washington, D.C.); Philadelphia was fifth; and Chicago eighth. By 1920, they were ranked first, second and fourth respectively. A total of some 200,000 Negroes migrated from the South and to the North and West, primarily to cities, between 1890 and 1910.⁸ In the decade 1900–1910, for the first time since their establishments as states in the early nineteenth century, Mississippi and Louisiana lost Negro population through emigration.⁹ Practically every southern state showed the first significant deficit in its Negro birth-residence index (the index that measures population increase and decrease through migration) for the decade 1890–1900. "Prior to 1890," observes one student of population movement, "the migration of Negroes was not great and seems to have been local, from state to state, and only to a slight extent out of the South. But after 1890, the northward direction of the movement has been steadfastly maintained and has increased in amount decade after decade."[10] The number of Negroes migrating to the principal southern cities declined significantly in the years 1890–1900. The Negro population in these cities increased 38.7 per cent between 1880 and 1890, but the growth amounted to only 20.6 per cent in the next ten years.[11] Northern cities were draining off the residents of, and prospective migrants to, the larger southern cities at the turn of the century.

A few discerning analysts were aware of this new shift in Negro migration in the 1890's. Working with census data, Frederick J. Brown pointed to the new northward migration from the Border States in 1897.[12] In 1898, W. E. B. DuBois noted the decline of Negro population in Farmville, Virginia, and explained it as "a fact due doubtless to the large emigration to Northern cities."[13] In his pioneering study of Philadelphia Negroes (1899), DuBois showed a significant increase in southern immigration since 1887,[14] and later depicted the "typical colored man" of Philadelphia as a young person "from the South, from twenty to forty years of age. . . ."[15] Similar conclusions were made by a student of New York City's Negro community in 1898,[16] and the United States Department of Labor undertook a detailed analysis of the movement of Negroes to urban areas in these same years.[17]

By the first decade of the twentieth century the migration was well recognized: "It needs no long argument to prove the existence of a large movement of Negroes northward," a social scientist recorded in 1905.[18] An entire issue of the social service magazine *Charities* was devoted to a survey of the migration and the problems that arose from it in the first decade of the twentieth century.[19] New York's leading Negro journal, *The New York Age,* carried innumerable articles in the early 1900's on the "marvelous increase of Afro-American population," "the enormous and steady growth in the Negro population," "the young people in New York City from our

Southern States who are constantly coming,"[20] and so on. In 1901 a Negro minister delivered a public lecture on what seemed to him to be "The Wholesale Exodus of the Negro from the South."[21]

This pre-World War I exodus has sometimes been characterized as the "Migration of the Talented Tenth." Politicians, businessmen, the educated, and especially skilled workmen, are supposed to have constituted the majority of people who left the South in these years. Southern Negroes, it has been said, were robbed of their leadership as the talented fled north.[22]

It is undoubtedly true that many educated and gifted Negroes did come north then. William Lewis Bulkley, for example, a South Carolinian born a slave, became a principal in the New York school system and a leader of the Negro community during these years. P. B. S. Pinchback, for a time Reconstruction governor of Louisiana and thereafter an active Republican politician, worked in the New York City Custom House a short while. He used the influence of Booker T. Washington and the Negro Republican leader of New York City, Charles W. Anderson, to get the position.[23] Pinchback's friend, J. Ross Stewart, a former member of the Louisiana legislature, worked there too.[24] North Carolinian George Henry White, member of Congress 1897–1901, practiced law and became a banker in Philadelphia when Negroes were disfranchised in his state. White later established an all-Negro communiy in New Jersey.[25] T. Thomas Fortune, editor of *The New York Age,* was a Floridian by birth. There were, in fact, *very few* prominent Negroes in New York City in the early twentieth century—lawyers, physicians, businessmen, clergymen, politicians—who were not born in the South.

These people were not typical urban Negro migrants, however. The majority, like all migrant populations, were young people, generally unskilled and unmarried, the earliest Negro generations born in freedom. W. E. B. DuBois described them as "the Southern freedman's sons and daughters," "untrained and poorly educated countrymen, rushing from the hovels of the country or the cottages of the country towns. . . ."[26] Most contemporaries spoke of them as such.[27]

In one group of 240 Negroes interviewed in New York City in 1907, for example, only eighteen were born in New York, and just three of the 222 others were over forty when they migrated. The vast majority were between the ages of fifteen and thirty, and 96 per cent had arrived in New York City after 1887.[28] Another survey of 365 workers found that 68 per cent were born in the South, the largest number single young men and women.[29]

III

There were as many individual and varied reasons for migration as there were people who moved. The less respectable as well as the educated came north. Negroes themselves characterized some as a "hoodlum element," "rovers," "wanderers," "vagrants," "criminals in search of a sporting life."[30] "Many of the worthless people of the race are making their way northward," said *The New York Age* in an editorial.[31] Some wayward husbands—the "travelin' men" of Negro folk songs—abandoned their families and responsibilities and sought the anonymity of a city: "I was raised in the country, I been there all my life/Lord I had to run off and leave my children and my wife."[32]

Others came north on excursion trains to get a look at the big city and never returned.[33] One man "heard so much of this town," he said, "that he decided to look it over." Another stated that he "didn't want to remain in one little place all my days. I wanted to get out and see something of the world."[34] Migratory laborers found work on New Jersey, Pennsylvania and New York farms every spring and summer. Some traveled back and forth each year; others simply went to the nearest city when winter came.[35] "Tired of the South," "Wanted to make a change," "Ran away from home," were some of the reasons advanced by Negroes for coming north.[36] All received nominally higher wages in the North, and this was certainly a great attraction. One woman who came to New York City from Virginia, for example, said she was "willing to live anywhere, if the wages were good."[37]

There were also those who fled social proscription and violence in the South. C. Vann Woodward has described the "Capitulation to Racism" that characterized the southern attitude toward the Negro from the late 1880's through the early twentieth century. Vast numbers of Jim Crow laws were passed in these years as the forces which held virulent southern racism in check suddenly crumbled. The conservative, *noblesse oblige* attitude of former Whig leaders ("it is a mark of breeding to treat Negroes with courtesy") was replaced by a violently racist white supremacy movement; the paternalism of a

Wade Hampton was followed by the viciousness of a Ben Tillman (whose racist tirades even embarrassed his southern colleagues). Free rein was given to mass aggressions as all forces joined together in an active program of "keeping the Negro down." The great heresy that proclaimed the Negro capable of attaining equality with the white had to be rooted out at all costs, it was argued. There were more Negroes lynched, burned, tortured and disfranchised in the late eighties, nineties and first decade of the twentieth century than at any other time in our history. The militant Negro Ida B. Wells graphically and sadly described this *Red Record* in 1895.[38] It was not surprising to find that the American Colonization Society, organized in 1817, experienced a long-hoped-for revival in the 1890's,[39] and various other plans to colonize Negroes in Africa were rekindled in these years. "I used to love what I thought was the grand old flag, and sing with ecstasy about the stars and stripes," wrote Negro Bishop Henry McNeal Turner of Georgia, "but to the Negro in this country today the American flag is a dirty contemptible rag. . . . Hell is an improvement upon the United States when the Negro is involved." "No man hates this Nation more than I do," Turner said on another occasion. He looked longingly to Africa as the only possible place of Negro freedom.[40]

Negro leaders and the Negro press continually stressed their belief that migration was primarily a movement away from racism: "The large cities of the North and West have had a marvelous increase of Afro-American population in the last ten years, and the increase is growing . . . because of the conditions in the Southern States which make for unrest"; "the terrors of mob wrath."[41] When T. Thomas Fortune, William Lewis Bulkley, and North Carolina educator and politician Edward A. Johnson came north, each emphasized he could no longer live under Jim Crow and racial violence.[42] George Henry White said he left North Carolina because he "couldn't live there and be a man and be treated like a man." He believed that thousands of others would follow him.[43] Booker T. Washington told the Board of Trustees of Tuskegee, in 1903, that "for every lynching that takes place . . . a score of colored people leave . . . for the city."[44]

In general, however, the migration could best be considered not so much a flight from racial violence, as it was a desire for expanded opportunity. This is best summarized in a phrase commonly used by the migrants themselves—the attempt "to better my condition."[45]

People moved away from the South in search of a better and more fulfilling life. A Negro shoemaker came north, for example, because he felt "choked" by the "narrow and petty life" he was forced to lead in a small Virginia town. To him, the great attraction of New York City was the "wider scope allowed the Negro."[46] One woman who "never could work . . . in a menial way" was proud that she could earn a living as an independent seamstress in New York.[47] Moving north, wrote DuBois in 1907, offered "the possibility of escaping caste at least in its most aggravating personal features. . . . A certain sort of soul, a certain kind of spirit, finds the narrow repression and provincialism of the South simply unbearable."[48]

> Where I come from
> folks work hard
> all their lives
> until they die
> and never own no part
> of earth nor sky.[49]

The *possibilities* for such movement resulted from two basic changes in American life. One was the overwhelming industrial expansion of the late nineteenth century. The Industrial Revolution created economic opportunities for rural people, Negro and white, and both migrated to industrial and urban centers in the North. For the Negro, hedged about by union restrictions and racial antagonism, employment was usually found in the fringe jobs that an industrial and commercial society creates—as janitors, elevator operators, general laborers of all kinds, longshoremen, servants. Negro women almost always worked as domestics. During periods of labor disputes, Negroes commonly found among the strikebreakers.[50]

There was, however, an added factor that influenced Negro migration and distinguished it from the general rural migration to cities. Why, it might be asked, had Negroes not moved in similar numbers in response to industrializaton in the 1870's—the period of great social upheaval and dislocation that followed the destruction of slavery? The answer undoubtedly lies in an understanding of the differences between the slave and post-slave generations. The Negroes who came north now were the first descendants of former slaves. They had listened to tales of slavery, gentle and harsh, but had not experienced and lived its blight—the denial of full manhood.[51] To them, *"War, Hell, and Slavery were but childhood tales. . . ."*[52] Their parents and grandparents, psychologically and economically unprepared to enter what contemporaries called the "competition for life," tended to remain as tenants, sharecroppers or laborers on their former plantations or on places similar to them. They continued in freedom to live the only life they had knowledge of. "There were great upheavals in political and labor conditions at the time of emancipation, but there was little shifting in the populations. For the most part, the freedmen stayed on in the states and counties where they had formerly existed as slaves," writes one historian of Negro life.[53] In 1900, practically all southern Negroes continued to work on the land and some 75 per cent remained sharecroppers, tenants and   laborers.[54] On one Georgia plantation in 1901, as on others, lived many Negroes who had been slaves there: "I have men," the white owner testified, "who were slaves on the place. . . . They have always lived there and will probably die there, right on the plantation where they were born." "It was predicted [during the Civil War] that the Negroes would leave the . . . fields and fill the towns in case of emancipation," said a southern planter at the turn of the century. "That prediction has not been realized suddenly as we anticipated it would be, but it seems to be approaching."[55]

Those who migrated to the North in the 1890's were a new generation. Many Negroes no longer felt any strong attachment to the soil. They could at least *conceive* of life in a new and different way. For some, the discontented and restless, there was now both the ability and willingness to move. They left a South in which their futures were sealed: "There is absolutely nothing before them on the farm. . . . Working year in and year out with . . . no prospect . . . but to continue until they die."[56] In many rural communities of the South, it was reported in 1907, a "number of youths have expressed their conviction that since their fathers and mothers have accumulated nothing after years on the land, they did not intend to stay on the plantation to repeat the process."[57] A leading Republican politician and defender of Negro civil rights, James S. Clarkson, took a trip to the South in the 1890's and "saw many a grey head . . . talking to the young people . . . encouraging the young people to become content," he wrote a Negro confidant.[58] The migrants who came north were aptly described by George Edmund Haynes as "groping seekers for something better. . . ."[59]

IV

To southerners this seemed to be a different and puzzling kind of Negro—not a people especially educated or skilled, but a group willing to make some change in the traditional patterns of its life. To the stereotype of the docile, irresponsible, immoral, dishonest Negro was now added a new "racial" characteristic—"a migratory disposition."[60] Philip A. Bruce, Virginia historian, called the "new generations" worthless. They "rarely remain long enough under the supervision of any planter to allow him sufficient time to teach them," he wrote.[61] "Habits of diligence, order, faithfulness"—all the qualities of a good slave—were absent in the "new generation," said another. There exists "a certain unrest and discontent," a white planter commented.[62] "Under its influence the boys and girls are beginning to drift to the cities." To contrast the supposedly "faithful old darkies" with "the new generation, which has become restless, dissatisfied, and worthless" (and "migrated from the plantations to the cities") was a standard and hackneyed statement found throughout the racial literature of the time.[63]

This attitude toward the Negro was accepted in popular thought as well: "The superiority of the older farm-hands to the younger generation is so universally asserted throughout the South," wrote Thomas Nelson Page in 1904, "that it must be given some of the validity of general reputation. The Negro has retrograded as a workman," he concluded.[64] There existed, said a Georgia Negro minister, "among a large number of older people, both white and black, the definite conviction that the present generation of Negroes is hopelessly degenerate. . . ."[65]

Most southern farmers who testified before the United States Industrial Commission in 1899–1901 expressed similar opinions. They spoke of the differences in attitudes between the freed slave and his children. The "good old negroes, as we call them . . . negroes about grown before the war," "old-time negroes" ("before-the-war negroes," they were sometimes called), were touted as the best farm workers and tenants. "The younger ones" are "discontented and want to be roaming." "The older class of colored labor," repeated a West Virginia farmer, "men that are pretty well up in years—are a first rate class of labor. The younger class . . . are . . . very trifling.

. . ." The Negro "is not as steady as he was," thought another. "The South laments to-day the slow, steady disappearance of a certain type of Negro—the faithful, courteous slave of other days, with his dignified . . . humility," W. E. B. DuBois commented at the turn of the century.[66] "He is passing away just as surely as the old type of Southern gentleman is passing. . . ."

Related to the belief of the emergence of a new and different Negro generation was the revival of scientific attempts to prove the Negro a degraded being. During this same period Darwinism invaded the South (as well as the North) to revive the debate over the place of the Negro in the human community. Arguments strikingly similar to the old proslavery diatribes of natural Negro inferiority were dressed up in the new scientific garb and presented to the public by "objective social scientists" who claimed to be uninfluenced by "preconceived ideas."[67] The improvident, dishonest, immoral, lazy, lascivious Negro was shown to be incapable of education: "he is a fungus growth that the white man will totally destroy. . . . The only race that has never made any progress in any respect," more similar in mind to the chimpanzee than to man.[68] The greatest menace and curse to our Anglo-Saxon civilization, some thought, was its pollution with the blood of the "depraved Ethiopian." Aryan supremacy could only be achieved, it was argued, after total separation, by colonization or extermination, of the entire Negro race.[69]

This ideology combined with the reality of Negro migration and encouraged southerners to attempt to replace Negro laborers with European immigrants. The substitution of immigrants for Negroes was an integral part of the philosophy that preached southern progress through industrialization—the New South. It was in these very years that the South attempted to rejuvenate its efforts, first begun in Reconstruction, to attract European immigrants.[70] State immigration bureaus were created and offices established in the principal port cities to direct the newest arrivals to southern farms. Southern emigration agents were even sent abroad.[71] There was more myth than reality in the conception of a New South—a South where factories were to spring up "like stars after twilight."[72] The movement to encourage settlement of immigrants to replace Negro labor was an almost total failure.[73]

This reality presented southerners with a major paradox. The new generation of Negroes seemed unreliable (even inhuman) and yet, at the same time, it was also clearly recognized that the southern economy was largely dependent upon them: "I think the Negro is a necessity in the South as a farm laborer," stated a South Carolinian. *"We have no other. . . ."* "I do not know how the South could live without negro labor," a Georgia plantation owner said. "It is the life of the South; it is the foundation of its prosperity. . . . God pity the day when the negro leaves the South. . . ."[74] "Think twice, before committing the State to a policy which may strip the land of its best . . . laborers," editorialized a North Carolina newspaper opposed to European immigration.[75] In the minds of most southerners, Negroes seemed racially adapted to agricultural life, permanently tied to the soil. To forsake farm life would necessarily lead to their degradation. This was their only "proper calling," their "proper place."[76]

Negro farmers in the South cultivated twice as much acreage as did all the farmers in New England combined. Nearly one-half of all farms under fifty acres in the South Atlantic states and one-fourth of those between fifty and one hundred were operated by Negroes. Negroes were also the most important farm laborers throughout the South.[77]

If Negroes began leaving the South in great numbers, Senator George F. Hoar of Massachusetts predicted, "there would be a general alarm on the part of the men who now depend on their labor, and they would find themselves pretty earnestly solicited to change their minds."[78] It was the reality of this practical dependence on Negro farm labor that produced a series of laws limiting the free movement of Negro workers and tenants and heavily taxing all labor agents sent south to "entice" them away. From the late 1880's through the first decade of the twentieth century such legislation was passed in Alabama, Arkansas, Florida, Georgia, Kentucky, Mississippi, North Carolina, South Carolina, Louisiana, Tennessee and Virginia.[79] Southern courts generally interpreted these laws for the benefit of the white farm owner, forcing Negro workers to remain on the land. The Department of Justice in 1907, for example, received eighty-three complaints from Negroes protesting what they considered to be their practical peonage.[80] Although the Supreme Court outlawed peonage in 1911, the practice continued through subterfuge for decades. (As late as 1947 the President's Committee on Civil Rights documented a case of forced labor.)[81]

Exaggerated accounts of the destitute conditions of migrants were commonly published in the press and every hint of failure was described as destitution. The high Negro mortality rate in northern cities was presented as absolute proof that the Negro could not live in cold climates: "they will take colds and develop pneumonia and consumption . . . and will die there."[82] The Southern Negro Anti-Exodus Association was founded in Virginia in 1905 to "preach the gospel of contentment to the colored people South of Mason and Dixon's line. . . ." When a labor agent was arrested in Georgia, an editorial in the *Age* said: "If there is one thing the Southern man preaches all the time it is that the young Negro is worthless and is not to be mentioned in the same breath with the older. . . . The young Negro is pictured as worthless and a general nuisance that has been tolerated too long. . . . But as yet no one can be found to deny the cold fact that this agent was arrested to put a stop to the exodus. . . . In spite of all this talk, there is a desire to keep the Negro help in the South."[83]

These reactions were a reflection of a basic dichotomy in southern thought. On the one hand, it was believed that the Negro was worthless, inefficient, untrustworthy, less faithful than the slave. The failure to use improved agricultural machinery and in industrialization in general was often blamed on his ignorance.[84] On the other hand, the Negro was encouraged to remain in the South (and sometimes forced to do so) as the only source of labor available—"the backbone of the South when it comes to labor"; "the best labor we could have in the South."[85] With the failure of attempts to attract European immigrants the reliance of the South on Negro farmers and laborers became even more evident. In reality, Southern society fundamentally distrusted the very people it seemed most hopelessly dependent upon. It was caught in a vise of restricting the migration of Negroes who, at the same time, were looked upon with the utmost disdain, even denied fully human qualities. This paradox in southern thought provided a seedbed for bitter racial antagonism. It added an emotionalism to the racial hatreds of these years that make them stand out, above all others, as a period of great violence.

V

Most of the Negro migrants who came to New York City prior to the 1930's settled in Manhattan. The Negro population of that borough increased by 24,288 between 1900 and 1910, whereas that of

Brooklyn expanded by 4,341. Seventy-eight per cent of the city's industry was located in Manhattan in the early twentieth century and the migrants filled many of the unskilled jobs that these factories created.[86]

The typical Negro migrant to the metropolis originally came from some rural area in the South. Most grew up on farms or in small southern towns. In 1913 a study was made of thirty-five Negroes in Harlem. Thirty-four came from the rural South, and only one grew up in a town whose population exceeded 10,000. Of the twenty-one born on farms, only three were children of parents who owned their land outright. The others were sons and daughters of sharecroppers and farm laborers. The majority of Negroes in this group were indirect migrants—they had lived in some large town or city for a time before coming to New York. All but four were presently employed as domestics, servants or laborers.[87] Similar findings were made in other surveys of northern cities.[88]

Among the immigrants who settled in New York City were young women who came north on what were sometimes called "Justice's Tickets."[89] These were tickets supplied to them by employment and labor agents. In exchange for transportation and the guarantee of a job on arrival, the women signed contracts to work where the agent placed them and swore to pay a fee usually equal to one or two months' wages. These employment agents thus collected money from both employers and workers. The following is a typical labor contract:

> In consideration of my expenses being paid
> from Richmond to _____ and a situation
> provided for me, I agree to give _____
> services after arrival as _____ to party
> or persons paying my expenses. And I further agree
> that all my personal effects may be subject to their
> order until I have fulfilled that contract, forfeiting
> all claims to said personal effects after sixty days
> after this date should I fail to comply with agreement.[90]

Social service organizations founded to assist Negroes in the city were vitally interested in protecting these girls from "the agents with oily tongues [who] come about and offer flattering inducements. . . ."[91] "Many of them," concluded one report, "are brought from the South, consigned like merchandise to Northern agents." Trunks, "slender satchels," clothing, trinkets—personal possessions of all kinds—were often kept as security until fees were paid.[92] Migrants commonly complained of extortionate charges and generally shoddy treatment.[93]

These women who worked as domestics and most of the Negroes who came to the city prior to World War I made the trip on boats that ran along the Atlantic Coast. "Negroes," observed one man in 1898, "are coming on every boat from southern waters." "Nobody knows how it happened," an old resident of the Tenderloin recalled, "but [on] every old Dominion Steamship that docked there [were] from two to three hundred negroes landed in New York."[94] This was the cheapest means of transportation from the South, and New York's migrant population was, and would continue to be, primarily composed of Virginians or people from states bordering the Atlantic. Steerage fare, with meals, from Norfolk or Richmond cost $5.50 or $6.00—the approximate equivalent of a week's wages in New York City. Cabin fares were $9.00. The Old Dominion Steamship Company (migrants called it the "O.D. Line") had a bi-weekly service between Virginia and New York. The Baltimore, Chesapeake and Atlantic Railway ran steamers from Washington and Baltimore, and others went as far south as Florida. Many of the waiters and seamen on these ships were Negroes, some of whom lived in New York City.[95] Negroes were generally berthed in separate quarters, ate at separate tables, and were served food inferior to that given white passengers. Some migrants complained that, besides these indignities, the Negro sections of the boats were also reserved for the dogs and pets of other travelers.[96]

It was common practice for migrants, who lived within a day's journey of their former homes, to shuttle back and forth for regular visits. If European immigrants found the Atlantic no great barrier to such journeys (as evidenced by what contemporaries called the "birds of passage"), the Negro migrant was even less restricted by distance and cost. Practically every issue of *The New York Age* carried some report of such movement: "R. C. Turner the barber, is back in the city after two months' vacation to his old home, Hillsboro, North Carolina"; "Mrs. Mary E. Swan . . . has gone to Virginia to bury her niece. . . . She will soon return."[97] Many migrants wrote home of their supposedly glowing successes in the North. Some returned to their birthplaces dressed in the latest fashion, pockets full of cash, to tell the rural folk of their exploits. George Edmund Haynes described "the exaggerated stories of prosperity which relatives and friends in these cities write to friends at home and the prosperity shown by those returning home in their display of clothes and cash."[98] Negro students and teachers from the South regularly came to study in New York City during their summer vacations. Some attended the summer session at Columbia University and lived in segregated quarters in Hartley Hall. Others came in search of summer jobs, lived at the Negro YMCA and YWCA, saved their money and returned south when school began: "New York is . . . crowded with a host of young men and women students from . . . southern schools. . . . These young [people] come North every season and work. . . ."[99]

For those who remained permanently, the city was a strange and often hostile place—it was so noisy and unfriendly, so cold, so full of "temptations and moral perils," a "pernicious influence," a "fast and wicked place." "Many of those who have come North complain of cold and chills from the like of which they had not previously suffered," wrote one scholar.[100] The oft-told tale of the sale of the Brooklyn Bridge to the rural hayseed had a basis in fact. One naive migrant wanted to know how it was done: "I heard about 'selling the Brooklyn Bridge,' " he said, "and I wondered how it was sold, and asked questions about it."[101] In 1902 Paul Laurence Dunbar published a novel, *The Sport of the Gods,* which described the dissolution and eventual destruction of a southern Negro family in the "fast life" of the "great alleys of New York."[102] Southern Negroes were commonly subject to intraracial as well as interracial prejudice.

Confronted with this estrangement and antagonism many migrants banded together to try to retain as much contact with the patterns of their former lives as possible:

> I'm a poor boy and I'm a stranger blowed in your town,
>   Yes I am,
> I'm a poor boy and I'm a stranger blowed in your town,
> I'm a poor boy and I'm a stranger blowed in your town,
> I'm goin' where a friend can be found.[103]

Negroes, foreign-born and native, established benevolent, fraternal and protective societies to keep up old friendships and provide insurance for themselves and families in sickness and death. The vast majority of New York's Negro population belonged to insurance and fraternal societies. The largest Negro insurance company of Virginia, the True Reformers, had a branch office in the city.[104] Prior to

World War I, New York City had its Sons and Daughters of South Carolina, Sons of North Carolina, Sons of Virginia, Sons of the South, Southern Beneficial League. When one North Carolinian was appointed Assistant District Attorney of New York County a celebration was given for him "in the fullness of the North Carolinian pride."[105] Storefront churches revived the spirit of southern preaching. These and other churches held special services and celebrations in honor of communicants from individual southern states. There were regular South Carolina days, Virginia days, and so on.[106] When the World War drew migrants in greater numbers from the Deep South and the West Indies, new societies were founded by Floridians, Georgians and the varieties of West Indians.

The entire Negro community of New York City took on a southern flavor. Businesses expanded to service the wants of a growing population: "The great influx of Afro-Americans into New York City within recent years from all parts of the South has made . . . possible a great number and variety of business enterprises," editorialized *The New York Age* in 1907.[107] Negro restaurants, undertaking establishments, saloons, barbershops—the plethora of small businesses necessary to satisfy a community's needs—catered to the newcomers. Restaurants advertised special "southern-style" breakfasts and dinners. Negro grocers specialized in Virginia fruits, vegetables and chickens. Migrants asked friends to send them special southern delicacies.[108]

New York was also the center of Negro philanthropy.[109] The offices of the Armstrong Association which supported Hampton Institute, the Board of Trustees of Tuskegee, Rockefeller's General Education Board, the Phelps-Stokes Foundation and the John F. Slater Fund were all located in the city. Many wealthy New Yorkers contributed individually to the support of southern Negro schools. Southern ministers and educators arrived in town regularly in search of financial assistance. Many of the clergymen preached "southern-style" sermons in local Negro churches that were "not soon forgotten." Southern Negro school principals, including Booker T. Washington in the 1890's, held mass meetings "to request race support." Fisk University Jubilee Singers and the Hampton Quartet came north to give concerts. "As the recently arrived Richmonder meanders along," commented one man, he "recognizes so many familiar faces [that] he readily concludes there is some . . . relationship between his city and this."[110]

Migration to the city created possibilities for economic mobility that were largely absent from southern life. Many of the businesses which provided services for Negroes were owned by migrants themselves. Some recent arrivals began as small entrepreneurs but made modest fortunes in a relatively short time.

Perhaps the most interesting and among the most successful was Lillian Harris, born in a shanty on the Mississippi Delta in 1870. She came north as a teenager and, in 1901, after having knocked around many northern cities for a decade, hitched her way from Boston to New York City on hay, milk and vegetable wagons. Miss Harris had $5.00, and with this capital went into business. She spent $3.00 for an old baby carriage and boiler and $2.00 for pigs' feet. This was the beginning of her career as New York's most widely known Negro peddler. Her converted buggy became a "traveling restaurant."

Hawking her wares in Negro sections, specializing in southern cooking (hog-maws, chitterlings), Lillian Harris was popularly called "Pig Foot Mary." She lived in a tiny room and scrimped and saved for years: "Saving for a respectable old age," she always said. When Negroes began moving to Harlem this astute street-corner saleswoman grasped at opportunity and invested her savings in Harlem property. By the First World War "Pig Foot Mary" (now Mrs. Lillian H. Dean) was a wealthy landlord—"one of the wealthiest women in Harlem"; "one of the most successful colored business women in New York." "Send it and send it damn quick," she wrote tenants who fell behind in their rent. "Pig Foot Mary" spent her "respectable old age" in retirement in California, where she died in 1929.[111]

William Mack Felton was another southern Negro who made good in New York. He arrived in the city in 1898 with a dollar tucked away in his shoe: "Heeding the call to the Big City," he said. Felton grew up on a small farm in Georgia with little opportunity for formal education. He was naturally bright, however, and gifted with mechanical ability. When he came to New York he worked as a longshoreman long enough to save some money to open a repair shop. The first big job that came his way called for the repair of dozens of clocks left in a Manhattan pawnshop. Most of them had simply stopped running because they had picked up dust and dirt lying around the shelves. Felton realized this, bought a large washtub, filled it with gallons of kerosene and oil and cleaned all the stripped-down clocks in one day. He used this same ingenuity to fix watches, pistols, bicycles—anything that needed repairing. In 1901, when wealthy New Yorkers began to buy the new automobile, Felton opened an auto school and garage. He later invented a device that washed cars automatically. By 1913 his Auto Transportation and Sales Company employed fifteen people and was housed in a seven-story building which he owned. Felton rode back to Georgia in his new car to visit his family and old friends and tell them of life in the "Big City."[112]

Success came to other southern migrants who arrived in New York City in these years. Madame C. J. Walker, born in Louisiana in 1867, was a laundress before she discovered a hair-straightening process (the "Walker System") which brought her great fortune. In 1913 she built a mansion for herself on West One Hundred and Thirty-sixth Street and four years later built a magnificent country estate, Villa Lewaro, in exclusive Irvington-on-the-Hudson.[113] H. C. Haynes, formerly a southern barber, founded a company which manufactured razor strops; Edward E. Lee, a Virginian, was Negro Democratic leader of New York County for fifteen years; J. Franklin Smallwood became chief collector of the State Bank of New York; J. S. Montague ran a mortgage and loan company on Wall Street; Ferdinand Q. Morton, of Macon, Mississippi, was prominent in Democratic politics and ruled "Black Tammany" from the First World War through the Great Depression.[114]

Practically all of these migrants were born in the direst southern poverty and achieved their positions, as the Reverend Dr. Adam Clayton Powell, Sr., later wrote, "Against the Tide."[115] Very few southern Negroes had such fortune, however. The majority of those who came to New York City ended in the ranks of the poor and swelled the slum populations of the Tenderloin, San Juan Hill or Harlem. To many northern Negroes, who had never known or had since forgotten the restrictive conditions in the South, the life of the typical migrant seemed no great improvement on his former condition.

The average Negro migrant to New York City obviously found life harsh and difficult. For those who came, however, conditions in the North did offer a measure of self-respect and the possibility for future advancement that was generally denied the Negro in the South. "To many of them oppressed within the limitations set up by the South," wrote Ray Stannard Baker, "it is indeed the promised land."[116]

CHAPTER 3

Alienation: New York and the Negro

"And the Nation echoed . . . : Be content
to be servants, and nothing more; what
need of higher culture for half-men."
—W. E. B. DuBois, 1903

"Assaults . . . upon innocent colored people
and the growing insolence of race prejudice
in the freest of all American cities have
become alarming."
—The Reverend Dr. W. H. Brooks, 1911

I

For the Negroes of New York City the years after 1900 marked not
only a new century but a breaking point in a way of life. As the
Negro population of New York and other northern cities increased,
so did racial antagonism, violence and patterns of social and residential segregation. "One of the striking developments of very recent
years," one white northerner noted in 1906, "is the recrudescence
of . . . prejudice against people of African descent. . . ."[1]
    At no period in the history of New York City were Negroes
accepted as full American citizens. Restrictions on Negro voting,
equal access to public facilities and education were maintained even
after emancipation was proclaimed in the early nineteenth century.
Jim Crow street stages, with "For Colored People Only" signs hung
over their sides, ran along Manhattan streets until the eve of the Civil
War. Colored people sat in special Negro pews (whites called them
"Nigger Pews") or in the balconies of white churches: "Negroes were
not permitted to sit in any public assembly, court or church, except in
the particular quarter set apart for them, [and] generally in the most
remote and worst situation." In 1837, *The Colored American* denounced the "Negro Pew" as a technique which whites used to
degrade Negroes.[2] The only minority group to suffer franchise re-

35

strictions in the state was the Negro. Negroes were forced to meet property qualifications for voting after these had been abolished for all other New Yorkers in 1821, and they were further subject to longer residential requirements for voting than whites.[3] Although racial prejudice was never absent from city life, it was not always uniformly intense. The attitudes of New Yorkers toward Negroes— sometimes eased, at other times hardened—wavered with national trends of racial adjustment.

In the late nineteenth century, and especially in the 1870's and 1880's, most northern communities made significant progress in attacking *institutionalized* racial prejudice. Laws were passed in most state legislatures, including New York's, which attempted to guarantee equal rights for Negroes. The motivating force for this liberal attitude toward the Negro was undoubtedly a spirit for racial reform which came in the aftermath of the Civil War and Reconstruction. Serious restrictions on Negro rights that had existed in some form since colonial times were done away with. In New York State, Negroes were given the right to vote without impediment by the Civil Rights Act of 1873, and this was followed by two other civil rights acts before the end of the century. New legislation permitted Negroes to travel on transportation facilities, attend theaters, eat at restaurants, and be buried in all cemeteries which served the public. Acts which had previously outlawed intermarriage were repealed, and insurance companies were specifically prohibited from charging Negroes rates higher than those paid by white clients.[4] The first Negro to serve as a juryman in Manhattan did so in the 1880's.[5] In 1884, the last three Negro public schools in the city were made ward schools, thus ending the tradition of separate education which had existed in New York City since the eighteenth century. In 1895 the first permanent appointment of a Negro teacher to a predominantly white public school was made. Susan Elizabeth Frazier, a graduate of Hunter College, won an extended legal battle with the school board. After Miss Frazier's breakthrough other Negroes received similar appointments. Statewide, the *coup de grâce* to separate Negro education came through a general education act passed in 1900.[6]

Negro and white people in New York were aware of the change in racial status typified by these acts. Cases of discrimination in public places continued to occur,[7] but it was generally recognized that significant progress was made in the area of race relations subject to law since the end of the Civil War. Jacob A. Riis commented on the "wavering color line" in New York City in 1890,[8] and Samuel R. Scottron later wrote of the "decline of color prejudice" in these years.[9] When southern Negro politicians passed through New York City in the 1880's they lived in the most exclusive hotels. P. B. S. Pinchback regularly stayed at the Hoffman House, John Mercer Langston at the Fifth Avenue Hotel, John R. Lynch at the Metropolitan Hotel.[10] The Negro *New York Freeman,* in an 1887 editorial, said that "Now in many of the best restaurants, hotels and churches decent colored people receive courteous treatment."[11] "Respectable colored men have little trouble in finding accommodations in the very best hotels," a Negro New Yorker indicated in the 1880's.[12] It was the easing of racial tensions in the North in these years that rekindled the traditional drive of the Negro middle class for total acceptance as Americans, not Negroes, within our society: "From the earliest times the attitude of the free negroes has been opposed to any organization or the segregation of the negroes as such," W. E. B. DuBois wrote in 1901. "Men like Fortune, McCune Smith, and Redmond [*sic*] insisted that they were American citizens, not negroes. . . ."[13]

II

In spite of the attack on institutionalized discrimination, however, there was very little (if any) change in the stereotyped conception of the Negro that most white Americans held. With rare exception, even in the North during the late nineteenth century, there was general agreement on what contemporaries called the "peculiar genius" of the Negro people.[14] The stereotyped image of the "sensuous," "lazy," "good-natured," "childlike," "faithful" Negro was presented by defenders as well as critics of the race—both Negro and white. The literature of the time abounds with relevant examples of this image. A New York rabbi, for example, in a sermon at Temple Emanu-El in 1906, attacked the vicious racism embodied in the Reverend Thomas Dixon, Jr.'s, novel, *The Clansman.* (Dixon's trilogy on race relations, of which *The Clansman* was a part, was the basis for the successful movie *The Birth of a Nation,* a film which Negroes have protested against for five decades.)[15] The rabbi defended "the faithful, loyal Negro—his humor, his pathos, his geniality, his shrewdness, his love of his master . . . his sympathy and charity, his even childlike patriotism, and love of freedom."[16] An Episcopal clergyman advocated the extension of church services to Negroes in the city in 1884: "The negro is exacting," he said, "therefore, let the Church . . . arouse him. If he is emotional, let the Church meet these emotions with a lively service, and thus subdue them. The negro is imitative," he concluded.[17] Train and hire Negro workers and they will always be loyal and never strike, a southern Negro educator told a group of northern businessmen in 1902: "Look at the great strikes you are having, and every time you have to make concessions," he said. "But if you educate this million and a half colored boys and girls and make skilled laborers of them they will take the place of these strikers."[18] "The negroes are . . . good-natured and happy under all circumstances," concluded a late-nineteenth-century writer.[19]

Negroes of prominence of New York City were often considered dark counterparts of white leaders. The Negro abolitionist Samuel Ringgold Ward was popularly known as a "Black Daniel Webster" prior to the Civil War.[20] After the war, a well-known Negro singer was called "Black Patti," and another "Colored Jenny Lind."[21] Three local colored politicians were respectively: "Black Depew," "Colored Croker," Negro "Mark Hanna."[22]

Popular images of the Negro were portrayed to New Yorkers in the numerous vaudeville and minstrel shows which regularly appeared in the city. New York City was the theater capital of America at the turn of the century and Negro vaudeville reached the height of its popularity then.[23] Many of the performances, including the Creole shows which specialized in presenting scantily clad and beautiful Negro women, were hits.[24] The hackneyed themes running almost without exception through all these plays were, in exaggerated form, a reflection of the generally accepted attitudes of white America toward Negro life. For the most part, they presented a comic and derisive caricature of an entire people: "The 'darky' to the white man is grotesquely amusing," Mary White Ovington wrote.[25]

The Negro of these plays was a ludicrous figure of a man—he was "darky," he was "coon." Williams and Walker, for example, were billed as the "Two Real Coons."[26] Such plays as the *Gentlemen Coons' Parade* (Chorus: "You'll find no common second-class nigs/ In the gentlemen coons' parade"), *The Coon at the Door, The Coon Musketeers, Dat Famous Chicken Debate* ("Resolved, That Stealing Chickens Ain't No Crime"), *Dat Watermillyon, The Coonville 'Ristocrat Club, The Coon and the Chink, Jes' Like White Folks, The*

Irishman and the Coon, The Policy Players, The Sons of Ham, In Bandanna Land, In Dahomey, In Abyssinia and dozens of others were performed on the stage in New York City and cities throughout the country.[27] Songs such as "All Coons Look Alike to Me," "Coon, Coon, Coon," "I Wish My Color Would Fade," had "wide currency" in New York City in the 1890's. "It was no longer the 'darkey melody' [that was popular in the 1890's] but the 'coon song.'" New York historian Henry Collins Brown noted. These songs presented a "ribald school of 'babies,' 'honies,' mercenary wenches . . . and sundry 'no account niggers.'"[28] Characters like "Useless Peabody," "George Washington Jones," "Moses Abraham Highbrow," "John Jacob Astor House" (crushed silk hat, big bow tie, long white gloves, worn-out shoes), were always about to steal a chicken or a watermelon, or pretending to be something they were not. "Sam Lightfoot," the waiter in *Badly Sold,* changed his attitudes to suit the customer, or lied to get a bigger tip.[29] "Careless Cupid" applied for a job in a bakery and listed the following qualifications to his prospective employer: "I kin eat an' I kin sleep, and de res' ob de time jes' lay round. Say, boss, whar's yo lounge? I's gettin' tired standin' yere. . . . I'm a straight out nigger, I am, yessir."[30] Sam Caesar, Pompey Ducklegs, Julius Crow, Doolittle Black, were waiters, porters, servants, butlers, confidence men, who shuffled along in baggy pants, liberally used ungrammatical language, loved whiskey, shot dice, seemed eternally shiftless or carefree. The covers of *Denison's Black-Face Series* showed a broadly smiling, white-toothed Negro woman whose hair was always tied with white bows and curlers, or a white-haired old Negro man strumming on a banjo. James Weldon Johnson, who was personally involved in the production of some of these shows in New York City, summed up the themes that ran throughout them: "The Negro songs then the rage were known as 'coon songs,'" he wrote, "and were concerned with jamborees of various sorts and the play of razors, with the gastronomical delights of chicken, pork chops and watermelon, and with the experiences of red-hot 'mammas' and their never too faithful 'papas.' These songs were for the most part crude, raucous, bawdy, often obscene."[31]

Many Negroes seriously objected to these ludicrous characterizations of Negro life. "It is humiliating to be regarded as a curiosity," wrote one man in 1895. *The New York Age* angrily denounced "plays which burlesque the character of a people and tend to degrade them in the estimation of their fellow citizens." It proposed that they "be prohibited."[32] Negro performers attempted to gain recognition for themselves as true artists, not hacks, but they were unable to convince theater managers that anything but the standard fare was profitable: "Every show had to be studied carefully for anything that might offend white prejudices. . . ."[33] In speaking of his friend Bert Williams, the most famous Negro comic of the early twentieth century (whites called him "the darky comedian"), James Weldon Johnson later wrote that he expressed "only certain conceptions about Negro life that his audience was willing to accept and ready to enjoy."[34] "My job," said Bert Williams simply, "is to make them laugh."[35]

> Why should the world be otherwise,
> In counting all our tears and sighs?
> Nay, let them only see us, while
> We wear the mask.[36]

What was most striking about the Negro stereotype was the way it portrayed a people in an image so totally the reverse of what Americans considered worthy of emulation and recognition. The major and traditional American values were all absent from the Negro stereotype. The Negro was conceived of as lazy in an ambitious culture; improvident and sensuous in a moralistic society; happy in a sober world; poor in a nation that offered riches to all who cared to take them; childlike in a country of men. He seemed more fit to be a servant, a "half man," than anything else: "And the Nation echoed . . . : Be content to be servants, and nothing more; what need of higher culture for half-men."[37] "Let the Negro learn," said a *New York Times* editorial in 1900, "to clean stables, care for horses, feed and harness and drive them, run lawn mowers, make and keep gardens, and also keep engagements. . . ."[38] Negroes hoped for full acceptance in a culture which mocked their aspirations.[39]

III

With the increased migration of Negroes from the South, the brighter side of race relations in the city—the softening of institutionalized prejudices—came to an end. Among white people, Kelly Miller remarked in 1906, there was a "prevailing dread of an overwhelming influx from the South."[40] Even during the late nineteenth century

Negroes argued that most white northerners knew little, and cared even less, about Negro life: "The Northern white man knows practically nothing of the Negro; he is looked upon more as a problem than as a factor in the general weal, with the same desires, passions, hopes, ambitions as other human creatures," a journalist concluded.[41] "Do we ever think of how such people live?" a reviewer of Dunbar's *The Sport of the Gods* wrote. "It is a . . . whole stratum of society of which all of us are densely ignorant and of whose very existence most of us are wholly unaware."[42] As the population increased, however, the city became more aware of its Negro residents, and responded by reversing the trend in formal race relations that had typified the 1870's and 1880's. The early twentieth century in New York City and in the North generally was a period of intensified racial alienation.

Racial antagonism was rekindled in a variety of ways. White churches, for example, which had formerly allowed small numbers of Negroes to participate in regular services, now attempted to ease their Negro members out: "In each of these churches when the number of Negro communicants was small the colored brother was accorded a hearty welcome, but as the Negro population steadily increased . . . from the white members would be heard generous suggestions that the Negro members get a place of worship of their own."[43] An Episcopal church in the area of San Juan Hill resolved its problem by holding separate services for Negroes.[44] Once the Negro population of Harlem expanded, the pastor of one white church told Negro members they were "Not Welcome," and then gave them an ultimatum to join one of the Negro institutions moving into the neighborhood: "When there were few black and colored communicants in the Harlem district the white . . . churches received them," a Negro New Yorker observed in 1913. "Of late years conditions have greatly changed. . . ."[45] "Trinity Vestry, in New York City, is making arrangements to provide a separate place of worship for the colored members," the NAACP journal *Crisis* recorded in 1914. "At present all worship at the same place."[46]

The separation that was evident in the churches was true of many other areas of racial contact in the city. When the "Colored Men's YMCA" was opened on West Fifty-third Street, it was taken for granted that Negroes would use these facilities exclusively rather than those Y's which catered to white people.[47] White fraternal organizations brought suit against Negro societies which used the same names.[48] The New York State Boxing Commission outlawed bouts between Negro and white fighters, and American society longed for a "White Hope" to defeat Negro heavyweight champion Jack Johnson.[49] There were innumerable legal suits brought by Negroes against white hotels, restaurants and theaters for refusing them service in the early twentieth century: "Northern Negroes believe this discrimination in public places against the black man [is] increasing in New York," Mary White Ovington noted.[50] Union restrictions and racial barriers in industry were so widespread that Negroes were largely excluded from "employment along lines other than those of beggarly paid menials."[51] As a result of these exclusions, the urban Negro continually represented a large group of unemployed workers readily available for strikebreaking: "In this matter of excluding colored men from unions, skilled mechanics must remember that they run the risk of building up in the United States a great body of justly indignant and always available STRIKE BREAKERS," a white journalist wrote in 1910. In 1895, 1904, 1907, 1910, 1911, 1912, 1916 and 1920 Negro strikebreakers were used to help break strikes of New York City longshoremen, laborers, street cleaners, baggage handlers, hod carriers, waiters, and garment workers.[52] There was even an unsuccessful attempt in 1910 to re-establish the state law barring intermarriage. The proposed "Act to Amend the Domestic Relations Law, in Relation to Miscegenation," proposed to void all marriages *"contracted between a person of white or Caucasian race and a person of the negro or black race."*[53] Negroes organized to oppose these new "Black Codes."[54] Assemblymen were urged to defeat the miscegenation bill. It was, a Negro New Yorker thought, but one part of a general "sentiment . . . that would 'Jim Crow' us at every turn, and that sentiment is growing in this State."[55] Negro Harlem was created in these years. It was a world within a world that reflected the subtle and radical changes then taking place in many areas of life in major cities of the North.

Was there any solution to the problems created by the migration and the intensified racial hatreds? With almost no exception the only opinion that was publicly stated was that it was necessary to convince Negroes their proper place was in the South. Booker T. Washington made a tour of the tenement districts of New York City in 1904. One journalist said that his trip would be of great value because Washington could then return south and describe the poverty he saw. He would tell the "country negroes [to remain] on the farms in the South rather than [come] to an overcrowded city" where they certainly would die.[56] "Northern men visiting southern colored industrial schools advise[d] the pupils to remain where they [were]," a white reformer noted in 1910.[57]

IV

The migration of southern Negroes also created antagonisms which were intraracial in nature. Negroes who had lived in the city for generations, especially those who gloried in the easing of racial tensions during the late nineteenth century, blamed the southern migrant for reversing this trend. Similar antagonisms were evident among most immigrant groups—Jews, Italians, Greeks, and others—when earlier generations seemed overwhelmed by the problems of later arrivals from their countries. Negroes of "the old Knickerbocker stamp," "the old time aristocracy bearing Knickerbocker names" ("the best people," "aristocratic dark race circles"), some of whom were members of the Negro Society of the Sons of New York, railed against the lower-class southern Negro with the virulence of good white racists: "The taint of slavery was far removed from these people," Mary White Ovington remarked, and they "looked with scorn upon arrivals from the South."[58] "These people are thoroughly embarrassed by the raucousness, vulgarity, and violence with which they find themselves surrounded," a Negro clergyman concluded. "They do everything possible to disassociate themselves from it." Middle-class Negroes in Chicago, Philadelphia and Boston reacted in a similar manner.[59]

To many New York Negroes the migrants were "riff-raff," "illiterate," "thoughtless," "lazy," "overdemonstrative," "boastful," "uncouth," "undesirable," "common." It was the southerner, they said, who created the "epidemic of negrophobia," the recent "spread of race antipathy in the North."[60] They listened too readily to "Tramp Preachers," and were too dirty—they were "the low element to our race . . . the class who own a lot of dirty rags and dogs and crowds of children," a correspondent of Booker T. Washington said.[61] The "Old Settlers" struck out against "the lower masses of their people" with an automatic, instinctive drive for "self-defense and self-preservation," DuBois wrote.[62] "We have too much unwarranted

criticism to fight to be handicapped in this way," a Negro New
Yorker complained in 1905.[63]

> God knows
> We have our troubles, too—
> One trouble is you:
> you talk too loud,
> look too black,
> don't get anywhere,
> and sometimes it seems
> you don't even care.[64]

The only solution that these people had to offer was basically the
one that white New Yorkers proposed—keep the migrants in the
South. In the 1880's, prior to any significant migration, *The New
York Age* encouraged Negroes to flee the social and economic
proscriptions of the South: "Why should they not seek in other
sections to better their social, material and civil condition," it said.
When migrants came in larger numbers, however, the *Age* changed its
tune: "It will well repay them to consider whether it will not be better
to bear some of the ills they now do, than fly to others they know not
of." "We believe the South is the best place for the great masses of
the Afro-American people."[65] This same theme was emphasized and
re-emphasized in a whole spate of articles, editorials and speeches
printed in Negro journals in the years preceding the First World War.
The interracial Committee for the Industrial Improvement of the
Condition of the Negro in New York, established in 1906, sent
circular letters to southern newspapers, churches and schools dis-
couraging any thoughts of migration to New York City.[66] Kelly
Miller and Booker T. Washington wrote numerous articles on "The
Farm" as the "Negro's Best Chance," and on the evils and destructive-
ness of life in northern cities. Only "country life" and "working on
the soil" would "uplift" the Negro, it was argued. "There should be
organized . . . a bureau of information which should furnish the
masses of the race . . . accurate knowledge of the evil of indis-
criminate influx to the North," Miller thought.[67] But "even while
they exclaimed," Paul Laurence Dunbar said, "they knew there was
no way, and that the stream of young negro life would continue to
flow up from the South. . . ." ("I was born and raised in the
country/But Mamma I'm stayin' in town.")[68]

V

This negative view of the migration expressed by Negroes and whites was felt most intensely in the working-class districts of the city into which migrants moved. Interracial conflicts became so common at the turn of the century, it will be remembered, that San Juan Hill was named as a parody on them. Small but regular clashes ordinarily involving Negroes and the Irish were recorded in the New York press then. The antagonism between these two peoples was undoubtedly one of the harshest intergroup hatreds in American history. The deep strain of nativism that traditionally runs through American Negro thought was especially evident during this period of overwhelming foreign immigration. The Negro, born in the United States, commonly expressed his antagonism for foreigners in general and for the Irish immigrant in particular: "It is to be regretted," the Negro journalist John E. Bruce said, "that in this land of Bibles where the outcasts—the scum of European society—can come and enjoy the fullest social and political privileges, the Native Born American with woolly hair and dark complexion is made the Victim . . . of Social Ostracism." Such statements as "These low-foreheaded, beetle-browed fellows . . . driven from Europe"; "tens of thousands of aliens are being landed on these shores and freely given the employment which is denied Negro citizens"; "his brogue was so heavy it sounded like he had marbles in his mouth"; "the time is upon us when some restriction will have to be placed upon the volume and character of European immigration," were written by Negroes. A Negro journal spoke of "the open dislike of the Irish and colored people. . . ." One man put it tersely. Whatever the Negro is, he said, "he is no hyphenate."[69]

The Irish immigrant, in turn, was given full leeway by American society to look with disdain upon the Negro. A European traveler to the city in the 1860's maintained that Irish immigrants considered Negroes "a soulless race." "I am satisfied that some of these people would shoot a black man . . . as they would a hog," he concluded. "Pat O'Flannagan does not have the least thing in the world against Jim from Dixie," a Negro educator remarked in 1909, "but it didn't take Pat long after passing the Statue of Liberty to learn that it is popular to give Jim a whack." "It is quite remarkable how easily

. . . foreigners catch on to the notion . . . to treat Afro-Americans disdainfully and contemptuously," *The New York Age* noted.[70]

Throughout the nineteenth century this mutual antipathy erupted into violence many times. Since the Draft Riots of 1863, however, there were no major clashes between Negroes and Irish in New York City. Now, with increased racial tensions pervading the city, especially in the neighborhoods where the two groups had closest contact, there was a revival of bitterness. The Tenderloin was a common battleground.

A major race riot occurred in New York City in 1900. It was the first serious outbreak of racial violence since the Draft Riots. The riot of 1900 was a symbol of the entire new trend of increasing racial alienation and violence taking place throughout the city. The generally apathetic response of the white community to the demands Negroes made after the riot for justice was a reflection of the growing lack of concern of white New Yorkers for the increasingly serious impediments to Negro equality.

VI

In August 1900 New York City was in the midst of a heat wave. The weather bureau recorded stifling temperatures throughout the month: "The warmest August since the Local Bureau kept track of it." At noon on August 12, the temperature reached 91 degrees. New Yorkers spilled out of their tenements seeking relief. Stoops in the Tenderloin were crowded throughout the night. Local saloons were packed to capacity.[71]

Arthur J. Harris left his house at 241 West Forty-first Street on the evening of August 12 to buy some cigars and pass some time at McBride's Saloon. Harris, twenty-two, was typical of many young Negroes who came to New York City at that time. Born in Richmond, Virginia, of an unstable family (his mother lived in Washington, D.C., in 1900, his father in Cranford, New Jersey), he had left home at fourteen and lived in Washington for seven years. In 1899 he came north to visit his father and find work. The Washington police never had any trouble with him, his record showed "No Prior Convictions." When asked about his previous education, he responded "Yes"; he could read and write.[72] He called himself a Protestant.[73]

In Jersey City in 1899, he had picked up money working at odd jobs—as a cook, baker, carpenter and poolroom attendant—and lived with 20-year-old May Enoch, who had left the husband she had married at sixteen. Harris and "his woman," or, as he often referred to her, "my wife," came to Forty-first Street at the beginning of August 1900, rented a room at Annie Johnson's, and said they were looking for work. At 2 A.M. on August 13, May came down to McBride's: "I says to Harris, 'Kid come on up home.' "[74] While she waited for him at the corner of Forty-first Street and Eighth Avenue, Robert J. Thorpe, a plain-clothes policeman, approached her and charged her with "soliciting." To Harris he looked like a white man who was mishandling his woman: "The policeman grabbed my girl. I didn't know who he was and thought he was a citizen like myself," he maintained later at his trial. Harris was clubbed in a struggle with the policeman. He said the policeman pummeled him with his club and shouted, "Get up you black son-of-a-bitch." "I thought the man was trying to kill me, and I believed that he would kill me if I didn't protect myself." Harris pulled out a knife and "cut him twice." May ran home where she was later picked up and arrested; Harris took a train to his mother's home in Washington; Thorpe died in Roosevelt Hospital the next day.[75]

Little more was needed to set off the racial tensions that now lay so near the surface of everyday life in the Tenderloin. A Negro, a recent southern migrant, had killed a "cop"—the son-in-law to be of the acting captain of the local police station. Rumors of violence spread throughout the Negro sections. One woman went to the police and begged for protection: "the tenants of her house were terror-stricken," she said. "They had been warned of an attack in the late night."[76] "Feelings against the Negroes in the neighborhood of Thorpe's late home had been at white heat for a couple of days," it was reported. Large crowds, including sixty members of the Thirty-seventh Street station house, gathered at the home of the Thorpe family to pay their respects.[77]

The immediate cause for the outbreak was a fight between a Negro, Spencer Walters, and a white man, Thomas J. Healy. The Police Board, in its official findings on the riot, claimed that Walters attempted to shoot Healy on the night of August 15. The fight took place near Thorpe's home the evening before the burial. Negroes said that Walters had been set upon by some hysterical people who just visited the Thorpe family.[78] It makes little difference who was right. If it was not this, there would have been some other excuse for violence.

The entire neighborhood went wild with rage. Walters was immediately attacked by a mob. He "was a wreck when placed under arrest." "If there had been a carefully arranged plot and this had been the agreed signal, the outbreak could not have been more spontaneous," a journalist reported. "Men and women poured by the hundreds from the neighboring tenements. Negroes were set upon wherever they could be found and brutally beaten."[79] The word spread that a "nigger chase" was on.[80] Up and down the streets, through hotels and saloons, in cellars and streetcars, Negroes were attacked and beaten. White street gangs mobbed the electric cars on Eighth Avenue ("Nigger, nigger never die, black face and shiny eye"), pulled Negroes off at random and beat them: "Every car passing up or down Eighth Avenue . . . was stopped by the crowd and every negro on board dragged out. . . . The police made little or no attempt to arrest any of [the] assailants," *The New York Times* noted. One man brought a clothesline, tied it to a lamppost, and looked for someone to lynch.[81]

A group of Negro waiters at a midtown hotel remained there all night rather than tempt the mob. Stephen Small and Adolphus Cooks were beaten by the police and decided to hide in a cellar all night. Zeb Robinson, a Negro barber, was attacked on the streets and taken to Bellevue in a disheveled state. Charles Mitchell became hysterical after repeated "blows on the head."[82] A friend of James Weldon Johnson never fully recovered from the beating he received with a lead pipe.[83] Affidavits were later collected from eighty Negroes—waiters, porters, elevator operators, chimney sweeps, laborers, longshoremen—attesting to police and mob brutality. Although there are no reliable estimates of the number of persons injured in the riot, any Negro who happened to be on the streets of the Tenderloin that night was attacked and beaten. That serious injury was done to many is attested in the individual complaints collected in *Story of the Riot* (1900). Others never bothered to protest.

Acting Captain Cooney of the Twentieth Precinct called out the reserves to quell the trouble. However, the predominantly Irish police force hardly acted as detached enforcers of the law. Some did protect Negroes, but most, at the height of the frenzy, encouraged the rioters:

"It was said freely by witnesses of the disorderly scenes of Wednesday night that the police had done as much as anybody to encourage and promote the abuse of inoffensive negroes," a reporter indicated. Policemen often led mobs that attacked Negroes. Some dragged Negroes off streetcars and beat them. Others looked the other way rather than witness trouble. A white woman, Mrs. Davenport, sheltered a few Negroes in her home on the night of August 15. When she refused to turn them over to the police, they replied: "What kind of woman are you to be harboring niggers?" It seemed their ambition to "club the life out of a nigger," a witness said.[84]

William J. Elliott, a Negro waiter, was arrested for carrying a revolver. Reporters saw him entering the Thirty-seventh Street station house uninjured. When he left the next morning he was beaten and bloody. Elliott told the Police Commissioners that as he passed through the muster room the lights were turned out and he was kicked, punched and clubbed into insensibility.[85] As he could not identify any specific assailant, however, the Commissioners found this evidence "contradictory," and ruled that "no conviction of a violation of the Rules of the Department could be sustained [on it]."[86]

At about 2 A.M. on August 16 a providential summer thunderstorm drenched the city. It ended the initial violence. Emergency staffs on all-night duty at Roosevelt, Bellevue and New York hospitals handled the many cases of battered heads. The local police courts were jammed to capacity—with Negroes. One of the magistrates criticized the police and asked to see "some of the white persons who participated in this riot." By 1:30 A.M. his request was fulfilled. A teenager, Frank Minogue, was brought in and charged with trying to trip a policeman who was dispersing a crowd of rioters.

VII

Although the riot had ended, the neighborhood remained tense. Negroes began to arm. Revolvers and other weapons were easily purchased at local pawnshops and hardware stores. In a survey made of the Tenderloin, just one day after the riot, it was found that 145 revolvers and a substantial amount of ammunition had been sold— "all had gone to negroes."[87] Lloyd Williams, a Negro bartender, was seen leaving one store with an arsenal of weapons. When asked what he was going to do with them, he replied: "I understand they're knocking down negroes 'round here. The first man tries it on me gets this. . . ." Other Negroes warned that no white men were going to bother them. As policemen patrolled the Negro blocks they were showered with bricks, bottles and garbage from rooftops and tenement windows. They fired back with revolvers. It seems miraculous that no one was killed then.

Orders went out to keep the Negroes off the streets. Paul Laurence Dunbar went into the Tenderloin, visited Negro homes and attempted to restore peace. Innumerable arrests were made, practically all of Negroes, on the charge of carrying concealed weapons. For more than a month after the riot there were almost daily clashes between individual Negroes and whites. At least two people were killed in these fights. Slowly, the Tenderloin returned to its normal state of semipeace.

VIII

The white community was shocked.[88] Editorials appeared throughout the press criticizing the police for their brutality and the vicious for their violence. The tone of the responses, however, lacked sympathy for the injured Negroes. The riot was made a political issue as the Republican press and the Good Government Society attacked Tammany Hall. The *New York Daily Tribune* printed a cartoon of a massive Tammany tiger in police uniform swinging a club. Huddled on the floor in the background was a bloody Negro. The caption read: "He's On the Police Force Now." The "Respectable Citizenry" attacked the "white trash" and advised Negroes to vote Republican.[89]

Negro leaders demanded punishment of the guilty and compensation for the injured. The Reverend Dr. W. H. Brooks of St. Mark's Methodist Episcopal Church led the protest. Brooks, born on a Maryland plantation, had been at St. Mark's since 1897—well equipped with a voice that could drown out the clatter of elevated trains that ran near his church.[90] One of the most important leaders of the city's Negro community, he later became a founder of the NAACP and the National Urban League. From his pulpit, and from the pulpits of all the Negro churches in the city, the mobs and police were vilified. An honest public investigation was demanded,[91] and prominent members of the Negro community—lawyers, clergymen, politicians, businessmen—were urged to use their influence to seek justice.[92] An *ad hoc* defense committee, the Citizens' Protective League, was organized at a meeting in St. Mark's on September 3. Two lawyers, Frank Moss and Israel Ludlow, were hired. Moss vowed never to let the riot "fade into forgetfulness." Suits were filed for damages against the city in the names of persons injured by the police.[93] At a mass meeting at Carnegie Hall to raise money and gain public support, some speakers urged caution and peaceful agitation. D. Macon Webster, a Negro lawyer, wanted justice done for the "humblest citizen." "One might think we [were] all aliens" from the manner in which we were treated, he concluded.[94] Others, more belligerent, urged Negroes to arm and defend their homes.[95] All agreed that right must be done.

The protests were militant and idealistic, the results cold and bleak. There was no mass response to the appeal for public support: "I heard many native Americans . . . say after the riot," a contemporary noted in *Harper's Weekly*, "that they would have been glad if many of the negroes had been killed." "This is a mass in the midst of what is . . . an alien and hostile people," another believed.[96] The August Grand Jury refused to indict a single policeman, alleging that accusations were brought against groups rather than individuals. When cases were presented against individual policemen, they too were dismissed.[97] The Police Board set up a committee of investigation, which refused Moss and Ludlow permission to cross-examine witnesses, and concluded in its report that "there is nothing in the evidence taken by your committee which will justify preferment of charges against any officer. . . ."[98] The *Tribune* quipped: "The Police Board wants it understood that the riot inquiry is to be full and impartial, only no evidence against the police will be admitted."[99] Arthur J. Harris was arrested in Washington for killing policeman Thorpe, tried in New York, found guilty of murder in the second degree, and "sentenced to the State Prison at Sing Sing at hard labor for the term of his natural life."[100] The Reverend Dr. Brooks created "The Arthur J. Harris Liberation Fund" and continued to fight for his release, but Harris died in prison on December 20, 1908.[101] The Citizens' Protective League simply ceased to exist. It accomplished nothing. The little power it could wield ran into an almost solid wall of indifference and opposition. "It is like sheep proclaiming the law of righteousness to a congregation of wolves," Kelly Miller commented on another occasion. "A complaint is effective only in so far as there is power to enforce it."[102]

And the Police Department, in its *Annual Report,* provided its own conclusion to the sad affair: "In the month of August the west side of the city was threatened with a race war between the white and colored citizens. . . . Prompt and vigorous action on the part of the Police . . . kept the situation under control, and . . . quiet was restored in districts . . . which were affected."[103]

Was the riot and the reaction to it a sign of intensified racial alienation in New York City, as some people claimed? No, said a columnist for *The New York Times* in an emphatic rejoinder. There is no "settled race hatred . . . in New York. There are no signs that the citizen of African descent is distrusted or disliked. . . . His crude melodies and childlike antics are more than tolerated in the music halls of the best class."[104]

Urban Progressives: Negro and White

"To my amazement I learned that
there was a Negro problem in my
city. I had never honestly thought
of it before."
—Mary White Ovington, 1900

"We seem to be doing things in the
same old unprogressive ways as when
society was less complex. . . ."
—Frances A. Kellor, 1907

I

The emergence of racial violence and antagonism and the increasing number of complex social problems created by the urbanization of the Negro produced a need for racial reform in the North in the early twentieth century. The movement for social and economic reform in northern cities, a vital part of the national Progressive movement, showed deep concern for the welfare of the Negro people.[1] The years preceding World War I found a revitalization of interest in Negro life among urban reformers in every major northern city to which migrants came in large numbers. When "Race was against the colored man," a Negro New Yorker recalled, "the reformers turned out. . . ." These Progressives were, in the words of a Negro businessman, the "doers," not the "talkers," of American society.[2]

The white people involved in this movement were primarily social workers and urban reformers who attempted to improve living conditions in the industrial and tenement house areas of northern cities. Those who established settlement houses for immigrants in the 1890's also founded similar institutions for Negroes. In the first decade of the twentieth century, Progressives organized the Frederick Douglass Center in Chicago, the Robert Gould Shaw House in

53

Boston, the Eighth Ward Settlement in Philadelphia, the Stillman House and two Lincoln Settlements in New York City. Frances Bartholomew, Carl Kelsey and R. R. Wright, Jr., in Philadelphia; Isabel Eaton, who had worked with DuBois on his study of Philadelphia Negroes, in Boston; Celia Parker Woolley, Sophonisba Breckinridge, Mary E. McDowell and Louise DeKoven Bowen in Chicago; Mary White Ovington, Elizabeth Walton, Victoria Earle Matthews and William Lewis Bulkley in New York City were all actively engaged in social work among Negroes.[3] Perceptive studies of Negro society were undertaken as well in these years, in the first major scholarly effort to analyze America's racial problems since the abolitionist era. In typical Progressive fashion, volumes of facts and statistics were gathered to learn how best to improve living conditions. "We must not forget," W. E. B. DuBois wrote in 1903, "that most Americans answer all queries regarding the Negro *a priori,* and that the least . . . human courtesy we can do is to listen to evidence."[4] Between 1899 and 1915 a number of books on race problems appeared, among them DuBois' *Philadelphia Negro* (1899), Ray Stannard Baker's *Following the Color Line* (1908), R. R. Wright, Jr.'s, *The Negro in Pennsylvania* (1908), Mary White Ovington's *Half A Man: The Status of the Negro in New York* (1911), George Edmund Haynes' *The Negro at Work in New York City* (1912), Louise DeKoven Bowen's *The Colored People of Chicago* (1913), Frank U. Quillin's *The Color Line in Ohio* (1913), John Daniel's *In Freedom's Birthplace: A History of the Boston Negro* (1914), William A. Crossland's *Industrial Conditions Among Negroes in St. Louis* (1914), and Frances Blascoer's *Colored School Children of New York* (1915). Numerous articles on Negro life were printed in contemporary periodicals early in the century. In 1909–1911 the first national Negro defense and improvement agencies were founded—the NAACP and the National League on Urban Conditions Among Negroes—both in New York City.

II

Concern for the welfare of Negroes among white people in New York City had traditionally been associated with religious groups, and most particularly with the Society of Friends. Quakers, leading abolitionists in New York City, played an important role in founding free schools for Negro children. After the Civil War, the only white organization that continued its works among the city's Negroes was the New York Colored Mission, founded by the Quakers. A few Negro churches in these years gave some assistance "to needy persons who find themselves in the great city without a home for a few days," but this effort was not highly organized.[5]

The "Friends' Mission," as some contemporaries called it (more vituperative observers christened it "Nigger School"),[6] offered missionary work and "Christian Fellowship"[7] to Negroes, distributing religious tracts, temperance literature and Bibles by the thousands to the city's Negro population.[8] Before its incorporation in 1871, the society was called the "African Sabbath School Association," and its first home was over a stable. When incorporated, it conceived of its task basically as a religious one: "To conduct in the City of New York a Sabbath School for Religious Instruction," and hold "Social, Religious Meetings."[9] Whatever practical assistance the organization would give Negroes was considered secondary to its religious obligation. The City Mission and Tract Society contributed enough money to the Colored Mission to permit it to purchase a building of its own in the Tenderloin, its motto: "Inasmuch as ye have done it unto one of the least of these my brethren, ye have done it unto me."[10]

But, as the Negro population of Manhattan increased, slightly in the 1870's and 1880's, more rapidly in the 1890's, the Colored Mission was slowly transformed into a social service agency. It conducted an employment bureau, provided temporary housing and inexpensive meals for migrants (a "Sunday bowl of soup and slice of bread"), opened a small "infant school" which cared for and fed Negro children for five cents a day, and bought glasses for Negroes who wanted to learn how to read (most wished to read the Bible). Destitution was so widespread in the depression winter of 1893–1894 that the Colored Mission distributed tons of coal and barrels of food to Negro families—flour, corn meal, oatmeal, hominy, rice, bread, beans, pork, milk. "The records of those months are so sad that one shrinks from recurring to them," the society's missionary recorded in his journal. "No fire, no food, dispossession impending, illness, death . . . confronted us. [People] were found actually dying of want."[11] Between the Civil War and the 1890's, with this one modest exception, no organizations in New York City were concerned with the welfare of Negroes. By 1915 there were more than a dozen.

III

Increasing interest in Negro life developed in the 1890's and first decade of the twentieth century among white and Negro reformers. The movement was widespread and involved people who disagreed with one another on the over-all methods of improving the status of the Negro in American society. Some were avid supporters of the gradualism of Booker T. Washington, others more militant followers of W. E. B. DuBois. Mary White Ovington, for example, considered herself "an ardent disciple of the DuBois School."[12] Whatever theoretic differences existed among them, they held basic agreement on the need for immediate practical reforms to improve the generally harsh lives of Negroes in the city. Urban reformers' primary concern was to find jobs and decent homes for Negro migrants, to open playgrounds for Negro children, to break the color barrier in businesses and unions, to improve health, educational and sanitary conditions in the Tenderloin, San Juan Hill and Harlem, and to protect Negro domestics from the exploitations of city employment bureaus.

The first organization this spirit of "social justice" produced, founded in 1897, was the White Rose Industrial Association; the "White Rose Working Girls' Home," as the sign which hung over its door read. A Negro, Mrs. Victoria Earle Matthews, the youngest daughter of a Georgia slave,[13] organized the society. Born in slavery herself just one month after the Civil War began, she came to New York City with her mother and family in the 1870's. She was young enough to attend the Negro public schools; after graduation she became a writer, and her stories and articles were published in white and Negro journals. She thought of herself as an emancipated woman, founded a Negro protest and women's rights society in the city (the "Women's Loyal Union of New York and Brooklyn"), supported Ida B. Wells' antilynching crusade, and delivered lectures on "The Awakening of the Afro-American Woman." When she learned of the "unscrupulous employment agents who deceived the unsuspecting girls desiring to come North," "those unprincipled men who haunted the wharves," she decided to "check the evil."[14]

Mrs. Matthews' association provided lodgings and meals for women until they could find work. The society kept agents at piers— "meeting the boats" it was called—in Norfolk as well as New York

City to answer questions, escort women to their places of employment or, instead, to the White Rose Home: "Our principal object is to protect our girls, to direct and help them amid the dangers of our great city." The White Rose Home became a settlement house as well as a temporary lodging place for migrants. The classes presented there in domestic training and "race history," the library of books on Negro life, and the facilities for recreation admitted the public as well as residents of the home. Paul Laurence Dunbar and Booker T. Washington gave lectures at the settlement. The White Rose Home continued its work among Negroes even after Mrs. Matthews' death in 1907, and finally moved to larger quarters in Harlem in 1918.[15]

The fear of exploitation of Negro women by "intelligence agents" that motivated Victoria Earle Matthews also led to the founding of an organization which attempted to do on a national scale what the White Rose Home did for Negro migrants who came to New York City. The initiator of this movement, a white reformer, Frances A. Kellor, wrote a perceptive series of articles on criminality among Negroes, one of the earliest sociological analyses of racial problems in the city.[16] She also spent a good part of her early crusading career attacking the corruptions of private employment bureaus. In 1903, the Woman's Municipal League of New York hired Miss Kellor to collect as much data on employment agencies as a thorough investigation could produce.[17] She gathered information from 732 private employment bureaus, published her findings in 1904 in an important book of the Progressive era, *Out of Work: A Study of Employment Agencies,* and bombarded municipal officials with the information she uncovered. Her criticisms and prodding led to the creation of the Office of Commissioner of Licenses in New York City, and helped establish the first state-controlled employment bureau in New York in 1911.[18]

Frances A. Kellor and other municipal reformers interested in job placement believed that many employment agents were dishonest and treated their clients in a shoddy manner, and, even worse, that many agencies served as subtle guises to draw women into the arms of "the alluring procuresses of the city."[19] Some Negro women found their jobs as maids and cooks to be in what Miss Kellor called "sporting houses." "They are often threatened until they accept positions in questionable places and are frequently sent out without knowing the character of their destination," she wrote in *Out of Work.*[20] In

Chicago also, Louise DeKoven Bowen discovered that "most of the maids employed in houses of prostitution were colored girls. . . ."[21] The recruitment of women for "immoral purposes" by "intelligence agents" was the first point the New York City Commissioner of Licenses listed in a memorandum which explained why the office had been created.[22] "The southern states, especially Virginia and Georgia, are honey-combed with the slick agents of these employment bureaus," Miss Kellor said in 1905. ". . . Good wages, easy work . . . and good times, are promised. . . . To them, going to Philadelphia or to New York seems like going to Heaven, where the streets will be paved with gold, all will be music and flowers!"[23]

The disparity between image and reality led Miss Kellor to establish a society for the protection of Negro women—the National League for the Protection of Colored Women. The League had offices in New York City and Philadelphia and agents in many southern port cities. It distributed literature to southern Negro pastors and schools urging them to "educate the women on these conditions."[24] Like the White Rose Home, and sometimes in conjunction with it, the League stationed workers at the major depots within the city and offered general fellowship and advice to country strangers who came to town for the first time: "It is the aim of the League to furnish helpful information to colored girls who are intending to come North, to protect them during the journey . . . and to find work or friends or homes for them [when they arrive]."[25] The National League for the Protection of Colored Women continued this work until 1911, when it became one of three Negro reform agencies to consolidate into the National League on Urban Conditions Among Negroes.

IV

Reformers Victoria Earle Matthews and Frances A. Kellor had concentrated on a single aspect of the problem—the exploitation of Negro domestic workers. Mary White Ovington became the first prominent New Yorker to devote herself to the improvement of all aspects of Negro life in New York City, and eventually in the entire nation.

Miss Ovington, like many other urban reformers of her generation, grew up in comfort and gentility. She was the daughter of a well-to-do New York merchant. Her home in an exclusive section of Brooklyn lay not far from the working-class districts, but it was as separate from them in spirit as two distinct worlds could be: "In my youth," she recalled in an autobiographical sketch, "no place was more remote than the section of the city in which persons of different caste lived."[26]

With the typical education of a young woman of refinement, Miss Ovington had studied as a child exclusively in private schools, and then went to Radcliffe. Her family expected her to take her proper place in society—"what we called 'going into society,'" she remarked. But the quiet, secure and stable world into which Miss Ovington was born seemed too remote in the America of the 1880's and 1890's. Massive industrialization and urbanization created major social dislocations on a scale unequaled in the previous history of the nation. It created urban slums, and the immigrants who lived in them often experienced poverty, distress, illness and a sense of hopelessness difficult for the socially conscious to overlook: "I found out about conditions in my own city of which I was utterly ignorant."[27]

Miss Ovington's reaction to these new conditions, similar to the responses of other Progressives, was positive and optimistic. Involvement in a movement for social reform also gave added meaning and fulfillment to her own life. There was, she recalled, a "fervor for settlement work in the nineties, for learning working-class conditions by living among the workers and sharing to some small extent in their lives. . . . The desire for such knowledge was in the air—*hope was in the air.*" In 1896, with the financial assistance of civic leader Frederick B. Pratt, Miss Ovington opened a settlement house "among white working-class people" in Greenpoint, Brooklyn. Her five-room home grew into a forty-room settlement in the seven years she remained there. "That I should later work for the Negro never entered my mind," she wrote.[28]

Her first awareness of the seriousness of urban problems among Negroes came at a lecture given by Booker T. Washington. The "Social Reform Club," of which she was a member (she was also a member of the Socialist Party), invited Washington to speak before it: "To my amazement I learned that there was a Negro problem in my city. I had honestly never thought of it before." At that time she decided to find out more about these conditions and, from 1904 till her death in 1951, devoted her life to improving them.[29]

Although Washington's descriptions may have appeared new and shocking to her as an adult, Mary White Ovington had heard similar stories as a child. The Ovington family was one of those ubiquitous New England families that controlled much of New York commerce, and much of the mercantile operations of all the seaboard cities, for a good part of the nineteenth century. William Lloyd Garrison had been a friend of her grandmother's and Miss Ovington, born in 1865, grew up when memories of the "Great Rebellion" were very much alive. She listened attentively to her grandmother's tales of abolitionism, the Underground Railroad, anti-abolitionist rioting in Boston, and the preaching of Garrison's close friend and follower, the Reverend Dr. Samuel J. May. She was taught to despise Daniel Webster and Henry Clay for compromising on the slavery issue. When Frederick Douglass came to speak at Plymouth Congregational Church, Miss Ovington went to see one of her idols. "I was," she wrote, "a sympathetic listener." Garrison "was my childhood's greatest hero."[30]

Mary White Ovington's parents were abolitionists too. Her father told her he severed connections with Plymouth Congregational Church because Henry Ward Beecher supported a missionary association which dealt with a slaveholder. He joined a Unitarian congregation, and his daughter continued in this religion, led by an abolitionist "of the strictest brand." Her brother later became a lifetime member of the NAACP. "Ours was an abolition family."

The Ovington family, like many other supporters of abolitionism, lost contact with Negro life after the Civil War. Slavery had been the great evil, they thought, and it was now destroyed. The Thirteenth, Fourteenth and Fifteenth Amendments were passed and Negroes were *legally* made equal American citizens. It seemed to them that nothing was left to be done: "Slavery was ended," she said. "That was the great point."

Booker T. Washington reawakened Miss Ovington's interest in the Negro people. She decided to open a settlement house for Negroes in New York City and asked Mary Kingsbury Simkovitch of Greenwich House for advice. They both decided the first step was to gather as much specific information as possible on Negro urban problems. Miss Ovington was appointed Fellow of Greenwich House in 1904 and began the studies which led to the publication of *Half A Man* seven years later.[31]

One of the enduring problems of the twentieth-century city has been its inability to supply decent and inexpensive living accommodations to Negroes: "The need for model tenements for colored people is perhaps the greatest of all . . . our's city's population," a group of tenement house reformers indicated in the early twentieth century. Miss Ovington, impressed with the desire of urban Negroes for "wholesome homes," decided to do something about it. She sought to contact Henry Phipps, steel magnate and philanthropist, who previously constructed model tenements for immigrants in New York. The City and Suburban Homes Company, incorporated in 1896, managed the houses built by Phipps and other patrician reformers—Alfred T. White, the Phelps Stokes family, and others—and they accepted a modest profit of five per cent on their investments.[32] It seemed an artful combination of philanthropy and sound business. Miss Ovington and Phipps had a mutual friend, John E. Milholland,[33] whom she went to see. Milholland was another early supporter of the civil rights cause and a good friend of W. E. B. DuBois. In 1904 he founded the Constitution League in New York City, and the League tried to breathe some life into the dormant post-Civil War constitutional amendments.[34] Milholland, convinced of the need for the project, in turn persuaded Phipps to construct a model tenement for the Negroes of San Juan Hill. When the new Phipps Houses were completed on West Sixty-third Street in 1907 they seemed an incongruity in the neighborhood. These fireproof, steam-heated, roof-gardened, six-story houses stood out against the older rundown tenements on the West Side. (The Phipps apartment houses have somehow survived a half-century of urban renewal and may be seen today.) Miss Ovington also hoped that Phipps would support a settlement house for Negroes in the building, and decided to live there herself: "I hoped by quietly renting on my own account, to persuade him to add social work," she wrote to a Negro friend.[35]

Mary White Ovington moved into the model tenement, the only white person in the entire house, in January 1908. There she gathered information for her book, became a close friend of the Reverend Dr. George H. Sims of Union Baptist Church on the block, attended his services occasionally, and read *Peter Rabbit* and other stories to the Negro youngsters who knocked at her door. (She later published stories for Negro children.) Miss Ovington lived on West Sixty-third Street for eight months, but failed to get the philanthropist to support a Negro settlement house.

In September 1908, after having attended meetings of the Negro

Niagara Movement, she read an article in *The Independent* which diverted her attention to national civil rights problems, and redirected the course of her life. William English Walling's since-famous article, "The Race War in the North," attacked the growing racial antipathy and apathy evident in the North and called for a revival of "the spirit of the abolitionists. . . ."[36] Miss Ovington responded to this appeal and called a small meeting of her friends to discuss what could be done to counteract this burgeoning racism. A National Negro Conference met in 1909 at the Henry Street Settlement and the National Negro Committee was established at this gathering. The NAACP had been born. Mary White Ovington spent the rest of her career within this organization.[37]

Although her main energies were channeled into the NAACP—she was called "Mother of the New Emancipation"—she remained active in social work among the city's Negroes. She was an executive of the Committee for Improving the Industrial Condition of the Negro in New York City, chairman of its "Neighborhood Work" subcommittee, president and main fund-raiser of the Lincoln Settlement, which she helped found for Negroes in Brooklyn, and organizer of the West End Workers' Association, active among the Negroes on San Juan Hill.[38] Her Negro secretary from 1905 to 1951 remembers Miss Ovington as a person totally dedicated to the struggle for Negro rights and honestly devoid of any racial prejudice.[39] Negro poet and novelist Claude McKay, in florid tones, wrote that "her personality radiated a quiet silver shaft of white charm which is lovely when it's real."[40] "No white woman's life in America has been colored more by the clash of color and race," concluded a Negro newspaper in an editorial.[41] "That the sincerity of my friendship has never been doubted has been my greatest joy," Miss Ovington said on her resignation as Chairman of the Board of Directors of the NAACP.[42]

V

The reforming zeal evident in Mary White Ovington reached a high point with the founding of the Committee for Improving the Industrial Condition of the Negro in New York (CIICN) in 1906. The primary motivation for the creation of the CIICN was the desire to broaden employment opportunities for the city's Negroes. Its members, supporters, directors and subcommittee chairmen were the most important municipal reformers in New York in the Progressive era, many later active in founding the NAACP. Interracial in structure, the CIICN included social workers, philanthropists, educators, clergymen, writers, publishers, physicians, supporters of Hampton and Tuskegee and businessmen.[43] The founder of the CIICN was a Negro principal in the New York City school system, Dr. William Lewis Bulkley. Bulkley decided to organize the Committee, he said in 1906, after seeing Negro students leaving his schools "to open doors, run bells or hustle hash" for the rest of their lives. "On every hand avenues of employment are shut tight, discouragement begins and [Negro children] leave school to work at any menial employment that offers itself," Bulkley observed. "The constant cry of the negro," another man wrote, "is for 'a white man's chance.' "[44]

Bulkley was the leading Negro educator in New York City in the early twentieth century, a bright, idealistic and ambitious man who rose from the slavery in which he was born in 1861 to earn a doctorate in ancient languages and literature from Syracuse University. As a boy he attended the local log cabin school in Greenville, South Carolina, and finally was graduated from Claflin University, in his home state, in 1882. Bulkley came north to Wesleyan University in Connecticut and continued his studies in France and Germany. In 1893, after completing his master's degree, he earned the Ph.D. at Syracuse.[45]

For a time, Bulkley taught as professor of Latin and Greek at Claflin, but as a student, he worked as janitor, steward, cook and salesman. To save the little money he earned this way he scrimped wherever he could. His meals often consisted of oatmeal and water, he washed and darned his own clothing, and pressed socks and handkerchiefs between the pages of books or under the mattresses on which he slept. William Lewis Bulkley, in the language of his day, achieved "Success Under Difficulties." The "Slave Boy Now a Professor" was "A Noble Example of the Triumph of Perseverance."[46]

Bulkley thought of himself as a southerner driven from his home by racism: "There is not one of us who would not gladly go back home if we did not know that every right dear to any full man has been ruthlessly torn from our grasp," he said in 1909. He longed to share the "soul-refreshings that only a [southern] Negro revival can give."[47] Bulkley came to New York City in the 1890's and was appointed seventh grade teacher in a lower Manhattan public school. In 1899 he became principal of P.S. 80 on West Forty-first Street in the Tenderloin.[48] This school, in the heart of the Negro district, had formerly been an all-Negro institution which was made a ward school in the integration of 1884. In 1909, despite protest meetings and petitions from the teachers of P.S. 125, Bulkley became the first Negro principal of a predominantly white school in city history.[49]

William Lewis Bulkley insisted that Negroes be given full equality in American society—constitutional, political, social, economic— immediately. He supported the demands made by W. E. B. DuBois along these lines, and became a founder of the NAACP. During his summer vacations he was a temporary expatriate who lived in Switzerland and France with his wife and children. His family sometimes remained in Europe when he returned to resume his duties in the fall. On retiring from the New York City school system in 1924 he left the country and established a private school in France. He died in Paris in 1933.[50] That a supporter of DuBois should found an organization to foster practical, industrial employment for the Negroes in the city seemed the height of inconsistency to Booker T. Washington's supporters. "You will see that this opponent of indus- trial education is not practicing what he preaches," one of them wrote. "This is inconsistency with a vengeance." Washington even had agents attend meetings of the CIICN to check the activities of "Bulkley and his crowd. . . ." "It is hard to carry out plans if our friends are in the minority," Washington observed.[51] White social workers, like Mary White Ovington, Jane Addams and Julia Rich- man, on the other hand, thought highly of Bulkley's work.[52]

A pragmatist, Bulkley met conditions in the city as he saw them and tried to improve them immediately as best he could. He "set out to make his school a social center," a contemporary journal com- mented. Soon after becoming principal of P.S. 80, for example, he opened a kindergarten to relieve the working mothers of the neigh- borhood. He delivered special lectures to parents and students five times a semester on proper nutrition and sanitation, health and other social problems. He visited homes, addressed church groups, at- tended parents' meetings, wanted "to awaken [Negroes] to a larger self respect and aspiration for better living."[53] In 1903 he started an evening school in the building which specialized in industrial and commercial training. Some of the most diligent students in the school were elderly Negro men and women, some in their seventies and eighties, who had no opportunity for education as youngsters but now wanted to learn to read and write.[54] Bulkley invited friends and associates to visit the school.[55] Members of the Board of Education, on one inspection tour, described it as "the most successful evening school that ever was established in New York. . . ."[56]

The idea of a permanent industrial organization to assist Negroes in New York City apparently originated with William H. Baldwin: President of the Long Island Railroad, philanthropist, and one of Booker T. Washington's key financial supporters. Bulkley, however, initiated the movement which led to the creation of the CIICN.

Bulkley had agitated since 1902 for an organization to do on a broad scale what he attempted to do as an individual at his school: "With an Afro-American population in New York increasing yearly at a very great, I had almost said alarming rate," he maintained in one speech, "it behooves every thoughtful man and woman in this city to stop long enough to think what it may mean to us and to them."[57] Early in 1906 he began a series of local meetings to discuss the subject. He, Mary White Ovington and others lectured these gatherings on the harsh facts of Negro urban life. Finally, in May 1906, at a meeting of some sixty Negro and white New Yorkers, Bulkley's hope became reality. The CIICN was founded and issued a public statement on its goals. "Here at home," the report maintained, "conditions are piling up which must be met at once." The Committee would endeavor to provide equal "economic opportunities" for all citizens: "A square deal in the matter of getting a livelihood is held to be fundamental."[58] William Jay Schieffelin, philanthropist, urban reformer, heir to the Jay family abolitionist tradition, and president of the Board of Trustees of Hampton's Armstrong Association, was appointed chairman. Schieffelin immediately began to contact friends to mobilize support for the new organization. With "seventy thousand Negroes in New York," he wrote in a letter, "we ought to feel a responsibility concerning them."[59]

The CIICN was divided into subcommittees, each headed by an eminent specialist in a particular area of service—"Employment," "Neighborhood Work," "Craftsmen," "Publication," "Trade Schools," "Social Centers," "Legal Affairs," "Public Meetings." They canvassed Negro streets in the city to gather information on social problems which seemed most pressing. Regular public meetings in Negro churches stimulated interest in the Committee's work and provided a sounding board for local discontent. An employment bureau located and helped create jobs for Negroes. The names of skilled Negro workers were collected and these craftsmen were organized into small trade units for dressmakers, printers, mechanics, waiters, carpenters and the like. The policies of racial restriction normally adhered to by unions cracked a bit when, under prodding from the CIICN, the Grand United Brotherhood of Carpenters and Joiners of America issued a charter to a Negro local in the city. Plumbers, construction workers, painters, bricklayers, masons, decorators, found jobs. Subway companies were asked to hire Negro motormen. The subcommittee on Trade Schools, headed by a New York City school superintendent, collected a thousand names on a petition for new night schools in the Negro districts. Two more evening schools primarily for Negroes began in these years. The City and Suburban Homes Company was encouraged to build additional model tenements for Negroes.[60]

The CIICN also co-operated with the other Negro reform agencies in the city. In 1908, for example, it began to send people to the docks to assist Frances A. Kellor's organization. When the Committee on Urban Conditions Among Negroes was established in New York in 1910, the CIICN sent spokesmen to the new organization to map out lines of co-operation with it. The problems which emerged from Negro migration grew more complex each year. In response to the obvious waste of a number of separate bodies' defining their spheres as particular aspects of what was really one broad and interrelated problem, a general agreement for consolidation in 1911 merged the CIICN, the National League for the Protection of Colored Women, and the Committee on Urban Conditions Among Negroes. A new and stronger society, which is still operating today, resulted—the National League on Urban Conditions Among Negroes (National Urban League). William Lewis Bulkley was its first vice-chairman. He probably originated in one of his speeches the phrase "Not Alms, But Opportunity," which became the organization's motto. "We do not ask for charity," he said in 1909, "all we ask is opportunity. We do not beg for alms; we beg only for a chance."[61]

The founding of the two most prominent national Negro organizations, the NAACP and the National Urban League, was a culmination and fulfillment of individual local reform efforts begun in the North in the first decade of the twentieth century. The serious revitalization of concern with racial problems this demonstrated was evident in New

York City in a variety of other ways as well. Each year brought to spontaneous life some new Negro welfare institution. Two settlement houses, one a branch of the Henry Street Settlement, were founded for Negroes in 1904 and 1907. In 1911 they consolidated into one large unit, the Lincoln Settlement House. Lillian D. Wald sent Negro nurses into the Tenderloin, San Juan Hill, and Harlem to help these communities with their medical problems; they still offer free nursing service today. A Negro Music School Settlement, numerous free nurseries, kindergartens, homes for delinquent girls and two new Negro Y's began. Housing bureaus attempted to clean up the streets of Negro slums and locate clean, respectable and inexpensive homes for Negro families. New York City's Board of Health conducted special evening classes for colored people in tuberculosis prevention.[62] Some migrants, fresh from the country, received rudimentary lessons in the use of modern sanitary and plumbing devices.[63] A Negro Fresh Air Committee was established in 1905; playgrounds and summer camps for Negro children were opened.

When the new century began the prevailing attitude toward the Negro in New York City had been one of hostility and increasing alienation. And as far as the majority of the population was concerned, there was no change in this dominant reaction of the city to the Negro people. The racial antagonism of the majority made necessary the creation of segregated communities like Harlem. But a sense of renewed promise and hopefulness among Negroes was born of the important reform movements that coped with the problems of rapid Negro urbanization. In 1900 Booker T. Washington and W. E. B. DuBois would have agreed that American reform seemed to overlook the Negro. Ten years later, both recognized a new "awakening" of interest in Negro life.[64] Some may question the degree of commitment and success this basically middle-class reform movement reflected. It obviously could not end the deep strains of racism that pervaded American culture, and it remained a minority movement. Yet these urban reformers were the first major group of Americans to manifest a serious concern with racial inequities since the abolitionist era. To some Negroes they were "a veritable god-send to the colored people."[65]

PART TWO

The Making of a Ghetto

CHAPTER 5

A Genteel Community: Harlem, 1890

"A great city is developing north
of Central Park."
—*Harlem Local Reporter*, 1889

"It is evident to the most superficial
observer that the centre of fashion,
wealth, culture, and intelligence,
must, in the near future, be found in
the ancient and honorable village of
Harlem. . . ."
—*The Harlem Monthly Magazine*, 1893

I

In the last three decades of the nineteenth century Harlem was a community of great expectations. During the previous quarter century it had been an isolated, poor, rural village. After the 1870's, however, it was transformed into an upper- and upper-middle-class residential suburb—Manhattan's first suburb.

Prosperity had come to Harlem before.[1] Throughout the colonial period its lands brought wealth to farmers. The estates of some of America's most illustrious colonial families were located there—Delanceys, Beekmans, Bleeckers, Rikers, Coldens, Hamiltons and others.[2] The stamp of respectability and distinction colored Harlem's name and later settlers recalled its past glories proudly: "Who among [you] then," a lecturer on the history of the community said in 1882, "with Harlem's . . . history before you, and the goodly prospects in store, are not proud of being called Harlemites. . . . The spirit which animated their [the founders'] breasts," he concluded romantically, "is rooted in the soft rich soil of Harlem. . . ."[3]

For some two hundred years the village of New Harlaem remained remarkably stable. Most of its small population, following the general ethnic patterns of New York City's population (as it would continue

71

to do in the future), descended from Dutch, French and English pioneers. The surnames of Harlem's residents in the late eighteenth century recall those of the seventeenth century.[4] Generations quietly passed into generations: ". . . Old Resolved Waldron built himself a house . . . where his children were born and where he finally died. His son inherited the home . . . reared his family under its roof, and was likewise buried from it. This homestead has been in the possession of the lineal descendants of Mr. Waldron ever since," a journalist recorded in 1883.[5]

There was no need for town government in a community of this size and social structure. Committees and magistrates appointed at town meetings settled matters of public concern. So it had been in 1667, so in 1774 and again in 1820. The commission appointed to lay out the streets of New York City in 1811 did not think Harlem would be "covered with houses for centuries to come."[6] In the 1820's the ninety-one families of the "delightful village" of Harlem had one church, one school, one library.[7]

And this tradition was not completely extinct in the late nineteenth century. Harlem always remained a strange combination of the old and new. A fifth-generation descendant of a man who came to Harlem in 1667 continued proudly to live on part of the family estate at the turn of the century.[8] At least four other heirs to seventeenth-century land titles lived in Harlem in 1882: Bensons, Montagnes, Hoppers, Raubs.[9] The Watt Mansion, originally built by John Delancey in the eighteenth century, was standing to meet the twentieth.[10] Hamilton Grange, completed in 1803–1804, may still be seen today, and the Hamilton Estate owned Harlem land in the 1890's. (In 1904, a hundred years after Hamilton's death, the community publicly honored his memory.)[11] Scattered throughout the area were other formerly stately colonial homes, two erected prior to 1670,[12] others "yet in good repair."[13] A boy fishing in Harlem Creek could still find a button from the uniform of a soldier of the American Revolution.[14] In 1910, the Collegiate Reformed Church, founded in 1660, celebrated its 250th anniversary, a solid reminder to newcomers of Harlem's distinguished past.[15]

II

To most residents of Harlem in the 1840's and 1850's, however, these were skeleton remains of a never-known age. Harlem's decline began when its lands, worn out after centuries of use, lost their former productivity. Hamilton's widow, for example, had abandoned the Grange because the farm was "yielding trifling returns."[16] Others, rather than eke out a grudging existence in an America of great opportunity, simply deserted the seemingly worthless property and went elsewhere. Formerly great estates were sold at public auction.[17] The city acquired much property and resold it.[18] In 1838 the New York City Board of Aldermen described Harlem as a "third or fourth-rate country village."[19]

Into this decaying community came groups of people to whom the once productive soil seemed less forbidding. Those in search of cheap property bought land there and built one- and two-story frame houses. Others, including many newly arrived and destitute Irish immigrants—some of whom remained in Harlem to see the twentieth century—squatted on the forsaken land or lived in mud flats at the river's edge. They created Harlem's shantytowns and lived in two-room cottages pieced together with any material that could be found: bits of wood, twigs, barrel staves, old pipes, tin cans hammered flat.[20] In the backwash of a growing metropolis, Harlem's squatters made money by raising animals and vegetables for local markets. Geese, cows, horses and "genus goat of the Harlem species" roamed over the area. There were so many hogs in one section of One Hundred and Twenty-fifth and One Hundred and Twenty-sixth Streets that it came to be known as Pig's Alley.[21] Parts of Harlem Plains[22] were marshes, which reeked so badly that they could "knock the breath out of a mule!"[23] Harlem at midcentury was largely "a village of shanties and huts with here and there a farm house. . . ."[24] And so it remained until the pressure of urban population growth and the subsequent need for living space restored value to Harlem lands.

With the exception of the marshes, Harlem's topography maintained much of its earlier beauty. Relatively untouched for centuries, it had the physical possibilities of becoming the country retreat of a burgeoning metropolis: "Everything that is lovely and much that is grand are assembled in a moderate space. Hill and dale, stream and wood, rock and meadow . . . river views . . . of surpassing magnificence," a historian noted in the 1890's. "The walks through the woodland shade . . . are always charming. . . . The clear brooks, the yellow leaves of autumn, the birds . . . lead one to forget the city and all its toils. . . . "[25]

Of a Sunday, from the 1860's on, the residents of Harlem shanties would find "downtowners" wandering about on country jaunts. They could walk to Harlem Lane (St. Nicholas Avenue) and watch men of the "exclusive class," "the horse-racing fraternity," "swells"—Commodore Vanderbilt was probably the most prominent—working out their "fast trotters": "Any fine afternoon you could see the wealthy horse-fanciers driving their . . . sulkies through Central Park on their way to 'the road' as they called Harlem Lane."[26] After a day in the country these "fashionable people" might stop at Toppy McGuire's Clubhouse or sip wine at the intriguing Brossi's Tunnel, bored out of rock at One Hundred and Twenty-second Street. "Harlem had become the rural retreat of the aristocratic New Yorker," an old Manhattanite recalled, and its "chief charm [was] its well-bred seclusion. . . ."[27]

In the late nineteenth century, this remoteness from city life served as the one great barrier to Harlem's development as a residential community. Harlem was approximately eight miles from City Hall and, under no great urgency to be otherwise, its transportation facilities remained rudimentary. The New York and Harlem Railroad ran trains from lower Manhattan to Harlem after 1837.[28] Horsecars started opposite City Hall and stopped at Forty-second Street. At this junction the horses were replaced by a locomotive and the train went directly to One Hundred and Twenty-ninth Street. The entire trip, scheduled to take forty minutes,[29] often took much longer. Young boys ran alongside the tracks and jeered:

> The Harlem Road is a smashing line,
> It starts at four and stops at nine,
> And if you want to go to town,
> The quickest way is to foot it down.[30]

There were other means of transportation to the city. Stage lines on the east and west sides operated after the 1830's as well ("Murphy's Economical Accommodation Line" was one), but they were even less reliable than the Harlem Railroad. Under ideal conditions they took an hour and forty minutes to the city but in the winter often bogged down in the snow.[31] After 1856 the picturesque steamboats of Sylvan Line, remembered with great fondness by Harlem's older residents, made the trip to Manhattan in thirty minutes, but closed during the winter months as ice clogged the East River.[32] Such a transportation system obviously did little to encourage settlement in Harlem.

III

The phenomenal growth of Harlem in the late nineteenth century was a by-product of the general development of New York City. From the 1870's on, the foundations of the modern metropolis were laid. This urban revolution was characterized by improvements in methods of sanitation, water supply, transportation, communication, lighting and building.[33] As the city expanded, so did its population. In 1880, for the first time in its history, and in the history of any American city, the population of Manhattan alone passed the one million mark (1,164,673),[34] and "New Immigrants" had just begun to arrive. This increase in population coincided with an expansion of commercial and industrial activity and both made serious inundations on living quarters in formerly staid residential sections. The only way for the island city to grow was northward. Many older residents and older immigrants, attempting to avoid the bustle of the new metropolis and escape contact with its newest settlers, looked to Harlem as the community of the future: "In our family, we were always careful to explain that we lived in Harlem, not in New York City," a man whose family moved uptown in these years recalled. "It was our way of avoiding contact with such uncouth citizens as might be found downtown. . . ."[35] The neighborhood would become "the choicest residential section of the city," predicted another resident. "Upper Seventh Avenue in Harlem has become one of the finest streets in New York. . . . Rows of trees and pretty gardens . . . lend to it a semi-suburban aspect."[36]

Harlem expanded gradually in the 1860's and was annexed to New York City in 1873.[37] The city filled some 1,350 acres of marshland in 1870, sold them to the public, and constructed houses over them. A few city fathers in the heyday of the Tweed Ring appropriated promising lands for themselves and built fashionable homes there.[38] The turning point in Harlem's history came in 1878–1881. During these years three lines of the elevated railroad came as far north as One Hundred and Twenty-ninth Street and, by 1886, the elevated line came even further north.[39] Rows of brownstones and exclusive apartment houses appeared overnight: "Business grows, blocks and flats go up with apparently so little effort, that the average Harlemite is in a continuous swim of development and prosperity," the local newspaper commented in 1890.[40] Practically all the houses that stand in Harlem today were built in a long spurt of energy that lasted from the 1870's through the first decade of the twentieth century. Electric lights were first installed in 1887 and the telephone followed the next year.[41] Shanties, doomed by "the wilderness of brownstone, brick and mortar . . . ,"[42] took with them Harlem's celebrated goat, the subject of much newspaper lampooning. An irate "Harlem Goat" begged the *New York Herald* to leave it in peace: "I feel as if my browsing days in Harlem are over, and I can hardly find a . . . blade of fresh grass. . . ."[43] "No more goats in Harlem/There's prosperity in Harlem," sang the Harlem Board of Commerce at a neighborhood fete. "When Harlem was a Prairie," echoed the motto of the Harlem Old-Timers Association.[44] An Irish resident of the community since the 1840's saw a "one horse town . . . turned into a teeming metropolis. . . ."[45]

Speculators made fortunes buying Harlem land, holding it for a short while, and reselling at great profit. Builders purchased land, constructed houses and sold them as soon as they were completed. They used the profits for reinvestment. Oscar Hammerstein I, Henry Morgenthau, and August Belmont were among them. "Hammerstein bought and sold properties in that area with great speed and generally at a profit," his biographer wrote.[46] Edward H. W. Just, another speculator, born in Eisleben, Germany, in the 1830's, came to New York City as a young man when the ready-made clothing industry was becoming a major source of city wealth. He became a successful shirt manufacturer and invested heavily in Harlem property. When he died in 1893 he left an estate worth more than $2,000,000.[47] One plot of land purchased in 1852 for $3,000 was worth $200,000 in 1890.[48] "When I see the prices that real estate is now bringing in Harlem," one old-timer bemoaned in 1889, "it makes me feel that I was a fool for not making . . . investments years ago when property was so cheap. Twenty years [ago] the meadow lands of Harlem were not considered worth paying taxes for. . . ."[49]

IV

If this man thought himself a fool, those who previously abandoned or sold their Harlem property felt cheated: "The country town grew, until this . . . almost valueless land has become worth millions." Descendants of Harlem settlers, some tracing their rights to the earliest seventeenth-century grants, now attempted to reclaim what they maintained was still their property. The first man to do so, Alfred E.

Tilton, gathered his old land titles and brought suit against the city in the 1870's, but he died in 1876 before any settlement was made. His idea, however, was exploited for more than a generation as the heirs of other settlers organized and tried to do in grand style what Tilton attempted to do as an individual. The movement to reclaim Harlem lands had all the overtones of a great land grab: "the Great Harlem Land Claim," newspapers called it.[50]

In 1883, the Harlem Commons Syndicate was organized and incorporated. Descendants of earlier residents, sought throughout the country, were made shareholders, for a price, in the great scheme. General John C. Frémont, a Harlem heir himself, became president of the corporation. Schuyler Colfax, former Vice-President of the United States, was a claimant. Every available scrap of information—genealogical data, wills, letters—was gathered to prove that descendants still held valid rights in the old commons land and in the recently filled marshes. The Syndicate pressured for congressional intervention and brought suit against New York City, but all efforts proved unsuccessful. The corporation finally collapsed in 1895.

The fortune-hunting temptation outlived the Harlem Commons Syndicate in the Harlem Associated Heirs Title Company, founded immediately after the demise of the Syndicate, in another group active at the turn of the century and still another as late as 1932.[51] Each, of course, sold shares to Harlem heirs. Genealogical information collected by researchers went for a price—$10 to $15. Stock was sold to some 1,400 persons. Two claimants of a family sued each other over contested rights to property neither legally owned. Provisions in old leases and sales were carefully checked for possible discrepancies, and many were supposedly uncovered. Books were written to show these claims valid and one man even tried to demonstrate by scripture that the cause was a righteous one: that "divine direction constituted the sole motive for the recovery of . . . Harlem rights and properties. . . ." Terrestrial forces, however, proved obdurate in their refusal to share Harlem's new-found prosperity, and these efforts were as unsuccessful (for all save the promoters, perhaps) as those of the Harlem Commons Syndicate.[52]

V

People generally took it for granted that Harlem would develop into an exclusive, stable, upper- and upper-middle-class community: "a neighborhood very genteel." The newly built elevator apartment houses, many equipped with servants' quarters, rented for prices that could be paid only by the wealthy. The most magnificent was a group of spacious, luxurious brownstones built on One Hundred and Thirty-eighth and One Hundred and Thirty-ninth Streets in 1891. Stanford White, the well-known architect so closely associated with the architectural history of the city (he designed Madison Square Garden, Washington Arch, Grand Central Station), had been commissioned to build one hundred and six distinguished homes, each with ten to sixteen rooms and flower-bedecked driveways. They were advertised to be as "distinctive as a suburban colony but with all the advantages of city life": "These driveways are ornamented at their intersections by circular beds of flowers, making a decorative feature even of their utility. Great care is taken of the property to preserve its exclusive appearance, and a general air of being well-looked-after pervades the surroundings." Houses set back twelve feet from the street added privacy and rear entrances "permitted the business of housekeeping to be kept out of sight." In a society whose working-class families paid an average of $10–18 a month rent, the rents for these homes *started* at just under $80, and ranged between $900 and $1700 a year.[53]

Another group of twenty-eight three-story exclusive homes, Astor Row, constructed in the 1890's on West One Hundred and Thirtieth Street, provided large porches and shade trees. They were known "as one of the most attractive and exclusive home centres" in Harlem, and "presented a picture of domestic tranquility and comfort which few other . . . blocks in the city possess," a *New York Times* reporter noted. In spite of high rentals Astor Row had a long waiting list of prospective tenants.[54]

Prosperity and optimism seemed the order of the day. One merchant built a large department store on One Hundred and Twenty-fifth Street in 1890 and had such confidence in Harlem's future that he offered to pay half the rent for five years of any businessman who followed him.[55] Local citizens could attend the Harlem Opera House, built by Oscar Hammerstein I in 1889, or go to one of Harlem's many theaters.[56] In 1900 they might dine at the luxurious German Pabst Harlem: "Where Gentlemen and Ladies can enjoy good music and a perfect cuisine amid surroundings which have been rendered as attractive to the eye and senses [as] good taste, combined with expenditure, could make them."[57]

The people attracted to this "residential heaven" were obviously older and wealthier New Yorkers—"people of taste and wealth."[58] Few neighborhoods in the entire city at the turn of the century had so disproportionate a number of native Americans or immigrants from Great Britain, Ireland and Germany, including German Jews, living in it. In 1902, of the 103,570 families in the Twelfth Ward, only 10,786 could be classified as "New Immigrants."[59] Many late-nineteenth-century Harlemites were born in downtown Manhattan or immigrated to America in the years 1830–1850, and subsequently moved to the community after 1870.[60] One man came to visit a friend in Harlem in 1889 and was surprised "to see so many downtowners who have come here to live. It looks as if everybody will be rushing up here from downtown before long," he said.[61] A future director of the Harlem Board of Commerce moved to the neighborhood in the 1880's and was surprised to meet so many Greenwich Village friends there.[62] The homes of municipal and federal judges, mayors, local politicos (including Tammany boss Richard Croker), prominent businessmen and state politicians (Chauncey M. Depew, for example), were scattered throughout Harlem.[63] Their children attended Grammar School 68, "referred to as the 'Silk Stocking School' of the City" because its "pupils were practically all from American families, and . . . more or less prosperous people."[64] Their daughters could go to "Mme. De Valencia's Protestant French and English Institute for Young Ladies," one of the many private schools for the wealthy that flourished in the nineteenth-century city.[65] A young Jewish boy moved to Harlem from the Lower East Side in the first decade of the twentieth century and recalled seeing rich German Jews, "Uptown Jews," strutting down Seventh Avenue in top hats, black coats and canes.[66]

Among the institutions developed to service Harlem's newest residents was Calvary Methodist Episcopal Church, organized in 1883 with forty members, but ten years later the congregation worshiped in a magnificent Gothic structure. Its membership had increased to over a thousand and two missions were in the process of being established.[67] Nor was this a unique story. New churches proliferated in Harlem in these years. Between 1870 and 1894, for example, six

Presbyterian churches were founded there.[68] Harlem had a First
German Baptist Church, a Temple Israel of Harlem, and a St.
Charles Borromeo Roman Catholic Church, to mention just a few.[69]
There were German *Turnvereins,* cafés and choirs, German-Jewish
fraternal societies, a Harlem Catholic Club, the elite Harlem Club
(initiation fee $100), a Harlem Yacht Club, a Harlem Literary So-
ciety, active local Democratic and Republican clubs, a branch of the
YMCA, a Harlem Philharmonic Orchestra, and even Harlem orders
of the Daughters of the Revolution and Loyal Women of American
Liberty: created "to defend our free institutions."[70] The Twelfth
Ward Savings Bank, founded in 1889, moved to larger quarters three
times by 1896.[71] Harlem supported a monthly literary magazine, a
weekly magazine of Harlem doings, and bi-weekly newspaper.[72] It
was a vital, ever-growing, genteel community of great promise whose
future seemed boundless.[73]

To the generation that remembered only this Harlem, those who
had never known the Harlem of squatters, shanties and mud flats
(and would little understand the causes for its future changes), its
memory remained warm and bright. It was a neighborhood "old-
timers have cherished," a resident wrote years later. Few could dis-
agree with the editor of *The Harlem Monthly Magazine* who saw
Harlem developing as a "district . . . distinctly devoted to the man-
sions of the wealthy, the homes of the well-to-do, and the places of
business of the tradespeople who minister their wants. . . ."[74] "We
have no adequate idea of . . . the greatness that lies in store for
Harlem," another thought in 1890.[75]

CHAPTER 6

The Other Harlem:
Roots of Instability

"Foreigners are crowding up the whole
length of the island."
—*The Harlem Local Reporter*, 1893

"The existing speculation in flats and
tenements surpasses . . . anything of the
kind which has previously taken place
in the real estate history of the city."
—*Real Estate Record and Builders' Guide*, 1904

I

Within the general prosperity and optimism characteristic of the Harlem community in 1890 a few sources of possible instability could be noted. Much of the neighborhood was rebuilt in the 1870's and 1880's but some sections along the waterfront and others inaccessible to transportation remained undeveloped. One Hundred and Thirty-eighth to One Hundred and Forty-eighth Streets west of Eighth Avenue was unfilled marshland, known locally as "Canary Island." A gang of youths who lived nearby called themselves the "Canary Island Gang," and guarded their territory like an armed brigade when Negroes began moving into the Canary Island neighborhood in the early twentieth century. "The Irish boys on Eighth Avenue wouldn't let the other races come on Eighth Avenue at all," an early Negro resident recalled. "Up here . . . we had the Canary Island gang. . . ."[1]

Other low and marshy sections of what were then the fringes of the community served as garbage dumps, one on West One Hundred and Forty-first Street between Fifth and Lenox Avenues and another at West One Hundred and Twenty-ninth Street. In the early 1890's it was generally believed that apartment houses would be constructed on these grounds in the near future, and that the garbage piled ten to twelve feet high would act as filler and save future work.[2] Residents of the neighborhood complained to municipal officials about these health hazards, spawning grounds for all kinds of disease. One prominent local businessman admonished the city fathers for failing to clean up the dumps: "You must remember, gentlemen," he protested, "that Harlem is no longer a country village."[3] "Fill in the Flats," a local newspaper said in an editorial.[4]

When the flats were filled in the late 1890's, they helped initiate another wave of land and property speculation in Harlem. In the aftermath of the collapse of this second speculative mania, during the first decade of the twentieth century, Negroes moved to Harlem in considerable numbers.

II

Near the less attractive areas of Harlem, on the periphery of the middle-class community, lived people by-passed by Harlem's late-nineteenth-century affluence. Italian immigrants crowded in "common tenements"[5] from One Hundred and Tenth to One Hundred and Twenty-fifth Streets, east of Third Avenue to the river. This section, the future bailiwick of La Guardia and Marcantonio, was "as thoroughly Italian as Rome, Naples, Palermo or Messina," a journalist noted. In the 1890's the poverty of "Harlem's Little Italy" seemed a glaring incongruity in a neighborhood known as the home of "the great middle-class population, the very cream of our citizenship."[6] Italians were the first New Immigrant group to come to Harlem and a source of embarrassment and displeasure to the richer people who lived nearby. The smells that emanated from their "vile tenements," one critic said in 1894, "annoyed their brownstone neighbors."[7]

The "Italian Colony" appeared like a "Foreign Village" to one man. Inquisitive Harlemites would stroll across town on religious holidays and feast days to gaze at the strange doings. They could see a marionette show or men grinding their street organs: the "boxes full of music that come around on four wheels everyday."[8] Pushcart peddlers hawking their wares upset the quiet demeanor of the neighborhood and a campaign was waged by local businessmen and street cleaners to keep them off the streets. In 1891 the city opened an area along the East River for use as a produce market: "Adieu! Peddlers Forever!"[9] The poorest of the poor groveled for leftover food in garbage dumps and trash cans: "Here can be found the refuse of Italy making a poor living on the refuse from Harlem ashbarrels," a caustic reporter commented.[10]

Those who lived through the transition of Harlem to a Negro ghetto tended to forget that substantial numbers of Negroes were also scattered throughout the neighborhood in the late nineteenth century. It seemed to many that Negroes came to Harlem suddenly in the twentieth century; older white residents never really understood the nature of the change that reshaped their entire community.[11] In reality, the Negro sections of Harlem predated those of its late-nineteenth-century residents. The first Negroes to live and work in Harlem were slaves and references to them are found in seventeenth-century documents. The original wagon road constructed between New Amsterdam and Harlem was built by the "Dutch West India Company's Negroes."[12] Slaves worked on farms and estates in Harlem in the seventeenth and eighteenth centuries and colonial Harlem even had its own "Negro Burying Ground." One local farmer bequeathed his slaves to his children in 1752.[13] The New York Census of 1790 listed 115 slaves for the "Harlem Division," just under one-third of its total population.[14]

With freedom Negroes continued to live in the general area. A white Methodist church in Harlem had some Negro communicants in 1832,[15] and Negro squatters and farmers settled in the community at the time Irish immigrants came in the 1840's and 1850's.[16] Harlem African Methodist Episcopal Zion Church ("Little Zion") was constructed as a mission to Harlem's Negroes by the downtown "Mother Zion" Church. In 1843 its sixty-six members worshiped in a small brick building on East One Hundred and Seventeenth Street. "Little Zion," a center of Negro life in Harlem throughout the nineteenth century, became an independent church in the twentieth.[17] There was a branch of Bethel African Methodist Episcopal Zion Church in Harlem in the 1840's,[18] and a Negro public school there in the 1850's.[19] Draft Rioters tramped through Harlem in 1863 destroying Negro cottages in their rage: "Many of them went through 125th Street carrying clubs toward the east side where they burned almost an entire block at 130th Street and the Harlem River," a white resident remembered.[20]

Harlem's small Negro community gradually increased in size in the late nineteenth century as colored servants worked in homes of the wealthy who moved into the neighborhood. One family paid for the passage of a Negro woman from Virginia in 1875 ("a genuine Virginia darkey," they recalled),[21] and later brought her daughter to Harlem also. Occasional advertisements for jobs by Negroes appeared in local periodicals: "Colored woman wants family washing."[22] William H. Butler, a Negro musician, offered lessons to the public.[23] A Harlem tenement house, "Hooker's Building," which had once been occupied by Irish refugees of the Famine, "fell an easy prey to the negro" in the 1890's, a white Harlemite recalled.[24] Salem Church, a mission of St. Mark's Methodist Episcopal Church, was founded in a Harlem store at the turn of the century.[25] Other Methodist and Baptist storefront missions "up in Harlem [were] doing much-needed work for colored servants" in 1900, the *New York Sun* observed.[26]

In fact, a substantial Negro population lived in Harlem at the turn of the twentieth century. Though much smaller but more disparate than the Negro sections in the Tenderloin and San Juan Hill, it included occasional Negro blocks distributed throughout Harlem: "they are found clear across the city from river to river," a Columbia University student wrote in 1898.[27]

In the 1880's and 1890's Negroes lived on East One Hundred and Twenty-second, One Hundred and Twenty-fourth and One Hundred and Twenty-sixth Streets, and on West One Hundred and Twenty-fourth, One Hundred and Twenty-fifth, One Hundred and Twenty-sixth and One Hundred and Thirty-fourth Streets.[28] There were two Negro apartment houses, the Garrison and the Sumner, of One Hundred and Twenty-fifth Street and Broadway in 1890.[29] West One Hundred and Forty-sixth Street had "a large colony of the poorest colored people" in the 1890's, and was popularly known by the choice epithet "Nigger Row."[30] The "Negro tenements" on West One Hundred and Thirtieth Street were called Harlem's "Darktown."[31] Colored Knights of Pythias had a lodge in Harlem, Negro churches used the Harlem and East Rivers for baptisms, public outings were held in Sulzer's Harlem Park.[32] In 1891 a Negro political organization conducted public meetings in a Harlem assembly hall.[33] "Colored Tenants Preferred," "The Neatest Apartments in Harlem," "Desirable Properties for Colored People," and similar signs appeared on tenements in Harlem in the 1890's.[34] In 1902 the New York City Tenement House Commission made a block-by-block sur-

Woods and meadows, Harlem Plains, 1812; lithograph by G. Hayward for *D. T. Valentine's Manual,* 1856 *(Brown Brothers)*

Boating on the Harlem River, around 1900 *(Brown Brothers)*

On the way to the Harlem Speedway, around 1905-1910 (*Brown Brothers*)

The WATT ESTATE—An Entire City Block
From Lenox to Seventh Avenues, 139th to 140th Streets

THE PINCKNEY HOMESTEAD

A Natural Playground Site in the Heart of Harlem

Endorsed by City Officials, The Harlem Board of Commerce, The Boys' and Girls' "Get-What-You-Want" Club and others, as one of Harlem's most needed public improvements.

¶ If you want the City to acquire this property for a play ground, *NOW* is the time to act.—Write to the Mayor, Presidents of the Borough and Board of Alderman, how badly you need this play-ground for your children.

The eighteenth-century Watt Mansion, which was later a cafeteria, The Lybia, and finally torn down (*"Harlem Magazine," October 1913*)

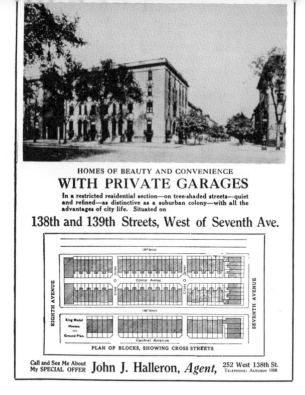

"Restricted" residential area in "quiet and refined" section, central Harlem, 1917, advertisement in the organ of the white Harlem Board of Commerce (*"Harlem Magazine," April 1917*)

Harlem Board of Commerce dinner, 1913 (note "Boost Harlem" sign), at Pabst Harlem Restaurant, which by 1920 was a Kress 5 & 10 cents store (*"Harlem Magazine," February 1913*)

"United we stand, divided we are at the mercy of the 'clever buyer' " —white Harlem, 1914 ("*Harlem Magazine,*" October 1914)

Anti-Litter League, part of the campaign for "desirable" citizens ("*Harlem Magazine,*" April 1917)

A CAMPAIGN FOR A CLEANER HARLEM

The Anti-Litter League, with Co-Operation of the Harlem Board of Commerce, Seeks Block Captains to Assist in Educating Public to Keep the Streets, Sidewalks and Parks Free of Rubbish and Litter

With the aid of the Harlem Board of Commerce and several other organizations in Harlem the Anti-Litter League proposes to preach the gospel of cleanliness to the residents of Harlem from now on. The gospel is a very easy one for them to live up to, and the co-operation of the Harlem Board of Commerce eventually hopes to bring about better street conditions as regards cleanliness.

The aim of the Anti-Litter League, of which Mr. Clarkson Cowl is founder and Mr. John C. Eames is president, and Mr. Robert J. Kennedy, secretary, is to raise an army of "block captains" in Harlem among the boys and girls attending the parochial and public schools and adults as well, whose duty it will be to point out to all they see throwing newspapers, burnt matches, cigar and cigarette stubs, discarded envelopes and a thousand and one other varieties of litter on the sidewalks, roadways and parks that they are violating the city ordinances and can be sent to prison or fined. The "block captain" will also point out that it is wrong to sweep refuse from the sidewalk to the roadway. Section 53 of the Sanitary Code permits the sweeping of the sidewalk between the hours of six and eight A. M. each day. The fault with a great many residents of Harlem is that they sweep their sidewalks at any time they feel like doing so, and rather than gather up their filth and place it into a receptacle they sweep it into the roadway where it is blown around, the result being that Street Cleaning Department is not on the job.

At a recent conference and luncheon held under the auspices of the Anti-Litter League the Harlem Board of Commerce and other organizations were represented, the Board of Commerce being represented by Mr. John A. Wilbur, secretary; Mr. Charles

A Block Captain's Warning

H. Fuller and Mr. Edward W. Forrest. Mr. Wilbur when called upon by Mr. Eames said that he would do all in his power to aid the work of the Anti-Litter League and would bring the matter up at the next meeting of the Harlem Board of Commerce.

What the Anti-Litter League wants everyone to do is a very simple matter. It simply requests that the residents of Harlem do all in their power to prevent the littering of the sidewalks, roadways and parks. No one in Harlem would like to have his front walk, or his porch, or his parlor messed up with newspapers, fruit peelings, burnt matches, cigar and cigarette stubs, discarded envelopes and a thousand and one other varieties of litter. Any person who would do this would be regarded as a very undesirable guest, and looked at from the standpoint of the community at large he is not a desirable citizen.

The aim of the Anti-Litter League is to make every citizen in Harlem as jealous of the orderly and tidy appearance of Harlem streets, sidewalks and public places as they would be of their own lawns and yards, their sidewalks and even their own living rooms. A roadway may be swept out each day. It may be thoroughly cleaned at frequent intervals; but it will not remain neat or tidy for any length of time if pedestrians habitually use the sidewalks, roadways and lawns as they would garbage receptacles for material they have no longer any use for.

The Anti-Litter League can be useful in a great many ways in the cause of public safety. Piles of all kinds contribute more accidental deaths and injuries than any other single type of mishap. A great many falls are occasioned by slipping. Fruit peelings under any conditions, cigar or cigarette stubs or bits of paper on a day are fertile causes of dangerous accidents, and the Anti-Litter League is, therefore, a co-worker in the great cause of public safety.

Anyone in Harlem can become a "block captain." There is no fee charged. Anyone who volunteers to become a "block captain" is doing a patriotic service. Everyone interested in the block in which he lives, and he pledges himself to refrain from throwing waste materials of every nature on sidewalks, streets, avenues, and other public places premises, to call the attention of offenders to the laws against throwing or sweeping rubbish upon streets and highways.

125th Street, Harlem's principal thoroughfare, side streets avenues and the parks of Harlem are in a badly littered condition and no criticism can be directed at Commissioner Fetherston of the Street Cleaning Department for he is doing all he possibly can to keep Harlem streets clean.

It is entirely up to the residents of Harlem themselves. If they want clean streets they had but to refrain from making them so. Cleanliness costs nothing.

Homes of Negroes who had moved north from Greenwich Village to San Juan Hill district, the West 60's, midway to Harlem (*Brown Brothers*)

Opposite: "For Respectable Colored Families Only," Harlem street scene, around 1915–1920 (*Brown Brothers*)

Afro-American Realty Company

OF THE

THE Afro-American Realty Company recently incorporated under the laws of the State of New York for $500,000 to operate in New York City Real Estate, had its origin in ten men, who over a year ago, joined themselves together, into co-partnership for the above mentioned purpose. They began by taking five year leases on flat houses and renting them to people of their own race. The success that met their efforts by far exceeded the expectation of the most optimistic of the co-partnership. In less than six months they were in control of ten flat houses, with an earning capacity of over $5,000 per annum.

Prejudice of White Owner and Agent Cause of Present Condition.

The reason for the present condition of the colored tenancy in New York City to-day, is because of the race prejudice of the white owner and his white agent. When the owner becomes colored and his agent colored, then there is compelled to come an improvement of the condition.

Race Prejudice Turned into Dollars and Cents.

Race prejudice is a luxury and like all other luxuries, can be made very expensive in New York City, if the Negroes will but answer this call of the Afro-American Realty Company. With a cash capital of $500,000, the Afro-American Realty Company can turn race prejudice into dollars and cents. The very prejudice which has heretofore worked against us can be turned and used to our profit.

From the prospectus for Afro-American Realty Company, 1904 (bankrupt in 1908), organized by Negro realtor Philip A. Payton, Jr., known as the "Father of Colored Harlem"

Successor to the ill-fated Afro-American Realty Company seeking "desirable tenants" through the NAACP magazine (*"The Crisis,"* January 1911)

Harlem family, around 1915 (*Brown Brothers*)

Shack at Fifth Avenue and 140th Street, 1927 (*United Press International photo*)

"Striver's Row," spacious brownstones at 139th Street, designed in 1891 by Stanford White (*photo by Roy DeCarava*)

Paul Laurence Dunbar Apartments, at 150th and 151st Streets, between Seventh and Eighth Avenues, built by Rockefeller in the 1920's for middle-class Negroes, sold by Rockefeller in 1937 (*The Schomburg Collection, New York Public Library*)

vey of Manhattan's population. Its records present an exact description of the *distribution* of Harlem's Negro population at the turn of the century.

DISTRIBUTION OF NEGRO FAMILIES IN THE TWELFTH WARD, 1902[35]

Families	Streets	Avenues
50	88th and 89th	2nd and 3rd
24	94th and 95th	2nd and 3rd
77	96th and 97th	2nd and 3rd
50	97th and 98th	Lexington and 4th
72	97th and 98th	3rd and Lexington
19	97th and 98th	2nd and 3rd
40	99th and 100th	3rd and Lexington
15	99th and 100th	2nd and 3rd
11	102nd and 103rd	2nd and 3rd
29	103rd and 104th	2nd and 3rd
17	114th and 115th	Madison and 5th
11	121st and 122nd	1st and 2nd
46	122nd and 123rd	1st and 2nd
13	123rd and 124th	7th and 8th
16	123rd and 124th	Pleasant and 1st
51	124th and 125th	7th and 8th
56	124th and 125th	Pleasant and 1st
16	125th and 126th	Amsterdam and Broadway
28	125th and 126th	Columbus and Amsterdam
27	125th and 126th	8th and Columbus
16	126th and 127th	Columbus and Amsterdam
46	126th and 127th	2nd and 3rd
14	127th and 128th	2nd and 3rd
12	130th and 131st	Broadway and West to River
39	133rd and 134th	Lenox and 7th
30	133rd and 134th	5th and Lenox
74	134th and 135th	Lenox and 7th
101	134th and 135th	5th and Lenox
48	135th and 136th	5th and Lenox
56	146th and 147th	7th and 8th
23	147th and 148th	8th and Bradhurst

III

The Negro and Italian sections of Harlem seemed, when thought of at all, curiosities, sources of minor annoyance or objects of charity to the typical Harlemite of the 1880's and 1890's. Women's clubs and religious organizations offered varieties of assistance to the poor of these neighborhoods. A young Negro educator from the South, known even then as a level-headed fellow, visited the Lenox Avenue Unitarian Church in 1893. He gave a lecture and appealed to Harlem's "substantial citizenry" to raise money for his small school in Alabama, and undoubtedly left the community with a sizable contribution.[36] He was Booker T. Washington.

The Republican Ladies Auxiliary of Harlem gave lessons in American democracy and voting to residents of the "Italian Quarter." (It was reported they taught immigrants to make the "X" next to the Republican column.)[37] In the Depression of 1893, the Harlem Relief Society, composed of volunteer workers from the local branch of the Charity Organization Society, was founded. The Society distributed food, clothing and fuel to the poor in the winter of 1893. (Winters in the city were always harshest for the poverty-stricken who lived in cold-water flats.)[38] In response to widespread economic distress churches in the neighborhood took up collections for the needy.[39] A Society for Befriending the Poor Catholic Children of Harlem was organized.[40] Tammany politicians opened "People's Restaurants" to offer decent five-cent meals to the hungry.[41] (Make the "X" next to the Democratic column.) With the growth of the Negro population of Harlem, the Relief Society boosted its work among colored people and eventually hired a Negro nurse and social worker to visit their homes. "No white person can quite understand the underlying thoughts and actions of this race," the Society said in explaining its reasons for hiring a Negro assistant. "Our work among Negroes increases year by year."[42]

The concern of Harlemites for the lower classes, Negro or white, was not always charitable. Newspapers mocked what they considered the peculiar social and religious lives of Negroes and Italians. *The Harlem Local Reporter,* typical of its age, made light of the "colored pussons" who attended the wedding of a Negro janitor, spoofed the Negro "ristocrats" who danced the Cake Walk (a cake or pie was given to the winning couple).[43] Harlemites who laughed at *A Trip to Coontown* and *In Old Kentucky* made them highly successful vaudeville shows.[44] Italian immigrants seemed to some knife-wielding members of the Mafia. Articles described "Harlem's Bowery Sights."[45] No one suspected that these minority groups and others who settled in Harlem in the early twentieth century would eventually become a serious threat to the stability of the community.

IV

Harlem life altered radically in the first decade of the twentieth century. The construction of new subway routes into the neighborhood in the late 1890's set off a second wave of speculation in Harlem land and property. Speculators who intended to make astronomic profits when the subway was completed bought the marshes, garbage dumps and lots left unimproved or undeveloped in the 1870's and 1880's. Between 1898 and 1904, the year that the Lenox Avenue line opened at One Hundred and Forty-fifth Street, "practically all the vacant land in Harlem" was "built over," the *Real Estate Record and Builders' Guide* noted in 1904. "The growth of . . . Harlem . . . has been truly astonishing during the last half dozen years."[46]

The real estate boom created a wave of new building activity in Harlem dominated primarily by speculators, although some individuals made long-term investments. It was taken as business gospel that investments would be doubled and trebled after the completion of the "tunnel road." "Even a 5-story single flat in Harlem would net . . . at the end of . . . three to five years . . . at the utmost . . . a very handsome unearned increment," a realtor concluded. "It would be impossible to err."[47] Another supposed expert in urban real estate maintained that no "other class of public improvements had such a great, immediate and permanent effect upon land values as rapid transit lines. . . ."[48]

Speculation in Manhattan land along the routes of new transportation facilities originally occurred when charters were granted to horsecar companies in the early nineteenth century.[49] Trafficking in city lots throughout urban America proved often more lucrative than speculation on the western frontier. At the turn of the century the "grey wolves" who dominated so many other urban commercial and industrial enterprises in the Gilded Age controlled New York City's building industry: "expert professional operators [who raised] amounts of money varying between a few thousand and many million dollars. They . . . eagerly scan . . . New York real estate values, and . . . make a rush for any section in which they see possibilities of profit."[50] The Equitable and Metropolitan Life insurance companies invested heavily in Harlem land. "The existing speculation in flats and tenements," an observer wrote at the turn of the century, "surpasses . . . anything of the kind which has previously taken place in the real estate history of the city."[51]

This real estate fever "seized upon [the Jewish] Ghettos of Greater New York" too. Offices were set up in people's homes, investments were discussed in Lower East Side restaurants, as workers with modest savings conceived themselves as budding realtors. Abraham Cahan, the well-known Jewish newspaper editor and novelist, graphically described the "boom atmosphere" which even pervaded the immigrant ghettos of the city: "Small tradesmen of the slums, and even working-men, were investing their savings in houses and lots. Jewish carpenters, house-painters, bricklayers, or instalment peddlers became builders of tenements or frame dwellings, real-estate speculators. Deals were being closed and poor men were making thousands of dollars in less time than it took to drink a glass of tea or the plate of sorrel soup over which the transaction took place. Women, too, were ardently dabbling in real estate. . . ."[52]

In the section of Harlem north of Central Park to One Hundred and Twenty-fifth Street, and west of Lexington Avenue to Seventh Avenue, new tenements and apartment houses went up in the late 1890's. These properties seemed to offer "good profit on investments," as East European Jews spilled out of the Lower East Side in search of better homes[53]—part of the migration to lower Harlem and other boroughs that reflected their economic mobility. The disintegration of the Jewish sections on the Lower East Side that began in the first decade of the twentieth century continued for thirty years. As Russian and Polish Jews replaced German Jews in the garment industry in these years, they now began to encroach on the residential center of "Uptown Jewry." To live in lower Harlem became a symbol of good times to many East European Jews. Some families who moved into the neighborhood, one contemporary recorded, "speak apologetically and at times are actually embarrassed when their former residence in the lower parts of the city is mentioned." The newspapers called this section of Harlem "Little Russia."[54]

The University Settlement, founded on the Lower East Side, followed its people to Harlem. An "Experimental School in Harlem" established in 1902[55] became the "Harlem Guild of the University Settlement" in 1903.[56] Maurice H. Harris, a social worker, started another settlement on East One Hundred and Fifth Street in 1906. "It is from the inspiration . . . I obtained from your Settlement that I have been enabled to start a humble venture of my own," he wrote his mentor Lillian D. Wald.[57] Jewish synagogues bought property in the neighborhood: "Calvary Presbyterian Church is now one of the prettiest little Jewish synagogues in . . . New York."[58] A variety of social institutions arose: the Harlem Home of the Daughters of Israel, Harlem Hebrew School, Harlem Hebrew Educational Institute, Harlem Hebrew Retail Grocers' Association, and so on. Local libraries began to acquire books of Jewish history and Yiddish literature for their newest readers.[59]

Older residents objected to the "migration of the better class of East Side Jews into the district north and east of the Park, then the new quarter of the most prosperous Russian Jews,"[60] in terms similar to those previously reserved for Italian immigrants and Negroes. "Foreigners are crowding up the whole length of the island," the *Harlem Local Reporter* said in an editorial.[61] Elmer Rice and his family, like many of their Harlem neighbors, moved away from One Hundred and Sixth Street in 1903 because the "neighborhood had been growing less 'refined'. . . ."[62] The sometimes bitter response of German Harlemites to the settlement of East European Jews in their community was symbolized by a to-let sign which hung on one building: *Keine Juden, und keine Hunde.* [No Jews, No Dogs.][63]

V

More luxurious apartment houses were built around 1900 in West Harlem, along Seventh and Lenox Avenues in the One Hundred and Thirties and One Hundred and Forties, the first section of the neighborhood to become Negro Harlem. Contemporaries called these blocks "the best of Harlem." This section of the community suffered most from inaccessibility in the 1880's and 1890's,[64] and hardly an edition of the local newspaper in the 1890's failed to demand improved transportation facilities there. To contemporaries this "old, old story of rapid transit" would make Harlem "even more popular than it is as a place of residence. . . ."[65]

Speculation in these properties was probably more widespread and involved larger expenditures than realty manipulations in other sections of Harlem or the city. Two brothers, John D. and Thomas F. Crimmins, for example, bought the entire blocks of One Hundred and Forty-fourth and One Hundred and Forty-fifth Streets between Lenox and Seventh Avenues in 1895, thinking the "Lenox Avenue electric car" would "greatly enhance the value of the property."[66] In keeping with the traditions of the neighborhood and the type of homes constructed in the 1880's, it was believed richer people who wanted "high-class flats," "costly dwellings," and who earned enough to afford them, would come to West Harlem. Many of the newly constructed buildings were equipped with elevators, maid's rooms and butler's pantries.[67] In 1899 William Waldorf Astor erected an apartment house on Seventh Avenue at a cost of $500,000.[68] Sunday real estate sections of New York City newspapers at the turn of the century bristled with full-page advertisements and pictures of the elegant homes in West Harlem.[69] The revived building activity of these years created the physical foundations for what became the most luxurious Negro ghetto in the world.

Speculation in West Harlem property led to phenomenal increases in the price of land and the cost of houses there—increases inflated out of all proportion to their real value. John M. Royall, Negro realtor, recalled that "from 1902 to 1905 real estate speculative fever seized all New York City. The great subway proposition . . . permeated the air. Real estate operators and speculators [imagined] becoming millionaires, and bought freely in the West Harlem district in and about the proposed subway stations. Men bought property on thirty and sixty day contracts, and sold their contracts . . . and made substantial profits. I have known buyers to pay $38,000 and $75,000 for tenements which showed a gross income of only $2600 and $5000 a year. On they went buying, buying. . . ." Houses continually changed hands. Each time a house was sold, Royall said, it brought a higher price. In the urge to get rich quick on Harlem property, few persons realized how artificial market values had become.[70]

The inevitable bust came in 1904–1905. Speculators sadly realized afterward that too many houses were constructed at one time. West Harlem was glutted with apartments and "excessive building . . . led to many vacancies."[71] No one knew exactly how long it would take to construct the subway and many houses built four and five years in advance of its completion remained partly unoccupied. The first of them to be inhabited by Negroes, for example, was never rented previously.[72] Rents were too high for the general population ($35–$45 per month) and precluded any great rush to West Harlem even after the subway was completed.[73] There was a widespread "overestimation of . . . rental value," a contemporary remarked. When the market broke, landlords competed with each other for

tenants by reducing rents, or offering a few months' rent-free oc-
cupancy to them. Local realtors unsuccessfully attempted to eliminate
these cutthroat practices.[74]

By 1905 financial institutions no longer made loans to Harlem
speculators and building-loan companies, and many foreclosed on
their original mortgages. The inflated prices asked for land and property in West Harlem "solemnly settled beneath a sea of depreciated
values."[75] In the aftermath of the speculative collapse, and as a
consequence of the initiative of Negro realtors, large numbers of
colored people began to settle in West Harlem.

CHAPTER 7

Race Enterprise: The Afro-American Realty Company

"The books of the Afro-American Realty Company
are now open for stock subscription. Today is
the time to buy, if you want to be numbered
among those of the race who are doing something
toward trying to solve the so-called 'Race
Problem.' "
—The Afro-American Realty Company, *Prospectus,* 1904

"In numerous conversations with you both, I have
urged that the very least the Company could do,
since it has ceased to do business, is to make . . .
an Explicit statement giving the reasons which
led to . . . failure. . . ."
—Emmett J. Scott to Philip A. Payton, Jr., and Fred R. Moore, 1908

I

The individuals and companies caught in Harlem's rapidly deflated real estate market were threatened with ruin. Rather than face "financial destruction" some landlords and corporations opened their houses to Negroes and collected the traditionally high rents that colored people paid.[1] Others used the threat of renting to Negroes to frighten neighbors into buying their property at higher than market prices. Shrewder operators (contemporaries called them "clever buyers" and "white blackmailers," present-day realtors refer to them as "blockbusters") hoped to take advantage of the unusual situation by "placing colored people in property so that they might buy other parcels adjoining or in the same block [reduced in price by] fear on the part of whites to one-half of the values then obtaining," John M. Royall noted. By using these techniques "a great number" of property owners were able "to dispose of their property or . . . get a . . .

92

more lucrative return from rents paid by colored tenants," he concluded.[2]

The existence of a loosely rooted Negro population ready to settle in Harlem was primarily the result of ever-increasing Negro migration to the city. Further, the destruction of many all-Negro blocks in the Tenderloin when Pennsylvania Station was built in the first decade of the twentieth century, part of a more general commercial expansion in midtown Manhattan, dislocated the Negro population. Negro businessmen who owned property in the Tenderloin made substantial fortunes by selling and moving uptown. Negro tenants, offered decent living accommodations for the first time in the city's history, "flocked to Harlem and filled houses as fast as they were opened to them."[3]

This situation offered unusual money-making opportunities to a Negro realtor, Philip A. Payton, Jr. Payton was keenly aware of the housing needs of New York City's growing Negro population. His plan seemed foolproof, and guaranteed to satisfy Harlem's white landlords, the Negro people and himself. Payton offered to lease Harlem apartment houses from white owners and assure them a regular annual income. He, in turn, would rent these homes to Negroes and make a profit by charging rents ten per cent above the then deflated market price.[4] Many Negroes were willing to scrimp to live in beautiful apartments in an exclusive section of the city and Payton's initial operations were highly successful. His name became a respected one in Negro New York.

II

Phil Payton, as his friends called him, was born and brought up in Westfield, Massachusetts. His father, a southerner by birth, was an educated man—a graduate of Wayland Seminary in the District of Columbia. The elder Payton came north in 1872 and earned his living as a merchant and barber. His barber shop was a gathering place for the small Negro community in Westfield. In 1873, he married a Baltimore girl, and Phil was born three years later.[5]

The younger Payton's career started in similar fashion. He went south for his education and was graduated from Livingston College in Salisbury, North Carolina, in 1898. When he married and came to seek his fortune in New York in 1899 he worked at odd jobs to support himself. At first he was a handyman at six dollars a week, then a barber (a trade he learned in his father's shop), and finally a janitor in a real estate office. Payton became intrigued with the real estate business in the boom atmosphere that pervaded the housing market at the turn of the century, and also picked up a touch of the speculator's urge himself.[6] In 1900 the twenty-four-year-old Philip A. Payton, Jr., decided to go into business for himself: "Management of Colored Tenements A Specialty."[7]

At first the nascent entrepreneur was far from successful. In fact, he did so little business initially that he could not pay rent on his office and was evicted from his apartment. Payton's first break came as a result of a dispute between two landlords. In an interview in 1912 he described the incident: "I was a real estate agent, making a specialty of the management of colored tenement property for nearly a year before I actually succeeded in getting a colored tenement to manage," he said. "My first opportunity came as a result of a dispute between two landlords in West 134th Street. To 'get even' one of them turned his house over to me to fill with colored tenants. I was successful in renting and managing this house, and after a time I was able to induce other landlords to . . . give me their houses to manage."[8] Within a short time Payton began to advertise his services in white real estate journals:

Colored Tenements Wanted[9]

Colored man makes a specialty of managing colored tenements; references; bond. Philip A. Payton, Jr., agent and broker, 67 West 134th.

By 1904 the young man who four years earlier could not afford a decent meal[10] became the most prominent Negro realtor in New York City.

Payton was a light-skinned man of medium height and build. He wore pince-nez glasses and could easily have passed for a young teacher or clergyman, but his physical appearance belied his personality.[11] Friends knew him as an ambitious and impetuous man, the archetype of a hard-driving salesman. When it was rumored that he was going to visit Liberia, for example, one of them wrote: "You had better cause the Liberians to be notified of his approach that they might get out their padlocks, and nail down everything that's lying around loose."[12]

Payton's business success brought him public recognition. By the first decade of the twentieth century he was an intimate of Negro politician and Internal Revenue Collector Charles W. Anderson, and a friend of Fred R. Moore, editor of *The New York Age*[13] and general manager of the National Negro Business League. He was on the closest terms with practically every other member of the small Negro business and professional community in the city. Payton corresponded with Booker T. Washington and Washington's secretary, Emmett J. Scott. He was president of a short-lived local Negro defense society organized to protest police brutality in 1905, and a respected member of Washington's National Negro Business League.[14] Payton certainly conceived himself as a leader of the race and his public and private statements tended to foster this impression. When Emmett J. Scott learned that white landlords in Harlem were organizing to prevent the settlement of Negroes there, Payton told him not to worry: *"The fight that I am making,"* he replied, *"has got to be made sooner or later and I see no better time than now."*[15] Four of the apartment houses he rented to Negroes in 1906 were called "The Washington," "The Langston," "The Douglass," "The Dunbar."[16] When asked about his role in securing homes for Negroes in Harlem, Payton emphasized his personal importance: "By opening for colored tenants first a house on one block and then a house in another I have finally succeeded in securing . . . over two hundred and fifty first-class flats and private dwellings," he said in 1912.[17] The letters "P A P," in red and black, appeared on all the houses Payton controlled. Philip A. Payton, Jr., has been called the "Father of Colored Harlem."[18]

There is no serious question of Payton's personal honesty, although he was later sued for fraud by some stockholders in the Negro real estate company he founded—the Afro-American Realty Company. He was, however, a young man who clearly saw the possibilities of exploiting Harlem's depressed real estate market for his own as well as for the race's interest. He seemed to have complete confidence in his own business judgments. He got rich almost overnight, and made deals involving large sums of money before he had much practical business experience. Sometimes his activities as a businessman were less than exemplary. He could, for example, forget to file his corporate financial statements at the proper time, as he did in 1910, and thereby make himself liable to penalties of $1,000 to $10,000. His friend, Collector of Internal Revenue Charles W. Anderson, got him out of this jam by extending the filing date: "Payton went away without arranging for any report of his corporations, as required by the corporation tax law," Anderson wrote. "Learning of this, I availed myself of the authority conferred on collectors in the law to extend the time . . . thirty days."[19]

Nor could Payton hold on to money once he made it. One of his properties, at One Hundred and Thirty-second Street and Lenox Avenue, was hopefully to become the site of the "Payton Building." He confessed to a friend that he sold the land for $10,000 in cash instead, and quickly spent it all: ". . . It is all gone," he lamented, "and now I need some more." Alluding to a commonly held stereotype that Negroes spent money freely, he concluded sadly, "I am colored, too."[20]

III

Payton's activities in Harlem real estate reached a high point in 1904 with his founding of the Afro-American Realty Company. The company had its genesis in a partnership of ten Negroes organized by Payton. This partnership specialized in acquiring five-year leases on Harlem property owned by whites and subsequently renting them to Negroes. In 1904, Payton conceived of reorganizing this small concern into a regular real estate corporation, capable of buying and constructing homes as well as leasing them. The company, incorporated on June 15, 1904, was permitted to "buy, sell, rent, lease, and sub-lease, all kinds of buildings, houses . . . lots, and other . . . real estate in the City of New York. . . ." It was capitalized at $500,000 and authorized to issue 50,000 shares at $10 each. Ten of the eleven original members of the all-Negro Board of Directors subscribed to 500 shares each. The company began with an estimated capital of $100,000.[21]

Some of the important backers of the Afro-American Realty Company were Negroes who succeeded in what the Negro press called "Race Enterprise." Wealth in the Negro community came principally from businesses which provided services to Negroes, or larger extensions of such businesses. Real estate men, undertakers, lawyers, barbers, hair stylists—small entrepreneurs of all kinds—were the leading figures in the Negro business world. They supported the new corporation.

James C. Thomas, first president of the company, was probably

Payton's key backer initially. (Payton, the real power of the corporation, held the offices of vice-president and general manager.) Thomas was born in Harrisburg, Texas, on Christmas Day in the year of Emancipation, 1863. As a young man he worked as a cabin boy on steamers that plied their way between Galveston and ports of the northeast. In 1881, at the age of eighteen, he came to New York City and never left.[22] He worked as a steward in some of Manhattan's private clubs; like many other Negro businessmen of his generation he found it necessary to accept service positions in the early years of his career. (Payton, a college graduate, was a porter and barber; the Reverend Dr. Adam Clayton Powell, Sr., was employed as a waiter in Atlantic City even after his ordination;[23] a Negro public school teacher earned her education by working as a janitress;[24] Negro educator William Lewis Bulkley was a cook, janitor and waiter.)[25] While working as steward Thomas attended a local embalming school and was graduated as registered undertaker.

After a short-lived partnership with another Negro undertaker in the 1890's, Thomas opened his own business in the Tenderloin. A good funeral was all that many Negroes could look forward to—death was often the high point of life—and Thomas, tall and distinguished-looking in his Vandyke beard, was known as the man to do a proper job. His business was so successful that he purchased two buildings on Seventh Avenue at the turn of the century. Thomas' luck was with him in the selection of these houses—they were near the site of the future Pennsylvania Station. He later sold them for $103,000 and, shortly afterward, moved his establishment to Harlem. By 1907 he was known as "the richest man of African descent in New York. . . ."[26]

James E. Garner and Wilford H. Smith also served as officers in the Realty Company. Garner, corporation secretary and treasurer, had been born a slave in Charles County, Maryland. He grew up in the District of Columbia and worked as a porter in a drugstore and as a waiter when he came to New York City. In 1880 he established a small janitorial service in the Tenderloin. By the turn of the century, Garner's Manhattan House Cleaning and Renovating Bureau regularly employed thirty to thirty-five workers. When the National Negro Business League was founded in 1900, he was appointed treasurer of its New York branch.[27] Smith, another southern migrant, was the corporation's lawyer, a close friend of Booker T. Washington, and one of the most esteemed Negro lawyers in Manhattan in the early twentieth century. Initially, Smith, Garner, Thomas and Payton held all the offices in the Afro-American Realty Company. In the next few years other well-known Negroes became directors and investors: Emmett J. Scott, the Reverend Dr. W. H. Brooks, Fred R. Moore and Charles W. Anderson.[28]

IV

The Afro-American Realty Company was founded with high hopes of success—hopes which proved unfounded. At first, the corporation seemed to have sound financial backing and the support of eminent members of the Negro community. "The personnel of the Board of Directors of the company is bound to commend it to the respect, trust and confidence of even the most skeptical of our race," its prospectus stated. "Most of them are men who have made a success in their individual lines and are well-known in New York City for their ability, worth and integrity."[29] Early company transactions were profitable and tended to verify Payton's optimistic judgments. In 1904, for instance, the Afro-American Realty Company sold three of its newly acquired houses on West One Hundred and Thirty-fifth Street to a white real estate concern, the Hudson Realty Company. Hudson Realty proceeded to evict its Negro tenants in order to replace them with whites. Payton, in turn, "blocked the game" by buying two other houses on the same street and evicting the white tenants in them. Within a short time, he was able to repurchase the original three (at 40, 42 and 44 West One Hundred and Thirty-fifth Street), "filling the houses with Afro-Americans." These first highly publicized transactions boosted the reputation of the Realty Company. They "gave great publicity to the existence of the Afro-American Realty Company," *The New York Age* concluded in 1905.[30]

Payton did not let the company rest on its laurels. To attract financial support from the Negro working class he advertised regularly in the Negro press and promised the average investor much more than he was able to fulfill later. (The prospectus offered profits of seven to ten per cent, the weekly advertisements omitted the seven.)[31] Investment would not only yield "Tempting Profit," Negroes were told, but it was also their obligation to support an enterprise which would help end "relentless race prejudice": "To-day is the time to buy, if you want to be numbered among those of the race who are doing something toward trying to solve the so-called 'Race Problem,' " it was argued. The anticipated success of the company would become a symbol of Negro business acumen and would end racial segregation in urban housing: "A respecting, law-abiding Negro will find conditions can be so changed that he will be able to rent, wherever his means will permit him to live," the *Prospectus* maintained. Race prejudice would be turned into "dollars and cents" for *Negroes,* not whites.[32] Although public reports showed stocks being sold rapidly, privately the company found it necessary to hire a salesman to drum up business at a commission of 20 per cent. And stocks were sold, usually to individuals who could afford only a few shares at a time.[33]

The Realty Company promised the world and delivered little. It had hopefully been incorporated for fifty years, but folded after four. During its short and hectic existence it was wracked with internal dissension. In four years there were three major reorganizations of its Board of Directors and officers. James C. Thomas and James E. Garner severed connections with the company in its first year. Wilford H. Smith was later influential in bringing suit against Payton for fraud. The final reorganization, in 1906, left Payton as president and general manager. It was formal recognition of the power he had wielded since the founding of the corporation.

V

In September 1905 Fred R. Moore, then secretary and treasurer of the corporation, wrote that the "Realty Company is coming on slowly. . . . If a conservative policy is followed profits can be made. : . ."[34] Payton played for bigger stakes. As general manager, he finally leased or purchased on loans and mortgages, at high interest rates, some twenty-five houses, the majority in Harlem.[35] The paper value of this property was estimated at $1.1 million and its annual rental income at $114,500.[36] Some members of the company objected to Payton's management, but they apparently had little say in the day-to-day operations of the corporation. The "directors," Wilford H. Smith wrote in 1906, "exercise no control. I think the near future will reveal all that I do not care to say."[37] Booker T. Washington, on close terms with all the officers of the Afro-American Realty Company, received regular reports of its progress. He was also a sounding board for the internal opposition to Payton's control. In May 1906, for example, Smith informed him he was severing connections with the corporation. "I still believe that if the Company is properly handled, it will pay each investor well," he wrote, "but I do not believe it will ever be handled in the interest of the stockholders as long as the present manager is in control."[38]

The dissension came into the open in October 1906 when forty-three dissatisfied stockholders, represented by Smith, sued Payton and the Realty Company for having issued a "fraudulent prospectus"; one which "intended to mislead and deceive, and to cheat and defraud the general public, and especially the colored people. . . ." The specific charge leveled at Payton was that he held absolute control of the company and was therefore personally liable for any misrepresentation. All the initial statements of the corporation's financial stability and the amount of property it owned were highly exaggerated, the accusation ran. Charles J. Crowder, the stockholder in whose name the suit was filed, charged that $100,000 in stock "had not in fact been honestly subscribed for," but issued to Payton and his associates on "fictitious values"; that the contracts for the ten apartment houses the Realty Company claimed to control on five-year leases contained sixty- and ninety-day cancellation clauses, and that "nearly all of them had been cancelled" when the prospectus was issued; and, finally, that most of the houses the company claimed to own were, in reality, mortgaged nearly to their "full value." Crowder and another litigant, Frank S. Armand, each held one hundred shares of the corporation's stock. Practically all the others involved in the suit owned one to ten shares.[39]

A touch of the ludicrous ran through the case. Payton, arrested in January 1907, immediately won release in the custody of one of his lawyers. The order of arrest was itself declared illegal and vacated when the judge ruled the suit a civil not a criminal action.[40] The lawyer for the plaintiff, Wilford H. Smith, had been the corporation's lawyer at the time of the writing of the supposedly fraudulent prospectus. During the trial, Payton's attorney introduced a manuscript copy of the original prospectus containing penciled corrections and revisions by Smith himself. The specific charge of fraud against Payton was dismissed on the grounds that he was only one of the officers in the corporation. The Realty Company itself, however, was found

guilty of misrepresentation and Crowder and other stockholders recovered their initial investments plus damages and legal costs. Justice
Victor J. Dowling cited the company for claiming it owned property
without restriction, when all its houses were heavily mortgaged.[41]

VI

The Afro-American Realty Company, with Payton as president, continued to do business through 1907 and the early part of 1908. After
some prodding from stockholders, and in an attempt to restore confidence in the company's name, the first (and last) dividend was
declared in June 1907.[42] Further attempts to stimulate interest in the
company after the bad press it received from Crowder's suit—letters
sent to officers and stockholders asking them to encourage friends to
invest, a stockholders' meeting in Mercy Baptist Church at which
participants were "requested to bring any friends whom you think
will be interested in subscribing to our Capital Stock"[43]—were unsuccessful. Before the end of the year the Afro-American Realty
Company floundered and, by 1908, it ceased to do business.

The corporation had been confronted with the first organized effort
of white property owners in Harlem to prevent the sale of houses or
the rental of apartments to Negroes, but this movement itself did not
do any serious damage to the company. Payton himself scoffed at its
importance. "I have taken no steps," he told his friend Emmett Scott,
"without serious talks with some of the *large Real Estate interests in
our City.*" Any fear on this account, he concluded, "is ground-
less. . . ."[44] Payton's connections must have been solid for, once
the company was in financial trouble and no longer met its mortgage
payments, some of the receivers gave it leeway. They initially permitted the Realty Company to collect rents and apply this money to
its indebtedness: "the receiverships are friendly," Fred Moore wrote
in the winter of 1907.[45] The suit against Payton, however, was certainly harmful for the company's reputation. He and his friends said
that *all* the troubles of the company were caused not by any opposition to his business methods but by personal enmity. "The purpose of
the action seems only to be to harass and discredit me," Payton
claimed. "The past grand masters of the United Orders of Envy and
Jealousy are arraying themselves against Mr. Payton," one of his
friends wrote.[46] When Payton was asked about the higher rents he
charged Negroes, he justified them on the grounds that he was forced

to borrow money at higher interest rates and had to pay more for his options than white realtors did.[47]

In spite of charges and countercharges the major burden for the failure of the Afro-American Realty Company was Phil Payton's speculations. He had continued to buy property at a rapid pace even after Crowder's suit, and refused to listen to those who counseled a more moderate policy of acquisition. Rather than encourage interest in the corporation, this tended to further alienate other stockholders: "No matter how friendly we may feel for Mr. Payton there seems to be an opposition in the Company against him as its head that prevents it from making any progress," Fred Moore told Emmett Scott in 1907.[48] Payton's management and continued purchases finally led to an overextension of the company's holdings. The success of the Afro-American Realty Company, as with all Race Enterprise, was inextricably tied to the earning capacity of the city's Negro community. This predominantly lower-class group was always hardest hit by economic recessions. The recession of 1907–1908 coincided with Payton's speculations and left the company with many new tenements, but few tenants. "The cause of . . . the trouble," Fred Moore explained privately, "was due to taking on some property which remained unoccupied for months, and the money received from the property which was occupied had to go toward keeping up the unoccupied property. . . ."[49] The Realty Company could not generate enough income to meet its mortgage and interest payments in 1907. It needed the comparatively small sums of $10,000 to $20,000 to keep solvent, but simply could not raise the money. In November 1907 Moore wrote: "The Realty Co. is [in] a bad way, am trying to help straighten it out by persuading Payton to resign."[50]

By the end of 1907 it was evident to the officers, only Moore and Payton then, that the corporation was on the verge of collapse. Payton tried desperately to keep the company from going under. Since he could no longer borrow any money on his name ("He has tried all the white folks who have money without result"),[51] he wrote Booker T. Washington for a letter of introduction to Andrew Carnegie. "The Doctor," as Washington was known to intimates, refused to intercede in what was a business not a philanthropic matter.[52] Payton went to see Carnegie anyway and Oswald Garrison Villard as well, but he won no support from either of them. Their response might have been different, Moore told him, if the Realty Company charged Negroes modest rents: "If, as I told him, we could show that we were housing these people at a nominal rent, and the rents were very much lower than those charged by the white people, then perhaps they might look into it."[53]

In a final gesture to keep the corporation in business Booker T. Washington himself was asked to underwrite the company's notes due on January 1, 1908. "I have promised to advise all parties as soon as I hear from you," Moore told him. Washington rejected this proposal and the last thread of hope was cut.[54] By 1908 the Afro-American Realty Company collapsed, and all its properties were lost.[55]

The underlying causes for the failure of the company were never made public—they have remained hidden in private correspondence for more than half a century. Emmett J. Scott, who fully supported Payton throughout "his hour of trial," and who lost $500 in the corporation's demise, addressed an angry letter to the officers. He criticized them for permitting the company to fail without "a single word" of explanation to the stockholders. "In numerous conversations with you both," he told Payton and Moore, "I have urged that the very least the Company could do, since it has ceased to do business, is to make a statement, to be signed by you both . . . an Explicit statement giving the reasons which led to the failure of the Company. As honorable men I do not see how the Company could do less than this."[56]

Payton was out of town when Scott's letter arrived in July 1908. Moore promised to issue such a statement "if I have to do it my-self. . . ."[57] By October, Moore was still promising to do so "at the very first opportunity."[58] No public statement was ever issued.

Payton was "down but not out."[59] He continued to operate in Harlem real estate as a private businessman and seems to have been successful in later ventures. His public reputation remained untainted, for all except those who lost their investments in the Realty Company. In one Negro encyclopedia he is remembered as "without a doubt the greatest Negro real estate dealer that ever lived."[60]

The Afro-American Realty Company played a significant part in opening homes for Negroes in Harlem. Philip A. Payton, Jr., owned and managed apartment houses and brownstones in sections never previously rented to Negro tenants. His holdings were scattered throughout Harlem from One Hundred and Nineteenth to One Hundred and Forty-seventh Streets. When the company folded, white realtors and mortgagors took over its property but the Negro tenants remained. The new owners continued to advertise the Negro company's former houses in the colored press.[61] The speculations of Philip A. Payton, Jr., led to the downfall of the Afro-American Realty Company, but they also helped lay the foundations of the largest Negro ghetto in the world.

CHAPTER 8

A Neighborhood Transformed

"The agents promise their tenants
that these houses will be rented
only to WHITE people."
—Harlem realtors, 1910

"The colored [people] are in Harlem
to stay, and they are coming each year by the thousands."
—John M. Royall, Negro realtor, 1914

I

The pressing need and desire for accommodations to house an expanding Negro population made the founding of the Afro-American Realty Company possible. This need continued to exist with greater intensity after the company's demise, and Negroes found other means to buy or rent homes in Harlem. The "border line" which separated whites and Negroes "rapidly receded" each year, and by 1914 some 50,000 Negroes lived in the neighborhood.[1]

But not all property owners were ready to open their houses to colored people. It seemed unbelievable to some that theirs, one of the most exclusive sections in the entire city, should become the center of New York's most depressed and traditionally worst-housed people. Some owners banded together in associations to repulse what they referred to as the Negro "invasion" or the Negro "influx." The language used to describe the movement of Negroes into Harlem— the words "invasion," "captured," "black hordes," "invaders," "enemy," for example, appear repeatedly in denunciations of Negroes—was the language of war.[2]

In the 1880's and 1890's Harlemites annually celebrated the historic Revolutionary Battle of Harlem Heights. These patriotic fetes were symbols of community pride and pamphlets were widely distributed informing the neighborhood of the dignitaries participating in them.[3] In the early twentieth century, however, Harlem's residents gathered not to preserve the memory of a Revolutionary conflict, but to fight their own battle—to keep their neighborhood white.

Most of the formal opposition to Negro settlement in Harlem centered in local associations of landlords. Some were committees representing individual blocks, others were community-wide in structure. Property owners on West One Hundred and Fortieth, One Hundred and Thirty-seventh, One Hundred and Thirty-sixth, One Hundred and Thirty-fifth, One Hundred and Thirty-first, One Hundred and Thirtieth, One Hundred and Twenty-ninth Streets, and so on, in descending order as the Negro community spread southward, and along the avenues, signed restrictive agreements. Each swore not to rent his apartments to Negroes for ten or fifteen years—till when, it was thought, "this situation . . . referred to . . . will have run its course": "The premises, land, and buildings of which we . . . are the owners . . . shall not be used as a . . . Negro tenement, leased to colored . . . tenants, sold to colored . . . tenants . . . or all [other] persons of African descent," one agreement reads. "Each of the parties," another maintains, "does hereby covenant and agree [not] to . . . hereafter . . . cause to be suffered, either directly or indirectly, the said premises to be used or occupied in whole or in part by any negro, quadroon, or octoroon of either sex whatsoever. . . ." Some covenants even put a limitation on the number of Negro janitors, bellboys, laundresses and servants to be employed in a home. Following a pseudo-legal procedure which was supposed to make these agreements binding, each signer paid all the others a fee of one dollar. The finished products were notarized and filed at the County Clerk's Office in the New York City Hall of Records where they may be read today.[4] The streets covered by such restrictive codes were known in the Negro community as "Covenant Blocks," and Negroes took pride in being the first colored landlords or tenants to live in them: "to knock [the covenants] into a cocked hat," one said. "Although organizations to prevent the settling of colored citizens in certain . . . sections of Harlem mushroom overnight," the *Age* quipped, "the colored invasion goes merrily along."[5]

Other community groups led by white realtors, businessmen, journalists, clergymen, members of the Board of Commerce and local citizens tried to hold back the Negro's "steady effort to invade Harlem." One realty company dealing in upper-Manhattan property was called the Anglo-Saxon Realty Corporation. Such organizations as the West Side Improvement Corporation, the West Harlem Property Owners' Association, the Save-Harlem Committee, the Committee of Thirty and the Harlem Property Owners' Improvement Corporation were formed. Each planned to arouse the interest of all white Harlemites in what they called "the greatest problem that Harlem has had to face."[6]

The Harlem Property Owners' Improvement Corporation (HPOIC), active from 1910 to 1915, was the most forceful of these organizations. "We are approaching a crisis," its founder, John G. Taylor, said in 1913. "It is the question of whether the white man will rule Harlem or the negro." Taylor hoped to organize the entire white community "to fight the common enemy." "We believe," he wrote on another occasion, "that real friends of the negroes will eventually convince them that they should buy large tracts of unimproved land near the city and there build up colonies of their own." "Drive them out," Taylor shouted in an angry tirade at another time, "and send them to the slums where they belong. . . ."[7]

The HPOIC found active support in the local press. *"When will the people of Harlem wake up to the fact that they must organize and maintain a powerful anti-invasion movement if they want to check the progress of the black hordes that are gradually eating through the very heart of Harlem?"* the *Harlem Home News* said in an editorial in 1911. "They must wake up and get busy before it is too late. . . . Are we to give Harlem over to the negroes altogether?"[8] Stories about Negroes in the *Home News* were generally accompanied by such abusive epithets as "coon," "darkey," "nigger," "black plague," "black hordes." Its journalists quoted Negroes in exaggerated dialect.[9] Meetings of property owners were held, some in white churches, and programs introduced which proposed evicting all Negroes in Harlem and outlawing future sale and rental of property to colored people. At one session, Taylor suggested that whites who lived on streets bordering Negro blocks build twenty-four-foot fences to separate themselves from Negro neighbors.[10] Advertisements for white tenants were printed in dailies with city-wide distribution, and *Harlem Magazine,* organ of the white Harlem Board of Commerce, publicized the activities of the HPOIC. It pleaded with whites to join the anti-Negro crusade: "Will You Help Yourself?"; "Help Protect Your Property"; "Will you do a little to save yourself?"; "Do you wish the influences which have tended to depreciate your realty values to be removed?" To participate in the restrictive movement, it maintained, would "be the most vital and useful thing that you have ever done."[11]

Negro realtors were contacted and told not to try to find houses on certain streets: "We herewith resolve that every colored real estate broker be notified as to the following: That the owners of this section have unanimously agreed not to rent their houses for colored tenancy. . . ."[12] Like an enemy negotiating a line of truce, whites called a meeting of Negro real estate men to attempt to draw a voluntary boundary line that would permanently separate the white and Negro communities—a "dead line," it was called.[13] Four members of Harlem's Church of the Puritans attended meetings of the New York Presbytery to protest the proposed movement of the Negro St. James Presbyterian Church into the neighborhood.[14] Others called on city fathers to try to prevent the licensing of a Negro-owned movie house on Lenox Avenue.[15] The Lafayette Theatre, on Seventh Avenue, permitted Negroes to sit only in its balcony.[16] People who signed restrictive covenants and subsequently broke them were brought to court.[17]

These movements permitted whites the opportunity to vent their anxieties and the chimerical hope that restrictive agreements "safeguarded the neighborhood . . . for all time," but they did not end Negro settlement in Harlem. All the organizations failed. That it was necessary to found so many in a relatively short period of time was a reflection of the general failure of each. Private housing covenants had not, during the life of the HPOIC, been ruled constitutional (from 1917 to 1948 the United States Supreme Court barred segregation by public ordinance but not separation in private agreements). Although at least two people were sued in New York City for violating their original commitments, local courts never convicted them. Negro realtors, like John M. Royall, ridiculed the proposal for a voluntary line of segregation as an agreement to "capitalize on prejudice," and "a joke."[18] In spite of protests of Harlemites—"can *nothing* be done to put a restriction on the invasion of the Negro into Harlem?"—St. James was permitted to move into the area and even granted a large loan from the Presbytery to build a new church.[19] Its success forced it to move to larger quarters twice in the next decade. In 1913 the Lafayette Theatre was sold to promoters who realized it was foolish to run a segregated theater in "what is destined to become a colored neighborhood." The new owners encouraged Negro patronage—"Our Doors Are Open To All"—and even contributed regularly to Negro charities. The large basement of the building in which the theater was housed, Lafayette Hall, was later leased as a temporary armory to Harlem's Negro National Guard unit. For a short time the entire building, including the theater, was controlled by a group of Negro businessmen. In the twenties, the Lafayette was advertised as the "Most Widely Known Negro Theatre in America"; "America's Leading Colored Theatre."[20]

The basic cause of the collapse of all organized efforts to exclude Negroes from Harlem was the inability of any group to gain total and unified support of all white property owners in the neighborhood. Without such support it was impossible to organize a successful neighborhood-wide restrictive movement. Landlords forming associations by blocks had a difficult time keeping people on individual streets united. There also continued to be speculators, Negro and white, who, as in 1904 and 1905, sought to exploit the situation for their own profit. They bought tenements and opened them to Negroes to try to force neighbors to repurchase them at higher prices.[21] Nor was it possible, and this is the major point, to create a well-organized and well-financed movement of Negro restriction (the HPOIC plan called for the contribution of one-half of one per cent of the assessed valuation of all property to a community fund)[22] in the disrupted and emotional atmosphere that pervaded Harlem in the first two decades of the twentieth century. The very setting in which whites were confronted with Negro neighbors for the first time led to less than level-headed reasoning. The first impulse of many "in a rather panicky state of mind"[23] was to sell at whatever price their property would bring and move elsewhere. Realtors called this "panic selling" and, in spite of efforts to prevent it, it continued.[24] Between 1907 and 1914, two-thirds of the houses in or near the Negro section were sold—practically all at substantial losses to the original owners. Since the already weak real estate market was flooded with property in a short time, and only a relatively few Negroes were wealthy enough to buy—"there was no market for real estate among the newcomers"—prices continued to depreciate rapidly: "realty values have tumbled by leaps and bounds." "The coming of Negroes to this locality without any financial backing brought about a decided change, as the colored people . . . were unable to adhere to the standard formerly observed by the whites," a Harlem banker wrote. "Hence there was a deterioration in values. . . ."[25] In the 1870's and 1880's fortunes were made in soaring Harlem land prices; by 1917 white realtors tried to encourage interest in the neighborhood by advertising how cheap property had become: "Changes in the character of Harlem population," a member of the Harlem Board of Commerce wrote, have led "to remarkable bargains, both for rental and purchase. . . . Such properties in good condition can now be purchased at less than the assessed value of the land alone."[26] In the 1920's, as will be shown, this situation changed radically.

The minority of Harlem landlords who adhered to their original restrictive covenants suffered serious economic consequences. Many were unable to find white people willing to rent their apartments. To encourage white tenants already in them to remain, some were forced to reduce rents drastically: "The introduction of negro tenants . . . has caused . . . many white tenants to move and [has] required a substantial reduction of rents to those who remained," a group of Harlem landlords complained.[27] Those who had mortgage payments to meet were threatened with foreclosure by banks and other lending institutions, and many found it "impossible . . . to hold out."[28] The opponents of Negro settlement faced the dilemma of maintaining a "White Only" policy and probably losing everything, or renting to Negroes at higher prices and surviving. Most chose what seemed to them the lesser of two evils. The following "Notice," one of many, appeared on a Harlem tenement in 1916:[29]

NOTICE

We have endeavored for some time to
avoid turning over this house to
colored tenants, but as a result of . . .
rapid changes in conditions . . . this
issue has been forced upon us.

II

The creation of Negro Harlem was only one example of the general development of large, segregated Negro communities within many American cities in the years *preceding* and following World War I. Harlem was New York's equivalent of the urban ghettos of the nation. "The Negroes are being relegated to the land of Goshen in all our great cities," Kelly Miller commented.[30] "Niggertowns," "Buzzard's Alleys," "Nigger Rows," "Black Bottoms," "Smoketowns," "Bronzevilles," and "Chinch Rows" developed elsewhere, North and South, by 1913—and they would continue to emerge in the future. The District of Columbia was noted for its supposedly decadent Negro alleys: "Tin Can Alley," "Coon Alley," "Hog Alley," "Moonshine Alley," and "Goat Alley." (Life in "Goat Alley," was the subject of a play by that name in the 1920's.) "So closely have the terms Alleys and Negroes been associated," a historian of Washington's Negro section wrote, "that in the minds of the older citizens they are inseparable." "There is growing up in the cities of America a distinct Negro world," George Edmund Haynes said in 1913. These were neighborhoods "isolated from many of the impulses of the common life and little understood by the white world," he concluded.[31]

Among these urban ghettos Harlem was unique. Initially, its name was a symbol of elegance and distinction, not derogation; its streets and avenues were broad, well-paved, clean and tree-lined, not narrow and dirty; its homes were spacious, replete with the best modern facilities, "finished in high-style."[32] Harlem was originally not a slum, but an ideal place in which to live. For the first and generally last time in the history of New York City, Negroes were able to live in decent homes in a respectable neighborhood, "the best houses that they have ever had to live in": "It is no longer necessary for our people to live in small, dingy, stuffy tenements," *The New York Age* said in an editorial in 1906.[33] Harlem was "a community in which Negroes as a whole are . . . better housed than in any other part of the country," an Urban League report concluded in 1914.[34] "Those of the race who desire to live in grand style, with elevator, telephone and hall boy service, can now realize their cherished ambition."[35]

It was expensive to live in "grand style." The rents paid by Harlem's Negroes were higher than those charged in any other Negro section of New York City and they continued to rise rapidly after World War I. In 1914 the average Negro family paid $23.45 per month for apartments in Harlem, and rents in the most elegant houses were much higher.[36] As Negroes moved into the neighborhood they complained of being overcharged by landlords and, as a rule, most were paying higher rents than their incomes would warrant.[37] Although the cost of living was certainly high by the standards of a low-income group, few of Harlem's rentals, *prior to World*

War I, were extortionate. Houses were originally constructed for the well-to-do, "the class above the ordinary." "Harlem tenements," one Negro wrote, "were built for persons of larger incomes than Negroes receive."[38] Since the beginning of the century, however, rents steadily declined, and they were usually lowered even further immediately before Negroes occupied a house. When homes were opened to Negroes it was the general practice to increase rents, but rarely prior to the First World War did prices return to their original levels.[39]

Those Negroes who could afford to pay high rents began moving into the neighborhood at the turn of the century. William H. Smith, caterer, businessman and member of Negro Manhattan's social set, bought a home on West One Hundred and Thirty-fourth Street in the 1890's. Another Negro merchant owned property on the same block at the turn of the century[40] and one wealthy Negro clergyman lived in Harlem in 1895—attended by white servants and chauffeured about in an expensive carriage.[41] As the housing market deteriorated in the early twentieth century other private homes were made available to "respectable colored people." By 1910 many of the city's most prominent Negroes lived in Harlem—the Reverend Dr. Adam Clayton Powell, Sr., Bert Williams, James C. Thomas, Charles W. Anderson and others. Madame C. J. Walker built her mansion on West One Hundred and Thirty-sixth Street in 1913.[42] A student of the Negro Tenderloin found every colored pastor of the churches he visited "living in Harlem" in 1912.[43] The less respectable middle class—gamblers, prostitutes and the like—could also afford high rents. One house was occupied by individuals who represented such an inordinate variety of occupations that Negroes called it "Noah's Ark."[44]

As Harlem became a Negro section its "modern houses" and "better homes" attracted many people from the older Negro sections of Manhattan. Negro women in the Tenderloin hoped "to marry and go get a home in Harlem."[45] Negro businessmen, finding customers moving uptown, sold their property and moved northward. "The massing of the large Negro population in the Harlem district," a journalist observed in 1910, "has been the making of many successful Negro . . . businessmen."[46] San Juan Hill (usually called Columbus Hill after the First World War) "was fast pouring its people into Harlem [as the] exodus from the downtown districts continues with great activity."[47] By 1920, the former Negro sections of Manhattan were terribly rundown backwash communities inhabited by Negroes who, as a rule, desired to live in Harlem but could not afford to pay the high rents charged there. A survey of Columbus Hill in the early 1920's classified 63 per cent of its houses as "absolutely undesirable," and 21 per cent as "passable." "Tenements show thirty to forty years of hard wear," T. J. Woofter recorded in *Negro Problems in Cities.* "Paving is noisy granite block, sidewalks are broken, and fire escapes are hung with bright garments. . . . On the avenue . . . are filthy stores, poolrooms filled with boys and men from morning to late night, with drunks and frowsy street-women. Families are shiftless. . . ." The older model tenements built early in the century were surrounded by houses noted for their congestion, filth and vice. "In regard to the Tuskegee," the City and Suburban Homes Company noted, "the caretaker reports that she cannot interest respectable colored persons in even looking at the vacancies. This has become a very bad street frequented by a most undesirable class of people and our tenants fear for their safety in going through it." One Negro woman, ashamed that she was left behind in a downtown tenement, proudly told an investigator: "I'd like to show you Harlem."[48]

III

After the collapse of the Afro-American Realty Company, Negro churches played a more important role in the development of Harlem than all other institutions in the Negro community. The primary reason for this was that the church had traditionally been the most stable and wealthy Negro institution. As the Negro population expanded rapidly in the early twentieth century the influence and wealth of the church increased phenomenally. Membership in older churches doubled and trebled, and they continually moved to larger quarters; little missions which began in storefronts or in private homes became independent and built or bought stately structures in which to worship; new churches were founded. Mercy Street Baptist Church, for example, was organized in Harlem by seven Negroes at the turn of the century. At first the small congregation met in a house owned by the Baptist City Mission. By July 1907 the congregation, supported by eight hundred communicants, moved to a new building. Population pressure made these facilities inadequate—"Standing room is always at a premium"—and the congregation, under its new name,

Metropolitan Baptist, negotiated the sale of a white Presbyterian church in 1918. Harlem Presbyterian had been "one of the finest church buildings in Harlem." Metropolitan Baptist has remained there ever since.[49]

Salem Memorial Mission, founded in a small room in Harlem in 1902 by the Reverend F. A. Cullen, foster father of the gifted poet Countée Cullen, had a similar history. The first service was attended by three women and the Reverend Mr. Cullen received nineteen cents for his efforts. Ten years later Salem Memorial Methodist Episcopal Church moved into quarters vacated by a white congregation and, in 1923, it moved again. Its final home, the former Calvary Methodist Episcopal Church, was a plush structure, the old meeting place of "one of the most prosperous congregations of the denomination in Manhattan." "The white people have moved away to such an extent," the minister of Calvary Church explained shortly before its sale, "that it is difficult now to continue the most limited church activities or finances. . . ."[50]

Similar changes occurred throughout Harlem in the early twentieth century. Exclusive white denominations left the neighborhood and sold their property to Negro Baptists, Methodists and others. "Little Zion," the uptown branch of "Mother Zion," remained in a small wooden building on Harlem's east side for three-quarters of a century before it constructed a new church on the west side in 1911. "Not in seventy years has there been so much real enthusiasm in the Harlem A.M.E. Zion Church," one member commented.[51] Ministers in all the churches preached in quarters inadequate to seat those who wished to attend, and some were forced to hold five or six services each Sunday.[52] New Negro Moravian, Seventh Day Adventist, Roman Catholic and evangelical churches were established in Harlem prior to and after the First World War. Before all the downtown congregations moved to Harlem they too opened branch Sunday schools and Bible classes in public halls and theaters. Mass services were sometimes held in "gospel tents," "mammoth tents," pitched on Harlem's empty lots, as clergymen sought to "Harvest the Souls" of the ungodly.[53]

Pastors of Negro churches, as they had done in the nineteenth century, planned to follow their congregations to the new Negro neighborhood. The Reverend Dr. Adam Clayton Powell, Sr., repeatedly preached his sermon "A Model Church," encouraging his congregation to move Abyssinian Baptist to Harlem and to purchase property there while prices were low. "It was apparent as early as 1911," he later wrote, "that Harlem would be the final destination of the Abyssinian Church."[54] "On to Harlem"[55] movements began in downtown churches and, prior to 1914, three of the oldest and most distinguished Negro churches, Bethel African Methodist Episcopal, African Methodist Episcopal Zion ("Mother Zion") and St. Philip's Protestant Episcopal Church moved into the section. By the early 1920's practically every established Negro church in Manhattan was located in Harlem, and most occupied exceptionally beautiful buildings.

But the Negro churches did more than simply follow their members to Harlem. Many were able to realize large profits by selling property in the midtown area at high prices and moving uptown where land and property had depreciated in value before World War I. The more important and wealthy congregations not only built new churches in Harlem, but invested heavily in local real estate. Negro churches became the largest Negro property owners in Harlem. St. Mark's Methodist Episcopal, Abyssinian Baptist, and "Mother Zion" owned houses in Harlem prior to 1915. After the war, they and other Negro churches continued to invest heavily in land and homes. Some of the houses purchased by churches were on blocks covered by restrictive covenants, but nothing could be done to prevent such transactions. By becoming landholders, Negro churches helped transform Harlem to a Negro section.

The Negro church most actively engaged in buying Harlem real estate was St. Philip's Protestant Episcopal Church. Throughout the nineteenth century St. Philip's was reputed to be the most exclusive Negro church in New York City. Its members were considered "the better element of colored people," and its services were dignified and refined. This reputation as a fashionable institution made membership in St. Philip's a sign of social recognition and many of the more prominent Negroes of the city were its communicants. It was the only Negro church in Manhattan with a "Pew System" in the nineteenth century—by which members outbid each other for choice seats in the chapel.[56] St. Philip's was also recognized as the "wealthiest Negro church in the country," and this reputation has continued to the present.[57]

The growth of St. Philip's was similar to that of many other important Negro churches. Founded by a small group of Negroes in the Five Points districts in 1809, it held its first formal services in 1819 in a wooden building, 60 feet by 50 feet, on what is now Centre Street. In 1856 St. Philip's moved to a former Methodist church on Mulberry Street and, in 1889, following the Negro population to the Tenderloin, it came to West Twenty-fifth Street. St. Philip's remained in the Tenderloin until 1910, when it moved to a newly constructed church in Harlem.[58]

Because of the opposition of Harlem property owners, the first transactions in the developing Negro section were made in subterfuge. The Reverend Dr. Hutchens C. Bishop, pastor of the church, came to New York City from Charleston, South Carolina, in 1886. He was a tall, thin and almost bald man who easily passed for white. From 1906 through 1910 the Reverend Dr. Bishop bought houses and land in Harlem in his name, including a site for a new church. Some white landlords were happy to sell him their houses and told him they would never sell to Negroes. In 1910 the pastor turned all the property he bought over to the church and prepared to move his congregation to Harlem.[59]

Aside from the church building which St. Philip's owned on West Twenty-fifth Street, it also acquired a number of lots on West Thirtieth Street in the 1830's. This property, originally donated to the church as a cemetery, was valued at the time of acquisition at $9,000. As real estate prices rose in mid-Manhattan the value of St. Philip's holdings skyrocketed. In 1909 the church sold its building on West Twenty-fifth Street for $140,000; the cemetery land was put on the market two years later and brought in $450,000.[60]

When the church site in the Tenderloin was sold in 1909, the Reverend Dr. Bishop attempted to purchase a white Protestant Episcopal church in Harlem. He offered the Church of the Redeemer $50,000 for its property on West One Hundred and Thirty-sixth Street. The neighborhood around the church was obviously changing, its members were moving away, and it would have been to the church's advantage to sell then at a reasonable price: ". . . the coming of so many negroes to the locality had made the property undesirable," its pastor said, "most of the members of the congregation having moved away."[61] West One Hundred and Thirty-sixth Street was a Covenant Block, however, and many of the vestrymen of the white church felt morally bound (if that is the proper term) to their original agreement. They rejected the offer and St. Philip's built its new church a few blocks away. (In 1913 the Church of the Redeemer put its property on the market for sale. For one year the vestrymen unsuccessfully tried to find a white buyer. In 1914, adhering to the letter not the spirit of the Covenant, the Church of the Redeemer was sold to a white woman who immediately resold it to the African Methodist Episcopal Zion ["Mother Zion"] Church for $22,000.[62] Within ten years "Mother Zion" outgrew the premises.)

The new St. Philip's, designed by Negro architects, as Madame Walker's mansion had been, was completed in Harlem in 1911. The church was always moderately wealthy, but it never before controlled the vast sums accumulated through the sale of its property in the Tenderloin. Taking advantage of the depressed condition of the real estate market, the decision was made to invest the church's capital in Harlem apartment houses. In 1911 St. Philip's bought a row of ten new apartment houses on West One Hundred and Thirty-fifth Street between Seventh and Lenox Avenues for $640,000—the largest single real estate transaction, involving Negroes, in the city's history at that time. Before the sale, signs which hung in renting offices of the white realtors who managed these buildings read:

> The agents promise their tenants that
> these houses will be rented only to
> WHITE people.

Shortly after the transfer of this property to St. Philip's and after its remaining white tenants were evicted, a new sign was displayed, telling prospective Negro tenants to contact colored real estate agents:

> *For Rent, Apply to Nail and Parker*[63]

IV

John E. Nail and Henry C. Parker handled the transactions which led to the sale of St. Philip's downtown property and the purchase of its One Hundred and Thirty-fifth Street holdings. They continued to act as agents for the church after 1911 when St. Philip's invested more heavily in Harlem real estate. Jack Nail, as he was known to his friends, was a member of the church and undoubtedly played a vital role in advising the Reverend Dr. Bishop on possibilities of making money in Harlem property. The firm of Nail and Parker, through these and other major transactions (for example, they acted as agents for the downtown YMCA when that body decided to move to Harlem, and later handled the transfer of the Stanford White houses), became the most important Negro real estate company in Harlem. Nail, president of the corporation, was an active participant in community affairs. He was first president of Harlem's Negro Board of Trade, vice-president of the exclusive and predominantly white Republican Business Men's Club of New York City, a member of the Mayor's Housing Committee and the first Negro elected to the Real Estate Board of New York. When President Hoover created a national commission to investigate American urban housing, Nail was brought in as consultant. Throughout his life he raised money for the New York Urban League and was elected one of its officers. John E. Nail was one of the most respected businessmen in New York City.[64]

Nail was the son of a well-known Negro saloon owner. The elder Nail, John B., migrated to the city from Baltimore in 1863, and began his career as an attendant in white gambling houses. Apparently more successful than most patrons, he saved enough money to open a café in the Tenderloin in the 1880's—a gathering place for theatrical people.[65] John B. Nail was another Negro businessman who made substantial profits from selling his downtown property and moving to Harlem in the early twentieth century: "Mr. Nail had been in business for about thirty years when he found that his community was on its way to Harlem and better housing," a student recorded. "Noting this trend—especially from his dwindling income—he sold his business and the building it occupied." He used the money to buy five newly built apartment houses.[66]

Henry C. Parker was a North Carolinian by birth and, like many other southern migrants, returned to Rocky Mount each year to visit his family and friends. The younger Nail and Parker learned about the real estate business as salesmen for Philip A. Payton, Jr. When, in December 1907, it was obvious the Afro-American Realty Company would fold, John E. Nail and Henry C. Parker established their own real estate corporation. Their business was highly successful (until the Great Depression) and they have sometimes been called the "Little Fathers" of Negro Harlem.[67]

The success that Nail and Parker achieved was typical of many other Negro realtors. As each year passed it became more evident that Harlem was to become a Negro section permanently: "The colored [people] are in Harlem to stay, and they are coming each

year by the thousands." White landlords and corporations hired
Negro managers to deal with their new Negro tenants. By 1914, 37
per cent of the Negro tenements in Harlem were managed by "colored agents," although less than five per cent of these houses were
owned by Negro landlords. In 1920 there were twenty-one Negro real
estate firms with offices in Harlem, specializing in uptown property,
and real estate dealers composed the largest single Negro professional
group at the time of the 1930 census.[68]

Compared with holdings of white landlords, insurance companies
and business firms, Negro ownership of Harlem property was, and
always remained, limited. After 1914, however, when houses were
made available to Negroes in larger numbers, a significant increase in
the amount of Negro capital invested in the area took place. Negro
businessmen from the South and other sections of the country,
smelling success and opportunity in Harlem, sent agents there. Local
realtors, like the dogged Philip A. Payton, Jr., closed deals involving
more than a million dollars. A month before his death, in August
1917, Payton and his associates, many of them Negro businessmen
from the South, bought six elevator apartment houses, "the last word
in high-class apartment house construction," and immediately opened
them to Negroes:

> The World's Finest Housing Proposition
> Catering Exclusively to
> Refined Colored Tenants

Each house bore the name of a distinguished Negro, and at the center
of every hall was a picture of the dignitary: Toussaint, Wheatley,
Attucks, Dunbar, Washington, Douglass.[69] Watt Terry, a successful
Negro businessman from Brockton, Massachusetts ("Watt Terry of
Brockton and New York"), came to New York City and founded
another Negro realty corporation in Harlem—the Terry Holding
Company. Terry, a Virginian who came north in 1901, was reputed
to be one of the wealthiest Negroes in America—if not *the* wealthiest.
In story-book fashion his original "capital stock" of fifteen cents, as
he once described it, was somehow transformed into a sizable fortune
through speculation in Massachusetts land. He came to New York
City in 1917 and made it his permanent residence. In the 1920's
Terry built a real estate empire in Harlem.[70] Wealthy Negroes from
Georgia, Florida, Pennsylvania, and the District of Columbia followed his path. The Sarco Realty Corporation, controlled by a man

who originally owned a house-cleaning business, bought the stately Smithsonian Apartment House, constructed in 1899. In 1919 the Equitable Life Assurance Society, after restricting ownership to whites for two decades, put the lovely brownstones designed by Stanford White on the market. The Negro press was plastered with advertisements for their sale; within eight months practically all were sold to well-to-do Negroes. They were called "the finest group of Negro residences in the country." Since then, within the Negro community, the Stanford White houses have been known as "Striver's Row." Buildings of the old Astor Estate, second in reputation and quality only to "Striver's Row," were also sold to Negroes in the early twenties.[71]

Practically every major Negro institution moved from its downtown quarters to Harlem by the early 1920's: the United Order of True Reformers; Odd Fellows, Masons, Elks, Pythians and other fraternal orders; the Music School Settlement; the Coachmen's Union League; the African Society of Mutual Relief; *The New York Age*; West Fifty-third Street YMCA and YWCA; almost all the Negro social service agencies, including local offices of the Urban League and NAACP; the AME Home and Foreign Missionary Society; all the major churches.[72] The virtual monopoly *The New York Age* had for generations as the city's only leading Negro journal was broken, and two other weeklies were established: the *New York News* and the *Amsterdam News* ("boasting local sheets," the *Age* called them). The *Age* continued to be a staid newspaper in the tradition of nineteenth-century journalism, although it too began to change in the 1920's. Its competitors were tabloids whose blaring and sensational headlines appealed to mass audiences and mirrored the highly successful white dailies. P.S. 89, on Lenox Avenue, three-quarters Negro by 1915, opened a night school, reading room and a community center for Negro youth. Within a short time it became one of the most run-down public schools in the city. P.S. 68, the former "Silk Stocking" school, was now noted for its regular skirmishes between white and Negro pupils. The *Harlem Home News* moved to the Bronx in 1913. A historic landmark of an earlier Harlem, Watt Mansion, was first transformed into a cafeteria, "the Lybia," and finally torn down. The famous Pabst Restaurant became a Kress five-and-ten-cent store in 1920, and Horton's Ice Cream Parlor, a well-known meeting place owned by the "Grand Old Man" of white

Harlem, was transformed into a shoestore. The most famous institution of white Harlem, Collegiate Reformed Church (Second Dutch Reformed Church), held out against the inevitable longer than most—in 1930, however, it became the Negro Ephesus Seventh Day Adventist Church, and has remained that to the present.[73]

Those who remembered the expectations of previous generations— Germans, German-Jews, Irish, and others—sadly moved away. "Harlem has been devastated as a result of the steady influx of Negroes," an old resident bemoaned in 1913. "The best of Harlem was gone," another thought in the same year, and it "will be all colored in ten years." In 1922, *The New York Times* reported that "very few of the old families remain which made . . . Harlem . . . a delightful . . . residential locality a quarter of a century ago. . . ." Harlem's Old-Timers changed their tune. When they met in their midtown clubhouse they no longer sang of Harlem's prosperity, but of how "everything has changed except our friendship."[74]

Merchants left behind as their former clientele departed attempted to adjust to new conditions, although a few refused to accept the change. H. C. F. Koch, for example, owned one of the largest department stores in Harlem. Koch moved into the German section of the community and opened a business on One Hundred and Twenty-fifth Street in 1890. When Negroes came to Harlem, Koch and his children ignored their trade or treated them discourteously: "The Koch family paid scant attention to colored . . . customers," a Negro wrote. Rather than continue business in a Negro section the family sold the store in 1930.[75]

Most businessmen remained. L. M. Blumstein, a German-Jew, opened his store in Harlem in 1896. Blumstein was as much opposed to Negro settlement as Koch, and refused to hire Negroes for other than menial positions until 1930. In that year he employed Negro elevator operators but still refused to hire Negro salesmen, clerks and cashiers. Negroes forced him to change his mind through the pressure of a successful boycott during the Great Depression. Blumstein remained in the neighborhood and the department store founded in 1896 remains one of Harlem's most successful businesses.[76]

As merchants saw it, the problem was to change the neighborhood's image to attract new industry. The Harlem Board of Commerce conducted an "elaborate campaign to advertise Harlem . . . telling of the advantage of Harlem from a business standpoint. . . ."

The community advertised as a place of exclusive residence in the 1880's and 1890's was now claimed to be the perfect area in which to locate factories. Land was cheap, it was argued in 1917, transportation good, and the neighborhood overflowing with unskilled, low-income families willing to accept any kind of employment. The heterogeneity of Harlem's population was then seen as one of the community's principal assets: "Only 17 per cent of its people are native white of native parents," a survey of the Harlem Board of Commerce concluded in 1917. "Racial colonization shows distinctly." "Let us consider Harlem as it is to-day," Charles H. Fuller of the Board of Commerce noted. "The zenith of its prosperity and utility as a residential section has . . . passed. . . . The hope of the future lies in the development of its manufacturing." Carnivals, pageants, fairs and parades were held regularly to stimulate public interest in Harlem's business opportunities. The community which formerly denounced street-hawkers and peddlers seemed to have gone into business for itself.[77]

The larger the Negro population became, the more often businessmen spoke of their community as "Greater Harlem"—an undefined term which apparently included surrounding white areas. In the 1920's, when Americans came to know Harlem as the "Negro Capital of the World," *Harlem Magazine* argued the impression was "erroneous." Negroes occupied only "a small fraction of *Greater Harlem,*" it maintained. By 1932 the Harlem Board of Commerce gave up its mirage. It changed its name, and the name of its journal. "While the decision of the Board to adopt a new name . . . is certain to cause deep regret," the final issue of *Harlem Magazine* editorialized, "it must be apparent to all . . . that such a step was inevitable. [Harlem has] a new and entirely different meaning to the present generation." "How our old Dutch burghers would writhe," an old resident commented, "if they could be reincarnated for just long enough to grasp the modern idea of what once was their cherished "Nieuw Haarlem!"[78]

In 1914 Negroes lived in some 1,100 different houses within a twenty-three-block area of Harlem. After a house-to-house survey in that year, the Urban League estimated Harlem's population at 49,555—the entire Negro population of Manhattan in 1910 was 60,534. *Prior to World War I,* the neighborhood was already the "largest colony of colored people, in similar limits, in the world"—

and it continued to expand. By 1920 the section of Harlem bordered approximately by One Hundred and Thirtieth Street on the south, One Hundred and Forty-fifth Street on the north and west of Fifth to Eighth Avenue was predominatly Negro—and inhabited by some 73,000 people. Two-thirds of Manhattan's Negro population lived there in 1920. "If my race can make Harlem," one man said, "good lord, what can't it do?" Harlem had become "the Mecca of the colored people of New York City."[79]

PART THREE

Harlem Slum

CHAPTER 9 ⚀

Harlem Tragedy:
An Emerging Slum

"I sit on my stoop on Seventh
Avenue and gaze at the sunkissed
folks strolling up and down and
think that surely Mississippi is
here in New York, in Harlem, yes,
right on Seventh Avenue."
—*The Messenger*, 1923

"I have been in places where cattle
and dogs sleep with masters, but
never before have I been in such a
filthy house."
—Judge William Blau's description of a Harlem tenement, 1922

I

The creation of a Negro community within one large and solid geographic area was unique in city history. New York had never been what realtors call an "open city"—a city in which Negroes lived wherever they chose—but the former Negro sections were traditionally only a few blocks in length, often spread across the island and generally interspersed with residences of white working-class families. Harlem, however, was a Negro world unto itself. A scattered handful of "marooned white families . . . stubbornly remained" in the Negro section, a United States census-taker recorded, but the mid-belly of Harlem was predominantly Negro by 1920.[1]

And the ghetto rapidly expanded. Between the First World War and the Great Depression, Harlem underwent radical changes. When the twenties came to an end Negroes lived as far south as One Hundred and Tenth Street—the northern boundary of Central Park; practically all the older white residents had moved away; the Russian-Jewish and Italian sections of Harlem, founded a short generation earlier, were rapidly being depopulated; and Negro Harlem, within the space of ten years, became the most "incredible slum" in the entire city. In 1920 James Weldon Johnson was able to predict a glowing future for this Negro community: "Have you ever stopped to think what the future Harlem will be?" he wrote. "It will be the greatest Negro city in the world. . . . And what a fine part of New York City [the Negro] has come into possession of!"[2] By the late 1920's and early 1930's, however, Harlem's former "high-class" homes offered, in the words of a housing expert, "the best laboratory for slum clearance . . . in the entire city." "Harlem conditions," a *New York Times* reporter concluded, are "simply deplorable."[3]

II

The Harlem slum of the twenties was the product of a few major urban developments. One of the most important was the deluge of Negro migration to New York City then. The Negro press, now largely dependent on the migrant community for support, changed its former critical attitude of migration to one openly advocating urban settlement. (The exodus was so large, a Negro minister preached, that it must have been "inspired by Almighty God.")[4] If one is looking for a dramatic turning point in the history of the urbanization of the Negro—"a race changing from farm life to city life"—it was certainly the decade of the twenties. Between 1910 and 1920 the Negro population of the city increased 66 per cent (91,709 to 152,467); from 1920 to 1930, it expanded 115 per cent (152,467 to 327,706). In the latter year less than 25 per cent of New York City's Negro population (79,264) was born in New York State. There were more Negroes in the city in 1930 than the combined Negro populations of Birmingham, Memphis and St. Louis. Similar population increases occurred in urban areas throughout the country.[5]

Negro migration in the twenties drew on areas of the South that had previously sent few people to New York City. The seaboard states of the Upper South—especially Virginia and the Carolinas—continued to be the main sources of New York's migrant Negro population, but people from Georgia and Florida and other Deep South states formerly under-represented also came in greater numbers: "Harlem became the symbol of liberty and the Promised Land to Negroes everywhere," the Reverend Dr. Powell wrote. "There was hardly a member of Abyssinian Church who could not count on one or more relatives among the new arrivals."[6] In 1930, some 55,000 foreign-born Negroes added to the growing diversity of the city's Negro population.

The following chart presents an exact description of the geographical origins of Negro migrants to New York City in 1930. I have selected states with 900 or more residents in the city:[7]

NEGRO IN-MIGRATION, NEW YORK CITY, 1930

Born in:

Virginia	44,471
South Carolina	33,765
North Carolina	26,120
Georgia	19,546
Florida	8,249
Maryland	6,656
Pennsylvania	6,226
New Jersey	5,275
District of Columbia	3,358
Alabama	3,205
Massachusetts	2,329
Louisiana	2,182
Ohio	1,721
Tennessee	1,651
Texas	1,592
Kentucky	1,216
Mississippi	969
Foreign-born	54,754

The rapid settlement of a heterogeneous Negro population coincided with another important population change—the migration of whites from all sections of Manhattan to other boroughs. For the first time since Dutch settlement Manhattan's population *declined* in the 1920's as first- and second-generation immigrants moved to nicer residential areas in the Bronx, Brooklyn and Queens. Many of the homes they left behind had deteriorated significantly. By 1930 a majority of New York City's foreign-born and second-generation residents lived outside Manhattan.[8] As whites moved out of Manhattan, Negroes moved in. The population of that borough declined 18 per cent in the 1920's as its Negro population increased 106 per cent. By 1930 Negroes represented 12 per cent of Manhattan's population—although they composed only 4.7 per cent of the population of the entire city.[9]

Harlem was the New York neighborhood most radically revamped by the population movements of the 1920's, although the Lower East Side also changed rapidly. Harlem underwent a revolution—what one contemporary accurately called a "stupendous upheaval." Between 1920 and 1930, 118,792 white people left the neighborhood and 87,417 Negroes arrived.[10] Second-generation Italians and Jews were responding to the same conditions of prosperity that promoted mobility in all the immigrant neighborhoods of Manhattan—they were not *only* moving away because Negroes settled near them. Conditions of life which satisfied immigrant parents were often unacceptable to children: "The tenements which housed their parents," immigration expert Edward Corsi wrote in 1930, "are being left behind by the children. . . ." "East Harlem used to have a great deal larger population," a survey of the Mayor's Committee on City Planning during the Great Depression concluded. "Like others of the older residential districts, it has suffered by the exodus of families to newer surroundings. . . ."[11]

The city's newest migrants moved into the Harlem flats vacated by Italians and Jews. Puerto Ricans came to live in East Harlem, created community organizations, and laid the foundations for "El Barrio" of today. By 1930 some 45,000 Puerto Ricans resided in New York City and most were heavily concentrated in East Harlem.[12] Negroes moved north along St. Nicholas Avenue—"On the Heights," they called it—and south into the heart of "Little Russia," the former Jewish section. "Just Opened for Colored" signs were common in the neighborhood. Mount Olivet Baptist Church occupied, and still occupies, the once exclusive Temple Israel of Harlem. Prince Hall Masons bought a building that "was formerly a home for aged Jews." Graham Court, a magnificent block-length apartment house on One Hundred and Sixteenth Street, with eight separate elevators and apartments of seven to ten rooms, was opened to Negroes in 1928.[13] By 1930, 164,566 Negroes, about 72 per cent of Manhattan's Negro population, lived in Harlem.[14] The Negro ghetto remained and expanded as the other ethnic ghettos disintegrated. The economic and residential mobility permitted white people in the city was, and would continue to be, largely denied Negroes. Most Negroes were "jammed together" in Harlem—even those who could afford to live elsewhere—with little possibility of escape.[15] "One notable difference appears between the immigrant and Negro populations," an important federal study of Negro housing concluded. "In the case of the former, there is the possibility of escape, with improvement in economic status, in the second generation, to more desirable sections of the city. In the case of Negroes, who remain a distinguishable group, the factor of race and certain definite racial attitudes favorable to segregation, interpose difficulties to . . . breaking physical restrictions in residence areas."[16] A rather ponderous paragraph, but a significant truth.

III

The settlement of West Indian Negroes in Harlem in the 1920's added another complicating dimension to the racial problems of this community—one that fostered discord rather than harmony among the city's Negroes. There were ten times as many foreign-born Negroes in New York City as in any other American urban area. In 1930, 54,754 foreign Negroes lived in the city—39,833 of whom resided in Manhattan. Miami, the next largest American city in terms of immigrant Negroes, was settled by only 5,512 people; Boston ranked third with 3,287 West Indians. About 25 per cent of Harlem's population in the twenties was foreign-born. Harlem was America's largest Negro melting pot.[17]

In the era of immigration restriction, West Indian Negroes came to America through what a contemporary called the "side door." The immigration laws of the 1920's seriously restricted the migration of Europeans and totally excluded Orientals but had little effect on peoples of the Caribbean. At first there were no restrictions on West Indian Negroes. After 1924, they could enter the country under quotas set aside for their mother countries. Since these quotas were never filled there was, in reality, a free flow of people from the islands to the United States in the 1920's.[18]

Although American Negroes tended to lump all the migrants together in a uniform image—"There is a general assumption," one migrant wrote, "that there is everything in common among West Indians"—it is important to recognize that Harlem's Negro immigrants represented a diverse group of peoples from dozens of different islands in the Caribbean.[19] Most Negro immigrants felt a strong attachment to their homeland. They demonstrated an "exaggerated" nationalism in America—a buffer against the strangeness of the new culture and the hostility they experienced—which was typical of white immigrant groups. It was common, for example, to find former British subjects at the office of the British consul protesting some difficulty they experienced in America.[20] Nationalistic organizations kept close check on American foreign policy in the Caribbean and often gave banquets for and listened to addresses by West Indian dignitaries. West Indian Negroes from all countries had the lowest rate of naturalization of all immigrant groups. The people white Americans and American Negroes called "West Indians" were really individuals from Jamaica, Trinidad, Barbados, Martinique, St. Vincent, St. Lucia, Dominica, British Guiana, St. Kitts, Nevis, Montserrat, Antigua, Virgin Islands, Bermuda, the Bahamas, and so on. Although the majority spoke English, some considered French their first tongue; others Spanish; a few Dutch. The fraternal and benevolent associations they founded were not inclusive organizations for all Negro immigrants, but exclusive ones—*landsmannschaften*—for people from specific islands. Danish settlers kept pictures of the King of Denmark in their homes; former British subjects held coronation pageants and balls ("Boxes, 12s. 6d.—Loges, 8s. 4d.") and flew the Union Jack in Harlem; Frenchmen had annual Bastille Day dances.[21]

Negro immigrants differed from each other in origin, yet in a broader sense they shared general experiences, desires and mores which set them apart *as a group* from their American brethren. Most came from societies in which class distinctions played a more important role in one's life than the color line—although the latter was certainly significant. Unaccustomed to common American racial slurs, they often refused to accept them without protest. The Pullman Company, for example, hesitated to employ West Indian Negroes, it was said, "because of their refusal to accept insults from passengers quietly."[22] Out of this heightened class consciousness came a small group of political and economic radicals in Harlem—"foreign-born agitators," local Negroes called them.[23] Many of Harlem's street-corner orators in the 1920's, though not all, were West Indian migrants. Hubert H. Harrison, a Virgin Islander, was among the most prominent. Harrison was a socialist, an expert in African history, a militant critic of American society and a proud defender of the "Negro's racial heritage." He conducted formal lectures in what he called the "Harlem School of Social Science," and others from street corners—his "outdoor university." A Harlem church, the Hubert H. Harrison Memorial Church, honors his memory. Others presented talks on "Socialism vs. Capitalism," organized tenants' leagues, published Marxist journals and tried to make Harlemites labor-conscious. Richard B. Moore, Frank R. Crosswaith and the Reverend Ethelred Brown—all Negro immigrants—were prominent local candidates for Board of Aldermen, Assembly and Congress on Socialist and Communist tickets—they usually polled an exceedingly small vote. Some organized rent strikes, "rent parades," lobbied for social legislation at City Hall and Albany and distributed radical literature in Harlem. "There is no West Indian slave, no American slave," the short-lived radical magazine *Challenge* commented. "You are all slaves, base, ignoble slaves."[24]

This concern with "class" led to the emergence of a broader tradition in America. What is striking about the Negro immigrant is the way his response to American conditions, such as his exaggerated sense of nationalism, was similar to the typical reactions of most European immigrants. The Negro immigrant "did not suffer from the local anesthesia of custom"[25] and he tried to create a meaningful economic position for himself within American society. Menial labor was, among most first-generation Negro immigrants, considered a sign of social degradation and looked upon with "disgust." Most were forced to accept such jobs initially, but were strongly motivated by their traditions to improve themselves. As a group, West Indians became noted for their ambition, thrift and business acumen. They were called "pushy," "the Jews of the race," "crafty," "clannish."[26] Negro journalist George S. Schuyler "admired their enterprise in business, their pushfulness."[27] "The West Indians [are] legendary in Harlem for their frugalness and thrift," one student noted. When a West Indian "got ten cents above a beggar," a common local saying ran, "he opened a business." Contemporary surveys of Negro business in Harlem and Columbus Hill demonstrate that a disproportionate number of small stores—the traditional "Race Enterprise"— were owned by Negro immigrants. Dr. P. M. H. Savory, one of the leading spokesmen of New York's foreign-born Negro community from the 1920's to his death in June 1965, owned and published the *Amsterdam News*. Many others achieved economic success within the racial barrier.[28]

Another significant distinction between the foreign-born Negro and the American was their attitude toward family life. Slavery initially destroyed the entire concept of family for American Negroes and the slave heritage, bulwarked by economic conditions, continued into the twentieth century to make family instability a common factor in Negro life. This had not been true for most West Indians, and they arrived in America with the orthodox respect for family ties that was traditional of rural people. The West Indian family was patriarchal in structure—contrasted with the typically matriarchal American Negro home. The father, as key worker and wage earner in the islands, ruled the household with a solid hand. It was beneath his dignity to help with domestic chores. (This led American Negroes to brand West Indian men "cruel.")[29] Children were supposed to obey their parents rigidly—American Negroes considered them strait-laced; have long and formal courtships; and receive parental approval before marriage. Illicit sexual relations were considered the worst form of moral evil.[30] These traditions began to change in the second generation, but throughout the 1920's family solidarity was a pervasive force among New York's Negro immigrants.[31]

These differences in style of life were also evident in another important institution—the church. The majority of Harlemites were Baptists and Methodists; the immigrants were predominantly Episcopalian and Catholic.[32] The beautiful St. Martin's Episcopal Church was founded in Harlem in 1928 to minister to the needs of West Indian migrants. Services in immigrant churches were generally staid and quiet; Sunday a day of prayer, rest and visiting—as it had been on the islands. Observers were impressed with the differences between the emotionalism of a typical Harlem religious service and the moderation and restraint shown in churches of the foreign-born. Negro immigrants also objected to the general frivolity and "fast ways" that were part of a typical Sunday in Harlem.[33]

All these factors combined to make Harlem in the 1920's a battleground of intraracial antagonism. American Negro nativism spilled over to taint Harlemites' reactions to the West Indian. The Negro immigrant was ridiculed; his tropical clothing was mocked; children tossed stones at the people who looked so different; foreigners were taunted with such epithets as "monkey-chaser," "ring-tale," "king Mon," "cockney." "When a monkey-chaser dies/Don't need no undertaker/Just throw him in de Harlem River/He'll float back to Jamaica," was a verse from a Harlem ditty of the twenties. West Indians came to Harlem, ran another common saying, "to teach, open a church, or start trouble." "Bitter resentment grew on both sides." Each group called the other "aggressive." "We have . . . in Harlem," NAACP director Walter White wrote, "this strange mixture of reactions not only to prejudice from without but to equally potent prejudices from within." "If you West Indians don't like how we do things in this country," an American Negro said tersely, "you should go back where you came from. . . ."[34]

The obvious hostility of American Negroes forced Negro immigrants to unite in defense organizations larger than their individual national groups. The West Indian Committee on America, the Foreign-Born Citizens' Alliance and the West Indian Reform Association were founded in the twenties to soften these intraracial tensions and promote "cordial relations between West Indians and colored Americans." Radio programs were devoted to discussions of "Intra-Race Relations in Harlem," and immigrants were urged to become naturalized citizens. American Negroes, in turn, were asked to tone down their "considerable prejudice against West Indians." A semblance of co-operation was achieved as mass meetings were held in Harlem churches. The hatreds of the 1920's did not die, however, until West Indian Negroes stopped migrating to New York. During the Depression more immigrants left New York than entered and intraracial tensions slowly eased. Young Harlemites today, even third-generation descendants of Negro immigrants, are often unaware of these old divisions. The unique type of intraracial hostility so prominent in the twenties has never reappeared. While it lasted, however, it served to weaken a Negro community in great need of unity. A divided Harlem confronted major social problems that desperately called for the co-operation of all.[35]

IV

The most profound change that Harlem experienced in the 1920's was its emergence as a slum. Largely within the space of a single decade Harlem was transformed from a potentially ideal community to a neighborhood with manifold social and economic problems called "deplorable," "unspeakable," "incredible." "The State would not allow cows to live in some of these apartments used by colored people . . . in Harlem," the chairman of a city housing reform committee said in 1927. The Harlem slum of today was created in the 1920's.[36]

The most important factor which led to the rapid deterioration of Harlem housing was the high cost of living in the community. Rents, traditionally high in Harlem, reached astounding proportions in the 1920's—they skyrocketed in response to the unprecedented demand created by heavy Negro migration and settlement within a restricted geographical area. "Crowded in a black ghetto," a sociologist wrote, "the Negro tenant is forced to pay exorbitant rentals because he cannot escape." In 1919 the average Harlemite paid somewhat above $21 or $22 a month for rent; by 1927 rentals had *doubled* and the "mean average market rent for Negro tenants in a typical block" was $41.77. In 1927 Harlem Negroes paid $8 more than the typical New Yorker for three-room apartments; $10 more for four rooms; and $7 more for five rooms, an Urban League survey noted.[37] Another report concluded that the typical white working-class family in New York City in the late twenties paid $6.67 per room, per month, while Harlem Negroes were charged $9.50.[38]

Realty values which had declined significantly prior to World War I *appreciated* in Harlem in the twenties.[39] Harlem experienced a slum boom. "The volume of business done in the section . . . during the last year is . . . unprecedented," *Harlem Magazine* announced in 1920. "Renting conditions have been very satisfactory to the owners and the demand for space . . . is getting keener every year [due] to the steady increase in the negro population," a *New York Times* reporter wrote in 1923. There was, in the language of a Harlem businessman, an "unprecedented demand for Harlem real estate."[40] For landlords—Negro and white (Negro tenants continually complained that Negro landlords fleeced them with equal facility as whites)—Harlem became a profitable slum.[41]

High rents and poor salaries necessarily led to congested and unsanitary conditions. The average Negro Harlemite in the 1920's, as in the 1890's, held some menial or unskilled position which paid low wages—work which was customarily "regarded as Negro jobs." There were generally two types of businesses in New York in terms of Negro hiring policy, E. Franklin Frazier wrote: "Those that employ Negroes in menial positions and those that employ no Negroes at all." Macy's, for example, hired Negroes as elevator operators, escalator attendants and cafeteria workers; Gimbels used none. "We have felt it inadvisable to [hire] colored people," a Metropolitan Life Insurance Company executive explained in 1930, "not because of any prejudice on the part of the company, but because . . . there would be very serious objection on the part of our white employees. . . ."[42] Throughout the city the vast majority of Negro men worked as longshoremen, elevator operators, porters, janitors, teamsters, chauffeurs, waiters and general laborers of all kinds. Negro women continued to work as domestics ("scrub women"), although in the 1920's an increasing number were employed as factory operatives in the garment industry and in laundries. Less than 20 per cent of Harlem's businesses were owned by Negroes.[43] The average Harlem family, according to President Hoover's Conference on Home Building and Home Ownership, earned $1,300 a year in the twenties; the typical white family in the city, $1,570. A variety of social investigations noted that working-class whites expended approximately 20 per cent of their income for rent, considered the proper amount by economists; Harlemites, 33 per cent and more.[44] An Urban League study of 2,160 Harlem families demonstrated that almost half (48 per cent) spent 40 or more per cent of their earnings on rent. A 1928 sample of tenement families found that Harlemites paid 45 per cent of their wages for housing. Similar conclusions were reached in a variety of local community studies.[45] Whatever the exact figure, few Negroes looked to the first of the month with expectancy.

Added to the combination of "high rents and low wages"[46] was the fact that Harlem's apartment houses and brownstones were originally built for people with a radically different family structure from that of the new residents. Seventy-five per cent of Harlem's tenements had been constructed before 1900.[47] The Negro community of the twenties, like all working-class peoples in times of great migration, continued to be most heavily populated by young adults— men and women between the ages of 15 and 44. Family life had not yet begun for many Negro Harlemites—as it had for older Americans and earlier immigrants who lived in the community previously. In 1930, 66.5 per cent of Harlem Negroes were between the ages of 15 and 44, contrasted with 56.5 per cent for the general population of Manhattan and 54.4 per cent for New York City at large. Harlemites who were married had few children. In 1930, 17.5 per cent of Harlem's population was under 14; the corresponding figure for New

York City was 24.5 per cent. The number of Harlemites under the age of 15 declined 14 per cent between 1920 and 1930, as whites left the neighborhood. There was a corresponding decrease of 19 per cent for those over 45 years of age.[48]

What all these statistics mean is simply that apartments of five, six, and seven rooms were suitable for older white residents with larger families and larger incomes—they obviously did not meet the needs of the Negro community in the 1920's. "The houses in the section of Harlem inhabited by the Negro were not only built for another race," E. Franklin Frazier noted, "but what is more important, for a group of different economic level, and consisting of families and households of an entirely different composition from those which now occupy these dwellings." "Unfortunately," Eugene Kinckle Jones of the Urban League stated, "the houses built before [the Negroes'] arrival were not designed to meet the needs . . . of Negroes." "The class of houses we are occupying today are not suited to our economic needs," John E. Nail said in 1921. Negro Harlemites desperately needed small apartments at low rentals: "One of the community's greatest needs [is] small apartments for small families with a reasonable rent limit. . . ."[49] Few realtors were philanthropic enough to invest their capital in new construction; older homes, properly subdivided, produced sufficient income. Only a handful of new houses were built in Harlem in the 1920's.[50]

A variety of makeshift solutions were found to make ends meet: "What you gonna do when the rent comes 'round," had been an old Negro song. The most common solution was to rent an apartment larger than one's needs and means and make up the difference by renting rooms to lodgers—"commercializing" one's home. In the twenties, approximately one white Manhattan family in nine (11.2 per cent) took in roomers, contrasted with one in four (26 per cent) for Negroes. Most lodgers were strangers people let into their homes because of economic necessity. It was difficult to separate "the respectable" from "the fast." "The most depraved Negroes lived side by side with those who were striving to live respectable lives," a contemporary complained. Urban reformers blamed many of Harlem's social problems on this "lodger evil."[51]

Every conceivable space within a home was utilized to maximum efficiency: "Sometimes even the bathtub is used to sleep on, two individuals taking turns!" Negro educator Roscoe Conkling Bruce wrote. Boardinghouses were established which rented beds by the week, day, night or hour. A large number of brownstones were converted to rooming houses: "Private residences at one time characteristic of this part of the city have been converted into tenements. . . ." One landlord transformed apartments in nine houses into one-room flats, a state commission investigating New York housing reported. Space which formerly grossed $40 a month now brought in $100 to $125. People were said to be living in "coal bins and cellars." In an extreme case, one social investigator discovered seven children sleeping on pallets on the floor of a two-room apartment. More common was the "Repeating" or "Hot Bed System"—as soon as one person awoke and left, his bed was taken over by another.[52]

An additional Harlem method devised to meet the housing crisis of the twenties was the "Rent Party." Tickets of admission were usually printed and sold for a modest price (25¢). All who wanted to come were invited to a party. Here is an example:[53]

> If you're looking for a good time,
>   don't look no more,
> Just ring my bell and I'll answer
>   the door.
> Southern Barbecue
> Given by Charley Johnson and Joe
> Hotboy, and How hot!

Chitterlings, pigs' feet, coleslaw and potato salad were sold. Money was raised in this way to pay the rent: "The rent party," *The New York Age* editorialized in 1926, "has become a recognized means of meeting the demands of extortionate landlords. . . ." The white world saw rent parties as picturesque affairs—in reality they were a product of economic exploitation and they often degenerated into rowdy, bawdy and violent evenings.[54]

A significant part of the deterioration of the neighborhood was caused by the migrants themselves. Some needed rudimentary training in the simplest processes of good health and sanitation (Booker T. Washington, it will be remembered, preached the "gospel of the toothbrush").[55] E. Franklin Frazier called many Negro Harlemites "ignorant and unsophisticated peasant people without experience [in] urban living. . . ." They often permitted homes and buildings to remain in a state of uncleanliness and disrepair. Landlords complained that apartments were looted and fixtures stolen, that courtyards and hallways were found laden with refuse. Clothes and bedding were hung out of windows; trash sometimes thrown down air shafts; dogs walked on rooftops; profanities shouted across streets; "ragtime" played throughout the night. "Ragtime is a sufficient infliction of itself," one wag complained, "but when it keeps up all night, it becomes unbearable." "Since the so-called 'Negro invasion,' " a colored woman noted, "the streets, the property and the character of everything have undergone a change, and if you are honest, you will frankly acknowledge it has not been for the . . . improvement of the locality. . . . Are we responsible for at least some of the race prejudice which has developed since the entry of Negroes in Harlem?" Negro journals criticized "boisterous" men who laughed "hysterically" and hung around street corners, and those who used "foul language on the streets." An editorial in the *Age,* one of many, attacked "Careless Harlem Tenants": "A great deal might be said about the necessity for training some of the tenants in the matter of common decency," it suggested. The absence of a sense of social and community responsibility, characteristic of urban life, obviously affected Negro Harlemites.[56]

All these factors combined to lead to the rapid decline of Harlem. The higher the rents, sociologists said, the greater the congestion: "Crowding is more prevalent in high-rent cities than in cities in which rent per room is more reasonable." In 1925, Manhattan's population density was 223 people per acre—in the Negro districts it was 336. Philadelphia, the second most congested Negro city in the country, had 111 Negroes to an acre of land; Chicago ranked third with 67. There were two streets in Harlem that were perhaps the most congested blocks in the entire world.[57]

People were packed together to the point of "indecency."[58] Some landlords, after opening houses to Negro tenants, lost interest in caring for their property and permitted it to run down—halls were left dark and dirty, broken pipes were permitted to rot, steam heat was cut off as heating apparatus wore out, dumb-waiters broke down and were boarded up, homes became vermin-infested. Tenants in one rat-infested building started what they called "a crusade against rats." They argued that the rats in their house were "better fed" and "better housed" than the people. Some common tenant complaints in the 1920's read: "No improvement in ten years"; "Rats, rat holes, and roaches"; "Very very cold"; "Not fit to live in"; "Air shaft smells";

"Ceilings in two rooms have fallen"; "My apartment is overrun with rats"; and so on.[59] There were more disputes between tenants and landlords in Harlem's local district court—the Seventh District Court —than in any municipal court in the five boroughs. Traditionally, municipal courts were known as "poor-men's courts"; Harlemites called the Seventh District Court the "rent court." Occasionally, socially conscious judges of this court made personal inspections of local tenements that were subjects of litigation. Without exception what they saw horrified them: "Conditions in negro tenements in Harlem are deplorable"; "Found few fit for human habitation"; "Negro tenants are being grossly imposed upon by their landlords"; "On the whole I found a need for great reformation"; were some of their comments. One municipal official accurately called the majority of Harlem's houses "diseased properties."[60]

V

And the disease did not confine itself to houses. To touch most areas of Harlem life in the 1920's is to touch tragedy. This was especially true of the health of the community. Theoretically, a section of the city inhabited by relatively young people should have ranked below the general population in mortality and sickness rates. Just the reverse was true. Undertaking was a most profitable Harlem business.[61]

From 1923 to 1927 an Atlanta University professor made an intensive study of Harlem health. His findings were shocking. During these years Harlem's death rate, for all causes, was 42 per cent in excess of that of the entire city. Twice as many Harlem mothers died in childbirth as did mothers in other districts, and almost twice as many Harlem children "passed" as did infants in the rest of New York. Infant mortality in Harlem, 1923–1927, was 111 per thousand live births; for the city, 64.5. Families wept at the processions of "so many little white caskets." Similar statistics are recorded for deaths from tuberculosis (two and a half to three times the city rate), pneumonia, heart disease, cancer and stillbirths.[62] An astounding number of Harlemites had venereal diseases. Negro children commonly suffered from rickets—a disease of malnutrition. More women than ever reported themselves "widows" to census-takers. Negro deaths by violence increased 60 per cent between 1900 and 1925.[63] With the single exception of the Lower West Side Health District,

Health center districts, 1930	Infant mortality per 1,000 live births	TB mortality per 100,000 population	Pulmonary TB new case rate per 100,000 population	Other infectious diseases, rate per 100,000 population	Venereal disease new case rate per 100,-000 population	General mortality rate per 1,000 population
Manhattan						
Central Harlem	98	251	487	987	2,826	15.3
Lower East Side	62	116	302	1,160	892	14.0
Kips Bay–Lenox Hill	73	75	184	937	629	12.7
East Harlem	75	137	311	1,326	913	12.0
Lower West Side	83	156	391	1,201	1,318	16.7
Riverside	64	75	196	827	778	12.3
Washington Heights	52	72	203	937	668	10.5
Total	73	122	294	1,049	1,455	13.3

which included the old San Juan Hill neighborhood, Harlem was the most disease-ridden community in Manhattan.[64]

Whatever the causes of Harlem's health problems—and medical investigators continue to search for all the answers—a good deal can be laid at the door of slum environment. Urban reformers consistently showed a high correlation between poverty and congestion on the one hand and disease and death on the other. Mortality rates for infants whose mothers worked away from home, for example—and twice as many Negro women as white women in the city did—was higher than for children whose mothers remained at home; working-class families in old-law tenements (pre-1901) died at a higher-rate than those in newer houses; poverty led to the consumption of the cheapest foods, and this in turn fostered diseases of poor diet; working mothers died more readily in childbirth than unemployed women; and so on.[65] Added to all these considerations, however, was a deep strain of peasant ignorance and superstition embedded in the minds of thousands of migrants—foreign-born as well as native— who settled in Harlem. Quackery abounded in the community in the 1920's.[66]

Harlem had the reputation of a "wide-open city." Whatever you wanted, and in whatever quantity, so the impression went, could be bought there. This was certainly true for the variety of "spiritualists," "herb doctors," "African medicine men," "Indian doctors," "dispensers of snake oils," "layers-on-of-hands," "faith healers," "palmists," and phrenologists who performed a twentieth-century brand of necromancy there: "Harlem sick people are flocking to all sorts of Quacksters," an *Age* reporter noted. One man, "Professor Ajapa," sold a "herb juice" guaranteed "to cure consumption, rheumatism, and other troubles that several doctors have failed in." Powders could be purchased to keep one's wife home at night, make women fertile and men sexually appealing. "Black Herman the Magician" and "Sister P. Harreld" held séances and sold "blessed handkerchiefs," "potent powders," love charms, lodestones, amulets and "piles of roots." "Ignorance, cherished superstitions and false knowledge often govern Negroes in illness and hamper recoveries," a colored physician with the Board of Health wrote in 1926. Nine wood lice gathered in a little bag and tied around a baby's neck, some believed, would end teething. An egg fried brown on both sides and placed on a woman's abdomen would hasten labor. If a mother in the course of childbirth kicked a Bible from her bed to the floor, either she or her child would die. People had faith in the medicinal qualities of dried cobwebs, rabbit brains, "dirt-dauber tea," and something called "cockroach rum." In spite of efforts of physicians, health agencies and the Negro press to bring modern-day medical information to the community, quackery "continued to thrive with impunity in Harlem." It aggravated an already tragic situation.[67]

Accompanying the proliferation of healers, and rooted in the same rural consciousness which made quackery possible,[68] was the host of storefront churches founded in Harlem in the twenties. These were places that healed one's soul: "Jesus is the Doctor, Services on Sunday," read a sign which hung over one door. An investigator found 140 Negro churches in a 150-block area of Harlem in 1926. "Harlem is perhaps overchurched," W. E. B. DuBois said modestly. Only about a third—fifty-four—of Harlem's churches were housed in regular church buildings—and these included some of the most magnificent and costly church edifices in New York City. The rest held services in stores and homes and appealed to Harlem's least educated people. "Jack-leg preachers," "cotton-field preachers," as their critics called them, hung out their poorly printed signboards and "preached Jesus" to all who wanted to listen. One self-appointed pastor held meetings in the front room of his home and rented chairs from the local undertaker to seat his small congregation. In Harlem in the twenties one could receive the word of the Lord through such nondenominational sects as: "The Metaphysical Church of the Divine Investigation," "The Temple of the Gospel of the Kingdom," "The Church of the Temple of Love," "Holy Church of the Living God," "Temple of Luxor," "Holy Tabernacle of God," "Royal Fraternity Association," "Knights of the Rose and Cross," "Sons of God," "Sons of Christ," "Sons of Jehovah," "Sanctified Sons of the Holy Ghost," and the "Live-Ever-Die-Never" church. People not only had their worries removed in these places, a Negro clergyman wrote, but "their meager worldly goods as well."[69]

The ministers of these churches preached a fundamentalism which centered around the scheming ways of Satan, who was everywhere, and the terror and joy of divine retribution, with an emphasis on terror. One congregation expelled members who attended the theater or movies. "The devil runs every theatre," its pastor said. "He collects a tax on the souls of men and robs them of their seat in heaven." Services were fervent, loud and boisterous as members felt the spirit of the Lord and shouted and begged for His forgiveness. Tambourines sometimes kept up a rhythmic beat in the background and heightened the emotionalism to a state of frenzy. Neighbors of one storefront church sued the congregation for "conducting a public nuisance." The "weird sounds" which emanated from the building, they complained, seemed like a "jazz orchestra."[70]

> Are you ready-ee? Hah!
> For that great day, hah!
> When the moon shall drape her face in mourning, hah!
> And the sun drip down in blood, hah!
> When the stars, hah!
> Shall burst forth from their diamond sockets, hah!
> And the mountains shall skip like lambs, hah!
> Havoc will be there, my friends, hah!
> With her jaws wide open, hah!
> And the sinner-man, hah!
> And cry, Oh rocks! Hah!
> Hide me! Hah!
> Hide me from the face of an angry God, hah!
> Hide me, Ohhhhhh! . . .
> Can't hide, sinner, you can't hide.[71]

Contemporaries were uniformly critical of these evangelists—there were many Harlem "Prophets"—and most of these preachers were probably charlatans in some form. There was at least one exception, however. A new denomination, the Church of Christ, Apostolic Faith, was founded on the streets of Harlem by the Reverend Mr. R. C. Lawson in 1919. The Reverend Mr. Lawson, of New Iberia, Louisiana, "the only real Apostolic–Holy Ghost–Bible Preacher," presented what he called the "Full Gospel" on street corners of Harlem's worst blocks. He decried the lack of emotionalism in the more established urban churches—copying "the white man's style," he said—and offered recent migrants a touch of fire and brimstone and personal Christianity characteristic of religion in the rural South:

> I have found it, I have found it,
> the meaning of life, life in God,
> life flowing through me by the
> Holy Spirit, life abundant, peace,
> joy, life in its fullness.

Lawson started preaching on One Hundred and Thirty-third Street, east of Lenox Avenue. This area "was to Harlem what the Bowery is to the lower East Side," a Negro journalist recorded. From the streets, the Reverend Mr. Lawson moved into a small building and held services for those "fast drifting to a life of eternal darkness" every day and every night of the week. His Refuge Church of Christ became the founding church of the new denomination, and the Reverend Mr. Lawson its first bishop. By 1930 the Apostolic Church had some forty branches throughout the country and ran an orphanage, elementary school and "Bible Supply House"; it continues to prosper today. Annual conventions met in Refuge Church, "the most honored in the sisterhood of the Apostolic Church," and local leaders praised and publicized its good works for Harlem Negroes: "This church has had one of the most remarkable growths of any religious organizations in the country."[72]

Harlem was also a "wide-open city" in terms of vice and gambling.[73] The annual reports of the anti-vice Committee of Fourteen, founded in 1905, showed Harlem as the leading or near-leading prostitution center of Manhattan throughout the twenties. The Committee hired a Negro doctor, Ernest R. Alexander, to do a secret study of Harlem vice in 1928. His report emphasized the "openness of vice conditions in this district." Dr. Alexander personally found sixty-one houses of prostitution in the neighborhood—more than the combined totals of four other investigators hired at the same time to survey other districts. "There is a larger amount and more open immorality in Harlem than this community has known in years," Negro alderman George W. Harris noted in 1922. "It is a house of assignation . . . this black city," Eric D. Walrond wrote bitterly in the Negro journal *The Messenger*.[74]

> Her dark brown face
> Is like a withered flower
> On a broken stem.
> Those kind come cheap in Harlem,
> So they say.[75]

The Committee of Fourteen also disclosed that more than 90 per cent of these "daughters of joy" institutions were owned and managed by whites. Other evidence verifies this.[76]

Gambling also prevailed in the neighborhood: "Bootleggers, gamblers, and other panderers to vice have found it profitable to ply their vicious trades in this section." The poorest of the poor sought instant riches through the numbers racket. No sum was too small to bet—starting with pennies. "One can bet with plenty of takers on anything from a horse race to a mule race," the *Age* editorialized. Many Harlemites "would rather gamble than eat," it concluded. People selected numbers to coincide with birthdays, dreams, hymns or chapters and verses of Scripture in expectation that they would coincide with the clearing-house figures of the day. The odds were thousands to one against success, yet the smallest hope for a richer life was better than none and Negroes continued to play "policy" avidly. "The chief pastime of Harlem seems to be playing the numbers," George S. Schuyler wrote in 1925.[77]

"Buffet flats," "hooch joints," "barrel houses," and cabarets supplied Harlemites with illegal liquor, and occasionally other things, in the Prohibition era. Drugstores, cigar stores, sweetshops and delicatessens were used as "fronts" for speakeasies. "Harlem can boast of more drugstores than any similar area in the world," one Negro commented. "A plethora of delicatessen stores may be found in the Negro sections of New York, most of which are simply disguised bootlegging stores," a Harlemite concluded in 1924. "And so many confectioners! One never dreamed the Negroes were so much in need of sugar." "Speakeasies downtown are usually carefully camouflaged," a *New York Tribune* reporter noted. "In Harlem they can be spotted a hundred yards off."[78]

Poverty and family instability also led to a high incidence of juvenile delinquency. A community with fewer young teenagers should have shown a proportionally lower juvenile crime rate; as with Negro health, just the reverse was true. "The records of the Children's Court of New York for every year from 1914 to 1927 show a steady increase in the percentage of all crimes committed by Negro boys and girls," Owen R. Lovejoy of the Children's Aid Society reported. In 1914 Negro children represented 2.8 per cent of all cases before the juvenile court of New York City; in 1930 this figure rose to 11.7 per cent.[79]

Working mothers had little time to care for their children. Youngsters "with keys tied around their necks on a ribbon" wandered around the streets until families came home at night. A substantial portion were products of broken homes—families without a male head. One Harlem school principal testified that 699 of his 1,600 pupils came from families whose fathers were not living at home. Nor did the majority of Harlem schoolchildren ever have time to accustom themselves to the regularity of school life; many families were rootless. Three-fourths of all the Negro pupils registered in one Harlem school, for example, transferred to some other before the end of one school year; some schools actually experienced a 100 per cent turnover. Pupils from the South were seriously deficient in educational training: "They are at times 14 to 15 years of age and have not the schooling of boys of eight," a Harlem principal wrote. "We cannot give a boy back seven years of wasted life. . . ." The typical Harlem school of the twenties had double and sometimes triple sessions. The "usual class size" was forty to fifty and conditions were generally "immensely over-crowded": "The school plant as a whole is old, shabby, and far from modern." In some schools 25 per cent and more of the children were overage or considered retarded.

Negro children in Harlem often led disrupted and harsh lives from the earliest years of their existence: "Testimony has been given before us as to the moral conditions among children, even of tender age," a municipal agency investigating Harlem schools recorded, "which is not to be adequately described by the word 'horrifying.' " These conditions were obviously reflected in high rates of juvenile crime but more subtly, and worst of all, in a loss of respect for oneself and for life in general. Harlem youngsters developed "a sense of subordination, of insecurity, of lack of self-confidence and self-respect, the inability . . . to stand on their own feet and face the world with open eyes and feel that [they have] as good a right as anyone else."[80]

This then was the horror of slum life—the Harlem tragedy of the 1920's. "Court and police precinct records show," a municipal agency maintained, "that in arrests, convictions, misdemeanants, felons, female police problems and juvenile delinquencies, these areas are in the lead. . . ." It was no wonder that narcotics addiction became a serious problem then and that Harlem became "the center of the retail dope traffic of New York"; nor that local violence and hatred for the police were continually reported in the press.[81] The majority of Harlemites even during normal times lived "close to the subsistence level." Many were "under care" of charitable agencies in the period of relatively full employment. Those who needed money quickly and had no other recourse were forced to turn to loan sharks,

Mary White Ovington (in 1940) and W. E. B. DuBois (in 1915), two of the founders of the NAACP *(United Press International photos)*

Model tenements at West 63rd Street built by steel magnate Henry Phipps and others in 1907, still there today; occupied in 1908 by Mary White Ovington, only white person in these Negro houses

("The Crisis," November 1910)

Do You Want a Position?

Best Places
Best Families

The New York and New Jersey Industrial Exchange, through its Employment Agency Department, furnishes more Colored Help to the leading families in the city and in the suburban towns than any other medium in New York.

It is located in the acknowledged best section of the city, being in the Henry Phipps' Model Tenements for Colored Families. No other Exchange is so well patronized by the foremost families, many of whom have never employed Colored Help before.

Our demand for competent Southern Help exceeds the supply many times over. Call and register. No charge. Bring your references. We can place you in a good position. If inconvenient to pay our required office fee, you are at liberty to take advantage of our Credit System. This new feature has proven extremely beneficial to many worthy persons seeking employment.

N.Y. & N. J. Industrial Exchange
237-239 West 63d Street
Telephones 5016-4546 Columbus

HENRY PHIPP'S MODEL TENEMENTS FOR COLORED FAMILIES

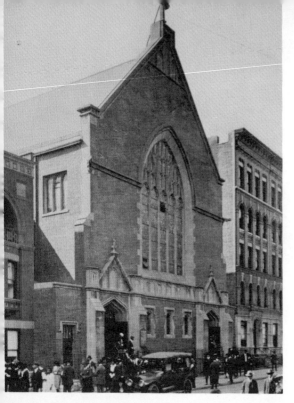

A Sunday morning in the 1920's, St. Philip's Protestant Episcopal Church (133rd Street near Seventh Avenue), most exclusive Negro church in New York City, founded in 1809 in the Five Points District; followed the Negro migration to Mulberry Street in 1856, to West 25th Street in 1889, and to Harlem in 1910 (*Brown Brothers*)

Cornerstone-laying ceremony, April 9, 1922, of the Abyssinian Baptist Church, 138th Street between Lenox and Seventh Avenues, organized in 1808 at present-day Worth Street (*courtesy, Abyssinian Baptist Church*)

The Reverend Dr. Adam Clayton Powell, Sr., famous pastor of the Abyssinian Baptist Church, undated, but probably in late 1920's (*Underwood & Underwood*)

Charles W. Anderson, noted Republican politician, named Collector of Third New York Internal Revenue Collection District, 1923 (*Underwood & Underwood*)

Dr. P. M. H. Savory, owner and publisher of the *Amsterdam News* from the 1930's until his death in 1965, one of many Negro leaders of West Indian origin (*The Schomburg Collection, New York Public Library*)

The Lafayette Theatre, Seventh Avenue between 131st and 132nd Streets, where Negroes were restricted to the balcony in the early 1900's, integrated in 1913; known in the 1920's as "America's Leading Colored Theatre" (*United Press International photo*)

Advertisements from *The New York News,* April 27, 1929, showing Negro entertainment widely patronized by whites, for whom Harlem was an exotic experience

OPPORTUNITY
Journal of Negro Life

JULY 1925

15 CENTS the copy

Symbols of the "New Negro Renaissance": Langston Hughes (above left), around 1927 (*photo by James L. Allen*), and Countée Cullen, on cover of National Urban League journal (*"Opportunity," July 1925*)

Social notes, *The New York News*, April 27, 1929

Harlem block dance, around 1915–1920   (*Brown Brothers*)

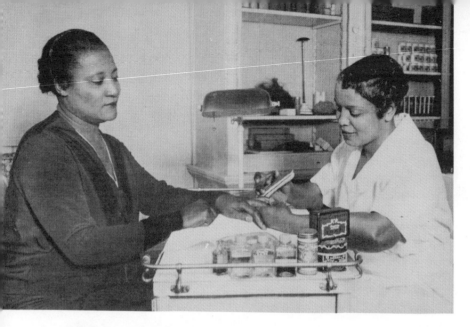

Madame C. J. Walker, former laundress, made wealthy by "Walker System" of hair straightening ("permanent straight," the opposite of "permanent wave") and other beauty preparations, in one of her many beauty parlors (*Underwood & Underwood*)

Ad for Mrs. C. J. Walker's Tan-Off—"will bleach" face, hands, neck, "make them a clear, light part of your body you'll be proud to show" (*"The Crisis," December 1930*)

Advertisement showing pride in Negro heritage (*"The Crisis," December 1923*)

Students, Public School #119, West 133rd Street, 1924, learning cooking, part of program to train Negroes for "suitable" jobs (*United Press International photo*)

The Dunbar National Bank, opened in 1928 in the Dunbar Apartments complex to encourage thrift and "to help the Negro help himself" (*Underwood & Underwood*)

AMERICAN LOGIC.

THIS MAN is not responsible for THIS MAN even if they do belong to the same race.

THIS MAN is responsible for all that THIS MAN does because they belong to the same race.

Cartoon from the NAACP magazine (*"The Crisis," June 1913*)

Negroes (including W. E. B. DuBois, second row, third from right) in the famous Silent Parade of muffled drums on July 28, 1917, up Fifth Avenue, protesting the East St. Louis race riots (*Underwood & Underwood*)

Negro and white, who charged 30 to 40 per cent interest: Harlem "has been infested by a lot of loan sharks," a municipal magistrate who dealt with such cases stated. In one form or another the sorrow and economic deprivation of the Depression had come to Harlem in the twenties: "The reason why the Depression didn't have the impact on the Negroes that it had on the whites," George S. Schuyler said, "was that the Negroes had been in the Depression all the time."[82]

CHAPTER 10 🔟

"Harlem Must Be Saved": The Struggle for Survival

"The development of playgrounds has
lagged far behind the development of
poolrooms. . . ."
—Winfred B. Nathan, *Health Conditions in North Harlem* (1932)

"The agencies established are inadequate
to meet the needs of this teeming section."
—Owen R. Lovejoy, *The Negro Children of New York* (1932)

I

"Harlem must be saved," the Reverend Dr. Adam Clayton Powell, Sr., wrote in 1923. "It deserves the jealous protection of all good men."[1] But it was simpler to recognize Harlem's difficulties and reduce them to series of statistical reports than it was to resolve them. Social and economic disorders of such "stupendous proportions" taxed the ability of society to deal with them. The combined efforts of all the traditional welfare and charity organizations acted as little more than holding operations, and often not even this, in the struggle to alleviate the poverty, slum housing, crime, vice and poor health that seemed embedded in the community's life: "The development of playgrounds," a Negro educator observed, "has lagged far behind the development of poolrooms. . . ." When a social worker asked a group of unemployed young men to join a youth club, they asked her to "join their crap game."[2]

Nor was American society willing to concern itself with the often tragic lives of Harlem Negroes. Small groups of socially conscious people, Negro and white, devoted their energies to the attempt to soften the hardships of rapid Negro urbanization; the city as a whole, however, and American society generally, lived basically unaware that Harlem had any misfortunes at all. At the very time Harlem was transformed into the city's worst slum its image for most white

150

Americans, and some Negroes as well, was just the reverse—a gay place inhabited by "a singing race," one man thought. "The attitude of the average white New Yorker to Harlem is one of tolerant amusement," a journalist concluded. "He thinks of it as a region of prosperous night clubs; of happy-go-lucky Negroes dancing all night to jazz music. . . ." White slummers visited Harlem's speakeasies in the 1920's and concluded that "Cabaret life was the true essence of Harlem."[3] Had these people arrived at noon and inspected a rat-infested tenement, their image of the gay Negro might have been changed; yet American racial consciousness refused to recognize any but the supposedly joyous side of Negro culture. It was impossible to mobilize any massive support for racial reform in the 1920's because American society voluntarily blinded itself to the harsh realities of Negro existence.

II

Some forty or fifty social service agencies were active in Harlem in the 1920's.[4] The varieties of institutions founded in the Progressive Era continued their existence, accompanied the movement of Negroes to Harlem, and constantly expanded in size once they got there. Harlem's YMCA's and YWCA's, for example, became the largest Negro Y's in America in the twenties. The old Fifty-third Street YMCA "quietly passed" from the scene in 1919. New York's Visiting Nurse Service employed some twenty-five or thirty Negro nurses in Harlem in the 1920's. These women, supervised by a Negro social worker, made an amazing total of some 35,000 home visits annually. The White Rose Home, New York Colored Mission, Sojourner Truth and Katy Ferguson Homes "for lifting fallen young colored women," Hope Day Nursery, Utopia Neighborhood Club, Circle for Negro Relief—and many others—continually appealed to the public for larger contributions to meet the slum crisis of the twenties. "Harlem's Trouble Doctor," as Negroes called the local office of the Charity Organization Society, received an increasingly large number of applications for aid from Negroes. It was forced to open a second office in the neighborhood in the 1920's, and established closer liaison with the Negro community through a committee of colored volunteers. Varieties of local Negro groups were formed, like the North Harlem Community Council and the North Harlem Vocational Guidance Committee, which concentrated on improving local schools, housing and health. Weekly discussions covering every possible type of social problem met at the One Hundred and Thirty-fifth Street public library—the library which later became the famous Schomburg Collection. "Block Beautiful Associations" distributed posters urging residents to show greater pride in their neighborhood.[5]

One of the most publicized institutions founded in the 1920's was the Harlem Tuberculosis and Health Committee. The Committee, organized in 1922, was a branch of the New York Tuberculosis and Health Association. The "ravages of the white plague" killed such an inordinate number of black New Yorkers—it was, a Negro physician wrote, "Public Enemy Number One in Harlem"—that the parent association decided to establish a separate unit in the Negro ghetto. The Committee concentrated its major efforts on eradicating TB but conceived of its task broadly and eventually set up health clinics to cover everything from "social hygiene" and nutrition to prenatal care. When twelve Negro dentists volunteered their services, the Harlem Committee opened a much-needed and much-used free dental clinic.[6]

Committee doctors visited homes without charge in an effort to locate Harlemites with pretubercular conditions. Children from particularly dangerous situations—especially those suffering from malnutrition and others in extremely congested homes—were sent to the country for fresh air and wholesome food. Public lectures were given in churches, schools and fraternal organizations: "Why the Babies Die"; "What Harlem Can Do for Her Children"; "A Proper Diet"; "The Negro and Tuberculosis"; "The Care of the Baby"; "Quackery in Harlem"; "How Tuberculosis Spreads"; "The Value of Early Diagnosis." A Health Institute trained local general practitioners in the latest techniques of diagnosing and treating tubercular patients. Health exhibits, posters, movies ("Peter Meets the Menace" was one), public demonstrations ("Chew Chew the Health Clown" described the proper care and handling of the toothbrush), appeared throughout Harlem in annual "Save-A-Life" campaigns. The Committee also published a significant number of health pamphlets for local distribution. "The aim of our entire work is to make Harlem as healthy a community as possible," the Committee's chairman noted in 1927.[7]

And all this effort certainly did some good. The over-all rates of death from tuberculosis in Negro Harlem declined slightly each year in the 1920's—it is frightening to imagine how high they would have been without the Harlem Committee and other public medical agencies.[8] Yet tubercular deaths remained shockingly high nonetheless and showed a tendency to decline more slowly for Negroes than for whites. The gap separating the two groups widened rather than narrowed in these years. Between 1929 and 1933, for example, four times as many Negroes died of this disease in Harlem as did whites in other New York neighborhoods—earlier in the century the ratios were never higher than 2 to 1 or 3 to 1. Tuberculosis was Harlem's "Number One" killer throughout the Great Depression and remains a serious urban problem today.[9]

The failure of the Harlem Committee, for all its good will and effort, to root out TB more successfully was reflected in the similar inabilities of social workers to end unusually high rates of infant and maternal mortality, juvenile delinquency, illegitimacy, dope addiction and all the other yardsticks of urban maladjustment. It seemed the more reformers pushed against the rock of Harlem's troubles, the more it rolled back upon them.

At least two basic reasons explain the relative failure of social reform in Harlem in the 1920's. One was the constant state of flux in which the community lived. Those familiar with the urban settlement of other minority groups will recall that the peak years of immigration were always accompanied by the most difficult periods of social adjustment—high crime and disease rates, slum housing, juvenile crime and so on.[10] Lillian D. Wald's New York, Jane Addams' Chicago, Robert A. Woods's Boston or Paul U. Kellogg's Pittsburgh were far from pleasant places for European immigrants to live despite the important efforts of an entire generation of municipal reformers. The tensions and problems created by the rapid urbanization of rural people never eased significantly until the years of greatest migration ended.

Harlem, like many other urban Negro communities, underwent its most radical years of transformation and Negro settlement in the 1920's. Community efforts were simply overwhelmed by the magnitude of the population change that took place. The generation of Negro migrants that had come north since the 1890's and adjusted as best it could to urban living had to make room for the latest initiates from the South. Continual Negro migration acted, and continues to act, as a disruptive force and served to prevent the development of a more stable, secure and promising pattern of community life. The constant renewal of Negro population through migration made Harlem, in the words of a prominent social worker, a "perpetual frontier." In spite of all efforts, an urban reformer wrote, "the agencies established are inadequate to meet the needs of this teeming section."[11]

Neither was it possible to resolve the complex hardships of Harlem by isolating one problem from the maze of interrelated and inseparable difficulties Negroes experienced in the city. The Harlem Committee, for example, hoped to end TB through health education. Tuberculosis, however, was largely an urban disease that spread fastest under congested conditions. It simply could not be cured without a concerted attack on the over-all circumstances that made Harlem the most overcrowded neighborhood in the nation: "Socioeconomic problems involved in tuberculosis control . . . are no doubt the greatest," a local physician wrote, "and a satisfactory control will never be attained until they are solved. . . . It takes more than a Health Department, a hospital or a clinic to eradicate disease."[12] This was true of other areas of reform. The Children's Aid Society did some good by centering its efforts on building playgrounds in Harlem, but this was obviously no solution for the disorders that produced juvenile crime. Negro and white educators organized interesting programs of vocational training for Harlem's schools in the 1920's, but these could not open jobs for Negro youngsters in New York's predominantly lily-white corporations and unions.

What the situation demanded was a sympathetic full-scale attack on all the conditions that made Harlem the tragic community it was: "The task of alleviation in North Harlem is impossible without the active participation of the public."[13] A very small group of Negro socialists, those who met weekly in the offices of *The Messenger,* recognized this. A. Philip Randolph, Grace P. Campbell and Frank R. Crosswaith, for example, realized that social conditions in Harlem would never improve unless the economic base of the community was broadened. They created the Trade Union Committee for Organizing Negro Workers and had some success in opening jobs for Negroes in the clothing trades, but most major economic barriers remained intact. When they demanded a large-scale program of housing reform in the neighborhood, they were denounced as radicals.[14] American society was unwilling to make a full commitment to a program of racial justice that the situation called for. This, and the planlessness that historically typified American urban growth, especially in New York City, permitted Harlem to become the horrible slum it remains today.

III

The inadequacy of individual good will as a solution to Harlem's social problems was demonstrated in the history of the most ambitious project for community improvement undertaken in the 1920's— the Paul Laurence Dunbar Apartments. John D. Rockefeller, Jr., who gave millions of dollars for Negro social welfare and education throughout the country, was a regular contributor to Harlem agencies and charities. He gave $250,000 to help build the local YWCA; $72,000 for the New York City Welfare Council's anti-juvenile-delinquency program in Harlem; $37,500 to help pay the mortgage of a neighborhood youth club; $15,000 for the relief of Harlem unemployed.[15]

In 1925 the philanthropist was approached by the director of the New York Urban League, James H. Hubert, and a number of local leaders, and urged to lend his financial support to one of the community's greatest needs—a major program of housing reform: "A delegation of Harlemites conferred with Mr. Rockefeller . . . and urged that he lend his aid to solving the housing problems of the community," a Negro journal recorded. Rockefeller agreed that a "housing crisis" existed in the ghetto and immediately began to purchase land for a complex of new apartments. Negroes hailed the "New Philanthropy."[16]

The aim was excellence. Careful consideration was given every detail of planning to insure the eventual success of the project. Earlier model tenements, like those on San Juan Hill, sometimes failed when the neighborhoods surrounding them deteriorated so badly that decent people refused to live there.[17] The new Rockefeller project guaranteed against this by creating a neighborhood of its own in miniature—six apartment houses covering more than five acres of land, surrounded by parks, gardens and playgrounds. The majority of the 511 apartments ranged in size from two to five rooms, although some were larger, and thus met the requirements of the typically small Harlem family of the 1920's. To eliminate the "lodger evil," roomers were not permitted in the new Rockefeller houses. Because more Negro than white mothers in the city worked away from home, the Dunbar Apartments had its own nursery—equipped with Lilliputian furniture, Mother Goose friezes and a dozen cribs—where women could leave children for a modest fee. A clubroom was provided for teenagers.[18] One of the "best known Negroes in the country," Roscoe Conkling Bruce, was hired as resident manager of the houses. Bruce, son of the United States Senator from Mississippi during Reconstruction, Blanche K. Bruce, was a prominent educator in his own right. His name added prestige to the project within the Negro community. The architect's plan for the Dunbar Apartments was basically simple and functional. He used the best materials available to build apartments that were decent to live in, light and airy: "Every room has abundant access to sunlight and fresh air." The New York chapter of the American Institute of Architects awarded the Dunbar houses its first prize for design in 1927. The finished product was all that Rockefeller had hoped for, an architectural achievement of high order: "the most attractive model tenement in America," two experts in urban housing concluded. "The work speaks for itself," the journal *Architecture* commented, "and its eloquence should bring more of its kind to . . . other cities."[19]

Every physical aspect of the new project was obviously arranged with great care. The next step was to provide a reliable tenantry. Bruce and his wife personally interviewed every applicant for an apartment. Three references were taken from each prospective resident and these were carefully checked. "We let it be widely known," the manager wrote, "that the sporting fraternity, the daughters of joy, and the criminal element, [would] not be tolerated." When the houses were occupied in 1928 the tenants could best be described as middle-class Negroes—clerks, civil service employees, Pullman porters ("the aristocrats of Negro labor") and so on. The median wage of Dunbar residents was about $149 a month—some $40 a month higher than the income of the average Harlem family.[20]

The entire project may have seemed a "New Philanthropy" to contemporaries but it was cast conceptually in an earlier tradition of American tenement house reform—the nineteenth-century "limited-dividend" tradition of Brooklyn's pioneer builder of working-class homes, Alfred T. White, or the houses constructed in slum areas of New York City by the City and Suburban Homes Company. The Dunbar project certainly outdid its predecessors in size and beauty but it was, like them, what nineteenth-century reformers called "philanthropy on a business basis." Philanthropy, it was then argued, was most "gratifying" when it became a proper combination of good works and good business. The City and Suburban Homes Company, for example, hoped "to offer capital what is believed to be a safe and permanent five per cent investment, while furnishing wage-earners wholesome homes at current rates."[21] "The capitalist has here an altogether safe, gratifying, long-term investment," one man wrote of the Dunbar houses.[22]

Apartments were rented on a co-operative basis. Initially, each tenant made a down payment of $50 per room and then was charged a monthly assessment of $11.50 to $17.50 a room. When deductions were made for maintenance and the 5½ per cent interest on Rockefeller's investment, about 50 per cent was left in principal. At this rate, it was believed, every tenant would own his apartment in twenty-two years. Rockefeller was assured absolute control of the houses by holding the only preferred stock in the corporation. To encourage thrift furthermore, "to help the Negro help himself," as Rockefeller said, the Dunbar National Bank was opened as part of the housing complex in 1928.[23]

The high hopes surrounding the new undertaking lasted an exceedingly short time. The houses were completed on the eve of the Great Depression, and the Depression forced the management to modify its original plans radically. Within six months of the Dunbar's opening, a free placement service had to be established for tenants who lost their jobs. Shortly afterwards, arrangements were made to reduce the initial down payment for new tenants—it was eventually done away with altogether. Substantial reductions in rent were made in 1932 "to relieve those whose income had been cut due to the depression." The few larger apartments remained unoccupied because they were too expensive for most single families. The rule banning lodgers was modified to permit relatives to share these homes; in 1935 the six- and seven-room apartments were divided into two and three. So many tenants failed to meet their obligations by 1936 that Rockefeller foreclosed on the first mortgage he held. It was a business venture, he argued, and the business was singularly unsuccessful. Residents had their original investments returned and the Dunbar Apartments became Rockefeller's privately owned corporation. He sold the project to a group of realtors in 1937 and withdrew his support of the

Dunbar National Bank the next year. Harlem's "noble experiment," "the adventure in community building," had proved a failure.[24]

The Great Depression was the most obvious cause for the collapse of the Dunbar Apartments. Yet Rockefeller's plan for housing reform in Harlem had serious limitations from its inception. It provided middle-class housing at relatively high rentals to a population that was predominantly lower class. The Harlem families most desperately in need of new housing were bypassed by the Dunbar houses. It was a measure of the hopelessly weak economic position of the city Negro that even the small group of middle-class families chosen after the most careful processes of selection were unable to earn a steady income during the Depression. Hard times always seemed hardest on Negroes.

Nor was private "philanthropy on a business basis"—a nineteenth-century blend of Christian charity and free enterprise—an adequate social philosophy for the complex problems of twentieth-century urban life. Had the Dunbar Apartments succeeded they would have provided housing for 511 middle-class Negro families at the cost, to them, of $3.3 million. But there were more than 50,000 families in Harlem[25]—the large majority seriously in need of better homes and unable to afford even a modest investment to get them. A problem of this magnitude involved expenditures that were obviously beyond the resources of private charity or individual social reform, and beyond the interest of private capital.

The earliest public recognition of the failure of "limited-dividend" tenement house reform came with the New Deal's program of low-rent municipal housing as an obligation of government; when Rockefeller sold the Dunbar Apartments, the city's Harlem River Houses were nearing completion a few blocks away. This was certainly a more advanced concept than the earlier reliance on philanthropy, but society assumed its obligation hesitantly and, as the ghettos of the 1960's attest, inadequately.

CHAPTER 11

A Taste of Honey: Ward Politics

"Where are the leaders up there
[Harlem]? Who will point the way
for the thousands there?"
—*The New York Age*, 1910

"The New York Negro has learned to
play the game [of politics] in a
realistic fashion."
—Francis E. Rivers, Negro Assemblyman, 1930

I

Politics proved a more rewarding form of community activity. While the urbanization of the Negro obviously caused great difficulties, it also provided the base for significant political power—political power unprecedented in the history of the Negro in the North. As the Negro population increased in numbers, the cynical and apathetic attitudes that typified the reactions of white politicians in the late nineteenth century came to an end. The Negro did not become a major political force in New York City in the first thirty years of the new century, but there were signs of public recognition after 1900—and especially after the creation of Negro Harlem—that were never evident previously. Requests for offices which Negroes made in the 1880's and 1890's, and which were ridiculed or ignored then, were renewed and granted. Negro spokesmen arose at all levels of municipal politics and demanded greater recognition of the Negro community: "The Negro wants his manhood recognized and encouraged," one of them wrote.[1]

Politics is a practical business. Political recognition and patronage would be granted Negroes, Tammany sachem Richard Croker said in the 1890's, in "proportion to their works and numbers."[2] In the late nineteenth century, a small and disorganized Negro community was forced to accept the lowest offices that white politicos would offer.

159

Negroes received appointments as street cleaners, assistant janitors, laborers. An early Negro political leader held the office of "street inspector," and another Negro appointee was "Detailed Inspector of Garbage."[3] At election time, it was often said, Negro votes were sold for a few dollars: "The flagrant manner in which votes were bought . . . on election day," *The New York Age* editorialized in 1887, "was shameful."[4]

What further weakened the political position of the Negro in New York City in the late nineteenth century was an almost solid adherence to the Republican Party. Those few Negroes who questioned the political efficacy of supporting the party of the Union then were branded traitors: "Truly," a Republican politician wrote, "the black Dem. is a strange animal."[5] Negro Democrats were sometimes pelted with bricks and garbage, drenched with water and debris, attacked by mobs.[6] "The Tammany Hall Society of New York," a Negro said in 1890, "is the rankest nest of political crookedness anywhere . . . in the United States."[7] To vote Democrat was to label yourself a Judas.[8]

This almost religious devotion to the Republican Party minimized the importance of the already weak political position of the Negro. In 1897, for example, Negro Republicans in the city attempted to have James D. Carr appointed Assistant District Attorney. Carr, born in Baltimore in 1868, had outstanding qualifications for the position. He graduated Phi Beta Kappa from Rutgers University and received an LL.B. from Columbia University Law School in 1895.[9] His appointment was rejected, however. The "time had not come," he was told, "to appoint a negro to such . . . high office," and the District Attorney hired a colored messenger instead. The Colored Republican County Committee also endorsed a Negro for the office of coroner in 1897 but were again turned down: "I know the negroes better than they know themselves," Lemuel Eli Quigg, Republican county leader, told a Negro delegation. "You couldn't drive them out of the Republican Party with a sledgehammer."[10] "The Negro ballot has almost lost its potency," a Negro scholar concluded, "on account of the unconcerned cocksureness of one political party that the other side will not get the benefit of it."[11]

Those Negro Republicans who left the meeting with Quigg resolved to break with the party. They supported the Tammany candidate for mayor in 1897 and formed the earliest regular Negro

Democratic organization in the nation, the United Colored Democracy, in January 1898.[12] Members of the UCD were pariahs within the Negro community. They were socially ostracized and denounced. Edward E. Lee, "Chief" Lee, first Negro Democratic leader, was ridiculed by local Negro groups. For their decision to break with the Republican Party, however, the small group of Negro Democrats was given a measure of political patronage immediately. James D. Carr was appointed Assistant District Attorney, "Chief" Lee was made sheriff, and his successors held more important and lucrative jobs.[13]

Bipartisanship brought some minimal rewards in the 1890's but the United Colored Democracy remained an anomalous branch of the Democratic Party—it never became an integral part of the regular machinery of city politics. The Negro Democratic organization existed as a separate and segregated unit. The Negro boss theoretically supervised *all* the Negro wards in the city. His power rose and fell at the disposition of the white Democratic county leader or mayor, not at the will of his constituency. The UCD's structure *prevented* the emergence of grass-roots ward leaders and centered Negro Democratic influence in the hands of a single, often autocratic, boss. No similar political organization existed for any other minority group in New York City. In politics, as in other areas of urban life in the 1890's, the Negro was a second-class citizen.

II

The situation began to change in the early twentieth century when the first Negro politician of any significance in the entire history of the city arose in the Republican Party—Charles W. Anderson. Charlie, as his friends knew him, was a self-educated and self-made man. His only formal education was some tentative training—"he took some courses"—in high school and in business college.[14] Like so many prominent New York Negroes of his time, Anderson came to the metropolis to seek his fortune as a young man from a rural town. He was born in Oxford, Ohio, a year after the Civil War ended and came to Manhattan, at the age of twenty, in 1886. Anderson immediately became active in local Republican politics and stumped for the party in Negro wards in the late 1880's. In 1890 he was elected president of the Young Men's Colored Republican Club of New York County and rewarded for his services with a low-rung patronage position—gauger in a district office of the Internal Revenue Service. From then until his retirement in 1934, with the exception of a few months in 1915, Anderson remained in public office. He became "the recognized colored Republican leader of New York"; "the race political leader."[15]

Charlie Anderson was an exceptionally bright, cultured, perceptive man and a gifted leader—"the unfailing observer," he was once called. His friend James Weldon Johnson recalled that Anderson was "much more than an ordinary orator," and could intelligently discuss English poetry and the state of world affairs. And Anderson, a member of the Metropolitan Museum of Art, preferred to talk over a glass of champagne. Shakespearean allusions are occasionally found in his speeches. Charles W. Anderson was obviously no hack politician.[16]

Anderson's letters are full of keen insights and predictions about contemporary politics—and he was rarely wrong. Throughout his life he paid the closest attention to detail. He could, for example, quote statistics on the exact number of registered voters in each assembly district or list the positions held by Negroes in the federal service and the salaries each job paid. In the first two decades of the twentieth century Anderson organized and supervised Negro Republican captains in every election district of Manhattan and was on the closest terms with most Negro religious and business leaders. He showed himself to be "a cool, calculating player in the game of politics." In 1908, for example, it was rumored that New York Negroes would not support William Howard Taft for President. Anderson issued orders to plaster windows in the Negro districts with pictures of Taft: "We are . . . putting lithographs in the windows of every colored man's house in the various black belts of the city," he wrote. "Any man passing through . . . will surely be convinced that the alleged disaffection of the negro voters is all moonshine." If you needed a job, wood in the winter, some contributions for Harlem charity or boxes of candy for a children's Christmas party, Charlie Anderson was the man to see. He worked quietly, efficiently—without the usual guffaw common to ward politics—and most often successfully, to get what he wanted. He was the complete politician.[17]

Political preferment was Anderson's natural reward. He quickly rose from gauger, to private secretary of New York State's Treasurer (1893–1895), to Chief Clerk in the State Treasury (1895–1898), to Supervisor of Accounts for the New York Racing Commission

(1898–1905). When Admiral Dewey returned from the Philippines and the Cuban fleet arrived in triumph at New York port after the Spanish-American War, Anderson was among the dignitaries to greet them. In 1905 he was appointed to what was undoubtedly the most responsible and important federal office held by any Negro politician in the early twentieth century: Collector of Internal Revenue for the Second New York District—the Wall Street District. Employees threatened to leave when they heard of their new Negro boss, but most remained on the job. "Strangely enough, the bottom did not drop out of Manhattan and the sun did not refuse to shine," *The New York Age* scoffed. "None of the employees left their employment and bolted for the door. They stuck to their desks *and* to their salaries." The young man from the small Ohio town had come a long way in fifteen years. "I doubt when we both left Ohio," a successful friend of his wrote, "that either of us believed that you would be in a position to collect, and I with a pressing need of paying, income tax. . . ."[18]

Anderson was certainly qualified for the post and his administration was noted for its honesty and thoroughness: "Capacity, courtesy . . . and high efficiency have been the qualities most remarked in his conduct of [the] office. . . ." He handled without a flaw the complicated new procedures made necessary by the passage of the income tax amendment in 1913. On his own initiative, he accepted checks rather than cash from local corporations during the Recession of 1907 and thus helped ease what he called the "financial stringency": "I accepted checks in payment of internal revenue tax, and I believe, [I] was the only collector in the country to do so," he told Booker T. Washington. "This materially assisted in relieving the situation here, and helped the merchants greatly. . . ." When the economic crisis ended, thankful businessmen offered him a personal gift. It would have been unethical for a collector to accept, so Anderson rejected the offer: "I have never permitted a private interest to interfere in the remotest way with my performance of any public duty," he said on a later occasion. Instead, he suggested that any money raised be sent to Tuskegee as a contribution to Negro education. Shortly afterwards Washington received a gift of $900, presented in Anderson's honor, from the Collector's clients.[19]

Charles W. Anderson had risen to his unique position in New York politics as a result of his own energy and ability, but his appointment as Collector in Theodore Roosevelt's administration was made through the all-pervasive political influence of Booker T. Washington.[20] Anderson was a devoted supporter of Washington and perhaps Washington's most trusted lieutenant. He guarded his mentor's interests with a religious fervor: "I am not easily frightened," he once wrote, "and when I believe in a man, no opposition . . . can swerve me by as much as a hair's breadth." "Always remember," he said at another time, "that absolute loyalty is more desired in a lieutenant than brains, experience or power. . . . Without this, all [else is] worse than useless." When Washington died, Anderson wrote of "how dearly I loved him." "It is a priceless thing to remember such loyal and disinterested friendship," Washington's personal secretary, Emmett J. Scott, replied.[21]

Anderson could be ruthless in guarding Washington's interests or doing Washington's bidding. He kept constant check on the activities of Negro Democrats, the followers of W. E. B. DuBois, and all persons who even remotely threatened Washington's authority or name. Anderson's voluminous correspondence with Washington constantly warns him of "men who play double," "the enemy," and urges their ouster. "It is high time that these crooks should be exposed," he wrote of two Negro Democrats. "What do you think about it?" If anyone in public office stepped out of line, he tried to use his influence in New York City or Washington to have him quieted or removed.[22]

A glaring case in point was that of the militant Negro Socialist and black nationalist Hubert H. Harrison. Harrison worked in the New York City post office early in the century and, in 1911, published some disparaging remarks about Booker T. Washington's leadership. Charlie Anderson dealt with him swiftly and efficiently. With obvious pride, he explained the situation to Washington: "Do you remember Hubert H. Harrison? He is the man who wrote two nasty letters against you in the New York 'Sun.' He is a clerk in the Post Office. The Postmaster is my personal friend. . . . Can you see the hand? I think you can. Please destroy this, that it may not fall under another eye. . . . If he escapes me, he is a dandy." Six weeks later Washington received the following note: "I am sure you will regret to learn that Mr. Hubert H. Harrison has been dismissed from his position as clerk in the New York Post Office." As long as he lived Harrison wondered whose influence had been used to arrange his dismissal.[23]

Anderson participated actively in the often bitter internecine warfare that split Negro leadership in the early twentieth century between the supporters of the Niagara Movement—W. E. B. DuBois, William Monroe Trotter, J. Max Barber and many others—and the followers of Booker T. Washington. To him, the Niagara people were visionaries who demanded full racial equality too quickly in a society unwilling to grant it. Anderson hoped for future gains but was willing to settle for something concrete in the present: "We do not belong to that group to whom nothing is desirable but the impossible," he once commented. "Some of us are trying to provide opportunities for members of the race. . . ."[24]

When one considers the long range interests of the Negro people in full equality, Anderson's views were certainly questionable. They did, however, prove an important immediate boon to Harlemites and to New York's Negro community generally. To Charlie Anderson, improving the race most often meant using his influence to find more and better-paying jobs for New York's Negro community. Anderson's correspondence dealing with questions of political patronage alone was voluminous. He found positions for Negroes as mechanical draftsmen, state examiners of auto chauffeurs, deputy collectors and gaugers in the Internal Revenue Service, customhouse inspectors and clerks ("I pulled off another colored inspector of Customs"), messengers, post office employees, immigration inspectors ("directed from Washington, at my request"), attorneys to examine election frauds ("This will throw a few hundred dollars . . . his way"), referees in foreclosure suits, assistant superintendents in the post office ("the first time it has been done in this state"), assistant district attorneys ("my man McDougald"), deputy United States marshals, stenographers ("she realizes $200 per year more than the white stenographers in the office"). When Judge Lorenz Zeller, a former counsel for the Brewers' Association, came before the city's Bar seeking approval for a higher position, Anderson scotched his hopes. He presented the Bar Association with documentary evidence that Zeller, as judge, refused to find bartenders guilty of violating the State's Civil Rights Act for failing to serve Negroes. As a result of Anderson's disclosures Zeller's candidacy was disapproved.[25] In 1914 Charles S. Whitman, whom Anderson first met as New York County District Attorney, was elected Republican governor of the state. Charlie used his influence with Whitman to win more jobs for Negroes, including one for himself later on, and arranged to have state legislative documents printed in the Negro press.[26] Samuel J. Battle applied to the New York police force for an appointment as patrolman. Battle, a giant of a man in perfect condition, was somehow unable to pass the department's physical examination. He asked the editor of the *Age,* Fred R. Moore, for assistance, and Moore spoke to Anderson. Charlie went to see the mayor, who immediately arranged for a new examination. In 1911 Samuel J. Battle was appointed the first Negro policeman on the New York City force. (People were taken on guided tours to see the strange phenomenon— a Negro policeman patrolling his beat. Battle recalled children taunting him: "There goes the nigger cop, there goes the nigger cop!" they shouted.) More Negroes received appointments to municipal and federal positions through Anderson's intercession than at any previous time in city history.[27]

Charles W. Anderson was a fine politician and a recognized votegetter, but his position as Collector primarily rested on Booker T. Washington's influence in the Republican Party. When Woodrow Wilson was elected President, Anderson, along with almost every other Negro federal office-holder, lost his job. After Washington's death in 1915, Anderson's political future seemed uncertain.[28]

That his power was not solely the gift of Washington was demonstrated in his public career after 1915. Charlie Anderson was unemployed only a few months. W. E. B. DuBois, obviously not on the closest terms with Anderson, was so impressed with his public record that he recommended his appointment as Minister to Haiti in the new Democratic administration. (DuBois supported Wilson in 1912.) "I do not know that Anderson would accept," DuBois wrote, "but it would be a graceful thing if he is offered this position after his remarkable service as Internal Revenue Collector."[29] Anderson did not get this job, but he received another offer from Albany. Governor Whitman, he was told, "wanted him placed." The governor appointed him Supervisory Agent of the State Agriculture Department in New York City—a well-paying patronage position. From his new post Anderson directed all state marketing operations and inspectors within the city.[30]

His career continued to blossom. In the presidential election of 1916 Anderson, as Chairman of the Colored Advisory Committee, directed the Republican Party's national campaign among Negroes. Gubernatorial, congressional and mayoralty candidates sought his support at election time. As an influential member of Harlem's Republican organization in the Nineteenth Assembly District he helped nominate, manage campaigns for and elect assemblymen and aldermen—white and Negro. He represented the ward as delegate to Republican state and national conventions and, in 1920, toured Negro communities throughout the Northeast in the interests of the national ticket. (In a speech at Newport, Rhode Island, he declared the easiest way to convert a Negro Democrat was to take "him on a little excursion through certain Southern States.") As a member of the Mayor's Committee on Receptions to Distinguished Guests, Anderson greeted the many dignitaries who visited the city, and he also attended all major local political functions. In 1923 a new federal Internal Revenue district was created in New York City—the Third District, which included Harlem. Anderson, the obvious man for the post, was appointed Collector. Although no manuscript records survive to tell the inside story of Anderson's influence on this job, the newspapers reported a surprising number of Harlem ward-heelers employed in the Internal Revenue Service. A Nineteenth AD election district captain was Charlie's secretary. An attendant in Harlem's public bathhouse, active in local politics, found himself promoted to Deputy Collector. The same old magic was apparently working again.[31]

A number of factors helped Charlie Anderson remain in political power. His earlier career provided him with influential friends, like Whitman, and an unimpeachable reputation for loyalty—"a party man"—honesty and efficiency. More important, however, was the fact that Anderson's career luckily extended into a new era of Negro urban politics. The doors of political preferment did not open to Negroes until their numbers and voting strength had increased considerably through migration; and especially after their concentration in Harlem. By the second decade of the twentieth century, Harlem's Negro community was large enough for all politicians to see. Anderson reaped the benefits of the growing importance of the Negro vote within the city. His appointment as Collector in the new revenue district was the "biggest job held by a Negro," but it was only one of many opportunities that brought greater political recognition to the colored community. The Republican boss of New York County, Samuel S. Koenig, apparently pushed hard for Anderson's appointment, and when it was made, Koenig said "it was with the definite idea of securing recognition for colored voters to which they are justly entitled."[32]

Anderson directed the Third District until his retirement in 1934—he died four years later. His importance in Harlem politics was restricted after 1927, however, when he became seriously ill and could no longer continue to work actively: "Nowadays he is rarely seen." Subordinates, it was reported, assumed the more burdensome duties of the collectorship until his retirement. Up to the time of his illness he was certainly a dynamic political figure. He was the first leader in city history to push open the doors of political opportunity for Negroes; and he had the good fortune to see other forces keep them open—wide enough, in fact, to provide room for himself at a crucial time in his political career. The rise of Charlie Anderson in many ways typified the political awakening of Negro New York: "I regarded him as being, beyond any doubt, the very ablest Negro politician," James Weldon Johnson wrote. "You just can't think of Republicanism in New York," a Negro newspaper editorialized, "without remembering Charlie Anderson."[33]

III

The unprecedented concentration of Negroes in Harlem permitted the entire community to take a more active role in politics. Unfortunately for Negro politicians, an accident of political geography divided the Negro vote between two assembly districts, the Nineteenth and Twenty-first. The Negro ghetto was one solid residential unit, but the Negro vote was split between districts which included substantial numbers of whites—Jews in the Nineteenth and Irish in the Twenty-first, although other ethnic groups were represented in smaller numbers. In 1930, after a decade of mass migration, Negroes composed 70 per cent of the population in each district.[34] This unintentional gerrymander tended to somewhat limit the political power of Negroes and forced them to share influence with white politicians and district leaders. Despite this, however, Negroes made significant political advances in Harlem in the 1920's. Too long, it was argued, had the Negro been treated as a pawn in the city politics; too often had Negroes been forced to accept "crumbs from the patronage table": such "fine, lucrative and honorable positions of spittoon cleaning and floor sweeping." The time has come, a Negro leader wrote, for "Official Recognition of the Negro's Interest."[35]

Negroes were aided in their struggle for power by the operation of an active two-party system in Harlem, especially in the 1920's. The United Colored Democracy continued its existence as a special Negro organization within the city's Democratic Party. Its leader after 1915, Harvard-educated Ferdinand Q. Morton, worked sympathetically with the white Democratic bosses of Harlem through the early 1930's. In exchange for his assistance Morton was recognized as the most powerful Negro Democrat in the city and was given almost dictatorial control of Negro patronage. Although Harlem Negroes unwaveringly supported Republican presidential candidates until 1932,[36] and usually cast their votes for Republican governors,[37] they showed greater political independence in local politics after the First World War.[38] In 1921, for example, Democratic mayoralty candidate John F. Hylan, known as an honest leader among Negroes, polled an amazing (for a Democrat) 73.6 per cent of Negro Harlem's vote. Negro Democrats represented Harlem in the state assembly and on the city's Board of Aldermen at varying times throughout the twenties. In 1922 Harlemites, for the only time, supported Al Smith for governor—he won in a landslide that year. Although the Republican tradition remained the stronger, Harlem became the first Negro community in the nation to lend significant support to the Democratic Party. "The Negro in Harlem," James Weldon Johnson commented in 1924, "has in very large degree emancipated himself from [single-party domination], and become an intelligent voter."[39]

And the Negro community reaped the benefits of its emerging political independence. No longer would "cocksure" Republican politicians say, as they had in the 1890's, that the Negro vote could not be driven from the party of Lincoln "with a sledgehammer." "Your race has too long segregated itself politically," Mayor Hylan wrote a Harlem supporter in 1921. "I can think of nothing which will contribute more effectively towards [your] progress . . . than this removal of the barriers behind which [you] so long remained in political isolation." Shortly after his victory in 1921, Hylan proved his point by selecting Ferdinand Q. Morton, who actively campaigned for him, to a lucrative and important city office, Chairman of the Municipal Civil Service Commission: "the first appointment in the history of our city of a colored man to head this or any other department."[40] Hylan's successor, James J. Walker, reappointed Morton to this municipal cabinet-rank position. After prodding from

Morton, Republican aldermen, the NAACP and the North Harlem
Medical Society, five Negro physicians were appointed for the first
time to the regular staff of Harlem Hospital in 1925, and a training
school for Negro nurses was established there. A sweeping reorganization of the hospital took place in 1930, in Jimmy Walker's
administration, and Harlem Hospital was opened without restriction
to Negro doctors. In 1932 more than seventy Negro interns and
physicians worked there. This was, an NAACP memorandum concluded, "the most decisive step ever taken anywhere in the United
States for recognition of . . . colored doctors and nurses."[41] Both
Hylan and Walker, New York's only mayors in the 1920's, were
regular visitors to Harlem; attended plays in Negro theaters; greeted
conventioning Negro organizations; lectured before fraternal and
church groups: "No Discrimination in the Administration of the
Government of New York City"; "Mayor's Attitude on Ku Klux
Klan"; "Discrimination Against Negroes." They dedicated new Negro parks, playgrounds and churches and had some of the more
objectionable features cut out of the film *Birth of a Nation* before it
was shown in the city. Al Smith campaigned in Harlem each time he
ran for office: "Call on me and I will help, either in word or deed,"
Smith said. "What the negro is entitled to and should receive is a
square deal and equal opportunities in civic life," Hylan told Urban
League director James H. Hubert. "These are rights guaranteed to
him under the constitution." Never before had Democratic politicians
shown as much interest in the Negro's welfare—and his vote.[42]

The most significant political advance made by the Negro community was the election of Harlemites to legislative offices. In 1917, for
the first time in city history, a Negro was nominated by a regular
district organization for the state assembly. (Negro independents ran
in Harlem, and lost, in 1913 and 1915.) The Republicans of
Harlem's Nineteenth AD selected Edward Austin Johnson for the
office. They chose a well-qualified man, a politician whose career
symbolized a major transition in American Negro and urban history:
the loss of Negro political power in the South, and its reacquisition in
northern metropolitan centers.

Johnson, born in Raleigh, North Carolina, in 1860, received his
earliest education from books sent south in barrels by sympathetic
northerners after the Civil War. He became a lawyer, Professor of
Law and Dean at Shaw University in Raleigh. As an active southern

Negro Republican of the late nineteenth century, he served as alderman, assistant district attorney and delegate to three national Republican conventions.[43] He was also well-known as the author of books on
Negro history and a rather unique, poorly written utopian novel,
Light Ahead for the Negro (1904). This novel visualized racial
harmony in a future South. In "Phoenix," Georgia, 2206, Johnson
foresaw a "high-minded" and "sympathetic" South; a South in which
"the spirit of helpfulness to Negroes [became] so popular that it
permeated all classes"; a section in which "the subdued look of the
old-time Negro" had disappeared forever. "I silently prayed," he
concluded, "God bless the New South!" But the Phoenix was a
mythical bird and in the harsher reality of his present, shortly after
completing *Light Ahead,* Negroes were practically disfranchised in
North Carolina and men like Johnson stripped of political power.
Rather than accept a proscribed life, Johnson, like his fellow North
Carolinian George Henry White, migrated from his home state. He
came to New York City in 1907, practiced law and bought some
property in Harlem. When he was elected in 1917 he became the first
Negro to sit in the state legislature.[44] Five other Negroes, four
Republicans and one Democrat, followed him to the state assembly
from the Nineteenth and Twenty-first AD's in the 1920's. In 1919
Republican Charles H. Roberts became New York City's first Negro
alderman. Other Negroes were elected in the next decade. A clergyman noted, "Political opportunity has knocked on the door of the
Harlem Negro."[45]

These men acted as spokesmen for their community. Through their
initiative, in a political structure now willing to recognize Negro
demands, Harlem Negroes received the "solid benefits which ac-
crued" from "an awakening political consciousness."[46] Johnson as
assemblyman, for example, drafted and helped pass a new civil rights
law for New York State in 1918. It extended the "equal accommodations" privileges of earlier acts to include every conceivable type of
public business—skating rinks, billiard parlors, bowling alleys, ice
cream parlors. The white press congratulated Johnson on the quality
and thoroughness of his legislation. He also arranged to have a state
employment office opened in Harlem: "an additional public employment office . . . which . . . would best serve the interest of the
negro population."[47] In 1916 Harlem's National Guard unit, the
"Fighting Fifteenth" (later the 369th), was outfitted. Negroes had

unsuccessfully requested a military organization for themselves since the Spanish-American War. Harlem's "Hell Fighters" made a distinguished record in France during World War I: the entire outfit was awarded the *Croix de guerre* for bravery by the French government, and the "Fifteenth" spent more days in combat (191) than any other American unit. A "Happy Harlem," a "proud Harlem," greeted the soldiers on their return, and the "Fifteenth's" exploits became part of the ghetto's folklore. In the 1920's the largest National Guard armory in the state was constructed in Harlem for New York's "Black Watch." Everyone claimed to be responsible for the legislation which organized the "Fifteenth" and built its new armory: Republicans and Democrats, mayors, aldermen, assemblymen, congressmen, white and Negro politicians. Whatever the exact truth, the most important point is that the legislation passed and politicians were interested enough to try to claim some part in it.[48]

Other acts beneficial to the Negro community were sponsored by Harlem's representatives. After a decade of pressure, two Negro Republicans in the state assembly, with the "particularly arduous" and "helpful" efforts of the white county chairman, forced the passage of an act which divided Harlem's Seventh District Municipal Court into a new administrative entity—the Tenth District. This *intentional* gerrymander guaranteed the election of two Negro judges —another city first—to the municipal bench in 1930. "The lines of the district were deliberately redrawn . . . to assure the elections of two colored judges," Francis E. Rivers, who drafted the bill, wrote. Republican sponsors of the bill were dismayed when two Negro Democrats were elected to fill the posts. A Harlem assemblyman was also responsible for introducing a state housing act—which passed— that protected tenants from "unjust" and "unreasonable" evictions or rent increases, and from landlords who failed to make necessary repairs. Harlem's aldermen, Republicans and Democrats, arranged to have playgrounds, parks and "bathhouses for the poor" built in the neighborhood in the 1920's. A once politically voiceless people had begun to find leaders who worked for the "realization of the hopes of the race." "The New York Negro," a colored assemblyman noted, "has learned to play the game [of politics] in a realistic fashion."[49]

But political leadership often inherently involves questions of personal ambition and power that sometimes conflict with, rather than supplement, the interests of a community. Competition for power among individual Negroes sometimes impeded the progress of the entire group. The accepted structure of the United Colored Democracy, for example, precluded any struggle for leadership in the Democratic ward organizations of Harlem. Ferdinand Q. Morton was recognized by all Democratic mayors and county chairmen as the sole spokesman of Negro Democracy. He used his authority to quiet local demands for the election of Negro Democratic leaders in the Nineteenth and Twenty-first AD's; this could only weaken his seemingly absolute control of "Black Tammany." Dissident Democrats complained that he was "haughty," "secretive," "exclusive," and acted as an "overlord." "Morton is utterly without the social qualities which make a leader easily accessible to his constituents and responsive to their needs," one of them commented. Others called him "arrogant," "cynical" and "vindictive." The UCD—"a segregated party in the County of New York for colored voters, headed by a leadership over which the colored voters have no control nor power of removal"— might have been acceptable to an earlier generation, a Negro Democrat said, but it "has outlived its usefulness" in the 1920's.

As long as Democratic mayors used Morton as the vehicle of city patronage, local Negro Democrats were unable to do more than voice their complaints and pray for change—he who held the jobs controlled the party. In fact, those who shouted defiance too often and too loud found themselves unemployed. A clerk in Harlem's municipal court, a superintendent of Harlem's state employment office and a New York County deputy sheriff were suddenly dismissed for "incompetency" after criticizing Morton's leadership or refusing to contribute ten per cent of their salaries to the UCD. Morton remained the virtual dictator of Negro Democracy until Republican Fiorello H. La Guardia was elected mayor in 1933. The liberal mayor cut the taproot of Morton's strength—patronage—and this caused the UCD to "cease functioning." La Guardia agreed to reappoint Morton Civil Service Commissioner on condition that he break with the Democratic Party. The Negro boss, who always regarded politics "as a selfish, desperate game," saved himself and left the Democratic Party: "Mr. Morton gave up his Tammany affiliations and announced he had joined the American Labor Party, with which the Mayor is affiliated," the *Age* recorded. In the twilight of his career Morton continued to practice the dictum he always relied upon as the only true source of political power: "We should take this political situation as a cold-blooded business proposition," he once said. "We should treat it as an honest-to-goodness shopping trip. Politics . . . is but a theoretical bargain counter, to buy wares and get the best we can in bargains. . . . " As Morton closed a deal for himself, Harlem Democrats, freed from his control, took over local district organizations from the old white bosses—the Nineteenth AD in 1935; the Twenty-first AD in 1939.[50]

Negro Republicans traditionally operated within the confines of regular party structure. Their struggle to elect Negro district leaders was thus less difficult than it had been for Democrats, but dissension was evident in Republican ranks too. Although Negro Republicans composed the majority of voters in the Nineteenth and Twenty-first AD's through most of the 1920's, and also the majority of county committeemen in each district—whose votes determine district leadership—it took an unusual effort to unseat the "real Harlemites," the men "born and raised in this section," who had control of the party when whites represented a majority in the neighborhood.

Leaders were powerful men. They alone distributed the patronage of the party—and this included enticing and sometimes lucrative positions. When necessary, it was reported, they could run "well-oiled" campaigns. Politics was a key source of mobility in every lower-class community and the influence of the district leader could mean the making or breaking of a young career. It was he, for example, who largely determined nominees for local office; and nomination or election to the state legislature or Board of Aldermen often carried unanticipated dividends with it. Take the case of Myles A. Paige. Paige, born in Montgomery, Alabama, graduated from Columbia University Law School in 1924 and was admitted to the Bar the next year. He was selected to run for the State Senate in August 1926. On September 5, Corporal Myles A. Paige went to summer camp with Harlem's 369th Infantry. Within a week the twenty-nine-year-old corporal had somehow been promoted second lieutenant; a week later, first lieutenant; and three days after that, captain and company commander. He must have performed unusual heroics in those two and a half weeks. Paige later became a municipal judge.[51]

District leaders had a wide source of influence and many local Negro politicians—lawyers, government clerks, election district captains, deputy sheriffs, secretaries to judges, election inspectors, Prohibition agents, postal employees, deputy collectors of Internal Revenue, varieties of municipal workers—hesitated to question their authority. When dissatisfied Negro Republicans demanded that white leaders step down—"Get rid of Conklin," "Grenthal must go"—the whites refused, and used a barrage of threats, dismissals and bribes to keep their positions as long as possible. In the midst of one battle, Robert S. Conklin, boss of the Twenty-first AD, sent letters to district captains telling them to support him or "get out." He "was fighting for his political life," he said. Prior to 1929 all efforts to elect Negro Republican leaders in the Nineteenth and Twenty-first AD's were defeated when a majority of colored committeemen joined with the white minority to vote against Negro insurgents: "As usual," the *Age* commented after one of these fights, "Negroes were pitted against each other. . . ."[52]

The breakthrough came in 1929 after a resolute effort on the part of Negro politicians, clergy and press. Abraham Grenthal, Republican leader of the Nineteenth AD and assemblyman 1924–1928, was the target of attack. Grenthal lived in the Jewish section of lower Harlem. He had attended the neighborhood public schools, City College, and graduated from New York Law School in 1914. As an active club politician, he was appointed election district captain, and rose from there to leader. He seemed to have been a conscientious ward boss who voiced the demands of his Negro constituency as well as his white. As assemblyman, for example, he fought for low-income housing legislation and rent control; he introduced bills to allow bootblacks to keep their stands open on Sundays, and to have a monument built honoring the 369th; he lectured on local problems in Negro churches. The Jewish leader even dressed as Santa Claus to distribute mittens and stockings to Harlem's poor in the winter. That he was popular in the community was demonstrated by his re-election to the assembly on five successive occasions—even against the opposition of Negro Democrats.[53]

The demand that Grenthal resign, then, rested not so much on his past record as on the fact that Negroes were the new majority in Harlem and wanted the political leadership their numbers warranted. Negroes urged Grenthal to "gracefully withdraw." "The time is ripe for the assertion of racial independence," a Negro politician said. "The idea of white men picking leaders for Negroes will no longer be tolerated." "There is an overwhelming sentiment among members of my group that one of their number should be the leader and another a member of the Assembly of the 19th District," Fred R. Moore told the white politician. "All racial groups throughout the city advance a similar argument—the Italian, the Jew, etc. It is the only way by which [minority] groups get elective representation."[54]

But politicians rarely "gracefully withdraw" from power, and Grenthal refused. Fred R. Moore, then alderman of the district, organized a slate of independent Republicans—including a Negro district leader—to run against Grenthal and the regular party's candidates for state and city offices in the 1929 primaries. He kept the contest on the front page of his newspaper, equated a vote for Grenthal with race disloyalty and arranged for Negroes of local and national prominence—Chicago's congressman Oscar DePriest, A. M. E. Bishop Reverdy C. Ransom, the Reverend Dr. Adam Clayton Powell, Sr.—to speak in Harlem for the insurgents' cause: "The fight is on and we are in it heart and soul." *Advance,* a Harlem church newspaper, printed scathing attacks on Grenthal's leadership and predicted his defeat in the primaries: "He has had his political day in the 19th," an *Advance* editorial maintained. "His winding sheets have been made. The hearse is backed up ready to receive his expiring corpse. His requiem will be said in the Primaries."[55]

And it was. The concerted effort was successful. The insurgent ticket defeated Grenthal's by large majorities and subsequently went on to win in the 1929 election. Lieutenant Colonel Charles W. Fillmore, officer in the 369th and auditor in the New York State Tax Bureau, became the first Negro district leader in city history. At about the same time a quiet agreement for "dual leadership" was reached in the Twenty-first AD. The white section of the district, the "Hill," continued to be represented by the white leader, Robert S. Conklin; the Negro part of the neighborhood, the "Valley," was turned over to Negro architect and politician Charles W. B. Mitchell. "Harlem Has Redeemed Itself," the headlines of the Negro press shouted. "It has freed itself of alien leadership. . . ."[56]

The Negro community obviously made significant political advances, but higher elective offices remained closed to this generation of Harlemites. The fact that Harlem contained more people in less space than any other area in the nation gave Negroes local political recognition, but paradoxically, it also prevented the election of a Negro congressman. No effort was spared to elect a Harlemite to the

House of Representatives. In 1924 the Republican Party avoided a threatened Negro revolt in Harlem by nominating and actively supporting Charles H. Roberts for congress. (The former white Republican candidate was encouraged to step down with a nomination to a judicial post.) Roberts was defeated then, and so were two other Negro congressional candidates in later elections—Edward A. Johnson in 1928, and Hubert T. Delany in 1929. The basic problem was not lack of Negro support, as more Negroes registered and voted in these campaigns than in others, but the difficulty caused by political geography. The Nineteenth and Twenty-first AD's were part of a larger congressional district—the Twenty-first CD—which included three solidly white and traditionally Democratic assembly districts. The importance of the Negro vote, although substantial enough to warrant nominations, was restricted by its very concentration. Chicago Negroes, partially because their population was spread across a wider geographic and political area, were able to elect a Negro congressman in 1928. The Nineteenth and Twenty-first AD's contained 25 per cent of the vote of the congressional district, and though these sections voted heavily for Negro congressmen each time they ran, their numbers were insufficient to offset the white Democratic vote in surrounding neighborhoods. Democrats, hesitant to chance defeat in a "safe" district, refused to run a Negro candidate. It was not until Harlem's political boundaries were redrawn, in 1944, that New York elected its first Negro member of the House of Representatives—the present occupant, Adam Clayton Powell, Jr.[57]

Although the Negro's political progress in New York City was not an unqualified success, there obviously was greater advance in this sphere of community activity than in all others. While the social and economic position of the city's Negroes tended to remain stable or, with the Great Depression, even retrogressed, there was significant political mobility. In the 1890's Negroes were an almost powerless minority group; the least influential minority group in the metropolis. Their role, if any, was on the farthest periphery of municipal affairs. Within the next generation, the generation that settled in Harlem, Negroes became an integral part of city government and politics— and politics proved a wedge for economic advancement. In the 1890's there were *no* Negro policemen and firemen; in the 1920's these departments not only hired Negro applicants but promoted them to supervisory positions. Similar strides were made in municipal hospitals, the Board of Education, the sanitation department, the Board of Health, city courts and public agencies generally. Negroes tasted the sweetness of political power for the first time, and this power grew as their population expanded. At the turn of the century they argued their cause from a position of weakness: "The black, poor, weak, helpless [citizen]," a Negro lawyer said plaintively at the time of the 1900 riot, should be treated as the equal of "the most influential official. . . . Life is as dear to us as it is to . . . the most exalted."[58] Within the next generation the indifference that characterized the reactions of municipal officials in the 1890's ended and they openly competed for and courted Negro support. Political problems obviously remained to be dealt with in the future, but the apathy of the 1890's was never repeated. The question: "Where are the leaders up there [Harlem]? Who will point the way for the thousands there?" had, in part, been answered.

Epilogue:
Symbols of the Jazz Age—
The New Negro and
Harlem Discovered

"You don't know, you don't know my mind,
When you see me laughin', I'm laughin'
to keep from cryin'. . . ."
—Negro folksong

"Within the past ten years Harlem has
acquired a world-wide reputation.
. . . It is . . . known as being exotic,
colourful, and sensuous; a place
where life wakes up at night."
—James Weldon Johnson, *Black Manhattan* (1930)

I

The dominant patterns of Harlem life were largely set in the 1920's, and have remained remarkably unchanged ever since. The intensity of most Harlem social problems has gradually diminished in the last generation, but two surveys of the community in the 1960's, *Youth in the Ghetto* and *A Harlem Almanac,* depict a neighborhood strikingly similar to the ghetto of the twenties.[1] The present generation has inherited the unsolved problems of the past.

If the 1920's added anything to our knowledge of social conditions in Harlem, it presented a distorted and negative image of reality. The Negro community was "discovered" in the twenties, and its reputation was not that of a tragic slum, but a "place of laughing, swaying, and dancing"; and this image spread not only throughout the nation but throughout the world. European visitors considered a trip to Harlem a "must" on their itineraries of American sights, and European journals carried articles on the community's "exotic" night spots.[2] "Within the past ten years," James Weldon Johnson noted in

179

1930, "Harlem has acquired a world-wide reputation." It would be difficult to find a better example of the confusions, distortions, half-truths and quarter-truths that are the foundations of racial and ethnic stereotypes than the white world's image of Harlem in the 1920's.

The portrayal of Harlem that developed in the twenties was *primarily* a product of broader changes in American society. The 1920's, as is well known, was a remarkable age in American intellectual history. A cultural rebellion of the first order erupted from beneath the complacency and conservatism that were dominant characteristics of American society and politics then. It was the time writers, artists, scholars, aesthetes and bohemians became aware of the standardization of life that resulted from mass production and large-scale, efficient industrialization—the "Machine Civilization," that "profound national impulse [that] drives the hundred millions steadily toward uniformity."[3] These intellectuals declared war on tenets of American thought and faith that had remained sacrosanct for three hundred years. As a by-product of their attack on traditional American middle-class values, which were constantly called "Puritanical," literary rebels and others discovered the Negro, America's "outcast," and created a semimythical dreamland which they came to idealize— "storied Harlem."[4]

In some part, this growing national awareness was caused by significant changes within Negro society. There seemed to be a new militancy in the Negro world during and after World War I—reflected in Harlem's well-known Silent Parade to protest the 1917 East St. Louis race riots, in the racial program and consciousness of Marcus Garvey, in A. Philip Randolph's struggling movement to found the Brotherhood of Sleeping Car Porters and Maids, in the numerous little leftist groups active in Harlem, in the national campaign to promote federal antilynching legislation. Yet American society did not really take these movements seriously in the 1920's— Garvey was considered a comical figure; an antilynching law was never enacted; riots continued; Randolph's union made little headway before the Great Depression; the leftists were largely ignored or considered crackpots.[5]

The twenties also saw the rise of a noteworthy group of Negro writers and scholars, and America gave *them* considerable recognition. Some of the novels, plays, poems, books and articles of Countée Cullen, James Weldon Johnson, George S. Schuyler, Claude McKay,

Wallace Thurman, Zora Neale Hurston, Jessie Fauset, Rudolph Fisher, Jean Toomer, Charles S. Johnson, E. Franklin Frazier and others were good enough in their own right to justify public acclaim. The poetry of Langston Hughes continues to be widely read. Harlem was the center of this "New Negro Renaissance" and, like an "ebony flute," it lured Negro writers to it: "Harlem was like a great magnet for the Negro intellectual, pulling him from everywhere," Langston Hughes wrote.[6] Claude McKay came to Harlem from Jamaica, after two years at an agricultural college in Kansas; Jean Toomer originally came from an Alabama plantation; Langston Hughes arrived in 1921 after a sojourn in Mexico. "I can never put on paper the thrill of the underground ride to Harlem," Hughes recalled. "I went up the steps and out into the bright September sunlight. Harlem! I stood there, dropped my bags, took a deep breath and felt happy again."[7] Wherever they wandered in the twenties, and many went to Paris or Africa for a time ("The cream of Harlem was in Paris"), the Negro literati always returned *Home to Harlem* (to use the title of a McKay novel). Little theater, art and political-discussion groups flourished in the community. Negro literary and political magazines made their appearance: *Fire, The Messenger, Voice of the Negro, The Negro Champion, Harlem.* The One Hundred and Thirty-fifth Street library became Harlem's cultural center. "The Schomburg Collection," George S. Schuyler remembered, "used to be a great gathering place for all the people of the Renaissance."[8] In the 1920's one could hear lectures there by such prominent people as Franz Boas, W. E. B. DuBois, Carl Van Doren, James Weldon Johnson, Carter G. Woodson, Kelly Miller, Melville J. Herskovits, R. R. Moton and Arthur A. Schomburg. Harlem became what contemporaries called the "Mecca of the New Negro."[9]

Some observers, Negro and white, looked to this outburst of literary and artistic expression as a significant step toward a more general acceptance of Negroes by American society. Alain Locke, gifted writer and Howard University professor, argued that social equality would result from the recognition of the Negro as an "artist class." "It seems that the interest in the cultural expression of Negro life . . . heralds an almost revolutionary revaluation of the Negro," he wrote in 1927. It was "an augury of a new democracy in American culture."[10] Heywood Broun, well-known journalist and critic, addressed the New York Urban League at a Harlem church.

He believed "a supremely great negro artist, [an artist] who could catch the imagination of the world, would do more than any other agency to remove the disabilities against which the negro race now labors." "This great artist may come at any time," Broun concluded, and he asked his audience to remain silent for ten seconds to imagine the coming of the savior-genius.[11] This same theme of a broad cultural acceptance evolving from the recognition of the "New Negro" as "a creator" dominates the writings of James Weldon Johnson in the twenties. Johnson and others somehow believed that American racism was a process that could be reasoned with; a phenomenon that would crumble when whites recognized that Negroes had extraordinary artistic talents. "I am coming to believe," Johnson wrote his close friend Carl Van Vechten, "that nothing can go farther to destroy race prejudice than the recognition of the Negro as a creator and contributor to American civilization."[12] "Harlemites thought the millennium had come," Langston Hughes remembered. "They thought the race problem had at last been solved though Art. . . ."[13]

There was an element of realism in the romantic hopes of Johnson, Broun and Locke. For white Americans to grant that the Negro was capable of making *any* contribution to American culture was in itself a new idea—"that the Negro is a creator as well as creature . . . a giver as well as . . . receiver."[14] A new and more liberal vision of democracy developed among social scientists in the twenties. Scholars like Robert E. Park, Herbert A. Miller, Franz Boas, Melville J. Herskovits, Charles S. Johnson, Bruno Lasker, E. Franklin Frazier and Horace M. Kallen attacked traditional American attitudes toward assimilation and "Americanization." A more vital and beautiful democracy would arise, they argued, by permitting ethnic groups to maintain their individuality, rather than conceiving them as swallowed up, or melted down, in the one dominant American culture. Each group, given freedom of expression and development, would then make valuable contributions to American society. Diversity, cultural pluralism, should be fostered and encouraged, they wrote, not stifled.[15]

A spate of articles and books published in the twenties seriously analyzed and attempted to understand the Negro's place in the nation. The dozens of volumes about Negroes written by pseudo-scientists and racists at the turn of the century were replaced by works which attempted to cut through racial stereotypes ("generalized theories about racial qualities") and tried to find some viable program of "interracial cooperation." "The American Negro can no longer be dismissed as an unimportant element in the population of the United States," one man concluded. Bruno Lasker's *And Who is My Neighbor?* and *All Colors* were among the earliest serious studies of American interracial attitudes.[16] *The Annals* of the American Academy of Political and Social Science printed a thick volume of studies on Negroes by the nation's leading scholars.[17] *The World Tomorrow,* a fascinating Christian-Pacifist journal, devoted two full issues to similar articles in the 1920's.[18] Most of the major periodicals of the decade contained many serious and important studies of Negro life. The artistic and human value of Negro spirituals, folk songs, folk legends and music was first seriously recognized in the twenties (many considered them America's most important contributions to world culture); Darius Milhaud, after listening to Negro music in Lenox Avenue cafés, composed pieces which made use of jazz rhythms and instruments; *In Abraham's Bosom,* one of Paul Green's many plays of southern Negro life, won the Pulitzer Prize in 1927; Eugene O'Neill and Robert E. Sherwood constructed plays and novels around Negro characters and themes.[19] As important as this new recognition was, however, it was a minor trend in American thought. The generation that advocated cultural pluralism was also the generation that revived the Ku Klux Klan, and permanently restricted foreign immigration into the United States.

Had intellectuals like Johnson and Locke looked more critically at the stereotype of the "New Negro" that developed in the writings of most white commentators of the twenties, they would have further questioned the extent of interracial understanding that existed then. White literary rebels created a "vogue in things Negro," "an enthusiasm for Negro life and art" that bordered on being a cult.[20] They saw Negroes not as people but as symbols of everything America was not. The concept of the existence of a "New Negro" and the publicity given to it in the 1920's was primarily the result of this new awareness and interest in Negro society by what one writer called the "New White Man."[21] The generation that discovered "newness" all around itself—New Humanism, New Thought, New Women, New Criticism, New Psychology, New Masses, New Poetry, New Science, New Era, New Words, New Morality and so on—also found a "New Negro"; and the concept became a cultural weapon: "Another

Bombshell Fired into the Heart of Bourgeois Culture." "Negro stock is going up," novelist Rudolph Fisher wrote, "and everybody's buying."[22]

In the literature of the twenties, Negroes were conceived as "expressive" ("a singing race") in a society burdened with "unnatural inhibitions"; their lives were "primitive" and "exotic" (these two words appear repeatedly) in a "dull," "weary," and "monotonous" age; they could laugh and love freely in a "land flowing with Socony and Bryan and pristine Rotary purity." Negroes were presented as people who lived an "entire lifetime of laughs and thrills, [of] excitement and fun"—they had an "innate gayety of soul." "Ecstasy," Joseph Wood Krutch noted in *The Nation,* "seems . . . to be his [the Negro's] natural state."[23] The stereotype of the Negro that existed in American society in the nineteenth century, and which I described earlier, was largely untouched by the new interest in Negro life. It continued in such "all-talking melodramas" as "Lucky Sambo," "Hearts in Dixie," and "Hallelujah," or in the new radio hit "Amos and Andy." In the twenties, however, the ludicrous image of the Negro as "darky" became a subordinate theme, eclipsed by the conception of the Negro as sensuous and rhythmic African. Negroes were still thought to be alienated from traditional American virtues and values, as they had been since colonial times, but this was now considered a great asset. "To Americans," a perceptive contemporary wrote in 1929, "the Negro is not a human being but a concept."[24]

II

This was the background against which white America and the world came to know Harlem: "with our eyes focused on the Harlem scene we may dramatically glimpse the New Negro." A large Negro community had gathered in Harlem prior to World War I, but aside from small numbers of dedicated social workers, American society seemed willing to overlook its existence. In the twenties, however, Harlem was made a national symbol—a symbol of the "New Negro"; a symbol of the Jazz Age. It was seen as the antithesis of Main Street, Zenith and Gopher Prairie. Whatever seemed thrilling, bizarre or sensuous about Harlem life became a part of the community's image; whatever was sad or tragic about it, ignored. "White folks discovered black magic there," Claude McKay said.[25]

Harlem of the twenties was presented as a "great playground,"

America's answer to Paris.[26] The institution that best describes this aspect of Harlem's image was the white slumming party: "it became quite a rage . . . to go to night clubs in Harlem," Carl Van Vechten recalled.[27] Cabarets were filled nightly with handsomely dressed white slummers who danced the Charleston or Black Bottom, listened to jazz or watched risqué revues. Some night spots, like the Cotton Club (which had "the hottest show in town") and Connie's Inn (which competed for the honor), catered exclusively to whites. They were, a journalist commented, dives "where white people from downtown could be entertained by colored girls."[28] If one were looking "to go on moral vacation," or wished to soften "the asperities of a Puritan conscience," Harlem's cabarets promised to do the job. The following is an advertisement, written especially for "white consumption," and distributed by a man who supplied "Slumming Hostesses" to "inquisitive Nordics" (each card was said to have a suggestive picture on it):[29]

Here in the world's greatest city it would both amuse and also interest you to see the real inside of the New Negro Race of Harlem. You have heard it discussed, but there are very few who really know. . . . I am in a position to carry you through Harlem as you would go slumming through Chinatown. My guides are honest and have been instructed to give the best service. . . . Your season is not completed with thrills until you have visited Harlem.

"White people," the *Age* commented, "are taking a morbid interest in the night life of [Harlem]."[30]

And the interest continued to grow throughout the decade. Carl Van Vechten's novel of Harlem life, *Nigger Heaven* (1926), sold 100,000 copies "almost immediately," and brought its author a substantial fortune. It was translated into French, Swedish, Russian and Japanese.[31] Van Vechten's book contained some interesting commentaries on the structure and problems of Negro society—the role of the middle class; "passing"; prejudice; color-consciousness— but its plot was contrived, sensationalistic and melodramatic; replete with orgies, drugs and seduction; a hodgepodge of *True Confessions* and the front pages of a tabloid. Its characters were unbelievable as people.[32] "The squalor of Negro life, the vice of Negro life," Van Vechten said, "offer a wealth of novel, exotic, picturesque materials to the artist." *Nigger Heaven* was "recognized in every quarter . . . as *the* portrayal of contemporary life in Harlem," its publisher said (and it undoubtedly was).[33] The white world looked curiously at the success of Marcus Garvey, whose movement basically reflected a profound Negro desire for racial pride and respect in a society that denied them, and concluded that Negroes in Harlem "have parades almost every day."[34] White intellectuals and bohemians knew Harlem through the cabarets, or at the famous parties in the salon of the "joy-goddess of Harlem," A'Lelia Walker's "Dark Tower": "dedicated to the aesthetes, young writers, sculptors, painters—a rendezvous where they may feel at home."[35] Bessie Smith, the great blues singer, toured America with her "Harlem Frolic" company. Josephine Baker ("Josephine of the Jazz Age") wowed them in Harlem as a young chorus girl, and went on to international acclaim in Europe. "From a world of stone with metal decoys/Drab stone streets and drab stone masses/New York's mold for the great middle-classes, Africa passes/With syncopated talking the Congo arouses."[36]

White audiences, like gluttons at a feast, vicariously tasted the "high yallers," "tantalizin' tans," and "hot chocolates" that strutted around in the Blackbird Revues, or in such plays as *Lulu Belle* (1926) and *Harlem* (1928)—and made them top box-office successes. *Black Boy* and *Deep River,* dramas which emphasized a more serious side of Negro life, were failures.[37] "Ten years ago," one Negro reviewer of *Lulu Belle* commented, "this play would have been unprofitable. Twenty years ago it would have caused a riot."[38] The following is a handbill distributed to advertise the play *Harlem,* "A Thrilling Play of the Black Belt":[39]

> Harlem! . . . The City that Never Sleeps! . . .
> A Strange, Exotic Island in the Heart of
> New York! . . . Rent Parties! . . . Number
> Runners! . . . Chippies! . . . Jazz Love! . . .
> Primitive Passion!

"How soon this common theme shall reach the nauseating state," a caustic critic remarked, "is not easy to tell."[40]

The Great Depression brought an abrupt end to the concept of a "New Negro" and the image of Harlem as an erotic utopia. A nation sobered by bread lines no longer searched for a dreamland inhabited by people who danced and loved and laughed for an "entire lifetime." America found the "New Negro" less enticing in the 1930's. Connie's Inn, the Lafayette Theatre and other places of entertainment went out of business. Leading figures of the Renaissance: Wallace Thurman, Richard B. Harrison, A'Lelia Walker, Rudolph Fisher, Charles S. Gilpin, Florence Mills and Arthur A. Schomburg died in the late twenties or thirties. Miss Walker's famous Villa Lewaro, another gathering place of the Renaissance, was sold at public auction. Most of the Negro literati, though not all, stopped writing or, if they continued to do so, found a less responsive American audience for their works.[41] All the Negro literary magazines folded.

And, as the exotic vision of the twenties passed, a new image of Harlem emerged—a Harlem already known to stolid census-takers, city health officers and social workers. "The rosy enthusiasms and hopes of 1925," Alain Locke said ten years later, "were . . . cruelly deceptive mirages." The ghetto was revealed in the thirties as "a nasty, sordid corner into which black folk are herded"— *"a Harlem that the social worker knew all along but had not been able to dramatize. . . . There is no cure or saving magic in poetry and art for . . . precarious marginal employment, high mortality rates, civic neglect,"* Locke concluded.[42] It was this Harlem, the neighborhood not visible "from the raucous interior of a smoke-filled, jazz-drunken cabaret," the Harlem hidden by the "bright surface . . . of . . . night clubs, cabaret tours and . . . arty magazines," that was devastated by the Depression; and has remained a community with an inordinate share of sorrow and deprivation ever since. "The depression brought everybody down a peg or two," Langston Hughes wrote. "And the Negroes had but few pegs to fall." The myth-world of the twenties had ended.[43]

Bibliographical Essay

The following is a select bibliographical essay of the works I found most valuable in the preparation of this book, and others that may be useful to scholars.

General Historical Studies of Negro New York

There are only two published books which attempt to survey the history of Negroes in New York City from colonial times to the early twentieth century: James Weldon Johnson's *Black Manhattan* (New York, 1930), and Mary White Ovington's *Half A Man: The Status of the Negro in New York* (New York, 1911). Johnson's study is primarily a popular and impressionistic history—he did not intend it to be otherwise. I found it most valuable for Johnson's sketches and recollections of Negroes in the theater and arts in the early twentieth century. *Half A Man* was written in the years 1904–1910. Although Miss Ovington tries to summarize the early history of Negro New York, she is most successful in describing life in the Tenderloin and San Juan Hill in the first decade of the twentieth century. The first chapter of her *The Walls Came Tumbling Down* (New York, 1947) is largely a repetition of the material she published in *Half A Man,* but it does include some new and interesting facts. George Edmund Haynes's *The Negro At Work in New York City: A Study in Economic Progress* (New York, 1912) originated as a Columbia University doctoral dissertation. Haynes later became a Negro leader of national prominence. His information on nineteenth-century economic life is sketchy, but his detailed material on Negro employment and small business in the early twentieth century, often derived from personal investigation and interviews, is enlightening.

The best over-all history of Negro New York is an unpublished study completed during the Great Depression under the auspices of the WPA. The three drafts of this social history are located in the Schomburg Collection. Each of the research papers written for the project is also at the Schomburg. I benefited from these throughout my research but used the utmost caution in double-checking the information they contained. Few were totally free of error, and many were simply exercises in research and writing. Seth M. Scheiner has recently published *Negro Mecca* (New York, 1965), a revision of his 1963 New York University dissertation.

Statistical Sources

It is possible to obtain the most exact information relating to Negroes in New York City, and elsewhere, through various publications of the United States Bureau of the Census. *Negro Population in the United States, 1790–1915* (Washington, D.C., 1918) and *Negroes in the United States, 1920–1932* (Washington, D.C., 1935) are the two most important general works. I have thoroughly surveyed each census volume on *Population, Occupations* and *Vital Statistics* for the years 1890–1930. These compilations not only provide a breakdown of Negro population by state, city and ward, but also present exact data on the numbers of Negroes employed in every occupation in each borough in New York City. A special volume on New York City, the results of an intensive investigation in the 1880's, was published with the *Eleventh Census, 1890: Vital Statistics of New York City and Brooklyn* (Washington, D.C., 1894). *Statistics of Women at Work, 1900* (Washington, D.C., 1907) also contains important information on Negro life.

Unfortunately, the published New York State Censuses of 1905 and 1915 omit data on the racial composition of the population. In the nineteenth century, however, the state census did record such information. Franklin B. Hough's *Statistics of Population of the City and County of New York. . . .* (New York, 1866), derived from the state census of 1865, is a handy abstract of statistical information on the Negro in the city from the seventeenth century to the Civil War. Walter Laidlaw's *Population of the City of New York, 1890–1930* (New York, 1932) and his massive *Statistical Sources for Demographic Studies of Greater New York, 1910* (New York, 1913), 2 Vols., are guides to twentieth-century conditions.

A number of reports of municipal agencies and local reform and social work organizations provided specific information which could not be obtained from other works. Annual Negro mortality and birth statistics are published in the *Annual Report of the New York City Health Department*. Articles on the health problems of the Negro community regularly appeared in the *Monthly Bulletin* of the Department of Health. One of the most important sources of municipal statistics is the *First Report of the Tenement House Commission of New York City* (New York, 1902), Vol. II. The Commission compiled data on the number of families on each block in Manhattan in 1902. Every block is numbered, and can be located on maps printed in this volume. The ethnic composition of every Manhattan street—by numbers of families—can be derived from this source. Statistics on Negro population, wages, rent, the cost of living generally, and many other things may be found in The Federation of

Churches and Christian Workers of New York City, *First, Second, Third* and *Fourth Sociological Canvasses* [each a separate volume] (New York, 1896–1899); Louise Bolard More, *Wage-Earners' Budgets: A Study of Standards and Cost of Living in New York City* (New York, 1907); and Robert Coit Chapin, *The Standard of Living Among Workingmen's Families in New York City* (New York, 1909).

Negro Migration and Settlement

Negro migration to the North prior to the First World War has largely been overlooked by historians and social scientists. World War I is usually considered the starting point of significant Negro migration to northern urban areas. Thomas J. Woofter, however, in his *Negro Problems in Cities* (New York, 1928), links Negro migration to the general trend of rural movement to urban centers since 1900. Woofter's *Negro Migration: Changes in Rural Organization and Population of the Cotton Belt* (New York, 1920) primarily deals with migration within Georgia. I was made aware of the earlier movement of Negroes northward through the maps in C. Warren Thornthwaite, *Internal Migration in the United States* (Philadelphia, 1934). Contemporary recognition of the movement of southern Negroes during and after World War I led to a voluminous literature on the subject. Louise Venable Kennedy's and Frank Ross's book-length bibliography, *Bibliography of Negro Migration* (New York, 1926), is an extraordinary source that lists the major contemporary studies and articles on migration. This book was completed as part of a general survey of Negro migration undertaken at Columbia University in the 1920's. Three other volumes were produced as a result of this project: Louise Venable Kennedy, *The Negro Peasant Turns Cityward: Effects of Recent Migrations to Northern Centers* (New York, 1930); Edward E. Lewis, *The Mobility of the Negro: A Study in the American Labor Supply* (New York, 1931); and Clyde Vernon Kiser, *Sea Island to City: A Study of St. Helena Islanders in Harlem and Other Urban Centers* (New York, 1932). Carter G. Woodson's *A Century of Negro Migration* (Washington, D.C., 1918), is now outdated. There is interesting information in Arna W. Bontemps and Jack Conroy, *They Seek A City* (New York, 1945). Charles S. Johnson traces the increase in Negro migration to the decline of European immigration in "Substitution of Negro Labor for European Immigrant Labor," *Proceedings of the National Conference of Social Work* (New York, 1926), 317–327. The standard work on West Indian immigration is Ira De Augustine Reid, *The Negro Immigrant: His Background, Characteristics and Social Adjustment, 1899–1937* (New York, 1939).

Difficulties confronted by the earliest generation of southern Negroes in New York City are studied in the following: Paul Laurence Dunbar, *The Sport of the Gods* (New York, 1902); the entire issues of *Charities*, XV (October 7, 1905), and *The Annals*, XXVII (May 1906); George Edmund Haynes, "The Movement of Negroes from the Country to the

City," *The Southern Workman,* XLII (April 1913), 230–236. A few contemporary masters' essays in sociology proved exceptionally helpful: William Fielding Ogburn, "The Richmond Negro in New York City: His Social Mind As Seen in His Pleasures" (1909); Robert Zachariah Johnstone, "The Negro in New York—His Social Attainments and Prospects" (1911); Seymour Paul, "A Group of Virginia Negroes in New York City" (1912); and Ernest Jasper Hopper, "A Northern Negro Group" (1912). All were written at Columbia University.

C. Vann Woodward's *The Strange Career of Jim Crow* (New York, 1955) is the starting point for any analysis of southern reaction to the Negro in the late nineteenth and early twentieth centuries. It is a groundbreaking work, but the thesis is somewhat overstated. Excellent articles on the subject are: Guion Griffis Johnson, "The Ideology of White Supremacy, 1876–1910," in Fletcher Melvin Green, ed., *Essays in Southern History* (Chapel Hill, 1949), 124–156; Bert James Loewenberg, "Efforts of the South to Encourage Immigration, 1865–1900," *South Atlantic Quarterly,* XXXIII (October 1934), 363–385; and Rowland T. Berthoff, "Southern Attitudes Toward Immigration, 1865–1914," *Journal of Southern History,* XVII (August 1951), 328–360.

Of the dozens of racist volumes produced at the turn of the century, the following are representative and gory: Charles Carroll, *The Negro A Beast, or, In the Image of God* (St. Louis, Mo., 1900); William P. Calhoun, *The Caucasian and the Negro in the United States. They Must Separate. If Not, Then Extermination . . .* (Columbia, S.C., 1902); Robert Wilson Shufeldt, *The Negro: A Menace to American Civilization* (Boston, 1907); Carlyle McKinley, *An Appeal to Pharaoh: The Negro Problem and Its Radical Solution* (Columbia, S.C., 1907); William P. Pickett, *The Negro Problem: Abraham Lincoln's Solution* (New York, 1909). Popular attitudes of southern white farmers toward the Negro, 1899–1901, are preserved in hundreds of pages of testimony in *Report of the Industrial Commission on Agriculture and Agricultural Labor* (Washington, D.C., 1901), Vol. X.

Negro New York—Pre-Harlem

There are a few published articles on the Negro population of New York City in the nineteenth century: Arnett G. Lindsay, "The Economic Condition of the Negroes of New York Prior to 1861," *Journal of Negro History,* VI (April 1921), 190–199; Aaron Hamlet Payne, "The Negro in New York Prior to 1860," *The Howard Review,* I (June 1923), 1–64; Leo H. Hirsch, Jr., "New York and the Negro, from 1783 to 1865," *Journal of Negro History,* XVI (October 1931), 382–471; Monroe N. Work, "The Life of Charles B. Ray," *ibid.,* IV (October 1919), 361–371; Herman D. Bloch, "The New York City Negro and Occupational Eviction, 1860–1910," *International Review of Social History,* V (1960), 26–38, and Bloch, "The New York Negro's Battle for Political Rights, 1777–

1865," *ibid.*, IX (1964), 65–80; Seth M. Scheiner, "The New York City Negro and the Tenement," *New York History*, XLV (October 1964), 304–315. Biographical sketches of prominent nineteenth-century New York Negroes are in the WPA research papers. Leon F. Litwak's *North of Slavery: The Negro in the Free States, 1790–1860* (Chicago, 1961) is primarily a study of interracial relations and institutional prejudice, but it does contain some interesting descriptive material on Negroes in northern cities.

A more thorough understanding of nineteenth-century Negro life may be derived from masters' essays and doctoral dissertations. Leslie H. Fishel, Jr., "The North and the Negro, 1865–1900: A Study in Race Discrimination" (Ph.D. dissertation, Harvard University, 1954), and August Meier, "Negro Racial Thought in the Age of Booker T. Washington, Circa 1880–1915" (Ph.D. dissertation, Columbia University, 1957), are works of high quality and thoroughness. Meier's excellent dissertation was published in somewhat abbreviated form as *Negro Thought in America, 1880–1915: Racial Ideologies in the Age of Booker T. Washington* (Ann Arbor, 1963). The following Columbia University masters' essays all contain solid information: John P. Clyde, "The Negro in New York City" (1899); Lucille Genevieve Lomax, "A Social History of the Negro Population in the Section of New York City known as Greenwich Village" (1930); Philmore L. Groisser, "The Free Negro in New York State, 1850–1860" (1939); and Joan Cohen, "The Social Conditions of the Negro in New York City, 1830–1865" (1951). Robert S. Dixon's "Education of the Negro in the City of New York, 1853–1900" (M.A. thesis, City College, 1935) has useful data.

There are a few primary sources which describe nineteenth-century Negro life in New York City. Among the most important are: Charles C. Andrews, *The History of the New-York African Free Schools . . .* (New York, 1830), and the extant copies of the New York Negro newspaper *The Colored American* for 1837 and 1838. Both are at the New-York Historical Society. The Schomburg Collection has microfilms of *The New York Globe* (1883–1885), *The New York Freeman* (1885–1887), and *The New York Age* (1887–1891, and scattered issues in the 1890's).

Two manuscript collections at the Schomburg, the John Edward Bruce and the Reverend Dr. Alexander Crummell Manuscripts, contain some relevant data. Waring Cuney, "Interview with Jerome B. Peterson: An Account of Wealthy Negroes, 1880–1890" (WPA research paper); "Wealthy Negroes," *The New York Times*, July 14, 1895, and "New York's Rich Negroes," *The Sun*, January 18, 1903, present biographical sketches of colored businessmen and professionals. All of Jacob Riis's books on New York City mention Negroes, as does his "The Black Half," *The Crisis*, V (April 1913), 298–299. Perceptive commentaries by W. E. B. DuBois may be found in a series of articles he wrote in 1901: *The New York Times*, November 17, 24, December 1, 8, 15, 1901. The reminiscences of Samuel R. Scottron were published in "The Industrial and Professional Pursuits of Colored People of Old New York," *The*

Colored American Magazine, XIII (October 1907), 265–267, and in many issues of *The New York Age* in 1905. Samuel J. Battle, the first Negro policeman in Manhattan, describes Negro life in the Tenderloin and San Juan Hill in "The Reminiscences of Samuel J. Battle" (Oral History Research Office, Columbia University, 1960). Some personal papers of John B. Nail, the Negro café owner, are preserved in the James Weldon Johnson Collection, Yale University. (Mrs. James Weldon Johnson, Grace Nail Johnson, is Nail's daughter.) Other material is recorded in James Weldon Johnson, *The Autobiography of an Ex-Coloured Man* (New York, 1960); Reverend Dr. Adam Clayton Powell, Sr., *Against the Tide: An Autobiography* (New York, 1938); Bishop Alexander Walters, *My Life and Work* (New York, 1917); Bishop Reverdy C. Ransom, *The Pilgrimage of Harriet Ransom's Son* (Nashville, 1950?); and James Weldon Johnson, *Along This Way* (New York, 1933).

Interracial Relations

The softening of institutionalized racial prejudices in New York City and in the North in the late nineteenth century is documented in Fishel's "The North and the Negro, 1865–1900." Magnificent collections of plays and vaudeville shows, from which I attempted to draw a characterization of the stereotype of the Negro at the turn of the century, are in the Schomburg Collection, and in the Atkinson Collection at the University of Chicago. The same image emerges in stories about Negroes in the white press, and in the newspaper clippings compiled in scrapbooks at the Gumby Collection, Columbia University. Manuscripts relating to the race riot of 1900—letters of protest, transcripts of the trials of policemen, the police commissioners' report to the mayor—are in the Van Wyck Papers, Municipal Archives. The case of "The People vs. Arthur J. Harris," including summaries of the testimony of witnesses, is on file at the Municipal Court Building. A few papers of the Citizens' Protective League are among the Miscellaneous Manuscripts, Schomburg Collection. [Frank Moss], *Story of the Riot: Persecution of Negroes by Roughs and Policemen in the City of New York, August, 1900* (New York, 1900), contains the notarized statements of eighty Negroes beaten during the riot.

As racial antagonism increased in New York City, municipal reformers attempted to improve the position of the Negro. Practically all the social service agencies that came into existence by 1915 are discussed in Frances Blascoer's *Colored School Children in New York* (New York, 1915). The *Annual Reports* of the New York Colored Mission are in the Schomburg Collection, and the Certificate of Incorporation of that society is in the New York City Hall of Records—along with the papers of incorporation of most other social service agencies. A director of the Urban League, L. Hollingsworth Wood, wrote on the organization in "The New York Colored Mission—Good Samaritan Inn," *Opportunity,* V (March 1927), 82–83. A biographical sketch of Victoria Earle Matthews and a summary of her work at the White Rose Home appeared in her obituary, *The New York Age,* March 14, 1907. Also see Mary L. Lewis, "The White Rose Industrial Association," *The Messenger,* VII (April 1925). On Frances A. Kellor and the National League for the Protection of Colored Women see: Kellor, *Out of Work: A Study of Employment Agencies. . . .* (New York, 1904); Kellor, "Assisted Emigration from the South: The Women," *Charities,* XV (October 7, 1905), 12–13; "Conditions Existing in the City of New York prior to May 1st 1904, Which Led to the Creation of this Office," a statement by the Commissioner of Licenses, in the Municipal Archives; and E. M. Rhodes, "The Protection of Girls Who Travel: A National Movement," *The Colored American Magazine,* XIII (August 1907), 114–115. Mary White Ovington's "Reminiscences" were published in the Baltimore *Afro-American,* September 1932–February 1933. Other information on her activities may be found in *Half A Man; The Walls Came Tumbling Down; How the NAACP Began* (New York, 1914); "The National Association for the Advancement of Colored People," *Journal of Negro History,* IX (April 1924), 107–116; "Beginnings of the NAACP," *The Crisis,* XXXII (June 1926), 76–77. Miss Ovington's secretary, Mrs. Richetta G. Wallace, was helpful in supplying details about her life that were unclear in the sources. Manuscript material on the CIICN is in the J. G. Phelps Stokes Collection, Columbia University. "The Reminiscences of William J. Schieffelin," president of the CIICN and supporter of Booker T. Washington, are in the Columbia University Oral History Research Office. It would have been impossible to re-create the life of William Lewis Bulkley without the assistance of the New York City Board of Education. I was permitted to see Bulkley's files, which contained valuable biographical information as well as an outline of his public school career. The archivist of Syracuse University sent me photostatic copies of Bulkley's graduate school records.

The political power of the Negro community increased as the population expanded. White politicians and municipal officials began to court Negro support and accede to demands that Negroes made for political recognition and patronage. The voluminous correspondence of Charles W. Anderson and Booker T. Washington, covering the years 1904–1915, often deals with questions of patronage and local Negro politics. It is a key manuscript source. These letters are in the Washington Papers, Library of Congress. The mayoralty papers of John F. Hylan, James J. Walker and Fiorello H. La Guardia are the major sources for a study of the changed attitudes of white politicians. Also see the Oral History reminiscences at Columbia University of Martin C. Ansorge (1949) and Samuel S. Koenig (1950). The *Official Canvass of Votes,* published each year in the *City Record,* records votes by election districts. The Schomburg Collection has files of newspaper clippings on Anderson's and Morton's careers, as it does for many other prominent Negroes. Other than this, it is necessary to turn to articles which appeared in *The New York Age* over decades to reconstruct the political history of Negro New York. On the rise of the

Negro National Guard Unit see: Arthur W. Little, *From Harlem to the Rhine: The Story of New York's Colored Volunteers* (New York, 1936); Emmett J. Scott, *Scott's Official History of the American Negro in the World War* (Chicago, 1919); Addie W. Hunton and Kathryn M. Johnson, *Two Colored Women with the American Expeditionary Forces* (Brooklyn, 1920); and Wilmer F. Lucas, "The 369th Infantry, New York National Guard," *The Crisis*, XXXVII (April 1930), 120–123. Unfortunately, the papers of Charles S. Whitman, the New York governor so active in Negro affairs, have not been preserved in the state archives.

White Harlem

There is no general history of New York City that would stand the test of modern scholarship. The nineteenth-century multi-volumed tomes, such as James Grant Wilson's *The Memorial History of the City of New-York* (New York, 1893), 4 Vols., are the works of antiquarians. They peripherally discuss Harlem in the colonial period, devote many pages to the Revolutionary Battle of Harlem Heights, but never re-create or develop an organized history of this section of Manhattan. James Riker, *Revised History of Harlem (City of New York): Its Origin and Early Annals* (New York, 1904), is the most significant secondary source. Its main concern is the history of Harlem in the seventeenth century. The 1904 edition (the first edition appeared in 1881) contains some 400 pages of genealogical data. Riker's diffuse footnotes often include information on Harlem in the nineteenth century, and I found them as valuable as the text. Colonel Alonzo B. Caldwell, *A Lecture: The History of Harlem* (New York, 1882), and Herbert Manchester, *The Story of Harlem and the Empire Savings Bank, 1889–1929* (New York, 1929), were helpful pamphlets.

To find out about white Harlem in the late nineteenth and early twentieth centuries, it was necessary to turn almost exclusively to primary sources. A number of local magazines and newspapers have survived. The New-York Historical Society has a file of the biweekly *Harlem Local Reporter* which is practically complete for the 1890's. This newspaper, along with the *Harlem Monthly Magazine* (1893, 1902), *Harlem Life* (1899–1900), *Harlem Magazine* (1912–1933), and the *Harlem Home News* (1911–1913), provides the best information on the history of the white population of Harlem.

Reminiscences of white Harlem by old residents contain fascinating information. Frederick A. Birmingham's *It Was Fun While It Lasted* (Philadelphia, 1960) is the only book-length memoir. The following were the most significant pamphlets and articles: Ella Bunner Graff, *Reminiscences of Old Harlem* (n.p., 1933); Richard Webber, Jr., "Historical Sketch of Harlem," *Harlem Magazine*, I (October 1912), 16–17; "Old-Timers' Tales of Harlem's Growth," *ibid.*, III (December 1914), 16–22; Samuel M. Brown, "Harlem's Early Transit Facilities," *ibid.*, IV (September 1915), 11; Michael C. O'Brien, "Memories of Hooker's Building," *ibid.*, IV (May 1916), 11, 17; Charles H. Fuller, "Harlem—from 'Cradle Days' to Now," *ibid.*, XV (October 1925), 6–7, 24; Berta Gilbert, "Morgenthau Reminisces About Harlem," *ibid.*, XX (May 1931), 4, 15–16; Elmer Rice, "A New York Childhood," *The New Yorker*, IV (September 22, 1928), 36–40; "The Reminiscences of John T. Hettrick" (Oral History Research Office, Columbia University, 1949).

Land and property speculation played an important part in the history of Harlem from the 1870's through the 1920's. The "Harlem Commons Syndicate" is an unpublished collection of newspaper clippings, letters, wills and other items relating to Harlem property. It, along with Walter H. Shupe's *First Annual Statement of the Harlem Commons Syndicate* (New York, 1884), and *Deduction of the Harlaem Commons* (New York, 1872), are at the New-York Historical Society. The New-York Historical Society also has a number of boxes of material on Harlem land transfers. Sections of Abraham Cahan's *The Rise of David Levinsky* (New York, 1960) magnificently re-create the mood of the turn-of-the-century real estate craze. The best source of information on speculation in Harlem land is the weekly *Real Estate Record and Builders' Guide*. It is possible to check each transfer of property in New York City through its columns, and every issue is voluminous. The *Record and Guide* also published *A History of Real Estate, Building, and Architecture in New York City During the Last Quarter of a Century* (New York, 1898). For an example of one speculator who made great profit in Harlem and built an opera house there, see Vincent Sheean, *Oscar Hammerstein I: The Life and Exploits of an Impresario* (New York, 1956). Henry Pennington Toler's *Arise Take Thy Journey* (New York, 1903) and Carl Horton Pierce's *New Harlem Past and Present: The Story of an Amazing Civic Wrong Now At Last To Be Righted* (New York, 1903) were written by men who tried to prove that descendants of colonial landholders still had legal claim to Harlem land.

The publications of many local institutions have survived—political clubs, social and charitable organizations, churches. See: Reverend Edgar Tilton, Jr., *The Reformed Low Dutch Church of Harlem: Historical Sketch* (New York, 1910); Collegiate Reformed Church of Harlem, *Two Hundred and Fiftieth Anniversary* (New York, 1910); William B. Silber, *A History of St. James Methodist Episcopal Church at Harlem, New York City, 1830–1880* (New York, 1882); Harlem Independent Schützen Corps, *Golden Jubilee, 1880–1930* (New York, 1930); *Harlem Library Bulletin* (1902–1905); Harlem Relief Society of the City of New York, *Annual Reports* (1893–1920); and the various publications of the Harlem Democratic and Republican clubs, the Harlem Regatta Association, and the Harlem Board of Commerce.

Organized opposition to Negro settlement may be traced through articles which appeared in *Harlem Magazine*, *The Crisis* and *The New York Age*, and the *Harlem Home News*. Some of the restrictive housing covenants were filed at the New York City Hall of Records. I knew of the existence of one covenant through press reports and located it and others by systematically checking the real estate records for each Harlem block. The city classifies each street by a specific number. With this number it is possible to locate separate "Libers" which record property transactions in New York City from colonial times to the present. The following "Libers," each in Section 7 at the Hall of Records, contained restrictive agreements: 127, pp. 365–368; 128, pp. 145–150; 151, pp. 134–146; 152, pp. 297–301; 159, pp. 7–15. *Harlem Survey* (New York, 1917?), published by the Harlem Board of Commerce, is a valuable document that depicts the radical ethnic changes that had taken place in Harlem by the First World War.

Negro Harlem

A substantial literature on the ghetto has accumulated in the last three years. A good starting point is Ernest Kaiser's bibliographical essay "The Literature of Harlem," *Freedomways,* III (Summer 1963), 276–291. This entire issue of *Freedomways* is devoted to Harlem and has appeared, in somewhat different form, as John Henrik Clarke, ed., *Harlem: A Community in Transition* (New York, 1965). Two exceptionally valuable studies are HARYOU, *Youth in the Ghetto: A Study of the Consequences of Powerlessness and a Blueprint for Change* (New York, 1964), and Columbia University Bureau of Applied Social Research, *A Harlem Almanac* (New York, 1964).

Claude McKay's *Harlem: Negro Metropolis* (New York, 1940) is primarily a popular history of Harlem in the 1930's. Myrtle Evangeline Pollard, "Harlem As Is: The Negro Business and Economic Community. . . ." (M.A. thesis, City College, 1937), also deals with the 1930's. It is a lengthy study, but rambling and disorganized. Information on the founding of Negro Harlem may be obtained from James Weldon Johnson's *Black Manhattan* (New York, 1930), and Robert C. Weaver's *Negro Ghetto* (New York, 1948).

The early history of Negro Harlem may best be studied through the thousands of articles and items that appeared in *The New York Age* (1905–1940) and *The Crisis* (1911–1940). Other helpful data were printed in *The Colored American Magazine* (1900–1909), *The Southern Workman* (1900–1920), *The Messenger* (1919–1929), and *Opportunity* (1923–1940).

Philip A. Payton, Jr.'s role in the founding of Negro Harlem has luckily been preserved in the Booker T. Washington Papers, Library of Congress. Emmett J. Scott, Washington's secretary, was a director of the Afro-American Realty Company and received regular reports of the corporation's activities from Fred R. Moore. Without their correspondence, it would have been impossible to uncover reliable information on the Realty Company. The "Certificate of Incorporation of the Afro-American Realty Company, June 15, 1904" is on file in the Hall of Records. "Crowder vs. Philip A. Payton, Jr. and the Afro-American Realty Company" (1907), the stockholders' suit against Payton, also threw valuable light on the company's operations. The plaintiff's charges, orders for the arrest of Payton, the final decision of the court and a copy of the original *Prospectus* of the corporation (New York, 1904) were all preserved with the papers of the case at the Hall of Records.

Most of the prominent people active in Harlem in the earliest years of Negro settlement are dead. The exact dates of their deaths may be checked in the annual *Negro Year Books*. A few contemporary records and statements are extant, however. An important interview with Payton was recorded in *The New York Age*, December 5, 1912. John M. Royall's description of the real estate boom, its collapse, and the subsequent movement of Negroes into Harlem is found in the *Age*, June 11, 1914. The role of the Reverend Dr. Hutchens C. Bishop in buying property for St. Philip's Protestant Episcopal Church is reviewed by his son in Waring Cuney, "Notes from an Interview with Reverend Shelton Bishop" (WPA research paper). A few letters of John E. Nail are in the James Weldon Johnson Collection, Yale University. The "John E. Nail Scrapbook," also at Yale, includes newspaper clippings of the Nail and Parker realty company, notices of Nail's death and material on Harlem in the Depression. Nail was also interviewed by a WPA researcher and described Negro Harlem in the first decade of the twentieth century in Odetta Harper, "Interview with John E. Nail." Powell's *Against the Tide* includes interesting recollections of Harlem, as does Battle's "Reminiscences."

Contemporary surveys and articles on Harlem proved to be of the utmost importance in tracing the emergence of the community as a slum. The most valuable were: National League on Urban Conditions Among Negroes, *Housing Conditions Among Negroes in Harlem, New York City* (New York, 1915); Benjamin H. Locke's "The Community Life of a Harlem Group of Negroes" (M.A. thesis, Columbia University, 1913); the New York Urban League's "Twenty-Four Hundred Negro Families in Harlem: An Interpretation of the Living Conditions of Small Wage-Earners" (typescript, Schomburg Collection, 1927); "Harlem: Mecca of the New Negro," *The Survey*, LIII (March 1, 1925), 629–724; E. F. Dycoff, "A Negro City in New York," *The Outlook*, CVIII (December 23, 1914), 949–954; Harlem Board of Commerce, *Harlem Survey* (New York, 1917?); Rollin Lynde Hartt, " 'I'd Like to Show You Harlem!' " *The Independent*, CV (April 2, 1921), 334–335; Eric D. Walrond, "The Black City," *The Messenger*, VI (January 1924), 13–14; Chester T. Crowell, "The World's Largest Negro City," *The Saturday Evening Post*, CXCVIII (August 8, 1925), 8–9, 93–94, 97; "The Negro City," *The American Review of Reviews*, LXXIII (March 1926), 323–324; Owen R. Lovejoy, "Justice for the Negro Child," *Opportunity*, VII (June 1929), 174–176; E. Franklin Frazier, "Negro Harlem: An Ecological Study," *The American Journal of Sociology*, XLIII (July 1937), 72–88; The Mayor's Commission on Conditions in Harlem, "The Negro in Harlem: A Report on Social and Economic Conditions Responsible for the Outbreak of March 19, 1935" (La Guardia Papers). Files on Negro life through the 1940's are included in the La Guardia Collection. James Ford, *et al., Slums and Housing: With Special Reference to New York City* (Cambridge, Mass., 1936), 2 Vols.; *Annual Reports of City and Suburban Homes Company* (1896–1930); Winfred B. Nathan, *Health Conditions in North Harlem, 1923–1927* (New York, 1932); Owen R. Lovejoy, *The Negro Children of New York* (New York, 1932); The President's Conference on Home Building and Home Ownership, *Report of the Committee on Negro Housing* (Washington, D.C., 1932); and Committee of Fourteen, *Annual Reports* (1905–1929), are exceptionally enlightening.

The revolutionary recognition of the Negro and Harlem in the twenties may best be traced through the periodicals. Practically all the major magazines, from the *Ladies' Home Journal* to *The American Mercury*, printed stories and articles on Negro life. The white journals that carried the most material on the Negro were: *The World Tomorrow, The Nation, The New Republic* and *The American Mercury*. The major theme I attempted to develop in the "Epilogue" is clearly typified by the following articles: Konrad Bercovici, "The Black Blocks of Manhattan," *Harper's Monthly Magazine*, CXLIX (October 1924), 613–623; Clement Wood, "Hosea Before the Rotary Club," *The World Tomorrow*, VIII (July 1925), 209–210; George S. Schuyler, "Blessed are the Sons of Ham," *The Nation*, CXXIV (March 23, 1927), 313–315; Joseph Wood Krutch, "Black Ecstasy," *ibid.*, CXXV (October 26, 1927), 456–458; and Hermann Keyserling, "What the Negro Means to America," *The Atlantic Monthly*, CXLIV (October 1929), 444–447. Diana N. Lockard's "The Negro on the Stage in the Nineteen Twenties" (M.A. thesis, Columbia University, 1960) analyzes the image of the Negro as "savage" in the drama. Perceptive contemporary criticisms of the distorted view of Negro life that emerged when the "Negro was in vogue" are Wallace Thurman's "Nephews of Uncle Remus," *The Independent*, CXIX (September 24, 1927), 296–298; and George Chester Morse's superb "The Fictitious Negro," *The Outlook and Independent*, CLII (August 21, 1929), 648–649.

The most valuable manuscript sources for a study of the Negro Renaissance are the papers of Carl Van Vechten, James Weldon Johnson and Langston Hughes in the James Weldon Johnson Memorial Collection, Yale University. Two excellent autobiographies by Negro writers discuss Harlem in the twenties: Langston Hughes, *The Big Sea* (New York, 1940); and Claude McKay, *A Long Way From Home* (New York, 1937). Wallace Thurman's *Infants of the Spring* (New York, 1932) is a novel about the Renaissance. The novels written by Negroes in the twenties are full of information on Harlem life, as are "The Reminiscences of Carl Van Vechten" (1960); "The Reminiscences of George S. Schuyler" (1960); and "The Reminiscences of Benjamin McLaurin" (1960). All these are in Columbia University's immensely valuable Oral History Collection. Alain Locke's *The New Negro: An Interpretation* (New York, 1925) is a classic statement of the views of the 1920's.

Notes

NOTES TO CHAPTER 1

1. Booker T. Washington and Robert E. Park, *The Man Farthest Down: A Record of Observation and Study in Europe* (New York, 1912), *passim*.

2. Bureau of the Census, *Negro Population in the United States, 1790–1915* (Washington, D.C., 1918), pp. 43–45; *Twelfth Census, 1900: Population* (Washington, D.C., 1901), I, 869, II, 193; Kelly Miller, "The Economic Handicap of the Negro in the North," *The Annals of the American Academy of Political and Social Science,* XXVII (May 1906), 547.

3. Mary White Ovington, *Half a Man: The Status of the Negro in New York* (New York, 1911), p. 148.

4. Bureau of the Census, *Statistics of Women at Work, 1900* (Washington, D.C., 1907), p. 146; W. E. B. DuBois, "The Black North," *The New York Times,* November 17, 1901; Federation of Churches and Christian Workers in New York City, *Second Sociological Canvass* (New York, 1897), p. 40.

5. *Twelfth Census: Occupations,* pp. 634–641.

6. Booker T. Washington, *The Negro in Business* (Boston, 1907), pp. 104–109; Samuel R. Scottron, "The Industrial and Professional Pursuits of Colored People of Old New York," *The Colored American Magazine,* XIII (October 1907), 265–266; *The New York Age,* July 27, 1905; *The New York Globe,* March 29, 1884; *The New York Times,* January 30, 1901; "The Negro Artisan," *Atlanta University Publications, No. 7* (Atlanta, 1902), p. 134.

7. Waring Cuney, "Interview with Jerome B. Peterson: An Account of Wealthy Negroes, 1880–1890" (WPA research paper, Schomburg Collection); Ovington, *Half A Man,* p. 29.

8. "Wealthy Negroes," *The New York Times,* July 14, 1895; "The Negro American Artisan," *Atlanta University Publications, No. 17* (Atlanta, 1912), p. 132.

9. Henry Collins Brown, *In the Golden Nineties* (New York, 1928), p. 84.

10. Ovington, *Half A Man,* p. 78.

11. Robert Ernst, *Immigrant Life in New York City, 1825–1863* (New York, 1949), pp. 66–67, 214–217.

12. *Ibid.,* p. 104.

13. James W. C. Pennington, *The Fugitive Blacksmith* (New York, 1849), p. 55.

14. Quoted in Lucille Genevieve Lomax, "A Social History of the Negro

Population Living in the Section of New York City known as Greenwich Village" (M.A. thesis, Columbia University, 1930), pp. 79–81.

15. "Our Friends Discourage Us," *The Colored American,* August 12, 1837; "Importance of the Mechanic Arts to Colored Youth," *ibid.,* December 22, 1838; Arnett G. Lindsay, "The Economic Condition of the Negroes of New York Prior to 1861," *Journal of Negro History,* VI (April 1921), 195.

16. "The Negro Artisan," pp. 29–30.

17. Quoted in Philmore L. Groisser, "The Free Negro in New York State, 1850–1860" (M.A. thesis, Columbia University, 1939), pp. 102–114.

18. Lomax, "A Social History," pp. 81–84.

19. The following are the exact numbers of Negroes in New York City who owned enough property to qualify for the franchise, 1825–1865. Adapted from Franklin B. Hough, *Statistics of Population of the City and County of New York. . . .* (New York, 1866), p. 240.

	Total Negro Population of New York City	Qualified to Vote
1825	12,559	68
1835	15,061	84
1845	12,913	255
1855	11,840	100
1865	9,943	44

20. Ernst, *Immigrant Life,* p. 67.

21. Hough, *Statistics of Population,* p. 230; *Negro Population, 1790–1915,* p. 64.

22. Bureau of the Census, *Vital Statistics of New York City and Brooklyn, 1890* (Washington, D.C., 1894), pp. 7 and *passim;* City of New York, *Annual Reports of the Department of Health* and *Monthly Bulletins of the Department of Health; Twelfth Census, 1900: Vital Statistics,* III, 458–464; R. R. Wright Jr., "The Migration of Negroes to the North," *The Annals of the Academy of Political and Social Science,* XXVII (May 1906), 563.

23. *Vital Statistics of New York City,* pp. 14, 441; New York Colored Mission, *Annual Report for 1905* (New York, 1906), p. 11; *The New York Age,* January 22, 1922.

24. For contemporary recognition of these medical problems and their continuing influence on Negro life see: "Mortality Among Negroes in Cities," *Atlanta University Publications, No. 1* (Atlanta, 1903); "Social and Physical Conditions of Negroes in Cities," *Atlanta University Publications, No. 2* (Atlanta, 1897); The New York Association for Improving the Condition of the Poor, *Health Work for Mothers and Children in a Colored Community* (New York, 1924); Ransom S. Hooker, *Maternal Mortality in New York City: A Study of all Puerperal Deaths, 1930–1932* (New York, 1933), pp. 57, 77, 91, 163–165; Jean Downes, *An Experiment in the Control of Tuberculosis Among Negroes* (New York, 1950); Janet B. Hardy and Miriam E. Brailey, *Tuberculosis in White and Negro Children* (Cambridge, Massachusetts, 1958), 2 Vols.

25. Mary White Ovington, *The Walls Came Tumbling Down* (New York, 1947), p. 51.

26. *The New York Globe,* February 16, 1884.

27. *Ibid.,* January 6, 1883.

28. The following sketches of Negro neighborhoods in the early nineteenth

century are primarily intended to describe them. Little information about them is extant and to find the exact causes for the decline of Five Points and the succession of Greenwich Village as Negro sections would involve a more detailed study of fugitive sources than I have been able to make.

29. Joan Cohen, "The Social Conditions of the Negro in New York City, 1830–1865" (M.A. thesis, Columbia University, 1951), pp. 6–12; Herbert Marshall and Mildred Stock, *Ira Aldridge: The Negro Tragedian* (London, 1958), p. 32; *The New York Freeman*, February 19, 1887; *The Colored American*, March 25, 1837; Caroline F. Ware, *Greenwich Village, 1920–1930; A Comment on American Civilization in the Post-War Years* (Boston, 1935), p. 12.

30. Charles Dickens, *American Notes* (London, 1900), pp. 102–105; Ernst, *Immigrant Life*, p. 39.

31. Charles C. Andrews, *The History of the New-York African Free Schools. . . .* (New York, 1830), pp. 57, 121–122.

32. Five Points House of Industry, *Monthly Record*, II (May 1858), 54–55.

33. "The Dens of Death," *New York Daily Tribune*, June 5, 1850; G. G. Foster, *New York by Gas-Light: With Here and There a Streak of Sunshine* (New York, 1850), pp. 56–57.

34. Ernst, *Immigrant Life*, p. 39; Groisser, "Free Negro," p. 88; Kate Holladay Claghorn, "The Foreign Immigrant in New York City," *Reports of the Industrial Commission on Immigration . . . and on Education* (Washington, D.C., 1911), XV, 453.

35. For a photograph of the Workingmen's House and the Negroes of the district see James Ford, *et al., Slums and Housing: With Special Reference to New York City* (Cambridge, Mass., 1936), II, 673.

36. Marshall and Stock, *Ira Aldridge*, pp. 28–47.

37. Wesley Curtwright, "Rise of Negro Churches in New York, 1827–1860" (WPA research paper, Schomburg Collection), p. 1; *The New York Age*, December 9, 1909, March 30, 1911, April 17, 1913; Monroe N. Work, "The Life of Charles B. Ray," *Journal of Negro History*, IV (October 1919), 361–371.

38. *The New York Age*, May 29, 1913; *The Crisis*, IX (February 1915), 166–167.

39. Andrews, *African Free Schools*, pp. 23–24.

40. *The New York Freeman*, January 31, 1885; "History of Our Schools in New York," *The New York Age*, July 13, 1905; Wesley Curtwright, "Life of James McCune Smith"; Simon Williamson, "The Life and Work of Henry Highland Garnet" (WPA research papers, Schomburg Collection); *Calendar of the Manuscripts in the Schomburg Collection of Negro Literature* (New York, 1943?), pp. 51–55. On the Downing family see Lorenzo T. Greene, "Protest Against Separate Schools in Rhode Island, 1859," *The Midwest Journal*, I (Summer 1949), 102–103; and *The Crisis*, XII (June 1916), 61.

41. Rev. Dr. Alexander Crummell, "Lecture Sermon on John Peterson, for 50 years a Teacher in An African School. . . ." Crummell Manuscripts, Schomburg Collection.

42. *The New York Age*, March 22, 1890; "For He Was a Good Man" (1886), Crummell Papers.

43. Five Points House of Industry, *Monthly Record*, IV (May 1860), 12–14.

44. *The New York Freeman*, February 19, 1887.

45. New York City Board of Health, *Annual Report, 1893* (New York, 1894), p. 164.

46. Charles W. Gardner, *The Doctor and the Devil: A Startling Exposé of Municipal Corruption* (New York, 1894), pp. 52, 57.

47. Henry Collins Brown, *In the Golden Nineties* (New York, 1928), p. 348.

48. Jacob A. Riis, *How the Other Half Lives: Studies Among the Tenements of New York* (New York, 1957), p. 117.

49. Lomax, "A Social History," pp. 91 ff; Jacob Riis, "The Black Half," *The Crisis*, V (April 1913), 298–299.

50. *The New York Age*, July 27, 1905.

51. Riis, *How the Other Half Lives*, p. 112.

52. John P. Clyde, "The Negro in New York City" (M.A. thesis, Columbia University, 1899), p. 3.

53. Bureau of the Census, *Eleventh Census, 1890: Population* (Washington, D.C., 1894), I, 564.

54. "Bruce Grits Column" (n.d.), Bruce Manuscripts, Schomburg Collection.

55. William McAdoo, *Guarding a Great City* (New York, 1906), pp. 91, 93 ff.

56. Ovington, *The Walls Came Tumbling Down*, p. 40; *The New York Age*, December 26, 1912; "Oldest New York's Past and Present Racial and Religious Conditions," *Federation*, III (December 1904), 4; George Edmund Haynes, *The Negro at Work in New York City: A Study in Economic Progress*, in Columbia University *Studies in History, Economics and Public Law*, XLIX (New York, 1912), p. 51.

57. "The Reminiscences of Samuel J. Battle" (Oral History Research Office, Columbia University, 1960), p. 22; Ovington, *The Walls Came Tumbling Down*, p. 35; William Fielding Ogburn, "The Richmond Negro in New York City: His Social Mind as Seen in His Pleasures" (M.A. thesis, Columbia University, 1909), p. 48; Niles Carpenter, *The Sociology of City Life* (New York, 1932), p. 78; *The New York Age*, January 13, 1916.

58. The Federation of Churches and Christian Workers in New York City, *Second Sociological Canvass* (New York, 1897), p. 85; *The New York Freeman*, March 7, 1885; Riis, *How the Other Half Lives*, pp. 113–114.

59. These were Mount Olivet Baptist, St. Mark's Methodist Episcopal, St. James Presbyterian, Union Baptist, St. Cyprian's Episcopal and St. Benedict the Moor's Roman Catholic.

60. Ovington, *The Walls Came Tumbling Down*, p. 40; Ogburn, "The Richmond Negro," pp. 49–52.

61. M. R. Werner, *It Happened In New York* (New York, 1957), pp. 36–116; Reverend Dr. Charles H. Parkhurst, *Our Fight With Tammany* (New York, 1895), *passim*; *New York Daily Tribune*, August 25, 1900; *The New York Times*, January 8, 1898, March 19, 1900, March 31, 1900; *The New York Age*, April 5, 1906, March 21, 1907; "The Terrible Tenderloin," *ibid.*, March 29, 1906.

62. Richard J. Latimer, "History of Negro Saloons" (WPA research paper, Schomburg Collection); James Weldon Johnson, *Along This Way* (New York, 1933), pp. 175–176; Riis, *How the Other Half Lives*, p. 117. At one place the management provided dusters for clients who bet themselves down to their bare essentials. James Weldon Johnson, *The Autobiography of an Ex-Coloured Man* (New York, 1960), pp. 96–97.

63. Reverend Charles S. Morris, "The Terrible Tenderloin," *The New York Age*, February 22, March 29, 1906.

64. Powell successfully campaigned to clean up West Fortieth Street. "The

last woman carried out of the block to serve four months in Blackwell's Island for prostitution was a member of the Abyssinian Church and one of the loudest shouters of the Sunday Morning Prayer Band," he remembered. Reverend Dr. Adam Clayton Powell, Sr., *Against the Tide: An Autobiography* (New York, 1938), pp. 49–57. See also Reverend Charles S. Morris to J. G. Phelps Stokes, December 6, 1902 (Stokes Manuscripts, Columbia University, Box 18).

65. Battle, "Reminiscences," p. 35.

66. "The Reminiscences of John T. Hettrick" (Oral History Research Office, Columbia University, 1949), pp. 46–47, 73; Wirt Howe, *New York at the Turn of the Century, 1899–1916* (Toronto, 1946), p. 27.

67. Bishop Reverdy C. Ransom, *The Pilgrimage of Harriet Ransom's Son* (Nashville, 1950?), p. 202.

68. St. Benedict's was partially founded on a legacy to Negro Roman Catholics bequeathed by Father Thomas Farrell. Father Farrell was a pastor of a church in Greenwich Village during the Civil War and a strong supporter of the Union. When the war began he nailed an American flag to the roof of his church and vowed to leave the country if the South won. St. Benedict's was opened in November 1883 on Bleecker Street and moved to West Fifty-third Street in 1898. It remains there today. *The New York Age*, February 20, 1913; "St. Benedict the Moor" (WPA research paper, Schomburg Collection); *The New York Globe*, July 28, 1883, November 10, 1883, March 8, 1884.

69. *New York Daily Tribune*, August 29, 1900.

70. A Negro YMCA had been established in 1867 but it was unsuccessful. Mount Olivet Baptist Church, *Mortgage Liquidation Journal* (New York, 1946), p. 9; Silas Xavier Floyd, *Life of Charles T. Walker, D.D.* (Nashville, 1902), pp. 104, 108–109; *The New York Age*, May 9, 1912, May 22, 1913. The title "Colored Men's YMCA" comes from a letterhead in the J. G. Phelps Stokes Manuscripts, Columbia University, Box 18.

71. Johnson, *Along This Way*, pp. 152, 170–183.

72. Haynes, *The Negro at Work*, pp. 80–81; Ernest Jasper Hopper, "A Northern Negro Group" (M.A. thesis, Columbia University, 1912), pp. 22–23, 34–35.

73. The Federation of Churches and Christian Workers in New York City, *First Sociological Canvass* (New York, 1896), pp. 88–90, 92, 97, 102–105; *Second Sociological Canvass*, pp. 16–17, 20–21, 25–27, 67–70, 73, 76, 85, 93–95; Frances Blascoer, *Colored School Children in New York* (New York, 1915); Robert Coit Chapin, *The Standard of Living Among Workingmen's Families in New York City* (New York, 1909), *passim;* Louis Bolard More, *Wage-Earners' Budgets: A Study of Standards and Cost of Living in New York City* (New York, 1907), *passim;* Tom McConnon, *Angels in Hell's Kitchen* (New York, 1959), p. 35; Ovington, *Half A Man*, p. 36.

74. W. E. B. DuBois, *The Souls of Black Folk: Essays and Sketches* (New York, 1953), p. 161.

NOTES TO CHAPTER 2

1. *The New York Age*, August 1, 1912.

2. There are two problems that confront anyone attempting to determine the increase in New York City's Negro population, 1890–1910. In 1890 the Census reported statistics for "Colored" people, including Chinese, Japanese and Indians. Another problem is the consolidation of counties into Greater New York

in 1898. "New York City" meant Manhattan and the Bronx in 1890, but Manhattan, Bronx, Queens, Richmond and Brooklyn in 1900 and 1910. I have corrected the statistics of 1890 for these two problems so that a more accurate comparison of population growth can be made. In doing so I have subtracted 5,000 (which is approximately accurate) from the 1890 figure to allow for Oriental population:

	1890	*1900*	*1910*
Manhattan	25,674	36,246	60,534
Bronx		2,370	4,117
Brooklyn	10,946	18,367	22,708
Queens	3,582	2,611	3,198
Richmond	981	1,072	1,152
	41,183		
	−5,000		
Approximately	36,183	60,666	91,709

United States Census Office, *Eleventh Census, 1890: Population* (Washington, D.C., 1895), I, 509, 543–545; *Twelfth Census, 1900: Population* (Washington, D.C., 1901), I, CXX, 631; *Thirteenth Census, 1910: Population* (Washington, D.C., 1913), I, 178.

3. William L. Bulkley, "Race Prejudice as Viewed from an Economic Standpoint," *Proceedings of the National Negro Conference* (New York, 1909?), p. 90.

4. Mary White Ovington, *Half A Man: The Status of the Negro in New York* (New York, 1911), p. 48.

5. Sources of New York State In-Migrant Population, 1910.

Born in:

Virginia	29,157
North Carolina	10,283
South Carolina	6,698
Georgia	3,792
Florida	1,257

There are no published statistics that give the exact states of birth for the Negro population of New York City in these years. These statistics are for the state as a whole. New York City was the center of the migrant population, however, and it is safe to assume that these figures would be even more heavily weighted on the side of southern migration there. They do present the general trend of migration to New York City typical of pre-World War I years. United States Census, *Negro Population in the United States, 1790–1915* (Washington, D.C., 1918), pp. 77, 78. In 1890, of the 68,543 Negroes in New York State, 40,177 were born there. United States Census, *Eleventh Census, 1890: Population* (Washington, D.C., 1895), I, 576–579.

6. *The New York Age*, June 5, 1913.

7. *Negro Population, 1790–1915*, p. 68.

8. The exact figure is 198,679. *Idem.* These statistics omit the migration of 1910–1914, which was considerable.

9. United States Census, *Thirteenth Census, 1910: Population* (Washington, D.C., 1913), IV, 707–709.

10. C. Warren Thornthwaite, *Internal Migration in the United States* (Philadelphia, 1934), p. 12 and map opposite p. 12.

11. George Edmund Haynes, *The Negro at Work in New York City: A Study in Economic Progress*, in Columbia University *Studies in History, Economics and Public Law*, XLIX (New York, 1912), p. 17.

12. Frederick J. Brown, *The Northward Movement of the Colored Population: A Statistical Study* (Baltimore, 1897).

13. W. E. B. DuBois, "The Negro in Farmville, Virginia: A Social Study," United States Department of Labor, *Bulletin No. 14* (Washington, D.C., 1895), p. 5.

14. W. E. B. DuBois, *The Philadelphia Negro: A Social Study*, in University of Pennsylvania Series in *Political Economy and Public Law*, XIV (Philadelphia, 1899), pp. 79–80.

15. W. E. B. DuBois, "The Black Vote of Philadelphia," *Charities: A Review of Local and General Philanthopy*, XV (October 7, 1905), 31.

16. John P. Clyde, "The Negro in New York City" (M.A. thesis, Columbia University, 1899), p. 3.

17. "The Condition of Negroes in Various Cities," United States Department of Labor *Bulletin*, II (May 1897), 257–369.

18. Carl Kelsey, "Some Causes of Negro Emigration: The Men," *Charities*, XV (October 7, 1905), 16.

19. *Ibid.* In 1906 *The Annals of the American Academy of Political and Social Science* also studied "The Industrial Conditions of the Negro in the North," XXVII (May 1906); and in 1913 "The Negro's Progress in Fifty Years," a book-length survey, in XLIX (September 1913).

20. *The New York Age,* June 10, 1907, July 4, 1912, November 16, 1911.

21. *The New York Times,* March 18, 1901.

22. Carter G. Woodson, *A Century of Negro Migration* (Washington, D.C., 1918), pp. 159–166.

23. "Hope something has been done regarding Pinchback." Booker T. Washington to Charles W. Anderson, July 4, 1905; Anderson to Washington, July 17, 1909, July 20, 1909, January 11, 1910, August 1, 1910. Washington Papers, Library of Congress.

24. *The New York Age,* October 6, 1910, May 22, 1913.

25. *Ibid.,* November 21, 1907; *New York Daily Tribune,* September 5, 1900; August Meier, "Negro Racial Thought in the Age of Booker T. Washington, Circa 1880–1915" (Ph.D. dissertation, Columbia University, 1957), p. 807.

26. DuBois, *Philadelphia Negro,* pp. 44–45.

27. Lillian Brandt, "The Make-Up of Negro City Groups," *Charities,* XV (October 7, 1905), 7–11.

28. Helen A. Tucker, "Negro Craftsmen in New York," *The Southern Workman,* XXXVI (October 1907), 545–551.

29. Haynes, *Negro At Work,* pp. 58–61.

30. W. E. B. DuBois, "The Northern Negro Problem," *The New York Age,* October 3, 1907; R. R. Wright, Jr., "The Migration of Negroes to the North," *The Annals,* XLIX (September 1913), 570.

31. *The New York Age,* April 6, 1905.

32. Paul Oliver, *Blues Fell This Morning: The Meaning of the Blues* (London, 1960), p. 23.

33. *The New York Freeman,* September 19, 1885.

34. *The New York Age,* September 22, 1910; William Fielding Ogburn, "The Richmond Negro in New York City: His Social Mind as Seen in His Pleasures" (M.A. thesis, Columbia University, 1909), p. 33.

35. *Report of the Industrial Commission on Agriculture and Agricultural Labor.* . . . (Washington, D.C., 1901), X, 351; R. R. Wright, Jr., "The Migration of Negroes," 564. *Report of Industrial Commission* hereafter cited as *USIC,* X.

36. R. R. Wright, Jr., "The Migration of Negroes," 566; Haynes, *Negro At Work,* pp. 31–32.

37. Seymour Paul, "A Group of Virginia Negroes in New York City" (M.A. thesis, Columbia University, 1912), p. 41.

38. C. Vann Woodward, *The Strange Career of Jim Crow* (New York, 1955), chapter II; C. Vann Woodward, *Origins of the New South, passim;* Woodson, *A Century of Negro Migration,* p. 161; NAACP, *Thirty Years of Lynching in the United States, 1889–1918* (New York, 1919); James Elbert Cutler, *Lynch Law: An Investigation into the History of Lynching in the United States* (New York, 1905), p. 161; Paul, "A Group of Virginia Negroes," p. 12; Ida B. Wells, *A Red Record: Tabulated Statistics and Alleged Causes of Lynching in the United States* (Chicago, 1895).

39. Meier, "Negro Racial Thought," pp. 157–158, 916.

40. There actually were some Negroes who did go to Africa in these years. An Abraham Lincoln African Aid and Colonization Society was established in Oklahoma in 1909. "Chief Sam" (Alfred Charles Sam), a bogus African chief, outfitted a steamer which left Galveston in 1914. T. McCants Stewart, Negro clergyman and lawyer of New York, finally settled in Liberia in 1906. *The New York Age,* April 27, 1905, November 30, 1905, February 26, 1906, September 20, 1906, January 3, 1907, July 11, 1907, September 16, 1909, January 22, 1914, January 29, 1914, April 2, 1914, July 9, 1914. William E. Bittle and Gilbert Geis, *The Longest Way Home: Chief Alfred C. Sam's Back to Africa Movement* (Detroit, 1964).

41. *The New York Age,* January 10, 1907, July 4, 1912.

42. *The New York Freeman,* February 28, 1885; Bulkley, "Race Prejudice," p. 90.

43. *New York Daily Tribune,* September 5, 22, 1900.

44. "Negro Exodus to Cities," *The New York Times,* May 28, 1903; Sutton E. Griggs, *Needs of the South* (Nashville, 1909), pp. 15, 28.

45. Tucker, "Negro Craftsmen," 550.

46. Paul, "A Group of Virginia Negroes," p. 35.

47. *Ibid.,* p. 31.

48. *The New York Age,* October 3, 1907; W. E. B. DuBois, "The Black North," *The New York Times,* December 15, 1901.

49. Langston Hughes, "New York," *Phylon,* XI (1950), 14.

50. R. R. Wright, Jr., "The Negro in Times of Industrial Unrest," *Charities,* XV (October 7, 1905), 69, 73; James Samuel Stemons, "The Industrial Color-Line in the North," *The Century Magazine,* LX (July 1900), 477–478; Mary White Ovington, "The Negro in the Trades Unions of New York," *The Annals,* XXVII (May 1906), 555–556.

51. Stanley M. Elkins has added great depth to our understanding of the personal psychological blight of the Peculiar Institution in his *Slavery* (Chicago, 1959).

52. W. E. B. DuBois, *The Souls of Black Folk* (New York, 1953), p. 68.

53. Edwin R. Embree, *Brown America* (New York, 1931), p. 37. "The Government by whom we were emancipated left us completely in the power of our former owners." Frederick Douglass, *Three Addresses on the Relations Subsisting between the White and Colored People of the United States* (Washington, D.C., 1886), p. 16. Also see Alrutheus Ambush Taylor, *The Negro in South Carolina During Reconstruction* (Washington, D.C., 1924), pp. 25, 55; Alrutheus Ambush Taylor, *The Negro in Reconstruction Virginia* (Washington, D.C., 1926), pp. 90–97.

54. W. E. B. DuBois, "The Negro Farmer," *Supplementary Analysis and Derivative Tables of the Twelfth Census* (Washington, D.C., 1906), *passim*.

55. *USIC*, X, 379, 820.

56. *Ibid.*, 428.

57. Haynes, *Negro at Work*, p. 30n.

58. J. S. Clarkson to J. E. Bruce, March 21, 1891. Bruce Manuscripts, Schomburg Collection.

59. George Edmund Haynes, "Conditions Among Negroes in the Cities," *The Annals*, XLIX (September 1913), 105–119.

60. *USIC*, xxi.

61. Philip A. Bruce, *The Plantation Negro as a Freeman: Observations on His Character, Condition, and Prospects in Virginia* (New York, 1889), p. 182.

62. John R. Rogers, *The Importance of Time as a Factor in the Solution of the Negro Problem* (New York, 1900?), p. 7; William Hannibal Thomas, *The American Negro: What He Was, What He Is, and What He May Become* (New York, 1901), p. 63.

63. John Ambrose Price, *The Negro: Past, Present and Future* (New York, 1907), pp. 101–103; Howard W. Odum, *Social and Mental Traits of the Negro: A Study in Race Traits, Tendencies, and Prospects* (New York, 1910), pp. 184ff; Thomas Nelson Page, "The Negro: The Southerner's Problem," *McClure's Magazine*, XXIII (May 1904), 100; *USIC*, X, 166–167.

64. Page, "The Negro," 100; Edgar Gardner Murphy, *The Task of The South* (n.p., 1903), pp. 29–34; Guion Griffis Johnson, "The Ideology of White Supremacy, 1876–1910," in Fletcher Melvin Green, ed., *Essays in Southern History* (Chapel Hill, 1949), 148, 154n., 156.

65. J. J. Watson, "Churches and Religious Conditions," *The Annals*, XLIX (September, 1913), 126. ". . . In the time of slavery the parents exercised a much stricter control over their children than they do now." *The Southern Workman*, XXIX (February 1900), 68.

66. *USIC*, X, 50; 504; 770; W. E. B. DuBois, *The Souls of Black Folk: Essays and Sketches* (New York, 1903), p. 310.

67. Frederick S. Hoffman, *Race Traits and Tendencies of the American Negro* (New York, 1896), p. 310.

68. William P. Calhoun, *The Caucasian and the Negro in the United States. They Must Separate. If Not, Then Extermination; A Proposed Solution: Colonization* (Columbia, S.C., 1902), pp. 139, 141–142.

69. Robert Wilson Shufeldt, *The Negro: A Menace to American Civilization* (Boston, 1907); Carlyle McKinley, *An Appeal to Pharaoh: The Negro Problem, and Its Radical Solution* (Columbia, S.C., 1907); Charles Carroll, *The Negro a Beast, or, In the Image of God* (St. Louis, Mo., 1900); William P. Pickett, *The Negro Problem: Abraham Lincoln's Solution* (New York, 1909).

70. Bert James Loewenberg, "Efforts of the South to Encourage Immigration, 1865–1900," *South Atlantic Quarterly*, XXXIII (October 1934), 363–385.

71. In 1907 the Attorney General of the United States ruled that states, but not individuals, could advertise for immigrants abroad and pay their passage to America without violating the Contract Labor Law. *The New York Age,* March 28, 1907, June 21, 1906, July 19, 1906, October 31, 1907.

72. C. Vann Woodward, *Origins of the New South, passim; The New York Age,* May 26, 1888.

73. Rowland T. Berthoff, "Southern Attitudes Toward Immigration, 1865–1914," *The Journal of Southern History,* XVII (August 1951), 328–360.

74. *USIC,* X, 382–383; 518.

75. *Raleigh Signal,* February 28, 1889, quoted in Frenise A. Logan, "The Movement of Negroes from North Carolina, 1876–1894," *The North Carolina Historical Review,* XXIII (January 1956), 54.

76. Price, *The Negro,* pp. 105–106.

77. DuBois, "Negro Farmer," pp. 523, 527, 532–533; Woofter, *Negro Migration, passim.*

78. Senator George F. Hoar to J. E. Bruce, February 25, 1895. Bruce Manuscripts, Schomburg Collection; "Italian Cotton vs. Negro Cotton in the Southern States," *The Colored American Magazine,* XIII (September 1907), 167.

79. Commissioner of Labor, *Labor Laws of the United States, with Decisions of Courts Relating Thereto,* in *Twenty-Second Annual Report* (Washington, D.C., 1908), *passim.*

80. Lafayette M. Hershaw, "Peonage," The American Negro Academy, *Occasional Paper, No. 15* (Washington, D.C., 1915), 10; Katherine Coman, "The Negro as a Peasant Farmer," *Quarterly Publication of the American Statistical Association,* IX (June 1904), 54; Thomas J. Edward, "The Tenant System and Some Changes Since Emancipation," *The Annals,* XLIX (September 1913), 38–46.

81. Jack Greenberg, *Race Relations and the American Law* (New York, 1960), p. 157. A Georgia plantation owner stated in an interview in 1903 that "the planters in the black belt will have to maintain their right to claim their contract labor, or else they will have to go out of business. . . ." Quoted in John R. Commons, *Races and Immigrants in America* (New York, 1920), p. 138. In *Bailey* vs. *State of Alabama,* the Supreme Court held such labor contracts in violation of the Thirteenth Amendment. Justice Hughes, delivering the opinion of the Court, concluded that the "words involuntary servitude have a 'larger meaning than slavery.' . . . The plain intention was to abolish slavery of whatever name and form . . . to make labor free, by prohibiting that control by which the personal service of one man is disposed or coerced for another's benefit. . . ." 219 *United States Reports,* 241.

82. *The Crisis,* XIII (December 1916), 89.

83. *USIC,* X, 429; *The New York Age,* May 11, June 8, 29, 1905; Logan, "The Movement of Negroes," 57–59.

84. *USIC,* X, 906–912.

85. *Ibid.,* 514; *The New York Age,* June 29, 1905. "Without the colored laborer," wrote Frederick Douglass, "the South would be a howling wilderness, given up to bats, owls, wolves, and bears." Douglass, *Three Addresses,* p. 13.

86. *Report of the New York City Commission on Congestion of Population* (New York, 1911), p. 11.

87. Benjamin H. Locke, "The Community Life of a Harlem Group of Negroes" (M.A. thesis, Columbia University, 1913), *passim.*

88. Ogburn, "The Richmond Negro," *passim;* Paul, "A Group of Virginia

Negroes," *passim;* R. R. Wright, Jr., "The Negro in Times of Industrial Unrest," 565; Clyde Vernon Kiser, *Sea Island to City: A Study of St. Helena Islanders in Harlem and Other Urban Centers* (New York, 1932), p. 219.

89. Ogburn, "The Richmond Negro," p. 47.

90. This is an exact copy of a typical labor contract. See Carl Kelsey, "Some Causes for Negro Emigration: The Men," *Charities,* XV (October 7, 1905), 16–17.

91. *USIC,* X, 428.

92. *Report of the New York Colored Mission, 1872* (New York, 1873), p. 8.

93. *The New York Age,* May 8, 1913.

94. Clyde, "Negro in New York City," p. 6; "Night Clubs," James Weldon Johnson Collection, Yale University.

95. *The Richmond Planet* carried regular advertisements for these companies. See, for example, February 23, 1895; Kelsey, "Some Causes for Negro Emigration," 17; *The New York Age,* September 11, 1913, February 5, 1914.

96. *The New York Globe,* July 7, 1883, October 18, 1884; *The New York Age,* August 17, December 28, 1905.

97. *The New York Age,* December 24, 1908, July 27, 1911.

98. "The Movement of Negroes from the Country to the City," *The Southern Workman,* XLII (April, 1913), 235.

99. DuBois, "The Black North," *The New York Times,* November 17, 1901; *The New York Age,* May 11, 1905.

100. Paul, "A Group of Virginia Negroes," p. 3.

101. The Reminiscences of Samuel J. Battle" (Oral History Research Office, Columbia University, 1960), p. 13.

102. Paul Laurence Dunbar, *The Sport of the Gods* (New York, 1902), pp. 112–113.

103. Folkways Records, Album No. FC7533.

104. Nellie M. Quander, "A Study of Insurance Among Negroes in the State of Virginia" (M.A. thesis, Columbia University, 1914), pp. 37 ff; "Some Efforts of American Negroes for their Own Social Betterment," *Atlanta University Publications, No. 3* (Atlanta, 1898), p. 19.

105. *The New York Age,* April 7, 1910.

106. Silas Xavier Floyd, *Life of Charles T. Walker, D.D.* (Nashville, 1902), pp. 105–106.

107. *The New York Age,* February 28, 1907.

108. "Dear Charlie—I find that the chitterlings went forward to you last week." Booker T. Washington to Charles W. Anderson, January 26, 1907. Washington Papers, Library of Congress, Box 35.

109. Box 18 in the J. G. Phelps Stokes Papers at Columbia University is full of requests for contributions from Negro institutions. Also see B. C. Caldwell, "The Work of the Jeanes and Slater Funds," *The Annals,* XLIX (September 1913), 173–176.

110. *The New York Freeman,* November 28, 1885; *The New York Age,* July 13, 1889, June 25, 1908, February 9, 1911.

111. Odette Harper, "Sketch of Pig Foot Mary" (WPA research paper, Schomburg Collection); *The New York Age,* November 12, 1927, July 20, 27, 1929.

112. *The New York Age,* February 13, 1913.

113. Mary McFadden, "Madame Walker" and Odette Harper, "Biographical Sketch of Madame C. J. Walker" (WPA research papers, Schomburg Col-

lection); *Baltimore Afro-American,* March 5, 1932. For pictures of the cabin in which Madame Walker was born and her villa in New York see *The Messenger,* VI (August, 1924), 255.

114. Biographical sketches of these and many other successful Negro migrants are scattered throughout the issues of *The New York Age.*

115. Reverend Dr. Adam Clayton Powell, Sr., *Against the Tide: An Autobiography* (New York, 1938).

116. Ray Stannard Baker, *Following the Color Line* (New York, 1908), *passim; The New York Age,* January 27, 1910.

NOTES TO CHAPTER 3

1. Linton Satterthwait, "The Color-Line in New Jersey," *The Arena,* XXV (April 1906), 394.

2. Joan Cohen, "The Social Conditions of the Negro in New York City, 1830–1865" (M.A. thesis, Columbia University, 1951), p. 38; Philmore L. Groisser, "The Free Negro in New York State, 1850–1860" (M.A. thesis, Columbia University, 1939), pp. 31–39; Dwight Lowell Dumond, *Antislavery: The Crusade for Freedom in America* (Ann Arbor, 1961), p. 300; Wilbur Young, "Plymouth Congregational Church" (WPA research paper, Schomburg Collection); *The Colored American,* June 3, 1837; Robert Ernst, *Immigrant Life in New York City, 1825–1863* (New York, 1949), p. 41; Charles Townsend Harris, *Memories of Manhattan in the Sixties and Seventies* (New York, 1928), p. 61.

3. Herman D. Bloch, "The New York Negro's Battle for Political Rights, 1777–1865," *International Review of Social History,* IX (1964), 65–80.

4. "Health and Physique of the Negro American," *Atlanta University Studies, No. 11* (Atlanta, 1906), p. 91; *The New York Age,* June 8, 1889, April 26, 1890, April 11, 1891; *The New York Globe,* February 9, 1884.

5. *The New York Freeman,* July 2, 1887.

6. The subject of Negro education in the North and in New York City is studied in great detail in Robert S. Dixon, "Education of the Negro in the City of New York, 1853–1900" (M.A. thesis, City College, 1935), and Leslie H. Fishel, Jr., "The North and the Negro, 1865–1900: A Study in Race Discrimination" (Ph.D. dissertation, Harvard University, 1954), pp. 183–248, 326–369, *passim.* The Fishel study is the most thorough history of race relations in the North in the late nineteenth century, and discusses all the specific points mentioned in this paragraph. It does not, however, emphasize the changing patterns of racial attitudes as I have attempted to do. Also see *The New York Age,* February 9, 1924, and June 27, 1925, for information on Miss Frazier.

7. *The New York Globe,* December 29, 1883; *The New York Freeman,* June 19, 1886, July 9, 1887; *The New York Age,* June 7, 1890.

8. Jacob A. Riis, *How the Other Half Lives: Studies Among the Poor* (London, 1891), p. 148.

9. *The New York Age,* January 4, 1900.

10. *The New York Globe,* June 30, August 25, September 1, 1883; *The New York Freeman,* July 25, 1885, July 16, September 3, 1887.

11. *The New York Globe,* July 28, 1883.

12. *The New York Freeman,* July 16, 1887.

13. W. E. B. DuBois, "The Black North," *The New York Times,* December 15, 1901. For an analysis of this attitude as a major theme in the Negro novel,

1890–1920, see Robert A. Bone, *The Negro Novel in America* (New Haven, 1958).

14. Benjamin Brawley, "The Negro Genius," *The Southern Workman*, XLIV (May 1915), 305–308.

15. The success of *The Clansman* and other of Dixon's works in the first two decades of the twentieth century must be set against the rise of racial antagonism in the North in these years. See *The Crisis*, LXII (January 1955), 37–38; Maxwell Bloomfield, "Dixon's *The Leopard's Spots*: A Study in Popular Racism," *American Quarterly*, XVI (Fall 1964), 387–401.

16. *The New York Age*, January 4, 1906.

17. *The Churchman*, L (September 20, 1884), 316.

18. *The Worker*, May 18, 1902.

19. Moses F. Sweester and Simeon Ford, *How to Know New York City* (New York, 1888), p. 11.

20. Dumond, *Antislavery*, p. 330.

21. *Harlem Local Reporter*, February 25, May 6, 1893; "Black Patti," in James Weldon Johnson Collection, Yale University.

22. *The New York Times*, October 4, 1900.

23. Diana N. Lockard, "The Negro on the Stage of the Nineteen Twenties" (M.A. thesis, Columbia University, 1960), chap. 1.

24. "Emma Harris" (WPA research paper, Schomburg Collection).

25. Mary White Ovington, *Half A Man: The Status of the Negro in New York* (New York, 1911), p. 135.

26. William L. Holler, "Bert Williams (Egbert Austin Williams), 1875–1922" (WPA research paper, Schomburg Collection), p. 3.

27. These plays and many others are collected in a special box of Negro vaudeville and minstrel shows at the Schomburg Collection, and in the extensive and magnificent Atkinson Collection at the University of Chicago.

28. Henry Collins Brown, *In the Golden Nineties* (New York, 1928), pp. 173–174; Howard W. Odum and Guy B. Johnson, *Negro Workaday Songs* (Chapel Hill, N.C., 1926), pp. 183–184.

29. George H. Coes, *Badly Sold: A Negro Act in Two Scenes* (Chicago, 1893).

30. F. E. Hiland, *Careless Cupid* (Boston, 1893), p. 5.

31. James Weldon Johnson, *Along This Way* (New York, 1933), pp. 152–153.

32. *The New York Age*, January 31, 1907; "Wealthy Negroes," *The New York Times*, July 14, 1895.

33. Johnson, *Along This Way, passim;* Holler, "Bert Williams," p. 8.

34. Johnson, *Along This Way*, p. 159. The game "Hit the Nigger" or "African Dodger"—in which vacationers threw baseballs at the head of a *real* person—was played in New York summer resorts until outlawed in 1917. *The Crisis*, X (July 1915), 114; *The New York Times*, October 2, 1916, May 3, 1917.

35. Lawrence Gelbert, "Bert Williams: Philosophical Tidbits Gleaned from His Songs and Stories" (WPA research paper, Schomburg Collection).

36. "We Wear the Mask," in *The Complete Poems of Paul Laurence Dunbar* (New York, 1921), p. 71.

37. W. E. B. DuBois, *The Souls of Black Folk: Essays and Sketches* (New York, 1953), p. 10.

38. "Raw Labor from the South," *The New York Times*, September 9, 1900.

39. There was a constant mockery of the so-called Negro aristocracy and

"400." See, for example, John Martin, "Dancing Through Two Centuries," Museum of the City of New York *Bulletin*, V (February 1942), 37.

40. Kelly Miller, "The Industrial Condition of the Negro in the North," *The Annals*, XXVII (May 1906), 543.

41. *The New York Freeman*, July 11, 1887.

42. A clipping of this review which appeared in *The Bookman*, XXIII (April 1906), was pasted on the back of an obituary of Dunbar in the Gumby Collection, Columbia University.

43. *The New York Age*, April 1, 1909.

44. Clyde Griffen, "An Urban Church in Ferment: The Episcopal Church in New York City, 1880–1900" (Ph.D. dissertation, Columbia University, 1960), p. 32.

45. *The New York Age*, April 17, 1913.

46. *The Crisis*, VIII (May 1914), 12.

47. *Ibid.*, IX (December 1914), 77–80.

48. *The New York Age*, April 9, June 21, 1906.

49. *Ibid.*, February 13, 1913. The depth of national racial hatred in the early twentieth century is clearly demonstrated in the longing and search for a "White Hope" to defeat Jack Johnson. Some of the anti-Negro legislation of these years, including those laws banning intermarriage, were partially stimulated by Johnson's second marriage to a white woman. See clippings under title "White Hope" in Gumby Collection, Columbia University. Florence Murray, editor, *The Negro Handbook, 1949* (New York, 1949), p. 350. The following, an article by Bill Corum in the *New York Journal American* at the time of Johnson's death in 1946, clearly demonstrates this racial antipathy: "Man alive, how I hated Jack Johnson in the Summer of 1910! Nor did I ever quite get over it. In recent years it became an aversion rather than a stronger feeling. But when he knocked out Jeffries at Reno I hated him. . . . I was 15 in a town of 4,000 people and until the Jeffries-Johnson fight . . . never heard of professional boxing." Clipping in Gumby Collection.

50. Ovington, *Half A Man*, p. 210. *The New York Age* and *The Crisis* carried dozens of articles and comments on this subject.

51. *The Crisis*, III (February 1912), 141.

52. *The New York Evening Journal*, December 12, 1910. Also see *The New York Times*, December 1, 1901; Mary White Ovington, "The Negro in the Trades Unions in New York," *The Annals*, XXVII (May 1906), 551–558; R. R. Wright, Jr., "The Negro in Times of Industrial Unrest," *Charities*, XV (October 7, 1905), 69–73; Mrs. Paul Laurence Dunbar, "Hope Deferred," *The Crisis*, VIII (September 1914), 238–242; Alma Herbst, *The Negro in the Slaughtering and Meat-Packing Industry in Chicago* (Boston and New York, 1932), pp. xviii–xix, 14–32, *passim; The New York Age*, June 13, 1907, August 19, 1909, January 20, 1910, November 30, 1911, June 6, 13, 1912, January 16, 1913.

53. Italicized in the original. Copy of act in Bruce Manuscripts, Schomburg Collection.

54. *The New York Age*, February 6, 1913.

55. Henry A. Spencer to John E. Bruce, March 22, 1910; Bruce to the Hon. Jesse S. Phillips, March 23, 1910. Bruce Manuscripts, Schomburg Collection.

56. Clippings from the *New York American*, September 30, 1904, in Stokes Manuscripts, Columbia University, Box 75.

57. Ovington, *Half A Man*, p. 76.

58. *Ibid.,* p. 34; *The New York Freeman,* July 18, 1885, January 16, 1886; *The New York Age,* January 31, 1907; "Certificate of Incorporation of the Society of the Sons of New York," November 28, 1891, in New York City Hall of Records.

59. See John H. Johnson, *A Place of Adventure: Essays and Sermons* (Greenwich, Conn., 1955), p. 10; "Boston, and Some Boston People," Bruce Manuscripts; W. E. B. DuBois, *The Philadelphia Negro: A Social Study* (Philadelphia, 1899), pp. 73n, 80; Roi Ottley, *The Lonely Warrior: The Life and Times of Robert S. Abbott* (Chicago, 1955), pp. 84–85; St. Clair Drake and Horace R. Cayton, *Black Metropolis: A Study of Negro Life in a Northern City* (New York, 1945), pp. 73–74, *passim.*

60. Charles Winslow Hall, "Racial Hatred," *The Colored American Magazine,* I (September 1900), 246; *The New York Age,* December 17, 1908, and *passim.*

61. *The New York Age,* June 22, 1905; Letter to the editor from Melvin J. Chisum, *The New York Times,* June 10, 1900.

62. DuBois, "The Black North," *The New York Times,* December 1, 1901.

63. *The New York Age,* April 6, 1905.

64. Langston Hughes, "High to Low," *The Midwest Journal,* I (Summer 1949), 26.

65. *The New York Freeman,* January 16, 1886; *The New York Age,* January 5, 1889, January 25, 1890, July 6, 1905, July 27, 1908.

66. *The New York Age,* May 14, 1908, July 7, 1910.

67. Miller, "Industrial Condition," 548; *The Boston Chronicle,* September 4, 1936. From 1900 to 1905 *The Southern Workman* printed an entire series of Miller's articles on this subject, and he continued to advocate a return to the farm until his death in 1939. See the excellent essay by Bernard Eisenberg, "Kelly Miller: The Negro Leader as Marginal Man," *Journal of Negro History,* XLV (July 1960), 182–187.

68. Paul Laurence Dunbar, *The Sport of the Gods* (New York, 1902), p. 213. The development of intraracial antagonism would be incomplete without mentioning the hostility that American Negroes, northern and southern, showed toward Negro immigrants from the West Indies. New York City was the largest urban center for foreign-born Negroes in the early twentieth century (12,851 in 1910). As this antagonism did not become a major theme in city history until the 1920's, I have saved discussion of it for Chapter 9.

69. John E. Bruce, "Practical Questions," Bruce Manuscripts, Schomburg Collection; *The Colored American Magazine,* XIII (July 1907), 68; "The Reminiscences of Samuel J. Battle" (Oral History Research Office, Columbia University, 1960), pp. 16–17; *The Crisis,* XII (August 1916), 166–167; *The New York Freeman,* May 15, 1886; *The New York Age,* May 25, 1905, October 5, 1916.

70. Florence E. Gibson, *The Attitudes of the New York Irish toward State and National Affairs, 1848–1892* (New York, 1951), p. 66; *The New York Age,* January 26, 1905; W. L. Bulkley, "Race Prejudice As Viewed from An Economic Standpoint," *Proceedings of the National Negro Conference, 1909* (New York, 1909?), 94.

71. This information and much that follows is derived from contemporary press reports.

72. Of the fifty Negro migrants studied by William Fielding Ogburn, all read the daily newspapers. "The Richmond Negro in New York City: His

Social Mind as Seen in His Pleasures" (M.A. thesis, Columbia University, 1909), p. 71.

73. The People vs. Arthur J. Harris, October 29, 1900. Transcript and summary of trial in New York City Magistrates Court.

74. *Ibid.*

75. *Ibid.; The World*, August 17, 1900.

76. *New York Daily Tribune*, August 17, 1900.

77. *Ibid.*, August 16, 1900.

78. Bernard J. York, Chairman of the Committee on Rules and Discipline, to Police Board, December 8, 1900 (Mayor Van Wyck Papers, Municipal Archives).

79. *New York Daily Tribune*, August 16, 1900.

80. *Ibid.*

81. *The New York Times*, August 16, 1900; *Autobiography of Dr. William Henry Johnson* (Albany, 1900), p. 148.

82. [Frank Moss], *Story of the Riot: Persecution of Negroes by Roughs and Policemen, in the City of New York, August, 1900* (New York, 1900), p. 5; Richard O'Connor, *Hell's Kitchen: The Roaring Days of New York's Wild West Side* (New York, 1958), p. 151.

83. *The New York Times*, August 20, 1900; Johnson, *Along This Way*, pp. 157–158.

84. *New York Daily Tribune*, August 16, 17, 1900.

85. Israel Ludlow to Bernard J. York, August 30, 1900 (Mayor Van Wyck Papers, Municipal Archives).

86. Bernard J. York to Police Board, December 8, 1900. *Ibid.*

87. *The World*, August 17, 1900.

88. Less than a month before the riot, the New York press had bitterly criticized the South for a race riot in New Orleans. Southerners now responded gleefully; stressed the universality of race hatred; made some comments about casting the first stone; and warned against the "young country negro" who flocks to the city to "lead a life of idleness." *Ibid.*, August 17, 18, 19, 1900.

89. *New York Daily Tribune*, August 19, 1900.

90. Clement Richardson, ed., *The National Cyclopedia of the Colored Race* (Montgomery, Alabama, 1919), I, 223; Mary White Ovington, *The Walls Came Tumbling Down* (New York, 1947), pp. 25–26.

91. *New York Daily Tribune*, August 27, 1900.

92. Some of the original postcards sent out by the Reverend Dr. Brooks may be found at the Schomburg Collection.

93. *New York Daily Tribune*, August 25, September 8, 1900; Israel Ludlow to Bernard J. York, President of Board of Police Commissioners, August 30, 1900 (Mayor Van Wyck Papers, Municipal Archives); Frank Moss to York, September 14, 1900, *ibid.*

94. "Notes of D. Macon Webster for a speech at protest meeting" (Miscellaneous Manuscripts, Schomburg Collection).

95. *The New York Times*, September 13, 1900.

96. J. G. Speed, "The Negro in New York: A Study of the Social and Industrial Condition of the Colored People in the Metropolis," *Harper's Weekly*, XLIV (December 22, 1900), 1249.

97. *New York Daily Tribune*, September 9, 1900.

98. John Hains vs. Herman A. Ohm, October 26, 1900; George L. Myers vs. John J. Cleary, October 26, 1900 (Mayor Van Wyck Papers, Municipal Archives).

99. Bernard J. York to Police Board, December 8, 1900 (Mayor Van Wyck Papers, Municipal Archives).
100. The People vs. Arthur J. Harris, October 29, 1900 (New York City Magistrates Court).
101. Harold W. Folletta, Acting Warden, Clinton Prison, to author, August 14, 1961.
102. Kelly Miller, "The American Negro as a Political Factor," *The Nineteenth Century*, LXVIII (August 1910), 297.
103. *Report of the Police Department of the City of New York* (New York, 1901), p. 10.
104. *The New York Times*, August 24, 1900.

NOTES TO CHAPTER 4

1. Historians have too often analyzed Progressivism primarily as a political movement. I define Progressivism as a national, broad-based movement—social, economic, industrial, medical, educational, religious, political, and so on. It was the *positive* national response to the shocking changes and inequities created by massive industrialization and unprecedented urbanization and the often-expressed awareness that American culture was being radically altered by them. The most enduring accomplishments of the Progressive movement, in my opinion, have been its social, industrial and economic reforms and these were most evident on the local, municipal and state levels. As any national reform movement in a democratic society would, it necessarily created issues which became influential in national political life. If one analyzes Progressivism only in its national political phase, however, it was often anti-Negro. Presidential candidates were sometimes willing to overlook the desires of a largely disfranchised group in hope of attracting white southern support. Theodore Roosevelt refused to seat southern Negro representatives at the 1912 Progressive convention in spite of protests by Jane Addams, Henry Moskowitz, Joel Spingarn and others. The segregationist and anti-Negro policies instituted during the Woodrow Wilson administrations are well-known. Progressivism as a political movement did therefore, as historians have pointed out, bypass the Negro. If, however, one includes social workers and industrial and municipal reformers in his definition of Progressivism, there was a serious, positive and hopeful interest expressed in Negro welfare by the Progressive movement. See Arthur S. Link, "The Negro as a Factor in the Campaign of 1912," *Journal of Negro History*, XXXII (January 1947), 81–99; Kathleen L. Wolgemuth, "Woodrow Wilson and Federal Segregation," *ibid.*, XLIV (January 1959), 158–173; Henry Blumenthal, "Woodrow Wilson and the Race Question," *ibid.*, XLVIII (January 1963), 1–21; Jane Addams, "The Progressive Party and the Negro," *The Crisis*, V (November 1912), 30–31.
2. *The New York Age*, November 3, 1910; "Night Clubs," James Weldon Johnson Collection.
3. A more thorough study of each of these cities would undoubtedly extend this list considerably.
4. W. E. B. DuBois, *The Souls of Black Folk: Essays and Sketches* (New York, 1953), p. 99.
5. *The New York Freeman*, May 23, June 6, 1885, January 9, February 13, April 3, 1886.
6. Augustus Taber, "New York Colored Mission: The Beginning of its Work," appended to the New York Colored Mission, *Twentieth Annual Report, 1885* (New York, 1886), p. 23.

7. *Report of the New York Colored Mission, 1904* (New York, 1905), p. 7.

8. *Report of the New York Colored Mission, 1880* (New York, 1881), p. 8.

9. "Certificate of Incorporation of the New York Colored Mission," August 3, 1871. New York City Hall of Records.

10. *Report on the New York Colored Mission, 1871* (New York, 1872), p. 3; and *Report, 1881* (New York, 1882), p. 8.

11. "The great ambition of the older people was to read the Bible before they died." Booker T. Washington, *Up from Slavery: An Autobiography* (New York, 1959), p. 21; *Report of the New York Colored Mission, 1893* (New York, 1894), pp. 13–15.

12. Mary White Ovington, "Beginnings of the N.A.A.C.P.," *The Crisis,* XXXII (June 1926), 76–77.

13. *New York Evening Post* as cited in *The New York Age,* July 6, 1905; Mary L. Lewis, "The White Rose Industrial Association," *The Messenger,* VII (April 1925), 158.

14. White Rose Industrial Association, *Annual Report for . . . 1911* (New York, 1912), p. 6.

15. See obituary in *The New York Age,* March 14, 1907; *The Crisis,* VII (December 1911), 51; Lassalle Best, "History of the White Rose Mission and Industrial Association" (WPA research paper, Schomburg Collection); Victoria Earle Matthews to Booker T. Washington, March 23, 1902. Washington Papers, Library of Congress, Box 1; August Meier, "Negro Racial Thought in the Age of Booker T. Washington, Circa 1880–1915" (Ph.D. dissertation, Columbia University, 1957), pp. 380–381.

16. Frances A. Kellor, "The Criminal Negro: A Sociological Study," *The Arena,* XXV (January–November 1901).

17. Frances A. Kellor, *Out of Work: A Study of Employment Agencies. . . .* (New York, 1904), p. vi.

18. For a detailed reply to Miss Kellor's charges see John N. Bogart to Mayor George B. McClellan, November 22, 1906, McClellan Papers, Municipal Archives. Also *Reports* of the Commissioner of Licenses and Bureau of Industries and Immigration; Kellor, "Report of the Research Department of the Woman's Municipal League," *Woman's Municipal League Bulletin,* IV (April 1906), 3–7.

19. *The New York Freeman,* May 16, 1885.

20. Agents "corral girls from the country districts." Kellor, *Out of Work,* pp. 73–74, 83, 97.

21. Louise DeKoven Bowen, *The Colored People of Chicago* (Chicago, 1913), n.p.

22. "Conditions Existing in the City of New York Prior to May 1st, 1904, Which Led to the Creation of this Office" (1909). Municipal Archives.

23. Frances A. Kellor, "Assisted Emigration from the South: The Women," *Charities,* XV (October 7, 1905), 12–13.

24. *Ibid.,* 14.

25. E. M. Rhodes, "The Protection of Girls Who Travel: A National Movement," *The Colored American Magazine,* XIII (August 1907), 114–115.

26. From September 1932 to February 1933, in twenty-four installments, Miss Ovington published her "Reminiscences" in *The Afro-American* of Baltimore. Most of the information for the following biographical sketch comes from there. *The Afro-American,* September 24, 1932.

27. *Ibid.,* September 17, 1932.

28. *Ibid.,* September 24, 1932.

29. *Idem.*

30. *Ibid.*, September 17, 1932; Mary White Ovington, *The Walls Came Tumbling Down* (New York, 1947), chap. 1; *The New York Age,* January 18, 1930.

31. *The Afro-American,* October 1, 1932; Mary White Ovington, *Half A Man: The Status of the Negro in New York* (New York, 1911), p. ix.

32. City and Suburban Homes Company, *Annual Report,* 1904–1905 (New York, 1905), p. 11; *Annual Report, 1906–1907* (New York, 1907), pp. 7–8.

33. On Phipps as philanthropist see Moses Rischin, *The Promised City: New York's Jews, 1870–1914* (Cambridge, 1961), p. 109; and "Reminiscences of William H. Allen" (Oral History Research Office, Columbia University, 1950), pp. 57–58; *Real Estate Record and Builder's Guide,* LXXV (March 4, 1905), 460; "Model Tenements," *The Outlook,* LXXIX (February 11, 1905), 364–365.

34. Arthur Gary, "Sketch of the Constitution League of the United States" (WPA research paper, Schomburg Collection); Ruth Worthy, "A Negro in Our History: William Monroe Trotter, 1872–1934" (M.A. thesis, Columbia University, 1952), p. 91. On Milholland's role in the NAACP see *The Crisis,* XXXIII (February 1927), 181–182, XXXV (April 1928), 124, XXV (May 1928), 166.

35. "I feel as though now that the tenement is promised us things are going pretty well for a settlement in it. Mr. Phipps, I know, is interested." Mary White Ovington to Fred R. Moore, February 23, 1905. Washington Papers, Library of Congress, Box 29. *The Afro-American,* October 15, 1932; *Half A Man,* pp. 41–42; *The Walls Came Tumbling Down,* pp. 33–34.

36. William English Walling, "The Race War in the North," *The Independent,* LXV (September 3, 1908), 529–534; William English Walling, "The Founding of the NAACP," *The Crisis,* XXXVI (July 1929), 228.

37. *The Afro-American,* November 26, December 10, 1932; *Then and Now: NAACP, 1909–1959* (New York, 1959?); Mary White Ovington, *How the NAACP Began* (New York, 1914).

38. *The Crisis,* V (February 1913), 163–164.

39. Interview with Mrs. Richetta G. Wallace, November 3, 1961; Richetta G. Wallace to author, November 7, 1961.

40. Claude McKay, *A Long Way From Home* (New York, 1937), p. 113.

41. *The Afro-American,* September 10, 1932; "A Tribute to Miss Ovington," *The New York Age,* July 2, 1932; Oswald Garrison Villard, *Fighting Years: Memoirs of a Liberal Editor* (New York, 1939), pp. 191–198.

42. *The Afro-American,* February 25, 1933.

43. For a list of members of the CIICN see "Committee on the Industrial Improvement of the Negro in New York," a small booklet in the Stokes Manuscripts, Columbia University, Box 18; *The New York Age,* May 17, July 12, 1906.

44. *The New York Age,* July 12, 1906; Bulkley, "The School as a Social Center," *Charities,* XV (October 7, 1905), 76.

45. J. Wayne Wrightstone, Director of the New York City Board of Educational Research to author, February 7, 1962; *The Crisis,* II (October 1911), 236; James K. Owens, Syracuse University Archivist, to author, January 8, 1963; *Alumni Record and General Catalogue of Syracuse University* (Syracuse, 1911), III, 1546.

46. "A Slave Boy, Now a Professor," *Success,* April 8, 1899.

47. William Lewis Bulkley, "Race Prejudice as Viewed from an Economic

Standpoint," *Proceedings of the National Negro Conference, 1909* (New York, 1909?), pp. 92–93.

48. Interview with Henry S. Coshburn of Board of Education, February 23, 1962.

49. *The New York Age,* July 22, 1909.

50. Ralph Ellison, "William Lewis Bulkley" (WPA research paper, Schomburg Collection); *The New York Age,* March 22, 1924, September 3, 1933.

51. "I wish very much that you could see your way clear to attend the meetings of the Commission for Improving the Industrial Condition of the colored people in Greater New York. I am very much afraid that unless you do attend that Bulkley and his crowd will get hold of this important organization." Booker T. Washington to Charles W. Anderson, October 1, 1907. Washington Papers, Library of Congress, Box 37.

52. Charles W. Anderson to Booker T. Washington, April 3, 1909. Washington Papers, Library of Congress, Box 43; *The New York Age,* April 6, 1905.

53. *Ibid.,* November 5, 1914; Bulkley, "The School as a Social Center," 77.

54. *Ibid.,* October 31, 1907. "A Square Deal for New York Negroes," *The Outlook,* LXXXIII (June 23, 1906), 398–399.

55. William Lewis Bulkley to J. G. Phelps Stokes, November 14, 18, 1906. Stokes Manuscripts, Columbia University, Boxes 18 and 77.

56. Charles W. Anderson to Booker T. Washington, March 23, 1906. Washington Papers, Library of Congress, Box 2; William Lewis Bulkley, "The Industrial Condition of the Negro in New York City," *The Annals,* XXVII (May 1906), 595.

57. *The New York Age,* May 17, 1906.

58. "CIICN," Stokes Manuscripts; "Committee for Improving the Industrial Condition of Negroes in New York," *The Colored American Magazine,* XII (June 1907), 459–64; *The New York Age,* April 26, 1906.

59. William Jay Schieffelin to J. G. Phelps Stokes, May 24, 1906. Stokes Manuscripts, Columbia University, Box 18. On Schieffelin see "The Reminiscences of William Jay Schieffelin" (Oral History Research Office, Columbia University, 1949), and "Harmful Rush of Negroes to the North," *The New York Times Magazine,* VI (June 3, 1917).

60. From 1906 to 1911 *The New York Age* regularly printed articles on the CIICN and this information is largely derived from them.

61. *Ibid.,* October 19, 1911; *The Crisis,* VIII (September 1914), 243–46; *The Urban League: Its Story* (New York, 1939); Bulkley, "Race Prejudice," 97.

62. *The New York Age,* June 22, 1905.

63. *Ibid.,* June 26, 1913; *The Colored American Magazine,* XIII (September 1907), 211.

64. *The Horizon: A Journal of the Color Line,* V (November 1909), 1–2.

65. *The New York Age,* July 22, 1908.

NOTES TO CHAPTER 5

1. There is no legally definable modern community of Harlem. The first settlement was made in the area in 1636, and the town of New Harlaem created in 1658. The last Harlem colonial patent was made in 1686. Its boundaries ran roughly from present-day Seventy-fourth Street to One Hundred and Twenty-ninth Street, East River to Hudson River. Subsequent grants made

in the general area of New Harlaem in colonial times outside these boundaries were also often referred to as Harlem grants. Sometimes the name Harlem was used to designate all upper Manhattan. Harlem in the late nineteenth century was part of the Twelfth Ward, which included all Manhattan above Eighty-sixth Street. At the turn of the nineteenth century its residents generally defined the community as bordered by One Hundred and Tenth Street on the south, One Hundred and Fifty-fifth Street on the north, East River on the east, and present-day Morningside and St. Nicholas Avenues on the west, but were never rigid in applying this definition. The same holds true today. This absence of legally designated boundaries presents no significant difficulty for this study because after this chapter I shall use an ethnic definition—the specific sections within the general area of Harlem occupied by Negroes, and these can be traced in the greatest of detail. In the 1920's Negro Harlem was most often called Central Harlem or North Harlem.

2. James Riker, *Revised History of Harlem (City of New York): Its Origin and Early Annals* (New York, 1904), *passim*.

3. Col. Alonzo B. Caldwell, *A Lecture: The History of Harlem* (New York, 1882), pp. 20, 30–31.

4. *Deduction of the Harlaem Commons* (New York, 1872), pp. 28–29. For extensive genealogical data on Harlem descendants consult Riker, *Revised History*, pp. 426–814.

5. *The New York Times*, November 17, 1883.

6. Richard Webber, Jr., "Historical Sketch of Harlem," *Harlem Magazine*, I (October 1912), 17.

7. New York Public Library, *Book of Charters, Wills, Deeds and Other Official Documents* (New York, 1905), pp. 307–325; *Constitution of the Harlaem Library Formed by a Convention of the Inhabitants* (New York, 1817); William B. Silber, *A History of St. James Methodist Episcopal Church at Harlem, New York City, 1830–1880* (New York, 1882), p. 22; James Ford, *et al., Slums and Housing: With Special Reference to New York City* (Cambridge, Massachusetts, 1936), I, 324.

8. This information is from a nonpaginated collection of typewritten material at the New-York Historical Society entitled "Harlem Commons Syndicate."

9. Caldwell, *A Lecture*, pp. 12, 18–19.

10. *Harlem Magazine*, II (October 1913), 11–13.

11. Broadus Mitchell, *Alexander Hamilton: The National Adventure, 1788–1804* (New York, 1962), pp. 499–500; *Harlem Local Reporter*, May 10, 1893, July 9, 1904.

12. Caldwell, *A Lecture*, p. 24.

13. Riker, *Revised History*, pp. 191n., 256n., 398n., 474, 530n., 588–589.

14. "Old Timers' Tales of Harlem's Growth," *Harlem Magazine*, III (December 1914), 16.

15. Rev. Edgar Tilton, Jr., *The Reformed Low Dutch Church of Harlem: Historical Sketch* (New York, 1910), p. 11; The Collegiate Reformed Church of Harlem, *Two Hundred and Fiftieth Anniversary* (New York, 1910), p. 1.

16. Mitchell, *Alexander Hamilton*, p. 552.

17. "Harlem Commons Syndicate"; Riker, *Revised History*, pp. 488–489.

18. Riker, *Revised History*, p. 298.

19. "Harlem Commons Syndicate."

20. "The Fall of Shantytown," *Harlem Local Reporter*, March 5, 1890; "A Shanty Scene in Harlem," *ibid.*, August 13, 1892; Kate Holladay Claghorn, "The Foreign Immigrant in New York City," *Reports of the Industrial Com-*

mission on Immigration . . . and on Education (Washington, D.C., 1901), XV, 457.

21. "Old Timers' Tales of Harlem's Growth," *Harlem Magazine*, III (December 1914), 16–22; Michael C. O'Brien, "Memories of Hooker's Building," *ibid.*, IV (May 1916), 11, 17; *Harlem Local Reporter*, September 21, 1892.

22. Harlem Plains, the area that became Negro Harlem, is made of limestone which eroded more readily than the schist of Harlem Heights. For a general geological history of the area see Edward Hagaman Hall, "A Brief History of Morningside Park and Vicinity," American Scenic and Historic Preservation Society, *21st Annual Report* (Albany, 1916), 537–598; *History and Commerce of New York, 1891* (New York, 1892?) p. 82.

23. Caldwell, *A Lecture*, p. 27.

24. Charles H. Fuller, "Harlem—from 'Cradle Days' to Now," *Harlem Magazine*, XIV (October 1925), 6–7; Charles H. Haswell, *Reminiscences of New York by an Octogenarian, 1816–1860* (New York, 1896), p. 459.

25. *The Harlem Monthly Magazine*, I (April 1893), 1–2; James Grant Wilson, ed., *The Memorial History of the City of New York* (New York, 1893), III, 453.

26. Lloyd Morris, *Incredible New York: High Life and Low Life of the Last Hundred Years* (New York, 1951), pp. 95–96; Reginald Pelham Bolton, *$5,000,000 Speedway: A Useless Driveway* (n.p., n.d.); Charles Townsend Harris, *Memories of Manhattan in the Sixties and Seventies* (New York, 1928), p. 78; Herbert Manchester, *The Story of Harlem and the Empire City Savings Bank, 1889–1929* (New York, 1929), pp. 13, 16, 19.

27. *Harlem Magazine*, XVIII (May 1929), 15; Charles Henry White, "In Up-Town New York," *Harper's Monthly*, CXII (January 1906), 220–228.

28. New York and Harlem Railroad, *Act of Incorporation and Subsequent Acts, 1831–1863* (New York, 1864), pp. 3–4.

29. *Taintor's Route and City Guides, Harlem Route* (New York, 1867), p. 6.

30. Samuel M. Brown, "Harlem's Early Transit Facilities," *Harlem Magazine*, IV (September 1915), 11; Joseph Warren Greene, Jr., "New York City's First Railroad, The New York and Harlem, 1832 to 1867," *The New-York Historical Society Quarterly Bulletin*, IX (January 1926), 107–123.

31. Ella Bunner Graff, *Reminiscences of Old Harlem* (n.p., 1933), p. 5; Caldwell, *A Lecture*, p. 28.

32. A. J. Wall, "The Sylvan Steamboats on the East River, New York to Harlem," *The New-York Historical Society Bulletin*, VII (October 1924), 59–72.

33. I. N. Phelps Stokes, *The Iconography of Manhattan Island, 1498–1909* (New York, 1918), III, 808–831; Thomas Adams, Harold M. Lewis and Theodore T. McCroskey, *Population, Land Values and Government* (New York, 1929), pp. 51 ff; James Austin Stevens, *The Physical Evolution of New York City in a Hundred Years, 1807–1907* (n.p., n.d.); James L. Bahret, "Growth of New York and Suburbs Since 1790," *The Scientific Monthly* (November 1920), 404–418.

34. Walter Laidlaw, *Population of the City of New York, 1890–1930* (New York, 1932), p. 51.

35. Frederic A. Birmingham, *It Was Fun While It Lasted* (Philadelphia, 1960), p. 39.

36. *Harlem Magazine*, II (April 1914), 17–18; *Harlem Local Reporter*, May 28, 1892.

37. *History and Commerce of New York, 1891* (New York, 1892?), p. 90.

38. "Harlem Commons Syndicate"; *The Harlem Local: Twelfth Ward News,* January 4, 1873.

39. *Harlem Magazine,* V (December 1916), 13; Manchester, *The Story of Harlem,* p. 21.

40. "During several years after the discovery of Harlem (from the stations on the elevated railroad) its growth was phenomenal. . . ." *Harlem Local Reporter,* March 1, 1890.

41. *Harlem Magazine,* XVIII (May 1929), 14.

42. *Harlem Local Reporter,* March 5, 1890.

43. Wirt Howe, *New York At The Turn of the Century, 1899–1916* (Toronto, 1946), pp. 2–3; *Harlem Local Reporter,* March 25, 1891; "Last Rites on Billy Goats," *ibid.,* March 30, 1895.

44. *Harlem Magazine,* IV (November 1915), 13, XV (July 1926), 4.

45. O'Brien, "Memories of Hooker's Building," 17.

46. Berta Gilbert, "Morgenthau Reminisces About Harlem," *Harlem Magazine,* XX (May 1931), 4, 15–16; Record and Guide, *A History of Real Estate, Building, and Architecture in New York City During the last Quarter of a Century* (New York, 1898), pp. 94–95, 112; *Harlem Local Reporter,* January 2, 1895; *Harlem Life,* XV (October 28, 1899), XVI (February 3, 1900), 6; Vincent Sheean, *Oscar Hammerstein I: The Life and Exploits of an Impresario* (New York, 1956), pp. 40 ff.

47. *Harlem Local Reporter,* March 1, 1893.

48. *Ibid.,* March 1, 1890, July 4, 1894.

49. *Ibid.,* December 28, 1889; Newspaper clipping in "Harlem Commons Syndicate."

50. The operations of these Harlem claimants are preserved in a collection of their official transactions, reports of annual meetings, letters, genealogical charts and newspaper clippings in the "Harlem Commons Syndicate," New-York Historical Society. See also Walter H. Shupe, *First Annual Statement of the Harlem Commons Syndicate* (New York, 1884).

51. *Harlem Magazine,* XXI (August 1932), 9, 16.

52. Henry Pennington Toler, *Arise Take Thy Journey* (New York, 1903), p. 48; Carl Horton Pierce, *New Harlem Past and Present: The Story of an Amazing Civic Wrong Now At Last to be Righted* (New York, 1903).

53. Charles C. Baldwin, *Stanford White* (New York, 1931), pp. 194–195, 200; Birmingham, *It Was Fun While It Lasted,* p. 41; *Harlem Library Bulletin,* I (March 1903), n.p.; *Harlem Magazine,* II (September 1913), 25; Robert Coit Chapin, *The Standard of Living of Workingmen's Families in New York City* (New York, 1909), p. 85; *The Hammer and the Pen,* I (August 1898), 3–4.

54. *The New York Times,* November 21, 1920.

55. *Harlem Magazine,* XVI (June 1927), 4–5.

56. Sheean, *Oscar Hammerstein I,* pp. 42–46, 57, 66.

57. *Harlem Magazine,* I (June 1912), 29.

58. Birmingham, *It Was Fun While It Lasted,* p. 14.

59. *First Report of the Tenement House Commission of New York City* (New York, 1902), II, 103.

60. This is taken from a survey of biographical sketches that appeared regularly in *Harlem Magazine.*

61. *Harlem Local Reporter,* December 28, 1889. "An army of downtowners [are] making their residences in this delightful section." *Ibid.,* May 2, 1891.

62. *Harlem Magazine,* II (April 1914), 17–18.

63. *Harlem Local Reporter,* January 7, 1890; *135th Anniversary of the*

Battle of Harlem Heights: With a History and Ready Reference Directory of Harlem (New York, 1911).
64. Graff, *Reminiscences of Old Harlem*, p. 4.
65. *The Local Reporter*, January 6, 1883.
66. Interview with Max Bollt, February 9, 1962.
67. *Harlem Local Reporter*, May 10, 1893.
68. Harlem Presbyterian Church, *Church Bulletin* (April 17, 1908), n.p.
69. *New York Street Directory and Shoppers' Guide for 1898* (New York, 1898), p. 73.
70. *Harlem Local Reporter*, February 15, 1890, October 19, 1892, November 26, 1892.
71. Manchester, *The Story of Harlem*, pp. 24–25.
72. Respectively: *The Harlem Monthly Magazine, Harlem Life* and *Harlem Local Reporter.*
73. The Independence Day Association of Harlem, *Celebration,* 1886 (New York, 1887), 17; Harlem Wohlthätigkeits Verein, *Constitution* (New York, 1896); Harlem Independent Schützen Corps, *Golden Jubilee, 1880–1930* (New York, 1930); Konrad Bercovici, *Around the World in New York* (New York, 1924), 215; Harlem Regatta Association, *Official Programme* (New York, 1902); Harlem Democratic Club, *Constitution, By-Laws, Rules. . . .* (New York, 1889), 5; Harlem Republican Club, *By-Laws and List of Members* (New York, 1892); *Harlem Evening High School News,* November 1907; Harlem Board of Commerce, *Constitution and By-Laws* (New York, 1896).
74. *The Harlem Monthly Magazine,* I (April 1893), 2; *Harlem Magazine,* XXI (December 1932), 8.
75. *Harlem Local Reporter,* April 16, 1890.

NOTES TO CHAPTER 6

1. "The Reminiscences of Samuel J. Battle" (Oral History Research Office, Columbia University, 1960), p. 21; *The Harlem Local Reporter,* April 4, 1894.
2. *The Harlem Local Reporter,* March 1, 1893.
3. *Ibid.,* April 20, 1895.
4. *Ibid.,* August 2, 1893.
5. *The Sun's Guide to New York* (New York, 1892), p. 26.
6. William McAdoo, *Guarding A Great City* (New York, 1906), p. 91.
7. *The Harlem Local Reporter,* December 26, 1894. "A Walk in Harlem Brings Surprises," *The New York Times,* January 2, 1921.
8. *Ibid.,* July 18, 1894, August 4, 1894; *The Harlem Local Reporter and Bronx Chronicle,* January 1, 1898; Frances Blascoer, *Colored School Children in New York* (New York, 1915), p. 75.
9. *The Harlem Local Reporter,* September 1, 1894; *Harlem Magazine,* IV (June 1915), 9; *Uptown New York* (May–June 1934), 9.
10. *Ibid.,* September 21, 1892, March 1, 1893.
11. Frederic A. Birmingham, *It Was Fun While It Lasted* (Philadelphia, 1960), p. 39.
12. James Riker, *Revised History of Harlem (City of New York): Its Origin and Early Annals* (New York, 1904), p. 189.
13. *Ibid.,* p. 287; Rev. Edgar Tilton, Jr., *The Reformed Low Dutch Church of Harlem: Historical Sketch* (New York, 1910), p. 31; "Harlem Commons Syndicate," n.p.; Col. Alonzo B. Caldwell, *A Lecture: The History of Harlem* (New York, 1882), p. 23.
14. *The Daily Advertiser* [New York], January 15, 1791.

15. William B. Silber, *A History of St. James Methodist Episcopal Church at Harlem, New York City, 1830–1880* (New York, 1882).

16. Robert S. Dixon, "Education of the Negro in the City of New York, 1853–1900" (M.A. thesis, City College, 1935), pp. 13–14.

17. Jonathan Greenleaf, *A History of the Churches, of All Denominations, in the City of New York from the First Settlement to the Year 1846* (New York, 1846), p. 322.

18. *Ibid.*, p. 330.

19. Dixon, "Education of the Negro," pp. 14, 19, 25.

20. Ella Bunner Graff, *Reminiscences of Old Harlem* (n.p., 1933), p. 8.

21. *Ibid.*, p. 11.

22. *The Harlem Local Reporter*, December 8, 1894.

23. *Harlem Library Bulletin, I* (September 1902), 10.

24. Michael C. O'Brien, "Memories of Hooker's Building," *Harlem Magazine*, IV (May 1916), 17.

25. *The New York Age*, March 6, 1913.

26. *Ibid.*, September 20, 1890; "The Negro in New York," *The Sun*, January 30, 1901.

27. John P. Clyde, "The Negro in New York City" (M.A. thesis, Columbia University, 1899), pp. 3–4.

28. This information is derived from advertisements and personal notices which appeared in the Negro and white press in the 1880's and 1890's.

29. *The New York Age*, February 21, 28, 1891, January 26, 1895.

30. *The Harlem Local Reporter*, November 4, 1893; Jacob A. Riis, *The Battle With the Slum* (New York, 1902), pp. 110–111.

31. *The Harlem Local Reporter*, December 26, 1894; *The New York Times*, December 26, 1901.

32. *The New York Age*, October 20, 1888, April 20, 1889; *The New York Globe*, May 12, June 2, June 30, 1883.

33. *The Harlem Local Reporter*, October 31, 1891.

34. *The New York Age*, May 17, 1890, February 21, 1891.

35. I have compiled these statistics by locating the exact blocks delineated by the Tenement House Commission on the ward maps which the Commission published. The selection I made was limited to blocks with ten or more Negro families. The statistics omit nonfamily groups and are therefore no accurate guide to the exact number of Negroes in Harlem in 1902. They do, however, present a description of the distribution of Negroes in the general area. *First Report of the Tenement House Commission of New York City* (New York, 1902), II, 103, and maps.

36. *The Harlem Local Reporter*, April 12, 1893.

37. *Ibid.*, October 26, 1895, March 1, 1894.

38. The Harlem Relief Society of the City of New York, *First Annual Report, 1893* (New York, 1894), and *Second Annual Report, 1894* (New York, 1895). James Baldwin, who obviously speaks for a later generation, writes of the "bitter expectancy with which, in my childhood, we awaited winter: It is coming and will be hard; there is nothing anyone can do about it." "The Harlem Ghetto," in *Notes of a Native Son* (Boston, 1955), p. 57.

39. *The Harlem Local Reporter*, December 13, 1893.

40. *Ibid.*, February 25, 1893.

41. *Ibid.*, December 23, 1893.

42. The Harlem Relief Society, *Twenty-Second Annual Report, 1914* (New York, 1915), pp. 2–3, 13.

43. For a wonderful description of the Cake Walk see *The New York Age*, September 1, 1934. *The Harlem Local Reporter*, February 28, 1891, March 29, 1890; Jacob A. Riis, *How the Other Half Lives* (New York, 1890), p. 154.

44. Vincent Sheean, *Oscar Hammerstein I: The Life and Exploits of an Impresario* (New York, 1950), pp. 58–59, 63; *Harlem Life*, XV, (October 21, 1899), 3.

45. *The Harlem Local Reporter*, May 20, 1893, August 4, 1894.

46. *Real Estate Record and Builder's Guide*, LXXIII (January 16, 1904), 105, and LXXIII (June 4, 1904), 1306.

47. *Ibid.*, LXV (January 27, 1900), 141.

48. John Martin, *Rapid Transit: Its Effects on Rents and Living Conditions* (New York, 1909), p. 13; James L. Bahret, "Growth of New York and Suburbs Since 1790," *The Scientific Monthly* (November 1920), 412.

49. Walter Stabler, "Development of the West Side: A Review of Past and Present Phases," *Record and Guide*, LXX (August 2, 1902), 157.

50. ". . . More than ever before the market is dominated by expert professional operations." *Ibid.*, LXIX (January 10, 1903), 37.

51. *Ibid.*, LXXIII (March 26, 1904). ". . . much of the remaining vacant land on the Upper East Side and in Harlem has passed into the hands of building loan operators. . . ." *Ibid.*, LXXV (January 14, 1905), 58.

52. Abraham Cahan, *The Rise of David Levinsky* (New York, 1960), p. 464.

53. *Record and Guide*, LXX (September 6, 1902), 328.

54. Howard Marion Lesourd, "A Harlem Neighborhood" (M.A. thesis, Columbia University, 1913), p. 6; Eleanor L. Symonds, "Population Shifting in Manhattan" (M.A. thesis, Columbia University, 1924), pp. 3 ff.

55. James Speyer to J. G. Phelps Stokes, September 30, 1903. Stokes Manuscripts, Columbia University, Box 4.

56. Lillian D. Wald to J. G. Phelps Stokes, September 30, 1903, *ibid.*

57. "There is no one whose presence in the Harlem Federation I will value more than yours. . . ." Maurice H. Harris to Lillian D. Wald, December 7, 1906. Wald Manuscripts, New York Public Library; Sarah Sussman, "A Settlement Club" (M.A. thesis, Columbia University, 1918).

58. *The Harlem Local Reporter*, September 10, 1900; "Liber 150," p. 124 and "Liber 127," p. 359, New York City Hall of Records.

59. *Harlem Library Bulletin*, I (September 1902), 4–6, I (July 1903), n.p.; *The New York Times*, November 3, 1913, February 21, June 8, 1914.

60. *Record and Guide*, LXXII (October 3, 1903), 574; Cahan, *Rise of David Levinsky*, p. 191.

61. *The Harlem Local Reporter*, May 10, 1893; *Record and Guide*, LXXII (August 29, 1903), 373.

62. Elmer Rice, "A New York Childhood," *The New Yorker*, IV (September 22, 1928), 36–40.

63. Konrad Bercovici, "The Black Blocks of Manhattan," *Harper's Monthly Magazine*, CXLIX (October 1924), 615.

64. "The district north of 125th Street has suffered most severely from inaccessibility." *Record and Guide*, XLVII (January 10, 1891).

65. *The Harlem Local Reporter*, July 5, 1893.

66. *Ibid.*, July 13, 1895.

67. "There is every reason to believe that the rapid transit railway will have the effect of reserving the better part of Manhattan Island as far north as Harlem . . . for elevator flats, costly dwellings, and business buildings. . . ." *Record and Guide*, LXV (February 24, 1900), 317; LXXV (June 25, 1905),

370. "Harlemites are naturally more interested in rapid transit than any others in the city. . . ." *The Harlem Local Reporter,* January 25, 1893.

68. *Harlem Life,* XV (October 28, 1899), 3, XVI (February 13, 1900), 6.

69. See, for example, *New York Daily Tribune,* August 26, 1900.

70. *The New York Age,* June 11, 1914.

71. *Record and Guide,* LXXIV (October 1, 1904), 667.

72. "Interview with John E. Nail" (WPA Research Paper, Schomburg Collection).

73. *Record and Guide,* LXXIV (October 31, 1903), 775.

74. *Ibid.,* LXXV (January 14, 1905), 287; James Weldon Johnson, "The Making of Harlem," *Survey Graphic,* VI (March 1925), 635.

75. *The New York Age,* June 11, 1914.

NOTES TO CHAPTER 7

1. *Real Estate Record and Builders' Guide,* LXXV (January 14, 1905), 58.

2. John M. Royall in *The New York Age,* June 11, 1914; *Harlem Magazine,* III (October 1914), 24.

3. *The New York Age,* June 11, 1914.

4. Wilfred R. Bain, "Negro Real Estate Brokers" (WPA research paper, Schomburg Collection), p. 1.

5. Obituary in *The New York Age,* October 22, 1908.

6. Clement Richardson, editor, *The National Cyclopedia of the Colored Race* (Montgomery, Alabama, 1919), I, 258.

7. From letterhead on Payton's stationery. See Philip A. Payton, Jr., to Emmett J. Scott, August 3, 1906. Booker T. Washington Papers, Library of Congress, Box 4.

8. *The New York Age,* December 5, 1912; Booker T. Washington, *The Negro in Business* (Boston, 1907), pp. 197–205.

9. *Record and Guide,* LXXI (January 31, 1902), 316.

10. Washington, *The Negro in Business,* pp. 197–205.

11. See photograph in E. F. Dycoff, "A Negro City in New York," *The Outlook,* CVIII (December 23, 1914), 951.

12. Charles W. Anderson to Booker T. Washington, January 5, 1910. Washington Papers, Box 49.

13. When Booker T. Washington bought a controlling interest in the *Age* in 1907, Moore was made editor. August Meier, "Booker T. Washington and the Negro Press," *Journal of Negro History,* XXXVIII (January 1953), 67–90.

14. *The New York Age,* December 28, 1905.

15. Underlined in original. Philip A. Payton, Jr., to Emmett J. Scott, August 3, 1906. Washington Papers, Box 4.

16. *The New York Age,* November 15, 1906.

17. *Ibid.,* December 5, 1912.

18. Bain, "Negro Real Estate Brokers," p. 2; Richardson, *National Cyclopedia,* p. 258; Arthur J. Gary, "Housing and Sanitary Conditions of Negroes in Harlem" (WPA research paper, Schomburg Collection), p. 1.

19. Charles W. Anderson to Emmett J. Scott, April 1, 1910. Washington Papers, Box 49.

20. Philip A. Payton, Jr., to Emmett J. Scott, January 16, 1914. Washington Papers, Box 12.

21. "Certificate of Incorporation of the Afro-American Realty Company Filed and Recorded June 15, 1904." New York City Hall of Records.

22. Wilbur Young, "Sketch of James C. Thomas" (WPA research paper,

Schomburg Collection); *The New York Age,* April 21, 1910.

23. Reverend Dr. Adam Clayton Powell, Sr., *Against the Tide: An Auto-biography* (New York, 1938).

24. Robert S. Dixon, "Education of the Negro in the City of New York, 1853–1900" (M.A. thesis, City College, 1935), p. 52.

25. "A Slave Boy Now a Professor," *Success,* April 8, 1899.

26. Young, "Sketch of James C. Thomas"; Washington, *The Negro in Business,* pp. 104–109.

27. Biographical sketch of Garner in *The New York Age,* September 21, 1905; W. E. B. DuBois, "The Segregated Negro World," *The World Tomorrow,* VI (May 1923), 136–138.

28. See stationery of Afro-American Realty Company with names of direc tors in Fred R. Moore to Emmett J. Scott, May 31, 1906. Washington Paper Box 33.

29. The Afro-American Realty Company, *Prospectus* (New York, 1904), p. 7. Original in New York City Hall of Records.

30. E. F. Dycoff, "A Negro City in New York," 949–950; *The New Yor. Age,* December 21, 1905; L. B. Bryan, "Negro Real Estate in New York (WPA research paper, Schomburg Collection), pp. 2–3.

31. See *The New York Age* in 1905 and 1906 for advertisements.

32. *Prospectus,* pp. 3–7.

33. Fred R. Moore to Emmett J. Scott, December 27, 1905. Washington Papers, Box 29.

34. Fred R. Moore to Emmett J. Scott, September 21, 1905. *Ibid.,* Box 29.

35. This estimate, probably a conservative one, is derived from advertisements which appeared in the Negro press under Payton's name and scattered references in the Washington Papers.

36. Fred R. Moore to Emmett J. Scott, December 12, 1906. Washington Papers, Box 33.

37. Wilford H. Smith to Emmett J. Scott, May 8, 1906. *Ibid.,* Box 5.

38. Wilford H. Smith to Booker T. Washington, May 17, 1906. *Ibid.,* Box 5. Moore also thought of resigning with Smith and advised Scott to join the Fred R. Moore to Emmett J. Scott, December 27, 1905. *Ibid.,* Box 29.

39. Charles J. Crowder vs. Afro-American Realty Company, a domestic corporation, and Philip A. Payton, Jr. Original in New York City Hall of Records.

40. Papers on Appeal from Order Vacating Order of Arrest. *Ibid.*

41. Crowder vs. Afro-American Realty Company, *passim; The New York Age,* January 31, February 7, 1907, November 19, 1908.

42. See Scott's prodding in Emmett J. Scott to Philip A. Payton, Jr., June 11, 1907; and Moore's reply, Fred R. Moore to Emmett J. Scott, no date. Washington Papers, Box 36.

43. Fred R. Moore to Emmett J. Scott, September 21, 1907. *Ibid.,* Box 36.

44. Underlined in original. Philip A. Payton, Jr., to Emmett J. Scott, August 3, 1906. *Ibid.,* Box 4.

45. Fred R. Moore to Emmett J. Scott, November 26, 1907. *Ibid.,* Box 36.

46. Melvin J. Chisum to Booker T. Washington, February 5, 1907. *Ibid.,* Box 6. Payton was interviewed during the course of the trial and declared: "The whole affair is a spite action brought against me by the former counsel of our company and several dissatisfied stockholders. . . ." *The New York Age,* January 31, February 7, 1907.

47. *The New York Age,* February 7, 1907.

48. Fred R. Moore to Emmett J. Scott, November 26, 1907. Washington Papers, Box 36.

49. *Ibid.*

50. Fred R. Moore to Emmett J. Scott, November 11, 1907. *Ibid.*, Box 36.

51. *Idem.* "I sincerely hope that a way out may be found. Payton can't borrow. . . ." Fred R. Moore to Booker T. Washington. *Ibid.*, Box 36.

52. Fred R. Moore to Emmett J. Scott, November 11, 1907; Booker T. Washington to Fred R. Moore, December 16, 1907. *Ibid.*, Box 36.

53. Fred E. Moore to Emmett J. Scott, November 26, 1907. *Ibid.*, Box 36.

54. Booker T. Washington to Fred R. Moore, December 16, 1907; Fred R. Moore to Booker T. Washington, December 23, 1907. *Ibid.*, Box 36.

55. The houses at 40, 42 and 44 West One Hundred and Thirty-fifth Street, the place where Payton and the Hudson Realty Company clashed in 1904, were advertised by a white corporation, Manheimer Brothers, in 1908. *The New York Age*, December 3, 1908.

56. "The company is allowed to lapse without one single word of explanation to the public or the stockholders. . . ." Draft of letter from Emmett J. Scott to Philip A. Payton, Jr., and Fred R. Moore, July 1908? Washington Papers, Box 41.

57. "Payton is out of the city. I shall take up your letter with him as soon as he returns—will see that a statement is issued if I have to do it myself. . . . Will send it to you as soon as prepared." Fred R. Moore to Emmett J. Scott, August 1, 1908. *Ibid.*, Box 41.

58. Fred R. Moore to Emmett J. Scott, October 19, 1908. *Ibid.*, Box 41.

59. *The New York Age*, July 30, 1908.

60. Richardson, *National Cyclopedia*, I, 258.

61. The houses that Payton controlled and their exact locations are derived from advertisements which appeared in *The New York Age* over a number of years.

NOTES TO CHAPTER 8

1. National League on Urban Conditions Among Negroes, *Housing Conditions Among Negroes in Harlem, New York City* (New York, 1915), p. 7. Hereafter cited as *Housing Conditions*.

2. Robert C. Weaver has pointed this out on a national scale in *The Negro Ghetto* (New York, 1948), *passim; The New York Times*, November 5, 1922.

3. The Independence Day Association of Harlem, *Celebration, 1886* (New York, 1887), p. 30.

4. At least five restrictive covenants were filed. See Section 7, Liber 127, pp. 365–368; Liber 128, pp. 145–150; Liber 151, pp. 134–146; Liber 152, pp. 297–301; Liber 159, pp. 7–15 at the New York City Hall of Records. The racial proviso in one agreement was also printed in *The Crisis*, IV (September 1912), 222.

5. *The New York Age*, June 8, December 4, 1911; *The Crisis*, III (January 1912), 99.

6. *Harlem Magazine*, II (February 1914), 21.

7. "Harlem Property Owners Discuss Negro Problem," *Harlem Home News*, April 7, 1911, July 31, August 28, 1913.

8. "Heart of Harlem Now Invaded by Negroes," "Harlem's Black Belt Is a Growing Menace," "Black Invaders Capture White Flat in 121st Street," *ibid.*, July 28, August 25, 1911, July 24, 1913.

9. *Ibid.*, June 2, June 23, August 25, September 22, 29, 1911.

10. *Ibid.*, April 7, 1911.

11. *Ibid.*, June 19, 1913; *The New York Times*, June 28, 1915; *Harlem Magazine*, II (February 1914), 24, II (April 1914), 25–28, II (August 1913),

17, 20, II (October 1913), 15, III (June 1914), 24; *The New York Age,* April 25, 1912.

12. *The New York Age,* October 3, 1912.

13. *Ibid.,* December 26, 1912, March 27, 1920; *Harlem Home News,* April 7, 1911.

14. *The New York Age,* June 11, 1914.

15. The theater was to be on One Hundred and Twenty-ninth Street and Lenox Avenue and the opponents argued that One Hundred and Thirtieth Street should be the permanent Negro-white dividing line. *The Crisis,* IX (February 1915), 12.

16. *The New York Age,* August 29, November 14, 1912, January 9, 1913.

17. *Ibid.,* August 14, 1913, August 20, 1921.

18. *Ibid.,* February 12, 1914.

19. *The New York Times* quoted in *The New York Age,* July 11, 1912; Section 7, Liber 184, p. 449; Richard J. Latimer, "History of St. James Presbyterian Church, New York City" (WPA research paper, Schomburg Collection); *The Crisis,* XXXIII (September 1927), 232.

20. *The New York Age,* February 6, 20, 1913, June 25, 1915, August 10, 1916, June 21, 1919, February 19, 1921; James Weldon Johnson, *Black Manhattan* (New York, 1930), p. 172.

21. ". . . Various parties have been purchasing different parcels of property in and about One hundred and thirty-seventh Street . . . and have leased or rented them to negro tenants for the purpose of compelling adjoining . . . owners to purchase the same to protect their holdings. . . ." Section 7, Liber 128, p. 145.

22. *Harlem Magazine,* III (July 1914), 24.

23. "Property Owners' Work Begun," *Harlem Magazine,* III (July 1914), 186.

24. Even Negro realtor John E. Nail advised whites against "panic selling": "If a Negro family gets in a house in your block . . . don't run away," he said. *The Crisis,* V (November 1912), 12.

25. *Housing Conditions,* pp. 13–14; *Harlem Magazine,* II (February 1914), 21; Meyer Jarmulowsky, "The Housing Problem of Negro Tenants from the Owner's Point of View," *The New York Age,* December 26, 1912.

26. Harlem Board of Commerce, *Harlem Survey* (New York, 1917?), p. 15.

27. Section 7, Liber 128, p. 146.

28. *The Crisis,* VII (February 1914), 175.

29. New York Urban League, "Twenty-Four Hundred Negro Families in Harlem: An Interpretation of the Living Conditions of Small Wage Earners" (typescript, Schomburg Collection, 1927), p. 7.

30. *The New York Age,* March 27, 1920.

31. George Edmund Haynes, "Conditions Among Negroes in the Cities," *The Annals,* XLIX (September 1913), 110; The President's Conference on Home Building and Home Ownership, *Report of the Committee on Negro Housing* (Washington, D.C., 1932), p. 25.

32. *The New York Age,* March 30, 1911.

33. *Ibid.,* November 22, 1906.

34. *Housing Conditions,* p. 8.

35. "Altogether, it is a healthful location." Seymour Paul, "A Group of Virginia Negroes in New York City" (M.A. thesis, Columbia University, 1912), pp. 20–21; *The New York Age,* June 27, 1912.

36. *Housing Conditions,* p. 16.

37. "The Negroes in Harlem . . . pay a much larger proportion of their income for rent than is paid by Negroes in . . . other cities. . . ." *Ibid.,* p. 17.

38. *Ibid.,* p. 29.

39. "Twenty-four Hundred Negro Families in Harlem," pp. 15–16.

40. Myrtle Evangeline Pollard, "Harlem As Is: The Negro Business and Economic Community. . . ." (M.A. thesis, City College, 1937), I, 172.

41. "Wealthy Negroes," *The New York Times,* July 14, 1895.

42. *The Messenger,* VI (August 1924), 255.

43. Ernest Jasper Hopper, "A Northern Negro Group" (M.A. thesis, Columbia University, 1912), pp. 40 ff.

44. *The New York Age,* May 12, 1934.

45. Robert Zachariah Johnstone, "The Negro in New York—His Social Attainments and Prospects" (M.A. thesis, Columbia University, 1911), p. 48.

46. "Eating places are springing up like mushrooms in Harlem." *The New York Age,* April 21, 1910, January 30, 1913.

47. Hopper, "A Northern Negro Group," pp. 17–18.

48. "Fifteen years ago a great stream of Negroes migrated from Chelsea to Harlem in search of better housing conditions." Charles William Nelson, "Social Activities of the Negro in Chelsea District, New York City" (M.A. thesis, Columbia University, 1921), pp. 4–7. "Downtown areas are being depleted of better classes." Reverend Ray Freeman Jenney, "A Sociological Study of a New York City Parish" (M.A. thesis, Columbia University, 1921), pp. 2–3. Norman L. Holmes, "Columbus Hill: The Story of a Negro Community," *Opportunity,* I (February 1923), 10–11; City and Suburban Homes Company, *Annual Report, 1930–1931* (New York, 1931), p. 8; Woofter, *Negro Problems in Cities* (New York, 1928), p. 101.

49. *The New York Age,* August 1, 1907, January 10, 1920; *The New York Times,* December 4, 1918.

50. George W. Hodges, *Touchstones of Methodism* (New York, 1947), pp. 50–62; *The New York Age,* March 30, 1911, February 6, March 17, 1923; *The New York Times,* March 17, 1923.

51. *The New York Age,* August 10, 1911.

52. Harold Cooke Phillips, "The Social Significance of Negro Churches in Harlem" (M.A. thesis, Columbia University, 1922), *passim.* By 1926 there were 140 Negro churches in Harlem. Ira De Augustine Reid, "Let Us Prey!" *Opportunity,* IV (September 1926), 274–278. In 1930, Harlem had 163 Negro churches. Greater New York Federation of Churches, *The Negro Churches of Manhattan* (New York, 1930), p. 19.

53. Lassalle Best, "Brief History of Seventh-Day Adventist Church Among Negroes in New York" (WPA research paper, Schomburg Collection), pp. 1–2; Ellen Terry, "Catholic Activities Among Negroes in New York City" (WPA research paper, Schomburg Collection), pp. 2–4; "The Reminiscences of Reverend George Barry Ford" (Oral History Research Office, Columbia University, 1956), pp. 2–3; *The New York Age,* November 3, 1910, June 13, October 12, 1912; *The Crisis,* IX (February 1915), 165.

54. Reverend Dr. Adam Clayton Powell, Sr., *Against the Tide: An Autobiography* (New York, 1938), pp. 67–70.

55. *The New York Age,* May 14, 1914.

56. *The New York Freeman,* April 17, 1886.

57. *The New York Age,* December 20, 1919, November 13, 1920.

58. *Ibid.,* March 30, 1911.

59. The Reverend Dr. Bishop's purchases can be traced, house-by-house and lot-by-lot, by checking the city's real estate records. See Section 7, Liber 124, p. 500; Liber 125, p. 470; Liber 127, pp. 15, 44; Liber 143, p. 410; Liber 154, p. 60; Liber 181, p. 487; Liber 184, p. 323.

60. Waring Cuney, "Notes From An Interview with Reverend Shelton Bishop" (WPA research paper, Schomburg Collection).

61. *Harlem Magazine,* II (February 1914), 24.

62. *The New York Age,* June 24, December 9, 1909, January 29, 1914.

63. "Million Dollar Deal," *The New York Age,* March 30, 1911, January 16, 1913; *The Crisis,* II (May 1911), 5.

64. Arthur Gary, "An Account of the Nail and Parker Business Enterprises"; Wilfred R. Bain, "Negro Real Estate Brokers"; Louis B. Bryan, "Brief History of the Chamber of Commerce" (WPA research papers, Schomburg Collection). For a picture of the business partners see *The New York Age,* March 30, 1911, February 10, 1916. "John E. Nail, *The Crisis,* XXIX (March 1925), 220–221; *The President's Conference,* p. 7 and *passim.*

65. Odetta Harper, "Interview with John E. Nail"; Waring Cuney, "Interview with Jerome B. Peterson: An Account of Wealthy Negroes, 1880–1890"; Richard J. Latimer, "History of Negro Saloons" (WPA research papers, Schomburg Collection); "John E. Nail Scrapbook," James Weldon Johnson Collection, Yale University.

66. This quotation is a paraphrase of an interview with John E. Nail in the 1930's. Pollard, "Harlem As Is," pp. 173–174. Also see description of Nail's bar in "Night Clubs," James Weldon Johnson Collection, Yale University.

67. *The New York Age,* February 10, 1916, January 4, 1917, March 15, 1947; "Nail Scrapbook," Johnson Collection, Yale University.

68. *Ibid.,* July 31, 1920; *Housing Conditions,* p. 12; Bureau of the Census, *Fifteenth Census, 1930: Population* (Washington, D.C., 1933), IV, 1130–1134; John E. Nail to James Weldon Johnson, July 9, 1914, Johnson Collection, Yale University.

69. *The Crisis,* XIV (September 1917), 260; *The New York Age,* July 12, 19, 1917. Payton's name was apparently a respected one at his death. Those who bought his interests called themselves the "Payton Apartments Corporation." See also John E. Nail to James Weldon Johnson, July 4, 1914. Johnson Collection, Yale University.

70. *Who's Who in Colored America* (New York, 1927), p. 199. When Terry returned to Virginia for visits he was showered with attention. "It seemed as if every other person I met had something to do with raising me," he said in a speech at Tuskegee. *The New York Age,* January 15, 1914, September 27, November 29, 1917, January 26, 1918. There are Terry letters in the Booker T. Washington Collection.

71. *The New York Age,* September 20, 1917, November 15, 29, December 6, 1919, February 28, March 13, April 3, 1920; Melvin J. Chisum to Booker T. Washington, September 10, 1906. Washington Papers, Library of Congress, Box 2; *The Crisis,* XXIX (March 1925), 220–221.

72. This information comes from items which appeared in *The Crisis* and *The New York Age* over the years. Also see Wilfred R. Bain, "Harlem Branch Y.M.C.A." and "West 137th St. Branch, Y.M.C.A." (WPA research papers, Schomburg Collection); Elbridge L. Adams, "The Negro Music School Settlement," *Southern Workman,* XLIV (March 1915), 161–165.

73. Frederick A. Birmingham, *It Was Fun While It Lasted* (Philadelphia, 1960), *passim; The New York Age,* July 20, 1911, January 30, 1926; *The New*

York Times, July 4, 1920, November 5, 1922; "Harlem's Astor Row for Colored Tenants," *ibid.,* November 21, 1920.
74. *Harlem Magazine,* I (April 1913), 22, II (August 1913), 17; "A Carnival and Pageant for Harlem," *ibid.,* III (August 1914), 16; *The New York Times,* November 5, 1922, April 23, 1924.
75. *Harlem Magazine,* XVI (June 1927), 4–5; *The New York Age,* October 4, 1930, June 9, 1934.
76. *Harlem Magazine,* XI (May 1921), XX (April 1931), 3–4; *The New York Age,* June 21, 1930, May 26, 1934.
77. Harlem Board of Commerce, *Harlem Survey* (New York, 1917?), pp. 1–3; *Harlem Magazine,* IV (December 1915), 14, VI (January 1917), 15–16; *The New York Times,* April 16, 1916, June 11, 1927.
78. *Harlem Magazine,* XIV (April 1925), 13, XXI (December 1932), 8; *Uptown New York,* XXII (January–February 1933), 10.
79. E. Franklin Frazier, "Negro Harlem: An Ecological Study," *The American Journal of Sociology,* XLIII (July 1937), 72–88; *The New York Age,* May 26, 1910, June 12, 1913; Reverend Dr. Alexander Walters, *My Life and Work* (New York, 1917), pp. 196–197.

NOTES TO CHAPTER 9

1. The Mayor's Commission on Conditions in Harlem, "The Negro in Harlem: A Report on Social and Economic Conditions Responsible for the Outbreak of March 19, 1935" (unpublished manuscript in La Guardia Papers, Municipal Archives), p. 53. This important study, prepared under the direction of E. Franklin Frazier, will hereafter be cited as "The Negro in Harlem."
2. "The Future Harlem," *The New York Age,* January 10, 1920.
3. John E. Nail to James Weldon Johnson, March 12, 1934, Johnson Collection, Yale University; "Harlem Conditions Called Deplorable," *The New York Times,* September 6, 1927.
4. "Let Them Come," "The New Exodus," *The New York Age,* March 3, 1923, October 16, 1920, September 14, 1929.
5. Bureau of the Census, *Fifteenth Census, 1930: Population* (Washington, D.C., 1933), II, 216–218; Walter Laidlaw, *Population of the City of New York, 1890–1930* (New York, 1932), p. 51.
6. Reverend Dr. Adam Clayton Powell, Sr., *Against the Tide: An Autobiography* (New York, 1938), pp. 70–71.
7. Bureau of the Census, *Fifteenth Census, 1930:* Population (Washington, D.C., 1933), II, 216–218. Note the difference in Chicago's migrant population. In order of greatest numbers Chicago Negroes came from Mississippi, Tennessee, Georgia, Alabama and Louisiana.
8. James Ford, *et al., Slums and Housing: With Special Reference to New York City* (Cambridge, Mass., 1936), II, 311–315.
9. *Ibid.,* p. 317; Bureau of the Census, *Negroes in the United States, 1920–1932* (Washington, D.C., 1935), p. 55.
10. Winfred B. Nathan, *Health Conditions in North Harlem, 1923–1927* (New York, 1932), pp. 13–14.
11. *Harlem Magazine,* XIX (June 1930), 8; Mayor's Commission on City Planning, *East Harlem Community Study* (typescript in New York Public Library, 1937), p. 16.
12. *Slums and Housing,* p. 370; Antonio T. Rivera to La Guardia, June 24, 1935, La Guardia Papers; "Harlem Puerto Ricans Unite to Prove Faith," *The*

New York Times, July 2, August 9, 16, 1926; *Opportunity,* IV (October 1926), 330.

13. *The New York Age,* August 27, 1927, March 31, 1928, January 11, 1930; *The New York Times,* October 19, 1924.

14. *Slums and Housing,* p. 314.

15. The attempt of Negroes to move into Washington Heights, Yonkers and Westchester was opposed in these sections as it had been in Harlem earlier. The Neighborhood Protective Association of Washington Heights urged landlords to sign racially restrictive covenants. Mortgage pressures from financial institutions closed down a Negro housing development in Yonkers. As a result of population pressure, however, another large ghetto was created in the Bedford-Stuyvesant section of Brooklyn in the 1920's. Of the 68,921 Negroes in Brooklyn in 1930, 47,616 lived in what is now called Bedford-Stuyvesant. "Negro Community Near Yonkers Abandoned," *The New York Age,* July 3, 1926, March 24, August 4, 1928, April 19, 26, 1930; *Slums and Housing,* p. 314. For a sketch of Brooklyn's Negro community see Ralph Foster Weld, *Brooklyn Is America* (New York, 1950), pp. 153–173.

16. The President's Conference on Home Building and Home Ownership, *Report of the Committee on Negro Housing* (Washington, D.C., 1931), p. 5.

17. Bureau of the Census, *Fifteenth Census, 1930: Population* (Washington, D.C., 1933), II, 70; Ira De Augustine Reid, *The Negro Immigrant* (New York, 1938), pp. 248–249; Barrington Dunbar, "Factors in the Cultural Background of the American Southern Negro and the British West Indian Negro that Condition their Adjustment in Harlem" (M.A. thesis, Columbia University, 1935), *foreword,* p. 4.

18. Reid, *The Negro Immigrant,* pp. 31–35; Reid, "Negro Immigration to the United States," *Social Forces,* XVI (March 1938), 411–417; W. A. Domingo, "Restricted West Indian Immigration and the American Negro," *Opportunity,* II (October 1924), 298–299.

19. W. A. Domingo, "Gift of the Black Tropics," in Alain Locke, ed., *The New Negro: An Interpretation* (New York, 1925), p. 343.

20. *The New York Age,* July 9, 1924, February 4, 1928; Harry Robinson, "The Negro Immigrant in New York" (WPA research paper, Schomburg Collection), p. 9.

21. Garrie Ward Moore, "A Study of a Group of West Indian Negroes in New York City" (M.A. thesis, Columbia University, 1923), pp. 19–20; Reid, *The Negro Immigrant,* pp. 126–128; *The New York Age,* February 28, 1931, July 29, 1933.

22. "The Negro in New York" (unpublished WPA manuscript, Schomburg Collection), pp. 25–27; Gardner N. Jones, "The Pilgrimage to Freedom" (WPA research paper, Schomburg Collection), p. 25.

23. Reid, *The Negro Immigrant,* p. 159.

24. *Ibid.,* p. 123; "Communists in Harlem," *The New York Age,* September 21, 1929, October 2, 9, 1926, December 24, 1927, January 21, May 12, December 8, 1928, September 21, 1929.

25. Domingo, "Gift of the Black Tropics," p. 347.

26. Robinson, "Negro Immigrant in New York," pp. 21–22; Moore, "West Indian Negroes in New York City," p. 26.

27. "The Reminiscences of George S. Schuyler" (Oral History Research Office, Columbia University, 1960), p. 73.

28. Robinson, "Negro Immigrant in New York," p. 9; "The Negro in New York," p. 25; Moore, "West Indian Negroes in New York City," p. 25; Reid,

The Negro Immigrant, p. 133; *The Messenger*, VII (September 1925), 326, 337–338; *The New York Age*, February 22, 1930; Baltimore *Afro-American*, January 9, 1932.

29. Moore, "West Indian Negroes in New York City," p. 5.

30. Dunbar, "Negro Adjustment in Harlem," pp. 14–25.

31. Reid, *The Negro Immigrant, passim.*

32. *Ibid.*, p. 125; Greater New York Federation of Churches, *Negro Churches in Manhattan* (New York, 1930).

33. Reid, *The Negro Immigrant*, p. 174; Moore, "West Indian Negroes in New York City," pp. 20–25; Dunbar, "Negro Adjustment in Harlem," chap. IV, pp. 22–23.

34. Roi Ottley, *'New World A-Coming': Inside Black America* (New York, 1943), pp. 47–48; Gardner Jones, "The Pilgrimage to Freedom" (WPA research paper, Schomburg Collection), p. 25; Beverly Smith, "Harlem—Negro City," *New York Herald Tribune*, February 14, 1930; Reid, *The Negro Immigrant*, p. 115; *The New York Age*, July 19, 1924, March 17, 1934; Dunbar, "Negro Adjustment in Harlem," chap. III, p. 4; Walter White, "The Paradox of Color," in Alain Locke, ed., *The New Negro: An Interpretation* (New York, 1925), p. 367.

35. *The New York Age*, March 3, 24, April 21, 1928; Domingo, "The Gift of the Black Tropics," p. 344–345; Reid, *The Negro Immigrant*, p. 235.

36. "Harlem Slums," *The Crisis*, XLVIII (December 1941), 378–381; *The New York Age*, January 22, 1927.

37. New York Urban League, "Twenty-four Hundred Negro Families in Harlem: An Interpretation of the Living Conditions of Small Wage Earners" (typescript, Schomburg Collection, 1927), pp. 16–18.

38. *Report of the Committee on Negro Housing*, p. 64.

39. "Appreciation" of prices "came [when owners] remained calm. . . ." T. J. Woofter, *et al.*, *Negro Problems in Cities* (New York, 1928), p. 75. *The New York Times* printed dozens of articles on Harlem's new business prosperity.

40. "Harlem Real Estate Increasing in Value," *Harlem Magazine*, VIII (February 1920), 18b; "Unprecedented Demand for Harlem Real Estate," *ibid.*, X (November 1920), 6; "Revival of Speculative Activity on Harlem's Main Thoroughfare," *The New York Times*, January 18, 1920, July 24, 1921, June 10, 1923, February 13, 1927.

41. "Of all the gouging landlords in Harlem, the colored landlords and agents are the worst, according to the records of the Seventh District Municipal Court." "Race Landlord is Hardest on His Tenants," *The New York Age*, November 20, 1920, June 16, September 22, 1923, May 29, 1926.

42. "The Negro in Harlem," pp. 27–32; *The New York Age*, April 26, 1930.

43. Bureau of the Census, *Fourteenth Census, 1920:* Population (Washington, D.C., 1923), IV, 366–367, 1157–1179; *Fifteenth Census, 1930: Occupations* (Washington, D.C., 1933), 1130–1134; Helen B. Sayre, "Negro Women in Industry," *Opportunity*, II (August 1924), 242–244.

44. *Report of the Committee on Negro Housing*, p. 64; *Negro Problems in Cities*, p. 122.

45. "Twenty-four Hundred Negro Families in Harlem," p. 19; Sidney Axelrad, *Tenements and Tenants: A Study of 1104 Tenement Families* (New York, 1932), p. 15; New York Building and Land Utilization Committee, *Harlem Family Income Survey* (New York, 1935), p. 3; James H. Hubert,

"Harlem—Its Social Problems," *Hospital Social Service,* XXI (January 1930), 44.

46. *Report of the Committee on Negro Housing,* p. vii.

47. William Wilson to La Guardia, October 6, 1944, La Guardia Papers.

48. *Health Conditions in North Harlem,* pp. 16–17; *Fifteenth Census, 1930: Population* (Washington, D.C., 1933), II, 733–734; "The Negro in Harlem," p. 20.

49. ". . . The greatest need is the construction of model tenements. These should consist of one, two, three and four room apartments." "Modern Housing Needs," *The New York Age,* February 12, 1921, January 20, 1923, January 26, 1926, January 29, 1927; "The Negro in Harlem," p. 53; Eugene Kinckle Jones, "Negro Migration in New York State," *Opportunity,* IV (January 1926), 9.

50. Victor R. Daly, "The Housing Crisis in New York City," *The Crisis,* XXXI (December 1920), 61–62.

51. National Urban League, *Housing Conditions Among Negroes, New York City* (New York, 1915), *passim;* Ford, et al., *Slums and Housing,* p. 338.

52. "Very often it is found that there are two shifts." William Wilson to La Guardia, October 6, 1944, La Guardia Papers; *The New York Age,* March 12, 1921, February 26, 1927; "Along Rainbow Row," *The New York Times,* August 15, 1921, January 27, 1922; "Twenty-four Hundred Negro Families in Harlem," *passim;* Roscoe Conkling Bruce, "The Dunbar Apartment House: An Adventure in Community Building," *The Southern Workman,* LX (October 1931), 418.

53. *New York Herald Tribune,* February 12, 13, 1930.

54. "I promoted a weekly party, to get money to pay rent." "Boisterous rent parties, flooded with moonshine, are a quick and sure resource." "The Reminiscences of Benjamin McLaurin" (Oral History Research Office, Columbia University, 1960), p. 155; *The New York Age,* August 11, 1923, June 21, December 11, 1926; Clyde Vernon Kiser, *Sea Island to City* (New York, 1932), pp. 44–45.

55. Booker T. Washington, *Up from Slavery: An Autobiography* (New York 1959), pp. 122–123. Note the following statement of a recent study: "There are many cases in which migratory workers do not understand or properly use ordinary living facilities, such as toilets, showers, bedding, kitchen appliances, and garbage cans. The result has been unnecessary damage to property and needless expense for repairs." 87th Cong., 1st Sess., *Senate Report 1098* (1961), p. 8.

56. *The New York Age,* August 1, 1912, June 5, 1920, September 16, 1922, July 14, 1928; National Urban League, *Housing Conditions Among Negroes,* pp. 9–10; "The Negro in Harlem," p. 113; Eslanda Goode Robeson, *Paul Robeson: Negro* (London, 1930), p. 46.

57. Woofter, *et al., Negro Problems in Cities,* pp. 79, 84; "The Negro in Harlem," p. 53; Ernest W. Burgess, "Residential Segregation in American Cities," *The Annals,* CXL (November 1928), 105–115; Ford, *et al., Slums and Housing,* p. 749.

58. Owen R. Lovejoy, *The Negro Children of New York* (New York, 1932), p. 15.

59. *The New York Age,* October 28, 1922, January 17, 1925; *Housing Conditions Among Negroes, passim;* "Twenty-four Hundred Negro Families in Harlem," *passim.*

60. "I do not think I need to say that our problem of Harlem is one of the

most serious we have to face." Langdon W. Post (Chairman of New York City Housing Authority) to La Guardia, April 30, 1936, La Guardia Papers. "The Negro families of the West Harlem section have undoubtedly the most serious housing problem in the City." Ford, *et al., Slums and Housing,* p. 326. *The New York Times,* September 16, 1920, October 17, 23, 1921, April 22, 1922, January 17, June 13, 1925; *The New York Age,* February 28, August 8, 1925, January 9, 1926; "Preliminary Report on the Subject of Housing (1935)," La Guardia Papers.

61. "High Cost of Dying," *The New York Age,* February 25, 1928.

62. *Health Conditions in North Harlem, passim; The Negro Children of New York,* p. 22; "Fighting the Ravages of the White Plague Among New York's Negro Population," *Opportunity,* I (January 1923), 23–24; Dr. Louis R. Wright, "Cancer as It Affects Negroes," *ibid.,* VI (June 1928), 169–170, 187; Louis I. Dublin, "The Effect of Health Education on Negro Mortality," *Proceedings of the National Conference on Social Work, 1924* (Chicago, 1924), 274–279. Hereafter cited as PNCSW.

63. ". . . Syphilitic infection is one of the most fruitful causes of still-births, miscarriages, and early death of infants." New York Association for Improving the Condition of the Poor, *Health Work for Mothers and Children in a Colored Community* (New York, 1924), p. 3; "The Negro's Health Progress During the Last Twenty-five Years," *Weekly Bulletin of the Department of Health,* XV (June 12, 1926), 93–96; *Fifteenth Census, 1930: Population* (Washington, D.C., 1933), II, 959; E. K. Jones, "The Negro's Struggle for Health," *PNCSW, 1923* (Chicago, 1923), 68–72.

64. Adapted from Godea J. Drolet and Louis Werner, "Vital Statistics in the Development of Neighborhood Health Centers in New York City," *Journal of Preventive Medicine,* VI (January 1932), 69.

65. In 1920, 30.3 per cent of white women in the city worked, and 57.9 per cent of colored women were employed. *Fourteenth Census, 1920: Population* (Washington, D.C., 1923), IV, 367. Robert Morse Woodbury, *Causal Factors in Infant Mortality* (Washington, D.C., 1925); L. T. Wright, "Factors Controlling Negro Health," *The Crisis,* XLII (September 1935), 264–265, 280, 284; Mildred Jane Watson, "Infant Mortality in New York City, White and Colored, 1929–1936" (M.A. thesis, Columbia University, 1938); Charles Herbert Garvin, "White Plague and Black Folk," *Opportunity,* VIII (August 1930), 232–235.

66. For "voodoo" and "devil worship" among West Indians see Reid, *The Negro Immigrant,* pp. 48–49, 136–138.

67. ". . . Many [are] bringing with them their simple faith in roots, herbs, home remedies, [and are] imposed upon by unscrupulous venders of worthless . . . remedies." Dr. Peter Marshall Murray, "Harlem's Health," *Hospital Social Service,* XXII (October 1930), 309–313; C. V. Roman, "The Negro's Psychology and His Health," *PNCSW, 1924* (Chicago, 1924), 270–274; *Opportunity,* IV (July 1926), 206–207; *The Crisis,* XLII (August 1935), 243; *The New York Age,* September 23, 1922, February 17, July 21, August 11, 25, 1923, January 6, April 5, 1924, February 21, March 14, 1925, January 18, July 23, 1927.

68. Note the striking similarities between the medical and healing superstitions of urban Negroes in the twentieth century and those of slaves in the early nineteenth century. The following is a description of slave superstition by an ex-slave: "There is much superstition among the slaves. Many of them believe in what they call 'conjuration,' tricking, and witchcraft; and some of

them pretend to understand the art, and say that by it they can prevent their masters from exercising their will over their slaves. Such are often applied to by others, to give them power to prevent their masters from flogging them. The remedy is most generally some kind of bitter root; they are directed to chew it and spit toward their masters. . . . At other times they prepare certain kinds of powders, to sprinkle their masters' dwellings." *Narrative of the Life and Adventures of Henry Bibb, An American Slave, Written by Himself* (New York, 1849), pp. 25-31.

69. Beverly Smith, "Harlem—Negro City," *New York Herald Tribune,* February 11, 1930: Ira De Augustine Reid, "Let Us Prey!" *Opportunity* IV (September 1926), 274-278; Reverend James H. Robinson, *Road Without Turning: An Autobiography* (New York, 1950), 231.

70. *The New York Age,* February 19, 1927; *The New York Times,* September 24, 1919.

71. Zora Neale Hurston, *Dust Tracks on a Road* (Philadelphia, 1942), pp. 279-280.

72. *The New York Age,* January 15, 1927, February 9, 1929, August 23, 1930, August 8, September 19, 1931, July 23, 1932, August 26, 1933, September 1, 1934.

73. "A Wide Open Harlem," *ibid.,* September 2, 1922.

74. Committee of Fourteen, *Annual Reports,* 1914-1930; *The Crisis,* XXXVI (November 1929), 417-418; *The Messenger,* VI (January 1924), 14.

75. Langston Hughes, "Young Prostitute," *The Crisis,* XXVI (August 1923), 162.

76. "Gambling is popular in Harlem, but the big shots of the racket are white." Fiorello La Guardia, "Harlem: Homelike and Hopeful" (unpublished manuscript, La Guardia Papers), p. 9; "A Summary of Vice Conditions in Harlem," Committee of Fourteen, *Annual Report for 1928* (New York, 1929), 31-34; *The New York Times,* February 13, 1922; *The New York Age,* February 28, 1925, May 18, 1929. Although whites seemed to control most of Harlem vice, Virgin Islander Casper Holstein—well-known as a philanthropist and café owner—was reputed to be a head of the numbers racket.

77. "Harlem—The Bettor," *The New York Age,* March 7, 1925, November 6, 20, 1926, June 4, 1927, June 23, 1928; *The New York Times,* June 12, 1922, March 11, 1927; "New York: Utopia Deferred," *The Messenger,* VII (October, November 1925), 344-349, 370.

78. *The New York Age,* September 16, 1922, April 21, 1923; *New York Herald Tribune,* February 13, 1930; *The Messenger,* VI (August 1924) 247, 262.

79. Lovejoy, *The Negro Children of New York,* p. 37; *New York Herald Tribune,* February 12, 1930; Joint Committee on Negro Child Study in New York City, *A Study of Delinquent and Neglected Negro Children Before the New York City Children's Court* (New York, 1927).

80. Jacob Theobald, "Some Facts About P.S. 89, Manhattan," *The New York Age,* January 17, 1920; "Report of Subcommittee on Education," La-Guardia Papers; "The Problem of Education and Recreation," *ibid.;* "The Negro in Harlem," p. 73; Lovejoy, *The Negro Children of New York,* p. 22; *The New York Age,* March 12, 1921.

81. "Results of the Crime and Delinquency Study," La Guardia Papers; *The New York Age,* January 6, February 17, June 23, 1923, June 12, 1926, December 3, 1927, July 28, 1928, January 4, 1930. A white Harlem policeman, at a later date, wrote the following: "Every one of [us] is made to feel like a soldier

in an army of occupation. He is engulfed by an atmosphere of antagonism."
The Crisis, LII (January 1945), 16–17.
82. Lovejoy, *The Negro Children of New York,* p. 15; "The Negro in Harlem," p. 110; *The New York Age,* February 9, 1929; "The Reminiscences of George S. Schuyler" (Oral History Research Office, Columbia University, 1960), p. 232.

NOTES TO CHAPTER 10

1. Reverend Dr. Adam Clayton Powell, Sr., "The Church and Social Work," *Opportunity,* I (January 1923), 15.
2. Owen R. Lovejoy, *The Negro Children of New York* (New York, 1932), p. 29; Marion Forrester, "Young Folks Sit Up and Take Notice," *Opportunity,* XVI (January 1938), 23; Winfred B. Nathan, *Health Conditions in North Harlem, 1923–1927* (New York, 1932), p. 57.
3. Beverly Smith, "Harlem—Negro City," *New York Herald Tribune,* February 10, 12, 1930.
4. James H. Hubert, "Social Work in New York City," *Opportunity,* IV (March 1926), 102–103; National Urban League, *What You Need, Where to Find It, How to Use It* (New York, 1916).
5. *Opportunity,* I (January 1923), 32; *The New York Times,* June 22, 1920; *The New York Age,* July 2, 1921, July 22, 1922, March 31, 1923, March 27, 1926; *The Crisis,* XXXVI (February 1929), 52.
6. The New York Tuberculosis and Health Association had itself originated as a committee of the Charity Organization Society. Forrester B. Washington, "Health Work for Negro Children," *Proceedings of the National Conference on Social Work, 1925* (Chicago, 1925), 229–230; Henry O. Harding, "Health Opportunities in Harlem," *Opportunity,* IV (December 1926), 386–387.
7. Drs. Peyton F. Anderson and Jerome S. Peterson, "Warring Against Tuberculosis in Harlem," *The Crisis,* XLIV (November 1942), 356–357, 359, 366; *The New York Age,* July 21, 1923, October 1, 1927; *Opportunity,* V (December 1927), 379; Katherine Z. Wells, "Health Education in Harlem," *ibid.,* I (December 1923), 361–363.
8. Louis I. Dublin, "The Effect of Health Education on Negro Mortality," *Proceedings of the National Conference on Social Work, 1924* (Chicago, 1924), 274–279.
9. Peyton and Peterson, "Warring Against Tuberculosis in Harlem," *passim.;* James Ford, *et al., Slums and Housing: With Special Reference to New York City* (Cambridge, Mass., 1936), pp. 334–335.
10. For early nineteenth century examples see Robert Ernst, *Immigrant Life in New York City, 1825–1863* (New York, 1949), *passim.*
11. George R. Arthur, *Life on the Negro Frontier* (New York, 1934), p. 14; Owen R. Lovejoy, *The Negro Children of New York* (New York, 1932), p. 31.
12. Peyton and Peterson, "Warring Against Tuberculosis in Harlem," 359.
13. Elise Johnson McDougald, "The School and its Relation to the Vocational Life of the Negro," *Proceedings of the National Conference of Social Work, 1923* (Chicago, 1923), 415–418; Nathan, *Health Conditions in North Harlem,* p. 11; McDougald, "The Task of Negro Womanhood," in Locke, *The New Negro* (New York, 1925), pp. 369–382.
14. *The New York Age,* September 4, 18, 1920, September 8, 1923, August 8, 1925, December 11, 1926, May 5, 1928; Frank R. Crosswaith, "The Trade

Union Committee for Organizing Negroes," *The Messenger,* VII (August 1925), 296–297, V (July 1923), 758, VII (July 1925), 261.

15. Daisy Cargile Reed, "For Harlem Negro Children," *Opportunity,* VI (August 1928), 246–247; *The New York Age,* May 7, 1927, June 30, 1928, March 28, 1931; *The Crisis,* XXXII (September 1926), 242–243.

16. "The New Philanthropy," *Opportunity,* VIII (January 1929), 5, IV (August 1926), 263; *The New York Age,* May 8, 15, 1926.

17. Ford, *et al., Slums and Housing,* pp. 744–748.

18. Alfred Alexander, "The Housing of Harlem," *The Crisis,* XXXV (October 1928), 333–335, 351–353; Roscoe Conkling Bruce, "The Dunbar Apartment House: An Adventure in Community Building," *The Southern Workman,* LX (October 1931), 417–428.

19. *Architecture,* LIX (January 1929), 5–12; Ford, *et al., Slums and Housing,* p. 745; *The Crisis,* XXXIV (December 1927), 340; Arthur J. Gary, "Interview with Roscoe Conkling Bruce" (WPA research paper, Schomburg Collection).

20. Roscoe Conkling Bruce, "The Idea of Cooperative Housing," in the President's Conference on Home Building and Home Ownership, *Report of the Committee on Negro Housing* (Washington, D.C., 1925), 245–248; *The Crisis,* XXXVI (February 1929), 53; *The New York Age,* January 26, 1929.

21. City and Suburban Homes Company, *First Annual Report, 1896–1897* (New York, 1897), p. 1.

22. T. J. Woofter, *et al., Negro Problems in Cities* (New York, 1928), p. 164; "The Idea of Cooperative Housing," 246.

23. "The Dunbar National Bank," *The Crisis,* XXXV (November 1928), 370–371, 387; *The New York Age,* February 15, 1930.

24. "Mr. Rockefeller Quits Harlem," *The New York Age,* November 5, 1932, February 16, 1935, October 17, December 5, 1936, January 9, 1937, April 23, 30, May 28, 1938.

25. The Mayor's Commission on Conditions in Harlem, "The Negro in Harlem: A Report on Social and Economic Conditions Responsible for the Outbreak of March 19, 1935" (unpublished manuscript in La Guardia Papers, Municipal Archives), pp. 26, 65.

NOTES TO CHAPTER 11

1. *The New York Age,* September 4, 1913, March 27, 1917.

2. Samuel Michelson, "History of the Democratic Party in Harlem, 1916–1932" (WPA research paper, Schomburg Collection), p. 1; *The New York Times,* October 20, 1898, January 12, 1900.

3. *The New York Freeman,* July 3, 1886; Frances Blascoer, *Colored School Children in New York* (New York, 1915), p. 125.

4. *The New York Age,* November 12, 1887; *The New York Globe,* January 6, 20, 1883; Robert Zachariah Johnstone, "The Negro in New York—His Social Attainments and Prospects" (M.A. thesis, Columbia University, 1911), p. 37.

5. Anderson to Washington, November 14, 1914, Washington Papers, Box 75.

6. M. Rothman, "Chief Lee"; Mr. Robinson, "Biography of Edward (Chief) Lee" (WPA research papers, Schomburg Collection).

7. *The New York Age,* May 31, 1890.

8. *The New York Globe,* January 6, 1883.

9. *The Crisis,* XXII (October 1921), 264.

10. "The United Colored Democracy—A Resumé," *The New York State Contender,* October 11, 1929; Waring Cuney, "The United Colored Democracy" (WPA research paper, Schomburg Collection); *The New York Age,* March 16, 1929.

11. John L. Love, "The Potentiality of the Negro Vote, North and West," The American Negro Academy, *Occasional Paper, No. 11* (Washington, D.C., 1905), p. 66.

12. Negroes occasionally supported Democratic presidents in the late nineteenth century but no stable and regular party organization continued its existence beyond election time.

13. "List of New York Negroes Appointed or Elected to Public Office, 1900–1939"; James Gardner, "Brief History of Ferdinand Q. Morton of New York" (WPA research papers, Schomburg Collection); *The Crisis,* XI (February 1916), 167. There is a collection of newspaper clippings on Morton in the biographical files of the Schomburg Collection.

14. There is a folder of newspaper clippings on Anderson's life at the Schomburg Collection. Hereafter cited as "Clippings." Also see biographical sketch in *National Cyclopedia of the Colored Race* (Montgomery, Ala., 1919), I, 447.

15. "Clippings"; *The New York Age,* January 11, April 12, 1890, March 30, 1911.

16. James Weldon Johnson, *Along This Way* (New York, 1933), pp. 218–223.

17. Anderson to Washington, November 14, 1931, Box 64; Washington to Anderson, March 2, 1906, Box 2; Anderson to Washington, April 1, October 7, 1908, Box 38, Washington Papers.

18. "Clippings"; *The New York Age,* March 23, 1918; Colored Citizens of New York, *Testimonial for Charles W. Anderson* (New York, 1915), in James Weldon Johnson Memorial Collection, Yale University.

19. Anderson to Washington, January 30, 1908; Anderson to Scott, March 18, 1908, Washington Papers, Box 38.

20. "Anderson confirmed, heartiest congratulations." P. B. S. Pinchback to Washington, March 14, 1904, *ibid.,* Box 4.

21. Anderson to Washington, October 31, 1904, Box 1; May 27, October 21, 1907, Box 35; Anderson to Emmett J. Scott, October 23, 1915, Box 68; Scott to Anderson, December 7, 1915, *ibid.,* Box 9.

22. Washington to Anderson, July 22, 1904, Box 1; Anderson to Washington, May 27, October 21, November 19, 1907, Box 35; March 24, 1908, *ibid.,* Box 38.

23. Anderson to Washington, September 10, October 30, 1911, *ibid.,* Box 15.

24. Anderson to Scott, November 1, 1905, *ibid.,* Box 27.

25. Anderson to Washington or Scott, September 25, 27, 1905, Box 27; June 1, 1906, Box 2; February 9, 16, 21, July 25, 1907, Box 35; April 23, 1908, Box 38; July 17, 20, December 14, 1909, Box 43; January 11, July 7, August 1, November 4, 1910, Box 49; October 24, 1913, Box 64; Scott to Anderson, November 5, 1913, *ibid.,* Box 64.

26. "Our people throughout the country, who admire and respect you, and are looking to you, would be very greatly encouraged if you could see your way clear to appoint two or three of our representative colored men to re-

sponsible places. . . ." Washington to Whitman, August 24, 1915; Anderson to Washington, September 22, 1915, *ibid.*, Box 9.

27. Anderson to Washington, July 5, 1911, *ibid.*, Box 52. "The Reminiscences of Samuel J. Battle" (Oral History Research Office, Columbia University, 1960), pp. 38–39.

28. Anderson to Washington, March 17, 1915, Box 68; Anderson to Scott, July 31, 1915, Box 9; October 23, November 16, 1915, Box 68, Washington Papers. For a list of Wilson's removals in New York City see *The New York Age,* March 25, 1915.

29. W. E. B. DuBois to Oswald Garrison Villard, March 31, 1915, Johnson Collection.

30. Anderson to Scott, October 14, November 2, 1915, Box 9, Washington Papers.

31. "Clippings"; *The Crisis,* XIX (April 1920), 340; *Opportunity,* I (May 1923), 25; *The New York Age,* November 6, 1920, April 26, 1924, September 12, October 17, 1925; *The New York Times,* September 14, 1920. I have used the term "ward" in this chapter for stylistic reasons, although there were technically no wards in New York City.

32. *The New York Age,* April 10, July 4, 1920, May 31, April 7, 1923, September 19, 26, 1925; Anderson to Scott, October 14, 1915, Box 9, Washington Papers.

33. "Clippings"; Johnson, *Along This Way,* pp. 218–223; *The New York Age,* April 22, 1933, July 14, 1934, January 19, 1935, February 5, 19, 1938.

34. John Albert Morsell, "The Political Behavior of Negroes in New York City" (Ph.D. dissertation, Columbia University, 1951), p. 25. Unfortunately, much of this study of Negro politics is questionable because the author uses statistics for Harlem's Assembly Districts as a basis for analysis—and these AD's included many white voters.

35. *Ibid.*, pp. 32–35; *The New York Age,* November 9, 1889, October 3, 1910, June 14, 1930.

36. As Assembly District returns include white voters it is necessary to analyze election district statistics in order to obtain accurate information on Negro voting in the 1920's. Election districts usually cover one or two blocks —and their boundaries within the Assembly District are often changed. In the 1920's election districts in the Nineteenth and Twenty-first AD's were altered five or six times. It was not possible, therefore, to get a uniform set of returns from the *same* districts throughout the decade. I selected eight ED's from the center of the ghetto at each election (from slides of districts in the New York City Municipal Library), however, and these sections were *at least* 90 per cent Negro at all times. All the following returns, and those in the body of the chapter, are drawn from the *Official Canvass of Votes* published annually in *The City Record* and the *Annual Reports of the Board of Elections:*

NEGRO PRESIDENTIAL VOTE, IN PERCENTAGES, 1920–1936

	Republican	Democratic	Other
1920	97.6	2.4	—
1924	85.3	11.5	3.2
1928	70.8	29.2	—
1932	47.4	50.3	2.3
1936	14.4	84.6	1.0

37.   NEGRO GUBERNATORIAL VOTE, 1920–1932

	Republican	Democratic	Other
1920	62.2	37.8	—
1922	34.5	65.5	—
1924	63.7	36.3	—
1926	58.6	41.4	—
1928	68.8	31.2	—
1930	53.1	45.7	1.2
1932	42.3	55.7	2.0

38.   NEGRO MAYORALTY VOTE, 1921–1932

	Republican	Democratic	Other
1921	26.4	73.6	—
1925	52.9	46.1	—
1929	56.5	37.4	6.1
1932	42.4	55.5	2.1

39. James Weldon Johnson, "The Gentleman's Agreement and the Negro Vote," *The Crisis,* XXVIII (October 1924), 264.

40. Hylan to Joseph S. McLane, October 26, 1921; Hylan to George E. Taylor, July 27, 1925; *Daily Star,* July 12, 1921, all in Hylan Papers, Municipal Archives.

41. Morton to John F. Smith, secretary to mayor, March 26, 1924, January 12, 1925, Hylan Papers; "N.A.A.C.P. Efforts for Negroes in New York City Hospitals," memorandum in La Guardia Papers.

42. This information is derived from clippings, speeches and memoranda in the Hylan and Walker Papers. Hylan was apparently the first mayor to keep a separate file on Harlem and Negroes. Also see J. S. McLane to Hylan, October 25, 1921; Hylan to Hon. John M. Parker, December 23, 1922; John R. Shillady to Hylan, February 21, 1918; Hylan to James H. Hubert, no date; *The New York Times,* November 20, 1923, August 19, Septmeber 4, 1925; *The New York Age,* December 4, 1926, February 4, 1928.

43. "The Life Work of Edward Austin Johnson," *The Crisis,* XL (April 1933), 81.

44. *Who's Who in Colored America,* 1927 (New York, 1927), pp. 105–106; Johnson, *Light Ahead for the Negro* (New York, 1904), pp. 17–19, 80, 88, 118.

45. *The New York Age,* August 23, 1924.

46. *The New York Age,* September 7, 1929, June 14, 1930.

47. *General Laws of the State of New York, 1918* (New York, 1919), pp. 44–45, 319.

48. Arthur W. Little, *From Harlem to the Rhine: The Story of New York's Colored Volunteers* (New York, 1936); Emmett J. Scott, *Scott's Official History of the American Negro in the World War* (Chicago, 1919), chap. 15; Addie W. Hunton and Kathryn M. Johnson, *Two Colored Women with the American Expeditionary Forces* (Brooklyn, 1920), pp. 69–72; *The New York Age,* May 25, 1918, February 14, 1919, February 28, 1931.

49. *General Laws of New York, 1930* (New York, 1931), pp. 215–216; *Opportunity,* VIII (December 1930), 380; *The New York Times,* July 30,

1917; *The New York Age,* February 14, May 22, 1920, December 18, 1926, January 18, April 19, May 3, 17, September 27, 1930; Francis E. Rivers, "Negro Judges in Harlem," *The Crisis,* XXXVII (November 1930), 377, 393.

50. *Who's Who in Colored America, 1938–1940* (Brooklyn, 1940), p. 383; "Ferdinand Q. Morton," *The Crisis,* XXX (July 1925), 115–116; *The New York Times,* April 3, 1925; *The New York Age,* May 28, 1927, February 8, 22, August 2, October 11, 18, 25, 1930, March 16, April 6, 13, 1935, August 6, 1938; Harlem Committee on Political Facts, *Whom the Gods Would Destroy—They First Make Newspaper Managers!* (New York, 1933?), p. 2, in La Guardia Papers; Edgar T. Rouzeau, "Harlem Seeks Political Leadership," *The Crisis,* XLII (September 1935), 268, 274.

51. *The New York Age,* April 5, 1924, August 7, 14, September 25, October 9, 1926.

52. *Ibid.,* July 24, September 11, 1926, September 8, November 3, 1928, August 19, 1929.

53. Abraham Grenthal, "Grenthal Advocates Extension of Rent Laws," *Harlem Magazine,* XIV (December 1925), 11, 22; *The New York Age,* February 9, August 16, 1924, January 3, 10, 1925, March 27, 1926, February 26, April 9, 16, June 24, 1927.

54. Public letter of Moore to Grenthal, *The New York Age,* July 25, 1929, March 3, 24, 1928.

55. "Grenthal on His Political Deathbed," *Advance* in *ibid.,* August 17, 1929; "Why Grenthal Should Go," February 25, August 18, 1928, March 9, June 22, August 31, 1929.

56. *Ibid.,* June 22, July 6, August 24, 31, September 14, 21, 1929.

57. "The Reminiscences of Martin C. Ansorge" (Oral History Research Office, Columbia University, 1949), *passim;* "The Reminiscences of Samuel S. Koenig" (Oral History Research Office, Columbia University, 1950), *passim; Official Canvass of the Votes* for returns in congressional elections.

58. "Notes of D. Macon Webster for Speech at Protest Meeting" (manuscript in Schomburg Collection).

NOTES TO EPILOGUE

1. HARYOU, *Youth in the Ghetto: A Study of the Consequences of Powerlessness and a Blueprint for Change* (New York, 1964); Columbia University Bureau of Applied Social Research, *A Harlem Almanac* (New York, 1964).

2. *The New York Age,* January 1, 1927.

3. Carl Van Doren, "The Negro Renaissance," *The Century Magazine,* III (March 1926), 637.

4. Gilbert Seldes, "The Negro's Songs," *The Dial,* LXXX (March 1926), 247–251.

5. As the Garvey movement has been discussed at length and competently in a number of sources I have avoided any lengthy analysis of it here. See: E. David Cronin, *Black Moses: The Story of Marcus Garvey and the Universal Negro Improvement Association* (Madison, Wisc., 1955); E. U. Essien-Udom, *Black Nationalism: A Search for an Identity in America* (Chicago, 1962); Essien-Udom, "The Nationalist Movements of Harlem," *Freedomways,* III (Summer 1963), 335–342; Richard B. Moore, "Africa-Conscious Harlem." *ibid.,* 315–334.

6. Langston Hughes, *The Big Sea* (New York, 1940), p. 240.

7. *Ibid.,* p. 81.

8. "The Reminiscences of George S. Schuyler" (Oral History Research Office, Columbia University, 1960), p. 208.

9. Claude McKay, *A Long Way From Home* (New York, 1937), chap. XXVII, *passim*, and *Home to Harlem* (1927); "Harlem: Mecca of the New Negro," *The Survey,* LIII (March 1, 1925), 629–724; Alain Locke, ed., *The New Negro: An Interpretation* (New York, 1925).

10. Alain Locke and Lothrop Stoddard, "Should the Negro Be Encouraged to Cultural Equality?" *The Forum,* LXXVIII (October 1927), 508; Locke, "Enter the New Negro," *The Survey,* LIII (March 1, 1925), 631–634; Locke, "Negro Contributions to America," *The World Tomorrow,* XII (June 1929), 255–257.

11. *The New York Times,* January 26, 1925.

12. James Weldon Johnson to Carl Van Vechten, envelope dated March 6, 1927. James Weldon Johnson Collection of Negro Arts and Letters, Yale University.

13. Hughes, *The Big Sea,* p. 228.

14. Johnson to Van Vechten, envelope dated March 6, 1927. Johnson Collection.

15. See, for example, Robert W. Bagnall, "The Divine Right of Race," *The World Tomorrow,* VI (May 1923), 149; Herbert A. Miller, "Democracy and Diversity," *ibid.,* VII (June 1924), 190–191; Robert E. Park, *The Immigrant Press and Its Control* (New York, 1922); Horace M. Kallen, *Culture and Democracy in the United States: Studies in the Group Psychology of the American Peoples* (New York, 1924).

16. "The Reminiscences of Bruno Lasker" (Oral History Research Office, Columbia University, 1957), p. 242 and chap. IX.

17. *The Annals of the American Academy of Political and Social Science,* CXL (November 1928).

18. *The World Tomorrow,* VI (May 1923) and IX (April 1926).

19. Laurence Buermeyer, "The Negro Spirituals and American Art," *Opportunity,* IV (May 1926), 158–159, 167; Harry Alan Potamkin, "African Sculpture," *ibid.,* VI (May 1929), 139–140, 147; James Weldon Johnson to Carl Van Vechten, envelope dated February 16, 1931, Johnson Collection; A. M. Chirgwin, "The Vogue of the Negro Spiritual," *The Edinburgh Review,* CCXLVII (January 1928), 57–74; Darius Milhaud, "The Jazz Band and Negro Music," *The Living Age,* CCCXXIII (October 18, 1924), 169–173.

20. Langston Hughes, "The Negro Artist and the Racial Mountain," *The Nation,* CXXII (June 23, 1926), 693; Charles S. Johnson, "The Balance Sheet: Debits and Credits in Negro-White Relations," *The World Tomorrow,* XI (January 1928), 13–16; Ernest Boyd, "Readers and Writers," *The Independent,* CXVI (January 16, 1926), 77; George Jean Nathan, "The Wail of the Negro," *The American Mercury,* XVIII (September 1929), 114–116; Claude McKay to James Weldon Johnson, April 30, 1928, Johnson Collection.

21. "The New White Man," *The World Tomorrow,* X (March 1927), 124–125.

22. Rudolph Fisher, "The Caucasian Storms Harlem," *The American Mercury,* XI (May 1927), 396.

23. Eugene Gordon, "The Negro's Inhibitions," *The American Mercury,* XIII (February 1928), 159–165; Clement Wood, "Hosea Before the Rotary Club," *The World Tomorrow,* VIII (July 1925), 209–210; Herman Keyserling, "What the Negro Means to America," *The Atlantic Monthly,* CXLIV (October 1929), 444–447; Joseph Wood Krutch, "Black Ecstasy," *The Nation,*

CXXV (October 26, 1927), 456–458; George S. Schuyler, "Blessed Are the Sons of Ham," *ibid.*, CXXIV (March 23, 1927), 313–315; "Black Voices," *ibid.*, CXIX (September 17, 1924), 278.

24. George Chester Morse, "The Fictitious Negro," *The Outlook and Independent*, CLII (August 21, 1929), 648.

25. McKay, *A Long Way From Home*, p. 322.

26. Beverly Smith, "Harlem—Negro City," *New York Herald Tribune*, February 10, 1930.

27. "The Reminiscences of Carl Van Vechten" (Oral History Research Office, Columbia University, 1960), p. 196.

28. *The Crisis*, XXXIX (September 1932), 293; *The New York Age*, August 6, 1927. For a survey of Harlem cabarets see Archie Seale, "The Rise of Harlem as an Amusement Center," *The New York Age*, November 2, 1935; and obituary of Moe Gale, owner of the Savoy Ballroom, *The New York Times*, September 3, 1964.

29. "The Slumming Hostess," *The New York Age*, November 6, 1926.

30. "Giving Harlem a Bad Name," "Is Harlem to be a Chinatown?", "In the Negro Cabarets," "Nordic Invasion of Harlem," *ibid.*, September 5, 1922, October 27, 1923, July 23, August 6, 1927; Committee of Fourteen, *Annual Report for 1926* (New York, 1927), pp. 31–32; and *Annual Report for 1928* (New York, 1929), pp. 31–34.

31. "The Reminiscences of Carl Van Vechten," p. 205.

32. Carl Van Vechten, *Nigger Heaven* (New York, 1926), *passim.*

33. "The Negro in Art—A Symposium," *The Crisis*, XXXI (March 1926), 219–220; *ibid.*, XXXIV (September 1927), 248.

34. Chester T. Crowell, "The World's Largest Negro City," *The Saturday Evening Post*, CXCVIII (August 8, 1925), 9; "The Caucasian Storms Harlem," 398.

35. "I am to be hostess at the Dark Tower Sunday Night April 21st, and I thought probably you and your friends would like to be present. . . ." A'Lelia Walker to Max Ewing, April 18, 1929. Ewing Collection, Yale University. A'Lelia Walker was the daughter and heir of Madame C. J. Walker. Eric R. Walrond, "The Black City," *The Messenger*, VI (January 1924), 14; *The New York Age*, October 29, 1927.

36. Paul Oliver, *Bessie Smith* (New York, 1959), p. 45. Ermine Kahn, "Lenox Avenue—Saturday Night," *The World Tomorrow*, VIII (November 1925), 337.

37. *The New York Age*, November 27, 1926.

38. Hubert H. Harrison, "The Significance of Lulu Bell," *Opportunity*, IV (July 1926), 228–229: *The Crisis*, XXXII (May 1926), 34; "Black Harlem Dramatized," *The Literary Digest*, C (March 16, 1929), 21–24; James Weldon Johnson to Carl Van Vechten, envelope dated April 4, 1930, Johnson Collection.

39. Quoted in Diana N. Lockard, "The Negro on the Stage in the Nineteen Twenties" (M.A. thesis, Columbia University, 1960), p. 38.

40. "The Fictitious Negro," 649; Charles S. Johnson, "Public Opinion and the Negro," *Proceedings of National Conference in Social Work, 1923* (Chicago, 1924), 497–502.

41. The most glaring exception to this generalization is Langston Hughes.

42. "Harlem had been too long the nighttime playground of New York. . . ." Alain Locke, "La Guardia and Harlem," manuscript in La Guardia Papers. Locke, "Harlem: Dark Weather-Vane," *Survey Graphic*, XXV (Au-

gust 1936), 457–462, 493–495. Quotations in the above text are from the manuscript of this article in the La Guardia Papers. Emphasis added.

43. Wallace Thurman, "Harlem Facets," *The World Tomorrow*, X (November 1927), 466; E. Franklin Frazier, "Negro Harlem: An Ecological Study," *The American Journal of Sociology*, XLIII (July 1937), 86; Hughes, *The Big Sea*, p. 247; George W. Harris, "Harlem Gets a New Jail," *The Nation*, CXXXIII (September 9, 1931), 258; "Negro Children in New York," *ibid.*, CXXXIV (May 25, 1932), 588.

Index

WORLD TALES

FOR CREATIVE DRAMATICS AND STORYTELLING

PRENTICE-HALL INTERNATIONAL, INC.
London • Tokyo • Sydney • Paris

PRENTICE-HALL OF CANADA, LTD.

PRENTICE-HALL DE MEXICO, S.A.

WORLD TALES

FOR CREATIVE DRAMATICS AND STORYTELLING

BURDETTE S. FITZGERALD
University of California, Los Angeles

1962

Prentice-Hall, Inc.   Englewood Cliffs, N.J.

PREFACE

This anthology presents a collection of world folk-tales that may be used for creative dramatics and storytelling. The tales, born in the spoken word of the entertainers of long ago, are readily adaptable as rich material for the creative drama leader and the storyteller of today.

Storytelling is one of the world's oldest entertainment forms. The old "vaquero" of Mexico or the "Outa Karel" of Africa were the actors of the past, who night after night brought to the eager dwellers of mountain forests, desert sands, or rocky sea coasts the adventurous, the fanciful, the excitement of the unknown—the story! Centuries have passed since these forefathers of dramatic literature told their stories, but their tales have been handed down by word of mouth and preserved as literature for the world by the scholars of folk-lore. They are a valuable source of material to be enjoyed through reading, telling, listening, and enacting.

There has been little attempt to alter or change the tales in this volume. If they are to be true to the cultures they represent, the original mode of expression must be preserved. It is for this reason that tales from certain cultures could not be included. These omissions are dictated by a realization that the cruelty of some ethnic customs, such as the infanticide of the Eskimo tribes, or the cannibalism of the races of southern Oceania, are subjects unsuitable for presentation to children. When material was altered or portions of stories deleted, it was done to heighten the dramatic structure of the plot or to eliminate unnecessary details. In some of the stories incidents must be re-arranged, telescoped, or eliminated in preparing a dramatization, and this procedure is fully explained.

Chapter 1 offers to the leader of creative dramatics and storytelling a consideration of the concept, approach, and methods applicable to the use of these stories. Suggestions are given for the selection, preparation, and telling of the stories, and the process of developing the educational values of the dramatic art is outlined with specific examples of the various activities that are helpful in stimulating the creativity of leader and child.

In this anthology the parent will find stories to read or tell to his children that will provide an opportunity for shared pleasure in the delight of the tale and the resulting thoughtful commentary or creative play. The recreation director will find a variety of stories for all ages which will assist in solving the ever-present group instability problem of the playground. The teacher, in a church, community theatre, or school, will find stories appropriate not only for storytelling and teaching creative dramatics, but also as a supplement and aid to the understanding of world cultures.

Although the purpose of this collection is to present material and methods for the storyteller and the creative dramatics leader, these stories have been selected for *children,* and their interests, desires, and likings have been a primary consideration. Here are fairies and leprechauns, ogres and giants, trolls and elves, witches and princesses, robbers and princes. Fantasy and actuality share the stage. Here are achievements and successes, punishments and disappointments. The right of the child to be shown life as it really is has been acknowledged. The constant struggle for existence, the adventure of life, the correction of wrong and the resulting justice, the beauty and joys of the fanciful and the factual are here in these folk-tales—for the children.

Acknowledgment is made to Frances Wishard, Curator, Human Relations Area Files in the library of the University of Southern California, whose assistance was invaluable in collecting part of the material for this anthology. Acknowledgment is also made to the library of the University of California, Los Angeles, for access to the folk-tale collection.

Grateful appreciation is given to June Coffing for her assistance in compiling the manuscript.

Burdette S. Fitzgerald

CONTENTS

1 CREATIVE DRAMATICS, 1

MOTIVATIONS · THE STORY · THE PLAYING OF THE STORY DRAMATIC KNOWLEDGE · MOVEMENT · CHARACTERIZA- TION DIALOGUE · DRAMATIC AWARENESS · DEVELOPING THE STORY INTO THE PLAY · CONCLUSION

2 AFRICA, 15

3 ASIA, 41

4 AUSTRALIA AND
THE SOUTHWEST PACIFIC, 75

5 EUROPE, 102

WORLD TALES

FOR CREATIVE DRAMATICS AND STORYTELLING

1
CREATIVE DRAMATICS

Creative dramatics is the theatre of the child, because it is a dramatic art form that allows the participants freedom of mind and movement. They are not restricted by the written drama, with the playwright's conception of dialogue, characterization, and action. Given a stimulus, such as a story, the children in a group act it out, using their own interpretation, words, and actions. It is their creative activity—their drama. Since they are not producing a play for an audience, they are not concerned with the techniques or disciplines of the adult stage. Their actions occur from a natural impulsive feeling; their stage is wherever they may be at the *moment*. It is this "moment," when thoughts are created and exchanged, when the emotions and inner feelings of people are sincerely felt, that is the child's drama. A group of twelve-year-olds, who had progressed to being allowed on the stage, and had learned terms and techniques for producing a play, were one day told the story of Ivan in "The Deserted Mine." As they developed the escape from the caved-in mine, they became so absorbed in the treacherous flight to safety that they forgot the stage completely and used the entire auditorium floor for the dark narrow passages of the tunnel. Adult standards were cast aside; they did not have to stay behind the proscenium arch, for there was no audience to inhibit or restrict their movements. This is the child's creative drama.

The role of the adult in creative dramatics is that of a leader who gives the proper stimulation for creative thinking. This process of the mind develops the ideas for active self-expression by the players. The leader prepares the mind or sets the mood, presents material for thinking, gives the opportunity for complete freedom of response, and guides intellectual appraisal. The purpose is to excite the mental and emotional state that manifests itself in bodily feelings and actions. Drama which presents the various and complex reactions of life readily offers an art form that challenges the mind. The leader who uses it wisely will achieve for the child and himself a feeling of self-confidence that comes only from the creative inner self.

The height and depth of this dramatic experience for the child depends first upon the leader's ability to establish the proper atmosphere and material for stimulation of the imagination. It is the imaginative mind that produces the various art forms. This is especially true of the drama, which is concerned with the portrayal of the feelings and actions of others. To stimulate the imagination, so that it will become active and creative, is the initial goal of the leader. Just as the teacher of the adult uses emotional and sensory devices, pantomimes and improvisations to train the mind and body, the leader of children also uses motivations to stir the mind and body of the child. Some of these motivating methods are dramatic play, imaginative situations and objects, and pantomimes.

MOTIVATIONS

Dramatic play is used primarily with the younger child, as it is a group activity based upon familiar experience that allows the child to just "be" in a situation, doing whatever he wants. A visit to the beach or going on a picnic are popular situations. The preparation for playing is simple. Certain plans are made, such as the location of the beach, or what they are taking on the picnic. As they play, they are recalling the memory of a past experience, using their imaginations to relive and extend those feelings and actions. A beginning class of six-year-olds took a walk around the room one day on the way to the planned picnic at the beach, and stopped to look at an imaginary tree. There were many faces looking up, but very little comment. On the way home from the beach, after they had dug in the sand, hunted shells, swam, ate their lunch, and listened to a story, the room became full of trees, flowers, cats, dogs, squirrels, and even a snake. The creative mood had been established.

As the child learns first through his five senses—hearing, seeing, smelling, tasting, and touching—it is natural that these abilities be used for beginning motivations. As he looks at the sky, the child might be asked what he sees, and if he can imagine anything else that might be there. A smell from the kitchen might be. . . . The chocolate drink which was going to be so good is. . . . A sound in the night storm is. . . . The sound of music suggests. . . . Not only does the child tell what his mind has created by the imagery of words, but he shows as well. Tommy's mind began to work one day as he sat looking skeptically at the rest of the class, which was having a good time feeling the gooey, sticky substance they imagined was on their hands. They were saying it was gum, tar, and honey, when he suddenly smiled and presented us with the best taffy pull ever beheld. When I commented upon the candy, he put his hands behind his back and said,

"It's not here, it's home." The imaginative moment of creative freedom was gone, but became much easier to arouse the next time. Motivational material based on the reaction of the senses is unlimited for the creative leader.

Imaginative situations or objects allow a wide range for development of the creative mind. A trip in a glass ball to the bottom of the ocean presents many ideas of sight and sound that may be formed into a story. Magic shoes may travel around the world in a few minutes, or they may go home with the child, as was once requested by a little girl. The telescope may see the faraway palace of the North Wind or the nest of the bird in the near-by tree. The floor of the room may become a lake, the desert sands, or a mountain top. Chairs can suddenly become the homes for sleeping elves, who will be awakened by the tap of their king's stick. There is a happy excitement about the imaginative land created by the child. The leader supplies the point of departure for the journey, going along only to encourage and stimulate further expansion.

The use of pantomime (action or gestures without words as a means of expression) generally enters into these creative situations, since it is largely by *doing* that the young child first expresses himself. The skilled leader, therefore, uses the art of bodily action as another form of motivation. An example is the act of eating something, which is a favorite with children. An imaginary tray holding things to eat may be passed around. Each child takes whatever he wants and holds it in his hands until all have been served. One by one they eat what they have taken, and the rest of the class tries to guess what it is. The one who guesses correctly gets the next turn. This becomes a game, which is what the pantomime should be in the first attempts. Other activities include showing what you like to do in the summer time; selecting a toy; finding an object you are looking for in the room; and any sports activity. After beginning experiences of this kind, the leader may introduce the next step in pantomimic action: feeling. The action should show how a person feels while he is doing it; the game of eating could be extended to find out if the person likes or dislikes what he eats. This opens up a variety of participation activities to stimulate the emotional state of mind and the physical response. If the movement is not accurate in detail, it is of no concern in this motivational period. The art of pantomime comes at a later stage in the child's progress. The purpose here is the stimulation of the imagination.

The selection of the motivation to be used will depend upon the age level of the group, the purpose or objective of the leader's planned session, or the story that is to be told. Whether the method used is dramatic play, sensory concepts, imaginary situations, pantomimic action, or other devices from the resources of the leader, such as music and rhythms, the result should be that the mind of the child is prepared for more extensive creativity.

THE STORY

When the imagination has been set to work, the happy recreation atmosphere established, it is time for the story, which may be either read or told. The tale will be enhanced by telling rather than reading; the responsive faces of the children will show this to be the preferred method.

Selection of the tale should be based primarily on finding something in the story of vital interest to the teller, as well as to the children. It is assumed that the leader of a children's class in creative dramatics will be aware of the interests, ages, and comprehensive abilities of the children concerned. To be able to see clearly the word pictures, to feel the intensity of the emotions of the people in the story, and to recreate them, requires an inner will that responds with understanding and a genuine liking for the story. It is the power of the spoken word that touches the feelings of children. A powerless teller will never reach the soul of the child. When the story is told with the self-possession that uses the imagination in recreating a work of art, there is beauty in the creative force . . . and there is response in the faces of the listeners. Whether it be fact or fantasy, the leader must enjoy the story in order to tell it with this result.

After selecting a story that will appeal, it should be carefully read for words that are unfamiliar, for secondary characters and sub-plots that may slow up the main action of the story, and for long passages of description. These should be eliminated, as the straight line of action is important in telling a story. It is the action that produces suspense, which is the keynote of listening to a story or play.

In preparing the story, it is helpful to memorize the structure of sequences of action. The entire story should not be memorized word for word because, if the mind refuses to remember, the story-teller is lost. The story must be so much a part of the teller that it flows like conversation. The chronological order of events in the story, and also the first and last sentences, should be memorized. This gives the teller a base around which he can weave the mental pictures through the imagery of the words. These should be selected carefully, since children like sensory impressions, color words, and the repetition of words. Each word is important in this art; there must be an economy which eliminates such unnecessary terms as ah, uh, so, and well-a. When dialogue is used, it should be placed in the present tense, which makes it more dramatic. If the words of the author are of a specific style, as many of them as possible should be mastered. The story should be practiced out loud; the sound of the voice is quite different from the quiet thought of mind.

When telling the story, a circle or semi-circle of children is the best physical arrangement, since eye contact is essential. It is easier to make each child feel the story is directed at him if he is at eye level. The approach must be enthusiastic and positive, with a quiet persuasiveness that lets the children know the story is for them. The voice quality should be pleasing, gestures used only when related to the story, and interpretation heightened by use of the dramatic techniques of the pause, variety of vocal pitch, and varying rates of speed.

Children do not need to have the story explained. The principal purpose of literature is to touch the feelings of the child, and to let him see the ideals, struggles, and values of life. Stories of literary quality will have this effect. Many of the folk tales emphasize the moral; the fable bases its form upon it. It is in acting out the story that the values of life will be emphasized through the dynamics of the living play.

THE PLAYING OF THE STORY

The leader guides the children in planning the part of the story to be acted by asking leading questions based upon the following: 1) the main points in the scene; 2) the setting; 3) the people in the scene; 4) general ideas for dialogue; 5) the necessary properties. After these have been discussed, with the leader clarifying and summarizing the ideas in order to give the players security of feeling, the parts are chosen. The leader must have an organized plan for selecting the children who are going to play, as every child must be given an opportunity. One simple method is to begin at one end of the semi-circle or row, allowing each child to choose the part he wants to play. The next time, the leader starts wherever he left off.

After the playing, evaluation or positive critical thinking about what has just happened takes place. This is the time for appreciation of what they have watched or done, and the time for suggestions for improvement. The scene is repeated again with different children playing the parts. It may be repeated a number of times; the leader extends the abilities of the children in dramatic art as the need and opportunities arise.

DRAMATIC KNOWLEDGE

As the children progress in confident freedom of expression, the leader guides them into using their abilities on a wider scope. Expansion and deepening of capabilities is part of the learning process in creative dramatics. It is accomplished, as in the stimulation of the imagination, through motivational devices, experiences which will make them more aware of other creative possibilities. These are not to be confused with acting techniques such as "sharing a scene" or "dressing the stage," which are theatrical disciplines for staging a play. Just as the adult actor in his training grows in bodily control, sensitivity to the feeling from within, and the mastery of the interpretive word, so the child learns more accurate movement, a greater power to express his feelings and the thoughts of others, and a more fluent speech skill.

The leader who is perceptive and accurately responsive to the children will know when to apply these experiences. The philosophy of children's librarians, "The right book for the right child at the right time," may well be used here. The creative spirit may be deadened if they are not applied at the right time. The leader must pick the moment when the children present a suggestion, question, or answer which opens the way for further exploration of the idea. As the impetus has come from them, there is no thought of inadequacy, disapproval, or unwanted direction which can close the creative mind. Generally, opportunities will arise during the evaluation period, when the children are discussing what they have just watched or played. In this atmosphere of talking over what can be done to improve the scene, the leader suggests things that will aid in understanding the situation. It is the right time for the intellectual appraisal.

MOVEMENT

The movements of children are delightful to watch; they are uninhibited and swing with abandon. In beginning work in creative drama, children tend to move together, to imitate, to crowd together in a small area. This is particularly true of the younger children. A favorite place to play is under the table. Such stories as "The Cat and the Mice" lend their settings to such a situation, but the need for movement around the room by the mice in this story makes it an excellent one for widening the concept of use of space. "How can the mice file past the cat if the table is used for the home?" is a leading question for the discussion. Exercises, such as movement to music, the large physical actions of horses, airplanes, kangaroos, and birds are some of the ways awareness of space and freedom of movement may be realized.

Although bodily action is easier for the young child than the spoken word, accuracy is still lacking. As the child progresses in his ability to act out a part, he needs to grow in this ability. The mother in "Salting the

Puddin' " must make the puddin' and place it in a believable manner. The actions must be detailed and correct for the rest of the plot. This fact, discovered by the children themselves, opens up the field of pantomime. If pantomimic exercises have been used earlier, they may be used again with the emphasis placed upon clarity and exactness of movement. There is a need to know immediately and convincingly what the person in the play is doing. Incidents from the story may be concentrated upon until the actions of everyone can be believed. The dishing up of the puddin' must be accurate, and the first bite must be real in order to give reason for the reaction of feeling that follows. A story such as "Juan[1] Goes to Heaven" presents the problem of opening the gates of Heaven, which gives an opportunity for the study of opening and closing doors in pantomime. Practice in detail of body movement is essential for dramatic growth.

CHARACTERIZATION

Development of the understanding of characterization may be encouraged through the asking of leading questions as to how the person feels, looks, talks, walks, and the reasons for his behaviour. After the discussion, a group activity should be presented, such as everyone sitting in his throne as the mighty King Kunz in "The Story of Kunz and His Shepherd," or dancing as the cats in "Another Haunted Mill," or as the body of armed men moving toward the Castle of Dunbar in the story, "Black Agnace of Dunbar." Following the group activity, there can be individual attempts at characterization, provided the leader knows that the children are ready for single flight. In order to deepen the intensity of feeling in the character of a little girl who was glued magically to her chair, a group of seven-year-olds was allowed to show individually what each one would do. All of the group of twenty struggled violently to get off the chair, many crying for their mothers. Three of them went beyond this initial step. The first asked for a pair of scissors to cut her dress and so get off. The second picked up the chair, went to an imaginary telephone, and phoned the magician; the third screamed, "Help! Help! Get me off this bloomin' thing!"

Absorption in the belief of the character is the drama of the child. Sincerity of feeling that can be sustained is the important part of characterization. This will not happen in the beginning, since children are easily distracted by the unusual, the funny, or the actions of others. As the child learns that each mood must not be broken as long as he is playing, his

[1] For the pronunciation of foreign names or terms, see the Glossary at the back of the book.

powers of concentration increase. One afternoon a group of sixth graders was playing out a story about a king. The boy who was the page held an imaginary tray in his two hands. The door of the room opened and a boy (not in the play) walked up to him and gave him a note. Instead of being distracted, he kept it in his hand and carried the tray across the room to the king. After bowing himself out of the room, he opened the note. This shows understanding of the feelings of others, and the ability to forget oneself in the pleasure of being someone else.

Short improvised scenes based upon the emotions or feelings of people may be used to train the will to respond when the imagination calls on it. Group situations, such as being cold, hot, thirsty, lonely, frightened, or happy, may be the mood around which a scene is played. Older groups like to develop their own plot line, after being given just the feeling. As characterization depends upon the inner-self and sensitivity to the understanding of a person's driving force, the development of this dramatic awareness will require a long period of time. The leader's encouragement is especially essential in intensifying this ability.

DIALOGUE

The child's capabilities in the art of dialogue run all the way from very little (in the very young) to too much dialogue in the advanced. The problem of encouraging the child to think and respond to the situation by speaking is difficult until he has become completely free. The child who can react as did the little girl of six who was playing the mother in the story of "The Three Bears" has learned this significant part of life. The bears had returned to find their porridge eaten and their chairs sat in. When the little bear cried, "Someone's broken my chair," the Mother said immediately, "Papa bear, you better fix that right away!"

It is only by first giving the child situations of group activity with a minimum of dialogue that the foundation for later creative powers in the spoken word will be created. Short exercises in situations that are familiar to them, such as an argument as to whose doll or train it is or buying an ice cream or a pair of shoes from the store, will aid in this development. A story such as "Ashiepattle and the Troll" is excellent material, not only strong in actions but so emotionally strong that the dialogue is easily remembered. To encourage original dialogue the leader may ask in the evaluation period if there was anything else the troll or the lads could have said. This is the help the child needs for growth in verbal expression.

The other aspect of dialogue is the period when everyone wants to talk at the same time, or the conversation stretched out merely for the sake of talking. These situations are readily apparent to the children in creative dramatics, and correction of the faults comes from them. The leader has only to ask what the trouble was. Situations can be given to illustrate the point: three friends are talking about a fourth, who suddenly appears; a family is taking an automobile ride; three friends are having lunch in a restaurant. The rest of the class listens for polite conversation and equality of the scene.

Another aspect of dialogue is quality of thought. This must be in keeping with the characterization. If silliness, unrelated or improbable ideas creep in, the leader must guide the group to a discussion of what is silly in contrast to humor, and the difference between the realistic and the unrealistic. In playing "Juan Goes to Heaven" (nineteenth century), one of the girls said she was Marilyn Monroe. The reply from a boy was, "That's silly! She's not dead yet!" The development of this quality is not difficult because children are sincere. They need the quick observance of the leader to encourage freedom of speech, knowledge of when to speak, and growth in the quality of the created dialogue.

DRAMATIC AWARENESS

An awareness of the total effect of the scene played becomes apparent to the group as learning progresses. They are stimulated by the well-done achievement or are impulsively honest when it is not a good one. A cooperative consciousness is felt, and they are ready for an understanding of what is drama. This may be accomplished by discussions, or by performing a scene showing the conflict necessary in a dramatic play. Two members of the class may be asked to approach each other from opposite sides of the room. They pass by without speaking. Is this drama? No, nothing happened. The next time they approach each other, they bump shoulders and go on their way. Is this drama? No, not enough happened. The next time they approach, they bump shoulders and react, their reactions involving spoken dialogue. Is this drama? Yes, because there was physical conflict which caused an emotional reaction. If their reactions caused the group to laugh, they had created a comic scene. If their reactions were so strong that one of them was hurt with the emotional response caused by pain, they had created a serious drama. Improvised scenes in groups of two or three will give practice in the understanding that drama depends upon the emotional and physical struggles of life. Suggestions for scenes should be based on subject matter within the comprehension of the group. Typical children's situations would include washing the dishes, flying a kite, playing ball, hiking, fishing, riding in an automobile, and going to the movies. The problem for the improvisation is to develop some action that will make the scene dramatic. Time is allowed for planning what is going to happen. After each group has participated, the action is evaluated in terms of plot structure. Did it have a good beginning, middle, and end? Was there suspense, and was it believable? A dramatic awareness has now been learned.

DEVELOPING THE STORY INTO THE PLAY

If it is necessary to present a story for an audience, as it is in certain situations, the creative dramatics approach is far more rewarding to the child than use of a written play. The introduction of the audience transposes the purpose from that of art for the child to art for the spectators. Such a transposition makes it necessary to observe the techniques required for staging a play, and may restrict naturalness of spirit. This is the reason it is better not to use the written script, as the memorization of words is a skill in itself. It becomes more important than interpretation of words and development of character. This danger may also occur in playing a story that has an unfamiliar name or song that cannot be left out of the plot. In the Mexican story of "The Hunchback," the song "Lunes, y martes y miércoles —tres" (Monday and Tuesday and Wednesday—three), is the keynote in the conflict. The words need to be chanted over and over in the planning period so that the attempt to remember will not stultify the children's joy in playing. In the created play the naturalness of speech will remain, as it has become spontaneous. Although this is not a problem, the performance for an audience requires observance of all of other stage disciplines which are comparable in every aspect to the adult theatre. The play is still the child's creation, but no longer just his.

The problems of developing the story into a stage play lie in the concern of dramatic action, change of scenes, time lapses, and keeping the story told by what the actors are saying and doing. This means there may have to be additional action for dramatic suspense, elimination of unnecessary incidents and characters, combining scenes or telescoping them into one incident, and maintaining time and space unity. The story, "Concerning Al-iot, The Spirit of Fire," is not a good one for creative dramatics or storytelling, since there is very little action. The value lies in the story of the ancient Siberian tribe's concept of fire. The student's adaptation which follows it shows how a more dramatic situation has been developed by the use of additional ideas and characters.

CONCERNING AL-IOT, THE SPIRIT OF FIRE

Until the arrival of the Tanguses, who pushed the Yakuts nearer the Northern Sea (Baikal is for them the South Sea), the Yakuts thought that besides themselves there were no other people on earth; land began at the upper part of the lena and finished at its outlet; that was the end. People, that is the Yakuts, at first had no knowledge of fire; they ate everything raw and suffered much from cold, for no good spirits taught them to get fire from stone.

The discovery of fire occurred thus: On a hot summer day an old man who was wandering among the mountains sat down to rest and, having nothing to do, struck one stone against another. Sparks issued from the blow and set alight the dry grass and next dry twigs. The fire extended, and people ran from all parts to gaze at the novel wonder. The farther it spread the larger it became and the more the fire bred fear and horror; but fortunately it was extinguished by a downpour of rain. Henceforth the Yakuts learned to kindle fire and to extinguish it. The Yakuts worship fire as a stupendous force; and whenever any sacrifice is offered, they sacrifice in the first place to fire; they give a spoonful of all food to the fire. Thus they throw into it a portion of the first spring kumyse; they worship Al-iot everywhere.

CONCERNING AL-IOT, THE SPIRIT OF FIRE. From *Siberian and Other Folk Tales,* by C. F. Coxwell. Permission granted by C. W. Daniel Co., Ltd.

CONCERNING AL-IOT, SPIRIT OF FIRE

Our story is about a group of people that lived years and years and years ago, in a country that is now called Siberia. They were a very primitive people; they lived in caves, wore animal skins, and at first had no knowledge of fire. They ate their food raw, and suffered terribly from the cold winters. They were called the Yakuts. Al-iot, the Spirit of Fire, was very unhappy about this, because he wanted so much to be discovered, partly because he felt sorry for the Yakuts, partly because he was impatient to be free to fly wherever he wished! So, Al-iot watched and waited for a long, long time, hoping that soon the Yakuts would learn to set him free. And then one hot summer day, when the Yakuts were busy about their usual work, the men searching for food, the women preparing it, and making their crude clothing out of skins, a certain Yakut boy got into trouble with his mother, be-

Susan Riskin, adaptation of "Concerning Al-iot, Spirit of Fire."

cause he hadn't remembered to bring home the fish for dinner. His mother scolded him loudly, and he went off to sulk by himself. Al-iot followed him (the boy couldn't see him, of course) thinking that maybe, just maybe, this was the chance he had been waiting for. The boy sat down on the ground near some dry, parched bushes. Al-iot saw some stones lying near by, and when the boy wasn't looking quickly pushed them where the boy could see them. The boy picked them up idly, Al-iot impatiently guided his hands until the boy had, unthinkingly, struck them together! The sparks flew to the dry grass and set it afire! Al-iot was freed! Gleefully, he gathered up more sparks and flew to the bushes, to the trees! Soon the whole side of the hill was afire! The boy was amazed. He called to his family and they all came and were amazed at this strange thing they had never seen before—what is it? What does it do? Where does it come from? Is it a danger to us, or a friend? The boy, curious, held out his hand to the fire, not knowing, and when it burned him, they all knew it could hurt and they began to be afraid. Al-iot went all over, and the fire spread, more people came to watch, and soon they too became more and more frightened. They saw trees fall, and felt the tremendous heat and saw the animals fleeing towards the river and they were horrified. At last, the rains poured down, and the fire was put out. Al-iot was contented though, because he would now be discovered and freed again and again and the Yakuts would realize that he was a power to be reckoned with. When the fire died away, all people gathered together, and talked about what had happened. They learned how the fire had started, and they had seen how it could be stopped. They discovered that the meat that had been scorched by the fire tasted better than when it was raw. And they had a great celebration, honoring Al-iot, and they sacrificed to him, and always gave the first spoonful of food to him, and worshipped Al-iot everywhere.

The story of "A Clever Lass"[2] presents the opposite problem, as there are eleven changes of time and place within the very short story. If the purpose is to develop it into a play for an audience, it must be condensed into as few scenes as possible. A succession of curtains being opened and closed leaves the audience with short, jerky ideas rather than sustained suspense. An incident that is only a few minutes in length is not sufficient material to warrant the effort of construction of scenery or change of sets during the play. The solution is in the combining and telescoping. One way of working out this story would be to combine the first five scenes into one act in the king's courtroom, and place the last six scenes on the road.

The play opens on the shepherd and his daughter (and added observers) standing before the king. The shepherd offers the mortar, and the king reacts as the daughter said he would. The shepherd tells the king about his

2 "A Clever Lass," page 102.

clever daughter; the king asks her if she could come to him neither walking nor riding, clothed nor unclothed, neither by day nor by night, neither at noon nor in the morning. She tells him how she would do it, and he asks her to marry him, if she will promise not to give advice to anyone after they are married.

The second act takes place outside of the king's palace. The two farmers are arguing over who owns the foal as the king and queen enter. The king gives his advice, which is wrong, and goes into the palace. The queen talks to the wronged farmer and advises him to use his fishnet right there in the road. The king enters again and sees what the farmer is doing. The farmer cleverly proves the king wrong, but the king is wise and knows his wife had advised him. He tells her to go back to her father's, but she can take with her the things she likes best. She immediately replies that she will take him, so he forgives her and says she can give advice from now on.

If at all possible, it is better to rearrange the incidents so that they may be played in one setting. In this story, the time elapsed, indicated by the marriage, and the necessity for the last part having to be played out of doors, eliminates such a possibility.

The leader approaches the development of the story into play form for an audience in the same method of question and answer discussion. The group plans together, with the leader summarizing its ideas. If there has been a true learning experience of the dramatic art, they will have no difficulty in putting the story into play form. When this has been accomplished, the first scene is discussed, following the steps of the planning period. The scene is played and evaluated over and over again until the group is satisfied with the incidents, dialogue, and characterizations. When the entire play is ready and the cast has been chosen, the leader becomes the director. This is the point when the play no longer belongs entirely to the child. It is now ready for the refinements necessary in a production for an audience. These must be done by someone who can look at the whole play objectively, with the eyes of the audience. This is the director, who focuses his attention upon the stage techniques, demanding that the actors utilize the skills of the theatre.

These skills are the details of any production which the director and the actors must plan and execute for clarity of the play and intensification of the emotions involved. Stage business, which is the visual activity of the actor other than movement, cannot just happen. Its purpose is to contribute action that will give emphasis or aid in telling the story. This demands that the stage business must be definite, motivated, varied, unified, accurately timed, and visibly clear. Creativity lies in the imagination and taste of the business selected by the director and the actors. Other skills, such as opening and closing doors, kneeling, gesturing, sitting and rising, falling, crying, and laughing require specific techniques. An audience not only expects pleasing and exciting stage pictures that have meaning, but also that the play be audible. This calls for the skills of speech and voice projection.

Although these are skills and not a creative process, they fit naturally into creative dramatics because they are needed to transmit the creation to an audience. They are not an end in themselves, but will have been assimilated into the genuine expression of each individual and of the group as a whole. This acquiring of knowledge aids in the creative imagination; it is the refining and verifying of the act. Creative play again proves its value as it gives the opportunity for extension and expansion of the learning possibilities of this dramatic art. Although the play is for an audience, the main purpose of creative dramatics should not be lost. It is an art that concerns itself with what is happening to the child while he is experiencing the art.

CONCLUSION

The child who experiences creative drama will be given an opportunity to develop the power to listen, concentrate, solve problems, speak and move freely and expressively with original ideas, to reason, synthesize, and evaluate. Beyond these abilities is the resulting condition of the mind. The happy person is the one who trusts himself, confident that he can create and express his ideas with freedom and vitality. This is the joy for the child in the happy moments of his own creation. This is the benefit for his future life. The leader has only stood by his side offering inspiration and the chance for the fullfillment of that inner urge "to be." It is as in this parable, ". . . often we told stories of the Father. I told them to the child and the child told them again to me. We told them, the child and I, over and over again. Sometimes we stopped to rest, leaning against one of the Father's trees, and letting His cool air cool our brows, and never speaking. And then, in the twilight, we met the Father. The child's eyes shone. He looked lovingly, trustingly, eagerly up into the Father's face. He put his hand into the Father's hand. I was for the moment forgotten. I was content."[3] The "moment" is the child's.

[3] Contributed by Margaret L. White, source unknown.

2

AFRICA

"What is it you say, my son, you want the moon?" asked the astonished king.

"Yes. Do get it for me at once, won't you?"

"But, my child, the moon is a long way up. How shall we ever be able to reach it?"[1]

The place was the village street or the forest camp. The day's work was done. It was the storyteller's time in southern Africa. The earth was the stage; the forest shadows cast by the moonlight, the scenery; the audience, hundreds of natives in whose blood ran the love of the story.

The tales told were numerous and covered every aspect of human life: animal stories, tales of victory of the small over the large through cunning and trickery, ogre tales, "how" tales, tales of imagination based on historical facts, and foreign tales such as found in the Malayan quarters of Cape Town.

THE STORY OF THE PRINCE WHO INSISTED ON POSSESSING THE MOON

The country now inhabited by the Basoko tribe of the Congo was formerly known as Bandimba. A king called Bahanga was its sole ruler. He married Bamana, the youngest daughter of his principal chief and became the father of a male child.

The prince grew up to be a marvel of strength and beauty and his father

THE STORY OF THE PRINCE WHO INSISTED ON POSSESSING THE MOON. From *My Dark Companions and Their Strange Stories,* by Henry M. Stanley. By permission of Sampson Low, Marston & Company Ltd.

[1] Henry M. Stanley, "The Story of the Prince Who Insisted on Possessing the Moon," from *My Dark Companions and Their Strange Stories.*

15

doted on him so much that he shared his power with the boy in a curious manner. The king reserved authority over all the married people, while the prince's subjects consisted of those not yet mated. It thus happened that the prince ruled over more people than his father, for the children, were, of course, more numerous than the parents. But with all the honour conferred upon him the prince was not happy. The more he obtained, the more he wished to possess.

One day the prince was playing with the youth of his court, and after the sport retired to the shade of a tree to rest, and his companions sat down in a circle at a respectful distance from him. He then felt a gush of pride stealing over him as he thought of his great power, and he cried out boastfully that there never was a boy so great, so rich and so favoured by his father, as he had become. "My father," said he, "can deny me nothing. I have only to ask, and it is given unto me."

Then one little slender boy with a thin voice said, "It is true, Prince. Your father has been very good to you. He is a mighty king, and he is as generous as he is great. Still, I know of one thing that he cannot give you —and it is certain that you will never possess it."

"What thing is that which I may not call my own, when I see it—and what is it that is not in the king's power to give me?" asked the prince, in a tone of annoyance.

"It is the moon," answered the little boy; "and you must confess yourself that it is beyond the king's power to give that to you."

"Do you doubt it?" asked the prince. "I say to you that I shall possess it, and I will go now and claim it from my father. I will not give him any peace until he gives it to me."

Now it so happens that such treasures as are already ours, we do not value so much as those which we have not yet got. So it was with this spoiled prince. The memory of the many gifts of his father fled from his mind, and their value was not to be compared with this new toy—the moon.

He found the king discussing important matters with the old.

"Father," said he, "just now, while I was with my companions I was taunted because I did not have the moon among my toys, and it was said that it was beyond your power to give it to me. Now, prove this boy a liar, and procure the moon for me that I may be able to show it to them, and glory in your gift."

"What is it you say, my son, you want the moon?" asked the astonished king.

"Yes. Do get it for me at once, won't you?"

"But, my child, the moon is a long way up. How shall we ever be able to reach it?"

"I don't know; but you have always been good to me, and you surely would not refuse me this favour, father?"

"I fear, my son, that we will not be able to give you the moon."

"But, father, I must have it; my life will not be worth living without it. How may I dare to again face my companions after my proud boast before them of your might and goodness. Now my soul is bent upon possessing this moon, and you must obtain it for me or I shall die."

"Nay, my son, speak not of death. It is an ugly word, especially when connected with my prince and heir. Let your mind be at rest. I will collect all the wise men of the land together, and ask them to advise me. If they say that the moon can be reached and brought down to us, you shall have it."

Accordingly the great state drum was sounded for the general palaver, and a score of criers went through the towns beating their little drums as they went, and the messengers hastened all the wise men and elders to the presence of the king.

When all were assembled, the king announced his desire to know how the moon could be reached, and whether it could be shifted from its place in the sky and brought down to the earth in order that he might give it to his only son, the prince. If there was any wise man present who could inform him how this could be done, and would undertake to bring it to him, he would give the choicest of his daughters in marriage to him and endow him with great riches.

When the wise men heard this strange proposal, they were speechless with astonishment, as no one in the Basoko Land had ever heard of anybody mounting into the air higher than a tree, and to suppose that a person could ascend as high as the moon was, they thought, simple madness. Respect for the king, however, held them mute, though what their glances meant was very clear.

But while each man was not yet looking at his neighbor in wonder, one of the wise men, who appeared to be about the youngest present, rose to his feet and said:

"Long life to the prince and to his father, the king! We have heard the words of our king, Bahanga, and they are good. I—even I—his slave, am able to reach the moon, and to do the king's pleasure, if the king's authority will assist me."

The confident air of the man, and the ring of assurance in his voice made the other wise men, who had been so ready to believe the king and prince mad, feel shame, and they turned their faces to him curiously, more than half willing to believe that after all the thing was possible. The king also lost his puzzled look, and appeared relieved.

"Say on. How may you be able to perform what you promise?"

"If it please the king," answered the man boldly. "I will ascend from the top of the high mountain near the Cataract of Panga. But I shall first build a high scaffold on it, the base of which shall be broad as the mountain top, and on that scaffold I will build another, and on the second I shall build a third, and so on and so on until my shoulder touches the moon."

"But is it possible to reach the moon in this manner?" asked the king doubtingly.

"Most certainly, if I were to erect a sufficient number of scaffolds, one above another; but it will require a vast quantity of timber, and a great army of workmen. If the king commands it, the work will be done."

"Be it so, then," said the king. "I place at your service every able-bodied man in the kingdom."

"Ah, but all the men in your kingdom are not sufficient, oh, king. All the grown-up men will be wanted to fell the trees, square the timber and bear it to the works; and every grown-up woman will be required to prepare the food for the workmen; and every boy must carry water to satisfy their thirst, and bark rope for the binding of the timbers; and every girl, big and little, must be sent to till the fields to raise cassava for food. Only in this manner can the prince obtain the moon for his toy."

"I say, then, let it be done as you think it ought to be done. All the men, women, and children in the kingdom I devote to this service, that my only son may enjoy what he deserves."

Then it was proclaimed throughout the wide lands of the Bandimba that all the people should be gathered together to proceed at once with the work of obtaining the moon for the king's son. And the forest was cut down, and while some of the workmen squared the trees, others cut deep holes in the ground, to make a broad and sure base for the lower scaffold; and the boys made thousands of rope coils to lash the timbers together out of bark, fibre of palm, and tough grass; and the girls, big and little, hoed up the ground and planted the cassava shrubs and sowed the corn; and the women kneaded the bread and cooked the greens, and roasted green bananas for food for the workmen. And all the Bandimba people were made to slave hard every day in order that a spoiled boy might have the moon for his toy.

In a few days the first scaffolding stood up as high as the tallest trees, in a few weeks the structure had grown until it was many arrowflights in height, in two months it was so lofty that the top could not be seen with the naked eye. In the sixth month the top of the highest scaffold was so high that on the clearest day people could not see half-way up; and it was said to be so tall that the chief engineer could tell the day he would be able to touch the moon.

In all the land, the countries adjoining it, there was found only one wise man who foresaw that if the moon was shifted out of its place what damage would happen, and that probably all those foolish people in the vicinity of the tower would be destroyed. Fearing some terrible calamity, he proposed to depart from among the Bandimba before it was too late. He then placed his family in a canoe, and, after storing it with sufficient provisions, he embarked, and in the night floated down the river and as fast as the current would take him—far far below any lands known to the Bandimba.

A week later, after the flight of the wise man and his family, the chief engineer sent down word to the king that he was ready to take the moon down.

"It is well," replied the king from below. "I will ascend, that I may see how you set about it."

Within twenty days the king reached the summit of the tower, and, standing at last by the side of the engineer, he laid his hand upon the moon, and it felt exceedingly hot. Then he commanded the engineer to take it down. The man put a number of cool bark coils over his shoulder and tried to dislodge it; but, as it was firmly fixed, he used such a deal of force that he cracked it, and there was an explosion, the fire and sparks from which scorched him. The timber on which the king and his chiefs were standing began to burn, and many more bursting sounds were heard, and fire and melted rock ran down through the scaffolding in a steady stream, until all the wood work was ablaze, and the flames soared upward among the uprights and trestles of the wood in one vast pile of fire; and every man, woman, and child was utterly consumed in a moment. And the heat was so great that it affected the moon, and a large portion of it tumbled to the earth; and its glowing hot materials ran over the ground like a great river of fire, so that most of the country of the Bandimba was burnt to ashes. Of those who were not smothered by the smoke, nor burnt by the fire, and who fled from before the burning river, the effect was very wonderful. Such of them as were grown up, male and female, were converted into gorillas, and all the children into different kinds of long-tailed monkeys.

Friends, if you doubt the truth of what I have said, all you have to do is to look at the moon when it is full, and you may see on a clear night a curious dark portion on its face, which often appears as though there were peaky mountains in it, and often the dark spots are like some kind of horned animals; and then again, you will fancy that on the moon you see the outlines of a man's face, but those dark spots are only the holes made in the moon by the man who forced his shoulders through it. By this you will know that I have not lied to you. Now ever since that dreadful day when the moon burst and the Bandimba country was consumed, parents are not in the habit of granting children all they ask for, but only such things as their age and experience warn them are good for their little ones.

But, what became of Bahanga and the little prince? Why, after the engineer of the works, the first who died were the king and prince whose folly had brought ruin on the land.

THE PARTNERSHIP OF RABBIT AND ELEPHANT, AND WHAT CAME OF IT

In Uganda, a Rabbit and an Elephant went on a little trading expedition to the Watusi shepherds. Now at a trade Elephant was not to be compared with Rabbit, for he could not talk so pleasantly as Rabbit, and he was not at all sociable. So Rabbit got a mighty fine cow in exchange for his little bale of cloth and the Elephant a year-old heifer.

Just as they began their return journey, Elephant said to Rabbit, "Now mind, should we meet anyone on the road, and we are asked whose cattle these are, I wish you to oblige me by saying that they are mine, because I should not like people to believe that I am not as good a trader as yourself. They will also be afraid to touch them if they know they belong to me; whereas, if they hear that they belong to you, every fellow will think he has as good a right to them as yourself, and you dare not defend your property."

"Very well," replied Rabbit, "I quite understand."

In a little while, as Rabbit and Elephant drove their cattle along, they met many people coming from market who stopped and admired them, and said, "Ah, what a fine cow is that! To whom does it belong?"

"It belongs to me," answered the thin voice of Rabbit. "The little one belongs to Elephant."

"Very fine indeed. A good cow that," replied the people, and passed on.

Vexed and annoyed, Elephant cried angrily to Rabbit, "Why did you not answer as I told you? Now mind, do as I tell you at the next meeting with strangers."

"Very well," answered Rabbit, "I will try and remember."

By-and-by they met another party going home with fowls, who, when they came up, said, "Ah, that is a fine beast, and in prime order. Whose is it?"

"It is mine," quickly replied Rabbit, "and the little scabby heifer belongs to Elephant."

This answer enraged Elephant, who said, "What an obstinate little fool you are. Did you not hear me ask you to say it was mine? Now, remember, you are to say so next time, or I leave you to find your own way home, because I know you are a horrible little coward."

"Very well, I'll do it next time," replied Rabbit in a meek voice.

In a short time they met another crowd, which stopped when opposite to them, and the people said, "Really, that is an exceedingly fine cow. To which of you does it belong?"

THE PARTNERSHIP OF RABBIT AND ELEPHANT, AND WHAT CAME OF IT. From *My Dark Companions*, by Henry M. Stanley. By permission of Sampson Low, Marston & Company Ltd.

"It is mine. I bought it from the Watusi," replied Rabbit.

The Elephant was so angry this time that he broke away from Rabbit, and drove his little heifer by another road, and to Lion, and Hyena, and Buffalo, and Leopard, whom he met, he said what a fine fat cow was being driven by cowardly little Rabbit along another road. He did this out of mere spite, hoping that someone of them would be tempted to take it by force from Rabbit.

But Rabbit was wise, and had seen the spite in Elephant's face as he went off; and was sure that he would play him some unkind trick; and, as night was falling and his home was far, and he knew that there were many vagabonds lying in wait to rob poor travelers, he reflected that if his wit failed to save him he would be in great danger.

True enough, it was not long before a big blustering lion rose from the side of the road, and cried out, "Hello, you there. Where are you going with that cow? Come, speak out."

"Ah, is that you, Lion? I am taking it to Mugassa (the deity) who is about to give a feast to all his friends, and he told me particularly to invite you to share it, if I should meet you."

"Eh? What? To Mugassa? Oh, well, I am proud to have met you, Rabbit. As I am not otherwise engaged I will accompany you, because everyone considers it an honour to wait upon Mugassa."

They proceeded a little further, and a bouncing buffalo came up and bellowed fiercely. "You Rabbit, stop," said he. "Where are you taking that cow?"

"I am taking it to Mugassa, don't you know? How would a little fellow like me have the courage to go so far from home if it were not that I am in service for Mugassa. I am charged to tell you, Buffalo, that if you like to join in the feast Mugassa is about to give, that he will be glad to have you as a guest."

"Oh, well, that is good news indeed. I will come along now, Rabbit, and am very glad to have met you. How do you do, Lion?"

A short distance off the party met a huge rogue elephant, who stood in the middle of the road, and demanded to know where the cow was being taken in a tone which required a quick answer.

"Now, Elephant, get out of the way. This cow is being taken to Mugassa, who will be angry with you if I am delayed. Have you not heard of the feast he is about to give? Bye the bye, as you are one of the guests, you might as well help me to drive this cow."

"Why, that is grand," said the Elephant. "I shall be delighted to feast with Mugassa. I will help you with pleasure."

Soon a leopard and then a hyena were met, but seeing such a powerful crowd behind the cow, they affected great civility, and were invited to accompany Rabbit's party to Mugassa's feast.

It was quite dark by the time they arrived at Rabbit's village. At the gate stood two dogs, who were Rabbit's chums, and they barked furiously; but hearing their friend's voice, came up and welcomed Rabbit.

"Well, my friends, do you hear what Dogs have just told me? Mugassa will come himself and give each his portion of the cow for the feast. But remember if the cow is touched before Mugassa arrives we are all ruined. Now each of you watch for falling leaves in order that we may have proper plates for Mugassa.

Having issued his instructions, Rabbit went to a secret hiding-place where he could watch all of the animals. Each watched the trees for the falling leaves but hyena who wanted the cow for himself. After he had made sure everyone was busy he crept up from behind a tuft of grass where the cow was busily eating and was just about to spring when Rabbit screamed, "Ah, you thief, Hyena. You thief, I see you. Stop thief, Mugassa is coming."

These cries so alarmed Hyena that he fled away as fast as his legs could carry him, and the others, Buffalo, Elephant, Lion, and Leopard, tired out with waiting, and hearing these alarming cries, also ran away, leaving Rabbit and his dog friends in quiet possession.

They laughed loud and long over the fun of it all.

My friends, Rabbit was the smallest of all, but by his wisdom he was more than a match for two Elephants, Buffalo, Leopard, Lion, Hyena, and all. And even his friends, the Dogs, had to confess that Rabbit's wit could not be matched. That is my tale.

THE SEARCH FOR THE HOME OF THE SUN

My tale is about King Masama and his tribe, the Balira, who dwelt far in the region. They were formerly very numerous, and many of them came to live among us, but one day King Masama and the rest of the tribe left their country and went eastward, and they have never been heard of since, but those who chose to stay with us explained their disappearance in this way.

A woman, one cold night, after making up her fire on the hearth, went to sleep. In the middle of the night the fire had spread, and spread, and began to lick up the litter on the floor, and from the litter it crept to her bed of dry banana leaves, and in a little time shot up into flames. When the woman and her husband were at last awakened by the fire, the flames had already mounted into the roof, and were burning furiously. Soon they broke through the top and leaped into the night, and a gust of wind

THE SEARCH FOR THE HOME OF THE SUN. From *My Dark Companions*, by Henry M. Stanley. By permission of Sampson Low, Marston & Company Ltd.

came and carried the long flames like a stream of fire towards the neighbouring huts, and in a short time the fire had caught hold of every house, and the village was entirely burned. It was soon known that besides burning up their houses and much property, several old people and infants had been destroyed by the fire, and the people were horror-struck and angry.

Then one voice said, "We all know in whose house the fire began, and the owner of it must make our losses good to us. He is a rich man and will be able to pay."

And he did so: his plantation of bananas and fruit trees, his plots of beans, yams, potatoes, ground-nuts, his slaves, spears, shields, knives, paddles and canoes. When he had given all, the hearts of the people became softened towards him, and they forgave him the rest.

After the elder's property had been equally divided among the sufferers by the fire, the people gained new courage, and set about rebuilding their homes, and before long they had a new village, and they had made themselves as comfortable as ever.

Then King Masama made a new law, a very severe law—to the effect that, in future, no fire should be lit in the houses during the day or night; and the people, who were now much alarmed about the fire, with one heart agreed to keep the law. But it was soon felt that the cure for the evil was as cruel as the fire had been. For the houses had been thatched with green banana leaves, the timbers were green and wet with their sap, the floor was damp and cold, the air was deadly, and the people began to suffer from joint aches, and their knees were stiff, and the pains traveled from one place to another through their bodies. The village was filled with groaning.

Masama suffered more than all, for he was old. He shivered night and day, and his teeth chattered sometimes so that he could not talk, and after that his head would burn, and the hot sweat would pour from him, so that he knew no rest.

Then the king gathered his chiefs and principal men together, and said:

"Oh, my people, this is unendurable, for life is with me now but one continuous ague. Let us leave this country, for it is bewitched, and if I stay longer there will be nothing left of me. Lo, my joints are stiffened with my disease, and my muscles are withering. Let us seek a warmer clime. Behold whence the sun issues daily in the morning, hot and glowing; there, where his home is, must be warmth, and we shall need no fire. What say you?"

Masama's words revived their drooping spirits. They looked towards the sun as they saw him mount the sky, and felt his cheering glow on their naked breasts and shoulders, and they cried with one accord: "Let us hence, and seek the place whence he comes."

And the people got ready and left their village.

Not until a long time afterwards did we hear what became of Masama and his people. It was said that they traveled until they came to the foot of the tall mountain which stands like a grandsire amongst the smaller mountains. Up the sides of the big mountain they straggled, and as the days passed, they saw that the world was cold and dark until the sun showed himself over the edge of the big mountain, when the day became more agreeable, for the heat pierced into their very marrow, and made their hearts rejoice. The greater the heat became, the more certain were they that they were drawing near the home of the sun. And so they pressed on and on, day after day, winding along one side of the mountain, and then turning to wind again still higher. Each day, as they advanced towards the top, the heat became greater and greater. Between them and the sun there was now not the smallest shrub or leaf, and it became so fiercely hot that finally not a drop of sweat was left in their bodies. One day, when not a cloud was in the sky, and the world was all below them —far down like a great buffalo hide—the sun came out over the rim of the mountain like a ball of fire, and the nearest of them to the top were dried like a leaf over a flame, and those who were behind were amazed at its burning force, and felt, as he sailed over their heads, that it was too late for them to escape. Their skins began to shrivel up and crackle, and fall off, and none of those who were high up on the mountain side were left alive. But a few of those who were nearest the bottom, and the forest belts, managed to take shelter, and remaining there until night, they took advantage of the darkness, when the sun sleeps, to fly from the home of the sun. Except a few poor old people and toddling children, there was none left of the once populous tribe of the Balira.

That is my story. We who live by the great river have taken the lesson, which the end of this tribe has been to us, close to our hearts, and it is this. Kings who insist that their wills should be followed, and never care to take counsel with their people, are as little to be heeded as children who babble of what they cannot know, and therefore in our villages we have many elders who take all matters from the chief and turn them over in their minds, and when they are agreed, they give the doing of them to the chief who can act only as the elders decree.

A TUG OF WAR

Leopard was dead, and the children of Leopard were still young; they had not grown to take their father's power and place. And Tortoise considered himself now a great personage. He said to people, "We three

A TUG OF WAR. From *Where Animals Talk*, West African Folk Lore Tales, by Robert H. Nassau; copyright by Richard G. Badger, The Gorham Press, Boston, 1912. By permission of Bruce Humphries, Inc.

who are left—I am Njâgu and Ngubu, are of equal power; we eat at the same table, and have the same authority." Every day he made these boasts; and people went to Elephant and Hippopotamus, reporting, " 'So and so,' says Ekâga." Elephant and Hippopotamus laughed, and disregarded the report, and said, "That's nothing, he's only to be despised."

One day Hippopotamus met Elephant in the forest; salutations were made, "Mbolo!" "Ai, Mbolo!" each to the other. Hippopotamus asked Elephant about a new boast that Tortoise had been making, "Have you, or have you not heard?" Elephant answered, "Yes, I have heard. But I look on it with contempt. For, I am Njâgu. I am big. My foot is as big as Ekâga's body. And he says he is equal to me! But, I have not spoken of the matter, and will not speak, unless I hear Ekâga himself make his boast. And then I shall know what I will do." And Hippopotamus also said, "I am doing so too, in silence. I wait to hear Ekâga myself."

Tortoise heard of what Elephant and Hippopotamus had been threatening, and he asked his informant just the exact words that they had used. "They said that they waited to hear you dare to speak to them; and that, in the meanwhile, they despised you."

Tortoise asked, "So! they despise me, do they?" "Yes," was his reply. Then he said, "So! indeed, I will go to them." He told his wife, "Give me my coat to cover my body." He dressed; and started to the forest. He found Elephant lying down; his trunk was eight miles long; his ears as big as a house, and his four feet beyond measure.

Tortoise audaciously called to him, "Mwěra! I have come! You don't rise to salute me? Mwěra has come!" Elephant looked, rose up and stared at Tortoise, and indignantly asked, "Ekâga! whom do you call 'Mwěra'?" Tortoise replied, "You! I call you 'Mwěra.' Are you not, Njâgu?" Elephant, with great wrath, asked, "Ekâga! I have heard you said certain words. It is true that you said them?"

Tortoise answered, "Njâgu, don't get angry! I did call you, just now, 'Mwěra'; but, you, Njâgu, why do you condemn me? You think that, because you are of great expanse of flesh, you can surpass Ekâga, just because I am small? Let us have a test. Tomorrow, sometime in the morning, we will have a lurelure (tug-of-war)." Said Elephant, "Of what use? I can smash you with one foot." Tortoise said, "Be patient. At least try the test." So, Elephant, unwillingly consented. Tortoise added, "But when we tug, if one overpulls the other, he shall be considered the greater; but if neither, then we are Mwěra."

Then Tortoise went to the forest, and cut a very long vine, and coming back to Elephant, said "This end is yours. I go off into the forest with my end to a certain spot, and tomorrow I return to the spot; and we will have our tug, and neither of us will stop, to eat or sleep until either you pull me over or the vine breaks." Tortoise went off far with his end of the vine to the town of Hippopotamus, and hid the vine's end at the outskirts of the town. He went to Hippopotamus and found him bathing, and going ashore, back and forth, to and from the water. Tortoise, shouted to him, "Mwĕra. I have come! You! Come ashore! I am visiting you!" Hippopotamus came bellowing in great wrath with wide open jaws, ready to fight, and said, "I will fight you today! For, whom do you call 'Mwĕra'?"

Tortoise replied, "Why! you! I do not fear your size. Our hearts are the same. But, don't fight yet! Let us first talk." Hippopotamus grunted, and sat down; and Tortoise said, "I, Ekâga, I say that you and I and Njâgu are equal, we are Mwĕra. Even though you are great and I small, I don't care. But if you doubt me, let us have a trial. Tomorrow morning let us have a lurelure. He who shall overcome, shall be the superior. But, if neither is found superior, then we are equals." Hippopotamus has claimed that the plan was absurd; but, finally, he consented.

Tortoise then stood up, and went out, and got his end of the vine, and brought it to Hippopotamus, and said, "This end is yours. And I now go. Tomorrow, when you feel the vine shaken, know that I am ready at the other end; and then you begin, and we will not stop to eat or sleep until this test is ended."

In the morning, Tortoise went to the middle of the vine, where at its half-way, he made on the ground a mark; and he shook it towards one end, and then towards the other. Elephant caught his end, as he saw it shake, and Hippopotamus did the same at his end. Tortoise was laughing in his heart as he watched the quivering vine.

He went away to seek food leaving those two at their tug.

Later in the afternoon he said to himself, "I'll go and see about the tug, whether those fools are still pulling." When he went there, the vine was still stretched taut; and he thought, "Assai! shame! let them die with hunger!" He sat there, the vine trembling with tensity, and he in his heart mocking the two tired beasts. The one drew the other toward himself; and then, a slight gain brought the mark back but neither was overcoming.

At last Tortoise nicked the vine with his knife; the vine parted; and, at their ends, Elephant and Hippopotamus fell violently back onto the ground. Tortoise said to himself, "So! that's done! Now I go to Elephant with one end of the broken vine; tomorow to Hippopotamus." He went, and came on to Elephant, and found him looking doleful, and bathing his leg with medicine, and "Mwĕra! How do you feel? Do you consent that we are Mwĕra?" Elephant admitted, "Ekâga, I did not know you were so strong! When the vine broke, I fell over and hurt my leg. Yes, we are really equal. Really! Strength is not because the body is large. I despised you because your body was small. But actually, we are equal in strength!"

So they ate and drank and played as chums; and Tortoise returned to this town.

Early the next morning, with the other end of the broken vine, he went to visit Hippopotamus, who looked sick, and was rubbing his head, and asked, "Ngubu! How do you feel, Mwĕra?" Hippopotamus answered, "Really! Ekâga! so we are equals! I, Ngubu, so great! And you, Ekâga, so small! We pulled and pulled. I could not surpass you, nor you me. And when the vine broke, I fell and hurt my head. So, indeed strength has not greatness of body." Tortoise and Hippopotamus ate and drank and played; and Tortoise returned to his town.

After that, whenever the three and others met to talk in council the three sat together on the highest seats. Were they equal? Yes, they were equal.

NUTS ARE EATEN BECAUSE OF ANGANGWE: A PROVERB

This is a proverb expressing the obligation we all owe to some superior protecting powers.

The Hogs had cleared a space in the forest, for the building of their town. They were many; men and women and children.

In another place, a Hunter was sitting in his town. Every day, at daybreak, he went out to hunt. And so, each day, he killed some animal. He never failed of obtaining something.

One day, his children said to him, "You always return with some animal; but you never have brought us Ngowa (hog)." He replied, "I saw many Ingowa today, when I was out there. But, I wonder at one thing; that, when they are all together eating, and I approach they run away. As to Ingowa they eat inkula nuts and I know where the trees are. Well, then, I ambush them; but, when I go nearer, I see one big Ngowa not eating, but going around and around the herd. Whether it sees me or does not see, sure when I get ready to aim my gun, then they all scatter. The reason that Ingowa escape me, I do not know."

When the Hogs heard that the other animals were being killed by Hunter they at first felt pity for all these other beasts. But, they began to soon mock them. "These are not people! They only die! But, as to us Ingowa, Hunter is not able to kill us. We hear only the report that there is such a person as Hunter, but he is not able to kill us."

When Hogs were thus boasting, their King laughed at them, saying, "You don't know, you Ingowa! You mock others, that Hunter kills them?" They answered, "Yes, we mock at them; for, we go to the forest as they do, but Hunter does not touch us." Their King answered, "When you thus

NUTS ARE EATEN BECAUSE OF ANGANGWE: A PROVERB. From *Where Animals Talk*, West African Folk Lore Tales, by Robert H. Nassau; copyright by Richard G. Badger, The Gorham Press, Boston, 1912. By permission of Bruce Humphries, Inc.

in the forest eat your inkula nuts, you each one eat them by his own strength and skill?" They answered, "Yes; ourselves we go to the forest on our own feet; we pick and eat the inkula. No one feeds us." The King said, "It is not so. Those inkula you eat are eaten because of a person." They insisted, "No, it is not so. Inkula have no person in particular to do anything about them." Thus they had this long discussion, the Hogs and their King; and they got tired of it, and lay down to sleep.

In the morning, when daylight came, the King said, "A journey for nuts! But, today, I am sick. I am not able to go to gather nuts with you. I will stay in town." The Hogs said, "Well! we do not mistake the way. It is not necessary for you to go."

They went jeering about their King who said they were eating nuts because of a certain person. They went to the inkula trees and found great abundance fallen to the ground during the night. The herd of Hogs jumped about in joy. They stooped down to pick up the nuts, their eyes busy with the ground. They ate and ate. No one of them thought of the Hunter, whether he was out or in the forest.

But, that very morning, Hunter had risen, taken his gun and ammunition-box, and had gone to hunt. And, after awhile, he had seen the Hogs in the distance. They were only eating and eating, not looking at anything but nuts.

Hunter said in his heart, "These Hogs, I see them often, but why have I not been able to kill them?" He crept softly nearer and nearer. Creeping awhile then he stood up to spy; and again stooping, and again standing up to spy. He did not see the big Hog which, on other days, he had always observed going round and around the herd. Hunter stooped close to the ground, and crept onward. Then, as he approached closer, the Hogs still went on eating. He bent his knee to the earth, and he aimed his gun! Ingowa still eating! his gun flashed! and ten Hogs died! The Hogs fled, some of them wounded.

When they had come clear on to the town, their King asked, "What news, from where you come?" They answered, "Evil news! But we do not know what is the matter. Only we know that the words you said are not really so, that 'nuts are eaten because of a certain person.' Because when we went, each one of us gathered by his own skill, and ate by his own strength, and no one trusted to anyone else. And when we went, we ate abundantly, and everything was good. Except that, Hunter has killed ten of us. And many are wounded." The King said to himself, "Ingowa have become great fools. They do not consent to admit that nuts are eaten by reason of a certain person. Tomorrow, I will go with them to the nuts."

So, in the morning, the King ordered, "Come all to nuts! But when we go for the nuts, if I say, 'Ngh-o-o!' then every one of you, who are eating them must start to town, and not come back, because I have seen or smelt Hunter; and I grunt to let you know." All the Hogs agreed. They went to the ground. But, the King, not eating, kept looking here and there.

He sniffed wind from the south and north, and assured them "Eat you all! I am here!" He watched and watched; and presently he saw a speck far away. He passed around to sniff the wind. His nose uplifted, he caught the odor of Hunter. He returned to the herd, grunted "Ngh-o-o." And he and they all fled. They arrived safely at town.

Then he asked them "Who is dead? Who is wounded?" They assured, "None." He said, "Good! But, when you went by yourselves to eat nuts, did not Hunter kill you? And since you obeyed my voice today, who has died?"

They then replied, "No one! No one! Indeed, you spoke truly. Nuts are eaten because of a certain person. It is so!"

WHO IS KING OF BIRDS?

Note

First—Ability to Speak is a greater gift than ability in Walking, Flying, or any other Force.
Second—Why Chickens live with Mankind.

All the Birds had their dwelling-place in a certain country of Njambi's Kingdom. The pelicans, chickens, eagles, parrots and all other winged kinds all lived together, separated from other animals, in that country under the Great Lord Njambi.

One day, they were discussing together on the question, "Who is King of the Birds?" They all, each one, named himself, e.g. the Chicken said, "I!" the Parrot, "I!" the Eagle, "I!" and so on. They were not able to settle it, so they agreed to go to Ra-Njambi (Lord and Master of all) and refer the question to him. When they all had arrived at Njambi's Town, he asked, "What is the affair on which you have come?" They replied, "We have come together here, not to visit, but for a purpose. We wish to know, of all the Birds, who is Head or Chief. Each one says for himself that he is the superior. This one, because he knows how to fly well; that one because he can speak well; and another one, because he is strong. But, of these three things, flight, speech, and strength, we ask you, which is the greatest?"

Immediately all the Birds began a competition, each one saying, "Choose me; I know how to speak!" Njambi silenced them, and bade them, "Well,

WHO IS KING OF BIRDS? From *Where Animals Talk,* West African Folk Lore Tales, by Robert H. Nassau; copyright by Richard G. Badger, The Gorham Press, Boston, 1912. By permission of Bruce Humphries, Inc.

then, come here! I know that you all speak. But, show me, each one of you, your manner of speaking."

So Eagle stood up to be examined. Njambi asked him, "How do you speak? What is your manner of speaking?" Eagle began to scream, "So-owe! so-o-we! so-os-we!" Njambi said, "Good! Now call me your wife!" The wife of Eagle came, and Njambi said to her, "You are the wife of Ngwanyani (Eagle); how do you talk?" The wife replied, "I say, So-s-we! So-o-we! so-o-we!" Ra-Njambi said to Eagle, "Indeed! you and your wife speak the same kind of language." Eagle answered, "Yes, I and my wife, we speak alike." They were ordered, "Sit aside."

Then Ra-Njambi directed, "Bring me here Ngozo" (Parrot). And he asked, "Ngozo, how do you talk? What is your way of speaking?" Parrot squawked, "I say, 'KoOdoko!' " Ra-Njambi ordered, "Well, call me your wife!" She came; and he asked her, "How do you talk? Talk now!" The wife replied, "I say, 'Ko-do-ko!' " Njambi asked Parrot, "So! your wife says, 'Ko-do-ko'?" Parrot answered "Yes; my wife and I both say, 'Ko-do-ko.' "

Njambi then ordered, "Call me here, Ugulungu" (Plantain-Eater). He came, and was asked, "And how do you talk?" He shouted, "I say, 'Mbu-kâ-kâ! mbru-kâ-kâ! mbru!' " Njambi told him, "Call me your wife!" She came, and when asked, spoke in the same way as her husband. Njambi dismissed them, "Good! you and your wife say the same thing. Good!"

So, all the Birds, in succession, were summoned; and they all, husband and wife, had the same mode of speaking, except one who had not hitherto been called.

Njambi finally said, "Call Njâgâni (Chicken) here!" The Cock stood up, and strutted forward. Njambi asked him, "What is your speech? Show me your mode of talking." Cock threw up his head, stretched forward his throat, and crowed, "Kâ-kâ-re-kââ." Njambi said, "Good! summon your wife hither." The wife came; and, of her, Njambi asked, "And what do you say?" She demurely replied, "My husband told me that I might talk only if I bore children. So, when I lay an egg, I say 'Kwâ-kâ! Kwâ-kâ!' " Njambi exclaimed, "So! you don't say, 'Kâ-kâ-re-kââ,' like your husband?" She replied, "No, I do not talk as he."

Then Njambi said to Cock, "For what reason do you not allow your wife to say, 'Kâ-kâ-re-kââ'?" Cock replied, "I am Njâgâni, I respect myself. I jeer at all these other birds. Their wives and themselves speak only in the same way. A visitor, if he comes to their towns, is not able to know, when one of them speaks, which is wife, because they both speak alike. But I, Njâgâni, as to my wife, she is unable to speak as I do. I do not allow it. A husband should be at the head; and in his wife it is not becoming for her to be equal with him or to talk as well as he does."

Njambi listened to this long speech; and then inquired, "Have you finished?" Chicken answered, "Yes."

Njambi summoned all the Birds to stand together in one place near him, and he said, "The affair which you brought to me I settle it thus: Njâgâni is your head; because you others all speak, husband and wife, each alike. But, he speaks for himself in his own way, and his wife in her way; to show that a husband has priority and superiority over a wife. Therefore, as he knows how to be Head of his family, it is settled that Njâgâni is Head also of your Tribe."

But, Njambi went on to say, "Though this is true, you, Njâgâni, don't go back again into the Forest, to your Kingship of the Birds. For the other birds will be jealous of you. You are not strong; you cannot fight them all. Lest they kill you, stay with me in my Town."

Cock went to get his wife and children, and returned and remained there with Ra-Njambi. Therefore, the original bird to dwell among Mankind was the Chicken.

When the other Birds scattered and went back to their own forest country without their King, they said, "Let it be so! We will not choose another King. Our King has left us, and emigrated to another country, and has sat down in Njambi's Town."

So, the Birds have lived in the forest without any King.

THE SUN, A BUSHMAN LEGEND

Long, long ago in the days of the Early race that were before even the Flat Bushmen, who were the first people we really know anything about, at a certain place lived a man, from whose armpits brightness streamed. When he lifted an arm, the place on that side of him was light; when he lifted the other arm, the place on *that* side of him was light; but when he lifted both arms, the light shone all around about him. But it only shone around the place where he lived; it did not reach to other places.

Sometimes the people asked him to stand on a stone, so that his light could go farther; and sometimes he climbed on a Kopje (hill) and lifted his arms: Ach! then the light streamed out far, far, and lighted up the veld (grass land) for miles and miles. For the higher he went, the farther the light shone.

Then the people said: "We see now, the higher he goes the farther his light shines. If only we could put him very high, his light would go out over the whole world."

So they tried to make a plan, and at last a wise old woman called the young people together and said: "You must go to this man from whose

THE SUN. From *Outa Karel's Stories*, South African Folk Lore Tales, by Sanni Meteler-kamp. By permission of Macmillan & Co., Ltd., London and St. Martin's Press, Inc.

armpits the light streams. When he is asleep, you must go; and the strongest of you must take him under the armpits, and lift him up, and swing him to and fro—and throw him as high as you can into the sky, so that he may be above the Kopjes, lifting his arms to let the light stream down to warm the earth and make green things to grow in summer."

So the young men went to the place where the man lay sleeping. Quietly they went, creeping along in the red sand so as not wake him. He was in a deep sleep, and before he could wake the strong young men took him under the armpits and swung him to and fro, as the wise old woman had told them. Then, as they swung him, they threw him into the air, high, high, and there he stuck.

The next morning, when he woke and stretched himself, lifting his arms, the light streamed out from under them and brightened all the world, warming the earth, and making the green things grow. And so it went on day after day. When he put up his arms, it was bright, it was day. When he put down one arm, it was cloudy, the weather was not clear. And when he put down both arms and turned over to go to sleep, there was no light at all: it was dark; it was night. But when he awoke and lifted his arms, the day came again and the world was warm and bright.

Sometimes he is far away from the earth. Then it is cold; it is winter. But when he comes near, the earth gets warm again; the green things grow and the fruit ripens; it is summer. And so it goes on to this day: the day and night, summer and winter, and all because the Old Man with the bright armpits was thrown into the sky.

"But the Sun is not a man, Outa," said downright Willem, "and he hasn't any arms."

"No, not now. He is not a man any more. But remember how long he has been up in the sky—spans, and spans of years, always rolling round, and rolling round, from the time he wakes in the morning till he lies down to sleep at the other side of the world. And with the rolling, he has got all rounder and rounder, and the light that at first came only from under his arms has been rolled right round him, till now he is a big ball of light, rolling from one side of the sky to the other. When it is a dark day, then he has put his arms out. He is holding them down, and spreading his hands before the light, so that it can't shine on the world. And sometimes, just before he goes to sleep at night, haven't you seen long bright stripes coming from the round ball of light? Those are the long fingers of the Sun. His arms are rolled up inside the fiery ball, but he sticks his long fingers out and they make bright roads into the sky, spreading out all round him. The Old Man is peeping at the earth through his fingers. The next time he sticks out his fingers you must count them and see if they are all there—eight long ones, those are the fingers; and two short ones for the thumbs. When he lies down, he pulls them in. Then all the world grows dark and the people go to sleep."

THE STAR AND THE STAR'S ROAD

Long, long ago, the sky was dark at night when the Old Man with the bright armpits lay down to sleep, but the people learned in time to make fires to light up the darkness; and one night a girl, who sat warming herself by a wood fire, played with the ashes. She took the ashes in her hands and threw them up to see how pretty they were when they floated in the air. And as they floated away she put green bushes on the fire and stirred it with a stick. Bright sparks flew out and went high, high, mixing with the silver ashes, and they all hung in the air and made a bright road across the sky. And there it is to this day. It is called the Milky Way, but Outa calls it the Star's Road.

Ai! but the girl was pleased! She clapped her hands and danced, shaking herself like Outa's people do when they are happy, and singing.

> The little stars! The tiny stars!
> They make a road for other stars.
> Ash of wood-fir! Dust of the Sun!
> They call the Dawn when Night is done!

Then she took some of the roots she had been eating and threw them into the sky, and there they hung and turned into large stars. The old roots turned into stars that gave a red light, and the young roots turned into stars that gave a golden light. There they all hung, winking and twinkling and singing. Yes, singing, and this is what they sang.

> We are children of the Sun!
> It's so! It's so! It's so!
> Him we call when Night is done!
> It's so! It's so! It's so!
> Bright we sail across the sky
> By the Star's Road, high, so high;
> And we, twinkling, smile at you,
> As we sail across the blue!
> It's so! It's so! It's so!

When the stars twinkle up there in the sky they are like little children nodding their heads and saying, "It's so! It's so! It's so!"

One star grew and grew till he was much larger than the others. He was the Great Star, and, singing, he named the other stars. He called each one

THE STAR AND THE STAR'S ROAD. From *Outa Karel's Stories,* South African Folk Lore Tales, by Sanni Metelerkamp. By permission of Macmillan & Co., Ltd., London, and St. Martin's Press, Inc.

by name, till they all heard their names, and in this way they knew that he was the Great Star.

Now, when the day is done, they walk across the sky on each side of the Star's Road. It shows them the way. And when the Night is over, they turn back and sail again by the Star's Road to call the Daybreak, that goes before the Sun. The Star that leads the way is a big bright star. He is called the Dawn's Heart Star, and in the dark, dark hour, before the Stars have called the Dawn, he shines—ah! he is beautiful to behold! The wife and the child of the Dawn's Heart Star are pretty, too, but not so big and bright as he. They sail on in front, and then they wait—wait for the other Stars to turn back and sail along the Star's Road, calling, calling the Dawn, and for the Sun to come up from under the world, where he has been lying asleep.

They call and sing, twinkling as they sing:

> We call across the sky,
> Dawn! Come, Dawn!
> You, that are like a young maid newly risen,
> Rubbing the sleep from your eyes!
> You, that come stretching bright hands to the sky,
> Pointing the way for the Sun!
> Before whose smile the Stars faint and grow pale,
> And the Star's Road melts away.
> Dawn! Come Dawn!
> We call across the sky,
> And the Dawn's Heart Star is waiting.
> It's so! It's so! It's so!

So they sing, because they know they are soon going out.

Then slowly the Dawn comes, rubbing her eyes, smiling, stretching out bright fingers, chasing the darkness away. The Stars grow faint and the Star's Road fades, while the Dawn makes a bright pathway for the Sun. At last he comes with both arms lifted high, and the brightness, streaming from under them, makes day for the world, and wakes people to their work and play.

THE ANIMAL'S DAM

"Ach! it was dry," said Outa. For a long time the Old Man in the sky shot down strong light and sucked all the water out of the veld. From morning to night he poured down hotness on the world, and when he

THE ANIMAL'S DAM. From *Outa Karel's Stories,* South African Folk Lore Tales, by Sanni Metelerkamp. By permission of Macmillan & Co., Ltd., London, and St. Martin's Press, Inc.

rolled round to sleep, a hot wind blew—and blew—and blew—till he woke up to shine again. The karroo bushes dried up, the rivers had no water, and the poor animals began to die from thirst.

At last Oom Leeuw [Uncle Lion] called the animals together to make a plan.

The Sun had gone under, and the Lady Moon was sailing in the sky—beautiful, as she always is, and looking down on the hot world. Oom Leeuw sat under a krantz [precipice] on the morning side of the kopje [hill], where it was a little cool, and the others sat round him like a watermelon slice. Leopard, Hyena, Baboon, Jakhals, Hare and Tortoise, Rabbit, Ostrich, and Zebra.

Oom Leeuw pulled in his tongue, which was hanging out because it was so dry, and rolled it around to get the dryness off. When it stopped rattling he began to talk.

"Friends and brothers and nephews, it is time to make a plan. If a land-rain comes, it will just sink into the ground because the ground is too loose and dry to hold it, so we must make a plan to keep the water, and my plan is to dig a dam. But it's no use for one or two to work; everyone must help. What do you say?"

"Certainly," said Leopard.

"Certainly," said Hyena.

"Certainly," said Baboon.

"Certainly," said Jakhals, but he winked his eye at the Lady Moon, and then put his nose into the warm sand so that no one could see his sly smile.

All the animals said, "Certainly," and then they began to talk about the dam. A person would never have said their throats were dry. Each had a different plan, and each one talked without listening to the other.

At last the Water Tortoise—he with the wise little head under his patch-work shell—said, "Let us go now while it is cool, and look for a place for the dam."

So they hunted about and found a nice place, and soon they began to make the dam. How those animals worked! They scratched, they dug, they poked, they bored, they pushed; and they all did their best, so that the dam could be ready when the rain came. Only lazy Jakhals did not work. He just roamed round saying to the others, "Why don't you do this?" "Why don't you do that?" till at last they asked, "Why don't you do it yourself?"

But Jakhals only laughed at them. "And why should I be so foolish as to scratch my nails off for your old dam?" he said.

"But you said 'Certainly,' too, when Oom asked us, didn't you?" they asked.

Then Jakhals laughed more than ever. "Ha-ha-ha! Ha-ha-ha! Am I a slave of my word? That was last night. Don't you know yet that a thing is one colour by moonlight, and quite another colour when the sun shines on it? Ha-ha-ha!"

So he went about bothering the poor animals that were working so hard, and laughing at them when they got hot and tired.

"What's the use of working so hard? Those who do not work will also drink."

"How do you know?" they asked.

"Wait a bit, you'll see," said Jakhals.

At last the dam was finished, and that very night the rain began. It kept on and on, till the dam was quite full and the water began to run away over the veld, down to the great big dam called the Sea. The milk-bushes grew green again, and the little veld flowers burst out of the hard ground, and opened their white, and blue, and pink, and purple eyes to look at the Sun. The Old Man in the sky was not fierce any more; he did not burn them with his hotness, but looked at them kindly.

And the animals were so glad for the water! From far and near they came to the dam to drink.

But Jakhals was before them all. Soon after the Sun went down—the wild animals sleep in the daytime and hunt in the night—he went to the dam and drank as much water as he wanted, and filled his clay pot with some to take home. Then he swam round and round to get cool, making the water muddy and dirty, and when the other animals came to drink, he slipped over the dam wall and was lost in the veld as if he had been a large pin.

My! but Oom Leeuw was very angry!

"Hoorr-rr-rr," he roared, "Hoo-rr-rr! What is this for a thing? Does the lazy one think he can share with the workers? Who ever heard of such a thing? Hoo-rr-rr! Here, Broer Babiaan (Brother Baboon), take this big stick and hide yourself by the dam tonight, so that you can catch this Vagabond, this Waterstealer."

Early that night, there was Jakhals again. He peeped this way and that way—and, yes truly, there was old Broer Babiaan lying amongst the bushes. But Jakhals was too sly for him. He made as if he didn't see him. He danced on his hind legs, round and round at the edge of the dam, singing:

> Hing-ting-ting! Honna-mak-a-ding!
> My sweet, sweet water!

He sang this over and over, every time he came to the end of the line, he dipped his fingers into his clay pot and sucked them.

"Aha! but my honey is nice," he said, licking his lips. "What do I want with their old dirty water, when I have a whole potful of nice sweet water!"

Now, baboons will do anything for honey, and when old Broer Babiaan heard Jakhals he forgot he was there to guard the dam. He crept out from his hiding place, a little nearer, and a little nearer, and at last he couldn't keep quiet any longer. When Jakhals came dancing along again, he called out in a great hurry, "Good evening, Jakhals! Please give me a little of your sweet water, too!"

"Oh," said Jakhals, jumping to one side and pretending to be startled. "What a scare you gave me! What are you doing here, Broer Babiaan?"

"I'm just taking a little walk. It's such a fine night."

"But why do you have that big stick?"

"Only to dig out some roots to eat."

"Do you really want some of my sweet water?"

"Yes, please Jakhals," said Broer Babiaan, licking his lips.

"And what will you give me for it?"

"I'll let you fill your pot with water from the dam."

"I don't want any of that dirty old dam water, but I know how fond you are of this sweet water, so I'll let you drink some. Here, I'll hold your stick while you drink."

Broer Babiaan was in such a hurry to get the honey that he just threw the stick to Jakhals, but as he was going to put his fingers into the pot, Jakhals pulled it away.

"No, wait a bit, Broer," he said. "I'll show you a better way. It will taste much nicer if you lie down."

"No! Really, Jakhals?"

"Yes, really," said Jakhals. "And if you don't lie down at once, you won't get a drop of my sweet water."

He spoke quite crossly, and Babiaan was so tame by this time that he was ready to believe anything, so he lay down, and Jakhals stood over him with his leather thong from his knapsack.

"Now, Brother, first I'll tie you with my thong, and then I'll feed you with the honey."

"Yes, yes," said Broer Babiaan quickly.

His mouth was watering for the honey; he couldn't think of anything else, and he had long ago forgotten all about looking after the dam. It goes so, when a person thinks only of what he wants and not of what he must. So he let Jakhals tie his hands and feet, and even his tail, and then he opened his mouth wide.

But Jakhals only danced round and round, sticking his fingers into the pot and licking them, and singing:

Hing-ting-ting! Honna-mak-a-ding!
My sweet, sweet water!

"Where's mine?" called Broer Babiaan. "You said you would feed me. Where's my sweet water?"

"Here's all the sweet water you'll get from me," said Jakhals, and he gave him a hit with the stick.

"Help! Help! Help!" screamed Broer Babiaan, and tried to roll away. But there was no one to help him, so he could only scream and roll over.

Jakhals squeezed the clay pot—and it had never had any honey in it at all—over Broer Babiaan's head, and ran off and drank as much water as he wanted. Then he took the clay pot off Broer Babiaan's head, filled it with water, and danced off, singing:

Hing-ting-ting! Honna-mak-a-ding!
My sweet, sweet water!

"Good-bye, Brother," he called out. "I hope you'll enjoy the sweet water you'll get from Oom Leeuw when he sees how well you have looked after the dam."

Poor Old Broer Babiaan was so miserable, but he was even more unhappy after Oom Leeuw had punished him by making him sit on a large stone for the other animals to mock at. They were so rude that the poor animal sat all in a heap, hanging down his head and trying not to see how they were mocking him.

When all the animals had passed on and drunk water, Oom Leeuw untied Broer Babiaan and let him go, and off he went as fast as he could with his tail between his legs.

And that is all for to-night. It is too long to finish now.

THE COCK

The Cock, it is said, was once overtaken by the Jackal and caught. The Cock said to the Jackal, "Please, pray first (before you kill me) as the white man does." The Jackal asked, "In what manner does he pray? Tell me." "He folds his hands in praying," said the Cock. The Jackal folded his hands and prayed. Then the Cock spoke again: "You ought not to look about you as you do. You had better shut your eyes." He did so; and the Cock flew away, upbraiding at the same time the Jackal with these words: "You rogue! do you also pray?"

There sat the Jackal, speechless, because he had been outdone.

THE COCK. From *Reynard the Fox in South Africa or Hottentot Fable and Tales,* by W. H. I. Bleek, Ph.D. Trubner and Co.

THE PATCHED CLOAK

A poor widow woman, who had only one son, named Abdullah, wanted very much to send him to school; but they had hardly enough to eat, and to buy clothes was quite out of the question. All that Abdullah had to wear was a tattered pair of trousers, and when it was cold the widow gave him a cloak patched with many colours.

Abdullah wished very much to go to school and could not understand why his mother grew so sad whenever he spoke of it. One cold morning he determined to ask the imam if he could join his classes.

"Of course, my son," said the imam. "Is not the Word of Allah proclaimed here, and are you not Abdullah? No doubt your mother was ashamed to send you here without pretty clothes. But here the poor and the rich are one, and I'll not allow anyone here to poke fun at poverty."

All went along splendidly at the imam's and Abdullah enjoyed his first lesson, but as soon as the other boys met him in the street they could not refrain from teasing him about his badly patched cloak.

One of the boys made a little song and they all sang it together, as soon as Abdullah, with patches all over him, appeared round the corner:

Lap, dit is lap,
Lap, dit is lap. . . .
[Patch, there is a patch]

That afternoon Abdullah wandered forlornly in the desert, for the children's mocking drove him out of the village.

At the foot of a date palm he came upon a dead dog, beside which its mate lay mourning.

"Poor creature!" said Abdullah to the little dog who was mourning. "You've lost your mate. If only I could, I'd give him back to you; but only Allah can do that."

The little dog looked up at him with beseeching eyes.

"Do you want me to pray for him? Maybe Allah will hear our prayer. I'll throw my cloak over your mate, so that the sun can't scorch him."

And Abdullah drew the patched cloak over the dead dog, knelt down near the date palm and begged Allah to give back the animal to its mate.

He had hardly finished when the cloak stirred and the dog crept out of it, licked Abdullah's hand and began to frolic with its mate.

The joy of those three was boundless as they went away.

Near one of the pale yellow sand dunes, which stretched out to the horizon, lay a dead cock and alongside mourned a little hen.

THE PATCHED CLOAK. From *Tales from the Malay Quarter*, by I. D. duPlessis. By permission of Maskew Miller, Ltd. publisher.

"Perhaps Allah will hear my prayer again," said Abdullah, and he threw his cloak over the cock before he began to pray.

He'd hardly finished when the cock crept out of the cloak.

The joy of those five was boundless as they went on further.

They then came to a palace with doors of pearl. A great multitude of people stood before it.

"Something must have happened!" said Abdullah, and he told the cock to have a look.

"Jump on to the wall," said Abdullah. "If you crow, I'll know there is sorrow, but if you only step about, I'll know it is joy."

Hardly had the cock got on top of the wall when he crowed loudly.

"Has someone died?" Abdullah asked.

"Yes," said a man at the gate. "Our Sultan has died and we are all very sad, for he was just and a good Prince."

"Let me pass!" cried Abdullah. "Maybe I can be of use."

At first the guards would not allow the boy in the patched cloak to pass, but he begged so earnestly that at last they let him in.

Abdullah drew his cloak over the Sultan and asked Allah if He would not give the Sultan back to his people.

Everybody was struck dumb and motionless as they saw the poverty-stricken boy, with the dogs and the fowls at his side, praying so earnestly at the Sultan's bed of state; but greater still was the astonishment when the cloak began to stir and the Sultan arose as if nothing had been the matter with him!

When the Sultan learnt what had happened, he would not allow Abdullah to depart.

"By your devout prayer," said the Sultan, "you gave me back to my people. Allah is great and good. He hearkens to the prayer of the pure in heart. Let me take you back to your mother, and I'll give her a house in my city. I shall want you to remain always near me."

Abdullah became a great man in the land, but although he was always dressed in silk and satin he never parted from his patched cloak, for by it he first learnt to know the mercy of Allah.

3
ASIA

Silver is his daïs, plastered o'er with gold;
In his ears are jewels, . . . some prince I must behold![1]

The darkness descended, the stars came out, the mosquito sang through the hot, heavy air, the dogs barked, and all voices were hushed except from the crowded huts where the voice of the story-teller was heard.

India is the home of the great masters of storytelling. The Hindu is alive with the beauty of poetry and the fantasy of fiction. The fables contained in their oldest literary piece, the *Pancha-Tantra,* are older than those of Aesop. It was the animal fable of India that Aesop carried to the West. In contrast to the African animal whose aspects are those of human beings, these stories are concerned with animals whose speech moralizes or teaches mankind their faults.

The Indian fable also traveled throughout Asia but only a few remain either in China or Japan. In China they became outmoded as the realistic Chinese preferred tales in which men played the important roles. There is also in the Chinese folk tales a restriction upon the imaginative powers and there is a lack of the dramatic construction or humourous sparkle of other countries.

The Japanese folk tales are similar to those of other lands. The relationships are those of ordinary folk, simple-hearted villagers, priests and strangers. They are mostly for adults and have too many strong characteristics which make them unsuitable for children. Yet the beauty of the land and the people is found in passages such as this from "Urashima Taro."[2]

Round it were wide gardens which reminded Urashima of the gardens of his own Japan, for maples and firs and plum and cherry-trees grew there, and wisteria climbed over arches, and little bridges of red lacquer spanned tiny torrents of foaming grey water.

[1] F. A. Steel and R. C. Temple, "The Jackal and the Iguana," from *Wide-Awake Stories.*

[2] Marjory Bruce, "Urashima Taro," from *A Treasury of Tales.*

41

THE JACKAL AND THE IGUANA

One moonlight night, a miserable half-starved jackal, skulking through the village, found a worn-out pair of shoes in the gutter. They were too tough for him to eat, so, determined to make some use of them, he strung them to his ears like earrings, and, going down to the edge of the pond, gathered all the old bones he could find together, and built a platform with them, plastering it over with mud.

On this he sat in a dignified attitude, and when any animal came to the pond to drink, he cried out in a loud voice, "Hi! stop! You must not taste a drop till you have done homage to me. So repeat these verses, which I have composed in honour of the occasion—

> Silver is his daïs, plastered o'er with gold;
> In his ears are jewels, . . . some prince I must behold!

Now, as most of the animals were very thirsty, and in a great hurry to drink, they did not care to dispute the matter, but gabbled off the words without a second thought. Even the royal tiger, treating it as a jest, repeated the jackal's rhyme, in consequence of which the latter became quite cock-a-hoop, and really began to believe he was a personage of great importance.

By-and-by, an iguana, or great lizard, came waddling and wheezing down to the water, looking for all the world like a baby alligator.

"Hi! you there!" sang out the jackal; "you mustn't drink until you have said

> Silver is his daïs, plastered o'er with gold;
> In his ears are jewels, . . . some prince I must behold!

"Pouf! pouf!" gasped the iguana. "Mercy on us, how dry my throat is! Mightn't I have just a wee sip of water first? and then I could do justice to your admirable lines; at present I am as hoarse as a crow!"

"By all means!" replied the jackal, with a gratified smirk. "I flatter myself the verses are good, especially when well recited."

So the iguana, nose down into the water, drank away, until the jackal began to think he would never leave off, and was quite taken aback when he finally came to an end of his draught, and began to move away.

"Hi! hi!" cried the jackal, recovering his presence of mind; "stop a bit, and say

THE JACKAL AND THE IGUANA. From *Wide-Awake Stories,* by F. A. Steel and R. C. Temple.

> Silver is his daïs, plastered o'er with gold;
> In his ears are jewels, . . . some prince I must behold!

"Dear me!" replied the iguana, politely, "I was very nearly forgetting! Let me see—I must try my voice first—Do, re, me, fa, sol, la, ti,—that is right! Now how does it run?"

> Silver is his daïs, plastered o'er with gold;
> In his ears are jewels, . . . some prince I must behold!

repeated the jackal, not observing that the lizard was carefully edging farther and farther away.

"Exactly so," returned the iguana; "now for it!" Whereupon he sang out at the top of his voice,

> Bones make up his daïs, with mud it's plastered o'er,
> Old shoes are his ear-drops: a jackal, nothing more!

And turning round, he bolted for his hole as hard as he could.

The jackal could scarcely believe his ears, and sat dumb with astonishment. Then, rage lending him wings, he flew after the lizard, who, despite his short legs and scanty breath, put his best foot foremost, and scuttled away at a great rate.

It was a near shave, however, for just as he popped into his hole, the jackal caught him by the tail, and held on. Then it was a case of "pull butcher, pull baker," until the lizard made certain his tail must come off, and the jackal felt as if his front teeth would come out. Still not an inch did either budge, one way or the other, and there they might have remained till the present day, had not the iguana called out, in his sweetest tones, "Friend, I give in! Just leave hold of my tail, will you? then I can turn round and come out."

Whereupon the jackal let go, and the tail disappeared up the hole in a twinkling; while all the reward the jackal got for digging away until his nails were nearly worn out, was hearing the iguana sing softly

> Bones make up his daïs, with mud it's plastered o'er,
> Old shoes are his ear-drops: a jackal, nothing more!

PRIDE GOETH BEFORE A FALL

In a certain village there lived ten cloth merchants, who always went about together. Once upon a time they had travelled far afield, and

PRIDE GOETH BEFORE A FALL. From *Indian Fairy Tales*, by Joseph Jacobs. By permission of G. P. Putnam's Sons, publishers.

were returning home with a great deal of money which they had obtained by selling their wares. Now there happened to be a dense forest near their village, and this they reached early one morning. In it there lived three notorious robbers, of whose existence the traders had never heard, and while they were still in the middle of it the robbers stood before them, with swords and cudgels in their hands, and ordered them to lay down all they had. The traders had no weapons with them, and so, though they were many more in number, they had to submit themselves to the robbers, who took away everything from them, even the very clothes they wore, and gave to each only a small loin-cloth a span in breadth and a cubit in length.

The idea that they had conquered ten men and plundered all their property now took possession of the robbers' minds. They seated themselves like three monarchs before the men they had plundered, and ordered them to dance for them before returning home. The merchants now mourned their fate. They had lost all they had, except their loin-cloths, and still the robbers were not satisfied, but ordered them to dance.

There was, among the ten merchants, one who was very clever. He pondered over the calamity that had come upon him and his friends, the dance they would have to perform, and the magnificent manner in which the three robbers had seated themselves on the grass. At the same time he observed that these last had placed their weapons on the ground, in the assurance of having thoroughly cowed the traders, who were now commencing to dance. So he took the lead in the dance, and, as a song is always sung by the leader on such occasions, to which the rest keep time with hands and feet, he thus began to sing:

> We are enty men,
> They are erith men:
> If each erith man,
> Surround eno men
> Eno man remains.
> Tâ, tai tôm, tadingana.

The robbers were all uneducated, and thought that the leader was merely singing a song as usual. So it was in one sense; for the leader commenced from a distance, and had sung the song over twice before he and his companions commenced to approach the robbers. They had understood his meaning, because they had been trained in trade.

When two traders discuss the price of an article in the presence of a purchaser, they use a riddling sort of language.

"What is the price of this cloth?" one trader will ask.

"Enty rupees," another will reply, meaning "ten rupees."

Thus, there is no possibility of the purchaser knowing what is meant unless he be acquainted with trade language. By the rules of this secret language erith means "three," enty means "ten," and eno means "one." So the leader by his song meant to hint to his fellow-traders that they were ten men, the robbers only three, that if three pounced upon each of the robbers, nine of them could hold them down, while the remaining one bound the robbers' hands and feet.

The three thieves, glorying in their victory, and little understanding the meaning of the song and the intentions of the dancers, were proudly seated chewing betel and tobacco. Meanwhile the song was sung a third time. Tâ tai tôm had left the lips of the singers; and, before tadingana was out of them, the traders separated into parties of three, and each party pounced upon a thief. The remaining one—the leader himself—tore up into long narrow strips a large piece of cloth, six cubits long, and tied the hands and feet of the robbers. These were entirely humbled now, and rolled on the ground like three bags of rice!

The ten traders now took back all their property, and armed themselves with the swords and cudgels of their enemies; and when they reached their village they often amused their friends and relatives by relating their adventure.

HOW SUN, MOON, AND WIND WENT OUT TO DINNER

One day Sun, Moon, and Wind went out to dine with their uncle and aunt Thunder and Lightning. Their mother (one of the most distant Stars you see far up in the sky) waited alone for her children's return.

Now both Sun and Wind were greedy and selfish. They enjoyed the great feast that had been prepared for them, without a thought of saving any of it to take home to their mother—but the gentle Moon did not forget her. Of every dainty dish that was brought round, she placed a small portion under one of her beautiful long fingernails, that Star might also have a share in the treat.

On their return, their mother, who had kept watch for them all night long with her little bright eye, said, "Well, children, what have you brought home for me?" Then Sun (who was eldest) said, "I have brought nothing home for you. I went out to enjoy myself with my friends—not to fetch a dinner for my mother!" And Wind said, "Neither have I brought anything home for you, Mother. You could hardly expect me to bring a collection

HOW SUN, MOON, AND WIND WENT OUT TO DINNER. From *Indian Fairy Tales,* by Joseph Jacobs. By permission of G. P. Putnam's Sons, publishers.

of good things for you, when I merely went out for my own pleasure."
But Moon said, "Mother, fetch a plate, see what I have brought you."
And shaking her hands she showered down such a choice dinner as never
was seen before.

Then Star turned to Sun and spoke thus: "Because you went out to
amuse yourself with your friends, and feasted and enjoyed yourself, without any thought of your mother at home—you shall be cursed. Henceforth, your rays shall ever be hot and scorching, and shall burn all that
they touch. And men shall hate you, and cover their heads when you appear."

(And that is why the Sun is so hot to this day.)

Then she turned to Wind and said, "You also who forgot your mother
in the midst of your selfish pleasures—hear your doom. You shall always
blow in the hot dry weather, and shall parch and shrivel all living things.
And men shall detest and avoid you from this very time."

(And that is why the Wind in the hot weather is still so disagreeable.)

But to Moon she said, "Daughter, because you remembered your
mother, and kept for her a share in your own enjoyment, from henceforth
you shall be ever cool, and calm, and bright. No noxious glare shall accompany your pure rays, and men shall always call you 'blessed.' "

(And that is why the moon's light is so soft, and cool, and beautiful
even to this day.)

THE FOUR SIMPLE BRÁHMANS

Introduction

In a certain district, proclamation had been made of a Samaradanam
being about to be held.[3] Four Bráhmans, from different villages going
thither, fell in upon the road, and, finding that they were all upon the
same errand, they agreed to proceed in company. A soldier, happening
to meet them, saluted them in the usual way, by touching hands and pro-
nouncing the words always applied on such occasions to Bráhmans,
"Dandamarya!" or "Health to my lord!" The four travellers made the
customary return, "Asirvadam!" and going on, they came to a well, where
they quenched their thirst and reposed themselves in the shade of some
trees. Sitting there, and finding no better subject of conversation, one of
them asked the others, whether they did not remark how particularly the
soldier had distinguished him by the polite salutation. "You!" said an-

THE FOUR SIMPLE BRÁHMANS. From *The Book of Noodles,* by W. A. Clouston.

[3] A Samaradanam is one of the public festivals given by pious people, and sometimes by those in power, at which the people assemble in great numbers.

other; "it was not you that he saluted, but me." "You are both mistaken," said a third; "for you may remember that when the soldier said, 'Danda-marya!' he cast his eyes upon me." "Not at all," replied the fourth; "it was I only he saluted; otherwise, should I have answered him as I did, by saying, 'Asirvadam'?"

Each maintained his argument obstinately; and as none of them would yield, the dispute had nearly come to blows, when the least stupid of the four, seeing what was likely to happen, put an end to the brawl by the following advice: "How foolish it is in us," said he, "thus to put our-selves in a passion! After we have said all the ill of one another that we can invent—nay, after going stoutly to fisticuffs, like Sudra rabble, should we be at all nearer to the decision of our difference? The fittest person to determine the controversy, I think, would be the man who occasioned it. The soldier, who chose to salute to one of us, cannot yet be far off: let us therefore run after him as quickly as we can, and we shall soon know for which of us he intended his salutation."

This advice appeared wise to them all, and was immediately adopted. The whole of them set off in pursuit of the soldier, and at last overtook him, after running a league, and all out of breath. As soon as they came in sight of him, they cried out to him to stop; and before they had well approached him, they had put him in full possession of the nature of their dispute, and prayed him to terminate it, by saying to which of them had he directed his salutation. The soldier instantly perceiving the charac-ter of the people he had to do with, and being willing to amuse himself a little at their expense, coolly replied, that he intended his salutation for the greatest fool of all four, and then, turning on his heel, he continued his journey.

The Bráhmans, confounded at this answer, turned back in silence. But all of them had deeply at heart the distinction of the salutation of the soldier, and the dispute was gradually renewed. Even the awkward de-cision of the warrior could not prevent each of them from arrogating to himself the preeminence of being noticed by him, to the exclusion of the others. The contention, therefore, now became, which of the four was the stupidest; and strange to say, it grew as warm as ever, and must have come to blows, had not the person who gave the former advice, to follow the soldier, interposed again with his wisdom, and spoke as follows: "I think myself the greatest fool of us all. Each of you thinks the same thing of himself. And after a fight, shall we be a bit nearer the decision of the question? Let us, therefore have a little patience. We are within a short distance of Dharmapuri, where there is a choultry, at which all little causes are tried by the heads of the village; and let ours be judged among the rest."

The others agreed in the soundness of this advice; and having arrived at the village, they eagerly entered the choultry, to have their business settled by the arbitrator. Thy could not have come at a better season. The chiefs of the district, Bráhmans and others, had already met in the choultry; and no other cause being brought forward, they proceeded immediately to that of the four Bráhmans, who advanced into the middle of the court, and stated that a sharp contest having arisen among them, they were come to have it decided with fairness and impartiality. The court desired them to proceed and explain the ground of their controversy. Upon this, one of them stood forward and related to the assembly all that had happened, from their meeting with the soldier to the present sad state of the quarrel, which rested on the superior degree of stupidity of one of their number. The detail created a general shout of laughter. The president, who was of gay disposition, was delighted no measure to have fallen in with so diverting an incident. But he put on a grave face, and laid it down, as the peculiarity of the cause, that it could not be determined on the testimony of witnesses, and that, in fact, there was no other way of satisfying the minds of the judges than by each, in his turn, relating some particular occurrence of his life, on which he could best establish his claim to superior folly. He clearly showed that there could be no other means of determining to which of them the salutation of the soldier could with justice be awarded. The Bráhmans assented, and upon a sign being made to one of them to begin, and the rest to keep silence, the first thus spoke:

Story of the First Bráhman

I am poorly provided with clothing, as you see; and it is not to-day only that I have been covered with rags. A rich and very charitable Bráhman merchant once made present of two pieces of cloth to attire me—the finest that had ever been seen in our village. I showed them to the other Bráhmans of the village, who all congratulated me on so fortunate an acquisition. They told me it must be the fruit of some good deeds that I had done in a preceding generation. Before I should put them on, I washed them, according to the custom, in order to purify them from the soil of the weaver's touch, and hung them up to dry, with the ends fastened to two branches of a tree. A dog, then happening to come that way, ran under them, and I could not discover whether he was high enough to touch the clothes or not. I asked my children, who were present, but they said they were not quite certain. How, then, was I to discover the fact? I put myself upon all-fours, so as to be of the height of the dog, and in that posture I crawled under the clothing. "Did I touch it?" said I to the children, who were observing me. They answered, "No," and I was filled with joy at the news. But after reflecting a while, I recollected that the dog had a turned-up tail, and that by elevating it above the rest of his body, it might well have reached my cloth. To ascertain that, I fixed a leaf in my loin-cloth, turning upwards, and then, creeping again on all-fours, I passed a second time under the clothing. The children immediately cried out that the point of the leaf on my back had touched the cloth. This proved to me that the point of the dog's tail must have done so too, and that my garments were therefore polluted. In my rage I pulled down the beautiful raiment, and tore it in a thousand pieces, loaded with curses both for the dog and the master.

When this foolish act was known, I became the laughing stock of all the world, and I was universally treated as a madman. "Even if the dog had touched the cloth," said they, "and so brought defilement upon it, might not you have washed it a second time, and so have removed the stain? Or might you not have given it to some poor Sudra, rather than tear it in pieces? After such egregious folly, who will give you clothes another time?" This was all true; for ever since, when I have begged clothing of any one, the constant answer has been, that, no doubt, I wanted a piece of cloth to pull to pieces.

He was going on, when a bystander interrupted him by remarking that he seemed to understand going on all-fours. "Exceedingly well," said he, "as you shall see"; and off he shuffled, in that posture, amidst the unbounded laughter of the spectators. "Enough! enough!" said the president. "What we have both heard and seen goes a great way in his favour. But let us now hear what the next has to say for himself in proof of his stupidity." The second accordingly began by expressing his confidence that if what they had just heard appeared to them to be deserving of the salutation of the soldier, what he had to say would change their opinion.

Story of the Second Bráhman

Having got my hair and beard shaved one day, in order to appear decent at a public festival of the Bráhmans, which had been proclaimed throughout the district, I desired my wife to give the barber a penny for his trouble. She heedlessly gave him a couple. I asked him to give me one of them back, but he refused. Upon that we quarrelled, and began to abuse each other; but the barber at length pacified me, by offering, in consideration of the double fee, to shave my wife also. I thought this a fair way of settling the difference between us. But my wife, hearing the proposal, and seeing the barber in earnest, tried to make her escape by flight. I took hold of her, and forced her to sit down, while he shaved her poll in the same manner as they serve widows.[4] During the operation she cried out bitterly; but I was inexorable, thinking it less hard that my wife should be close-shaven than that my penny should be given away for nothing. When the barber had finished, I let her go, and she retired immediately to a place of concealment, pouring down curses on me and the barber. He took his departure and meeting my mother in his way, told

---

[4] In a Sinhalese story, referred to on p. 68 of *The Book of Noodles*, it is curiously enough, the woman herself "Who has her head shaved, so as not to lose the services of the barber for the day when he came, and her husband was away from home."

her what he had done, which made her hasten to the house, to inquire into the outrage; and when she saw that it was all true she also loaded me with incivilities.

The barber published everywhere what had happened at our house; and the villain added to the story that I had caught her with another man, which was the cause of my having her shaved; and people were no doubt expecting, according to our custom in such a case, to see her mounted on an ass, with her face turned towards the tail. They came running to my dwelling from all quarter, and actually brought an ass to make the usual exhibition in the streets. The report soon reached my father-in-law, who lived at a distance of ten or twelve leagues, and he, with his wife, came also to inquire into the affair. Seeing their poor daughter in that degraded state, and being apprised of the only reason, they reproached me most bitterly, which I patiently endured, being conscious that I was in the wrong. They persisted, however, in taking her with them and keeping her carefully concealed from every eye for four whole years; when at length they restored her to me.

This little accident made me lose the Samaradanam, for which I had been preparing by a fast of three days; and it was a great mortification to me to be excluded from it, as I understood it was a most splendid entertainment. Another Samaradanam was announced to be held ten days afterwards, at which I expected to make up for my loss. But I was received with the hisses of six hundred Bráhmans, who seized my person, and insisted on my giving up the accomplice of my wife, that he might be prosecuted and punished, according to the severe rules of the caste.

I solemnly attested her innocence, and told the real cause of the shaving of her hair; when a universal burst of surprise took place, every one exclaiming, how monstrous it was that a married woman should be so degraded, without having committed the crime of adultery. "Either this man," said they, "must be a liar, or he is the greatest fool on the face of the earth!" Such, I daresay, gentlemen, you will think me, and I am sure you will consider my folly (looking with great disdain on the first speaker) as being far superior to that of the render of body-clothing.

The court agreed that the speaker had put in a strong case; but justice required that the other two should be heard. The third claimant was indeed burning with impatience for his turn, and as soon as he had permission, he thus spoke:

Story of the Third Bráhman

My name was originally Anantya; now all the world call me Betel Anantya, and I will tell you how this nickname arose. My wife, having been long detained at her father's house, on account of her youth, had cohabited with me but about a month when, going to bed one evening, I happened to say (carelessly, I believe), that all women were babblers. She retorted that she knew men who were not less babblers than women. I perceived at once that she alluded to myself; and being somewhat piqued at the sharpness of her retort, I said, "Now let us see which of us shall speak first." "Agreed," quoth she; "but what shall be the forfeit?" "A leaf of betel," said I. Our wager being thus made, we both addressed ourselves to sleep, without speaking another word.

Next morning, as we did not appear at our usual hour, after some interval, they called us, but got no answer. They again called and then roared stoutly at the door, but with no success. The alarm began to spread in the house. They began to fear that we had died suddenly. The carpenter was called with his tools. The door of our room was forced open, and when they got in they were not a little surprised to find both of us wide awake, in good health, and at our ease, though without the faculty of speech. My mother was greatly alarmed, and gave loud vent to her grief. All the Bráhmans in the village, of both sexes, assembled, to the number of one hundred; and after close examination, every one drew his own conclusion on the accident which was supposed to have befallen us. The greater number were of opinion that it could have arisen only from the malevolence of some enemy who had availed himself of magical incantations to injure us. For this reason, a famous magician was called, to counteract the effects of the witchcraft, and to remove it. As soon as he came, after steadfastly contemplating us for some time, he began to try our pulses, by putting his finger on our wrists, on our temples, on the heart, and on various other parts of the body; and after a great variety of grimaces, the remembrance of which excites my laughter, as often as I think of him, he decided that our malady arose wholly from the effect of malevolence. He even gave the name of the particular devil that possessed my wife and me and rendered us dumb. He added that the devil was very stubborn and difficult to allay, and that it would cost three to four pagodas for the offerings necessary for compelling him to try.

My relations, who were not very opulent, were astonished at the grievous imposition which the magician had laid on them. Yet, rather than we should continue dumb, they consented to give him whatever should be necessary for the expense of his sacrifice; and they further promised that they would reward him for his trouble as soon as the demon by whom we were possessed should be expelled. He was on the point of commencing his magical operations, when a Bráhman, one of our friends, who was present, maintained, in opposition to the opinion of the magician and his assistants, that our malady was not at all the effect of witchcraft, but arose from some simple and ordinary cause, of which he had seen several instances, and he undertook to cure us without any expense.

He took a chafing-dish filled with burning charcoal, and heated a small bar of gold very hot. This he took up with pincers, and applied to the soles of my feet, then to my elbows, and the crown of my head. I endured these cruel operations without showing the least symptom of pain, or making any complaint; being determined to bear anything, and to die, if necessary, rather than lose the wager I had laid.

"Let us try the effect on the woman," said the doctor, astonished at my resolution and apparent insensibility. And immediately taking the bit of gold, well heated, he applied it to the sole of her foot. She was not able to endure the pain for a moment, but instantly screamed out, "Enough!" and turning to me, "I have lost my wager," she said. "There is your leaf of betel." "Did I not tell you," said I, taking the leaf, "that you would be the first to speak out, and that you would prove that I was right in saying yesterday, when we went to bed, that women are babblers?"

Every one was surprised at the proceeding; nor could any of them comprehend the meaning of what was passing between my wife and me; until I explained the kind of wager we had made overnight, before going to sleep. "What!" they exclaimed, "was it for a leaf of betel that you have spread this alarm through your own house and the whole village?— for a leaf of betel that you showed such constancy, and suffered burning from the feet to the head upwards? Never in the world was there seen such folly!" And so, from that time, I have been constantly known by the name of Betel Anantya.

The narrative being finished, the court were of opinion that so transcendent a piece of folly gave him high pretensions in the depending suit; but it was necessary also to hear the fourth and last of the suitors, who thus addressed them:

Story of the Fourth Bráhman

The maiden to whom I was betrothed, having remained six or seven years at her father's house, on account of her youth, we were at last apprised that she was become marriageable; and her parents informed mine that she was in a situation to fulfill all the duties of a wife, and might therefore join her husband. My mother being at that time sick, and the house of my father-in-law being at the distance of five or six leagues from ours, she was not able to undertake the journey. She therefore committed to myself the duty of bringing home my wife, and counselled me so to conduct myself, of words and actions, that they might not see that I was only a brute. "Knowing thee as I do," said my mother, as I took leave of her, "I am very distrustful of thee." But I promised to be on my good behaviour; and so I departed.

I was well received by my father-in-law, who gave a great feast to all the Bráhmans of the village on the occasion. He made me stay three days, during which there was nothing but festivity. At length the time of our departure having arrived, he suffered myself and my wife to leave him, after pouring out blessings on us both, and wishing us a long and happy life, enriched with a numerous progeny. When we took leave of him, he shed abundance of tears, as if he had foreseen the misery that awaited us.

It was then the summer solstice, and the day was exceedingly hot. We had to cross a sandy plain of more than two leagues; and the sand, being heated by the burning sun, scorched the feet of my young wife, who, being brought up too tenderly in her father's house, was not accustomed to such severe trials. She began to cry, and being unable to go on, she lay down on the ground, saying she wished to die there. I was in dreadful trouble, and knew not what step to take; when a merchant came up, travelling the contrary way. He had a train of fifty bullocks, loaded with various kinds of merchandise. I ran to meet him, and told him the cause of my anxiety with tears in my eyes; and entreated him to aid me with his good advice in the distressing circumstances in which I was placed. He immediately answered, that a young and delicate woman, such as my wife was, could neither remain where she lay nor proceed on her journey, under a hot sun, without being exposed to certain death. Rather than that I should see her perish, and run the hazard of being suspected of having killed her myself, and being guilty of one of the five crimes which the Bráhmans consider as the most heinous, he advised me to give her to him, and then he would mount her on one of his cattle and take her along with him. That I should be a loser, he admitted; but, all things considered, it was better to lose her, with the merit of having saved her life, than equally to lose her, under the suspicion of being her murderer. "Her trinkets," he said, "may be worth fifteen pagodas; take these twenty and give me your wife."

The merchant's arguments appeared unanswerable; so I yielded to them, and delivered to him my wife, whom he placed on one of his best oxen, and continued his journey without delay. I continued mine, also, and got home in the evening, was exhausted with hunger and fatigue, and with my feet almost roasted with the burning sand, over which I had walked the greater part of the day. Frightened to see me alone, "Where is your wife?" cried my mother. I gave her a full account of everything that had happened down to the time I left her. I spoke of the agreeable and courteous manner in which my father-in-law had received me, and how, by some delay, we had been overtaken by the scorching heat of the sun at noon, so that my wife must have perished and myself suspected of having caused her death, had we proceeded; and that I had preferred to sell her to a merchant who met us for twenty pagodas. And I showed my mother the money.

When I had done, my mother fell into an ecstasy of fury. She lifted up her voice against me with cries of rage, and overwhelmed me with imprecations and awful curses. Having given way to these first emotions of despair, she sank into a more moderate tone: "What hast thou done! Sold thy wife, has thou! Delivered her to another man! A Bráhmanari has become the concubine of a vile merchant! Ah, what will her kindred and ours say when they hear the tale of this brutish stupidity—of folly so unexampled and degrading?"

The relations of my wife were soon informed of the sad adventure that had befallen their unhappy girl. They came over to attack me, and would certainly have murdered me and my innocent mother, if we had not both made a sudden escape. Having no direct object to break their vengeance upon, they brought the matter before the chiefs of the caste, who unanimously fined me in two hundred pagodas, as a reparation to my father-in-law, and issued a proclamation against so great a fool being ever allowed to take another wife; denouncing the penality of expulsion from the caste against any one who should assist me in such an attempt. I was therefore condemned to remain a widower all my life, and to pay dear for my folly. Indeed, I should have been excluded forever from my caste, but for the high consideration in which the memory of my late father is still held, he having lived respected by all the world.

Now that you have heard one specimen of the many follies of my life, I hope you will not consider me as beneath those who have spoken before me, nor my pretensions altogether undeserving of the salutation of the soldier.

Conclusion

The heads of the assembly, several of whom were convulsed with laughter while the Bráhmans were telling their stories, decided, after hearing them all, that each had given such absolute proofs of folly as to be entitled, in justice, to a superiority in his own way: that each of them, therefore, should be at liberty to call himself the greatest fool of all, and to attribute to himself the salutation of the soldier. Each of them having thus gained his suit, it was recommended to them all to continue their journey, if it were possible, in amity. The delighted Bráhmans then rushed out of court, each exclaiming that he had gained his cause.

THE STORY OF THE CAT AND THE MICE

Once upon a time there was a Cat who lived in a large farmhouse in which there was a great number of Mice. For many years the Cat found no difficulty in catching as many Mice as she wanted to eat, and she lived a very peaceful and pleasant life. But as time passed on she found that she was growing old and infirm, and that it was becoming more and more difficult for her to catch the same number of Mice as before; so

THE STORY OF THE CAT AND THE MICE. From *Folk-Tales from Tibet*, by Captain W. F. O'Connor. By permission of Hurst and Blackett, Ltd.

after thinking very carefully what was the best thing to do, she one day called all the Mice together, and after promising not to touch them, she addressed them as follows:

"Oh! Mice," said she, "I have called you together in order to say something to you. The fact that I have lead a very wicked life, and now, in my old age, I repent of having caused you all so much inconvenience and annoyance. So I am going for the future to turn over a new leaf. It is my intention now to give myself up entirely to religious contemplation and no longer to molest you, so henceforth you are at liberty to run about as freely as you will without fear of me. All I ask of you is that twice every day you should all file past me in procession and each one make an obeisance as you pass me by, as a token of your gratitude to me for my kindness."

When the Mice heard this they were greatly pleased, for they thought that now, at last, they would be free from all danger from their former enemy, the Cat. So they very thankfully promised to fulfill the Cat's conditions, and agreed that they would file past her and make a salaam twice every day.

So when evening came the Cat took her seat on a cushion at one end of the room, and the Mice all went by in single file, each one making a profound salaam as it passed.

Now the cunning old Cat had arranged her little plan very carefully with an object of her own; for, as soon as the procession had all passed by with the exception of one little Mouse, she suddenly seized the last Mouse in her claws without anybody else noticing what had happened, and devoured it at her leisure. And so twice every day, she seized the last Mouse of the series, and for a long time lived very comfortably without any trouble at all in catching her Mice, and without any of the Mice realizing what was happening.

Now it happened that amongst these Mice there were two friends, whose names were Rambé and Ambé, who were very much attached to one another. Now these two were much cleverer and more cunning than most of the others, and after a few days they noticed that the number of Mice in the house seemed to be decreasing very much, in spite of the fact that the Cat had promised not to kill any more. So they laid their heads together and arranged a little plan for future processions. They agreed that Rambé was always to walk at the very front of the procession of the Mice, and that Ambé was to bring up the rear, and that all the time the procession was passing, Rambé was to call to Ambé, and Ambé to answer Rambé at frequent intervals. So next evening, when the procession started as usual, Rambé marched along in front, and Ambé took up his position last of all. As soon as Rambé had passed the cushion where the Cat was seated and had made his salaam, he called out in a shrill voice.

"Where are you, Brother Rambé?" squeaked the other from the rear of the procession. And so they went on calling and answering one another until they had all filed past the Cat, who had not dared to touch Ambé as long as his brother kept calling to him.

The Cat was naturally very much annoyed at having to go hungry that evening, and felt very cross all night. But she thought it was only an accident which had brought the two friends, one in front and one in the rear of the procession, and she hoped to make up for her enforced abstinence by finding one particularly fat Mouse at the end of the procession next morning. What, then, was her amazement and disgust when she found that on the following morning the very same arrangement had been made, and that Rambé called to Ambé, and Ambé answered Rambé until all the Mice had passed her by, and so, for the second time, she was foiled of her meal. However, she disguised her feelings of anger and decided to give the Mice one more trial; so in the evening she took her seat as usual on the cushion and waited for the Mice to appear.

Meanwhile, Rambé and Ambé had warned the other Mice to be on the lookout, and to be ready to take flight the moment the Cat showed any appearance of anger. At the appointed time the procession started as usual, and as soon as Rambé had passed the Cat he squeaked out:

"Where are you, Brother Ambé?"

"Here I am, Brother Rambé," came the shrill voice from the rear.

This was more than the Cat could stand. She made a fierce leap right in the middle of the Mice, who, however, were thoroughly prepared for her, and in an instant they scuttled off in every direction to their holes. And before the Cat had time to catch a single one the room was empty and not a sign of a Mouse was to be seen anywhere.

After this the Mice were very careful not to put any further trust in the treacherous Cat, who soon after died of starvation owing to her being unable to procure any of her customary food; whilst Rambé and Ambé lived for many years, and were held in high honour and esteem by all the other Mice in the community.

THE SUN AND THE COCK

The Miao of South-West China are one of the child races of the world. "Though poor, thriftless and no lovers of fighting, they are simple and generous, honest and lovable. One of the child races of the world, they are as old as the China sea, and when Moses led the children of Israel through the wilderness, the Miao were hunting wild beasts on their beloved hills and at the close of day their birds would sing a Miao version

THE SUN AND THE COCK. From *Stone Gateway and the Flowery Miao*, by William H. Hudspeth. By permission of the Methodist Missionary Society, Cargate Press.

of the Creation, the Flood, and the Re-population of the World; and story-tellers would narrate quaint legends which have been handed down to this generation. Here is one. Would not Kipling have enjoyed it."

Long, long ago, instead of there being only one sun in the skies, there were six and in those days the world was beautifully warm. One year, however, the rain refused to come and by degrees vegetables and trees were withered. A meeting of the old men was held to discuss what could be done. One man said this and another that until it was finally decided that the suns must be shot. A famous archer called Yang Yah was called and ordered to shoot the suns. Bringing his cross-bow and arrows, Yang Yah looked up at the suns and observed they were a long distance away. Fortunately, near by, there was a small lake in which all six suns were reflected and the happy thought came to Yang Yah that if he could shoot the reflections the same purpose would be served as hitting the suns themselves. Adjusting an arrow and taking careful aim, he released the trigger and hit sun number one right in the centre, upon which sun number one promptly disappeared. He shot a second arrow and sun number two disappeared, and so on with suns number three, four, five, but as Yang Yah adjusted his arrow to shoot sun number six, this sun became vastly afraid and away it went beyond the horizon. The next morning—well, really there wasn't a next morning, as the sun refused to come out and day after day darkness was upon the face of the earth. To bring water from the springs people had to carry torches, and to plough the land, lights were suspended from the horns of the cows. What was to be done? A second gathering of the old men of the tribe was held; once more one man suggested this and another that, until finally it was proposed that some one should call to the sun and ask him to come out, assuring him that no one would shoot him. But how were they to call to the sun? It was thought that a tiger would be able to do this rather well; so one was brought and loudly it roared. "Dear me!" thought the sun, "the people are still angry with me, I won't go out yet." Then some one wondered whether it wouldn't be a good thing to use a cow to call to the sun. The lowing of a cow is far-reaching and yet not so frightening as the roar of a tiger. So a cow was brought and loudly it lowed. "Aha!" thought the sun, "they are not quite so displeased with me as they were, but they are still angry; so I won't go out yet." Then some one had the happy idea of using a cock; the crow of a cock is far-reaching yet pleasing, and being placed on a perch, it crowed lustily. "What a very nice sound that is," thought the sun, "I'll just look out to see what is happening," and he peeped over the horizon. People were so pleased to see him that they shouted for joy. The sun was quite as delighted as the people, and from the red of the morning he fashioned a little comb which he placed on the head of the cock. Now every morning, before the sun comes out, the cock crows to tell him it is alright, no one will shoot him.

LO-SUN, THE BLIND BOY

Lo-Sun was a blind boy and, like many others thus afflicted in China, he had no home, for his hard-hearted parents had driven him forth to beg his living. From morning till night he wandered along the city streets and country lanes, always carrying with him a blind man's staff. With the help of this stick he seldom missed his footing, and he learned to go from one part of the city to another, and to find his way around in the near-by villages very well.

Lo-Sun had one companion, a faithful dog named Fan, who helped him to many a stray copper. Whenever the little master snapped his fingers three times, the well-trained animal went down at once upon her knees and touched her head to the ground, thus making what is called in China a kotow, or mark of respect. So pleased were many passers-by with this polite trick on the part of a dog, that they often paused to hand the blind lad a bit of money. After a time he made many friends in the city, and not a few men spoke to him as he tapped his way about the narrow streets.

One evening as Lo-Sun and his dog were strolling along a country road they were overtaken by nightfall, and it became necessary for them to sleep out-of-doors. As this was nothing unusual for either, they had no fear, but at once began to search for a good spot in which to make their bed. It did not take Fan long to discover a large, leafy tree under which they might rest in comfort. She barked the good news to her master, who understood several words of the dog language, and led him to the haven of rest. Soon, curled up together like two kittens, the tired pair fell fast asleep.

In the night Lo-Sun had a strange dream. Some one addressed him softly, saying, "Lo-Sun, Lo-Sun, do you see me?"

"Alas!" answered the boy sadly, "I am blind."

"My poor little fellow, that is indeed a sore affliction, but perhaps I may be of some service to you."

"Oh," said Lo-Sun, his face brightening, "kind sir, can you, will you restore my sight?"

"No, my lad, I will not, but I shall make it possible for you to do it for yourself. Heed well what I say and then become your own healer. Henceforth each time you do a good action, no matter how small it may be, a little light shall enter your poor blind eyes. As the deeds of virtue multiply, greater and greater shall be the change which you will notice; until at last the scales that have hindered you from seeing shall fall off com-

LO-SUN, THE BLIND BOY. From *Chinese Fairy Tales* by Norman H. Pitman; copyright 1938 by Lucy A. Pitman. By permission of Thomas Y. Crowell Company and George G. Harrap and Co., Ltd., Publishers.

pletely and your sight be entirely restored. But, mark well my words. If, instead of doing deeds of kindness and of love, you should so far forget my promise as to soil your heart by a bad act, then shall your eyes be sealed the tighter and you shall lose twice as much as you are allowed to profit by a deed of virtue."

The strange voice was silent, and Lo-Sun, with a start, awoke from his slumber. The sun was shining in his face, and the whole world seemed brighter than it had ever been before. Fan also seemed happy, and licked her little master's hand in silent sympathy.

"Shall we do it, Fan?" asked Lo-Sun, speaking as if Fan had heard and understood the dream words as well as he.

The dog barked joyously at hearing her master's voice.

"All right, if you agree, I think I can get back my eyesight. You know I can't do much without your help, old fellow." Lo-Sun threw his arms about the great dog's shaggy neck and hugged her in a tight embrace.

The two then set out for the city, and Lo-Sun could think of nothing but the words of the good fairy in the dream. Oh, if he might only have back his eyesight, how happy he would be! He would like to show the cruel father who had cast him out of house and home that he would amount to something in the world, that he would rise above the lowly station which his parents occupied. Just outside the city wall, as he was about to enter by the large gate, he came near stumbling over an old beggar who was lying at the side of the road.

"Give a poor blind man a penny," mumbled the pauper; "for the love of mercy, do not pass me by."

"But we are both in the same boat, my friend," laughed Lo-Sun, "for I too am blind."

"Alas! kind youth, I am much more unfortunate than you; I am a cripple also."

With a cry of sympathy, and with no thought of the fairy's promise, Lo-Sun drew out the only coin he had, a tiny bit of copper, and handed it to the lame man, saying, "Take it; this is all I have."

Suddenly there seemed to come a flash of light before his eyes; the blackness that had so long robbed him of sight seemed to grow less dense.

"The dream was really true!" he exclaimed joyfully, and the people who heard him thus talking to himself, thinking the lad crazy, drew their garments aside as he passed by. Never had Lo-Sun been so light-hearted as he was that day. The whole world seemed to smile at him and fill his heart with summer.

That night he slept in the Beggars' Temple, an old tumble-down building just outside the North Gate, long since deserted by the priests, and given over by general consent for the use of the homeless creatures who had no other place of shelter. In one corner lay an aged hag, weak from starvation. Lo-Sun gave her willingly the stale bread which was to have served for his supper, and again to his surprise and delight noticed a faint glow which lightened up his vision. But as a consequence, he and Fan were compelled to go to bed hungry.

Awakened early in the morning by the cravings of an empty stomach, the blind boy set out along the dusty highway. It was yet too soon for travellers, and he was still puzzling his brains as to how he should satisfy his hunger when Fan solved the question by running down a fat hen which chanced to cross her pathway. Here was luck for a blind boy! No one in the neighbourhood, apparently, not even the sound of a distant cartwheel! Lo-Sun took the hen from the dog's mouth, and as the animal barked in noisy joy, praised her for showing such ability as a hunter. In twenty minutes he was at the market-place by the river, where he had very little trouble in selling his fowl at a good price.

No sooner, however, had the money been counted into his hands than the lad felt a dark veil descend over his eyes. The reward he had received for his two good deeds was thus in a moment snatched away, and he found his condition the same as when he had left the tree under which the dream had come to him.

Lo-Sun was not easily discouraged. Readily admitting the wrong of which he had been guilty, he resolved to retrace his steps and find the owner of the stolen hen. Throughout that whole day he trudged up and down the highway which passed by the Beggars' Temple, vainly inquiring of every passer-by if he knew of any one who had lost a fowl. By evening his little legs were weary, and his face, usually sunny, was covered with a veil of dust. The pangs of hunger which had annoyed him at daybreak now made him ravenous, yet sturdily he resisted the temptation to spend the ill-gotten gains. The next morning when he awoke he found to his great delight that his eyesight had improved once more as by magic. Evidently his sincere sorrow for wrong-doing had not been without avail.

For a number of weeks by a succession of good deeds Lo-Sun advanced so rapidly on his journey toward the goal of restored sight, that at last he could tell when some one was coming toward him in the road, not only by hearing, but by the actual power of vision, and he even fancied he could distinguish the glory of the sunset. When he had reached this stage in his healing, he was overjoyed, and at once resolved to save every cent possible, to supply himself with the glasses which he had been told people with weak eyesight sometimes wore.

But one day he again met the old lame man to whom he had once given his last money.

"Alas! I have nothing," said he to the latter's plea, although he was now quite well supplied with coppers, "nothing that I can give you."

"But I am starving," implored the beggar.

"I too," answered Lo-Sun.

A sudden twitch, a darkening shadow, and lo! the glory of the sunlight was denied him.

Now Lo-Sun was in despair. He had tried, oh, so hard, to lead a sinless life! He had denied himself many things. And for what reward?

"As fast as I gain," he reflected bitterly, "I lose, and thus go backward." He was discouraged. What could a blind boy do in China, a country where there are no schools for the afflicted, where those thus suffering are cast out upon the street?

Angry with the world, his neighbours, the evil fortune that had placed him at so great a disadvantage, he made his way finally to the bank of a roaring river. It was the rainy season, and a vast torrent of angry waters was rushing down a channel which usually was calm. He sat down on the bank of the noisy stream and pictured himself as a stick swept along by the raging flood, sometimes cast high upon the shore, and then again, as the level of the waters rose, picked up and dashed onward. Was not the only real friend he had in all the world a faithful dog? And do the best she might, what could such an ally do to bring her master back the visual powers denied him by the gods? Without sight, he could not hope to strive among men for money and position.

"Poor Fan!" he cried, "you do all for me that you can, and yet you cannot save me." The grateful animal licked her master's face. "You are all that I have; nothing shall ever separate us, for without you I should die."

Just at this moment a cry was raised along the river, "A man is drowning! See! within the rapids. His boat is capsized; he cannot swim!"

From all directions came the rush of hurrying footsteps. A crowd of excited people gathered in an instant. All were looking curiously at the struggling man, and yet no man dared to lift a hand to rescue.

"See! he is losing strength," they shouted. "His boat is swept away, and with it his last chance of reaching shore. Soon he will go down for the last time!"

The blind boy listened to the uproar with a sense of sadness in his heart. How could this crowd of strong men stand by and make no effort to save another from perishing before their very eyes? If he were only in their position, how quickly would he leap to the rescue, how quickly would he show the others they were cowards!

Suddenly his breast thrilled with emotion. Would it be possible? Yes, he would undertake it—he the blind boy would try to do what all those heartless people were failing to perform.

"Fan can do it!" he shouted wildly, springing to his feet. "My dog will save him!"

"Stop!" said one of the bystanders who had seen the boy on several occasions, and who out of sympathy for him wished to do him a friendly turn. "Stop! it is too late. You will only lose your dog, and do no good. Let the fellow drown; he is only a worthless beggar."

"That's all I am," was Lo-Sun's quick reply, "and like helps like, you know."

Quick as a wink he seized his dog by the neck and dragged her to the brink of the stream. "Fetch, Fan, fetch!" he shouted, as he pushed her into the torrent.

With a bark of intelligence, the animal seemed to take in the situation at a glance, and struck out with powerful strokes toward the struggler. The excitement on the bank grew intense. "It is too late," they said. "The man can't hold out a minute longer, and the dog will never reach him."

Never had Lo-Sun felt the need of sight so keenly as at that moment when his one friend was in danger of being swept away from him forever. In his mind's eye he seemed to see the whole picture.

A shout from the idlers at last told him plainly that the swimmer had seen the effort being made in his behalf, and was redoubling his own attempts to hold up until the dog had reached him. Nearer and nearer Fan fought her way through the foaming whitecaps. Her master had commanded; it was hers but to obey. With acute foresight did she make allowance for the distance which the swimmer would be carried downstream before she could reach him, and the crowd on shore shouted wildly as they saw the noble animal close her teeth in his ragged garments just as he was sinking. Now came the most heroic struggle of the dog's existence, a fight against the elements for her own life and that of him whom she had seized. Back she struggled, her great eyes fixed upon her master, who all the while running along the river bank with the crowd, was madly cheering her on to victory. At length a man on shore, who was carrying a boat-hook, was able to fix the barb in the drowning man's clothing. The dog, seeing that her life-saving work was over, released her hold, and the half-drowned beggar was drawn in to a place of safety. But, alas! poor Fan! At that very moment an undercurrent caught her and dragged her down. She was too weak to struggle and sank at once.

The cry of the crowd told the boy of this sad fate, and with a moan of anguish, Lo-Sun fell upon the sand and buried his face in the dirt. The curious onlookers eyed the grief-stricken little boy for a few moments, and then as the night began to fall, one by one departed. When morning dawned and Lo-Sun awoke, there was no devoted friend to lick his hands and bark his joyous welcome back to wakefulness. But to his astonishment, as he raised his head, his eyes were dazzled with a glorious light. He looked around and saw the things about him, was able to distinguish the outlines of the river, the willows fringing the banks, and behind, the walls of the city. True, he could not take in the smaller objects, but oh, how delightful it was to see these marvellous sights that had for so long a time been denied him. As he pondered the wonder of it all, he knew full well that his willing sacrifice of Fan for the drowning beggar had given him this priceless blessing.

As Lo-Sun thus sat upon the ground rejoicing in his new strength, he saw a man coming toward him. He could see the figure of the man but not his features. Closer and closer came the stranger, until at last he was standing directly over the boy.

"My lad, it was you who saved my life yesterday." Lo-Sun looked up eagerly, trying to make out the features of the one for whom he had lost his all.

"What! Is it you?" exclaimed the other. "Is it Lo-Sun, the boy whom I turned out from house and home?"

With a moan of bitterness, Lo-Sun covered his face with his hands. So it was his father, the man whom he had hated for his cruelty—his father for whom he had given up his faithful dog!

Angry words welled up within his breast, and in another minute he would have cursed the man who had mistreated him so shamefully. But just then a soft voice warned him and stretching out his hands, he said, "Father, I forgive you."

The man, touched to the quick by what had happened, clasped the little fellow in his arms and held him tightly to his breast. "The gods be merciful!" he cried, "for I have sinned most foully. My son, my son, I cast thee off, and lo! thou hast been the one to save my life."

And as Lo-Sun returned his father's embrace, the last scale fell from his eyes, and he looked freely out upon the whole beautiful world.

THE COUNTRY OF THE MICE

Once upon a time there was a King who ruled over a large tract of country in which there lived a great number of Mice. Generally the Mice were very prosperous and had plenty to eat, but it happened one year that the crops of the country were very poor, and the Mice, who subsisted chiefly on the spare grains left after the harvest, found that their stores were running short before the end of the winter. So the King of the Mice decided that he would make a petition to the King of the country, to lend the Mice what grain they required on condition that they repaid the whole amount the following year.

So he dressed himself up in his best clothes and set off one morning to the King's palace. When he got to the door of the palace the door-keeper asked him where he was going.

"Oh!" replied the Mouse, "I wish to see the King of the country, as I have a petition to make to him."

When the King heard that a Mouse wanted to see him he was very much amused, and he ordered that the little animal should be admitted.

When the Mouse entered the King's presence he walked slowly up the

THE COUNTRY OF THE MICE. From *Folk-Tales from Tibet*, by Captain W. F. O'Connor. By permission of Hurst and Blackett, Ltd.

Hall of Audience, carrying in his hand a little silk thread, which he presented to the King, instead of the usual ceremonial scarf.[5]

"Good-morning, Brother Mouse," said the King, "what can I do for you?"

"Oh! King," replied the Mouse, "you must know that this year our crops have fallen short, and we are threatened with a famine unless we can borrow sufficient grain to carry us through the winter; so I, who am King of the Mice, have come here to ask you if you can help us in this matter. If you can lend us the grain we require, we will repay you faithfully with interest at the next harvest."

"Well," said the King, "how much grain do you want?"

"I think that we shall require," said the Mouse, "one of your big barns full."

"But," said the King, "if I were to give you a barn full of grain how would you carry it away?"

"Leave it to me," said the Mouse; "if you will give us the grain we will undertake to carry it off."

So the King agreed to present the Mice with one of his granaries full of barley, and he ordered his officers to throw open the doors, and to let the Mice carry away as much as they wanted.

That night the King of the Mice summoned all his subjects together, and to the number of many hundreds of thousands they invaded the barn, and each one picked up as much grain as he could carry in his mouth, on his back, and curled up in his tail, and when they had all finished the barn was empty, and not a single grain of barley was left.

Next morning, when the King went out to look at his barn, he was very much astonished to find that the Mice had been able to empty it so effectually, and he conceived a very high opinion of their powers; and when, in the following spring, the King of the Mice redeemed his promise by repaying with interest the loan he had taken from the King of the country, the latter saw that they were trustworthy as well as clever.

Now it happened shortly after this that the King of the country went to war with a neighbouring kingdom, which lay on the opposite side of the river forming the frontier between the two countries. This other country was far more wealthy and powerful than the country where the Mice lived, and its King soon assembled a huge army on the opposite bank of the river and began making preparations for invasion.

When the Mice heard what was happening, they were much distressed, for they feared that if the enemy entered their country and destroyed their friend the King, they themselves would suffer considerable hardships under a strange ruler; so the King of the Mice set out again to visit the King of the country, and when he reached the palace he demanded an inter-

[5] This is in accordance with Tibetan custom, whereby a scarf is invariably presented upon all occasions of ceremony.

view with His Majesty. This was at once accorded to him, and finding the King looking very depressed, he addressed him as follows:

"I have come to you a second time, Oh King, in order to see whether I can be of any use to you. The last time I was here you did me and my people a great favour, for which we shall ever be grateful, and if it is now in our power to assist you in any way, we shall be very glad to do our best."

The King, in spite of his grief, was much amused on hearing these words from the Mouse.

"Why," said he, "what could the Mice do to help me in my present predicament? We are threatened with invasion by a foreign army, outnumbering mine by many thousands, and all the men I can muster will not be sufficient to enable me to repel the enemy. I don't see how the Mice can help me."

"Do you remember, Oh King!" replied the Mouse, "that on the last occasion I was here you doubted our ability to carry away the grain you had given us, or to repay you the loan? And yet we proved ourselves able to do both. All we ask you now is to trust us again, and if you will undertake to do one or two things which we ask of you, we on our part will undertake to rid you of the invading army."

The King was a good deal struck by this remark of the Mouse, and he replied:

"Very well, what you say is quite true; and if you will inform me what you wish me to do, I will undertake to carry out my share of the bargain."

"Well, then," answered the Mouse, "all we wish you to do is to provide us by to-morrow evening with one hundred thousand sticks, each about a foot long, and to have them laid in rows on the bank of the river. If you will undertake to do this, we on our side will undertake to stave off the threatened invasion and to put the opposing army into a state of confusion and panic. And if we succeed in carrying out all we promise, we will ask you for the future to safeguard us against the two principal dangers which threaten the existence of the Mice who live in our country."

"I will gladly do what I can," replied the King, "to safeguard you against these dangers if you will tell me how to proceed."

"The two dangers to which I refer," continued the Mouse, "are flood and Cats. You see the majority of our burrows are in the low-lying land near the river, and whenever the river rises a little it overflows this level country and floods our nests. What we would suggest to you is that you should build a strong dam all down the river bank so as to ensure that the water cannot overflow into our nests. And as to the Cats they are always the persecutors of Mice, and we ask you to banish them altogether from your kingdom."

"Very well," replied the King, "if you can succeed in averting the danger which now threatens us, I will undertake to do all that you ask of me in this respect."

On hearing this, the King of the Mice salaamed profoundly to the King, and returned as fast as he could to his own subjects.

On the following evening he marshalled all the fullgrown Mice of his kingdom, and about dusk, he led down a large army numbering several hundreds of thousands to the edge of the river, where he found the sticks all laid out as had been arranged with the King. In accordance with instructions they had received, the Mice at once proceeded to launch these sticks on the river, and they themselves embarked upon them two or three at a time; and so, pushing off from the bank, they sailed across the river and soon landed on the opposite side.

It was now quite dark, and the enemy's soldiers were all asleep in their camp, some lying in tents and some in the open air, with their arms beside them ready for any alarm. The Mice on a word of command from their King, scattered themselves without delay through the sleeping camp, and each one began to do as much destruction as he possibly could in the shortest possible space of time. Some nibbled at the bowstrings and the slings of the soldiers' muskets; others gnawed the slow-match and fuses; whilst others bit off the clothes and pigtails of the sleeping men. In fact, they attacked fiercely anything upon which their teeth could make an impression, and tents, stores, grain, and provisions of all kinds were soon reduced to shreds or scattered in confusion in every direction; and after a couple of hours' work they all collected upon the river banks, and, embarking again on their sticks, they sailed quietly over to their own shore without having been detected by the enemy, or even having caused any alarm.

Next morning at daybreak, a great outcry arose from the enemy's camp. Each man as he rose from his sleep found himself in a woeful plight—his clothes in rags, his pigtail cut off, his bow without a string, his rifle without a sling, and with no fuse or slow-match to fire it, and no provisions for breakfast. Each one began to accuse the other of theft and treachery, and before many minutes had passed the whole camp was in a state of wild confusion, comrade quarrelling with comrade, or accusing their officers of dishonesty and ill-faith.

In the midst of this uproar the sound of bugles was heard on the opposite bank, and a few shots were fired; and terrified at the thought of being taken unawares, the whole army took to flight, and in a few minutes not a man was to be seen.

When the King of the country of the Mice saw what had happened he was greatly elated, and, sending for the King of the Mice, he thanked him very sincerely for his good offices. And, in accordance with the bargain they had made, he at once had a strong embankment constructed all down his own side of the river to guard against floods, and he issued an edict forbidding all persons, on pain of death, to keep a Cat of any kind henceforth within the frontiers of his country, and so the Mice lived securely and happily ever afterwards.

And in order to insure against any more attempts at invasion from the side of the neighbouring kingdom, the King sent a herald across the river to the ruler of that country, to say that, on this occasion, he had only considered it worth while to employ his Mice to defeat his enemies; but that if he was again threatened, he was ready to employ first all the domestic animals of the country; and if they did not succeed, he would have to have recourse to the wild beasts; and in the event of their failing, he was prepared to come himself with his warriors in order to produce the desired results.

When the ruler of the other country heard this message he considered it wiser to make a treaty of peace, as he could not hope to defeat the warriors and wild beasts of a country whose Mice had shown such skill and courage. So the two countries remained on friendly terms for many years after; and the Mice, secured against flood and Cats, lived happily and safely, and received every year from the King of the country a barn full of grain as a free gift in thankful recognition of the services which they had rendered in time of need.

A LESSON FROM CONFUCIUS

Confucius once heard two of his pupils quarreling. One was of a gentle nature and was called by all the students a peaceful man. The other had a good brain and a kind heart, but was given to great anger. If he wished to do a thing, he did it, and no man could prevent; if anyone tried to hinder him, he would show sudden and terrible rage.

One day, after one of these fits of temper, the blood came from his mouth, and, in great fear, he went to Confucius. "What shall I do with my body?" he asked. "I fear I shall not live long. It may be better that I no longer study and work. I am your pupil and you love me as a father. Tell me what to do for my body."

Confucius answered, "Tsze-Lu, you have a wrong idea about your body. It is not the study, not the work in school, but your great anger that causes the trouble.

"I will help you to see this. You remember when you and Nou-Wui quarreled. He was at peace and happy again in a little time, but you were very long in overcoming your anger. You can not expect to live

A LESSON FROM CONFUCIUS. From *Chinese Fables and Folk Stories,* by Mary Hayes Davis and Chow Leung; copyright 1908 and 1934 by American Book Company. Reprinted by permission.

long if you do that way. Every time one of the pupils says a thing you do not like, you are greatly enraged. There are a thousand in this school. If each offends you only once, you will have a fit of temper a thousand times this year. And you will surely die, if you do not use more self-control. I want to ask you some questions:

"How many teeth have you?"

"I have thirty-two, teacher."

"How many tongues?"

"Just one."

"How many teeth have you lost?"

"I lost one when I was nine years old, and four when I was about twenty-six years old."

"And your tongue—is it still perfect?"

"Oh, yes."

"You know Mun-Gun, who is quite old?"

"Yes, I know him well."

"How many teeth do you think he had at your age?"

"I do not know."

"Two, I think. But his tongue is perfect, though he is very old.

"You see the teeth are lost because they are strong, and determined to have everything they desire. They are hard and hurt the tongue many times, but the tongue never hurts the teeth. Yet, it endures until the end, while the teeth are the first of man to decay. The tongue is peaceful and gentle with the teeth. It never grows angry and fights them, even when they are in the wrong. It always helps them do their work, in preparing man's food for him, although the teeth never help the tongue, and they always resist everything.

"And so it is with man. The strongest to resist, is the first to decay; and you, Tsze-Lu, will be even so if you learn not the great lesson of self-control."

URASHIMA TARO

Many hundreds of years ago, in a village on the craggy sea-coast of Japan, there dwelt a fisher-lad whose name was Urashima Taro. Of all the fishermen in the village he was the most skillful with his line and net, and he was also the kindest hearted. If one of his comrades had bad luck when his own was good, he always shared his "catch" with him. And he could not bear to see any creature, however lowly, tormented or hurt.

URASHIMA TARO. From *A Treasury of Tales,* by Marjory Bruce. By permission of George G. Harrap and Co., Ltd., and Thomas Y. Crowell Company, Publishers.

One fine evening, when Urashima was on his way home to his father's little cottage, he came upon a group of mischievous boys teasing an unlucky tortoise. One boy cast pebbles at its shell, another rapped it with a stick, a third tried to poke twigs inside. The sight made Urashima very angry.

"You cruel children," he said, "what evil has the poor thing done? Do you not know that unless you put it back into the sea it will die?"

"What then?" cried the bad boys. "It is only a silly old tortoise. It may die if it pleases. We do not care."

"Will you not give your tortoise to me?" asked Urashima.

"No, we will not," returned the bad boys. "It is ours. We want it."

Now Urashima had in his hand a small stock of money, slung on a string through the hole left for that purpose in the centre of each coin. It was his earnings for an entire week, hard-won with many hours of patient labour.

"Listen to me, boys," said Urashima, "if you will not give me your tortoise, perhaps you will sell it." And he jingled the string of coins before their eyes. The bad boys hesitated.

"Think," urged Urashima, "what a lot of things you could buy with this money—much better playthings than a poor tortoise."

"There is some truth in what Urashima Taro says," remarked the ringleader. "Let us take the money and give him the tortoise."

So they took Urashima's little store of coin, and ran off, laughing and jumping, and the fisher-lad was left alone with his purchase.

"Poor old fellow," said Urashima, stroking the hard, tawny-coloured shell, "I wonder if it is true that you tortoises live for a thousand years. Perhaps you are still young, and may have nine hundred and ninety years of life before you still. Anyhow, I am going to put you back into the sea. And I advise you, as a friend, not to allow yourself to get caught again!"

Then Urashima lifted the tortoise in his arms, went down to the beach, and let it slide softly into the water.

Next day the lad was early astir. He knew that he would have to work extra hard in order to make up for the money he had given the bad boys; all his earnings for a whole week had gone. The sea was as smooth as glass, and reflected the lovely turquoise colour of the cloudless sky. Urashima's slender boat drifted rapidly along, and soon left the craft of the other fishermen far behind.

Presently he heard a soft voice calling him by name.

"Urashima Taro—Urashima!"

Urashima stood up in the boat and shaded his eyes with his hand, but there was no human creature in sight.

"Urashima!" called the voice again.

It came from the sea. Looking down, he saw a tortoise swimming alongside his boat, and he thought it seemed remarkably like the one which he had befriended the day before.

"Honourable Mr. Tortoise," said Urashima, politely, "was it you who called me just now?"

"Yes," replied the tortoise, "do you not remember me? I have come to thank you for your kindness to me yesterday."

"That is very good of you," said Urashima. "Would you care to come into my boat and bask in the sun for a while? I know that you tortoises love to do that."

"Many thanks," responded the tortoise, and Urashima helped it to climb aboard.

Presently his queer passenger began to talk again.

"Have you ever seen the Rin-Gin, the palace of the Dragon-King, Urashima?"

Urashima shook his head. "All we fishermen have heard of that palace, but none of us has ever beheld it."

"If it would interest you to see it," said the tortoise, "I can show you the way thither."

"It would interest me very much," answered Urashima, "but I am only a human being. I could not swim anything like as far as you could."

"Swim?" repeated the tortoise. "But why should you swim? I can carry you on my back with ease."

"Perhaps I am heavier than you think," hinted the fisher-lad, who was afraid that if he were to say, "You are too small to carry me," he might hurt the feelings of his new friend.

"Not a bit of it," returned the tortoise, clambering over the edge of the boat and slipping down into the bright blue water. "Try and see! Perhaps I am larger than you think, honourable Mr. Urashima!"

Urashima looked, and it certainly seemed that the tortoise had grown much bigger since it went back into the sea.

"Come on," urged the tortoise.

"All right!" said Urashima Taro.

He jumped upon the tortoise's back, and away the creature swam, carrying him as easily as if he had been a baby.

"Honourable Mr. Tortoise," said Urashima presently, "I hope you are not going to dive, for if you do, I shall be drowned."

"I am going to dive," returned the tortoise, "but you are not going to be drowned."

And down, down, down it went, through the clear blue water.

To his astonishment Urashima found that he could breathe quite as well under the sea as above it. Fishes, great and small, of a thousand gorgeous colours and quaint forms, swam over his head as birds fly dry land, and lovely starry anemones, and delicately fringed seaweeds, grew like flowers on the bed of the sea.

Presently, far off, Urashima saw a great gateway, and beyond that the roofs of some magnificent buildings all glittering with brilliant green and blue tiles.

"We shall soon be there," remarked the tortoise, swimming faster than ever.

A few moments later the creature halted outside the great gateway, and the porter, who was a large and splendid-looking fish, opened the gate.

"This is the honourable Mr. Urashima Taro, from the land of Japan," explained the tortoise. "He has come to visit the Rin-Gin, the palace of the Dragon-King of the Sea."

"He is very welcome," said the fish.

Urashima now descended from the tortoise's back and the fish, floating slowly before him, led the way into the palace.

No words could possibly describe the beauty of that great palace in the depths of the sea. It was built of green and blue jewels, of coral and beryl, sapphire and pearl. Round it were wide gardens which reminded Urashima of the gardens of his own Japan, for maples and firs and plum and cherry-trees grew there, and wisteria climbed over arches, and little bridges of red lacquer spanned tiny torrents of foaming grey water.

In the eastern part of the garden it was always spring, and the fruit-trees were gay with unfading blossom. To the south was perpetual summer. To the west lay the autumn garden, where the maples were ruddy-golden and the chrysanthemums shone like fire. To the north was the realm of winter, and there the fir-trees were white with snow, and the torrents under the little bridges were frozen into long icicles as they fell.

All these marvels and glories took Urashima's breath away. But there remained one far beyond all the rest, and that was the lady Otohimé, the daughter of the Dragon-King of the Sea. When she approached Urashima he fell upon his knees, and bowed his head upon the sand, for never had he dreamt that any being could be so beautiful. Her robes were of green silk shot through with threads of silver and gold, and her long, fine black hair hung like a great mantle upon his shoulders.

"Welcome and greeting, Urashima Taro," said the lady Otohimé.

"Most humbly do I thank your honourable ladyship," stammered Urashima, not daring to raise his head.

"It is I who must thank you, Urashima Taro," returned the lady Otohimé. "Listen, and you shall learn why. Once a year, as we immortals reckon years, it is the will of my father, the Dragon-King of the Sea, that I should assume the form of some sea-creature, and allow myself to be caught by some mortal's net or snare. If that mortal be merciful, great is his reward. But if he be cruel, his punishment also is great. Urashima Taro, arise. Fear nothing, my friend. I was that tortoise whom you delivered from the hands of the cruel children who would have made me suffer much pain."

So Urashima arose, and he and the lady Otohimé went forth into the garden where it was always spring. And fish-servants brought them rice, and saké in cups of pearl, and fish-minstrels made music for them under the blossoming trees. Urashima found favour in the eyes of the lady

Otohimé. She sought leave of her father, the Dragon-King of the Sea, to take the fisher-lad for her husband. And so they were married, and even in the Rin-Gin, the sea-palace of many marvels, such rejoicings were never known as the rejoicings at the wedding of Urashima Taro and the beautiful daughter of the Dragon-King.

Urashima was very happy with his royal bride in the depths of the sea, and for a long time he forgot all about his father and mother, and his old home on the craggy coast of Japan. Then, one day Otohimé noticed that her husband was looking thoughtful and sad.

"What ails you, Urashima Taro?" she asked.

"I have just remembered," said Urashima, "that far away, in the land of mortals whence I come, I have a father and a mother. They are old. Unless I make haste, perchance I may never see them again. Surely they have wept for me, thinking that I had left them never to return."

"Alas, Urashima," cried the lady Otohimé, "have you ceased to love me? Are you no longer happy in the Rin-Gin?"

"No," said Urashima, sorrowfully, "I have not ceased to love your honourable ladyship. But I cannot be happy until I have beheld my father and my mother again. I am ashamed that I should have forgotten them so long. Let me go to them, even if it be for one day. Then I will return."

Then the lady Otohimé wept bitter tears. "If you wish to depart," she told him, "I cannot keep you here. Go, then. But take with you this casket, lest I, too, should be forgotten." With these words she placed in Urashima's hands a little box of golden lacquer tied tightly round with a cord and tassels of scarlet silk. "This casket," said the lady Otohimé, "holds something very precious and very rare. Take it with you, my husband, wherever you go. But remember, you must not open it. For if you do, great evil will befall you."

Urashima Taro promised that nothing would ever persuade him to open the golden lacquer box. He bade farewell very sadly to the lady Otohimé, cast a last regretful glance at the gardens of the four seasons, and then went down to the great gateway at which he had arrived, and where he found a tortoise waiting to bear him whence he had come.

The tortoise swam steadily, on and on, till at last the blue peaks of Japan arose upon the horizon. Urashima's heart began to beat faster. He recognized the coastline, the fir-woods and the craggy shore. Soon he would see his old home again, and kneel down before his father and mother imploring their forgiveness.

He jumped off the tortoise's back in his impatience and waded ashore. Coming toward him was an aged man whom he took for his father. A moment later Urashima realized his mistake. Then he ran in the direction where his father's house had stood.

What a change! The little hut had vanished, and a much larger house, with purple iris-flowers growing between the roof-tiles, occupied its place.

"Surely my family has grown rich in my absence," thought Urashima.

A man came out of the house, and Urashima approached him politely.

"Honourable Sir, can you tell me whether the parents of Urashima Taro the fisherman still live in this house?"

The man stared at him in amazement. "Who may you be, Mr. Stranger?" he asked.

"I am Urashima Taro."

The man burst out laughing at this. "You! Why, he has been dead for more than three hundred years, Urashima Taro!"

"Pardon me," said Urashima, "I am he. I have been absent for some time—I do not know exactly how long—perhaps one year, perhaps two— but I have returned because I am anxious to see my aged parents again before they die."

"If you are really Urashima Taro you have arrived three hundred years too late," returned the man. "Why, the house where he lived was pulled down in my great-grandfather's time, and even then it was many years since that fisher-lad vanished one fine morning. Either you are joking or you are a ghost."

"I am not a ghost," cried Urashima, stamping on the ground. "You know that ghosts have no feet! I am as much alive as you are—I am Urashima Taro!"

"Urashima Taro lived three hundred years ago," retorted the man. "It is all written in the village records, which are kept in the temple. Why do you repeat such a foolish jest?"

Feeling sick with fear and disappointment, Urashima continued his walk along the sea-shore. At every step he saw changes which showed only too plainly that the man had spoken truly, and that not one year, or two, but three centuries had come and gone since he last beheld that place.

"Every one whom I knew and loved in the land of the mortals has long since been dead," thought Urashima, sadly; "why should I tarry here? I must go back as quickly as I can to the beautiful land of the immortals, and to my wife, the lady Otohimé. He walked down to the edge of the sea and gazed anxiously across the waves. The tortoise which had brought him from the Rin-Gin had vanished. How was he to find his way back to the realm of the Dragon-King again?

Urashima sat down on a rock and buried his head in his hands. What could he do? He was alone in a strange, unfriendly world, and his only possession was the golden lacquer casket which he had promised that he would not open. He took it on his knee, and looked wistfully at the scarlet cords which had been knotted by the hands of the lady Otohimé.

"Surely," he said to himself, "if I break my vow, she will forgive me. Surely if I untie these cords, and open the lid, I shall find something that will tell me how to win my way back to her again!"

So Urashima set the casket upon the ground, and untied the scarlet cords, and lifted the lid. The casket was empty! Only there seemed to waft from it a faint purple cloud, which hovered over his head for a moment and then rose into the air and floated away across the sea.

Till that moment Urashima Taro had looked just as he did when he left Japan three hundred years before, a strong, dark-haired, well-built lad of twenty-one. But as he stood watching the purple cloud fading and receding, a great change came over him. His bright eyes grew dim, his black locks turned white, his sturdy limbs became suddenly withered and bent. Then, with a cry of despair, he fell upon his knees, with his face against the ground.

Next morning some fisherman going down to the sea with their nets found an aged man lying dead beside a casket of golden lacquer. They peeped into the casket, but there was nothing inside.

"Is this the man who spoke to you yesterday?" one of the fishermen asked the other.

"Oh, no," answered his comrade, "he was a sturdy young fellow, he who tried to make me believe that he was Urashima Taro."

4

AUSTRALIA AND THE
SOUTHWEST PACIFIC

Many thousands of years ago the inhabitants of the earth were all of one race and spoke but one language. Suddenly a fungus of enormous size made its appearance and continued to grow larger and higher every day and was looked upon by the people as a shelter from the sun and rain which had been sent them by the gods; but at last it grew to such a size that their crops, on which they depended entirely for food, suffered by being deprived of the blessings of the sun, rain, and dew, and they began to wish that they had stopped its growth before. Sacrifices were offered to the gods to remove the fungus from the face of the earth but their prayers were without effect. As time went on it became necessary for the preservation of life to cut it down whether the gods resented such action or not. So it was felled, cut up, and everybody ate of it with the result that they all fell of stupor and began to speak every man a different language, and confusion was so great that they scattered over the face of the earth, and it was in this way that the many languages now spoken in the world originated.[1]

This legend of the origin of the many languages of the world could be easily applied to the folklore of Australia and the islands of the Pacific. The subject matter is the same: animals, people, the creation, trickery, the supernatural, the struggle for existence. The difference lies in the language and the cultures adopted by each race.

The tales tell of the customs which grew from savagery and cannabalism to varying degrees of civilization, depending upon the government. The Australian tale is treated in a simple realistic manner; the Philippine tale has a spiritual quality because of the Spanish rule and the introduction of the Catholic religion; the themes of the Malayan and Korean stories, dealing mostly with the trickery of animal and man, always point to a moral; and the New Zealand tale is filled with people and allegories.

In these tales there is little of the desire for wealth or for the hand of

[1] "The Dyak Account of the Origin of the Different Languages of Mankind," from *The Sarawak Gazette,* Vol. 38–40, by W. Howell. By permission of The Government Printer, Kuching, Sarawak.

a princess—a marked contrast to the European tale of Cinderella or Prince Charming. The Pacific tales, little concerned with distinction of rank and without the complication of dramatic intrigue, tell of the beautiful birds, the native workers, and the mountain spirit.

THE BANK CAT

Because "Tent-Peg" on the Bogan isn't on the map of Australia, it must not be inferred that the little township does not exist. Indeed, any old colonist who knows his way about will tell you that the place is in the sister colony, and consists of one public-house, a blacksmith's shop, a store, a church (about the shape and size of a haystack), and a small branch bank.

The latter building presented nothing of the polish and artistic finish, or the magnificence of many of our metropolitan banks, but it was one of the most snug and cosy institutions in the whole country, within its walls. No doubt Toney Buck, the messenger, was of the same opinion, as he sat dozing before a warm coal fire, this severe winter night, with no other company than a large black cat, of the male gender, for his companion.

Toney Buck was an orphan, aged twelve years, or thereabouts, and acted in the dual role of servant to the manager and messenger to the bank. The boy slept on the premises, and the manager having gone to visit a neighbouring squatter, his servant had been ordered to sit up until he returned. There Toney sat in the manager's armchair, bowing and nodding to the fire, be this as it may. Every time he opened his heavy eyelids, he encountered the round, black, winking orbs of Tabby fixed full upon his face, with a strange expression stamped thereon. Indeed, more than once Toney felt certain that the cat actually laughed at him, and when discovered in the act, instantly attempted to compose its features and wink at the fire in a knowing way. It is not a very easy task for a sleepy boy, who feels as if his eyelids were freighted with four-pound weights, to rouse himself and his waking faculties all in a moment, but Toney managed to sit bolt upright after a time and to stare at his companion. Toney fancied he could stare. So he could without a doubt; but the cat could and did stare harder than Toney. Its eyes never moved, in their fixed look, from his face, yet he could see their colour change from black to pale sea-green, and from green to grey, and then turn flaming red as the fire. Toney feeling uncomfortable, removed his chair farther back, muttering, "Oh, bother the cat!"

"Whirr. You're another," replied a voice instantly.

THE BANK CAT. From *Australian Fairy Tales*, by Altha Westbury. By permission of Ward Lock & Co., Limited.

The messenger was in the act of sitting down again, but he gave a jump as if a snake had bitten him. He looked first at Tabby, and then at the fire bewildered, and said, "Who spoke?"

"I did," replied the cat.

"Good gracious! Are you sure now?" inquired Toney, with the scales—or the weights, rather—fallen from his eyeballs.

"I did say 'You're another'; and so you are. If you bother me I'll bother you!" replied Tabby, whisking his long tail.

"Oh, my! I never knew cats could talk, although I've heard their voices sometimes, of a night, to some tune."

"None of your sneers, Toney," interrupted Tabby quickly. "There are more wonderful things in Australia than a talking cat, and some noises to which our midnight concerts are as sweet music in comparison. Listen to me. The bank will be robbed this very night. There!"

"Talking cat—the bank robbed. I—I hope I'm awake," cried Toney, tugging at his unkempt hair in astonishment.

"I hope you are, for there are those coming who will soon arouse you," replied the cat, jumping on the back of a chair, and erecting his back in the form of a rainbow. "Hark! that noise is worse than our caterwauling. Hear them forcing in the door of the front office."

As the cat spoke there came upon their ears first a low grating noise, then followed a sound as if the heavy door of the bank had been wrenched off its hinges. "Lord help us! It's the bushrangers, and master's away. Oh! what shall I do?" and the poor boy began to cry bitterly.

"Stop crying. Wait and see!" Tabby hadn't time to say more, ere three men, with masks upon their faces, and armed with revolvers, rushed into the room.

"Hallo! only a boy here. Where's the manager?" inquired one of the robbers, grasping Toney.

"He isn't here, sir."

"Come, none o' that," cried the man gruffly. "Tell us where he is, or I'll shove you a-top of that fire."

Toney looked at the fire, and then at the bushranger, and began to cry afresh.

"Where's the manager?"

"Gone to Mr. Hilton's, the station on the river."

"Are you certain?"

"Yes, as certain as that you will be hanged."

The man let go his hold of Toney instantly, and stared first at the cat and then at the messenger, as if he was puzzled as to which had answered him. He appeared to decide in favour of the boy, for he said hoarsely, "No cheek, my fine kiddie, or I'll roast you like a chicken. Bring the keys of the safe, quick."

"Master has them in his pocket, sir."

The robber swore a frightful oath, then held converse with his companions in an undertone. After which they produced a cord, and having tied the lad hand and foot, left him in the room with the cat, locked the door on the outside, and proceeded to ransack the bank.

Poor Toney! What could he do against three armed men?

"Toney. Hi, Toney!" The boy jumped. He had forgotten all about the cat.

"You were always kind to me, Toney, and I'm going to help you now."

"How can a cat help anybody?" replied poor Toney.

"Ah! but I wasn't always a cat, Toney."

"Oh, bother; I suppose you mean when you were a little kitten," muttered the boy.

"No, I don't Toney Buck. I never was a kitten. I mean when I was a happy fairy in Elfland, before I was changed into a cat for being cruel and selfish."

"Snooks!" answered Toney sceptically.

"Who?"

"Snooks! It won't do, you know. There are no fairies, nor moonland, and such nonsense."

"Supposing my shape were to change again, here under your very nose; would you believe what you saw?"

"Rather! but you can't do it, puss."

"Can't I? You shall see," replied Tabby. "Say 'Sevle naila rtsua' very slowly. Now!"

" 'Sevle naila rtsua,' " cried the boy in a brisk tone; but he had no sooner uttered the words than the black cat vanished into thin air, and in its place he beheld a wee, thin, elderly gentleman dressed in hunting costume, seated astride the back of the chair, who bowed very politely and lifted his hat to the astonished messenger.

"Well I never!" cried Toney. "Who are you, pray?"

" 'Sevle naila rtsua!' " replied the little man, laughing.

"What is 'Sevle naila rtsua'?" demanded the boy.

"Read the letters backwards and join the first two syllables together."

"Ah! A–u–s–t–r–a–l–i–a–n—E–l–v–e–s—Australian Elves, eh?"

"That's it, Toney; I'm proud to be one of them, my boy. Now I'll show you how a cat can help you out of this scrape," answered the wee man, with a smile only to be seen on the face of a fairy. "I'm going out at that broken pane in the window there, straight to Dick Holmes' stable, take out the steeplechaser 'Nightwind,' ride as fast as he can go to the junction, return with half-a-dozen troopers by a short cut, and secure these ruffians red-handed with their booty."

"Hurrah!" cried Toney in his enthusiasm.

"Hush, boy. Not so loud," said the elfin; "they may hear you. I must away on my errand quickly; yet mind, Toney, if you don't see the bank cat here again, I'm always to be found on the banks of the Bogan. Keep good heart. Good-bye."

With a hop, skip, and a jump the wee man was through the broken pane and astride the horse "Nightwind" before the boy could realise that he was alone.

Meanwhile the strong-room of the bank resounded with the heavy blows dealt by the robbers upon the solid doors of the iron safe, which for a long time withstood their utmost attempts to break it open. Poor Toney sat in fear and trembling, and counted the minutes as they fled by, listening to the noises without, and wondering if the little elfin man would really do what he promised. It seemed hardly possible that he could sit a horse at all, much less guide the crack steeplechaser "Nightwind" across country on a dark night. Nevertheless, the confident tone of the fairy before he jumped out at the window reassured him, and hope began to gather in Toney the messenger.

Alas! that hope was dispelled the next moment by a loud shout from the bushrangers, which proclaimed that the safe had yielded. Had the robbers been less intent upon the bags of gold and silver which met their gaze, it is probable they would have seen the half-dozen police-troopers who entered, carbine in hand, and surrounded them. When the ruffians did see them, however, it was too late to resist, and they were taken away out into the darkened night, some of them never to see the light of the sun again as free men.

At the trial of the bushrangers the police couldn't swear who gave the information about the bank, and I believe it remains a mystery to this day.

TIM

The sinking sun cast a soft amber-tinted radiance over the little township of Wentworth, New South Wales, as a little boy, weary and footsore with travel, knocked at a farmer's door about two miles beyond the settlement.

A kind, motherly woman who answered the knock stared with astonishment at the juvenile tramp, who blurted out in a faint voice, "If you please, ma'am, will you give me a drink of water? I'm so hungry, I really don't know where I shall sleep to-night."

The good lady laughed heartily at the little fellow's quaint request. She took him into the house, and led him into a back room, where a great fat man was seated at tea.

"Who is this, Wife?" said he in a surly tone, looking at our hero.

"Only a poor boy begging some food, Mark; that's all," answered his wife meekly.

TIM. From *Australian Fairy Tales*, by Altha Westbury. By permission of Ward Lock & Co., Limited.

"I didn't beg, ma'am, please," said the boy quickly.

"Oh, you didn't beg?" rejoined the farmer in the same gruff voice. "Git down on that stool now."

"I came a very long way, sir, and I —" began the boy.

"Silence! Wife, take his bundle; pull off his old shoes; let him be washed; then give him his tea." The voice lost nothing of its coarse disagreeable ring as it gave the curt order, but the man's eyes looked kindly at the little wanderer, "What is your name?" he said gruffly.

"Tim, sir, please."

"Tim what? Hav'n't you another name?"

"No, sir. Nuggety Joe never called me anything else than Tim."

"And who is Nuggety Joe?" asked the farmer.

The boy played nervously with the edge of his tattered jacket for a moment, and then replied in a voice broken and unsteady with emotion, "Please, sir, father and Joe were mates on the diggings at Forbes. When the great dam broke and flooded the creek, and drowned father, mother, and little sister Jessie, Joe took care of me, and was a father to me—he was—until he took the fever, and died, and then I —" The child's quavering voice gave way to a fit of bitter wailing.

"Stop that!" cried the farmer, putting his handkerchief to his nose, and making that organ sound like a French horn. "Stop it at once. I'll have no snivelling here."

"Look here, boy, I think I can give you something to do on my farm. Mind, I'll set you a task the first thing in the morning; if you perform it to my satisfaction, and you likewise prove yourself an honest, trustworthy youngster, why, you shall never want a home or a friend while Mark Wilson lives. Now, Wife, put him to bed."

The good dame led Tim to a small attic bedroom, which contained, amongst other things, a beautiful parrot in a stout wire cage.

"Cockie" had evidently been enjoying a nap, for he shook himself at sight of the intruders, and sent forth from his bill a volley of strange sounds, in true imitation of a person just aroused from slumber. Mrs. Wilson retired, but she had hardly closed the door before the bird began to flap his wings and crow like a rooster.

"A funny parrot," muttered Tim. "I wonder if it can talk?"

"Of course it can," answered Cockie, eyeing him through the bars of the cage. The lad rubbed his eyes, and stared at the bird in the cage for fully three minutes without speaking a word, so great was his consternation. "Don't stare, Tim; it's very rude to stare," continued the bird gravely. "People in this colony have a bad habit of staring you out of countenance, I am sorry to say."

"Why, you can talk like a man," cried the boy in his astonishment.

"Certainly; much better than some men, I trust. Pray come here and scratch me, Tim," cried the parrot coaxingly.

Little Tim obeyed very cautiously, and in fear and trembling.

"That is delightful," said Cockie.

"It's wonderful," muttered poor Tim.

"What is wonderful, sir? Can't parrots talk?"

"Some of them can, but not like you."

"Oh! but I'm not a parrot, I'm a fairy."

"A fairy?" cried the boy, agape with wonder. "Are you really?"

"Truly I am. One of the Lake George fairies. Xanthine, our Queen, turned me into a parrot, five years ago, through her foolish jealousy, and here I've been caged up ever since with this great beak upon my face, which quite disfigures me."

"What a shame! Can't you get back again to your friend at Lake George?" cried the boy.

"Yes, for Queen Xanthine is dead, and I can now return in safety, if you will help me," replied the bird.

"Me! how can I help you?" answered little Tim.

"I will tell you," rejoined the elfin. "You must know, boy, that every one of us could help each other if we would. The rich can help the poor, and the poor the wealthy; yea, even the smallest can render assistance to the strong and powerful, as was the case with the lion and the mouse. Now, I can prove how I can render you a service. Judge. Didn't the master say he would set you a task in the morning?"

"He did," replied Tim in wonder.

"Very well. The task is to milk a bad-tempered, touchy old cow called 'Peggy.' The beast, who is a splendid milker, is the torment and plague of the farmer's life. She has kicked him until he is afraid to approach her, and every one, man, woman, and boy, who attempts to milk Peggy is sure to be upset. It has proved useless to tie her by the leg and the tail—the wicked rogue would find a way of defeating her enemies before the milking was ended."

"Are you sure that I shall have to try to milk Peggy in the morning?" inquired Tim.

"Quite certain," replied the elfin.

"Then I—I think I had better go away now, at once, before the morning, don't you?" said the lad ruefully.

"No, I don't, because I can tell you how to overcome the antics of this refractory cow."

"How?"

"I will tell you upon one condition," replied the fairy parrot, rubbing its beak reflectively.

"What condition?" asked Tim.

"That you set me free as soon as you have completed your task to-morrow."

"It's a bargain," replied little Tim readily. "I can easily get the farmer another parrot—a real bird, you know—and then there will be no harm done."

"Very good. Now listen. On the gable of this house there grows a creeper with a pale blue flower. In the morning, when they call you, go and gather a small wreath of this plant, and when the wicked cow is bailed up ready for milking, place the vine around her horns, and you may take the word of an Australian fairy that Peggy will stand as quiet as a mouse until you have drained her teats as dry as a corn cob."

"Lor! how simple!" replied Tim.

"All knowledge is simple, boy, when you once acquire it. You'll not forget my instructions?"

"No, I thank you. I shall remember."

"Kiss Cockie, then, say your prayers like a good boy, and go to bed. Good-night."

Tim wished to ask the fairy bird a hundred questions, but after it had said good-night it would not utter another word, so the boy went to bed and fell asleep.

The sun was up before him in the morning. Yet Tim managed to get down into the garden and cut a slender tendril from the creeper, which he formed into a small hoop, just as the farmer's voice was heard calling him.

Twenty cows had to be milked every morning at the farm, and Tim heard a great deal of shouting and bellowing, and clanking of milk-cans, which proceeded from a yard at hand, enclosed with a high fence and into which the cattle had been driven.

The boy went up to Peggy, who gave a loud bellow at sight of him. He placed the vine around her horns, then sat down to his task. Mark Wilson stood ready to pick the boy up in case the cow knocked him over; but the beast never moved until the boy had drawn every drop of milk from her teats. The good farmer was filled with amazement, and cried out, "Twenty-five boys and ten men have all tried to milk Peggy, and not one of them has succeeded but you. Therefore, from this moment, I will adopt you as my son, Tim, and you shall marry my little girl Amy, by-and-by, and I will leave you the farm as a wedding present." And the farmer kept his word.

When Tim went upstairs to set the parrot free, he found the bird transformed into a beautiful wee lady, whom he politely lifted out of the cage. She thanked him, and made him a graceful curtsey as she vanished out of the window.

WAYAMBEH THE TURTLE

Oolah, the lizard, was out getting yams on a Mirrieh flat. She had three of her children with her. Suddenly she thought she heard some one moving behind the big Mirrieh bushes. She listened. All of a sudden out jumped Wayambeh from behind a bush and seized Oolah, telling her not to make a noise and he would not hurt her, but that he meant to take her off to his camp to be his wife. He would take her three children too and look after them. Resistance was useless, for Oolah had only her stick, while Wayambeh had his spears and boondees. Wayambeh took the woman and her children to his camp. His tribe when they saw him bring home a woman of the Oolah tribe, asked him if her tribe had given her to him. He said, "No, I have stolen her."

"Well," they said, "her tribe will soon be after her; you must protect yourself; we shall not fight for you. You had no right to steal her without telling us. We had a young woman of our own tribe for you, yet you go and steal an Oolah and bring her to the camp of the Wayambeh. On your own head be the consequences."

In a short time the Oolahs were seen coming across the plain which faced the camp of the Wayambeh. And they came not in friendship or to parley, for no women were with them, and they carried no boughs of peace in their hands, but were painted as for war, and were armed with fighting weapons.

When the Wayambeh saw the approach of the Oolah, their chief said: "Now, Wayambeh, you had better go out on to the plain and do your own fighting; we shall not help you."

Wayambeh chose the two biggest boreens that he had; one he slung on him, covering the front of his body, and one the back; then, seizing his weapons, he strode out to meet his enemies.

When he was well out on to the plain, though still some distance from the Oolah, he called out, "Come on."

The answer was a shower of spears and boomerangs. As they came whizzing through the air Wayambeh drew his arms inside the boreens, and ducked his head down between them, so escaped.

As the weapons fell harmless to the ground, glancing off his boreen, out again he stretched his arms and held up again his head, shouting, "Come on, try again, I'm ready."

The answer was another shower of weapons, which he met in the same way. At last the Oolahs closed in round him, forcing him to retreat towards the creek.

Shower after shower of weapons they slung at him, and were getting at

WAYAMBEH THE TURTLE. From *Australian Legendary Tales*, collected by K. Langloh Parker.

such close quarters that his only chance was to dive into the creek. He turned towards the creek, tore the front boreen off him, flung down his weapons and plunged in.

The Oolah waited, spears poised in hand, ready to aim directly as his head appeared above water, but they waited in vain. Wayambeh, the black fellow, they never saw again, but in the waterhole wherein he had dived they saw a strange creature, which bore on its back a fixed structure like a boreen, and which, when they went to try and catch it, drew in its head and limbs, so they said, "It is Wayambeh." And this was the beginning of Wayambeh, or turtle, in the creeks.

BUNNYYARL THE FLIES AND WURRUNNUNNAH THE BEES

The Bunnyyarl and Wurrunnunnah were relations, and lived in one camp. The Wurrunnunnah were very hardworking, always trying to gather food in a time of plenty, to lay in a store for a time of famine. The Bunnyyarl used to give no heed to the future, but used to waste their time playing round any rubbish, and never thinking even of laying up any provisions. One day the Wurrunnunnah said, "Come out with us and gather honey from flowers. Soon will the winter winds blow the flowers away, and there will be no more honey to gather."

"No," said the Bunnyyarl, "we have something to look to here." And off they went, turning over some rubbish and wasting their time, knowing whatever the Wurrunnunnah brought they would share with them. The Wurrunnunnah went alone and left the Bunnyyarl to their rubbish. The Wurrunnunnah gathered the flowers and stored the honey, and never more went back to live with the Bunnyyarls, for they were tired of doing all the work.

As time went on the Wurrunnunnah were changed into little wild bees, and the lazy Bunnyyarls were changed into flies.

WEEDAH THE MOCKING BIRD

Weedah, the mocking bird was playing a great trick on the birds and beasts who lived near him. He had built himself a number of grass

BUNNYYARL THE FLIES AND WURRUNNUNNAH THE BEES. From *Australian Legendary Tales*, collected by K. Langloh Parker.

WEEDAH THE MOCKING BIRD. From *Australian Legendary Tales*, collected by K. Langloh Parker.

nyunnoos [grass huts], more than twenty. He made fires before each, to make it look as if some one lived in the nyunnoos. First he would go into one nyunnoo, and cry like a baby, then to another and laugh like a child, then in another sing like a young girl, corrobboree [dance] like a man, call out in a quavering voice like an old man, and in a shrill voice like an old woman: in fact imitate any sort of voice he had heard, and imitate them so quickly in succession that any one passing would think there was a great crowd in the camp. His object was to entice as many as he could into his camp and then kill them. In this way he would have the whole country to himself.

One day, when Beeargah [hawk] did not return, his cousin, Mullyan determined to find out what this mystery was. After following the track of Beeargah, he came at last through the bushes to hear the sounds of many voices, babies crying, women singing, men talking. Peering through the bush, he saw the grass huts. "Who can these be?" he thought. The track led him right into the camp, where alone Weedah was to be seen. Mullyan advanced towards him and asked where were the people whose voices he had heard as he came through the bush.

Weedah said: "How can I tell you? I know of no people; I live alone."

"But," said Mullyan the eagle hawk, "I heard babies crying, women laughing, and men talking, not one but many."

"And I alone am here. Ask of your ears what trick they played you, or perhaps your eyes fail you now. Can you see any but me? Look for yourself."

"And if, as indeed it seems, you only are here, what did you do with Beeargah my cousin, and where are my friends? Many are their trails that I see coming into this camp, but none going out. And if you alone live here you alone can answer me."

"What know I of you or your friends? Nothing. Ask of the winds that blow. Ask of Bahloo the moon, who looks down on the earth by night. Ask of Yhi the sun, that looks down by day. But ask not Weedah, who dwells alone, and knows naught of your friends." But as Weedah was talking he was carefully edging Mullyan towards the fire.

Mullyan, the eagle hawk, too, was cunning, and not easy to trap. He saw a blazing fire in front of him, he saw the track of his friend behind him, he saw Weedah was edging him towards the fire, and it came to him in a moment the thought that if the fire could speak, well could it tell where were his friends. But the time was not yet come to show that he had fathomed the mystery. So he affected to fall into the trap. But when they reached the fire, before Weedah had time to act his usual part, with a mighty grip Mullyan, the eagle hawk, seized him, saying, "Even as you served Beeargah the hawk, my cousin, and my friends, so now serve I you." And right into the middle of the blazing fire he threw him. Then he turned homewards in haste, to tell everyone that he had solved the fate of their friends, which had so long been a mystery. When he was some distance from the Weedah's camp, he heard the sound of a thunder clap. But it was not thunder, it was the bursting of the back of Weedah's head, which had burst with a bang as of a thunder clap. And as it burst, out from his remains had risen a bird, Weedah, the mocking bird; which bird to this day has a hole at the back of his head, just in the same place as Weedah the black fellow's head had burst, and whence the bird came forth.

To this day the Weedah makes grass playgrounds, through which he runs, imitating, as he plays, in quick succession, any voices he has ever heard, from the crying of a child to the laughing of a woman; from the mewing of a cat to the barking of a dog, and hence his name Weedah, the mocking bird.

THE STORY OF THE MOUSE-DEER AND OTHER ANIMALS WHO WENT OUT FISHING

Once upon a time the Mouse-Deer, accompanied by many other animals, went on a fishing expedition. All day long they fished, and in the evening returned to the little hut that they had put up by the river-side, salted the fish that they had caught, and stored it up in their jars. They noticed that somehow or other their fish disappeared day by day, and the animals held a council to decide what it was best to do. After some discussion the Deer said he would stay behind while the others went out to fish, so that he might catch the thief.

"I shall be able to master him, whoever he is," said the Deer. "If he refuses to do what I wish, I shall soon punish him with my sharp horns."

So the others went out fishing, leaving the Deer at home. Soon he heard the tramp of someone coming to the foot of the steps leading up into the hut, calling out:

"Is anyone at home?"

"I am here," said the Deer. Looking out, he saw a great Giant, and his heart failed him. He wished he had asked one of his companions to stay at home with him.

"I smell some fish," said the Giant. "I want some, and I must have it. I am hungry. Let me have what I want."

"It does not belong to me," said the Deer in great fear. "It belongs to the Pig, the Bear, the Tiger, and the Mouse-Deer. They would punish me severely if I gave any of it to you."

THE STORY OF THE MOUSE-DEER AND OTHER ANIMALS WHO WENT OUT FISHING. From *Seventeen Years among the Sea Dyaks of Borneo,* by Edwin H. Gomes. By permission of the Seeley Service & Co., Ltd.

"Don't talk to me in that way. If you do not let me have what I want, I will eat you up," said the Giant.

The Deer was too much awed by his visitor to attack the Giant, so he let him eat the fish and take some away with him.

When his companions returned, the Deer gave them his account of the Giant's visit. They blamed him for his cowardice, and the Wild Boar said he would keep watch the next day.

"If the Giant comes," said he, "I will gore him with my tusks and trample him underfoot."

But he fared no better than the Deer, for when he saw the Giant, who threatened to kill him if he refused to give him some fish, he was afraid, and let him take as much as he wanted.

Great was the disgust of the others to find on their return that their fish had again been stolen.

"Let me watch," said the Bear. "No Giant shall frighten me. I will hug him in my arms and scratch him with my sharp claws."

So Bruin was left in charge the next day, while the others went out to fish.

Soon he heard the Giant, who came to the foot of the steps and shouted: "Hullo! Who's there?"

"I am," said the Bear. "Who are you, and what do you want?"

"I can smell some nice fish, and I am hungry, and want some."

"I cannot let you have any," said the Bear. "It does not belong to me."

"Let me have some at once," said the Giant in a voice of thunder, "therefore I will kill and eat you."

The Bear was too much frightened to interfere while the Giant ransacked the jars. When he had enough, he bade the Bear goodbye and went off.

On the return of the other animals, the Tiger said he would put a stop to this state of things. He would stay at home the next day and keep watch. It would have to be a very strong Giant indeed that would dare to fight him.

The Giant paid his visit as before, and when he found the Tiger at home, he said that he was hungry, and asked for some fish. At first the Tiger refused to give any to him, but when he saw his formidable enemy he was afraid, and let him have as much as he wanted.

On their return again the animals found their fish had been stolen.

Then the Mouse-Deer spoke. "I see," he said, "that it is no use depending on you others. You boast, but when the time comes for action, you have no courage. I will stay at home and secure this Giant that you spoke of."

When his companions had gone away the next morning, the Mouse-Deer put a bandage round his forehead and lay down.

Soon came the Giant, and shouted: "Who's there?"

"Only me," said the Mouse-Deer, groaning with pain. "Come up, who-ever you may be."

The Giant climbed up the rickety steps, and saw the Mouse-Deer lying with his head bandaged.

"What is the matter with you?" asked the Giant.

"I have a headache," was the answer.

"Whatever has given you the headache?" asked the Giant.

"Can't you guess?" said the Mouse-Deer. "It is the smell of this fish in these jars. It's so strong it is enough to make anyone ill. Don't you feel ill yourself?"

"I think I do," said the Giant. "Cannot you give me some medicine?"

"I have no medicine with me," said the Mouse-Deer, "but I can bandage you, as I have done myself, and it is sure to do you good."

"Thank you," said the Giant. "It is good of you to take the trouble to cure me."

So the Giant lay down as he was bid, while the Mouse-Deer bandaged his head, and fastened the ends of the bandage to pegs which he drove in to the ground under the open flooring of the hut.

"Don't you feel a little pain in your ankles?" anxiously suggested the Mouse-Deer.

"I think I do," was the foolish Giant's reply.

So the Mouse-Deer bandaged his legs and made them secure, so that the Giant was quite unable to move.

By this time the Giant began to feel uneasy, and trying to get up, and finding himself securely bound, he struggled and roared in pain and anger.

The little Mouse-Deer sat before him and laughed, and said: "You were a match for the Deer, the Pig, the Bear, and the Tiger, but you are defeated by me. Don't make so much noise, or I shall drive a peg through your temples and kill you."

Just then the others returned from their fishing. Great was their joy to find their enemy securely bound. With cries of triumph they fell upon the Giant and killed him, and praised the Mouse-Deer for his cleverness in securing him.

THE MAGIC CAP

The goblins of Korea used to wear magic caps, called Horang Gamtĕ, which had the power of rendering them invisible.

Now there once lived a man who was most diligent in his worship of his

THE MAGIC CAP. From *Folk Tales from Korea*, by Zong In-Sob. By permission of Routledge & Kegan Paul Ltd.

ancestors. He was always holding services to their memory, with lavish offerings of delicious food and drink. One day, when he had held such a service, a group of goblins came to his house, and ate up all the good things set out on the altars. And on every following occasion they did the same. Of course they were invisible, for they wore their magic caps, and so the offerings just disappeared. The man was very gratified at first to see his offerings eaten, for it seemed to prove that his ancestors relished them. So he spent more and more money to provide even more lavish feasts until he was almost ruined.

At last his wife complained of his extravagance. "There must be something wrong," she said. "The spirits of our ancestors would never eat so much as to leave us almost ruined. There must be thieves coming in and stealing them while we are occupied with the ceremonial and bowing before the altar. In future I think we ought to keep a careful watch."

So one night the husband hid behind a screen by the altar. He held a stout cudgel in his hand. In the middle of the night he heard the sound of whispering and of food being eaten. He peeped over the screen and saw the food steadily disappearing from the dishes. Yet he could see no one by the table. So all of a sudden he rushed out brandishing his cudgel and rushed round the altar and into all the corners of the room. Alarmed by his violent onslaught the goblins ran away, but the man touched one of them with his cudgel and knocked his cap off. When the goblins had gone the man saw a red cap lying on the floor, the like of which he had never seen before. He picked it up curiously and put it on, and then began to shout "Thief! Thief!"

His wife heard his shouts and came into the hall. But she could not see her husband, though she could hear him beside her gasping breathlessly, "The thief got away, but he left a very strange cap behind. See?" His wife just stood there bewildered and said, "But where are you, my dear? I can't see you." Her husband took her by the hand and said, "I'm here. What's the matter?" She felt him take hold of her, and tried to grasp him. She chanced to knock off the cap which he had put on his head. No sooner had it fallen to the floor than she saw him standing beside her.

She picked up the cap and said, "Is this the cap you mean? It must have made you invisible. So that's how the thief got in unnoticed. Let me try it." She put it on her head and immediately vanished. "This must be Horang Gamtĕ, the magic cap. I'm sure of it!" she exclaimed. "The thief was no man, but a goblin."

Having made this remarkable find they determined that they would turn it to their profit. From that day on they went from house to house in the village, stealing all that they could lay their hands on. Many complaints were made to the authorities, but though a strict watch was kept not a single clue could be found, so stealthily were the thefts committed.

They continued their activities for more than a year, and became very rich. But one day the husband went to a jeweller's shop. It was not open yet, so he waited by the door. In a little while the jeweller came along and opened the door and the thief slipped in behind him. The jeweller took his money from the safe and began to count it. While he was counting it he was amazed to see the coins disappearing one by one. He searched the whole shop, on the floor, and in every corner, but could find no trace of them. Then he looked up, and saw a piece of thread moving slowly in the air. He grabbed it with his fingers, something dropped on the floor, and there beside him he saw a man. The magic cap was beginning to wear out, and a thread had come loose from one of the seams.

The jeweller seized him with both hands, but when he returned all the money he had stolen and offered him the magic cap he let him go. Then the jeweller neglected his business and began himself to use the magic cap as the other had done. One day in the harvest time he went to a rich farmer's house, wearing the magic cap on his head. The yard was full of labourers threshing rice with flails. As he passed through the yard to the house one of the flails knocked the cap off his head, and it fell in tatters to the ground. So he was discovered, and immediately arrested.

He was brought to trial, and the husband and wife as well. They were all condemned to imprisonment, and shortly afterwards died in prison.

THE RAT'S BRIDEGROOM

Once upon a time there lived a family of rats. When the eldest daughter grew up her parents decided that they must find the most powerful bridegroom in the world for her.

So one day they went and called on the Sun. "Good day, Mr. Sun," they said. "Our daughter has grown up and it is time she was married. So we are looking for the most powerful person in the world to ask him to be her husband. By your high position and great power you seem to be the most powerful of all, and so we have come to invite you to be her bridegroom."

But the Sun shook his head and said with a smile, "It may seem to you that I am the most powerful, but it is not so. Mr. Cloud is more powerful than I am, for he can cover my face and keep me from shining. So I recommend Mr. Cloud to you."

Mr. and Mrs. Rat thought over what the Sun had told them, and decided that Mr. Cloud must indeed be the most powerful of all. So they called on him and said, "Good day, Mr. Cloud. Our daughter has grown up, and it is time she was married. We wish to invite the most powerful person in the world to be her husband, and so we have come to welcome

THE RAT'S BRIDEGROOM. From *Folk Tales from Korea*, by Zong In-Sob. By permission of Routledge & Kegan Paul Ltd.

you as her bridegroom, for you can cover the face of the Sun and keep him from shining."

Mr. Cloud smiled and shook his head. "Yes, I can cover the face of the Sun and keep him from shining," he said. "Yet I am not the most powerful, for Mr. Wind blows me away, whether I wish to go or not. He is far more powerful than I, and so I recommend him to you."

Mr. and Mrs. Rat thought it over, and decided that Mr. Wind must indeed be more powerful than Mr. Cloud. So they went to him and said, "Good day, Mr. Wind. Our daughter has grown up and it is time she was married. We wish to invite the most powerful person in the world to be her husband, and so we have come to welcome you as her bridegroom, for you can blow Mr. Cloud away, whether he wishes to go or not."

But Mr. Wind shook his head and laughed. "I appreciate your kind offer," he said. "I am indeed very powerful, but there is one more powerful than I. It is the Stone Buddha, in Ŭnzin, in the Province of Zŏlla. His feet are planted so firmly on the ground that, blow how I will, I cannot budge him in the slightest. He has a hat on his head, but I cannot even blow that off. He is surely the most powerful of all, so I recommend him to you."

So Mr. and Mrs. Rat went off and called on the Stone Buddha of Unzin. Mrs. Rat said to him, "My daughter is old enough to marry now, and we invite you to be her bridegroom, as you are the most powerful of all."

The Stone Buddha smiled and answered in a gentle voice, "Thank you for the kind offer. But there is one yet more powerful than I. He is the young rat who lives beneath my feet. One day he will undermine me completely and I will fall. Mrs. Rat, I am at the mercy of the rats."

Mr. and Mrs. Rat were happy and realized at last that the only fitting bridegroom for their daughter was a young rat. So they returned home and married their daughter to a young rat.

A SELFISH HUSBAND

Once upon a time an old man lived with his wife. One day, after he had held a service in memory of his ancestors, one of their neighbours sent them a present of some food. He sent them cooked rice and vegetables, but only one cake. They were unwilling to divide it, and so they agreed that the first to speak should forfeit the cake. So they left it on the table, and sat gazing at it in silence.

Just then a thief broke into the house, and when he saw the old man and his wife sitting there in silence he concluded that they must be blind and deaf. So he calmly helped himself to everything he could find, and then

A SELFISH HUSBAND. From *Folk Tales from Korea,* by Zong In-Sob. By permission of Routledge & Kegan Paul Ltd.

began a violent assault on the old woman. But her husband just sat and watched in silence. At last his wife could stand it no longer. She shouted at him, "You heartless old man! You sit there quietly while this fellow beats me!"

Then the old man said, "The cake is mine," and coolly popped it into his mouth.

DADDY LONG-LEGS

The season was so dry that the rice crop failed; and the Long-leg family were sore put to it to get food, picking up occasionally a little rice, occasionally potatoes, sugar-cane, banana, and so on. At last came the wet weather and all folk went down to their rice-fields to clean ditches, repair broken dykes, plough up with buffaloes their patches of rice-fields till the soil was soft and good for planting, and the crop healthy and free from the danger of such pests as worms, rats, and pigs. Everybody worked except Daddy Long-legs, who did nothing but doze day and night in the house, very wretched at his poverty and unable to see his way to buy food on credit.

One day said Daddy Long-legs to his son: "Alas, in what a plight we are, without any food!" Said Long-legs, "Well, what can you think of, Daddy?" Quoth Daddy Long-legs, "You go and hide a pair of buffaloes that belong to those folk ploughing; hide them in the scrub. If the people clamour at their loss, say I have the gift of divination and can show them the place where their buffaloes are." They had finished their plotting. It was midday and all the rice-planting folk were tired, ceased work, and went into their shelters, ate, drank, and some fell asleep. Their buffaloes were tethered near the dykes in the shade, grazing, and half of them wallowing in pools. So Long-legs went alone, peeping and spying at the sleeping owners, seized two buffaloes by their cords, took them about a mile away and tied them up to a big tree. Then he went home and told his father, who was glad when he heard how his son had followed his teaching. When it was evening, all the rice-planters went back to their fields to fetch their buffaloes, and found two missing. In vain they searched and said, "We wonder if there is anyone who has the gift of divination? We want to get him to tell us where our lost buffaloes are." Just then, Long-legs was playing near and cried, "My father knows a little magic for finding lost goods." "Is it true?" asked the folk. "Yes," said Long-legs. Then said one of them, "Come my friend, let us all go to Daddy Long-legs and ask him to help us." So all the rice-planters went to see Daddy Long-

DADDY LONG-LEGS. From the *Papers on Malay Subjects,* by R. O. Winstedt. By permission of Malaya Publishing House, Ltd., Singapore.

legs. Daddy Long-legs was at home, his betel-crusher in his hand, and gave them greeting. "What purpose have ye, my sons?" They answered, "We've come to ask you to tell us where are the buffaloes we've lost and sought in vain." Quoth Daddy Long-legs, "I have little skill, but will try if you like," and he fetched a piece of shabby paper and wrote on it hapazard at a venture like the searching of a fowl, and he counted his fingers and closed his eyes, and exclaimed, "Ah, my sons, that pair of buffaloes is tied up to a bog tree of this shape towards the west, and ye must be quick or they'll die." As soon as they heard this, those folk were glad at heart; half went home and half went in search of the buffaloes and came in due time to the spot where Daddy Long-legs had tethered them. The buffaloes were nearly dead of thirst. So they took them and brought them home; sure and confident of Daddy Long-legs' skill: and they went to his house, with a number of presents, husked and unhusked, tobacco, and so on, worth about fifty pieces of money. Daddy Long-legs was delighted at the presents, and he and his family had food in plenty. And the rice planters all went off to their several places.

The following is a modern version of the ending of Daddy Long-legs:[2]

In due time they came to the spot where Long-legs had tethered the buffaloes, but both were dead of thirst. Just before their eyes started dimming with tears of sorrow, they discovered huge footprints around the tree in the soft ground, such as could only belong to a member of the Long-leg family. Also, the rope was tied up so high on the tree, that none but Long-legs could reach it. This was proof enough to the farmers to see Daddy Long-legs' evil scheme. Angrily they seized Long-legs and tied him to the tree and then hurried to get Daddy Long-legs and joined him to his son.

The next morning the villagers harnessed the two culprits in front of the plough the poor dead animals had to draw before, and made them do the work of the buffaloes all summer long, until a new pair could be purchased.

Some people in the next village believe the two are still ploughing fields to repay for the buffaloes, others say that Daddy Long-legs may have lost his gift for divination altogether by now.

RONGO AND THE LIZARD-GOD

On one of the Pacific Islands, in ancient days, there was a great feud between the adherents of Rongo, the god of cultivated crops, and

RONGO AND THE LIZARD-GOD. From *Maori Tales and Legends*, by Kate McCosh Clark.
[2] Walter Schmid, by permission.

Matarau, the eight-tailed lizard-god. During the fierce fight between the two parties, Rongo took prisoner a youth of high rank, named Vaioevé; he then changed him into a large sword-fish, which was laid for sacrifice on Rongo's altar. Great was the consternation of Matarau when he heard the tidings, for Vaioevé was a young brave, beloved by his tribe, and the lizard-god resolved himself to rescue the sword-fish even from the sacred altar of Rongo.

The hot day was ended, and the sudden darkness of the tropics fell upon the land. A cool night breeze sprang up, and as it swept over the calm sea, the sleeping waters shivered. The breeze rose with the rising tides up the dark creeks, hustling the twisted mangroves, rustling the fan-fronds of the palms, playing with the leafy fringes of the dark forest canopies.

In the dead of night the lizard-god came out of his hiding-place, a rocky cave, and, stealing through the dense undergrowth, gained the outskirts of the woods. Grey clouds hid the stars, and the glitter of his two hundred eyes was veiled in darkness. Keeping his eight heads and eight tails close to the ground, the monster slid along, so that no unusual movement of the long dry grass should be seen. He reached the open cultivated land of his enemy, and gliding cautiously through the large patches of Kumara (sweet potatoes), got near the altar of Rongo unnoticed by any of the followers of that god. "Ah, there is the captive," breathed Matarau, as he could just discern the sword-fish lying on the altar ready for the morning sacrifice. He darted forward, seized his prize and carried it in triumph through the forest to his cave. Rongo was filled with wrath when he heard that his sacrifice had been stolen, and was determined to recover it. So he called his swift messengers, the little birds, and said:

"Go, and find where the sword-fish is hidden; my enemy Matarau must have carried it off in the night. Bring the fish back to me. Such is my command."

There was a flash of jewel-colours, a soft whirr of many wings, and the birds were gone. They looked everywhere with their bright eyes for the sword-fish, and at last saw it in the entrance of the cave. But the dreaded lizard was guarding it, and the little birds were sore afraid, for his eight heads were ever on the move, and his two hundred eyes ever on the alert. They sat for a long time on the branches of some trees near, hoping they might get a chance to carry off the fish. But it was useless; the lizard's watch was unceasing, his eyes could see all around, and if perchance some closed in the slumbrous heat of noon, others were always open, and the snip-snap of his many restless jaws rang on the silence.

What could the little birds do against such a foe? They chirped and twittered, and twittered and chirped, but could settle on no stratagem by which to evade his vigilance. The lizard, hearing the unusual noise in the branches, waked and yawned, and yawned and slept, but troubled not. It was only the birds. At last they agreed to fly back and tell Rongo what they had seen, and that they could do nothing; and Rongo was angry at this, and told the little birds that they must try by some means to get back the sword-fish, and he ordered them to return at once to the cave.

There was again a flash of jewel-colours, a whirr of many wings, and the birds had gone. Once more they perched on the trees and chirped and twittered above the lizard. At last some of them ventured to fly down and try and carry off the sword-fish when they thought the terrible heads lay in sleep; but the lizard had one eye open, and his strong tails lashed them, and his terrible jaws snapped them up. More and more birds ventured down, but the terrible lizard seemed to be a very whirlpool of heads and tails; and in the end all the winged messengers were destroyed and eaten, except one which flew back to tell Rongo what had befallen the rest.

Then Rongo called other and larger birds to him, even sea-birds and birds of prey. "Go," he said, "and fail not to bring me back the fish."

There was a darkening of the sun, a beat of heavy wings, and the big birds were gone. But they too were knocked down by the lashing tails as they ventured near, and were eaten by the monster lizard-god, and the air was full of snapping jaws and flying feathers, and not one bird went back to tell Rongo the tidings.

When his servitors returned not, Rongo knew they also must have perished, and he waxed more and more wroth, but knew not what to do. Now some crimson and black butterflies were flitting from flower to flower near by, their rich colours gleaming in the sunshine. Rongo saw them, and he called them to him and said:

"All the birds are destroyed which I sent to get back my sacrifice. You must go and try to snatch the sword-fish from our enemy, the lizard-god."

"How can we succeed when all the birds, little and great, have failed?" said they. But Rongo replied, "Go."

There was a sigh from the flowers, a flutter in the air, and the butterflies had gone. But as the brave little fellows settled on a brilliant creeper, festooning the cave, in order to get near to the fish, the lizard spied them. There was a rapid sweep of a tail, and they lay on the ground, quivering spots of brightness, then, with closed wings, were still. Rongo was in despair, when the red and black butterflies returned not, and he knew not how to outwit his enemy. After a while two large yellow butterflies flitted about the flowers like gleams of golden light, and Rongo called to them, for he had at last thought of a good plan. "Go, O yellow butterflies," said he, "to the cave of Matarau, the lizard-god, and snatch from him my sword-fish which he has stolen."

"How can we succeed when so many others have failed?" asked they. "Speak not of a failure; I will tell you how to gain success," said Rongo.

"There is a large banyan tree growing outside the entrance of the cave, and its branches reach high overhead. On it there are some yellow leaves; hide under them and you will not be seen. I will send other moths and butterflies of different colours, and bid them conceal themselves also in places where they will not be noticed. Go and do what I have said, and afterward I will help you."

The two large yellow butterflies were plucky and clever; they flew swiftly toward the banyan tree and, lost to sight in the brilliant sunshine, hid under two yellow leaves, and the lizard saw them not. Rongo then sent other butterflies, and moths of all colours. They flitted round and round, settled on flower and leaf, now here, now there, then, rising, flew each time nearer and nearer, till at last they were close to the cave. The many-eyed lizard blinked in the sun, he heard the soft music of light wings and saw the bright moving specks of colour, but he said, "It is only the butterflies!" and he cared not. Then one by one the insects hid in places the colour of their wings, some on flowers and leaves, others in the crevices of loose bark. And the flutter of bright wings ceased, and butterflies and moths waited the promised help of Rongo.

The evening drew on with its changeful lights and cool, tremulous shadows, and the lizard-god roused himself. The hidden moths and flies watched his eight tails waving to and fro more and more vigorously, and saw the glitter of his two hundred eyes, which shone now yellow, now red, now green, as they reflected the lights and colours of flower on tree. The spines on his back stood up stiff and sharp, and his heads wagged, and his jaws snapped as he caught any unwary insects and reptiles which ventured too near! But the lizard saw not the hidden insects, and they chuckled with delight at having so far outwitted the dreaded monster. But when would Rongo help them?

As the last yellow rays of the setting sun slanted through the trees, Rongo made the west wind blow across the land, and a shower of leaves was blown down upon the lizard and the sword-fish. The lizard blinked and wriggled his heads and tails till he was free of the fallen leaves; but he did not know that underneath two were hidden the brave yellow servitors of his enemy. Again and again blew the west wind, showering down numberless leaves and twigs and loose bits of bark, with the insects hidden beneath them. And the dust and little pieces of dry bark were blown into the lizard's eyes till he could not see out of them, and he was nothing but an angry, writhing mass of heads and tails. At that moment the two yellow butterflies, who were close to the fish, uncurled their long slender trunks, and gave a soft signal call. Thereat the insects came quickly out of their hiding places, and all laid hold of the sword-fish, and rising suddenly together, they carried the captive away high up into the air. By the time the astonished lizard had blinked his eyes free of dust, the fish was high over his head; and he was mad with rage, and his eyes flashed fire, and his hot breath smoked as he made the forest ring with the furious snapping of his jaws. But what cared the triumphant little thieves? They were far out of reach. They flew off gaily with their prize, and nearing the abode of Rongo and his followers, they sang:

In triumph dance before the fish, that we
Now lift on high and bear so carefully.

When the twinkling stars came out, and the pale-lit torch of night gleamed through the forest tangle, Matarau, the lizard-god, heard the song of the war dance of Rongo, rising shrill and triumphant on the night air. He crept to his cave in despair, and his people wailed. And the swordfish, even their young, brave Vaioevé, was sacrificed on the altar of Rongo. This was the first human sacrifice on the island. And the place where the victim was killed is still called Vaioevé.

THE DANCING CROSSES

There was a little girl who lost her way in the woods.

The sun had sunk too quickly and the creatures of dusk played pranks on the little girl's eyes. Now one path looked like the right one and when she followed it she found herself lost deeper in the woods. Then another path seemed more familiar than the last but it was the wrong one just the same.

Soon it was dark. The birds had ceased to sing. The crickets had begun to chirp. Now and then an owl hooted. The girl was caught in brambles and stumbled over tree roots until she was ready to cry.

Then she saw a light in the woods.

Now it is known that fairies sometimes lead travelers astray. And that was how it happened with the little girl. For soon she discovered to her dismay that the lights in the woods were merely fireflies.

On and on she walked until she was very tired and could walk no more. Then she sat down on the ground and prepared to stay there for the night. But when she looked around her once more she saw another light.

This time it wasn't fireflies. She went on and out of the dark of the woods and she came into a clearing and in that clearing was a hut and at the foot of the steps she called out, "Tao po!" as any well brought up child will do.

But nobody answered. And again she called out, "Tao po!" And still no one answered. Entering the house she found food on the stove. After eating she looked around for a corner to sleep in.

Before curling up to sleep she made the sign of the cross. Then she drew crosses in the air all around her. And after that she fell soundly asleep.

THE DANCING CROSSES. From *Philippine Tales and Fables,* by Manuel and Lyd Arguilla. By permission of the Capitol Publishing House, Inc.

Toward midnight the goblins who inhabited the house came home. Something human smells! They cried all at once.

It has eaten of our food!

Here it is! They discovered the child curled up in a corner.

The goblins were ready to lay their hands on the child when crosses of fire began to dance all around the little girl.

So scared were the goblins that they ran away.

In the morning the little girl woke up refreshed. She ate the rest of the food on the stove and set forth on her way.

She found the right path with no trouble. So differently does everything look in the morning light from what it seems at night.

MANSUMANDIG

One day a man said to his wife: "My wife, we are getting very poor and I must go into business to earn some money."

"That is a good idea," replied his wife. "How much capital have you?"

"I have twenty-five centavos," answered the man; "and I am going to buy rice and carry it to the mines, for I have heard that it brings a good price there."

So he took his twenty-five centavos and bought a half-cavan of rice which he carried on his shoulder to the mine. Arriving there he told the people that he had rice for sale, and they asked eagerly how much he wanted for it.

"Why, have you forgotten the regular price of rice?" asked the man. "It is twenty-five centavos."

They at once bought the rice, and the man was very glad because he would not have to carry it any longer. He put the money in his belt and asked if they would like to buy any more.

"Yes," said they, "we will buy as many cavans as you will bring."

When the man reached home his wife asked if he had been successful.

"Oh, my wife," he answered, "it is a very good business. I could not take the rice off my shoulder before the people came to buy it."

"Well, that is good," said the wife; "we shall become very rich."

The next morning the man bought a half-cavan of rice the same as before and carried it to the mine and when they asked how much it would be, he said:

"It is the same as before—twenty-five centavos." He received the money and went home.

"How is the business today?" asked his wife.

MANSUMANDIG. From *Philippine Folk Tales,* by Mabel Cook Cole, McClurg & Co.

"Oh, it is the same as before," he said. "I could not take the rice off my shoulder before they came for it."

And so he went on with his business for a year, each day buying a half-cavan of rice and selling it for the price he had paid for it. Then one day his wife said that they would balance accounts, and she spread a mat on the floor and sat down on one side of it, telling her husband to sit on the opposite side. When she asked him for the money he had made during the year, he asked:

"What money?"

"Why, give me the money you have received," answered his wife; "and then we can see how much you have made."

"Oh, here it is," said the man, and he took the twenty-five centavos out of his belt and handed it to her.

"Is that all you have received this year?" cried his wife angrily. "Haven't you said that rice brought a good price at the mines?"

"That is all," he replied.

"How much did you pay for the rice?"

"Twenty-five centavos."

"How much did you receive for it?"

"Twenty-five centavos."

"Twenty-five centavos. Oh, my husband," cried his wife, "how can you make any gain if you sell it for just what you paid for it."

The man leaned his head against the wall and thought. Ever since then he has been called "Mansumandig," a man who leans back and thinks.

THE MALLET OF WEALTH

Long, long ago there lived a very poor boy. He used to go out into the mountains every day to cut firewood. His parents used to sell the wood he gathered to buy food.

One day he went out to the mountain to cut wood as usual. As the afternoon wore on he began to feel very hungry, and so he looked around for something to eat. By good fortune he soon found a walnut tree growing in the forest, and climbing it he began to pick the nuts.

He picked one and put it in his pocket. "This is for father," he said.
He picked another. "This is for mother," he said.
Then he picked a third. "This is for my brother," he said.
Picking a fourth he said, "This is for my sister."
"And now, one for me," he said, and picking the fifth nut he put

THE MALLET OF WEALTH. From *Folk Tales from Korea*, by Zong In-Sob. By permission of Routledge & Kegan Paul Ltd.

it in his mouth and ate it. Then he picked more, until his hunger was satisfied.

When he set out for home the sun had set and it was already growing dark. So he stopped to pass the night in a wayside shrine. He sat on the floor quite alone. It was eerie sitting there on the floor, and he felt quite frightened. So he climbed up into the rafters to await the dawn.

In the middle of the night he was surprised to hear the clamour of voices outside, and then a crowd of goblins rushed into the hall talking animatedly to one another.

"Where have you been to-day?"

"I hung on the tail of an ox."

"I have been looking for a filial son. But it's very hard to find one these days, isn't it?"

"I have spent the whole day teasing a bad boy."

"I have been jumping in a ditch and blowing bubbles in the mud."

"I have been sleeping in the crevices of a stone wall."

"I have been dancing under a floor."

Every goblin recounted his doings of the day. Then one of them who seemed to be the leader cried, "Enough! Let us have a drink. I suppose you are all very hungry, aren't you?"

One goblin took a mallet from his belt, and striking the floor with it· chanted, "Tudurag-tag-tag, come out, cooked rice."

Immediately a great dish of cooked rice appeared from nowhere.

"Tudurag-tag-tag, come out, wine."

At once a cask of wine appeared in the middle of the hall. In the same way they got fish, meat, eggs, cake, fruit, and as many delicacies as they wished. So they feasted on all the good things.

The boy hiding in the rafters looked down on the scene of revelry by the dim light that penetrated the paper windows, and he too began to feel hungry. So he took a walnut from his pocket and cracked it in his mouth. Startled by the noise he made all the goblins shouted, "Help! Help! The roof is falling. We must get out at once." They all rushed in a panic from the hall, abandoning all the food and their mallet.

The boy came down from the rafters and ate his fill. Then he picked up the magic mallet and tried it out. He struck the floor with it and said, "Tudurag-tag-tag, come out, clothes." Immediately there appeared a full suit of clothes. Then he struck with the mallet again and wished for a pair of shoes. These too appeared. The boy was thrilled by his unexpected find, for he guessed that this was the celebrated "Mallet of Wealth," of which he had often heard, though no man had ever seen it before.

At day-break next day he hastened home with the mallet. His parents and the neighbours had worried greatly over his failure to return home the previous night, and now with great relief they listened to his story: walnuts, shrine, goblins, mallet, and all. His parents were delighted to get the mallet, for now they could live at their ease, and in the end they became quite rich.

Now there was in the same village a greedy and selfish boy. When he heard that his friend had suddenly become rich he came to him and asked him the secret of his good fortune. The honest filial boy told him all about his experiences.

So the selfish boy, who was really quite well-off, and who had never in his life gone out into the mountains to cut wood, went out to look for the walnut tree. At last, after a long weary search, he found it, and, being by now very hungry, he picked a nut and ate it. Afterwards he picked some nuts for his father and mother, and then rushed off to the wayside shrine while it was still light, so impatient was he. He waited in the hall until it got dark, and then he climbed up and hid among the rafters.

In the middle of the night the goblins came in and, striking the floor with a mallet, began their feast. The selfish boy was too impatient to wait until the wine had befuddled their wits, and, taking out a walnut, cracked it in his mouth. This time the goblins were not at all alarmed by the sound, but merely looked up and said, "There he is up there. We are not going to be tricked a second time. Pull him down before he spoils our entertainment."

So the selfish boy was dragged down from the rafters. The goblins sat round him on the floor and put him on trial.

"What shall we do with this idle greedy fellow?" asked the leader of the goblins.

"Hang him! Hang him!" shouted the others.

"That would be too severe. After all he is only a boy. I suggest that we stretch his tongue."

The assembly agreed with this suggestion, and so one of the goblins tapped his tongue with a mallet and intoned, "Tudurag-tag-tag, come out this tongue, one hundred feet long." Immediately his tongue began to grow, until it was one hundred feet long. Then the goblins kicked him out of the hall.

In his pain and weariness he could hardly stagger along carrying his tongue on his back. He came to a river, and saw that there was no bridge. So he stretched out his tongue across the river, so that it formed a bridge that people could walk on. He had repented of his selfishness, and had made up his mind to serve others. Travellers walked gratefully across the bridge he had formed, but one man let some burning tobacco fall on his tongue. He jumped with the pain and fell into the river.

The filial boy heard the news and came to his rescue. With great difficulty he managed to save him, and then he took his mallet and tapped the enormous tongue. "Tudurag-tag-tag, draw in, tongue," he said, and at once the tongue returned to its proper size. Thus he was cured, and never again did he do anything selfish as long as he lived.

5

EUROPE

"What's a Brownie?" you say. Oh it's a kind of a sort of a Bogle, but it isn't so cruel as a Redcap! What! You don't know what's a Bogle or a Redcap? Ah, me, what's the world a-coming to?[1]

This is the spirit and fundamental nature of the European folk tales. Although there are the marked dissimilarities due to the differing elements of the countries, the imaginative quality of fantasy mixed with the reality of life is constant. The common folk tale themes are presented in each country according to the social customs and traditions of the people who have told them throughout the years.

CZECHOSLOVAKIA

Sadly she shut the window; she crossed herself, and prayed for her sister and her mother.[2]

Here is the religious quality found in the Czechoslovakian tale. It stresses a yearning for truth and justice. Another characteristic is the sense of honor such as is found in "The Clever Lass." Although the supernatural is a feature of "Grandfather's Eyes," and "The Twelve Months," it is not predominate in Czechoslovakian folklore.

A CLEVER LASS

Once upon a time there was a shepherd. He used to pasture his sheep upon a hill, and one day he saw something glittering on the opposite

A CLEVER LASS. From *Czech Folk Tales*, by M. R. I. A. Baudis. By permission of George Allen & Unwin Ltd.

[1] J. Jacobs, "The Cauld Lad of Hilton," from *English Fairy Tales*.
[2] M. R. I. A. Baudis, "The Twelve Months," from *Czech Folk Tales*.

hill. So he went to see what it was. It was a golden mortar. He took it up and said to his daughter: "I will give this mortar to our king."

But she said: "Don't do that. If you give him the mortar, you won't have the pestle, and he is sure to ask for it, and then you will get into trouble."

But the shepherd thought that she was only a silly girl. He took the mortar, and, when he came before the king, he said: "Begging your pardon, Mr. King, I want to give you this mortar."

The king answered him roughly: "If you give me the mortar, I must have the pestle as well. Unless the pestle is here within three days, your life will be forfeited."

The shepherd began to lament: "My daughter was right when she said that when you had the mortar you would want the pestle too. I wouldn't listen to her, so it serves me right."

"Have you such a clever daughter as that?" asked the king.

"Indeed I have," said the shepherd.

"Then tell your daughter that I will marry her, if she comes neither walking nor riding, clothed or unclothed, neither by day nor night, neither at noon nor in the morning. And I won't ask for the pestle either."

The shepherd went home and said: "You can get me out of this, if you go to Mr. King neither clothed nor unclothed," and the rest of it.

But the daughter wasn't a bit frightened. She came with the fall dusk (and that was neither at noon nor in the morning); she dressed herself in fishing-nets; she took a goat, and she partly rode on the goat and partly she walked.

And when the king saw that she had only a fishing-net on, that she came with the approach of dusk, and that she was partly walking, partly riding on the goat, he was bound to marry her. But he said to her: "You will be my wife so long as you don't give advice to anybody; but if you do, you must part with me."

Well, she didn't give advice to anybody until one day there was a market in town, and a farmer's mare had a foal at the market. The foal ran away to another farmer, who was there with a gelding, and the farmer said: "This foal belongs to me."

They went to law about it, and at last the matter came before the king. And the king, considering that every animal ought to run to its mother, decided that a gelding had a foal.

The farmer who owned the mare went down the stairs, saying over and over again: "The gelding has foaled! The gelding has foaled!"

The queen heard this, and she said: "Man, you are talking nonsense."

So he told her that he had been at the market, that his mare had foaled, but the foal ran to another farmer who was there with a gelding. "And now," he said, "it has been decided that the gelding has foaled." So he thought there could be no mistake; at any rate, he couldn't help it.

When the queen heard this story she said: "To-morrow, my lord the king will go out for a stroll. Take a fishing-net, and begin fishing on the road in front of him. The king will ask you: 'Why are you fishing on a dry road?' And you must answer: 'Why not? It's as hopeful as expecting a gelding to foal.' But you must not say who gave you this advice."

So it was. As the king was walking along he saw the farmer fishing on the dry road. He asked him why he was fishing there.

"Why not?" said he. "It's as hopeful as expecting a gelding to foal."

The king at once began to berate the farmer. "That's not out of your own head," he said, and he kept at the farmer until he let the secret out.

So the king came home, summoned the queen, and said to her: "You have been with me over a long time, and you have given advice in spite of all, so you must go tomorrow. But I will allow you to take with you the thing you like best."

It was no good arguing so the king invited all his courtiers and prepared a splendid banquet. When the banquet was finished, the queen said to the king: "Before we part, you must drink this glass of wine to my health," and she had put some opium into the wine on the sly.

The king drank the draught and fell asleep at once. A carriage was got ready, and the queen put the king in it and drove to her father's old hut. There she laid the king on the straw, and, when he woke up, he asked where he was.

"You are with me. Didn't you tell me that I could take the thing I liked best with me?"

The king saw how clever she was, and he said: "Now you can give advice to anybody you like."

And so they drove home again, and he was king and she was queen again.

GRANDFATHER'S EYES

Once upon a time there was a poor boy whom everybody called Yanechek. His father and mother were dead and he was forced to start out alone in the world to make a living. For a long time he could find nothing to do. He wandered on and on and at last he came to a little house that stood by itself near the edge of the woods. An old man sat on the doorstep and Yanechek could see that he was blind, for there were empty holes where his eyes used to be.

Some goats that were penned in a shed near the house began bleating and the old man said:

GRANDFATHER'S EYES. From *Czechoslovak Fairy Tales;* copyright 1919 by Parker Fillmore, renewed, 1947, by Louise Fillmore. By permission of Harcourt, Brace & World, Inc.

"You poor things, you want to go to pasture, don't you? But I can't see to drive you and I have no one else to send."

"Send me, Grandfather," Yanechek said. "Take me as your goatherd and let me work for you."

"Who are you?" the old man asked.

Yanechek told him who he was and the old man agreed to take him.

"And now," he said, "drive the goats to pasture. But one thing, Yanechek: don't take them to the hill over there in the woods or the Yezinkas may get you! That's where they caught me!"

Now Yanechek knew that the Yezinkas were wicked witches who lived in a cave in the woods and went about in the guise of beautiful young women. If they met you they would greet you modestly and say something like "God bless you!" to make you think they were good and kind and then, once they had you in their power, they would put you to sleep and gouge out your eyes! Oh, yes, Yanechek knew about the Yezinkas.

"Never fear, Grandfather, the Yezinkas won't get me!"

The first day and the second day Yanechek kept the goats near home. But the third day he said to himself: "I think I'll try the hill in the woods. There's better grass there and I'm not afraid of the Yezinkas."

Before he started out he cut three long slender switches from a blackberry bramble, wound them into small coils, and hid them in the crown of his hat. Then he drove the goats through the woods where they nibbled at leaves and branches, beside a deep river where they paused to drink, and up the grassy slopes of the hill.

There the goats scattered this way and that and Yanechek sat down on a stone in the shade. He was hardly seated when he looked up and there before him, dressed all in white, stood the most beautiful maiden in the world. Her skin was red as roses and white as milk, her eyes were black as sloe berries, and her hair, dark as the raven's wing, fell about her shoulders in long waving tresses. She smiled and offered Yanechek a big red apple.

"God bless you, shepherd boy," she said. "Here's something for you that grew in my own garden."

But Yanechek knew that she must be a Yezinka and that, if he ate the apple, he would fall asleep and then she would gouge out his eyes. So he said, politely: "No, thank you, beautiful maiden. My master has a tree in his garden with apples that are bigger than yours and I have eaten as many as I want."

When the maiden saw that Yanechek was not to be coaxed, she disappeared.

Presently a second maiden came, more beautiful, if possible, than the first. In her hand she carried a lovely red rose.

"God bless you, shepherd boy," she said. "Isn't this a lovely rose? I picked it myself from the hedge. How fragrant it is! Will you smell it?"

She offered him the rose but Yanechek refused it.

"No, thank you, beautiful maiden. My master's garden is full of roses much sweeter than yours and I smell roses all the time."

At that the second maiden shrugged her shoulders and disappeared.

Presently a third one came, the youngest and most beautiful of them all. In her hand she carried a golden comb.

"God bless you, shepherd boy."

"Good day to you, beautiful maiden."

She smiled at Yanechek and said: "Truly you are a handsome lad, but you would be handsomer still if your hair were nicely combed. Come, let me comb it for you."

Yanechek said nothing but he took off his hat without letting the maiden see what was hidden in its crown. She came up close to him and then, just as she was about to comb his hair, he whipped out one of the long blackberry switches and struck her over the hands. She screamed and tried to escape but she could not because it is the fate of a Yezinka not to be able to move if ever a human being strikes her over the hands with a switch of bramble.

So Yanechek took her two hands and bound them together with the long thorny switch while she wept and struggled.

"Help, sisters! Help!" she cried.

At that the two other Yezinkas came running and when they saw what had happened they, too, began to weep and to beg Yanechek to unbind their sister's hands and let her go.

But Yanechek only laughed and said: "No. You unbind them."

"But, Yanechek, how can we? Our hands are soft and the thorns will prick us."

However, when they saw that Yanechek was not to be moved, they went to their sister and tried to help her. Whereupon Yanechek whipped out the other two blackberry switches and struck them also on their soft pretty hands, first one and then the other. After that they, too, could not move and it was easy enough to bind them and make them prisoners.

"Now I've got the three of you, you wicked Yezinkas!" Yanechek said. "It was you who gouged out my poor old master's eyes, you know it was! And you shall not escape until you do as I ask."

He left them there and ran home to his master to whom he said: "Come, Grandfather, for I have found a means of restoring your eyes!"

He took the old man by the hand and led him through the woods, along the bank of the river, and up the grassy hillside where the three Yezinkas were still struggling and weeping.

Then he said to the first of them: "Tell me now where my master's eyes are. If you don't tell me, I'll throw you into the river."

The first Yezinka pretended she didn't know. So Yanechek lifted her up and started down the hill toward the river.

That frightened the maiden and she cried out: "Don't throw me into the river, Yanechek, and I'll find you your master's eyes, I promise you I will!"

So Yanechek put her down and she led him to a cave in the hillside where she and her wicked sisters had piled up a great heap of eyes—all kinds of eyes they were: big eyes, little eyes, black eyes, red eyes, blue eyes, green eyes—every kind of eye in the world that you can think of.

She went to the heap and picked out two eyes which she said were the right ones. But when the poor old man tried to look through them, he cried out in fright:

"I see nothing but dark tree tops with sleeping birds and flying bats! These are not my eyes! They are owls' eyes! Take them out! Take them out!"

When Yanechek saw how the first Yezinka had deceived him, without another word he picked her up, threw her into the river, and that was the end of her.

Then he said to the second sister: "Now you tell me where my master's eyes are."

At first she, too, pretended she didn't know, but when Yanechek threatened to throw her likewise into the river, she was glad enough to lead him back to the cave and pick out two eyes that she said were the right ones.

But when the poor old man tried to look through them, again he cried out in fright: "I see nothing but tangled underbrush and snapping teeth and hot red tongues! These are not my eyes! They are wolves' eyes! Take them out! Take them out!"

When Yanechek saw how the second Yezinka had deceived him, without another word he picked her up, and threw her also into the river, and that was the end of her.

Then Yanechek said to the third sister: "Now you tell me where my master's eyes are."

At first she, too, pretended she didn't know, but when Yanechek threatened to throw her likewise into the river, she was glad enough to lead him to the cave and pick out two eyes that she said were the right ones.

But when the poor old man tried to look through them, again he cried out in fright: "I see nothing but swirling waters and flashing fins! These are not my eyes! They are fishes' eyes! Take them out! Take them out!"

When Yanechek saw how the third Yezinka had deceived him, without another word he was ready to serve her as he had served her sisters. But she begged him not to drown her and she said:

"Let me try again, Yanechek, and I'll find you the right eyes, I promise you I will!"

So Yanechek let her try again and from the very bottom of the heap she picked out two more eyes that she swore were the right ones.

When the old man looked through them, he clapped his hands and said: "These are my own eyes, praise God! Now I can see as well as ever!"

After that the old man and Yanechek lived on happily together. Yanechek pastured the goats and the old man made cheeses at home and they ate them together. And you may be sure that the third Yezinka never showed herself again on that hill!

THE TWELVE MONTHS

Once upon a time there lived a mother who had two daughters. One was her own child, the other her stepdaughter. She was very fond of her own daughter, but she would not so much as look at her stepdaughter. The only reason was that Marusa, the stepdaughter was prettier than her own daughter, Holena. The gentle-hearted Marusa did not know how beautiful she was, and she could never make out why her mother was so cross with her whenever she looked at her. She had to do all the housework, tidying up the cottage, cooking, washing, and sewing, and then she had to take the hay to the cow and look after her. She did all this work alone, while Holena spent the time adorning herself and lazying about. But Marusa liked work, for she was a patient girl, and when her mother scolded and ranted her, she bore it like a lamb. It was no good, however, for they grew crueler and crueler every day, only because Marusa was growing prettier and Holena uglier every day.

At last the mother thought: "Why should I keep a pretty stepdaughter in my house? When the lads come courting here, they will fall in love with Marusa and they won't look at Holena."

From that moment the stepmother and her daughter were constantly scheming how to get rid of poor Marusa. But she bore it all, and in spite of all she kept growing prettier every day.

One day—it was in the middle of January—Holena felt a longing for the scent of violets.

"Go, Marusa, and get me some violets from the forest; I want to wear them at my waist and to smell them," she said to her sister.

"Great heavens! sister. What a strange notion! Who ever heard of violets growing under the snow?" said poor Marusa.

"You wretched tatterdemalion! How dare you argue when I tell you to do something? Off you go at once, and if you don't bring me violets from the forest I'll kill you!" said Holena threateningly.

The stepmother caught hold of Marusa, turned her out of the door, and slammed it after her. She went into the forest weeping bitterly. The snow lay deep, and there wasn't a human footprint to be seen. Marusa wan-

THE TWELVE MONTHS. From *Czech Folk Tales,* by M. R. I. A. Baudis. By permission of George Allen & Unwin Ltd.

dered about for a long time, tortured by hunger and trembling with cold. She begged God to take her from the world.

At last she saw a light in the distance. She went towards the glow, and came at last to the top of a mountain. A big fire was burning there, and round the fire were twelve stones with twelve men sitting on them. Three of them had snow-white beards, three were not so old, and three were still younger. The three youngest were the handsomest of them all. They were not speaking, but sitting silent. These twelve men were the twelve months. Great January sat highest of all; his hair and beard were as white as snow, and in his hands he held a club.

Marusa was frightened. She stood still for a time in terror, but, growing bolder, she went up to them and said: "Please, kind sirs, let me warm my hands by your fire. I am trembling with the cold."

Great January nodded and asked her: "Why have you come here, my dear little girl? What are you looking for?"

"I am looking for violets," answered Marusa.

"This is no time to be looking for violets, for everything is covered with snow," answered Great January.

"Yes, I know; but my sister Holena and my stepmother said that I must bring them some violets from the forest. If I don't bring them, they'll kill me. Tell me, fathers, please tell me where I can find them."

Great January stood up and went to one of the younger months—it was March—and, giving him the club, he said: "Brother, take the high seat."

March took the high seat upon the stone and waved the club over the fire. The fire blazed up, the snow began to melt, the trees began to bud, and the ground under the young beech-trees was covered with grass and the crimson daisy buds began to peep through the grass. It was springtime. Under the bushes the voilets were blooming among their little leaves, and before Marusa had time to think, so many of them had sprung up that they looked like a blue cloth spread on the ground.

"Pick them quickly, Marusa!" commanded March.

Marusa picked them joyfully till she had a big bunch. Then she thanked the months with all her heart and scampered merrily home.

Holena and the stepmother wondered when they saw Marusa bringing the violets. They opened the door to her, and the scent of violets filled all the cottage.

"Where did you get them?" asked Holena sulkily.

"They are growing under the bushes in a forest on a high mountain."

Holena put them in her waistband. She let her mother smell them, but she did not say to her sister: "Smell them."

Another day as she was wallowing near the stove she longed for some strawberries. And she called to her sister and said: "Go, Marusa and get me some strawberries from the forest."

"Alas! dear sister, where could I find any strawberries? Who ever heard of strawberries growing under the snow?" said Marusa.

"You wretched little tatterdemalion, how dare you argue when I tell you to do a thing? Go at once and get me the strawberries, or I'll kill you!"

The stepmother caught hold of Marusa and pushed her out of the door and shut it after her. Marusa went to the forest weeping bitterly. The snow was lying deep, and there wasn't a human footprint to be seen anywhere. She wandered about for a long time tortured by hunger and trembling with cold. At last she saw the lights she had seen the other day. Overjoyed, she went towards it. She came to the great fire with the twelve months sitting round it.

"Please, kind sirs, let me warm my hands by the fire. I am trembling with cold."

Great January nodded, and asked her: "Why have you come again and what are you looking for here?"

"I am looking for strawberries."

"But it is winter now, and strawberries don't grow on the snow," said January.

"Yes, I know," said Marusa sadly: "but my sister Holena and my stepmother bade me bring them some strawberries, and if I don't they will kill me. Tell me, fathers, tell me please, where I can find them."

Great January arose. He went over to the month sitting opposite to him —it was June—and handed the club to him, saying: "Brother, take the high seat."

June took the high seat upon the stone and swung the club over the fire. The fire shot up, and its heat melted the snow in a moment. The ground was all green, the trees were covered with leaves, the birds began to sing, and the forest was filled with all kinds of flowers. It was summer. The ground under the bushes was covered with white starlets, the starry blossoms were turning into strawberries every minute. They ripened at once, and before Marusa had time to think, there were so many of them that it looked as though blood had been sprinkled on the ground.

"Pick them at once Marusa!" commanded June.

Marusa picked them joyfully till she had filled her apron full. Then she thanked the months with all her heart and scampered merrily home. Holena and the stepmother wondered when they saw Marusa bringing the strawberries. Her apron was full of them. They ran to open the door for her, and the scent of the strawberries filled the whole cottage.

"Where did you pick them?" asked Holena sulkily.

"There are plenty of them growing under the young beech-trees in the forest on the high mountains."

Holena took the strawberries, and went on eating them till she could eat no more. So did the stepmother too, but they didn't say to Marusa: "Here is one for you."

When Holena had enjoyed the strawberries, she grew greedy for other dainties, and so on the third day she longed for some red apples.

"Marusa, go into the forest and get me some red apples," said she to her sister.

"Alas! sister dear, how am I going to get apples in the winter?" protested Marusa.

"You wretched little tatterdemalion, how dare you argue when I tell you to do a thing? Go to the forest at once, and if you don't bring me the apples I will kill you," threatened Holena.

The stepmother caught hold of Marusa and pushed her out of the door and shut it after her.

Marusa went to the forest weeping bitterly. The snow was lying deep: there wasn't a human footprint to be seen anywhere. But she didn't wander about this time. She ran straight to the top of the mountain where the big fire was burning. The twelve months were sitting round the fire; yes, there they certainly were, and Great January was sitting on the high seat.

"Please, kind sirs, let me warm my hands by the fire. I am trembling with cold."

Great January nodded, and asked her: "Why have you come here, and what are you looking for?"

"I am looking for red apples."

"It is winter now, and red apples don't grow in winter," answered January.

"Yes, I know," said Marusa sadly; "but my sister and my stepmother, too, bade me bring them some red apples from the forest. If I don't bring them, they will kill me. Tell me, father, tell me, please, where I could find them."

Great January rose up. He went over to one of the older months—it was September. He handed the club to him and said: "Brother, take the high seat."

Month of September took the high seat upon the stone and swung the club over the fire. The fire began to burn with a red flame, the snow began to melt. But the trees were not covered with leaves, the leaves were wavering down one after the other, and the cold wind was driving them to and fro over the yellowing ground. This time Marusa did not see any flowers. Only red pinks were blooming on the hillside, and meadow saffrons were flowering under the young beech-trees. But Marusa was only looking for red apples, and at last she saw an apple-tree with red apples hanging high among its branches.

Right gladly Marusa shook the tree, and one apple fell down. She shook it a second time, and another apple fell down.

"Now, Marusa, run home quickly!" shouted the month.

Marusa obeyed at once. She picked up the apples, thanked the months with all her heart, and ran merrily home.

Holena and the stepmother wondered when they saw Marusa bringing the apples. They ran to open the door for her, and she gave them two apples.

"Where did you get them?" asked Holena.

"There are plenty of them in the forest on the high mountain."

"And why didn't you bring more? Or did you eat them on the way home?" said Holena harshly.

"Alas! sister dear, I didn't eat a single one. But when I had shaken the tree once, one apple fell down, and when I shook it a second time, another apple fell down, and they wouldn't let me shake it again. They shouted to me to go straight home," protested Marusa.

Holena began to curse her: "May you be struck to death by lightning!" and she was going to beat her.

Marusa began to cry bitterly, and she prayed to God to take her to Himself, or she would be killed by her wicked sister and her stepmother. She ran away into the kitchen.

Greedy Holena stopped cursing and began to eat the apple. It tasted so delicious that she told her mother that she had never tasted anything so nice in all her life. The stepmother liked it too. When they had finished, they wanted some more.

"Mother, give me my fur coat. I'll go to the forest myself. That ragged little wretch would eat them all up again on her way home. I'll find the place all right, and I'll shake them all down, however they shout at me."

Her mother tried to dissuade her, but it was no good. She took the fur coat, wrapped a cloth round her head, and off she went to the forest. Her mother stood on the threshold, watching to see how Holena would manage to walk in the wintry weather.

The snow lay deep, and there wasn't a human footprint to be seen anywhere. Holena wandered about for a long time, but the desire of the sweet apple kept driving her on. At last she saw a light in the distance. She went towards it, and climbed to the top of the mountain where the big fire was burning, and round the fire on twelve stones the twelve months were sitting. She was terrified at first, but she soon recovered. She stepped up to the fire and stretched out her hands to warm them, but she didn't say as much as "By your leave" to the twelve months; no, she didn't say a word to them.

"Why have you come here, and what are you looking for?" asked Great January crossly.

"Why do you want to know, you old fool? It's no business of yours," replied Holena angrily, and she turned away from the fire and went into the forest.

Great January frowned and swung the club over his head. The sky grew dark in a moment, the fire burned low, the snow began to fall as thick as if feathers had been shaken out to blow through the forest. Holena couldn't see one step in front of her; she lost her way altogether, and several times she fell into snowdrifts. Then her limbs grew weak and began slowly to stiffen. The snow kept on falling and the icy wind blew more icily than ever. Holena began to curse Marusa and the Lord God. Her limbs began to freeze, despite her fur coat.

Her mother was waiting for Holena; she kept on looking out over the river, first at the window, then outside the door, but all in vain.

"Does she like the apples so much that she can't leave them or what is the matter? I must see for myself where she is," decided the stepmother at last. So she put on her fur coat, she wrapped a shawl round her head, and went out to look for Holena. The snow was lying deep; there wasn't a human footprint to be seen; the snow fell fast, and the icy wind was blowing through the forest.

Marusa had cooked the dinner, she had seen to the cow, and yet Holena and her mother had not come back. "Where are they staying so long?" thought Marusa as she sat down to work at the distaff. The spindle was full already and it was quite dark in the room, and yet Holena and the stepmother had not come back.

"Alas, Lord! what had come to them?" cried Marusa, peering anxiously through the window. The sky was bright and the earth was all glittering but there wasn't a human soul to be seen. Sadly she shut the window; she crossed herself, and prayed for her sister and her mother. . . . In the morning she waited with breakfast, she waited with dinner; but however much she waited, it was no good. Neither the mother nor her sister ever came back. Both of them were frozen to death in the forest.

So good Marusa inherited the cottage, a piece of plough land and the cow. She married a kind husband, and they both lived happily ever after.

ENGLAND

> Once upon a time when the pigs spoke rhyme.
> And monkeys chewed tobacco,
> And hens took snuff to make them tough,
> And ducks went quack, quack, quack, O![3]

The English tale is familiar in the field of children's literature due to the Joseph Jacobs collection arranged especially for children. His editing of the stories which eliminated the secondary plots and the brutal aspects of life makes them more suitable for storytelling.

[3] J. Jacobs, "The Story of the Three Little Pigs," from *English Fairy Tales*.

THE CAULD LAD OF HILTON

At Hilton Hall, long years ago, there lived a Brownie that was the contrariest Brownie you ever knew. At night, after the servants had gone to bed, it would turn everything topsy-turvy, put sugar in the salt cellars, pepper into the beer, and was up to all kinds of pranks. It would throw the chairs down, put tables on their backs, rake out fires, and do as much mischief as could be. But sometimes it would be in a good temper, and then!—"What's a Brownie?" you say. Oh, it's a kind of a sort of a Bogle, but it isn't so cruel as a Redcap! What! you don't know what's a Bogle or a Redcap! Ah, me! what's the world a-coming to? Of course a Brownie is a funny little thing, half man, half goblin, with pointed ears and hairy hide. When you bury a treasure, you scatter over it blood drops of a newly slain kid or lamb, or, better still, bury the animal with the treasure, and a Brownie will watch over it for you, and frighten everybody else away.

Where am I? Well, as I was a-saying, the Brownie at Hilton Hall would play at mischief, but if the servants laid out for it a bowl of cream, or a knuckle cake spread with honey, it would clear away things for them, and make everything tidy in the kitchen.

One night, however, when the servants had stayed up late, they heard a noise in the kitchen, and, peeping in, saw the Brownie swinging to and fro on the Jack chain, and saying:

> Woe's me! woe's me!
> The acorn's not yet
> Fallen from the tree,
> That's to grow the wood,
> That's to make the cradle,
> That's to rock the bairn,
> That's to grow the man,
> That's to lay me.
> Woe's me! Woe's me!

So they took pity on the poor Brownie, and asked the nearest henwife what they should do to send it away. "That's easy enough," said the henwife, and told them that a Brownie that's paid for its service, in something that's not perishable, goes away at once. So they made a cloak of Lincoln green, with a hood to it, and put it by the hearth and watched. They saw the Brownie come up, and seeing the hood and cloak, put them on and frisk about, dancing on one leg and saying:

> I've taken your cloak, I've taken your hood;
> The Cauld Lad of Hilton will do no more good.

And with that it vanished, and was never seen or heard of afterwards.

THE CAULD LAD OF HILTON. From *English Fairy Tales*, by Joseph Jacobs. By permission of G. P. Putnam's Sons.

HOW JACK WENT TO SEEK HIS FORTUNE

Once on a time there was a boy named Jack, and one morning he started to go and seek his fortune.

He hadn't gone very far before he met a cat.

"Where are you going, Jack?" said the cat.

"I am going to seek my fortune."

"May I go with you?"

"Yes," said Jack, "the more the merrier."

So on they went, jiggelty-jolt, jiggelty-jolt.

They went a little further and they met a dog.

"Where are you going, Jack?" said the dog.

"I am going to seek my fortune."

"May I go with you?"

"Yes," said Jack, "the more the merrier."

So on they went, jiggelty-jolt, jiggelty-jolt.

They went a little further and they met a goat.

"Where are you going, Jack?" said the goat.

"I am going to seek my fortune."

"May I go with you?"

"Yes," said Jack, "the more the merrier."

So on they went, jiggelty-jolt, jiggelty-jolt.

They went a little further and they met a bull.

"Where are you going, Jack?" said the bull.

"I am going to seek my fortune."

"May I go with you?"

"Yes," said Jack, "the more the merrier."

So on they went, jiggelty-jolt, jiggelty-jolt.

They went a little further and they met a rooster.

"Where are you going, Jack?" said the rooster.

"I am going to seek my fortune."

"May I go with you?"

"Yes," said Jack, "the more the merrier."

So on they went, jiggelty-jolt, jiggelty-jolt.

Well, they went on till it was about dark, and they began to think of some place where they could spend the night. About this time they came in sight of a house, and Jack told them to keep still while he went up and looked in through the window. And there were some robbers counting over their money. Then Jack went back and told them to wait till he gave the word, and then to make all the noise they could. So when they were all ready Jack gave the word, and the cat mewed, and the dog barked,

HOW JACK WENT TO SEEK HIS FORTUNE. From *English Fairy Tales*, by Joseph Jacobs. By permission of G. P. Putnam's Sons.

and the goat bleated, and the bull bellowed, and the rooster crowed, and altogether they made such a dreadful noise that it frightened the robbers all away.

And then they went in and took possession of the house. Jack was afraid the robbers would come back in the night, and so when it came time to go to bed he put the cat in the rocking chair, and he put the dog under the table, and he put the goat upstairs, and he put the bull in the cellar, and the rooster flew up on to the roof, and Jack went to bed.

By-and-by the robbers saw it was all dark and they sent one man back to the house to look after their money. Before long he came back in a great fright and told them his story.

"I went back to the house," said he, "and went in and tried to sit down in the rocking-chair, and there was an old woman knitting, and she stuck her knitting-needles into me." That was the cat, you know.

"I went to the table to look after the money and there was a shoemaker under the table, and he stuck his awl into me." That was the dog, you know.

"I started to go up-stairs, and there was a man up there threshing, and he knocked me down with his flail." That was the goat, you know.

"I started to go down cellar, and there was a man down there chopping wood, and he knocked me up with his axe." That was the bull, you know.

"But I shouldn't have minded all that if it hadn't been for that little fellow on top of the house, who kept a-hollering, 'Chuck him up to me-e! Chuck him up to me-e!'" Of course that was the cock-a-doodle-do.

THE STORY OF THE THREE LITTLE PIGS

> Once upon a time when the pigs spoke rhyme
> And monkeys chewed tobacco,
> And hens took snuff to make them tough,
> And ducks went quack, quack, quack, O!

There was an old sow with three little pigs, and as she had not enough to keep them, she sent them out to seek their fortune. The first that went off met a man with a bundle of straw, and said to him:

"Please, man, give me that straw to build me a house."

Which the man did, and the little pig built a house with it. Presently came along a wolf, and knocked at the door, and said:

"Little pig, little pig, let me come in."

To which the pig answered:

THE STORY OF THE THREE LITTLE PIGS. From *English Fairy Tales*, by Joseph Jacobs. By permission of G. P. Putnam's Sons.

"No, no, by the hair of my chiny chin chin."

The wolf then answered to that:

"Then I'll huff, and I'll puff, and I'll blow your house in."

So he huffed, and he puffed, and he blew his house in, and ate up the little pig.

The second little pig met a man with a bundle of furze and said:

"Please, man, give me that furze to build a house."

Which the man did, and the pig built his house. Then along came the wolf, and said:

"Little pig, little pig, let me come in."

"No, no, by the hair of my chiny chin chin."

"Then I'll huff, and I'll puff, and I'll blow your house in."

So he huffed, and he puffed, and he puffed, and he huffed, and at last he blew the house down, and he ate up the little pig.

The third little pig met a man with a load of bricks, and said:

"Please, man, give me those bricks to build a house with."

So the man gave him the bricks, and he built his house with them. So the wolf came, as he did to the other little pigs, and said:

"Little pig, little pig, let me come in."

"No, no, by the hair of my chiny chin chin."

"Then I'll huff, and I'll puff, and I'll blow your house in."

Well, he huffed, and he puffed, and he huffed and he puffed, and he puffed and huffed; but he could not get the house down. When he found that he could not, with all his huffing and puffing, blow the house down, he said:

"Little pig, I know where there is a nice field of turnips."

"Where?" said the little pig.

"Oh, in Mr. Smith's Home-field, and if you will be ready to-morrow morning I will call for you, and we will go together, and get some for dinner."

"Very well," said the little pig, "I will be ready. What time do you mean to go?"

"Oh, at six o'clock."

Well, the little pig got up at five, and got the turnips before the wolf came (which he did about six), who said:

"Little pig, are you ready?"

The little pig said: "Ready! I have been and come back again, and got a nice potful for dinner."

The wolf felt very angry at this, but thought that he would be up to the little pig somehow or other, so he said:

"Little pig, I know where there is a nice apple tree."

"Where?" said the pig.

"Down at Merry-garden," replied the wolf, "and if you will not deceive me I will come for you at five o'clock to-morrow and get some apples."

Well, the little pig bustled up the next morning at four o'clock, and went off for the apples, hoping to get back before the wolf came; but he had further to go, and had to climb the tree, so that just as he was coming down from it, he saw the wolf coming, which, as you may suppose, frightened him very much. When the wolf came up he said:

"Little pig, what! are you here before me? Are they nice apples?"

"Yes, very," said the little pig. "I will throw you down one."

And he threw it so far, that, while the wolf was gone to pick it up, little pig jumped down and ran home. The next day the wolf came again, and said to the little pig:

"Little pig, there is a fair at Shanklin this afternoon; will you go?"

"Oh yes," said the pig, "I will go; what time shall you be ready?"

"At three," said the wolf. So the little pig went off before the time as usual, and got to the fair, and bought a butter-churn, which he was going home with, when he saw the wolf coming. Then he could not tell what to do. So he got into the churn to hide, and by so doing turned it round, and it rolled down the hill with the pig in it, which frightened the wolf so much, that he ran home without going to the fair. He went to the little pig's house, and told him how frightened he had been by a great round thing which came down the hill past him. Then the little pig said:

"Hah, I frightened you, then. I had been to the fair and bought a butter-churn, and when I saw you, I got into it, and rolled down the hill."

Then the wolf was very angry indeed, and declared he would eat up the little pig, and that he would get down the chimney after him. When the little pig saw what he was about, he hung on the pot full of water, and made up a blazing fire, and, just as the wolf was coming down, took off the cover, and in fell the wolf; so the little pig put on the cover again in an instant, boiled him up, and ate him for supper, and lived happy ever afterwards.

FRANCE

"The sign of the cross never came amiss, wherever it may be," answered Bernet.[4]

The traditional tales, such as "Cinderella," "Sleeping Beauty," "Little Red Riding Hood," which were collected by Charles Perrault and published in 1697, represent the French folk tale. The well-contrived plot, the poetic justice, the humor and light heartedness of these stories, have made them favorites with children for storytelling and play acting. "The Stones of Plouvinec" represents the tale that appeals to the older child as it contains a more religious, adventuresome, and magical quality.

[4] Katherine Pyle, "The Stones of Plouvinec," from *Wonder Tales from Many Lands*.

THE STONES OF PLOUVINEC

In the little village of Plouvinec there once lived a poor stone-cutter named Bernet.

Bernet was an honest and industrious young man, and yet he never seemed to succeed in the world. Work as he might, he was always poor. This was a great grief to him, for he was in love with the beautiful Madeleine Pornec, and she was the daughter of the richest man in Plouvinec.

Madeleine had many suitors, but she cared for none of them except Bernet. She would gladly have married him in spite of his poverty, but her father was covetous as well as rich. He had no wish for a poor son-in-law, and Madeleine was so beautiful he expected her to marry some rich merchant, or a well-to-do farmer at least. But if Madeleine could not have Bernet for a husband, she was determined that she would have no one.

There came a winter when Bernet found himself poorer than he had ever been before. Scarcely anyone seemed to have any need for a stone-cutter, and even for such work as he did get he was poorly paid. He learned to know what it meant to go without a meal and to be cold as well as hungry.

As Christmas drew near, the landlord of the inn at Plouvinec decided to give a feast for all the good folk of the village, and Bernet was invited along with all the rest.

He was glad enough to go to the feast, for he knew that Madeleine was to be there, and even if he did not have a chance to talk to her, he could at least look at her, and that would be better than nothing.

The feast was a fine one. There was plenty to eat and drink, and all was of the best, and the more the guests feasted, the merrier they grew. If Bernet and Madeleine ate little and spoke less, no one noticed it. People were too busy filling their own stomachs and laughing at the jokes that were cracked. The fun was at its height when the door was pushed open, and a ragged, ill-looking beggar slipped into the room.

At the sight of him the laughter and merriment died away. This beggar was well known to all the people of the village, though none knew whence he came nor where he went when he was away on his wanderings. He was sly and crafty, and he was feared as well as disliked, for it was said that he had the evil eye. Whether he had or not, it was well known that no one had ever offended him without having some misfortune happen soon after.

"I heard there was a great feast here to-night," said the beggar in a humble voice, "and that all the village had been bidden to it. Perhaps, when all have eaten, there may be some scraps that I might pick up."

THE STONES OF PLOUVINEC. From *Wonder Tales from Many Lands,* by Katherine Pyle.

"Scraps there are in plenty," answered the landlord, "but it is not scraps that I am offering to anyone to-night. Draw up a chair to the table, and eat and drink what you will. There is more than enough for all." But the landlord looked none too well pleased as he spoke. It was a piece of ill-luck to have the beggar come to his house this night of all nights, to spoil the pleasure of the guests.

The beggar drew up to the table as the landlord bade him, but the fun and merriment were ended. Presently the guests began to leave the table, and after thanking their host, they went away to their own homes.

When the beggar had eaten and drunk to his heart's content, he pushed back his chair from the table.

"I have eaten well," said he to the landlord. "Is there not now some corner where I can spend the night?"

"There is the stable," answered the landlord grudgingly. "Every room in the house is full, but if you choose to sleep there among the clean hay, I am not the one to say you nay."

Well, the beggar was well content with that. He went out to the stable, and there he snuggled down among the soft hay, and soon he was fast asleep. He had slept for some hours, and it was midnight, when he suddenly awoke with a startled feeling that he was not alone in the stable. In the darkness two strange voices were talking together.

"Well, brother, how goes it since last Christmas?" asked one voice.

"Poorly, brother, but poorly," answered the other. "Methinks the work has been heavier these last twelve months than ever before."

The beggar, listening as he lay in the hay, wondered who could be talking there at this hour of the night. Then he discovered that the voices came from the stalls near by; the ox and the donkey were talking together.

The beggar was so surprised that he almost exclaimed aloud, but he restrained himself. He remembered a story he had often heard, but had never before believed, that on every Christmas night it is given to the dumb beasts in the stalls to talk in human tones for a short time. It was said that those who had been lucky enough to hear them at such times had sometimes learned strange secrets from their talk. Now the beggar lay listening with all his ears, and scarcely daring to breathe lest he should disturb them.

"It has been a hard year for me too," said the ox, answering what the donkey had just said. "I would our master had some of the treasure that lies hidden under the stones of Plouvinec. Then he could buy more oxen and more donkeys, and the work would be easier for us."

"The treasure! What treasure is that?" asked the donkey.

The ox seemed very much surprised. "Have you never heard? I thought every one knew of the hidden treasure under the stones."

"Tell me about it," said the donkey, "for I dearly love a tale."

The ox was not loath to do this. At once it began:

"You know the barren heath just outside of Plouvinec, and the great stones that lie there, each so large that it would take more than a team of oxen to drag it from its place?"

Yes, the donkey knew that heath, and the stones too. He had often passed by them on his journeys to the neighbouring town.

"It is said that under those stones lies hidden an enormous treasure of gold," said the ox. "That is the story; it is well known. But none has seen that treasure; jealously the stones guard it. Once in every hundred years, however, the stones go down to the river to drink. They are only away for a few minutes; then they come rolling back in mad haste to cover their gold again. But if anyone could be there on the heath for those few minutes, it is a wonderful sight that he would see while the stones are away. It is now a hundred years, all but a week, since the stones went down to drink."

"Then a week from to-night the treasure will be uncovered again?" asked the donkey.

"Yes, exactly a week from now, at midnight."

"Ah, if only our master knew this," and the donkey sighed heavily. "If only we could tell him! Then he might go to the heath and not only see the treasure, but gather a sack full of it for himself."

"Yes, but even if he did, he would never return with it alive. As I told you, the stones are very jealous of their treasure, and are away for only a few minutes. By the time he had gathered up the gold and was ready to escape, the stones would return and would crush him to powder."

The beggar, who had become very much excited at the story, felt a cold shiver creep over him at these words.

"No one could ever bring away any of it then?" asked the donkey.

"I did not say that. The stones are enchanted. If anyone could find a five-leaved clover, and carry it with him to the heath, the stones could not harm him, for the five-leaved clover is a magic plant that has power over all the enchanted things, and those stones are enchanted."

"Then all he would need would be to have a five-leaved clover."

"If he carried that with him, the stones could not harm him. He might escape safely with the treasure, but it would do him little good. With the first rays of the sun the treasure would crumble away unless the life of a human being had been sacrificed to the stones there on the heath before sunrise."

"And who would sacrifice a human life for a treasure!" cried the donkey. "Not our master, I am sure."

The ox made no answer, and now the donkey too was silent. The hour had passed in which they could speak in human voices. For another year they would again be only dumb brutes.

As for the beggar, he lay among the hay, shaking all over with excitement. Visions of untold wealth shone before his eyes. The treasure of Plouvinec! Why, if he could only get it, he would be the richest man in the village. In the village? No, in the country—in the whole world! Only to see it and handle it for a few hours would be something. But before even that were possible and safe it would be necessary to find a five-leaved clover.

With the earliest peep of dawn the beggar rolled from the hay, and wrapping his rags about him, stole out of the stable and away into the country. There he began looking about for bunches of clover. These were not hard to find; they were everywhere, though the most of them were withered now. He found and examined clump after clump. Here and there he found a stem that bore four leaves, but none had five. Night came on, and the darkness made him give up the search; but the next day he began anew. Again he was unsuccessful. So day after day passed by, and still he had not found the thing he sought so eagerly.

The beggar was in a fever of rage and disappointment. Six days slipped by. By the time the seventh dawned he was so discouraged that he hunted for only a few hours. Then, though it was still daylight, he determined to give up the search. With drooping head he turned back toward the village. As he was passing a heap of rocks he noticed a clump of clover growing in a crevice. Idly, and with no hope of success, he stooped and began to examine it leaf by leaf.

Suddenly he gave a cry of joy. His legs trembled under him so that he was obliged to sink to his knees. The last stem of all bore five leaves. He had found his five-leaved clover!

With the magic plant safely hidden away in his bosom the beggar hurried back toward the village. He would rest in the inn until night. Then he would go to the heath, and if the story the ox had told were true, he would see a sight such as no one living had ever seen before.

His way led him past the heath. Dusk was falling as he approached it. Suddenly the beggar paused and listened. From among the stones sounded a strange tap-tapping. Cautiously he drew nearer, peering about among the stones. Then he saw what seemed to him a curious sight for such a place and such a time. Before the largest stone of all stood Bernet, busily at work with hammer and chisel. He was cutting a cross upon the face of the rock.

The beggar drew near to him so quietly that Bernet did not notice him. He started as a voice suddenly spoke close to his ear.

"That is a strange thing for you to be doing," said the beggar. "Why should you waste your time in cutting a cross in such a lovely place as this?"

"The sign of the cross never came amiss, wherever it may be," answered Bernet. "And as for wasting my time, no one seems to have any use for it at present. It is better for me to spend it in this way than to idle it away over nothing."

Suddenly a strange idea flashed into the beggar's mind—a thought so strange and terrible that it made him turn pale. He drew nearer to the stone-cutter and laid his hand upon his arm.

"Listen, Bernet," said he; "you are a clever workman and an honest one as well, and yet all your work scarcely brings you in enough to live on. Suppose I were to tell you that in one night you might become rich —richer than the richest man in the village—so that there would be no desire that you could not satisfy; what would you think of that?"

"I would think nothing of it, for I would know it was not true," answered Bernet carelessly.

"But it is true; it is true, I tell you," cried the beggar. "Listen, and I will tell you."

He drew still nearer to Bernet, so that his mouth almost touched the stone-cutter's ear, and in a whisper he repeated to him the story he had heard the ox telling the donkey—the story of the treasure that was buried under the stones of Plouvinec. But it was only a part of the story that he told after all, for he did not tell Bernet that anyone who was rash enough to seek the treasure would be crushed by the stones unless he carried a five-leaved clover; nor did he tell him that if the treasure were carried away from the heath it would turn to ashes unless a human life had been sacrificed to the stones. As Bernet listened to the story he became very grave. His eyes shone through the fading light as he stared at the beggar's face.

"Why did you tell me this?" he asked. "And why are you willing to share the treasure that might be all your own? If you make me rich, what do you expect me to do for you in return?"

"Do you not see?" answered the beggar. "You are much stronger than I. I, as you know, am a weak man and slow of movement. While the stones are away we two together could gather more than twice as much as I could gather myself. In return for telling you this secret, all I ask is that if we go there and gather all we can, and bring it away with us, you will make an even division with me—that you will give me half of all we get."

"That seems only just," said Bernet slowly. "It would be strange if this story of the hidden treasure proved to be true. At any rate, I will come with you to the heath tonight. We will bring with us some large bags, and if we manage to secure even a small part of the gold you talk of I shall never cease to be grateful to you."

The beggar could not answer. His teeth were chattering, half with fear and half with excitement. The honest stone-cutter little guessed that the beggar was planning to sacrifice him to the stones in order that he himself might become a rich man.

It was well on toward midnight when Bernet and the beggar returned to the heath with the bags. The moon shone clear and bright, and by its light they could see the stones towering up above them, solid and motionless. It seemed impossible to believe that they had ever stirred from their places, or ever would again. In the moonlight Bernet could clearly see the cross that he had carved upon the largest stone.

He and the beggar lay hidden behind a clump of bushes. All was still except for the faint sound of the river some short distance away. Suddenly a breath seemed to pass over the heath. Far off, in the village of Plouvinec, sounded the first stroke of twelve.

At that stroke the two men saw a strange and wonderful thing happen. The motionless stones rocked and stirred in their places. With a rendering sound they tore themselves from the places where they had stood for so long. Then down the slope toward the river they rolled, bounding faster and faster, while there on the heath an immense treasure glittered in the moonlight.

"Quick! quick!" cried the beggar in a shrill voice. "They will return! We have not a moment to waste."

Greedily he threw himself upon the treasure. Gathering it up by handfuls he thrust it hurriedly into a sack. Bernet was not slow to follow his example. They worked with such frenzy that soon the two largest sacks were almost full. In their haste everything but the gold was forgotten.

Some sound, a rumbling and crashing, made Bernet look up. At once he sprang to his feet with a cry of fear.

"Look! look!" he cried. "The stones are returning. They are almost on us. We shall be crushed."

"You, perhaps; but not I," answered the beggar. "You should have provided yourself with a five-leaved clover. It is a magic herb, and the stones have no power to touch him who holds it."

Even as the beggar spoke the stones were almost upon them. Trembling, but secure, he held up the five-leaved clover before them. As he did so the ranks of stones divided, passing around him a rank on either side; then, closing together, they rolled on toward Bernet.

The poor stone-cutter felt that he was lost. He tried to murmur a prayer, but his tongue clove to the roof of his mouth with fear.

Suddenly the largest stone of all, the one upon which he had cut the cross, separated itself from the others. Rolling in front of them, it placed itself before him as a shield. Grey and immovable it towered above him. A moment the others paused as if irresolute, while Bernet cowered close against the protecting stone. Then they rolled by without touching him and settled sullenly into their places.

The beggar was already gathering up the sacks. He believed himself safe, but he wished to leave the heath as quickly as possible. He glanced fearfully over his shoulder. Then he gave a shriek, and turning, he held up the five-leaved clover. The largest stone was rolling toward him. It was almost upon him.

But the magic herb had no power over a stone marked with a cross. On it rolled, over the miserable man, and into the place where it must rest again for still another hundred years.

It was morning, and the sun was high in the heavens when Bernet staggered into the inn at Plouvinec. A heavy, bulging sack was thrown over one shoulder; a second sack he dragged behind him. They were full of gold—the treasure from under the stones of Plouvinec.

From that time Bernet was the richest man in Plouvinec. Madeleine's father was glad enough to call him son-in-law and to welcome him into his family. He and Madeleine were married, and lived in the greatest comfort and happiness all their days. But for as long as he lived Bernet could never be induced to go near the heath nor to look upon the stones that had so nearly caused his death.

GERMANY

"Ah," said he to himself, "where the key is, there, to be sure, will the lock be found.[5]

The Grimm brothers, in their scientific search of the folklore of Germany, have given stories to the world ranging from the dark and gloomy to the light and fanciful. The ones included here represent the humor found in these traditional German tales.

THE GOLDEN KEY

One cold winter's day, when the snow was thick upon the ground, a poor little lad was sent into the forest to gather wood, which he was to stack upon a little sledge and bring home for fuel. By the time he had collected enough, he was so cold that he thought he would make a fire and warm himself before he went home. So he scraped away the snow, and in so doing found a little golden key.

"Ah," said he to himself, "where the key is, there, to be sure, will the lock be found," and went on scraping away the snow until he found an iron chest. "Now," he said, "if only the key fits the lock, I shall no doubt find all sorts of precious things in the chest."

He searched for a long time, and at last he discovered a lock—so small, however, that one could scarcely see it.

He tried the key, and it fitted exactly; he turned it slowly, slowly, and —if only we wait patiently until he has turned it right round and opened the lid, why then we shall know what was inside the chest.

THE GOLDEN KEY. From *Grimms' Fairy Tales,* by the Brothers Grimm.
5 The Brothers Grimm, "The Golden Key," from *Grimms' Fairy Tales.*

THE GOLDEN GOOSE

There was once a man who had three sons. The youngest of them was called Dullhead, and was sneered and jeered at and snubbed on every possible opportunity.

One day it happened that the eldest son wished to go into the forest to cut wood, and before he started his mother gave him a fine rich cake and a bottle of wine, so that he might be sure not to suffer from hunger or thirst.

When he reached the forest he met a little old gray man who wished him "Good morning," and said: "Do give me a piece of that cake you have got in your pocket, and let me have a draught of your wine—I am so hungry and thirsty."

But this clever son replied: "If I give you my cake and wine I shall have none left for myself: you just go your own way"; and he left the little man standing there and went further into the forest. There he began to cut down a tree, but before long he made a false stroke with his ax, and cut his own arm so badly that he was obliged to go home and have it bound up.

Then the second son went to the forest, and his mother gave him a good cake and a bottle of wine as she had to his elder brother. He too met the little old gray man, who begged him for a morsel of cake and a draught of wine.

But the second son spoke most sensibly too, and said: "Whatever I give you I deprive myself of. Just go your own way, will you?" Not long after his punishment over-took him, for no sooner had he struck a couple of blows on a tree with his ax, than he cut his leg so badly that he had to be carried home.

So then Dullhead said: "Father, let me go out and cut wood."

But his father answered: "Both your brothers have injured themselves. You had better leave it alone; you know nothing about it."

But Dullhead begged so hard to be allowed to go that at last his father said: "Very well, then—go. Perhaps when you have hurt yourself, you may learn to know better." His mother only gave him a very plain cake made with water and baked in cinders, and a bottle of sour beer.

When he got to the forest, he too met the little old gray man, who greeted him and said: "Give me a piece of your cake and a draught from your bottle; I am so hungry and thirsty."

And Dullhead replied: "I've only got a cinder cake and some sour beer, but if you care to have that, let us sit down and eat."

So they sat down, and when Dullhead brought out his cake he found it had turned into a fine rich cake, and the sour beer into excellent wine.

THE GOLDEN GOOSE, by the Brothers Grimm.

Then they ate and drank, and when they had finished the little man said: "Now I will bring you luck, because you have a kind heart and are willing to share what you have with others. There stands an old tree; cut it down, and among its roots you'll find something." With that the little man took leave.

Then Dullhead fell to at once to hew down the tree, and when it fell he found among its roots a goose, whose feathers were all of pure gold. He lifted it out, carried it off, and took it with him to an inn where he meant to spend the night.

Now the landlord of the inn had three daughters, and when they saw the goose they were filled with curiosity as to what this wonderful bird could be, and each longed to have one of its golden feathers.

The eldest thought to herself: "No doubt I shall soon find a good opportunity to pluck out one of its feathers," and the first time Dullhead happened to leave the room she caught hold of the goose by its wing. But, lo and behold! her fingers seemed to stick fast to the goose, and she could not take her hand away.

Soon after the second daughter came in, and thought to pluck a golden feather for herself too; but hardly had she touched her sister than she stuck fast as well. At last the third sister came with the same intentions, but the other two cried: "Keep off! For Heaven's sake keep off!"

The younger sister could not imagine why she was to keep off, and thought to herself: "If they are both there, why should not I be there too?"

So she sprang to them; but no sooner had she touched one of them than she stuck fast to her. So they all three had to spend the night with the goose.

Next morning Dullhead tucked the goose under his arm and went off, without in the least troubling himself about the three girls who were hanging on to it. They just had to run after him right or left as best they could. In the middle of a field they met a parson, and when he saw this procession he cried: "For shame, you bold girls! What do you mean by running after a young fellow through the fields like that? Do you call that proper behavior?" And with that he caught the youngest girl by the hand to try and draw her away. But directly he touched her he hung on himself, and had to run along with the rest of them.

Not long after the clerk came that way, and was much surprised to see the parson following the footsteps of three girls. "Why, where is Your Reverence going so fast?" cried he; "don't forget there is to be a christening today"; and he ran after him, caught him by the sleeve, and hung on to it himself. As the five of them trotted along in this fashion one after the other, two peasants were coming from their work with their hoes. On seeing them the parson called out and begged them to come and rescue him and the clerk. But no sooner did they touch the clerk than they stuck on too, and so there were seven of them running after Dullhead and his goose.

128   E U R O P E

After a time they all came to a town where a king reigned whose daughter was so serious and solemn that no one could ever manage to make her laugh. So the king had decreed that whoever should succeed in making her laugh should marry her.

When Dullhead heard this he marched before the princess with his goose and its appendages, and as soon as she saw these seven people continually running after each other she burst out laughing, and could not stop herself. Then Dullhead claimed her as his bride, but the king, who did not much fancy him as a son-in-law, made all sorts of objections, and told him he must first find a man who could drink up a whole cellarful of wine.

Dullhead bethought him of the little gray man, who could, he felt sure, help him; so he went off to the forest, and on the very spot where he had cut down the tree he saw a man sitting with a most dismal expression of face.

Dullhead asked him what he was taking so much to heart, and the man answered: "I don't know how I am ever to quench the terrible thirst I am suffering from. Cold water doesn't suit me at all. To be sure I've emptied a whole barrel of wine, but what is one drop on a hot stone?"

"I think I can help you," said Dullhead. "Come with me, and you shall drink to your heart's content." So he took him to the king's cellar, and the man sat down before the huge casks and drank till he drank up the whole contents of the cellar before the day closed.

Then Dullhead asked once more for his bride, but the king vexed at the idea of a stupid fellow whom people called "Dullhead" carrying off his daughter, and began to make fresh conditions. He required Dullhead to find a man who could eat a mountain of bread. Dullhead did not wait to consider long, but went straight off to the forest, and there on the same spot sat a man who was drawing in a strap as tight as he could round his body, and making a most woeful face the while. Said he: "I've eaten up a whole oven full of loaves, but what's the good of that to anyone who is as hungry as I am? I declare my stomach feels quite empty, and I must draw my belt tight if I'm not to die of starvation."

Dullhead was delighted, and said: "Get up and come with me, and you shall have plenty to eat," and he brought him to the king's court.

Now the king had given orders to have all the flour in his kingdom brought together, and to have a huge mountain baked of it. But the man from the wood just took up his stand before the mountain and began to eat, and in one day it had all vanished.

For the third time Dullhead asked for his bride, but again the king tried to make some evasion, and demanded a ship "which could sail on land and water. When you come sailing in such a ship," said he, "you shall have my daughter without further delay."

Again Dullhead started off to the forest, and there he found the little gray man with whom he had shared his cake, and who said: "I have eaten and I have drunk for you, and now I will give you the ship. I have done all this for you because you were kind and merciful to me."

Then he gave Dullhead a ship which could sail on land or water, and when the king saw it he felt he could no longer refuse him his daughter.

So they celebrated the wedding with great rejoicings; and after the king's death Dullhead succeeded to the kingdom, and lived happily with his wife for many years after.

A RIDDLE STORY

Three women were once changed into three flowers, which grew in the fields; but one of them was allowed to spend the night in her own home.

Once, when the daylight was very near and she knew that she must return to her companions in the field, she said to her husband:

"If you were to come this morning and gather me, I should be released from the enchantment and could stay with you always."

This happened, and now comes the riddle:

How did the man know which flower was his wife, for all three were exactly alike?

You cannot guess? Then I will tell you.

Because she spent the night at home, instead of in the field as the others did, the dew which fell upon them did not touch her, and this was how her husband recognized her.

HUNGARY

May all these lightnings strike him who won't listen to my tale which I have brought from beyond the Operencian Sea.[6]

The Hungarian stories come from the Magyars, who in 900 settled in what was known as "The cockpit of eastern Europe." The influence of the various cultures is readily seen in the marked similarities of theme and plot with those of other countries.

A RIDDLE STORY. From *Grimms' Tales,* by the Brothers Grimm.

[6] Rev. W. Henry Jones and Lewis L. Kropf, "The Wishes," from *The Folk Tales of the Magyars.*

THE SPEAKING GRAPES, THE SMILING APPLE, AND THE TINKLING APRICOT

There was once, I don't know where, beyond seven times seven countries, a king who had three daughters. One day the king was going to the market, and thus inquired of his daughters: "What shall I bring you from the market, my dear daughters?" The eldest said, "A golden dress, my dear royal father"; the second said, "A silver dress for me"; the third said, "Speaking grapes, a smiling apple, and a tinkling apricot for me." "Very well, my daughters," said the king, and went. He bought the dresses for his two elder daughters in the market, as soon as he arrived; but, in spite of all exertions and inquiries, he could not find the speaking grapes, the smiling apple, and tinkling apricot. He was very sad that he could not get what his youngest daughter wished, for she was his favourite; and he went home. It happened, however, that the royal carriage stuck fast on the way home, although his horses were of the best breed, for they were such high steppers that they kicked the stars. So he at once sent for extra horses to drag out the carriage; but all in vain, the horses couldn't move either way. He gave up all hope, at last, of getting out of the position, when a dirty, filthy pig came that way, and grunted, "Grumph! grumph! King, give me your youngest daughter, and I will help you out of the mud." The king, never thinking what he was promising, and over-anxious to get away, consented, and the pig gave the carriage a push with its nose, so that carriage and horses at once moved out of the mud. Having arrived at home the king handed the dresses to his two daughters, and was now sadder than ever that he had brought nothing for his favourite daughter; the thought also troubled him that he had promised her to an unclean animal.

After a short time the pig arrived in the court-yard of the palace dragging a wheelbarrow after it, and grunted, "Grumph! grumph! grumph! King, I've come for your daughter." The king was terrified, and, in order to save his daughter, he had a peasant girl dressed in rich garments, embroidered with gold, sent down and had her seated in the wheelbarrow: the pig again grunted, "Grumph! grumph! grump! King, this is not your daughter"; and, taking the barrow, it tipped her out. The king, seeing that deceit was of no avail, sent down his daughter, as promised, but dressed in ragged, dirty tatters, thinking that she would not please the pig; but the animal grunted in great joy, seized the girl, and placed her in the wheelbarrow. Her father wept that through a careless promise he had brought his favourite daughter to such a fate. The pig went on and on with the sobbing girl, till, after a long journey, it stopped before a dirty pig-stye

THE SPEAKING GRAPES, THE SMILING APPLE, AND THE TINKLING APRICOT. From *The Folk Tales of the Magyars,* by Rev. W. Henry Jones and Lewis L. Kropf.

and grunted, "Grumph! grumph! grumph! Girl, get out of the wheel-barrow." The girl did as she was told. "Grumph! grumph! grumph!" grunted the pig again; "go into your new home." The girl, whose tears, now, were streaming like a brook, obeyed; the pig then offered her some Indian corn that it had in a trough, and also its litter which consisted of some old straw, for a resting-place. The girl had not a wink of sleep for a long time, till at last, quite worn out with mental torture, she fell asleep.

Being completely exhausted with all her trials, she slept so soundly that she did not wake till next day at noon. On awaking she looked round, and was very much astonished to find herself in a beautiful fairy-like palace, her bed being of white silk with rich purple curtains and golden fringes. At the first sign of her waking, maids appeared all round her, awaiting her orders, and bringing her costly dresses. The girl, quite enchanted with the scene, dressed without a word, and the maids accompanied her to her breakfast in a splendid hall where a young man received her with great affection. "I am your husband, if you accept me, and whatever you see here belongs to you," said he; and after breakfast led her into a beautiful garden. The girl did not know whether it was a dream she saw or reality, and answered all the questions put to her by the young man with evasive and chaffing replies. At this moment they came to that part of the garden which was laid out as an orchard, and the bunches of grapes began to speak "Our beautiful queen, pluck some of us." The apples smiled at her continuously, and the apricots tinkled a beautiful silvery tune. "You see, my love," said the handsome youth, "here you have what you wished for—what your father could not obtain. You may know now, that once I was a monarch but I was bewitched into a pig, and I had to remain in that state till a girl wished for speaking grapes, a smiling apple, and a tinkling apricot. You are the girl, and I have been delivered: and if I please you, you can be mine for ever." The girl was enchanted with the handsome youth and the royal splendour, and consented. They went with great joy to carry the news to her father, and to tell him of their happiness.

THE WISHES

There were 10,000 wagons rolling along the turnpike road; in each wagon there were 10,000 casks, in each cask 10,000 bags, in each bag 10,000 poppy seeds, in each poppy seed 10,000 lightnings. May all these thunderous lightnings strike him who won't listen to my tale, which I have brought from beyond the Operencian Sea!

THE WISHES. From *The Folk Tales of the Magyars,* by Rev. W. Henry Jones and Lewis L. Kropf.

There was once, it doesn't matter where; there was once upon a time, a poor man who had a pretty young wife; they were very fond of each other. The only thing they had to complain of was their poverty, as neither of them owned a farthing; it happened, therefore, sometimes, that they quarrelled a little, and then they always cast it in each other's teeth that they hadn't got anything to bless themselves with. But still they loved each other.

One evening the woman came home much earlier than her husband and went into the kitchen and lighted the fire, although she had nothing to cook. "I think I can cook a little soup, at least, for my husband. It will be ready by the time he comes home." But no sooner had she put the kettle over the fire, and a few logs of wood on the fire in order to make the water boil quicker, than her husband arrived home and took his seat by the side of her on the little bench. They warmed themselves by the fire, as it was late in the autumn and cold. In the neighbouring village they had commenced the vintage on that very day. "Do you know the news, wife?" inquired he. "No, I don't. I've heard nothing; tell me what it is." "As I was coming from the squire's maize-field, I saw in the dark, in the distance, a black spot on the road. I couldn't make out what it was, so I went nearer, and lo! do you know what it was?—A beautiful little golden carriage, with a pretty little woman inside, and four fine black dogs harnessed to it." "You're joking," interrupted the wife. "I'm not, indeed, it's perfectly true. You know how muddy the roads about here are; it happened that the dogs stuck fast with the carriage and they couldn't move from the spot; the little woman didn't care to get out into the mud, as she was afraid of soiling her golden dress. At first, when I found out what it was, I had a good mind to run away, as I took her for an evil spirit, but she called out after me and implored me to help her out of the mud; she promised that no harm should come to me, but on the contrary she would reward me. So I thought that it would be a good thing for us if she could help us in our poverty; and with my assistance the dogs dragged her carriage out of the mud. The woman asked me if I was rich. I replied, not at all; I didn't think, I said, that there were two people in our village who were poorer than we. That can be remedied, replied she. I will fulfill three wishes that your wife may propose. And she left as suddenly as if dragons had kidnapped her: she was a fairy."

"Well, she made a regular fool of you!"

"That remains to be seen; you must try and wish something, my dear wife." Thereupon the woman without much thought said: "Well, I should like to have some sausage, and we could cook it beautifully on this nice fire." No sooner were the words uttered than a frying-pan came down the chimney, and in it a sausage of such length that it was long enough to fence the whole garden. "This is grand!" they both exclaimed together. "But we must be a little more clever with our next two wishes; how well we shall be off! I will at once buy two heifers and two horses, as well as a sucking pig," said the husband. Whereupon he took his pipe from his hatband, took out his tobacco-pouch, and filled his pipe; then he tried to light it with a hot cinder, but was so awkward about it that he upset the frying-pan with the sausage in it. "Good heaven! The sausage; what on earth are you doing? I wish that sausage would grow on to your nose," exclaimed the frightened woman, and tried to snatch the same out of the fire, but it was too late, as it was already dangling from her husband's nose down to his toes. "My Lord Creator help me!" shouted the woman. "You see, you fool, what you've done, there! now the second wish is gone," said her husband, "what can we do with this thing?" "Can't we get it off?" said the woman. "Take off the devil! Don't you see that it has quite grown to my nose; you can't take it off." "Then we must cut it off," said she, "as we can do nothing else." "I shan't permit it: how could I allow my body to be cut about? not for all the treasures on earth; but do you know what we can do, love? there is yet one wish left; you'd better wish that the sausage go back to the pan, and so all will be right." But the woman replied, "How about the heifers and the horses, and how about the sucking pig; how shall we get those?" "Well, I can't walk about with this ornament, and I'm sure you won't kiss me again with this sausage dangling from my nose." And so they quarrelled for a long time, till at last he succeeded in persuading his wife to wish that the sausage go back to the pan. And thus all three wishes were fulfilled; and yet they were as poor as ever.

They, however, made a hearty meal of the sausage; and as they came to the conclusion that it was in consequence of their quarrelling that they had no heifers, nor horses, nor sucking pig, they agreed to live henceforth in harmony together; and they quarrelled no more after this. They got on much better in the world, and in time they acquired heifers, horses, and a sucking pig into the bargain, because they were industrious and thrifty.

IRELAND

Come, listen to a tale of times of old,
Come, listen to me. . . .[7]

The superstitions of the Gaelic-speaking people have colored their tales with the little people, the wee folk, the leprechauns, and the fairies. The dreamer, the ghost, the giant, and the mythical hero of the past are characteristic of the peasants' tales from Ireland and Scotland.

[7] T. Crofton Croker, "Legend of Bottle-Hill," from *Fairy Legends and Traditions of the South of Ireland.*

LEGEND OF BOTTLE-HILL

Come, listen to a tale of times of old,
Come, listen to me. . . .

It was in the good old days when the little people, most im-
pudently called fairies, were more frequently seen than they are in these
unbelieving times, that a farmer, named Mick Purcell, rented a few acres
of barren ground in the neighbourhood of the once celebrated preceptory
of Mourne, situated about three miles from Mallow, and thirteen from
"the beautiful city called Cork." Mick had a wife and family. They all
did what they could, and that was but little, for the poor man had no
child grow up big enough to help him in his work; and all the poor
woman could do was to mind the children, and to milk the one cow, and
to boil the potatoes, and carry the eggs to market to Mallow; but with all
they did, 'twas hard enough on them to pay the rent. Well, they did
manage it for a good while; but at last came a bad year, and the little
grain of oats was all spoiled, and the chickens died of the pip, and the
pig got the measles—she was sold in Mallow and brought almost nothing;
and poor Mick found that he hadn't enough to half pay his rent, and two
gales were due.

"Why, then, Molly," says he, "what'll we do?"

"Wisha, then, mavourneen, what would you do but take the cow to
the fair of Cork and sell her?" says she; "and Monday is fair day, and
so you must go to-morrow, that the poor beast may be rested again for
the fair."

"And what'll we do when she's gone?" says Mick, sorrowfully.

"Never a know I know, Mick; but sure God won't leave us without
him, Mick; and you know how good he was to us when poor little Billy
was sick, and we had nothing at all for him to take—that good doctor
gentleman at Ballydahin come riding and asking for a drink of milk; and
how he gave us two shillings; and how he sent the things and bottles for
the child, and gave me my breakfast when I went over to ask a question,
so he did; and how he came to see Billy, and never left off his goodness
till he was quite well?"

"Oh! you are always that way, Molly, and I believe you are right after
all, so I won't be sorry for selling the cow; but I'll go to-morrow, and
you must put a needle and thread through my coat, for you know 'tis
ripp'd under the arm."

Molly told him he should have everything right; and about twelve
o'clock next day he left her, getting a charge not to sell his cow except for

LEGEND OF BOTTLE-HILL. From *Fairy Legends and Traditions of the South of Ireland,* by T. Crofton Croker.

the highest penny. Mick promised to mind it, and went his way along the road. He drove his cow slowly through the little stream which crosses it, and runs under the old walls of Mourne. As he passed he glanced his eye upon the towers and one of the old elder trees, which were only then little bits of switches.

"Oh, then, if I only had half the money that's buried in you, 'tis n't driving this poor cow I'd be now! Why, then, is n't it too bad that it should be there covered over with earth, and many a one besides me wanting? Well, if it's God's will, I'll have some money myself coming back."

So saying he moved on after his beast. 'Twas a fine day, and the sun shone brightly on the walls of the old abbey as he passed under them. He then crossed an extensive mountain tract, and after six long miles he came to the top of that hill—Bottle-Hill 'tis called now, but that was not the name of it then, and just there a man overtook him. "Good morrow," says he. "Good morrow, kindly," says Mick, looking at the stranger, who was a little man; you'd almost call him a dwarf, only he wasn't quite so little neither: he had a bit of an old, wrinkled, yellow face, for all the world like a dried cauliflower, only he had a sharp little nose, and red eyes, and white hair, and his lips were not red, but all his face was one colour, and his eyes never were quiet, but looking at everything, and although they were red they made Mick feel quite cold when he looked at them. In truth he did not much like the little man's company; and he could n't see one bit of his legs nor his body, for though the day was warm, he was all wrapped up in a big great coat. Mick drove his cow something faster, but the little man kept up with him. Mick didn't know how he walked, for he was almost afraid to look at him, and to cross himself, for fear the old man would be angry. Yet he thought his fellow-traveller did not seem to walk like other men, nor to put one foot before the other, but to glide over the rough road—and rough enough it was—like a shadow, without noise and without effort. Mick's heart trembled within him, and he said a prayer to himself, wishing he had n't come out that day, or that he was on Fair-hill, or that he had n't the cow to mind, that he might run away from the bad thing—when, in the midst of his fears, he was again addressed by his companion.

"Where are you going with the cow, honest man?"

"To the fair of Cork then," says Mick, trembling at the shrill and piercing tones of the voice.

"Are you going to sell her?" said the stranger.

"Why, then, what else am I going for but to sell her?"

"Will you sell her to me?"

Mick started—he was afraid to have anything to do with the little man, and he was more afraid to say no.

"What'll you give for her?" at last says he.

"I'll tell you what, I'll give you this bottle," said the little one, pulling a bottle from under his coat.

Mick looked at him and the bottle, and in spite of his terror, he could not help bursting into a loud fit of laughter.

"Laugh if you will," said the little man, "but I tell you this bottle is better for you than all the money you will get for the cow in Cork—ay, than ten thousand times as much."

Mick laughed again. "Why then," says he, "do you think I am such a fool as to give my good cow for a bottle—and an empty one, too? Indeed, then, I won't."

"You had better give me the cow, and take the bottle—you'll not be sorry for it."

"Why, then, and what would Molly say? I'd never hear the end of it; and how would I pay for the rent? and what would we all do without a penny of money?"

"I tell you this bottle is better for you than money; take it, and give me the cow. I ask you for the last time, Mick Purcell."

Mick started.

"How does he know my name?" thought he.

The stranger proceeded: "Mick Purcell, I know you, and I have a regard for you; therefore do as I want you to do, or you may be sorry for it. How do you know but your cow will die before you go to Cork?"

Mick was going to say "God forbid!" but the little man went on (and he was too attentive to say anything to stop him; for Mick was a very civil man, and he knew better than to interrupt a gentleman, and that's what many people, that hold their heads higher, do n't mind now).

"And how do you know but there will be much cattle at the fair, and you will get a bad price, or may be you might be robbed when you are coming home? But what need I talk more to you, when you are determined to throw away your luck, Mick Purcell."

"Oh! no, I would not throw away my luck, sir," said Mick; "and if I was sure the bottle was as good as you say, though I never liked an empty bottle, although I had drank the contents of it, I'd give you the cow in the name—"

"Never mind names," said the stranger, "but give me the cow; I would not tell you a lie. Here, take the bottle, and when you go home do what I direct exactly."

Mick hesitated.

"Well, then, good-bye, I can stay no longer: once more, take it, and be rich; refuse it, and beg for your life, and see your children in poverty, and your wife dying for want—that will happen to you, Mick Purcell!" said the little man with a malicious grin, which made him look ten times more ugly than ever.

"May be, 'tis true," said Mick, still hesitating: he did not know what to do—he could hardly help believing the old man, and at length in a fit of desperation, he seized the bottle. "Take the cow," said he, "and if you are telling a lie, the curse of the poor will be on you."

"I care neither for your curses nor your blessings, but I have spoken truth, Mick Purcell, and that you will find tonight, if you do what I tell you."

"And what's that?" says Mick.

"When you go home, never mind if your wife is angry, but be quiet yourself, and make her sweep the room clean, set the table out right, and spread a clean cloth over it; then put the bottle on the ground, saying these words: 'Bottle, do your duty,' and you will see the end of it."

"And is this all?" says Mick.

"No more," said the stranger. "Good-bye, Mick Purcell—you are a rich man."

"God grant it!" said Mick, as the old man moved for the cow, and Mick retraced the road towards his cabin; but he could not help turning back his head, to look after the purchaser of his cow, who was nowhere to be seen.

"Lord between us and harm!" said Mick. "He can't belong to this earth; but where is the cow?" She too was gone, and Mick went homeward muttering prayers and holding fast the bottle.

"And what would I do if it broke?" thought he. "Oh! but I'll take care of that"; so he put it into his bosom, and went on anxious to prove his bottle, and doubting of the reception he should meet from his wife. Balancing his anxieties with his expectation, his fears with his hopes, he reached home in the evening, and surprised his wife, sitting over the turf fire in the big chimney.

"Oh! Mick, are you come back? Sure you were n't at Cork all the way! What has happened to you? Where is the cow? Did you sell her? How much money did you get for her? What news have you? Tell us everything about it."

"Why then, Molly, if you'll give me time, I'll tell you all about it. If you want to know where the cow is, 'tis n't Mick can tell you, for the never a know does he know where she is now."

"Oh! then, you sold her; and where's the money?"

"Arrah! stop awhile, Molly, and I'll tell you all about it."

"But what is that bottle under your waistcoat?" said Molly, spying its neck sticking out.

"Why, then, be easy now, can't you," says Mick, "till I tell you"; and putting the bottle on the table, "That's all I got for the cow."

His poor wife was thunderstruck. "All you got! and what good is that, Mick? Oh! I never thought you were such a fool; and what'll we do for the rent, and what . . ."

"Now, Molly," says Mick, "can't you hearken to reason? Didn't I tell you how the old man, or whatsomever he was, met me—no, he did not meet me neither, but he was there with me—on the big hill, and how he made me sell him the cow, and told me the bottle was the only thing for me?"

"Yes, indeed, the only thing for you, you fool!" said Molly, seizing the bottle to hurl it at her poor husband's head; but Mick caught it, and quietly (for he minded the old man's advice) loosened his wife's grasp, and placed the bottle again in his bosom. Poor Molly sat down crying, while Mick told her his story, with many a crossing and blessing between him and harm. His wife could not help believing him, particularly as she has as much faith in fairies as she had in the priest, who indeed never discouraged her belief in the fairies; may be he did n't know she believed in them, and may be he believed in them himself. She got up, however, without saying one word, and began to sweep the earthen floor with a bunch of heath; then she tidied up everything, and put out the long table, and spread the clean cloth, for she had only one, upon it, and Mick, placing the bottle on the ground, looked at it, and said, "Bottle, do your duty."

"Look there! look there, mammy!" said his chubby eldest son, a boy about five years old—"look there! look there!" and he sprung to his mother's side, as two tiny little fellows rose like light from the bottle, and in an instant covered the table with dishes and plates of gold and silver, full of the finest victuals that ever were seen, and when all was done went into the bottle again. Mick and his wife looked at everything with astonishment; they had never seen such plates and dishes before, and did n't think they could ever admire them enough, the very sight almost took away their appetites; but at length Molly said, "Come and sit down, Mick, and try and eat a bit: sure you ought to be hungry after such a good day's work."

"Why, then, the man told no lie about the bottle."

Mick sat down, after putting the children to the table, and they made a hearty meal, though they could n't taste half the dishes.

"Now," says Molly, "I wonder will those two good little gentlemen carry away these fine things again?" They waited, but no one came; so Molly put up the dishes and plates very carefully, saying, "Why, then, Mick, that was no lie sure enough; but you'll be a rich man yet, Mick Purcell."

Mick and wife and children went to their bed, not to sleep, but to settle about selling the fine things they did not want, and to take more land. Mick went to Cork and sold his plate, and bought a horse and cart, and began to show that he was making money; and they did all they could to keep the bottle a secret; but for all that, their landlord found it out, for he came to Mick one day and asked him where he got all his money—sure it was not by the farm; and he bothered him so much, that at last Mick told him of the bottle. His landlord offered him a deal of money for it, but Mick would not give it, till at last he offered to give him all his farm for ever: so Mick, who was very rich, thought he'd never want any more money, and gave him the bottle: but Mick was mistaken—he and his family spent money as if there was no end of it; and to make the story short, they became poorer and poorer, till at last they had nothing left but one cow; and Mick once more drove his cow before him to sell her at Cork fair, hoping to meet the old man and get another bottle. It was hardly daybreak when he left home, and he walked on at a good pace till he reached the big hill; the mists were sleeping in the valleys and curling like smoke wreaths upon the brown heath around him. The sun rose on his left, and just at his feet a lark sprang from its grassy couch, and poured forth its joyous mating song, ascending into the clear blue sky,

> Till its form like a speck in the airness blending,
> And thrilling with music, was melting in light.

Mick crossed himself, listening as he advanced to the sweet song of the lark, but thinking, notwithstanding, all the time of the little old man; when, just as he reached the summit of the hill, and cast his eyes over the extensive prospect before and around him, he was startled and rejoiced by the same well-known voice: "Well, Mick Purcell, I told you you would be a rich man."

"Indeed, then, sure enough I was, that's no lie for you, sir. Good morning to you, but it is not rich I am now—but have you another bottle, for I want it now as much as I did long ago; so if you have it, sir, here is the cow for it."

"And here is the bottle," said the old man, smiling; "you know what to do with it."

"Oh! then, sure I do, as good right I have."

"Well, farewell forever, Mick Purcell: I told you you would be a rich man."

"And good-bye to you, sir," said Mick, as he turned back; "and good luck to you, and good luck to the big hill—it wants a name—Bottle-Hill—Good-bye, sir, good-bye": so Mick walked back as fast he could, never looking after the white-faced little gentleman and the cow, so anxious was he to bring home the bottle. Well, he arrived with it safely enough, and called out as soon as he saw Molly—"Oh! sure I've another bottle!"

"Arrah! then, have you? why then, you're a lucky man, Mick Purcell, that's what you are."

In an instant she put everything right; and Mick, looking at his bottle, exultingly cried out, "Bottle, do your duty." In a twinkling, two great stout men with big cudgels issued from the bottle (I do not know how they got room in it), and belaboured poor Mick and his wife and all his family, till they lay on the floor, when in they went again. Mick, as soon as he recovered, got up and looked about him; he thought and thought, and at last he took up his wife and his children; and, leaving them to recover as well as they could, he took the bottle under his coat and went to his landlord, who had a great company: he got a servant to tell him he wanted to speak to him, and at last he came out to Mick.

"Well, what do you want now?"

"Nothing, sir, only I have another bottle."

"Oh! ho! is it as good as the first?"

"Yes, sir, and better; if you like, I will show it to you before all the ladies and gentlemen."

"Come along, then." So saying, Mick was brought into the great hall, where he saw his old bottle standing high up on a shelf: "Ah! ha!" says he to himself, "may be I won't have you by and by."

"Now," says the landlord, "show us your bottle." Mick set it on the floor, and uttered the words: in a moment the landlord was tumbled on the floor; ladies and gentlemen, servants and all, were running, and roaring, and sprawling, and kicking, and shrieking. Wine cups and salvers were knocked about in every direction, until the landlord called out, "Stop those two devils, Mick Purcell, or I'll have you hanged."

"They never shall stop," said Mick, "till I get my own bottle that I see up there at top of that shelf."

"Give it down to him, give it down to him, before we are all killed!" says the landlord.

Mick put his bottle in his bosom; in jumped the two men into the new bottle, and he carried them home. I need not lengthen my story by telling how he got richer than ever, how his son married his landlord's only daughter, how he and his wife died when they were very old, and how some of the servants, fighting at their wake, broke the bottles; but still the hill has the name upon it; ay, and so 'twill be always Bottle-Hill to the end of the world, and so it ought, for it is a strange story!

TEIGUE OF THE LEE

"I can't stop in the house—I won't stop in it for all the money that is buried in the old castle of Carrigrohan. If ever there was such a thing in the world!—to be abused to my face night and day, and nobody to the fore doing it! and then, if I'm angry, to be laughed at with a great roaring ho, ho, ho! I won't stay in the house after to-night, if there was not another place in the country to put my head under." This angry soliloquy was pronounced in the hall of the old manor-house of Carrigrohan by John Sheehan. John was a new servant; he had been only three days in the house, which had the character of being haunted, and in that short space of time he had been abused, and laughed at by a voice which

TEIGUE OF THE LEE. From *Fairy Legends and Traditions of the South of Ireland,* by T. Crofton Croker.

sounded as if a man spoke with his head in a cask; nor could he discover who was the speaker, or from whence the voice came. "I'll not stop here," said John; "and that ends the matter."

"Ho, ho, ho! be quiet, John Sheehan, or else worse will happen to you."

John instantly ran to the hall window, as the words were evidently spoken by a person immediately outside, but no one was visible. He had scarcely placed his face at the pane of glass, when he heard another loud "Ho, ho, ho!" as if behind him in the hall; as quick as lightning he turned his head, but no living thing was to be seen.

"Ho, ho, ho, John!" shouted a voice that appeared to come from the lawn before the house: "do you think you'll see Teigue?—oh, never! as long as you live! so leave alone looking after him, and mind your business; there's plenty of company to dinner from Cork to be here to-day, and 't is time you had the cloth laid."

"Lord bless us! there's more of it!—I'll never stay another day here," repeated John.

"Hold your tongue, and stay where you are quietly, and play no tricks on Mr. Pratt, as you did on Mr. Jervois about the spoons."

John Sheehan was confounded by this address from his invisible persecutor, but nevertheless he mustered courage enough to say—"Who are you?—come here, and let me see you, if you are a man"; but he received in reply only a laugh of unearthly derision, which was followed by a "Good-bye—I'll watch you at dinner, John!"

"Lord between us and harm! this beats all!—I'll watch you at dinner! —maybe you will!—'t is the broad day-light, so 't is no ghost; but this is a terrible place, and this is the last day I'll stay in it. How does he know about the spoons?—if he tells it I'm a ruined man!—there was no living soul could tell it to him but Tim Barrett, and he's far enough off in the wilds of Botany Bay now, so how could he know it?—I can't tell for the world! But what's that I see there at the corner of the wall!— 't is not a man!—oh, what a fool I am! 't is only the old stump of a tree!—But this is a shocking place—I'll never stop in it, for I'll leave the house tomorrow; the very look of it is enough to frighten any one."

The mansion had certainly an air of desolation; it was situated in a lawn, which had nothing to break its uniform level save a few tufts of narcissuses and a couple of old trees coeval with the building. The house stood at a short distance from the road, it was upwards of a century old, and Time was doing his work upon it; its walls were weather-stained in all colours, its roof showed various white patches, it had no look of comfort; all was dim and dingy without, and within there was an air of gloom, of departed and departing greatness, which harmonized well with the exterior. It required all the exuberance of youth and of gaiety to remove the impression, almost amounting to awe, with which you trod the huge square hall, paced along the gallery which surrounded the hall, or explored the long rambling passages below-stairs. The ball-room, as the large drawing-room was called, and several other apartments, were in a state of decay; the walls were stained with damp, and I remember well the sensation of awe which I felt creeping over me when, boy as I was, and full of boyish life and wild and ardent spirits, I descended to the vaults; all without and within me became chilled beneath their dampness and gloom—their extent, too, terrified me; nor could the merriment of my two school-fellows, whose father, a respectable clergyman, rented the dwelling for a time, dispel the feelings of a romantic imagination until I once again ascended to the upper regions.

John had pretty well recovered himself as the dinner-hour approached, and several guests arrived. They were all seated at table, and had begun to enjoy the excellent repast, when a voice was heard in the lawn.

"Ho, ho, ho, Mr. Pratt, won't you give poor Teigue some dinner? Ho, ho, a fine company you have there, and plenty of everything that's good; sure you won't forget poor Teigue?"

John dropped the glass he had in his hand.

"Who's that?" said Mr. Pratt's brother, an officer of the artillery.

"That is Teigue," said Mr. Pratt, laughing, "whom you must often have heard me mention."

"And pray, Mr. Pratt," inquired another gentleman, "who is Teigue?"

"That," he replied, "is more than I can tell. No one has ever been able to catch even a glimpse of him. I have been on the watch for a whole evening with three of my sons, yet, although his voice sometimes sounded almost in my ear, I could not see him. I fancied, indeed, that I saw a man in a white frieze jacket pass into the door from the garden to the lawn, but it could be only fancy, for I found the door locked, while the fellow, whoever he is, was laughing at our trouble. He visits us occasionally, and sometimes a long interval passes between his visits, as in the present case; it is now nearly two years since we heard that hollow voice outside the window. He has never done any injury that we know of, and once when he broke a plate, he brought one back exactly like it."

"It is very extraordinary," said several of the company.

"But," remarked a gentleman to young Mr. Pratt, "your father said he broke a plate; how did he get it without your seeing him?"

"When he asks for some dinner we put it outside the window and go away; whilst we watch he will not take it, but no sooner have we withdrawn than it is gone."

"How does he know that you are watching?"

"That's more than I can tell, but he either knows or suspects. One day my brothers Robert and James with myself were in our back parlour, which has a window into the garden, when he came outside and said, 'Ho, ho, ho! Masters James and Robert and Henry, give poor Teigue a lick of whiskey.' James went out of the room, filled a glass with whiskey, vinegar, and salt, and brought it to him. 'Here, Teigue,' said he, 'come for it now.' 'Well, put it down, then, on the step outside the window.' This was done, and we stood looking at it. 'There, now, go away,' he shouted. We retired, but still watched it. 'Ho, ho! you are watching Teigue! go out of the room, now, or I won't take it.' We went outside the door and when we returned, the glass was gone, and a moment after we heard him roaring and cursing frightfully. He took away the glass, but the next day the glass was on the stone step under the window, and there were crumbs of bread in the inside, as if he had put it in his pocket; from that time he was not heard till to-day."

"Oh," said the colonel, "I'll get a sight of him; you are not used to these things; an old soldier has the best chance, and as I shall finish my dinner with this wing, I'll be ready for him when he speaks next.—Mr. Bell, will you take a glass of wine with me?"

"Ho, ho! Mr. Bell," shouted Teigue. "Ho, ho! Mr. Bell, you were a Quaker long ago. Ho, ho! Mr. Bell, you're a pretty boy;—a pretty Quaker you were; and now you're no Quaker, nor anything else:—ho, ho! Mr. Bell. And there's Mr. Parkes; to be sure, Mr. Parkes looks mighty fine to-day, with his powdered head, and his grand silk stockings, and his bran new rakish-red waistcoat,—And there's Mr. Cole,—did you ever see such a fellow? A pretty company you've brought together, Mr. Pratt: kiln-dried quakers, butter-buying buckeens from Mallow-lane, and a drinking exciseman from the Coal-quay, to meet the great thundering artillery-general that is come out of the Indies, and is the biggest dust of them all."

"You scoundrel!" exclaimed the colonel: "I'll make you show yourself"; and snatching up his sword from a corner of the room, he sprang out of the window upon the lawn. In a moment a shout of laughter, so hollow, so unlike any human sound, made him stop, as well as Mr. Bell, who with a huge oak stick was close at the colonel's heels; others of the party followed on the lawn, and the remainder rose and went to the windows. "Come on, Colonel," said Mr. Bell; "let us catch this impudent rascal."

"Ho, ho! Mr. Bell, here I am—here's Teigue—why don't you catch him?—Ho, ho! Colonel Pratt, what a pretty soldier you are to draw your sword upon poor Teigue, that never did anybody harm."

"Let us see your face, you scoundrel," said the Colonel.

"Ho, ho, ho!—look at me—look at me: do you see the wind, Colonel Pratt?—you'll see Teigue as soon; so go in and finish your dinner."

"If you're upon the earth I'll find you, you villain!" said the colonel, whilst the same unearthly shout of derision seemed to come from behind an angle of the building. "He's round that corner," said Mr. Bell—"run, run."

They followed the sound, which was continued at intervals along the garden wall, but could discover no human being; at last both stopped to draw breath, and in an instant, almost at their ears, sounded the shout,—

"Ho, ho, ho! Colonel Pratt, do you see Teigue now?—do you hear him? —Ho, ho, ho! you're a fine colonel to follow the wind."

"Not that way, Mr. Bell—not that way; come here," said the colonel.

"Ho, ho, ho! what a fool you are; do you think Teigue is going to show himself to you in the field, there? But, colonel, follow me if you can:—you a soldier!—ho, ho, ho!" The colonel was enraged—he followed the voice over hedge and ditch, alternately laughed at and taunted by the unseen object of his pursuit,—(Mr. Bell, who was heavy, was soon thrown out)—until at length, after being led a weary chase, he found himself at the top of the cliff, over that part of the river Lee which, from its great depth, and the blackness of its water, has received the name of Hell-hole. Here, on the edge of the cliff, stood the colonel out of breath, and mopping his forehead with his handkerchief, while the voice, which seemed close at his feet, exclaimed—"Now, Colonel Pratt—now, if you're a soldier, here's a leap for you;—now look at Teigue—why don't you look at him?—Ho, ho, ho! Come along; you're warm, I'm sure, Colonel Pratt, so come in and cool yourself; Teigue is going to have a swim!" The voice seemed as descending amongst the trailing ivy and brushwood which clothes this picturesque cliff nearly from top to bottom, yet it was impossible that any human being could have found footing. "Now, Colonel, have you courage to take the leap?—Ho, ho, ho! what a pretty soldier you are. Good-bye—I'll see you again in ten minutes above, at the house—look at your watch, Colonel:—there's a dive for you"; and a heavy plunge into the water was heard. The colonel stood still, but no sound followed, and he walked slowly back to the house, not quite half a mile from the Crag.

"Well, did you see Teigue?" said his brother, whilst his nephews, scarcely able to smother their laughter, stood by,—"Give me some wine," said the colonel. "I never was led such a dance in my life; the fellow carried me all round and round till he brought me to the edge of the cliff, and then down he went into Hell-hole, telling me he'd be here in ten minutes: 't is more than that now, but he's not come."

"Ho, ho, ho! Colonel, isn't he here?—Teigue never told a lie in his life: but, Mr. Pratt, give me a drink and my dinner, and then good-night to you all, for I'm tired; and that's the colonel's doing." A plate of food was ordered; it was placed by John, with fear and trembling, on the lawn under the window. Every one kept on the watch, and the plate remained undisturbed for some time.

"Ah! Mr. Pratt, will you starve poor Teigue? Make every one go away from the windows, and Master Henry out of the tree, and Master Richard off the garden wall."

The eyes of the company were turned to the tree and the garden wall; the two boys' attention was occupied in getting down; the visitors were looking at them; and "Ho, ho, ho!—good luck to you, Mr. Pratt;—'t is a good dinner, and there's the plate, ladies and gentlemen—good-bye to you, Colonel!—good-bye Mr. Bell!—good-bye to you all"—brought their attention back, when they saw the empty plate lying on the grass; and

Teigue's voice was heard no more for that evening. Many visits were afterwards paid by Teigue; but never was he seen, nor was any discovery ever made of his person or character.

A LEGEND OF KNOCKMANY

What Irish man, woman or child has not heard of our renowned Hibernian Hercules, the great and glorious Fin McCoul? Not one, from Cape Clear to the Giant's Causeway, nor from that back again to Cape Clear. And, by the way, speaking of the Giant's Causeway brings me at once to the beginning of my story. Well, it so happened that Fin and his men were all working at the Causeway, in order to make a bridge across to Scotland; when Fin, who was very fond of his wife Oonagh, took it into his head that he would go home and see how the poor woman got on in his absence. So, accordingly, he pulled up a fir-tree, and, after lopping off the roots and branches, made a walking-stick of it, and set out on his way to Oonagh.

Oonagh, or rather Fin, lived at this time on the very tiptop of Knockmany Hill, which faces a cousin of its own, called Cullamore, that rises up, half-hill, half-mountain, on the opposite side.

There was at that time another giant, named Cucullin—No other giant of the day could stand before him; and such was his strength that, when well vexed, he could give a stamp that shook the country about him.

By one blow of his fists he flattened a thunderbolt and kept it in his pocket, in the shape of a pancake, to show to all his enemies, when they were about to fight him. Fin heard Cucullin was coming to the Causeway to have a trial of strength with him; and he was seized with a very warm and sudden fit of affection for his wife, poor woman, leading a very lonely, uncomfortable life of it in his absence.

"God save all here!" said Fin good-humoredly, on putting his honest face into his own door.

"Musha, Fin, avick, an' you're welcome home to your own Oonagh, you darlin' bully." Here followed a smack that is said to have made the waters of the lake at the bottom of the hill curl, as it were, with kindness and sympathy.

Fin spent two or three happy days with Oonagh, and felt himself very comfortable, considering the dread he had of Cucullin. This, however, grew upon him so much that his wife could not but perceive something lay on his mind which he kept altogether to himself.

"It's this Cucullin," said he, "that's troubling me. When the fellow gets

A LEGEND OF KNOCKMANY. From *Celtic Fairy Tales*, by Joseph Jacobs. Reprinted by permission of G. P. Putnam's Sons.

angry, and begins to stamp, he'll shake you a whole townland; and it's well known that he can stop a thunderbolt, for he always carries one about him in the shape of a pancake, to show to any one that might misdoubt it."

As he spoke, he clapped his thumb in his mouth, which he always did when he wanted to prophesy, or to know anything that happened in his absence; and the wife asked him what he did it for.

"He's coming," said Fin; "I see him below Dungannon."

"Thank goodness, dear! an' who is it, avick? Glory be to God!"

"That baste, Cucullin," replied Fin; "and how to manage I don't know. If I run away, I am disgraced; and I know that sooner or later I must meet him, for my thumb tells me so."

"When will he be here?" said she.

"To-morrow, about two o'clock," replied Fin, with a groan.

"Well, my bully, don't be cast down," said Oonagh; "depend on me, and maybe I'll bring you better out of this scrape than ever you could bring yourself, by your rule o'thumb."

She then made a high smoke on the top of the hill, after which she put her finger in her mouth, and gave three whistles, and by that Cucullin knew he was invited to Cullamore—for this was the way that the Irish long ago gave a sign to all strangers and travelers, to let them know they were welcome to come and take share of whatever was going.

In the meantime Fin was very melancholy, and did not know what to do, or how to act at all. Cucullin was an ugly customer to meet with; and the idea of the "cake" aforesaid flattened the very heart within him. What chance could he have, strong and brave though he was, with a man who could, when put in a passion, walk the country into earthquakes and knock thunderbolts into pancakes?

"Oonagh," said he, "can you do nothing for me? Where's all your invention? Am I to be skivered like a rabbit before your eyes, and to have my name disgraced forever in the sight of all my tribe, and me the best man among them? How am I to fight this man-mountain—this huge cross between an earthquake and a thunderbolt?—with a pancake in his pocket that was once . . ."

"Be easy, Fin," replied Oonagh; "troth, I'm ashamed of you. Keep your toe in your pump, will you? Talking of pancakes, maybe, we'll give him as good as any he brings with him—thunderbolt or otherwise. If I don't treat him to as smart feeling as he's got this many a day, never trust Oonagh again. Leave him to me, and do just as I bid you."

This relieved Fin very much; for, after all, he had great confidence in his wife, knowing, as he did, that she had got him out of many a quandary before. Oonagh then drew the nine woolen threads of different colors, which she always did to find out the best way of succeeding in anything of importance she went about. She then platted them into three plats with three colors in each, putting one on her right arm, one round her heart, and the third round her right ankle, for then she knew that nothing could fail with her that she undertook.

Having everything now prepared, she sent round to the neighbors and borrowed twenty-one iron griddles, which she took and kneaded into the hearts of twenty-one cakes of bread, and these she baked on the fire in the usual way, setting them aside in the cupboard according as they were done. She then put down a large pot of new milk, which she made into curds and whey. Having done all this, she sat down quite contented, waiting for his arrival on the next day about two o'clock, that being the hour at which he was expected—for Fin knew as much by the sucking of his thumb. Now this was a curious property that Fin's thumb had. In this very thing, moreover, he was very much resembled by his great foe, Cucullin; for it was well known that the huge strength he possessed all lay in the middle finger of his right hand, and that, if he happened by any mischance to lose it, he was no more, for all his bulk, than a common man.

At length the next day, Cucullin was seen coming across the valley, and Oonagh knew that it was time to commence operations. She immediately brought the cradle, and made Fin to lie down in it, and cover himself up with the clothes.

"You must pass for your own child," said she; "so just lie there snug, and say nothing, but be guided by me."

About two o'clock, as he had been expected, Cucullin came in. "God save all here!" said he; "is this where the great Fin McCoul lives?"

"Indeed it is, honest man," replied Oonagh; "God save you kindly— won't you be sitting?"

"Thank you, ma'am," says he, sitting down; "You're Mrs. McCoul, I suppose?"

"I am," said she; "and I have no reason, I hope, to be ashamed of my husband."

"No," said the other, "he has the name of being the strongest and bravest man in Ireland; but for all that, there's a man not far from you that's very desirous of taking a shake with him. Is he at home?"

"Why, then, no," she replied; "and if ever a man left his house in a fury, he did. It appears that some one told him of a big basthoon of a giant called Cucullin being down at the Causeway to look for him, and so he set out there to try if he could catch him. Troth, I hope, for the poor giant's sake, he won't meet with him, for if he does Fin will make paste of him at once."

"Well," said the other, "I am Cucullin, and I have been seeking him these twelve months, but he always kept clear of me; and I will never rest night or day till I lay my hands on him."

At this Oonagh set up a loud laugh, of great contempt, by the way, and looked at him as if he was only a mere handful of a man.

"Did you ever see Fin?" said she, changing her manner all at once.

"How could I?" said he; "he always took care to keep his distance."

"I thought so," she replied; "I judged as much; and if you take my advice, you poor-looking creature, you'll pray night and day that you may never see him, for I tell you it will be a black day for you when you do. But, in the meantime, you perceive that the wind's on the door, and as Fin himself is from home, maybe you'd be civil enough to turn the house, for it's always what Fin does when he's here."

This was a startler even to Cucullin; but he got up, however, and after pulling the middle finger of his right hand until it cracked three times, he went outside, and getting his arms about the house, turned it as she had wished. When Fin saw this he felt the sweat of fear oozing out through every pore of his skin; but Oonagh, depending upon her woman's wit, felt not a whit daunted.

"Arrah, then," said she, "as you are so civil, maybe you'd do another obliging turn for us as Fin's not here to do it himself. You see, after this long stretch of dry weather we've had, we feel very badly off for want of water. Now, Fin says there's a fine spring-well somewhere under the rocks behind the hill here below, and it was his intention to pull them asunder; but having heard of you, he left the place in such a fury that he never thought of it. Now, if you try to find it, troth I'd feel it a kindness."

She then brought Cucullin down to see the place, which was then all one solid rock; and, after looking at it for some time, he cracked his right middle finger nine times, and, stooping down, tore a cleft about four hundred feet deep, and a quarter of a mile in length, which has since been christened by the name of Lumford's Glen.

"You'll now come in," said she, "and eat a bit of such humble fare as we can give you. Fin, even although he and you are enemies, would scorn not to treat you kindly in his own house; and, indeed, if I didn't do it even in his absence, he would not be pleased with me."

She accordingly brought him in, and placing half a dozen of the cakes we spoke of before him, together with a can or two of butter, a side of boiled bacon, and a stack of cabbage, she desired him to help himself— for this, be it known, was long before the invention of potatoes. Cucullin put one of the cakes in his mouth to take a huge whack out of it, when he made a thundering noise, something between a growl and a yell. "Blood and fury," he shouted; "how is this? Here are two of my teeth out! What kind of bread is this you gave me?"

"What's the matter?" said Oonagh coolly.

"Matter!" shouted the other again; "why, here are the two best teeth in my head gone."

"Why," said she, "that's Fin's bread—the only bread he ever eats when at home; but, indeed, I forgot to tell you that nobody can eat it but himself, and that child in the cradle there. I thought, however, that as you were reported to be rather a stout little fellow of your size, you might be able to manage it, and I did not wish to affront a man that thinks himself able to fight Fin. Here's another cake—maybe it's not so hard as that."

Cucullin at the moment was not only hungry, but ravenous, so he accordingly made a fresh set at the second cake, and immediately another yell was heard twice as loud as the first. "Thunder and gibbets!" he roared. "Take your bread out of this, or I will not have a tooth in my head; there's another pair of them gone!"

"Well, honest man," replied Oonagh, "if you're not able to eat the bread, say so quietly, and don't be wakening the child in the cradle there. There, now, he's awake upon me."

Fin now gave a skirl that startled the giant, as coming from such a youngster as he was supposed to be. "Mother," said he, "I'm hungry—get me something to eat." Oonagh went over, and putting into his hand a cake that had no griddle in it, Fin, whose appetite in the meantime had been sharpened by seeing eating going forward, soon swallowed it. Cucullin was thunderstruck, and secretly thanked his stars that he had the good fortune to miss meeting Fin, for, as he said to himself, "I'd have no chance with a man who could eat such bread as that, which even his son that's but in his cradle can munch before my eyes."

"I'd like to take a glimpse at the lad in the cradle," said he to Oonagh; "for I can tell you that the infant who can manage that nutriment is no joke to look at, or to feed of a scarce summer."

"With all the veins of my heart," replied Oonagh; "get up, acushla, and show this decent little man something that won't be unworthy of your father, Fin McCoul."

Fin, who was dressed for the occasion as much like a boy as possible, got up, and bringing Cucullin out, "Are you strong?" said he.

"Thunder an' hounds!" exclaimed the other, "what a voice in so small a chap!"

"Are you strong?" said Fin again. "Are you able to squeeze water out of that white stone?" he asked, putting one into Cucullin's hand. The latter squeezed and squeezed the stone, but in vain.

"Ah, you're a poor creature!" said Fin. "You a giant! Give me the stone here, and when I'll show what Fin's little son can do, you may then judge of what my daddy himself is."

Fin then took the stone, and exchanging it for the curds, he squeezed the latter until the whey, as clear as water, oozed out in a little shower from his hand.

"I'll now go in," said he, "to my cradle; for I scorn to lose my time with anyone that's not able to eat my daddy's bread, or squeeze water out of a stone. Bedad, you had better be off out of this before he comes back; for if he catches you it's in flummery he'd have you in two minutes."

Cucullin, seeing what he had seen, was of the same opinion himself; his knees knocked together with the terror of Fin's return, and he accordingly hastened to bid Oonagh farewell, and to assure her that from that day out he never wished to hear of, much less to see, her husband. "I admit fairly that I'm not a match for him," said he, "strong as I am; tell him I will avoid him as I would the plague, and that I will make myself scarce in this part of the country while I live."

Fin, in the meantime, had gone into the cradle, where he lay very quietly, his heart at his mouth with delight that Cucullin was about to take his departure without discovering the tricks that had been played off on him.

"It's well for you," said Oonagh, "that he doesn't happen to be here, for it's nothing but hawk's meat he'd make of you."

"I know that," says Cucullin; "divil a thing else he'd make of me; but before I go, will you let me feel what kind of teeth Fin's lad has got that can eat griddle-bread like that?"

"With all pleasure in life," said she; "only, as they're far back in his head, you must put your finger a good way in."

Cucullin was surprised to find such a powerful set of grinders in one so young; but he was still much more so on finding, when he took his hand from Fin's mouth, that he had left the very finger upon which his whole strength depended behind him. He gave one loud groan, and fell down at once with terror and weakness. This was all Fin wanted, who now knew that his most powerful and bitterest enemy was at his mercy. He started out of the cradle, and in a few minutes the great Cucullin, that was for such a length of time the terror of him and all his followers, lay a corpse before him. Thus did Fin, through the wit and invention of Oonagh, his wife, succeed in overcoming his enemy by cunning, which he never could have done by force.

THE SPRIGHTLY TAILOR

A sprightly tailor was employed by the great Macdonald in his castle at Saddell, in order to make the laird a pair of trews, used in olden time. And trews being the vest and breeches united in one piece, and ornamented with fringes, were very comfortable, and suitable to be worn in walking or dancing. And Macdonald had said to the tailor, that if he would make the trews by night in the church, he would get a handsome reward. For it was thought that the old ruined church was haunted, and that fearsome things were to be seen there at night.

The tailor was well aware of this; but he was a sprightly man, and when the laird dared him to make the trews by night in the church, the

THE SPRIGHTLY TAILOR. From *Celtic Fairy Tales*, by Joseph Jacobs. Reprinted by permission of G. P. Putnam's Sons.

tailor was not to be daunted, but took it in hand to gain the prize. So, when night came, away he went up the glen, about half a mile distance from the castle, till he came to the old church. Then he chose him a nice gravestone for a seat and he lighted his candle, and put on his thimble, and set to work at the trews; plying his needle nimbly, and thinking about the hire that the laird would have to give him.

For some time he got on pretty well, until he felt the floor all of a tremble under his feet; and looking about him, but keeping his fingers at work, he saw the appearance of a great human head rising up through the stone pavement of the church. And when the head had risen above the surface, there came from it a great, great voice. And the voice said: "Do you see this great head of mine?"

"I see that, but I'll sew this!" replied the sprightly tailor; and he stitched away at the trews.

Then the head rose higher up through the pavement, until its neck appeared. And when its neck was shown, the thundering voice came again and said: "Do you see this great neck of mine?"

"I see that, but I'll sew this!" said the sprightly tailor; and he stitched away at his trews.

Then the head and neck rose higher still, until the great shoulders and chest were shown above the ground. And again the mighty voice thundered: "Do you see this great chest of mine?"

And again the sprightly tailor replied: "I see that, but I'll sew this!" and stitched away at his trews.

And still it kept rising through the pavement, until it shook a great pair of arms in the tailor's face, and said: "Do you see these great arms of mine?"

"I see those, but I'll sew this!" answered the tailor; and he stitched hard at his trews, for he knew that he had no time to lose.

The sprightly tailor was taking the long stitches, when he saw it gradually rising and rising through the floor, until it lifted out a great leg, and stamping with it upon the pavement, said in a roaring voice: "Do you see this great leg of mine?"

"Ay, ay: I see that, but I'll sew this!" cried the tailor; and his fingers flew with the needle, and he took such long stitches that he was just come to the end of the trews, when it was taking up its other leg. But before it could pull it out of the pavement the sprightly tailor had finished his task; and blowing out his candle, and springing from off his gravestone, he buckled up, and ran out of the church with the trews under his arm. Then the fearsome thing gave a loud roar, and stamped with both feet upon the pavement, and out of the church he went after the sprightly tailor.

Down the glen they ran, faster than the stream when the flood rides it; but the tailor had got the start and a nimble pair of legs, and he did not choose to lose the laird's reward. And though the thing roared to him to stop, yet the sprightly tailor was not the man to be beholden to a monster. So he held his trews tight, and let no darkness grow under his feet, until he had reached Saddell Castle. He had no sooner got inside the gate, and shut it, than the monster came up to it; and, enraged at losing his prize, struck the wall above the gate, and left there the mark of his five great fingers. Ye may see them plainly to this day, if ye'll only peer close enough.

But the sprightly tailor gained his reward: for Macdonald paid him handsomely for the trews, and never discovered that a few of the stitches were somewhat long.

ITALY

My legs, it is no shame
To run away when there is need.[8]

"Ciarpe Tales" are tales of gossip, in the sense that they concern the people and their affairs. The Roman tale has taken the basic myth and eliminated the superstitious beliefs in knight and dragon, horror stories, and monsters that appear in the northern countries.

BUCHETTINO

Once upon a time there was a child whose name was Buchettino. One morning his mama called him and said: "Buchettino, will you do me a favour? Go and sweep the stairs." Buchettino, who was very obedient, did not wait to be told a second time, but went at once to sweep the stairs. All at once he heard a noise, and after looking all around, he found a penny. Then he said to himself: "What shall I do with this penny? I have half a mind to buy some dates . . . but no! for I should have to throw away the stones. I will buy some apples . . . no! I will not, for I should have to throw away the core. I will buy some nuts . . . but no, for I should have to throw away the shells! What shall I buy then? I will buy—I will buy—enough! I will buy a pennyworth of figs," and he went to eat them in a tree. While he was eating, the ogre passed by, and seeing Buchettino eating figs in the tree said:

Buchettino,
My dear Buchettino,
Give me a little fig

[8] F. F. Crane, "Buchettino," from *Italian Popular Tales*.

With your dear little hand,
If not I will eat you!

Buchettino threw him one, but it fell in the dirt. Then the ogre repeated:

Buchettino,
My dear Buchettino,
Give me a little fig
With your dear little hand,
If not I will eat you!

Then Buchettino threw him another, which also fell in the dirt. The ogre said again:

Buchettino,
My dear Buchettino,
Give me a little fig
With your dear little hand,
If not I will eat you!

Poor Buchettino, who did not see the trick, and did not know that the ogre was doing everything to get him into his net and eat him up, what does he do? he leans down and foolishly gives him a fig with his little hand. The ogre, who wanted nothing better, suddenly seized him by the arm and put him in his bag; then he took him on his back and started for home, crying with all his lungs:

Wife, my wife,
Put the kettle on the fire,
For I have caught Buchettino!
Wife, my wife,
Put the kettle on the fire,
For I have caught Buchettino!

When the ogre was near his house he put the bag on the ground, and went off to attend to something else. Buchettino, with a knife that he had in his pocket, cut the bag open in a trice, filled it with large stones, and then:

My legs, it is no shame
To run away when there is need.

When the rascal of an ogre returned he picked up the bag, and scarcely had he arrived home when he said to his wife: "Tell me, my wife, have

BUCHETTINO. From *Italian Popular Tales*, by T. F. Crane. By permission of Houghton Mifflin Company.

you put the kettle on the fire?" She answered at once: "Yes." "Then," said the ogre, "we will cook Buchettino; come here, help me!" And both taking the bag, they carried it to the hearth and were going to throw poor Buchettino into the kettle, but instead they found only the stones. Imagine how cheated the ogre was. He was so angry that he bit his hands. He could swallow the trick played on him by Buchettino and swore to find him again and be revenged. So the next day he began to go all about the city and to look into all the hiding places. At last he happened to raise his eyes and saw Buchettino on a roof, ridiculing him and laughing so hard that his mouth extended from ear to ear. The ogre thought he should burst with rage, but he pretended not to see it and in a very sweet tone he said: "O Buchettino; just tell me, how did you manage to climb up there?"

Buchettino answered: "Do you really want to know? Then listen. I put dishes upon dishes, glasses upon glasses, pans upon pans, kettles upon kettles; afterward I climbed up on them and here I am." "Ah! is that so?" said the ogre; "wait a bit!" And quickly he took so many dishes, so many glasses, pans, kettles, and made a great mountain of them; then he began to climb up, to go and catch Buchettino. But when he was on the top—brututum—everything fell down; and that rascal of an ogre fell down on the stones and was cheated again.

Then Buchettino, well pleased, ran to his mama, who put a piece of candy in his little mouth.

THREE GREAT NOODLES

Once upon a time there were a husband and a wife who had a son. This son grew up, and said one day to his mother, "Do you know, mother, I would like to marry?" "Very well, marry! Whom do you want to take?" He answered, "I want the gardener's daughter." "She is a good girl—take her; I am willing." So he went, and asked for the girl, and her parents gave her to him. They were married, and when they were in the middle of the wedding meal, the wine gave out. The husband said, "There is no more wine!" The bride, to show that she was a good housekeeper, said, "I will go and get some." She took the bottles and went to the cellar, turned the cock, and began to think, "Suppose I should have a son, and we should call him Bastianelo, and he should die! Oh, how grieved I should be! oh, how grieved I should be!" And thereupon she began to weep and weep; and meanwhile the wine was running all over the cellar.

THREE GREAT NOODLES. From *The Book of Noodles,* by W. A. Clouston.

When they saw that the bride did not return, the mother said, "I will go and see what the matter is." So she went into the cellar, and saw the bride, with the bottle in her hand, and weeping. "What is the matter with you that you are weeping?" "Ah, my mother, I was thinking that if I had a son, and should name him Bastianelo, and he should die, oh, how I should grieve! oh, how I should grieve!" The mother, too, began to weep, and weep, and weep; and meanwhile the wine was running over the cellar.

When the people at the table saw that no one brought the wine, the groom's father said, "I will go and see what is the matter. Certainly something wrong has happened to the bride." He went and saw the whole cellar full of wine, and the mother and the bride weeping. "What is the matter?" he said; "has anything wrong happened to you?" "No," said the bride; "but I was thinking that if I had a son, and should call him Bastianelo, and he should die! oh, how I should grieve!" Then he, too, began to weep, and all three wept; and meanwhile the wine was running over the cellar.

When the groom saw that neither the bride, nor the mother, nor the father came back, he said, "Now I will go and see what the matter is that no one returns." He went into the cellar and saw all the wine running over the cellar. He hastened and stopped the cask, and then asked, "What is the matter that you are all weeping, and have let the wine run all over the cellar?" Then the bride said, "I was thinking that if I had a son and called him Bastianelo, and he should die, oh, how I should grieve! Oh, how I should grieve!" Then the groom said, "You stupid fools! Are you weeping at this and letting all the wine run into the cellar? Have you nothing else to think of? It shall never be said that I remained with you. I will roam about the world, and until I find three fools greater than you, I will not return home."

He had a bread-cake made, took a bottle of wine, a sausage, and some linen, and made a bundle, which he put on a stick and carried over his shoulder. He journeyed and journeyed, but found no fool. At last he said, worn out, "I must turn back, for I see I cannot find a greater fool than my wife." He did not know what to do, whether to go on or turn back. "Oh," said he, "it is better to try and go a little farther." So he went on, and shortly saw a man in his shirt-sleeves at a well, all wet with perspiration, and water. "What are you doing, sir, that you are so covered with water and in such a sweat?" "Oh, let me alone," the man answered; "for I have been here a long time drawing water to fill this pail, and I cannot fill it." "What are you drawing the water in?" he asked him. "In this sieve," he said. "What are you thinking about, to draw water in that sieve? Just wait!" He went to a house near by and borrowed a bucket, with which he returned to the well and filled the pail. "Thank you, good man. God knows how long I should have had to remain here!" —"Here," thought he, "is one who is a greater fool than my wife."

He continued his journey, and after a time he saw at a distance a man in his shirt, who was jumping down from a tree. He drew near, and saw a woman under the same tree, holding a pair of breeches. He asked them what they were doing, and they said that they had been there a long time, and that the man was trying on those breeches and did not know how to get into them. "I have jumped and jumped," said the man, "until I am tired out, and I cannot imagine how to get into those breeches." "Oh," said the traveller, "you might stay here as long as you wished, for you would never get into them this way. Come down and lean against the tree." Then he took his legs and put them in the breeches, and after he had put them on, he said, "Is that right?" "Very good; bless you; for it had not been for you, God knows how long I should have had to jump." Then the traveller said to himself, "I have seen two greater fools than my wife."

Then he went his way, and as he approached a city, he heard a great noise. When he drew near he asked what it was, and was told it was a marriage, and that it was the custom in that city for the brides to enter the city gate on horseback, and that there was a great discussion on this occasion between the groom and the owner of the horse, for the bride was tall and horse high, and they could not get through the gate; so that they must either cut off the bride's head or the horse's legs. The groom did not wish his bride's head cut off, and the owner of the horse did not wish his horse's legs cut off, and hence this disturbance. Then the traveller said, "Just wait," and came up to the bride and gave her a slap that made her lower her head, and then he gave the horse a kick, and so they passed through the gate and entered the city. The groom and the owner of the horse asked the traveller what he wanted, for he had saved the groom his bride and the owner of the horse his horse. He answered that he did not wish anything, and said to himself, "Two and one make three! that is enough. Now I will go home." He did so, and said to his wife, "Here I am, my wife; I have seen three greater fools than you;—now let us remain in peace, and think of nothing else." They renewed the wedding, and always remained in peace. After a time the wife had a son, whom they named Bastianelo, and Bastianelo did not die, but still lives with his father and mother.

THE HAPPY COUPLE

I can tell you a story, or two perhaps. What a number I used to know, to be sure! But what can I do? It is thirty years and more since

THE HAPPY COUPLE. From *Roman Legends,* by R. H. Busk.

anyone has asked me for them, and it's hard to put one's ideas together after such a time. You mustn't mind if I put the wrong part of the story before, and have to go backwards and forwards a little.

I know there was one that ran thus:—

There was a married couple who lived so happy and content and fond of each other, that they never had a word of dispute about anything the live-long day, but only thought of helping and pleasing each other.

The Devil saw this, and determined to set them by the ears; but how was he to do it? Such love and peace reigned in their home, that he couldn't find any way into the place. After prowling and prowling about, and finding no means of entrance, what did he do? He went to an old woman,—she must have been one of those who dabble with things they have no business to touch,—and said to her:

"You must do this job for me!"

"That's no great matter," answered the old hag. "Give me ten scudi for my niece and a new pair of shoes for me, and I'll settle the matter."

"Here are the ten scudi," said the Devil; "it will be time enough to talk about the shoes when we see how you do the business."

The bad old woman set off accordingly with her niece and the ten scudi, instructing her by the way what she was to do.

This husband and wife lived in a place where there was a house on one side and a shop on the other, so that through a window in the house where they lived they could give an eye to anything that went on in the shop.

Choosing a moment when the man was alone in the shop, she sent the girl in with the ten scudi; and the girl, who had been told what to do, selected a dress, and a handkerchief, and a number of fine things, and paid her ten scudi. Then she proceeded leisurely to put them on, and to walk up and down the shop in them. Meantime the bad old woman went up to the wife:—

"Poor woman!" she said. "Poor woman! Such a good woman as you are, and to have such a hypocrite of a husband!"

"My husband a hypocrite!" answered the wife. "What can you mean— he is the best man that ever was."

"Ah! he makes you think so, poor simple soul. But the truth is, he is very different from what you think."

So they went on conversing, and the bad old woman all the time watching what was going on in the shop till the right moment came. Just as the girl was flaunting about and showing herself off, she said:

"Look here, he has given all those things to that girl there."

And though the wife did not believe a word, curiosity prompted her to look, and there she saw the girl bowing herself out with as many thanks and adieus as if the poor man had really given her the things she had brought.

"Perhaps you will believe that!" observed the bad old woman.

"Indeed, I cannot help believing it," answered the wife, "but never

otherwise should I have thought it; and I owe you a great deal for opening my eyes"; and she gave her a whole cheese. "I know what I shall do,"
she continued, as she sobbed over her lost peace of mind; "I shall show
him I know his bad conduct by having no dinner ready for him when he
comes up by-and-by."

"That's right," said the bad old woman. "Do so, and show him you
are not going to be trampled on for the sake of a drab of a girl like that";
and she tied her cheese up in a handkerchief, and went her way.

Down she went now to the husband, and plied him with suspicions
of his wife, similar to those she had suggested to her against him. The
husband was even less willing to listen to her than the wife had been,
and when at last he drove her away, she said:

"You think she's busy all the morning preparing your dinner; but instead of that, she's talking to those you wouldn't like her to talk with. And
you see now if today she hasn't been at this game so long that she has
forgotten your dinner altogether."

The husband turned a deaf ear, and continued attending to his shop;
but when he went into the house and found no dinner ready, it seemed
as if all that the bad old woman had said was come true.

He was too sad for words, so they didn't have much of a quarrel, but
there could not but be a coldness after such an extraordinary event as a
day without dinner.

The husband went back to his shop and mused. The wife sat alone in
her room crying; presently the old hag came back to her.

"Well, did you tell him you had found him out?" she inquired.

"No! I hadn't courage to do that. And he was so patient about there
being no dinner, that I felt quite sorry to have suspected him. Oh, you
who have been so clever in pointing out my misery to me, can you tell me
some means of reconciliation?"

"Yes, there is one; but I don't know if you can manage it."

"Oh yes; I would do anything!"

"Then you must watch till he is quite sound asleep, and take a sharp
razor and cut off three hairs from the undergrowth of his beard, quite close
to the skin. If you do that it will all come right again."

"It seems a very odd remedy," said the wife; "but if you say it will do,
I suppose it will, and thank you kindly for the advice"; and she gave
another cheese.

Then the witch went back to the husband.

"I suppose I was mistaken, and you found your dinner ready after all?"
she said.

"No!" he replied; "you were right about there being no dinner; but I
am certain there was some cause for there being none, other than what
you say."

"What other cause should there be?" exclaimed the old woman.

"That I don't know," he replied. "But some other cause I am persuaded there must have been."

"Well, if you are so infatuated, I will give you another token that I am right," replied the old woman. "You don't deserve that I should save your life, but I am so goodnatured, I can't help warning you. To-night, I have reason to know, she intends to murder you. You just give some make-believe snoring, but mind you don't sleep, whatever you do; and you see if she doesn't take up one of your razors to stab you in the throat."

The good husband refused to believe a word, and drove her away. Nevertheless, when night came he felt not a little anxious; and if he had tried to sleep ever so much he could not, for he felt so excited. Then curiosity to see if the woman's words would come true overcame him, and he pretended to snore.

He had not been snoring thus long, when the wife took up the razor and came all trembling to the bedside, and lifted up his beard.

A cold sweat crept over the poor husband as she approached—not for fear of his life, which he could easily rescue, as he was awake—but because the proof seemed there that the old hag had spoken the truth. However, instead of taking it for granted it was so, and refusing to hear any justification—perhaps killing her on the spot, as she had hoped and expected,—he calmly seized her arm, and said:

"Tell me, what are you going to do with that razor?"

The wife sank on her knees by his side, crying:

"I cannot expect you to believe me, but this is really how it was. An old woman came and told me you were making love to a young girl in the shop, and showed me how she was bowing and scraping to you. I was so vexed, that to show you my anger I got no dinner ready; but afterwards, I felt as if I should like to ask you all about it, to make sure there was no mistake: only after what I had done, I didn't know how to begin speaking to you again. Then I asked the old woman if she couldn't tell me some means of bringing things straight again; and she said, if I could cut off three hairs from the undergrowth of your beard, all would come right. But I can't expect you to believe it."

"Yes, I do," replied the husband. "The same old wretch came to me, and wanted me in like manner to believe all manner of evil things of you, but I refused to believe you could do anything wrong. So I had more confidence in you than you had in me. But still we were both very nearly making ourselves very foolish and very unhappy; so we will take a lesson never to doubt each other again."

And after that there never was a word between them any more.

When the Devil saw how the old woman had spoilt the affair, he took the pair of shoes he was to have given her, and tied them on to a long cane which he fastened on the top of a mountain, and there they dangled before her eyes, but she could never get at them.

THE VALUE OF SALT

They say there was a king who had three daughters. He was very anxious to know which of them loved him most; he tried them in various ways, and it always seemed as if the youngest daughter came out best by the test. Yet he was never satisfied, because he was prepossessed with the idea that the elder ones loved him most.

One day he thought he would settle the matter once for all, by asking each separately how much she loved him. So he called the eldest by herself, and asked her how much she loved him.

"As much as the bread we eat," ran her reply; and he said within himself, "She must, as I thought, love me the most of all; for bread is the first necessary of our existence, without which we cannot live. She means, therefore, that she loves me so much she could not live without me."

Then he called the second daughter by herself, and said to her, "How much do you love me?"

And she answered, "As much as wine!"

"That is a good answer too," said the king to himself. "It is true she does not seem to love me quite so much as the eldest; but still, scarcely can one live without wine, so that there is not much difference."

Then he called the youngest by herself, and said to her, "And you, how much do you love me?"

And she answered, "As much as salt!"

Then the king said, "What a contemptible comparison! She only loves me as much as the cheapest and commonest thing that comes to table. This is as much as to say, she doesn't love me at all. I always thought it was so. I will never see her again."

Then he ordered that a wing of the palace should be shut up from the rest, where she should be served with everything belonging to her condition in life, but where she should live by herself apart, and never come near him.

Here she lived, then, all alone. But though her father fancied she did not care for him, she pined so much at being kept away from him, that at last she was worn out, and could bear it no longer.

The room that had been given her had no windows on to the street, that she might not have the amusement of seeing what was going on in the town, but they looked upon an inner court-yard. Here she sometimes saw the cook come out and wash vegetables at the fountain.

"Cook! cook!" she called one day, as she saw him pass thus under the window.

The cook looked up with a good-natured face, which gave her encouragement.

THE VALUE OF SALT. From *Roman Legends*, by R. H. Busk.

"Don't you think, cook, I must be very lonely and miserable up here all alone?"

"Yes, Signorina!" he replied; "I often think I should like to help you to get out; but I dare not think of it, the king would be so angry."

"No, I don't want you to do anything to disobey the king," answered the princess; "but would you really do me a favour, which would make me very grateful indeed?"

"O! yes, Signorina, anything which I can do without disobeying the king," replied the faithful servant.

"Then this is it," said the princess. "Will you just oblige me so far as to cook papa's dinner to-day without any salt in anything? Not the least grain in anything at all. Let it be as good a dinner as you like, but no salt in anything. Will you do that?"

"I see!" replied the cook, with a knowing nod. "Yes depend on me, I will do it."

That day at dinner the king had no salt in the soup, no salt in the boiled meat, no salt in the roast, no salt in the fried meat.

"What is the meaning of this?" said the king, as he pushed dish after dish away from him. "There is not a single thing I can eat to-day. I don't know what they have done to everything, but there is not a single thing that has got the least taste. Let the cook be called."

So the cook came before him.

"What have you done to the victuals to-day?" said the king, sternly. "You have sent up a lot of dishes, and no one alive can tell one from another. They are all of them exactly alike, and there is not one of them can be eaten. Speak!"

The cook answered:

"Hearing your Majesty say that salt was the commonest thing that comes to the table, and altogether so worthless and contemptible, I considered in my mind whether it was a thing that at all deserved to be served up to the table of the king; and judging that it was not worthy, I abolished it from the king's kitchen, and dressed all the meats without it. Barring this, the dishes are the same that are sent every day to the table of the king."

Then the king understood the value of salt, and he comprehended how great was the love of his youngest child for him; so he sent and had her apartment opened, and called her to him, never to go away any more.

ROUMANIA

It is the hour when the butterfly spreads his wing bathed in dew, and springing from his bed of flowers flies on a sunbeam towards the skies.[9]

[9] E. C. Grenville Murray, "Michaï the Brave and the Executioner," from *Songs and Legends of Roumania*.

The Roumanian peasant told tales of the animal kingdom, tales in which the elements of nature are personified—the wind, sun, moon, and rain—and "why" stories which represent the questioning of God about the creation of all things.

MICHAÏ THE BRAVE AND THE EXECUTIONER

It is the hour when the butterfly spreads his wing bathed in dew, and springing from his bed of flowers flies on a sunbeam towards the skies.

Michaï is kneeling before the Executioner. The first rays of the daylight fall broken upon his long hair. Near him is his daughter Florica. She trembles like a dew-drop in the rays of sun, and her lovely eyes shine beneath their long lashes, like two stars on the bosom of a cloud.

"Why dost thou weep, my daughter?" asks Michaï, with a noble reproach. "I die for my country, and for the faith of my fathers. Is not such a death as this honourable enough? Thou shouldst rejoice at it, and deck the tresses of thy hair with flowers. He who dies for his country should look upon the day of his death as a festival."

"On thy knees!" cries the pale Executioner. "The axe is raised above thy head, and it must fall."

Michaï gives the word. He looks steadily at the Executioner. The people murmur. Falls the axe? No! The blow is not yet struck. The headsman trembles, and kneels at the feet of Michaï, fascinated.

The people press round; they break the chains of their hero, and Michaï is carried home by them in triumph. And the young maidens dress their long hair with flowers, and every child in Roumania repeats the brave words of Michaï:

"He who dies for his country should look upon the day of his death as a festival."

HANS' ADVENTURE WITH THE SHADOWS

"Mother, where do all the shadows go to at night, when there is no more sun? They must stay somewhere, the poor shadows; they cannot be quite dead and come to life again every day."

MICHAÏ THE BRAVE AND THE EXECUTIONER. From *Songs and Legends of Roumania*, by E. C. Grenville Murray.

HANS' ADVENTURE WITH THE SHADOWS. From *A Real Queen's Fairy Tales*, by Carmen Sylva.

"The shadows have all gone into the one big shadow which night makes."

But that the little fellow would not believe, for the shadows all seemed to him so real, he could not think of them otherwise than as having their own life, and own thoughts, and particular purposes.

"Do they go to sleep?" he went on questioning.

"Yes, they sleep, and you must go to sleep, too," replied his mother.

But he could not fall asleep so easily, for it seemed to him as if shadows gathered round and beckoned to him—dark and light shadows, pretty ones and ugly ones—talking and laughing, and crying, just as if they were alive. So he sat up in his little bed and asked them why they were not asleep. His mother thought they slept, but then his mother certainly never paid so much attention to them as he did; he always watched, and saw how slowly and unwillingly they took their leave, trying to stop a little at the last minute, and drawing themselves out quite long, so as to make it all the more difficult to take them away.

"And why are you then always taken away, just when I want to play a little longer with you?" he asked, turning towards them as if they were old acquaintances.

"Are we then never to be allowed to rest?" asked a shadow.

"Rest? But you do not run about, and you have no lessons to learn!"

"And have you never noticed that everything you do we have to do it too, whether we like it or no?"

"But you have no weight at all, so you can never be tired."

"We are tired, just because we can never do what we like, but must always follow some one else."

"Besides," said another shadow, "we always have to suffer if our masters are not good, or if they are ill, or have any grief themselves, or if they simply neglect to take us out into the sun to get back our strength. If we are long, we shadows, without seeing the sun, we grow so weak we feel as if we should die."

"Where is my poor shadow?" cried Hans in consternation. "I would not go out at all to-day, although my mother wished it."

"Your shadow is so weak it cannot speak a word."

"And the other day when I was just stretching out my hand to take that apple I saw quite distinctly how the shadow shook its fist at me."

"Of course it did to warn you that the apple was not meant for you. And then the time you lifted your hand to strike your little sister, did you see what your shadow did?"

"It lifted up its hand to give me a blow!"

"Think what the world would be without us! What would a mountain look like that cast no shade? And who would care to sit under a shadow-less tree? The smallest flower has its own pretty little shadow, as neat and clearly outlined as a pencil sketch, in which the beetles can walk down and up. Only think how frightfully hot the world would be if there were no more shade. Neither human beings nor animals could bear it very long."

"But," said Hans, "does it not hurt you, then, to grow so small at midday?"

"Indeed it does; that is the dreadful time for us, for then we always think the sun is going to kill us, and we are so frightened we begin to shiver and shake, and shrink and shrivel, and the sun pursues us unpityingly, and scolds and threatens us: 'You foolish little shadows! You cannot escape me—I shall swallow you all!' "

"That is why people must rest at midday, when they have worked the whole morning, to let the shadows recover from the shock?"

"Exactly so; and we are so grateful to them when they lie down and we can hide ourselves under them, where the sun cannot reach us."

"But the evening is a good time for you, for you are all larger than life-size. And at night the whole world belongs to you."

"True we are beautiful in the evening, are we not? We are so glad to think that night is coming, and we only wish it could be much, much longer."

"What do you do, then, at night?"

"Shall we take you with us for once? But you must be very quiet, for shadows are not very robust, and are apt to take fright at the least sound. And if you make any noise they will fancy it is already day-break, and will be setting to work too early."

And Hans felt suddenly as if his eyes were opened so that he could see in the darkness, like an owl or cat. He seemed to feel himself grow lighter, too, as though he could fly, and the shadows took him with them, to dance and be merry with them. It was such fun, he felt inclined to shout for joy, but a hand was placed before his mouth, and a soft voice whispered: "Hush! Hush! No noise!" It seemed to him the strangest thing of all, that one should be quiet, and yet enjoy one's self.

It was bright moonlight, and the shadows, instead of sleeping, had met to hold their revels on the grass. They looked like great lovely nightmoths, as they danced their strange fantastic rounds.

And all at once he heard a sweet and well-known voice, and looking up he thought he saw his mother coming towards him. And though it was not herself, but only her shadow that had come to watch over him, yet from that moment he felt much safer and went fearlessly wherever the kind shadow led him.

"Do you see now, Hans," whispered his mother, "your shadow would be here among the rest if you had only been good enough, but you have spoiled its pleasure, and it may not play with the others."

"What is my poor shadow doing then?"

"It is doing what you neglected, thinking of that which you forgot, and learning what you would not learn, so that you may not again stand looking foolish when questions are put to you in the class. We little know how much we owe the shadows, who work for us while we sleep."

"But can I do nothing at all to make things pleasanter for my poor shadow?"

"You can do very much; it lies with you whether your shadow is to be as merry at night as you have been all day, or whether it is to have no pleasure at all."

Hans was quite grave for a few minutes, for he was really fond of his shadow that was such a faithful companion, and took part in all his games, and knew all his thoughts. The farther they went the better he understood to what an extent our shadows have to do and think as we do. They came upon one shadow who was struggling to carry a heavy load.

"Look, Hanschen, how that poor shadow toils to lift that weight, because its master is a miser, and never rests, day or night, from adding to his hoard. Now the shadow knows where there are riches to be found, and as its master cares for nothing else it thinks that it must help him, and so it comes at night to try to carry them off for him."

"But that is dreadful," said Hans, and he became quite thoughtful.

The moon shone in through a window where they saw a shadow hard at work sewing.

"What is it working at?" asked Hans.

"In that room lives a very poor girl who has her sick mother to keep, and when she is so tired she cannot work any longer her shadow goes on working for her to help her. Then in the morning when she comes to work quite early she finds some of it done and fancies that she must be dreaming still, or that she has gone on working in her sleep, and she is surprised not to feel more tired."

"But do the shadows never sleep?"

"They never require sleep—they have no bodies that must be rested. But look in at that other window. There sits a poor student, a young man who reads and writes till far into the night, and sometimes the whole night through. And then this shadow comes very quietly, and places itself before that lamp, so that he fancies it is going out, and his eyes close, and the shadow takes his place and works till dawn. But just before daybreak the shadow goes out into the open air, and jumps and runs with the others to refresh itself for the whole day, and the young student is refreshed, too, and wonders to find his brain so much clearer to continue his work. And when good children put their books under their pillows, so that they may know their lessons well in the morning, then the shadow comes and sits upon the bed beside them, and reads the passage over and over again, till there can be no doubt about its meaning."

"Our shadows really love us then?"

"Indeed they do; they are such good friends to us we must be very careful to do nothing that can hurt them."

Next they saw the shadow of a little girl searching for something and looking so distressed.

"It is looking for a penny which the little girl dropped yesterday, and if it can but find it it will lead her in the morning to the spot. There are not too many pence in that house, and the poor child cannot sleep for thinking of it, for unless this one is found it will mean so much less bread for all. But look, do you see what the shadow is doing now?"

Just then the shadow stopped and looked under a tuft of grass, where it spied the small coin lying. Then it pushed the blades of grass again a little on one side to mark the spot.

"Will the little girl see that in the morning?" asked Hans, anxiously.

"She will be sure to see it, for she goes about with her eyes fixed on the ground hunting everywhere for what she has lost. So her attention will be drawn to the spot, and the good shadow will again have proved itself a true friend."

Farther on there was a poor little shadow, all in rags, crying as if its heart would break.

"Why do you cry so, you poor little shadow?" asked Hans in great concern.

"Oh, Oh! They have put my little master in prison for stealing."

"For stealing?" said Hans. "But that is very bad to steal, and of course one goes to prison for it. Why did you not tell him it was wrong?"

"About that he knows nothing—about right and wrong. He lives with people who have taken great pains to teach him to pick pockets. They did not want me to see it—they always told him to beware of me—that I should some day betray him! I, his own shadow, who loves him so! And yet, it is true—I have betrayed him!"

"You have betrayed him? How, then?"

"I always have to do everything that he does, and he was not careful, and just as he was taking a purse out of a stranger's pocket I had to do the same, and the man saw me on the wall, and turned and took him by the collar, and marched him off to the police station! And he is so hungry—so dreadfully hungry! They would not give him anything to eat because he had brought nothing home for so long. And now they have locked him up, all alone in the dark, where I cannot even go in to comfort him! When he was hungry we played together—and then he forgot his hunger. But now it is so dark—I cannot go to him! And there he sits, and is so unhappy, and thinks that I betrayed him! For the old gentleman told the policeman he saw the shadow putting its hand into his pocket. Oh, what can I do? My poor, poor, little master!"

At that moment Hans felt his mother's shadow pass a hand gently over his hair, and he seemed to know what he ought to say.

"Tell me where I can find your little master, and I promise you shall both be taken in, first in my own house, then in another good house I know of where you will be taken care of and kindly treated. Trust me and do not cry any longer, for first thing in the morning we will go to the prison and fetch your little master out!"

"Ah, no! I am sure you will forget all about us."

"No, for I have a good, kind mother, whose shadow is with me now, and when I wake in the morning it will at once remind me of all that has happened this night, and we will both make haste to help you."

And onward the shadows led Hans in their midnight wandering through the beautiful wide world, and he saw everything as clearly as in the day-light—so keen had his sight become. Out of the flowercups new shadows poured every moment and began to dance and play with the shadows of pretty little children. Hans was delighted to recognize among these the shadows of his elder brother and little sisters playing together so nicely. But all at once they began to quarrel and dispute—all struggling to get possession of a moonbeam, which the smallest girl held in her hand.

"We want to shine like that!" cried the others, and tore it away from her.

Hans felt the serious, inquiring glance of his mother's shadow bent upon him. He grew very red.

"Yes, it is quite true," he said. "We did quarrel to-day and we were very cross and disagreeable—and at last we fought."

"Now look and see what the shadows are doing."

They were fighting together; they tore at one another, till the big shadows stepped in between them and separated them and ordered them off to bed.

"Away, you naughty little shadows, we cannot have you spoil sports here. Go home and tell those you belong to, in their sleep, how you are punished for their bad behavior during the day. Away! you wretched little shadows!"

And so saying the big shadow blew upon them and they were gone, like a puff of wind, nothing more was to be seen of them; they would not even be able to put themselves together again, until the children should go out into the morning sunshine.

The whole night long the musicians never tired of playing, and Hans felt happier than ever in his life before—it seemed to him as if he were in a little kingdom of his own, where everyone was trying to do some-thing or other for his special pleasure. He did not know what to say to it all, and at last, from sheer happiness, he fell asleep.

What happened to him then—how the deer carried him so carefully down the mountain, how his mother's shadow took him gently in her arms and laid him in his bed—of all that Hans knew nothing, for he slept soundly, and when he awoke very late next morning he was not so sure that it had not all been a dream, especially when he found that his mother remembered nothing either of the beautiful or sad things that had hap-pened, although he reminded her of them.

And, whenever his brothers and sisters were inclined to quarrel, he would call out: "Stop! Stop! You do not know how you will grieve the shadows!" And that always astonished them so much that he had to tell them, over and over again, the wonderful story of his night spent among the shadows.

WHY HAS THE STORK NO TAIL?

The Story of the Water of Life and Death

[This tale, though part of a longer fairy tale, is still complete in itself.]

The hero of the tale, Floria, having shown some kindness to a stork, who afterwards turns out to be the king of the storks, receives from him a feather, which when taken up at any time of danger would bring the stork to him and help him. And thus it came to pass that the hero, finding himself at one time in danger, remembered the gift of the stork. He took out the feather from the place where he had hidden it, and waved it. At once the stork appeared and asked Floria what he could do for him. He told him the king had ordered him to bring the water of life and the water of death.[10]

The stork replied that if it could possibly be got he would certainly do it for him. Returning to his palace, the stork, who was the king of the storks, called all the storks together, and asked them whether they had seen or heard or been near the mountains that knock against one another, at the bottom of which are the fountains of the water of life and death.

All the young and strong looked at one another, and not even the oldest one ventured to reply. He asked them again, and then they said they had never heard or seen anything of the water of life and death. At last there came from the rear a stork, lame on one foot, blind in one eye, and with a shrivelled-up body, and with half of his feathers plucked out. And he said, "May it please your majesty, I have been there where the mountains knock one against the other, and the proofs of it are my blinded eye and my crooked leg." When the king saw him in the state in which he was, he did not even take any notice of him.

Turning to the other storks, he said: "Is there any one among you who, for my sake, will run the risk and go to these mountains and bring the water?" Not one of the young and strong, and not even any of the older ones who were still strong replied. They all kept silence. But the

WHY HAS THE STORK NO TAIL? From *Rumanian Bird and Beast Stories*, by M. Gaster. By permission of The Folk-Lore Society, London.

[10] The water of death means a water which, poured over a body which has been cut in pieces, causes all these pieces to join together, and the wounds to heal. This restores life to the body thus joined.

lame stork said to the king, "For your sake, O Master King, I will again put my life in danger and go." The king again did not look at him, and turning to the others repeated his question; but when he saw that they all kept silence, he at last turned to the stork and said to him:

"Dost thou really believe, crippled and broken as thou art, that thou wilt be able to carry out my command?"

"I will certainly try," he said.

"Wilt thou put me to shame?" the king again said.

"I hope not; but thou must bind on my wings some meat for my food, and tie the two bottles for the water to my legs."

The other storks, on hearing his words, laughed at what they thought his conceit, but he took no notice of it. The king was very pleased, and did as the stork had asked. He tied on his wings a quantity of fresh meat, which would last him for his journey, and the two bottles were fastened to his legs. He said to him, "A pleasant journey." The stork, thus prepared for his journey, rose up into the heavens, and away he went straight to the place where the mountains were knocking against one another and prevented any one approaching the fountains of life and death. It was when the sun had risen as high as a lance that he espied in the distance those huge mountains which, when they knocked against one another, shook the earth and made a noise that struck fear and terror into the hearts of those who were a long distance away.

When the mountains had moved back a little before knocking against one another, the stork wanted to plunge into the depths and get the water. But there came suddenly to him a swallow from the heart of the mountain, and said to him, "Do not go a step further, for thou art surely lost."

"Who art thou who stops me in my way?" asked the stork angrily.

"I am the guardian spirit of these mountains, appointed to save every living creature that has the misfortune to come near them."

"What am I to do then to be safe?"

"Hast thou come to fetch water of life and death?"

"Yes."

"If that be so, then thou must wait till noon, when the mountains rest for half an hour. As soon as thou seest that a short time has passed and they do not move, then rise up as high as possible into the air, and drop down straight to the bottom of the mountain. There, standing on the ledge of the stone between the two waters, dip thy bottles into the fountains and wait until they are filled. Then rise as thou hast got down, but beware lest thou touchest the walls of the mountain or even a pebble, or thou art lost."

The stork did as the swallow had told him; he waited till noontide, and when he saw that the mountains had gone to sleep, he rose up into the air, and, plunging down into the depth, he settled on the ledge of the stone and filled his bottles. Feeling that they had been filled, he rose with them as he had got down, but when he had reached almost the top of the mountains, he touched a pebble. No sooner had he done so, when the two mountains closed furiously upon him; but they did not catch any part of him, except the tail, which remained locked up fast between the two peaks of the mountains.

With a strong movement he tore himself away, happy that he had saved his life and the two bottles with the waters of life and death, not caring for the loss of his tail.

And he returned the way he had come, and reached the palace of the king of the storks in time for the delivery of the bottles. When he reached the palace, all the storks were assembled before the king, waiting to see what would happen to the lame and blind one who had tried to put them to shame. When they saw him coming back, they noticed that he had lost his tail, and they began jeering at him and laughing, for he looked all the more ungainly, from having already been so ugly before.

But the king was overjoyed with the exploit of his faithful messenger; and he turned angrily on the storks and said, "Why are you jeering and mocking? Just look round and see where are your tails. And you have not lost them in so honourable a manner as this faithful messenger." On hearing this they turned round, and lo! one and all of them had lost their tails.

And this is the reason why they have remained without a tail to this very day.

WHY HAS THE THISTLE-FINCH RUFFLED FEATHERS?

When God created the world, he made all the creatures to be of one colour, or rather none of them of any colour at all. You see, God was too busy to bother about these little things. When he had finished making everything that he intended to make, he called all the birds together and said, "Now, I am going to paint you with nice colours."

When the birds heard that message, they came all overjoyed to God, who took his brush and dipped in various pots filled with paint and painted them one by one. When he had almost finished, who would come but the thistle-finch, with his feathers all ruffled and out of breath. When God saw the little bird, he said to him, "Well, little master, how do you look; where have you been; have you not heard my command; why did you not come in time? Now all the paint is gone, I cannot do anything for you, and it serves you right; you should have come in time like the others did." And

WHY HAS THE THISTLE-FINCH RUFFLED FEATHERS? From *Rumanian Bird and Beast Stories*, by M. Gaster. By permission of The Folk-Lore Society, London.

the little bird began to weep and said, "O God, I am quite innocent; just look at me and see what a state I am in; I was very hungry and tried to find something to eat, but could not find anything for a long time, until I espied at last a few grains of millet in a bush of thistles. So I got in and started picking. But, as soon as I moved, the thistles got hold of me and would not let me go, and the more I tried to get out, the more strongly did they hold me, and tore my feathers and dishevelled my hair, and it was only after a long tussle that I was able to get myself free and come here."

When God saw that the little bird had told the truth, and that it looked torn about and ruffled, he took pity on it and said, "Wait a little and I will see what I can do," and taking his brush he endeavoured to pick up the drops of paint which were left at the bottom of the various pots. Taking them all on the tip of his brush, he sprinkled the little bird all over with the drops of the various colours which he had picked up from the bottom of the pots, and that is the reason why the thistle-finch has so many spots and so many colours. His name has remained to this very day "little master" (domnisor in Rumanian) and also thistle-finch, because the thistles ruffled his feathers and tore at him.

RUSSIA

Ivashko, my son,
I have brought thee a bun!
Come nearer to me,
I have food here for thee![11]

The souls of men and the material facts of this world are linked together in a magic symbolism in many of the folk tales of the days of the Tzars. Facts appear to be the dominating characteristic. Humor or kindness has not been forgotten, however, as is shown in the Russian Christ of this old tale from the A. M. Afanas'ev collection.

One day St. Peter and Christ were out walking together. St. Peter was deep in thought and suddenly said: "How fine it must be to be God! If for half a day I might be God, then let me be Peter all the rest of my days!" The Lord smiled. "Your will shall be granted. Be God until nightfall." They were approaching a village and saw a peasant girl driving a flock of geese. She drove them to the meadow, left them there, and hurried back home. "Are you going to leave the geese by themselves?" St. Peter asked.

"Well, what?—guard them to-day? It's a feast day."

"But who will look after the geese?"

"God Almighty, maybe," she said, and ran away.

"Peter, you have heard her," said the Saviour. "I should have been delighted

[11] Edith M. S. Hodgetts, "Ivashko and the Witch," from *Tales and Legends from the Land of the Tzar.*

to go with you to the village feast, but then the geese might come to some harm. You are God until nightfall, and must stay and watch them." Poor Peter! He was angry; but he had to stay and guard the geese. He never again wished to be God.

THE DESERTED MINE

At the entrance of the new mine stood a group of miners. They wore leather jerkins and small lamps that flickered at their belts. The young overseer was talking to the oldest miner, whose gray beard fell untidily over his hollow chest. The old man's breath came in thin, whistling sounds; his black eyes burned like black holes shot through with strange, fantastic light; his feeble arms hung at his sides, his legs tottered under him. They called him Ivan the Silent.

"Listen, old man," said the overseer. "You can never manage the ladders. We'll put you in the bucket and lower you in."

The other miners laughed good-humoredly. "Think of old Father Ivan thinking he could go down the ladders with the best of us. Ho-ho!"

Ivan looked at the bucket they were making ready. He hadn't been lowered in a bucket since he was a baby, eighty years ago. He had been born in the old mine—the deserted one. His father had been killed in it; his mother had gone on working in his place so there might be food enough for two when he was born. He had been born down there in the eternal darkness. The first noises he remembered were sounds of picks and blasting rocks. He lay all through babyhood on an old blanket in a hole, sucking away at his milk rag. His eyes followed the flickerings of his mother's lamp. He learned to walk in the mine, his hand on the ledges of rock; and as he grew he came to know new sounds—rushing water, sudden crashing, swishing, hollow echoes. Sometimes a miner sang; sometimes he swore or groaned. Sometimes there was silence. The silences were terrible.

"Get in, old man," said the overseer.

He pushed him in and Ivan squatted down at the bottom.

"Now in the name of God you'll turn round a bit," said one.

"Look you, we'll get him down in the wink of an eye," said another.

Nevertheless, there was time for many memories as old Ivan swung and creaked down on the rusty chain. He watched the square of daylight over his head dim out until it was only a speck of gray. The lamp at his belt threw timid shadows on the damp trickling walls of the shaft. At last the daylight above him closed its gray eye and he was in the dark.

"Already the shaft is old. Old and rotten. Some day it will come crash-

THE DESERTED MINE. From *The Way of the Storyteller,* by Ruth Sawyer. Copyright 1942 by Ruth Sawyer. By permission of the Viking Press, Inc.

ing in with all the earth on top of it. Then those who are inside will stay in, and those that are out will stay out."

He said all this to himself. He never spoke aloud. No one had heard him speak in ten years. He stirred his memories about and pulled out one that he liked. He was still very little—talking some—walking as one does in such darkness—listening to everything. He had a friend, an old miner, old as he was himself now. Down there in what he called the comfortable darkness, he had told him about the Lord Jesus Christ.

"I tell you, Ivanovitch," he would say, "He has His Kingdom here, under the earth, the same as above. He is here, moving about us, often. Listen some day and you will see it is the truth. You will hear the rustle of His garments as He passes through the long galleries. If you are lucky you will see Him; if not today, why, then tomorrow."

"And do you see Him?"

At the question his friend had laughed in his throat. "Now why should I see Him! I am old—everything has grown too thick about me. But when I was little like you, Ivanovitch, I heard Him often—and saw Him. If I had not, how could I be telling you about Him now?"

One day his friend was telling him again about Jesus when there came a long sighing. And the sighing changed to a rumble and grumble, and there was a sense of tossing as if Mother Earth was shaking herself. "Pray, Ivanovitch," said the old man and he thrust him down on his knees.

So, for the first time in his life he had prayed. He did not know what this praying was supposed to be like, so all he said was: "Good Jesus, good old Jesus."

He said it over a great many times and after that he put his hands in his friend's and together they felt their way down to the other end of the pit where his mother had been working. All they found was a mountain of fresh earth and underneath her boots sticking out. He had tried to get those boots. He had tugged and tugged but the mine held them fast.

He had a playmate, a little boy like himself. One day they were playing at being miners, each with a pick of his own. Some way a stone became dislodged in the vault over them. It came crashing down, straight on top of the playmate, and that was the end of him. When Ivan was half grown he lost his old friend, too. He tripped on one of the ladders and came tumbling down the shaft. They buried him above ground in the churchyard. He was the only one of all Ivan knew who had been buried above ground.

Ivan grew up and became a miner. His eyes were all now for his pick and bright masses of ore he struck. He saw Jesus no longer and forgot how His garments sounded rustling through the long galleries. Long ago they had left the old mine, deserted it. The new mine held no memories.

Down went the bucket—down went Ivan. All round him now sounded rushing water. "There is too much water," he said to himself. "If Jesus comes into the new mine He will see it is not safe, that shaft. If He pays no attention to it, it will go quickly one day."

The bucket scraped on the bottom. The old miner got out and shouldered his pickax. He tottered forward, mumbling: "Earth—water—darkness— they are all in God's hands."

He passed other miners who spoke to him kindly but with humor: "See who comes here!" . . . "Good day, Father." . . . "Here's better walking." He answered them all alike—with a doffing of his old cap. He never spoke.

The gallery where he worked was high. He felt at home here. Sometimes when a terrible feeling of loneliness came over him he would sleep here all night. The comfortable security of the dark—that was the way he felt about it. The sun frightened him: it was too big and blazing. The stars he liked: they were small and friendly. He liked flowers. Sometimes he brought down clumps of sod with daisies growing in them. The water kept them alive for days; they gleamed like stars in the flicker of his lamp.

He began to work. Then he rested—he was tired. He looked out for rock that was not so hard to break. When he had a pile, he broke the metal out and put it on the wheelbarrow, to wheel into the main gallery. This was hard work. He stumbled and fell many times. It was exhaustion that felled him. When he passed his fellow-workers, one stopped him. "Here, wait a minute, I'll help you."

But another laughed. "What, do you think now that anyone is allowed to help old Father Ivan? He is the proud, ancient one."

Ivan brushed away angrily the one who had come to help. He lifted his shoulders, he straightened his tottering legs, he pushed on with his barrow.

The others watched him go, wagging their heads with approval. "He is as proud as Croesus," laughed one. "He is the ancient child," said another and tapped his forehead meaningly.

And then someone cried out: "God! What was that!"

A few paces ahead Ivan dropped his barrow and stood huddled over it. No one stirred. It began with a sound of deep breathing, not human but the earth's. It was as if the mountain over them was taking a gust of air into its lungs. Far off at first, then closer and closer. A rush of wind came upon them and blew out all their lights; water started gushing down on them from everywhere. Miners came running from other galleries like sheep in a pen. Only Ivan stood quite still.

The overseer came hurrying up—he had a lighted torch. They stumbled after him toward the shaft. There they came upon nothing but a mountain of fresh damp earth, and half of the bucket that had lowered Ivan into the mine. Under the earth one could see a face with eyelids set, and far from that a hand still clutching a slice of bread with salt on it. At the bottom of the pile the earth was changing fast to mud. At that rate, Ivan said to himself, it wouldn't take long to flood the mine.

"We are lost!" shouted one miner.

"Caught like rats in a trap!" screamed another.

Panic took them. They dug their nails into the rock that penned them in. They trod on each other; they clawed each other's faces. They cursed like madmen.

"Stop!" The overseer kept shouting at them. "It will not save your skins to kill your neighbors. Come! On to the long gallery—there may be a way out!"

The overseer led. They followed, quieted a little. But in the long gallery it was no better. Air was growing thin; water rushed at their heels. "Half an hour and we'll all be choking," groaned one. "If we knew the way into the old mine," said another. And another answered, crying out with hope: "Always as a boy I was told there was a way from the new into the old mine."

Hope was killed the next moment. "What of it? No one knows the way. Better die here where we know where we are than go wandering, lost into strange parts."

Behind them came another sound of shifting earth, soft, caressing. Then a crash: earth, rocks, driving water. Then a tumbling at their very backs. "We can't go back." . . . "We're shut off." . . . "God have mercy on our souls!"

A worse panic took them. They dug like beasts at the mass that shut them in until their nails hung torn and bleeding. They beat at one another with fists as hard as rock. They would have gone quite mad if something had not happened. Ivan took the torch from the overseer and spoke. It was the first time in ten years he had spoken, and the men in their amazement forgot their terror and stopped to listen.

"Hush," he was saying, "keep quiet, you men." His voice was strong, his eyes blazed. "How will we hear the rustle of His garments if you make such noise?"

"Look at him—he has gone mad," whispered one. But they kept listening to him just the same.

He was cocking his ear now, his eyes were searching the dark, narrow passage ahead. He kept sucking his lips in and out in a hushing sound. At last a look of foolish delight swept his face. "Ah, what did I tell you? Look! There He goes, the light about His head, just as I remember seeing it as a child. It is seventy years since I have seen Him."

He swung the torch above his head, beckoning. Then he stepped his way into the passage, crying: "I come, Lord, I come!"

"Stop!" cried the overseer. "What in the name of saints and devils do you see?"

Ivan turned. "See? What you yourself see. Come. It is Jesus. He will lead us safely out." He turned away and started along the passage again, repeating his cry: "I come, Lord, I come!"

Holding their breath, not daring to speak, they followed, to a man. At the end of the passage they came upon a blank wall. No way dismayed,

Ivan pointed to the loose earth at the bottom and bade the men dig. "See"—he pointed—"His shining footsteps. He marches through the darkness like the sun."

Amazed, doubting, the men plied their picks. The rock crumbled. In no time there was an aperture. Gusts of fresh air rushed through. The men crowded about the diggers, pulling bits of rock away with their bare hands. Ivan slipped through the opening; the others followed. He led them along winding galleries; he led them through fissures and around yawning chasms where they could hear water rushing forty feet below; along narrow ledges with sheer walls on one side and horrible precipices on the other, where they had to crawl on hands and knees; and always Ivan leading with his cry: "I come, Lord, I come!"

He was sobbing with eagerness now, like a child. In and out, through this gallery and that, he wound. The floor of rock under them now was dry. Water no longer dripped from roof and walls. Suddenly he stopped, stock-still, and looked above his head. The men crowded and looked. They saw a small gray eye. They had reached the shaft of the deserted mine.

A hoarse shout went up, but it died as quickly as it had been born.

"The ladders are rotten as dead fish."

"A man might as well try to climb to heaven on cobwebs."

"What good is it to us to see daylight if we cannot reach it!"

"Let one of us try the ladders," said the overseer. "If one can get to the top, he can fetch ropes for the rest."

They turned, one to another, appraising, comparing. Who was the lightest, the most agile? Who had courage to try? No one noticed Ivan. He was following the rise of the ladders, as if watching for a signal. Suddenly he placed his old tottering legs on the first rung. He was thirty feet up the shaft before the others saw him.

"Merciful God."

"He will fall in a second and come down like a bag of stones."

"Look you," said the overseer, "Ivan is climbing on faith."

They climbed after him. Quickly, breathlessly; so close they went it was as if each man mounted on the next man's shoulders. Up and up—they could hear Ivan's panting breath. At last they were above ground; strong Mother Earth was under their feet. Ivan scanned the blazing blue sky over him for an instant. He looked frightened, bewildered. Then he smiled suddenly, his face alight with the radiance of his Lord whom he had followed. Down he went like a tottering old tree. Only the overseer caught his last cry: "I come, Lord, I come!"

IVASHKO AND THE WITCH

In a pleasant little Russian village a long, long time ago, there lived an old peasant and his wife, who had an only son, by name Ivashko, whom they dearly loved.

One bright summer morning Ivashko asked his parents to let him go fishing in a little lake hard by.

"Fishing!" exclaimed his mother, "how can so small a boy as you go a-fishing? You would surely drown yourself!"

"No, mother dear!" replied the boy, "I will not drown myself, but will bring you some fish for supper. So please let me go!"

The old woman at last consented, and, dressing him up in a little white shirt and a red sash, let him go.

Ivashko, when he came to the lake, got into his father's little boat and cried,—

> Little boat, little boat, swim farther!
> Little boat, little boat, swim farther!

Away swam the little boat, far into the middle of the lake, and Ivashko began fishing. He caught so many fish that the little boat soon became quite full. Still he went on catching more, when he suddenly heard his father's voice calling to him,—

> Ivashko, my son,
> I have brought thee a bun!
> Come nearer to me,
> I have food here for thee!

So Ivashko said to the little boat,—

"Swim across, little boat, to the shore, for my father is calling me."

Back went the little boat to the side of the lake, where the father stood waiting. He gave his little son something to eat and drink, and then, taking all the fish out of the boat, let Ivashko go on with his fishing.

> Little boat, little boat, swim farther!

cried the boy.

When he had got to the middle he commenced fishing again, and caught still more fish than he had before.

After a little while he heard his mother's voice calling him,—

IVASHKO AND THE WITCH. From *Tales and Legends from the Land of the Tzar,* by Edith M. S. Hodgetts.

> Ivashko, my son,
> I have brought thee a bun!
> Come nearer to me,
> I have food here for thee!

Ivashko again told his boat to swim to the shore, and, giving his mother the fish, he took his food, and returned to fishing.

It so happened that a wicked old witch had been listening to the call of the boy's parents, and wondered whether she could imitate the peasants' voices, and get Ivashko and the fish, for she was very hungry. So she went to the shore, and called out in a thin voice,—

> Ivashko, my son,
> I have brought thee a bun!
> Come nearer to me,
> I have food here for thee!

The voice was so like that of Ivashko's mother that the boy thought it was she, and told the boat to swim towards the shore. But, alas! what was his horror when the witch suddenly seized him and his fish, and took them home to her hut, where she told her daughter, Alenka, to heat the stove and bake Ivashko for her dinner, while she went to invite some of her fellow-witches to make merry!

Alenka obeyed, and when the stove was heated she turned to Ivashko, and said,—

"Get on to this stove, so that I may push you in!"

"Alas!" answered the cunning boy, "I was born stupid, and know nothing, not even how to get into a stove; but if you will but show me, I daresay I shall be able to manage it then."

"All right!" replied the girl, as she jumped on to the stove.

Ivashko quickly pushed her in, and closed the stove door, letting the unfortunate girl bake in his stead! He then ran out, locking the door behind him, and climbed up an old tree that spread its leafy branches over the little hut.

Very soon Ivashko saw the witch march up to her little dwelling, accompanied by her friends, but, finding the door locked, the hag grumbled, and climbed in at the window, saying,—

"That bad girl has gone for a walk and locked the door; but no matter, as long as she has cooked the boy I don't care, for I am hungry."

She then opened the door, and asked her guests to walk in. Soon the witches were dancing around and singing. "We shall roll, and we shall play, with the boy Ivashko's bones!"

When Ivashko heard this he was greatly amused, and said, in a very low tone of voice,—

"You will roll, you will play, with the girl Alenka's bones!"

"We shall roll, and we shall play, with the boy Ivashko's bones!"
"I heard something very strange!" said one of the witches.
"Oh, no it was nothing but the leaves of the tree!" returned the hostess.
And they chanted as before,—
"We shall roll, and we shall play, with the boy Ivashko's bones!"
Still Ivashko continued,—
"You will roll, you will play, with the girl Alenka's bones!"
This time all the witches heard the voice, ran out of the house and looking up to the tree, the witch saw Ivashko sitting laughing at her, as though he enjoyed the joke! The witch, greatly enraged, flew to the tree and began biting it; but she soon broke her front teeth in doing so!
Ivashko was now at a loss what to do, when suddenly he beheld some black swans flying towards him, so he called out to them,—

> Swans of the air,
> Lift me with care,
> And carry me home
> O'er the water's foam!

But the swans replied,—
"Let the next set take the boy!"
And tossing up their proud heads, they flew haughtily away.
Soon the next set came flying: they were of the beautiful grey colour. When Ivashko saw them, he called out again,—

> Swans of the air,
> Lift me with care,
> And carry me home
> O'er the water's foam!

But these were as haughty as the first, and answered,—
"Let the other set take the boy!"
Soon a set of beautiful white swans came in sight, and Ivashko cried out to them,—

> Swans of the air,
> Lift me with care,
> And carry me home
> O'er the water's foam!

These, however, consented; they made him sit on their wings, and away they went, leaving the witch to storm and rage, and break her teeth as much as she pleased!
Away went the swans over the water, until they reached Ivashko's home. They put him down very carefully, and flew away.

Ivashko's mother was baking cakes, and while doing so she said sadly to her husband,—

"Would that I knew whither our darling boy has gone! I wish I could see him in my dreams!"

The old woman sighed, and after she had baked the cakes she began to divide them between herself and her husband, saying,—

"Well, old man—this is for you—this is for me—this is for you—and this for me!"

"And what is for me?" asked Ivashko, at the door; for he had heard everything that had been said. "You say, 'This is for you, and this for me' but you have quite forgotten me!"

The mother gave a cry of delight, and in another moment she and her little son were locked in a warm embrace. Ivashko then told his parents all that had happened to him since last he saw them.

The peasants lived very happily ever after with their little boy, and were troubled no more by his disappearance, and so ends the story of Ivashko and the witch.

THE CAT, THE COCK, AND THE FOX

Once there was an old man who had a cat and a cock. The old man went to work in the woods; the cat brought him some food and the cock was left to watch the house. Just then a fox came to the house.

> Cock-a-doodle-doo, little cock,
> Golden crest!
> Look out the window
> And I'll give you a pea.

Thus sang the fox as he sat under the window. The cock opened the window and poked out his head to see who was singing. The fox snatched the cock in his claws and carried him off to eat him for dinner. The cock cried out: "The fox is carrying me away, he is carrying the cock beyond dark forests, into distant lands, into foreign countries, beyond thrice nine lands, into the thirtieth kingdom and the thrice tenth empire! Cat Cotonaevich, rescue me!" In the field the cat heard the cock's voice, rushed after him, overtook the fox, rescued the cock, and brought him home. "Now mind, Petya," said the cat to the cock, "don't look out of the window again, don't trust the fox; he'll eat you up, bones and all!"

THE CAT, THE COCK, AND THE FOX. From *Russian Fairy Tales;* translated by Norbert Guterman. By permission of Pantheon Books Inc.

Once again the old man went to work in the woods and the cat went to bring him food. Before leaving, the old man told the cock to watch the house and not to look out of the window. But the fox was wily; he wanted very badly to eat the cock; so he came to the hut and began to sing:

> Cock-a-doodle-doo, little cock,
> Golden crest!
> Look out the window
> And I'll give you a pea—
> I'll give you seeds too.

The cock walked about the room and did not answer. Once again the fox sang his song and cast a pea in through the window. The cock ate the pea and said: "No, fox, you cannot fool me! You want to eat me, bones and all." "Don't say such things, Petya. I have no idea of eating you. I just wanted you to pay me a visit, to see my house and take a walk around my estate." And he sang again:

> Cock-a-doodle-doo, little cock,
> Golden crest!
> I gave you a pea,
> I'll give you seeds too.

The cock looked out of the window and at once the fox snatched him in his claws. The cock cried in a shrill voice: "The fox is carrying me off, carrying the cock beyond dark woods, beyond thick forests, along steep banks, up high mountains! He wants to eat me, bones and all!" In the field the cat heard him, rushed after him, rescued him, and brought him home. "Did I not tell you not to open the window, not to poke out your head, or the fox would eat you, bones and all? Listen now, heed my words! Tomorrow we shall be even farther away."

Again the old man went to work and again the cat went to bring him his food. The fox stole under the window and began to sing the same song; he sang it three times, but the cock remained silent. The fox said: "What's the matter, has Petya become dumb?" "No, fox, you cannot fool me, I won't look out of the window." The fox cast a pea and several wheat grains in at the window and again sang:

> Cock-a-doodle-doo, little cock,
> Golden crest,
> Butter head,
> Look out the window!
> I have a big mansion:
> In every corner
> There's a measure of wheat;
> Eat your fill!

Then he added: "And, Petya, you should also see my collection of curios! Don't believe the cat; if I wanted to eat you, I would have done so long ago. The truth is, I like you, I want to show you the world, to develop your mind, to teach you how to live. Now show yourself, Petya! I'll go behind a corner," and he concealed himself closer to the wall. The cock jumped up on a bench and looked through the window from a distance; he wanted to see whether the fox was still there. Then he poked his head out of the window, and at once the fox snatched him and darted off. The cock sang the same tune as before, but the cat did not hear him. The fox carried the cock away and ate him up behind a fir grove, leaving only his tail feathers for the wind to scatter. The old man and the cat came home and discovered that the cock was gone. They were deeply distressed and said to each other: "This is what comes of not heeding warnings!"

A SOLDIER'S RIDDLE

Two soldiers on a trip stopped to rest in an old woman's house. They asked for some food and drink, but the old woman said: "What shall I offer you? I have nothing, my boys." Yet in her oven she had a boiled cock in a pot under the roasting pan. The soldiers guessed this; one of them—who was a roguish fellow—went out into the yard, upset a cart full of sheaves of grain, returned to the house, and said: "Little grandmother, go out, the cattle are eating your grain." The old woman went out and the soldiers peered into the oven, took the cock out of the pot, put an old shoe in the pot instead, and hid the cock in their bag. The old woman came back and said: "My dear boys, didn't you set the cattle loose? Why do you cause mischief like that? Don't do that again, please." The soldiers sat in silence awhile, then asked again: "Please, little grandmother, give us something to eat." "Take some kvass and bread, my boys; that will do."

Then the old woman wanted to crow because she had cheated them and proposed a riddle to them: "Well, my boys, you've traveled a lot, you've seen the world. Now tell me—is Mr. Cock Cockson still living in Ovenia, at Potburg near Pantown?" "No, little grandmother." "Who, then, is living there?" "Mr. Shoe Shoeson." "And what has happened to Mr. Cock Cockson?" "He moved to Bagville, little grandmother." After that the soldiers left. The old woman's son returned from the field and asked her for some food. She said: "Imagine, my son, some soldiers came by here and asked me for something to eat. But instead of giving it to them I posed

A SOLDIER'S RIDDLE. From *Russian Fairy Tales;* translated by Norbert Guterman. By permission of Pantheon Books Inc.

them a riddle about the cock that I have in the oven, and they couldn't solve it." "And what riddle did you pose them, mother?" "This one—'Is Mr. Cock Cockson still living in Ovenia, at Potburg, near Pantown?' They did not solve it. They said: 'No, little grandmother.' 'But where is he?' I asked them. 'He has moved to Bagville,' they said. They never guessed what I had in my pot." She looked into the oven, but the cock had flown away; she dragged out only an old shoe. "Ah, my little son, those accursed fellows robbed me after all." "You should have known better, mother; a soldier knows the world, he cannot be cheated!"

THE TURNIP

Grandfather planted a turnip. The time came to pick it. He took hold of it, and pulled and pulled, but he couldn't pull it out. Grandfather called grandmother; grandmother pulled grandfather, and grandfather pulled the turnip. They pulled and pulled, but they couldn't pull it out. Then their granddaughter came; she pulled grandma, grandma pulled grandpa, grandpa pulled the turnip; they pulled and they pulled, but they couldn't pull it out. Then the puppy came; he pulled the granddaughter, she pulled grandma, grandma pulled grandpa, grandpa pulled the turnip; they pulled and they pulled, but they couldn't pull it out. Then a beetle came; the beetle pulled the puppy, the puppy pulled the granddaughter, she pulled grandma, grandma pulled grandpa, grandpa pulled the turnip; they pulled and they pulled, but they couldn't pull it out. Then came a second beetle. The second beetle pulled the first beetle, the first beetle pulled the puppy, the puppy pulled the granddaughter, she pulled grandma, grandma pulled grandpa, grandpa pulled the turnip; they pulled and they pulled, but they couldn't pull it out. (Repeated for a third beetle, and a fourth.) Then the fifth beetle came. He pulled the fourth beetle, the fourth beetle pulled the third, the third pulled the second, the second pulled the first, the first beetle pulled the puppy, the puppy pulled the granddaughter, she pulled grandma, grandma pulled grandpa, grandpa pulled the turnip; they pulled and they pulled, and they pulled out the turnip.

SCANDINAVIA

"If you cut down my trees, I'll kill you!" said the troll.

This is the antagonist of so many of the Norse tales—the troll, a supernatural being who lived in the rocky, barren cliff or the wild pine forest.

THE TURNIP. From *Russian Fairy Tales;* translated by Norbert Guterman. By permission of Pantheon Books Inc.

He was supposed to be the evil one who might have had a wish to cause death.

The other conflicting force is the giant, whose powers lie in his strength and size rather than in his cunning or wit. The action in these stories is strong and dramatic, with a sense of humor and carefree attitude that makes delightful storytelling.

ASHIEPATTLE AND THE TROLL

There was once upon a time a peasant who had three sons. He was badly off, and old and feeble, and the sons would not do any work.

To the farm belonged a large pine forest, and the father wanted his sons to cut timber in it, and try to get some of his debts paid off. At last he got them to listen to him, and the eldest one was to go out first and fell trees. When he got into the forest and began felling an old bearded pine, a great big troll came up to him.

"If you cut down my trees, I'll kill you!" said the troll.

When the lad heard this, he threw down the axe and set off home as fast as he could. He got there quite out of breath, and told what had happened to him, but the father said he was chicken-hearted; the trolls had never frightened him from felling trees when he was young, he said.

The next day the second son was to go, and the same thing happened to him. He had no sooner struck some blows at the pine than the troll came and said:

"If you cut down my trees, I'll kill you!"

The lad hardly dared to look at him; he threw down the axe and took to his heels, just like his brother, only rather quicker.

When he came home the father became angry, and said that the trolls had never frightened him when he was young.

On the third day Ashiepattle wanted to set out.

"You indeed!" said the two eldest; "you'll never be able to do anything, you who have never been outside the door!"

Ashiepattle did not answer, but only asked for plenty of food to take with him. His mother had nothing ready, and so she put on the pot and made a cheese for him, which he placed in his scrip, and then set out from home. When he had been felling trees awhile, the troll came to him and said:

"If you cut down my trees, I'll kill you!"

ASHIEPATTLE AND THE TROLL. From *Fairy Tales from the Far North,* by P. C. Asbjornsen.

But the lad was not slow; he ran into the forest for the cheese and squeezed it, so that the whey spurted from it.

"If you don't be quiet," he shouted to the troll, "I'll squeeze you just as I squeeze the water out of this white stone."

"Oh dear, oh dear! Spare me! You can cut all the trees you want!" and the troll ran off into the forest and was never seen again.

ANOTHER HAUNTED MILL

Once on a time there was a mill; this mill was not in these parts, it was somewhere up the country. No one could grind a grain of corn in it for weeks together, when something came and haunted it. But the worst was that, besides haunting it, the trolls, or whatever they were, took to burning the mill down. Two Whitsun-eves running it had caught fire and burned to the ground.

Well, the third year, as Whitsuntide was drawing on, the man had a tailor in his house hard by the mill, who was making Sunday-clothes for the miller.

"I wonder, now," said the man on Whitsun-eve, "whether the mill will burn down this Whitsuntide, too?"

"No, it shan't," said the tailor. "Why should it? Give me the keys: I'll watch the mill."

Well, the man thought that brave, and so, as the evening drew on, he gave the tailor the keys, and showed him into the mill. It was empty, you know, for it was just new-built, and so the tailor sat down in the middle of the floor, and took out his chalk and chalked a great circle round about him, and outside the ring all round he wrote the Lord's Prayer, and when he had done that he wasn't afraid—no, not if Old Nick himself came.

So at dead of night the door flew open with a bang, and there came in such a swarm of black cats you couldn't count them; they were as thick as ants. They were not there long before they had put a big pot on the fireplace and set light under it, and the pot began to boil and bubble, and as for the broth, it was for all the world like pitch and tar.

"Ha! ha!" thought the tailor, "that's your game, is it!"

And he had hardly thought this before one of the cats thrust her paw under the pot and tried to upset it.

"Paws off, pussy," said the tailor, "you'll burn your whiskers."

"Hark to the tailor, who says, 'Paws off, pussy,' to me," said the cat to the other cats, and in a trice they all ran away from the fireplace, and be-

ANOTHER HAUNTED MILL. From *Tales from the Fjeld,* by Sir George Dasent. By permission of G. P. Putnam's Sons.

gan to dance and jump round the circle; and then all at once the same cat stole off to the fireplace and tried to upset the pot.

"Paws off, pussy, you'll burn your whiskers," bawled out the tailor again, and again he scared them from the fireplace.

"Hark to the tailor, who says 'Paws off, pussy,'" said the cat to the others, and again they all began to dance and jump round the circle, and then all at once they were off again to the pot, trying to upset it.

"Paws off, pussy, you'll burn your whiskers," screamed out the tailor the third time, and this time he gave them such a fright that they tumbled head over heels on the floor, and began dancing and jumping as before.

Then they closed round the circle, and danced faster and faster: so fast at last that the tailor's head began to turn round, and they glared at him with such big ugly eyes, as though they would swallow him up alive.

Now just as they were at the fastest, the same cat which had tried so often to upset the pot, stuck her paw inside the circle, as though she meant to claw the tailor. But as soon as the tailor saw that, he drew his knife out of the sheath and held it ready; just then the cat thrust her paw in again, and in a trice the tailor chopped it off, and then, pop! all the cats took to their heels as fast as they could, with yells and caterwauls, right out at the door and were never seen again on Whitsun-eve.

THE CAT ON THE DOVREFELL

Once on a time there was a man up in Finnmark who had caught a great white bear, which he was going to take to the King of Denmark. Now, it so fell out that he came to the Dovrefell just about Christmas Eve, and there he turned into a cottage where a man lived, whose name was Halvor, and asked the man if he could get house-room there for his bear and himself.

"Heaven never help me, if what I say isn't true!" said the man; "but we can't give any one house-room just now, for every Christmas Eve such a pack of Trolls come down upon us that we are forced to flit, and haven't so much as a house over our own heads, to say nothing of lending one to any one else."

"Oh!" said the man, "if that's all, you can very well lend me your house; my bear can lie under the stove yonder, and I can sleep in the side-room."

Well, he begged so hard, that at last he got leave to stay there; so the people of the house went out, and before they went everything was got ready for the Trolls; the tables were laid, and there was rice porridge, and

THE CAT ON THE DOVREFELL. From *Popular Tales from the Norse*, by Sir George Dasent. By permission of G. P. Putnam's Sons.

fish boiled in lye, and sausages, and all else that was good, just as for any other grand feast.

So, when everything was ready, down came the Trolls. Some were great, and some were small; some had long tails, and some had no tails at all; some, too, had long, long noses; and they ate and drank, and tasted everything. Just then one of the little Trolls caught sight of the white bear, who lay under the stove; so he took a piece of sausage and stuck it on a fork, and went and poked it up against the bear's nose, screaming out,—

"Pussy, will you have some sausage?"

Then the white bear rose up and growled, and hunted the whole pack of them out of doors, both great and small.

Next year Halvor was out in the wood on the afternoon of Christmas Eve, cutting wood before the holidays, for he thought the Trolls would come again; and just as he was hard at work, he heard a voice in the wood calling out—

"Halvor! Halvor!"

"Well," said Halvor, "here I am."

"Have you got your big cat with you still?"

"Yes, that I have," said Halvor; "she's lying at home under the stove, and what's more, she has now got seven kittens, far bigger and fiercer than she is herself."

"Oh, then, we'll never come to see you again," bawled out the Troll away in the wood, and he kept his word; for since that time the Trolls have never eaten their Christmas brose with Halvor on the Dovrefell.

THE LAD WHO WENT TO THE NORTH WIND

Once on a time there was an old widow who had one son and as she was poorly and weak, her son had to go up into the safe to fetch meal for cooking; but when he got outside the safe, and was just going down the steps, there came the North Wind, puffing and blowing, caught up the meal, and so away with it through the air. Then the lad went back into the safe for more; but when he came out again on the steps, if the North Wind didn't come again and carry off the meal with a puff; and more than that, he did so the third time. At this the lad got very angry; and as he thought it hard that the North Wind should behave so, he thought he'd just look him up, and ask him to give up his meal.

So off he went, but the way was long, and he walked and walked; but at last he came to the North Wind's house.

THE LAD WHO WENT TO THE NORTH WIND. From *Popular Tales from the Norse*, by Sir George Dasent. By permission of G. P. Putnam's Sons.

"Good day!" said the lad, and "thank you for coming to see us yester-day."

"GOOD DAY!" answered the North Wind, for his voice was loud and gruff, "AND THANKS FOR COMING TO SEE ME. WHAT DO YOU WANT?"

"Oh!" answered the lad, "I only wished to ask you to be so good as to let me have back that meal you took from me on the safe steps, for we haven't much to live on; and if you're to go on snapping up the morsel we have there'll be nothing for it but to starve."

"I haven't got your meal," said the North Wind; "but if you are in such need, I'll give you a cloth which will get you everything you want, if you only say, 'Cloth, spread yourself, and serve up all kinds of good dishes!' "

With this the lad was well content. But, as the way was long he couldn't get home in one day, so he turned into an inn on the way; and when they were going to sit down to supper, he laid the cloth on a table which stood in the corner and said,—

"Cloth, spread yourself, and serve up all kinds of good dishes."

He had scarce said so before the cloth did as it was bid; and all who stood by thought it a fine thing, but most of all the landlady. So, when all were fast asleep, at dead of night, she took the lad's cloth and put another in its stead, just like the one he had got from the North Wind, but which couldn't so much as serve up a bit of dry bread.

So, when the lad woke, he took his cloth and went off with it, and that day he got home to his mother.

"Now," said he, "I've been to the North Wind's house, and a good fellow he is, for he gave me this cloth, and when I only say to it, 'Cloth, spread yourself, and serve up all kinds of good dishes,' I get any sort of food I please."

"All very true, I daresay," said his mother; "but seeing is believing, and I shan't believe it till I see it."

So the lad made haste, drew out a table, laid the cloth on it, and said,—

"Cloth, spread yourself, and serve up all kind of good dishes."

But never a bit of dry bread did the cloth serve up.

"Well," said the lad, "there's no help for it but to go to the North Wind again"; and away he went.

So he came to where the North Wind lived late in the afternoon.

"Good evening!" said the lad.

"Good evening!" said the North Wind.

"I want my rights for that meal of ours which you took," said the lad; "for as for that cloth I got, it isn't worth a penny."

"I've got no meal," said the North Wind; "but yonder you have a ram which coins nothing but golden ducats as soon as you say to it—

" 'Ram, ram! make money!' "

So the lad thought this a fine thing; but as it was too far to get home that day, he turned in for the night to the same inn where he had slept before.

Before he called for anything, he tried the truth of what the North Wind had said of the ram, and found it all right; but when the landlord saw that, he thought it was a famous ram, and, when the lad had fallen asleep, he took another which couldn't coin gold ducats, and changed the two.

Next morning off went the lad; and when he got home to his mother, he said,—

"After all, the North Wind is a jolly fellow; for now he has given me a ram which can coin golden ducats if I only say, 'Ram, ram! make money!' "

"All very true, I daresay," said his mother; "but I shan't believe any such stuff until I see the ducats made."

"Ram, ram! make money!" said the lad; but if the ram made anything it wasn't money.

So the lad went back again to the North Wind, and blew him up, and said the ram was worth nothing, and he must have his rights for the meal.

"Well," said the North Wind; "I've nothing else to give you but that old stick in the corner yonder; but it's a stick of that kind that if you say—

" 'Stick, stick! lay on!' it lays on till you say—

" 'Stick, stick! now stop!' "

So, as the way was long, the lad turned in this night too to the landlord; but as he could pretty well guess how things stood as to the cloth and the ram, he lay down at once on the bench and began to snore, as if he were asleep.

Now the landlord, who easily saw that the stick must be worth something, hunted up one which was like it, and when he heard the lad snore, was going to change the two, but just as the landlord was about to take it the lad bawled out—

"Stick, stick! lay on!"

So the stick began to beat the landlord, till he jumped over chairs, and tables, and benches, and yelled and roared,—

"Oh my! oh my! bid the stick be still, else it will beat me to death, and you shall have back both your cloth and your ram."

When the lad thought the landlord had got enough, he said—

"Stick, stick! now stop!"

Then he took the cloth and put it into his pocket, and went home with his stick in his hand, leading the ram by a cord round its horns; and so he got his rights for the meal he had lost.

THE THREE AUNTS

Once on a time there was a poor man who lived in a hut far away in the wood, and got his living by shooting. He had an only daughter, who was very pretty, and as she had lost her mother when she was a child, and was now half grown up, she said she would go out into the world and earn her bread.

"Well, lassie!" said the father, "true enough you have learnt nothing here but how to pluck birds and roast them, but still you may as well try to earn your bread."

So the girl went off to seek a place, and when she had gone a little while, she came to a palace. There she stayed and got a place, and the queen liked her so well that all the other maids got envious of her. So they made up their minds to tell the queen how the lassie said she was good to spin a pound of flax in four-and-twenty hours, for you must know the queen was a great housewife, and thought much of good work.

"Have you said this? Then you shall do it," said the queen; "but you may have a little longer time if you choose."

Now, the poor lassie dared not say she had never spun in all her life, but she only begged for a room to herself. That she got, and the wheel and the flax were brought up to her. There she sat sad and weeping, and knew not how to help herself. She pulled the wheel this way and that, and twisted and turned it about, but she made a poor hand of it, for she had never even seen a spinning-wheel in her life.

But all at once, as she sat there, in came an old woman to her.

"What ails you, child?" she said.

"Ah!" said the lassie, with a deep sigh, "it's no good to tell you, for you'll never be able to help me."

"Who knows?" said the old wife. "Maybe I know how to help you after all."

Well, thought the lassie to herself, I may as well tell her, and so she told her how her fellow-servants had given out that she was good to spin a pound of flax in four-and-twenty hours.

"And here am I, wretch that I am, shut up to spin all that heap in a day and a night, when I have never seen a spinning-wheel in all my born days."

"Well, never mind, child," said the old woman, "if you'll call me Aunt on the happiest day of your life, I'll spin this flax for you, and so you may just go away and lie down to sleep."

Yes, the lassie was willing enough, and off she went and lay down to sleep.

THE THREE AUNTS. From *Popular Tales from the Norse*, by Sir George Dasent. By permission of G. P. Putnam's Sons.

Next morning when she woke, there lay all the flax spun on the table, and that so clean and fine, no one had ever seen such even and pretty yarn. The queen was very glad to get such nice yarn, and she set greater store by the lassie than ever. But the rest were still more envious, and agreed to tell the queen how the lassie had said she was good to weave the yarn she had spun in four-and-twenty hours. So the queen said again, as she had said it she must do it; but if she couldn't quite finish it in four-and-twenty hours, she wouldn't be too hard upon her, she might have a little more time. This time, too, the lassie dared not say no, but begged for a room to herself, and then she would try. There she sat again, sobbing and crying, and not knowing which way to turn, when another old woman came in and asked,—

"What ails you, child?"

At first the lassie wouldn't say, but at last she told her the whole story of her grief.

"Well, well!" said the old wife, "never mind. If you'll call me Aunt on the happiest day of your life, I'll weave this yarn for you, and so you may just be off, and lie down to sleep."

Yes, the lassie was willing enough; so she went away and lay down to sleep. When she awoke, there lay the piece of linen on the table, woven so neat and close, no woof could be better. So the lassie took the piece and ran down to the queen, who was very glad to get such beautiful linen, and set greater store than ever by the lassie. But as for the others, they grew still more bitter against her, and thought of nothing but how to find out something to tell about her.

At last they told the queen the lassie had said she was good to make up the piece of linen into shirts in four-and-twenty hours. Well, all happened as before; the lassie dared not say she couldn't sew; so she was shut up again in a room by herself, and there she sat in tears and grief. But then another old wife came, and said she would sew the shirts for her if she would call her Aunt on the happiest day of her life. The lassie was only too glad to do this, and then she did as the old wife told her, and went and lay down to sleep.

Next morning when she woke she found the piece of linen made up into the shirts, which lay on the table—and such beautiful work no one had ever set eyes on; and more than that, the shirts were all marked and ready for wear. So, when the queen saw the work, she was so glad at the way in which it was sewn, that she clapped her hands, and said,—

"Such sewing I never had, nor even saw, in all my born days"; and after that she was as fond of the lassie as of her own children; and she said to her,—

"Now, if you would like to have the Prince for your husband, you shall have him; for you will never need to hire work-women. You can sew, and spin, and weave all yourself."

So as the lassie was pretty, and the Prince was glad to have her, the wedding soon came on. But just as the Prince was going to sit down with the bride to the bridal feast, in came an ugly old hag with a long nose— I'm sure it was three ells long.

So up got the bride and made a curtsey, and said,—

"Good-day, Auntie."

"That Auntie to my bride?" said the Prince.

"Yes, she was!"

"Well, then, she'd better sit down with us to the feast," said the Prince; but to tell you the truth, both he and the rest thought she was a loathsome woman to have next you.

But just then in came another ugly old hag. She had a back so humped and broad, she had hard work to get through the door. Up jumped the bride in a trice, and greeted her with "Good-day, Auntie!"

And the Prince asked again if that were his bride's aunt. They both said, Yes; so the Prince said, if that were so, she too had better sit down with them to the feast.

But they had scarce taken their seats before another ugly old hag came in, with eyes as large as saucers, and so red and bleared, 't was gruesome to look at her. But up jumped the bride again, with her "Good-day, Auntie," and her, too, the Prince asked to sit down; but I can't say he was very glad, for he thought to himself,—

"Heaven shield me from such Aunties as my bride has!" So when he had sat a while, he could not keep his thoughts to himself any longer, but asked,—

"But how, in all the world can my bride, who is such a lovely lassie, have such loathsome mis-shapen Aunts?"

"I'll soon tell you how it is," said the first. "I was just as good-looking when I was her age; but the reason why I've got this long nose is, because I was always kept sitting, and poking, and nodding over my spinning, and so my nose got stretched and stretched, until it got as long as you now see it."

"And I," said the second, "ever since I was young, I have sat and scuttled backwards and forwards over my loom, and that's how my back has got so broad and lumped as you now see it."

"And I," said the third, "ever since I was little, I have sat, and stared and sewn, and sewn and stared, night and day; and that's why my eyes have got so ugly and red, and now there's no help for them."

"So, so!" said the Prince, " 'twas lucky I came to know this; for if folk can get so ugly and loathsome by all this, then my bride shall neither spin, nor weave, nor sew all her life long."

THE THREE BILLY-GOATS GRUFF

Once on a time there were three Billy-goats, who were to go up to the hill-side to make themselves fat, and the name of all three was "Gruff."

On the way up was a bridge over a burn they had to cross; and under the bridge lived a great ugly Troll, with eyes as big as saucers, and a nose as long as a poker.

So first of all came the youngest billy-goat Gruff to cross the bridge.

"Trip, trap! trip, trap!" went the bridge.

"WHO'S THAT tripping over my bridge?" roared the Troll.

"Oh, it is only I, the tiniest billy-goat Gruff; and I'm going up to the hill-side to make myself fat," said the billy-goat, with such a small voice.

"Now, I'm coming to gobble you up," said the Troll.

"Oh, no! pray don't take me. I'm too little, that I am," said the billy-goat; "wait a bit till the second billy-goat Gruff comes, he's much bigger."

"Well, be off with you"; said the Troll.

A little while after came the second billy-goat Gruff to cross the bridge.

"Trip, trap! Trip, trap! Trip, trap!" went the bridge.

"WHO'S THAT tripping over my bridge?" roared the Troll.

"Oh, it's the second billy-goat Gruff, and I'm going up to the hill-side to make myself fat," said the billy-goat, who hadn't such a small voice.

"Now I'm coming to gobble you up," said the Troll.

"Oh, no! don't take me, wait a little till the big billy-goat Gruff comes, he's much bigger."

"Very well! be off with you," said the Troll.

But just then up came the big billy-goat Gruff.

"TRIP, TRAP! TRIP, TRAP! TRIP, TRAP!" went the bridge, for the billy-goat was so heavy that the bridge creaked and groaned under him.

"WHO'S THAT tramping over my bridge?" roared the Troll.

"IT'S I! THE BIG BILLY-GOAT GRUFF," said the billy-goat, who had an ugly hoarse voice of his own.

"Now, I'm coming to gobble you up," roared the Troll.

> Well, come along! I've got two spears,
> And I'll poke your eyeballs out at your ears;
> I've got besides two curling-stones,
> And I'll crush you to bits, body and bones.

That was what the big billy-goat said; and so he flew at the Troll, and poked his eyes out with his horns, and crushed him to bits, body and

THE THREE BILLY-GOATS GRUFF. From *Popular Tales from the Norse,* by Sir George Dasent. By permission of G. P. Putnam's Sons.

bones, and tossed him out into the burn, and after that he went up to the hill-side. There the billy-goats got so fat they were scarce able to walk home again; and if the fat hasn't fallen off them, why, they're still fat; and so—

> Snip, snap, snout,
> This tale's told out.

THE TWELVE WILD DUCKS

Once on a time there was a Queen who was out driving, when there had been a new fall of snow in the winter; but when she had gone a little way, she began to bleed at the nose, and had to get out of her sledge. And so, as she stood there, leaning against the fence, and saw the red blood on the white snow, she fell a-thinking how she had twelve sons and no daughter, and she said to herself—

"If I only had a daughter as white as snow and as red as blood, I shouldn't care what became of all my sons."

But the words were scarce out of her mouth before an old witch of the Trolls came up to her.

"A daughter you shall have," she said, "and she shall be as white as snow, and as red as blood; and your sons shall be mine, but you may keep them till the babe is christened."

So when the time came the Queen had a daughter, and she was as white as snow, and as red as blood, just as the Troll had promised, and so they called her "Snow-white and Rosy-red." Well, there was great joy at the King's court, and the Queen was as glad as glad could be; but when what she had promised to the old witch came into her mind, she sent for a silver-smith, and bade him make twelve silver spoons, one for each prince, and after that she bade him make one more, and that she gave to Snow-white and Rosy-red. But as soon as ever the Princess was christened, the Princes were turned into twelve wild ducks, and flew away. They never saw them again,—away they went, and away they stayed.

So the Princess grew up, and she was both tall and fair, but was often so strange and sorrowful, and no one could understand what it was that failed her. But one evening the Queen was also sorrowful, for she had many strange thoughts when she thought of her sons. She said to Snow-white and Rosy-red—

"Why are you so sorrowful, my daughter? Is there anything you want? If so, only say the word, and you shall have it."

THE TWELVE WILD DUCKS. From *Popular Tales from the Norse*, by Sir George Dasent. By permission of G. P. Putnam's Sons.

"Oh, it seems so dull and lonely here," said Snow-white and Rosy-red; "every one else has brothers and sisters, but I am all alone; I have none; and that's why I'm so sorrowful."

"But you had brothers, my daughter," said the Queen; "I had twelve sons who were your brothers, but I gave them all away to get you"; and so she told her the whole story.

So when the Princess heard that, she had no rest; for, in spite of all the Queen could say or do, and all she wept and prayed, the lassie would set off to seek her brothers for she thought it was all her fault; and at last she got leave to go away from the palace. On and on she walked into the wide world, so far, you would never have thought a young lady could have strength to walk so far.

So, once, when she was walking through a great, great wood, one day she felt tired, and sat down on a mossy tuft and fell asleep. Then she dreamt that she went deeper and deeper into the wood, till she came to a little wooden hut, and there she found her brothers; just then she woke, and straight before her she saw a worn path in the green moss, and this path went deeper into the wood; so she followed it, and after a long time she came to just such a little wooden house as that she had seen in her dream.

Now, when she went into the room there was no one at home, but there stood twelve beds, and twelve chairs, and twelve spoons—a dozen of everything, in short. When she saw that she was so glad, she hadn't been so glad for many a long year, for she could guess at once that her brothers lived here. She proceeded to cook their dinner, and to make the house as tidy as she could; and when she had done all the cooking and work, she ate her own dinner, and crept under her youngest brother's bed, and lay down there, but she forgot her spoon upon the table.

So she had scarcely laid herself down before she had heard something flapping and whirring in the air, and so all the twelve wild ducks came sweeping in; but as soon as ever they crossed the threshold they became Princes.

"Oh, how nice and warm it is in here," they said. "Heaven bless him who made up the fire, and cooked such a good dinner for us."

And so each took up his silver spoon and was going to eat. But when each had taken his own, there was one still left lying on the table, and it was so like the rest that they couldn't tell it from them.

"This is our sister's spoon," they said; "and if her spoon be here, she can't be very far off herself."

"If this be our sister's spoon, and she be here," said the eldest, "she shall be killed, for she is to blame for all the ill we suffer."

And this she lay under the bed and listened to:

"No," said the youngest, "twere a shame to kill her for that. She has nothing to do with our suffering ill; for if anyone's to blame, it's our own mother."

So they set to work hunting for her both high and low, and at last they looked under all the beds, and so when they came to the youngest Prince's bed, they found her, and dragged her out. Then the eldest Prince wished again to have her killed, but she begged and prayed so prettily for herself.

"Oh! gracious goodness! don't kill me, for I've gone about seeking you these three years, and if I could only set you free, I'd willingly lose my life."

"Well!" said they, "if you will set us free, you may keep your life; for you can if you choose."

"Yes; only tell me," said the Princess, "how it can be done, and I'll do it, whatever it be."

"You must pick thistle-down," said the Princes, "and you must card it, and spin it, and weave it; and after you have done that, you must cut out and make twelve coats, and twelve shirts, and twelve neckerchiefs, one for each of us, and while you do that, you must neither talk, nor laugh, nor weep. If you can do that, we are free."

"But where shall I ever get thistle-down enough for so many neckerchiefs, and shirts, and coats?" asked Snow-white and Rosy-red.

"We'll soon show you," said the Princes; and so they took her with them to a great wide moor, where there stood such a crop of thistles, all nodding and nodding in the breeze, and down all floating and glistening like gossamers through the air in the sunbeams. The Princess had never seen such a quantity of thistle-down in her life, and she began to pluck and gather it as fast and as well as she could; and when she got home at night she set to work carding and spinning, and all the while keeping the Princes' house, cooking, and making their beds. At evening home they came, flapping and whirring like wild ducks, and all night they were Princes, but in the morning off they flew again, and were wild ducks the whole day.

But now it happened once, when she was out on the moor to pick thistle-down,—and if I don't mistake, it was the very last time she was to go thither,—it happened that the young King who ruled that land was out hunting, and came riding across the moor, and saw her. So he stopped there and wondered who the lovely lady could be that walked along the moor picking thistle-down, and he asked her name, and when he could get no answer, he was still more astonished; and at last he liked her so much, that nothing would do but he must take her home to his castle and marry her. So he ordered his servants to take her and put her up on his horse. Snow-white and Rosy-red she wrung her hands, and made signs to them, and pointed to the bags in which her work was, and when the King saw she wished to have them with her, he told his men to take up the bags behind them. When they had done that the Princess came to herself, little by little, for the King was both a wise man and a handsome man too, and he was as soft and kind to her as a doctor. But when they got home to the palace, and the old Queen, who was his stepmother, set eyes on Snow-white and Rosy-red, she got so cross and jealous of her because she was so lovely, that she said to the King—

"Can't you see now, that this thing whom you have picked up, and whom you are going to marry, is a witch? Why, she can't either talk, or laugh, or weep!"

But the King didn't care a pin for what she said, but held on with the wedding, and married Snow-white and Rosy-red, and they lived in great joy and glory; but she didn't forget to go on sewing at her shirts.

So when the year was almost out, Snow-white and Rosy-red brought a Prince into the world; and then the old Queen was more spiteful and jealous than ever, and at dead of night she stole in to Snow-white and Rosy-red, while she slept, and took away her babe, and threw it into a pit full of snakes. After that she cut Snow-white and Rosy-red in her finger, and smeared the blood over her mouth, and she went straight to the King.

"Now come and see," she said, "what sort of a thing you have taken for your Queen; here she has eaten up her own babe."

Then the King was so downcast, he almost burst into tears, and said—

"Yes, it must be true, since I see it with my own eyes; but she'll not do it again, I'm sure, and so this time I'll spare her life."

So before the next year was out she had another son, and the same thing happened. The King's stepmother got more and more jealous and spiteful. She stole in to the young Queen at night while she slept, took away the babe, and threw it into a pit full of snakes, cut the young Queen's finger, and smeared the blood over her mouth, and then went and told the King she had eaten up her own child. Then the King was so sorrowful, you can't think how sorry he was, and he said—

"Yes, it must be true, since I see it with my own eyes, but she'll not do it again, I'm sure, and so this time too I'll spare her life."

Well, before the next year was out, Snow-white and Rosy-red brought a daughter into the world, and her, too, the old Queen took and threw into the pit full of snakes, while the young Queen slept. Then she cut her finger, smeared the blood over her mouth, and went again to the King and said—

"Now you may come and see if it isn't as I say; she's a wicked, wicked witch, for here she has gone and eaten up her third babe too."

Then the King was so sad, there was no end to it, for now he couldn't spare her any longer, but had to order her to be burnt alive on a pile of wood. But just when the pile was all ablaze, and they were going to put her on it, she made signs to them to take twelve boards and lay them round the pile, and on these she laid the neckerchiefs, and the shirts, and the coats for her brothers, but the youngest brother's shirt wanted its left arm, for she hadn't had time to finish it. And as soon as ever she had done that, they heard such a flapping and whirring in the air, and down came twelve wild ducks flying over the forest, and each of them snapped up his clothes in his bill and flew off with them.

"See now!" said the old Queen to the King, "wasn't I right when I told you she was a witch; but make haste and burn her before the pile burns low."

"Oh!" said the King, "we've wood enough, and to spare, and so I'll wait a bit, for I have a mind to see what the end of all this will be."

As she spoke, up came the twelve princes riding along as handsome well-grown lads as you'd wish to see; but the youngest prince had a wild duck's wing instead of his left arm.

"What's all this about?" asked the Princes.

"My Queen is to be burnt," said the King, "because she's a witch, and because she has eaten up her own babes."

"She hasn't eaten them at all," said the Princes. "Speak now, sister; you have set us free and saved us, now save yourself."

Then Snow-white and Rosy-red spoke, and told the whole story; how every time she was brought to bed, the old Queen, the King's stepmother, had stolen in to her at night, had taken her babes away, and cut her little finger and smeared the blood over her mouth; and then the Princes took the King, and showed him the snake-pit where three babes lay playing with adders and toads, and lovelier children you never saw.

So the King had them taken out at once, and went to his stepmother, and asked her what punishment she thought that woman deserved who could find it in her heart to betray a guiltless Queen and three such blessed little babes.

"She deserves to be fast bound between twelve unbroken steeds, so that each may take his share of her," said the old Queen.

"You have spoken your own doom," said the King, "and you shall suffer it at once."

So the wicked old Queen was fast bound between twelve unbroken steeds, and each got his share of her. But the King took Snow-white and Rosy-red, and their three children, and the twelve Princes; and so they all went home to their father and mother, and told all that had befallen them, and there was joy and gladness over the whole kingdom, because the Princess was saved and set free, and because she had set free her twelve brothers.

SCOTLAND

The extreme similarity of your fiction to ours in Scotland is very striking. . . . The beautiful superstition of the Banshee seems in a great measure peculiar to Ireland, though in some highland families there is a spectre, particularly in that of MacLean of Lochbury; but I think I could match all your other tales with something similar.——*Sir Walter Scott.*

The similarity between the Irish and the Scottish story is described in this part of a letter written by Sir Walter Scott to his friend, T. C. Croker, the author of *Irish Fairy Legends*.

BLACK AGNACE OF DUNBAR

> Some sing o' lords, and some o' knichts,
> An' some o' michty men o' war,
> But I sing o' a leddy bricht,
> The Black Agnace o' Dunnebar.

It was in the year 1338, when Bruce's son was but a bairn, and Scotland was guided by a Regent, that we were left, a household of women, as it were, to guard my lord's strong Castle of Dunbar.

My lord himself, Cospatrick, Earl of Dunbar and March, had ridden off to join the Regent, Sir Andrew Moray, and help him to drive the English out of the land. For the English King, Edward III, thought it no shame to war with bairns, and since he had been joined by that false loon, Edward Baliol, he had succeeded in taking many of our Scottish fortresses, including Edinburgh Castle, and in planting an English army in our midst.

Now the Castle of Dunbar, as all folk know, is a strong Castle, standing as it doth well out to sea, on a mass of solid rock, and connected with the mainland only by one narrow strip of land, which is defended by a drawbridge and portcullis, and walls of solid masonry. Its other sides need no defence, for the wild waters of the Northern Sea beat about them with such fury that it is only at certain times of the tide that even peaceful boatmen can find a safe landing. Indeed, 'tis one of the strongest fortresses in the country, and because of its position, lying not so far from the East Border and being guard as it were to the Lothians, and Edinburgh, it is often called "The Key of Scotland."

My lord deemed it impregnable, as long as it was well supplied with food, so he had little scruple in leaving his young wife and her two little daughters alone there, with a handful of men-at-arms, too old, most of them, to be of any further service in the field, to guard them.

She, on her part, was very well content to stay, for was she not a daughter of the famous Randolph, and did she not claim kinship with Bruce himself? So fear to her was a thing unknown.

I, who was a woman of fifty then, and am well-nigh ninety now, can truly say that in all the course of a long life, I never saw courage like to hers.

BLACK AGNACE OF DUNBAR. From *Children's Tales from Scottish Ballads*, by Elizabeth W. Grierson. By permission of A. & C. Black Ltd.

I remember, as though it were yesterday, that cold January morning when my lord set off to the Burgh Muir, where he was to meet with the Regent. When all was ready, and his men were mounted and drawn up, waiting for their master, my lady stepped forth joyously, in the sight of them all, and buckled on her husband's armour.

"Ride forth and do battle for thy country and thine infant King, poor babe," she said, "and vex not thy heart for us who are left behind. We deserve not the name we bear, if we cannot hold the Castle till thy return, even though it were against King Edward himself. Thinkest thou not so, Marian?" and she turned round to where I was standing, a few paces back, with little Mistress Marjory clinging to my skirts, and little Mistress Jean in my arms.

For though I was but her bower-woman, I was of the same clan as my lady, and had served in her family all my life. I had carried her in my arms, as I now carried her little daughter, and, at her marriage, I had come with her to her husband's home.

"Indeed, Madam, I trow we can, God and the Saints helping us," I answered, and at her brave words the soldiers raised a great cheer, and my lord, who was usually a stern man, and slow to show his feelings, put his arm round her and kissed her on the lips.

"Spoken like my own true wife," he said. "But in good troth, Sweetheart, methinks there is nothing to fear. For very shame neither King Edward nor his Captains will war against a woman, and, e'en if they do, if thou but keep the gates locked, and the portcullis down, I defy any one of them to gain admittance. And, look ye, the well in the courtyard will never run dry—'tis sunk in the solid rock—and besides the beeves that were salted down at Martinmas, and the meal that was laid in at the end of harvest, there are bags of grain hidden down in the dungeons, enough to feed a score of men for three months at least."

So saying, he leaped into his saddle, and rode out of the gateway, a gallant figure at the head of his troop of armed men, while we climbed to the top of the tower, and stood beside old Andrew, the watchman, and gazed after them until the last glint of their armour disappeared behind a rising hill.

After their departure all went well for a time. Indeed, it was as though the years had flown back, and my lady was once more a girl, so lighthearted and joyous was she, pleased with the novelty of being left governor of that great Castle. It seemed but a bit of play when, after ordering the house and setting the maidens to their tasks, she went round the walls with Walter Brand, a lame archer, who was gently born, and whom she had put in charge of our little fighting force, to see that all the men were at their posts.

And mere play it seemed to her still, when, some two weeks after my lord's departure, as she was sitting sewing in her little chamber, whose windows looked straight out over the sea, and I was rocking Mistress

Jean's cradle, and humming a lullaby, little Mistress Marjory, who was five years old, and stirring for her age, came running down from the watch-tower, where she had been with old Andrew, and cried out that a great host of men on horseback were coming, and that old Andrew said that it was the English.

We were laughing at the bairn's story, and wondering who the strangers could be, when old Andrew himself appeared, a look of concern on his usually jocund face.

"Oh, my lady," he cried, "there be a body of armed men moving towards the Castle, led by a knight in splendid armour. A squire rides in front of him, carrying his banner; but the device is unknown to me, and I fear it was never wrought by Scottish hands."

"Ah ha," laughed the Countess, rising, and throwing away her tapestry. "Thou scentest an Englishman, dost thou, Andrew? Mayhap thy thoughts have run on them so much of late, that the habit hath dimmed thine eyes."

"Nay, nay, my lady," stammered old Andrew, half hurt by her gentle raillery, "mine eyes are keen enough as yet, although my limbs be old."

" 'Tis but my sport, Andrew," she answered kindly. "I have always loved a jest, and I have no wish to grow old and grave before my time, even if I have the care of a whole Castle on my shoulders. But hark, there be the stranger's trumpets sounding before the gate. See to it that Walter Brand listens to his message, and answers it as befits the dignity of our house: and thou, do thou mount to thy watch-tower, and keep a good lookout on all that passes."

We waited in silence for some little space; we could hear the sound of voices, but no distinct words reached us.

At last Walter Brand came halting to the door and knocked. Like old Andrew, he wore an anxious look. He was devoted to the Countess, and was aye wont to be timorous where she was concerned.

" 'Tis the English Earl of Salisbury," he said, "who desires to speak with your Grace. I asked him to entrust his message to me, and I would deliver it, but he gave answer haughtily, that he would speak with no one but the Countess."

"Then speak with me he shall," said my lady, with a flash of her eye, "but he must e'en bring himself to catch my words as they drop like pearls from the top of the tower. Summon the archers, Walter, and let them stand behind me for a body-guard: no man need know how old and frail they be, if they are high enough up, and keep somewhat in the background. And thou, Marian, attend me, for 'tis not fitting that the Countess of Dunbar and March should speak with a strange knight in her husband's absence, without a bower-woman standing by."

Casting her wimple round her, she ascended the steep stone stairs, and, as we followed, Walter Brand put his head close to mine. "I like it not," he said in his sober way, "for this Earl of Salisbury is a bold, brazen-faced fellow, and to my ears his voice rings not true. I fear me, he wishes no good to our lady. They say, moreover, that he is one of the best Captains that the King of England hath, and he hath at least two hundred men with him."

"Trust my lady to look after her own, and her husband's honour," I said sharply, for, good man though he was, Walter Brand aye angered me; he seemed ever over-anxious, a character I love not in a man.

All the same my heart sank, as we stepped out on the flat roof of the tower, and glanced down over the battlements.

I saw at once that Walter had spoken truly. Montague, Earl of Salisbury, had a bold, bad face, and his words, though honeyed and low, had a false ring in them.

"My humblest greetings, fair lady," he cried; "my life is at thy service, for I heard but yesterday that thy lord, caitiff that he be, hath left thee alone among rough men, in this lonely wind-swept Castle. Methinks thou art accustomed to kinder treatment, and therefore am I come to beg thee to open thy gates, and allow me to enter. By my soul, if thou wilt, I shall be thy servant to the death. Such beauty as thine was never meant to be wasted in the desert. Let me enter, and be thy friend, and I will deck thee with such jewels,—with gold and with pearls, that thou shalt be envied of all the ladies in Christendom."

My lady drew herself up proudly; but even yet she thought it was some sport, albeit not the sport that should have been offered to a noble dame in her husband's absence.

"Little care I for gold, or yet for pearls, my Lord of Salisbury," she said in grave displeasure. "I have jewels enough and to spare, and need not that a stranger should give them to me. As for the gates, I am a loyal wife, and I open them to no one until my good lord returns."

Now, had my Lord of Salisbury been a true knight, or even a plain, honest, leal soldier, this answer of my lady's would have sufficed, and he would have parleyed no more, but would have departed, taking his men with him. But, villain that he was, his honeyed words rose up once more in answer.

"Oh, lady bright, oh, lady fair," he cried, "I pray thee have mercy on thy humble servant, and open thy gates and speak with him. Thou art far too beautiful to live in these cold Northern climes, among rough and brutal men. Come with me, and I will dress thee in cloth-of-gold, and take thee along with me to London. King Edward will welcome thee, for thy beauty will add lustre to his court, and we shall be married with all speed. I warrant the Countess of Salisbury will be a person of importance at the English court, and thou shalt have a retinue such as in this barren country yet little dream of. Thou shalt have both lords and knights to ride in thy train, and twenty little page boys to serve thee on bended knee; and hawks, and hounds, and horses galore, so thou wouldst join in the chase. Think of it, lady, and consider not thy rough and unkind lord. If he had loved thee in the least, would he have left thee in my power?"

Now the English lord's words were sweet, and he spoke in the soft Southern tongue, such as might wile a bird from the lift,[12] if the bird chanced to have little sense, and when he ceased I glanced at my lady in alarm, lest for a moment she were tempted.

Heaven forgive me for the thought.

She had drawn herself up to her full height, and her face of righteous anger might have frightened the Evil One himself; and, by my Faith, I am not so very sure that it was not the Evil One who spoke by the mouth of my Lord of Salisbury.

The Countess was very stately, and of wondrous beauty. "Black Agnace," the common folk were wont to call her, because of her raven hair and jet black eyes. Verily at that moment these eyes of hers burned like stars of fire.

"Now shame upon thee, Montague, Earl of Salisbury," she cried, and because of her indignation her voice rang out clear as a trumpet. "Open my gates to thee, forsooth! go to London with thee, and be married to thee there, and bear thy name, and ride in the case with thy horse and hounds, as if I were thy lawful Countess. Shame on thee, I say. I trow thou callest thyself a belted Earl, and a Christian Knight, and thou comest to me, the wife of a belted Earl—who, thank God, is also a Christian Knight, and a good man and true, moreover, which is more than thou art—with words like these. Yea," and she drew a dainty little glove from her girdle, and threw it down at the Earl's feet, "I cry thrice shame on thee, and here I fling defiance in thy face. Keep thy cloth-of-gold for thine own knights' backs; and as for thy squires and pages, if thou hast so many of them, give them each a sword, and set them on a horse, and bring them here to swell thy company. Bring them here, I say, and let them try to batter down these walls, for in no other way wilt thou ever set foot in Dunbar Castle."

A subdued murmur, as if of applause, ran through the ranks of the armed men, who stood drawn up in a body behind the English Earl. For men love bravery wherever they chance to meet it, and I trow we must have seemed to them but a feeble company to take upon us the defence of the Castle, and to throw defiance in the teeth of their lord.

But the bravery of the Countess did not seem to strike their leader; possibly he was not accustomed to receive such answers from the lips of women. His face flushed an angry red as his squire picked up my lady's little white glove and handed it to me.

"Now, by my soul, Madam," he cried, "thou shalt find that it is no light matter to jeer at armed men. I have come to thee with all courtesy, asking thee to open thy Castle gates, and thou hast flouted me to my face. Well, so be it. When next I come, 'twill be with other words, and other weapons. Mayhap thou wilt be more eager to treat with me then."

"Bring what thou wilt, and come when thou wilt," answered the lady

[12] Sky.

passionately, "thou shalt ever find the same answer waiting thee. These gates of mine open to no one save my own true lord."

With a low mocking bow the Earl turned his horse's head to the South, and galloped away, followed by his men.

We stood on top of the tower and watched them, I, with a heart full of anxious thoughts for the time that was coming, my lady with her head held high, and her eyes flaming, while the men stood apart and whispered among themselves. For we all knew that, although the English had taken themselves off, it was only for a time, and that they would return without fail.

When the last horseman had disappeared among the belt of trees which lay between us and the Lammermuirs, my lady turned round, her bonnie face all soft and quivering.

"Will ye stand by me, my men?" she asked.

"That will we, till the death, my lady," answered they, and one after another they knelt at her feet and kissed her hand, while, as for me, I could but take her in my arms, as I had done oft-times when she was a little child, and pray God to strengthen her noble heart.

Her emotion passed as quickly as it had come, however, and in a moment she was herself again, laughing and merry as if it had all been a game of play.

"Come down, Walter; come down, my men," she cried; "we must e'en hold a council of war, and lay our plans; while old Andrew will keep watch for us, and tell us when the black-faced knave is like to return."

And when we went downstairs into the great hall, and found that the silly wenches had heard all that had passed, and were bemoaning themselves for lost, and frightening little Mistress Marjory and Mistress Jean well-nigh out of their senses, I warrant she did not spare them, but called them a pack of chicken-hearted, thin-blooded baggages, and threatened that if they did not hold their tongues, and turn to their duties at once, she would send them packing, and then they would be at the mercy of the English in good earnest.

After that we set to work and made such preparations as we could. We set the wenches to draw water from the well, and to bake a good store of bannocks to be ready in time of need, for the men must not be hungry when they fought. Walter Brand and two of the strongest men-at-arms set to work to strengthen the gates, by laying ponderous billets of wood against them, and clasp these in their places by strong iron bars; while the rest, led by old Andrew, went round the Castle, looking to the loopholes, and the battlements, and examining the cross-bows and other weapons.

Upstairs and downstairs went my lady, overlooking everything, thinking of everything, as became a daughter of the great Randolph, while I sat and kept the bairns, who, poor little lassies, were puzzled to know what all the stir and din was about.

And indeed it was none too soon to look to all these things, for although

the country seemed quiet enough through the hours of that short afternoon, when night fell, and I was putting the bairns to bed, my lady helping
me—for, when one bears a troubled heart (and her heart must have been
troubled, in spite of her cheerful face), it aye seems lighter when the hands
are full—a little page came running in to tell us that there were lights
flickering to Southward among the trees.

"Now hold thy silly tongue, laddie," said I, for I was anxious that we
should at least get one good night's rest before the storm and stress of war
came upon us.

My lady looked up with a smile from where she was kneeling beside
Mistress Jean's cradle. "Let him be, Marian," she said; "the lad meant
it well, and 'tis good to know how the danger threatens. Come, we will go
up and watch with old Andrew."

So, as soon as the bairns were asleep, we threw plaids over our heads,
and crept up the narrow stairs to where old Andrew was watching in his
own little tower, which stood out from the great tower like a corbie's[13] nest,
and, crouching down behind the battlements to gain some shelter from the
cruel wind, we watched the flickering lights coming nearer and nearer from
the Southward, and listened to the shouting of men, and the tramp of
horses' hoofs, which we could hear at times coming faintly through the
storm.

For two long hours we waited, and then, as we could only guess what
was taking place, it being far too dark to see, we crept down the narrow
stairs again, stiff and chilled, and threw ourselves, all dressed as we were,
on our beds.

The gray winter dawn of next morning showed us that the English Earl
meant to do his best to reduce our fortress in good earnest, for a small
army of men had been brought up in the night, from Berwick most likely,
and they were encamped on a strip of greensward facing the Castle. They
must have spent a busy night, for already the tents had been pitched, and
fires lit, and the men were now engaged in cooking their breakfast, and
attending to their horses. At the sight my heart grew heavier and heavier;
but my lady's spirits seemed to rise.

" 'Tis a brave sight, is it not, Marian?" she said. "In good troth, my
Lord of Salisbury does us too much honour, in setting a camp down at our
gates, to amuse us in our loneliness. Methinks that is his own tent, there
on the right, with the pennon floating in front of it; and there are the
mangonells behind," and she pointed to a row of strange-looking machines,
which were drawn up on a hill a little way to the rear. "Well, 'tis a stony
coast; his lordship will have no trouble in finding stones to load them
with."

"What be they, madam?" I asked, for in all my life I had never seen
such things before.

13 Crow's.

My lady laughed as she turned her head to greet Walter Brand, who came up the stairs at that moment.

"Welcome, Walter," she said merrily. "We are just taking the measure of our foes, and here is Marian, who has never seen mangonells before, wondering what they are. They are engines for shooting stones with, Marian; for well the knaves know that arrows are but poor weapons with which to batter stone walls. But see, the fray begins, for yonder are the archers approaching, and yonder go the men down to the sea-shore to gather stones for the mangonells. Thou and I must e'en go down, and leave the men to brave the storm. See to it, Walter, that they do not expose themselves unduly; we could ill afford to lose one of them."

Then began the weary onslaught which lasted for so many weeks. In good faith it seems to me that, had we known, when that first rush of arrows sounded through the air, how long it would be ere we were quiet again, we scarce would have had the courage to go on. And when those infernal engines were set off, and their volleys of stones and jagged pieces of iron sounded round our ears, the poor silly wenches lost their heads, and screamed aloud, while the bairns clung to my skirts, and hid their chubby faces in the folds.

But even then my lady was not daunted. Snatching up a napkin, she ran lightly up the stairs, and before anyone could stop her, she stepped forward to the battlements, and there, all unheeding of the danger in which she stood from the arrows of the enemy, she wiped the fragments of stone, and bits of loose mortar daintily from the walls, as if to show my Lord of Salisbury how little our Castle could be harmed by all the stones he liked to hurl against it.

It was bravely done, and again a murmur of admiration went through the English ranks; and—for I was peeping through a loophole—I trow that even the haughty Earl's face softened at the sight of her.

The story of that first day is but the story of many more days that followed. Showers of arrows flew from the cross-bows, volleys of stones fell from the mangonells until we got so used to the sound of them that by the third week the veriest coward among the maidens would go boldly up and wipe the dust away where a stone had been chipped, or another displaced, as calmly as our lady herself had done on that first terrible morning.

Their archers did little harm, for our men were so few, and our places of shelter so many, that they ran small risk of being hurt, and although one or two poor fellows were killed, and half a dozen more had wounds, it was nothing to be compared with the loss which the English suffered, for our archers had the whole army to take aim at, and I wot their shafts flew sure.

In vain they brought battering-rams and tried to batter down the doors. Our portcullis had resisted many an onslaught, and the gates behind it were made of oak a foot thick, and studded all over with iron nails, and they might as well have thought to batter down the Bass Rock itself.

So, in spite of all, as the weeks went by, we began to feel fairly safe and comfortable, although my lady never relaxed her vigilance, and went her round of the walls, early and late. At Walter's request she began to wear a morion on her head, and a breast-plate of fine steel, to protect her against any stray arrow, and in them, to my mind, she looked bonnier than ever. In good sooth, I think the very English soldiers loved her, not to speak of our own men; for whenever she appeared they would rise their caps as if in homage, and hum a couplet which ran in some wise thus—

> Come I early, come I late,
> I find Annot at the gate

as if they would praise her for her tireless watchfulness. One day, Earl Montague himself, moved to admiration by the manner in which Walter Brand had sent his shaft through the heart of an English knight, cried out in the hearing of all his army, "There comes one of my lady's tire-pins; Agnace's love-shafts go straight to the heart." At which words all our men broke into a mighty shout, and cheered, and cheered again, till the walls rang, and the echoes floated back from far out over the sea.

In spite of their admiration at our lady's bravery, however, the English were determined to conquer the Castle, and after a time, when they saw that their battering-rams and mangonells availed little, they bethought them of a more dangerous weapon of warfare.

It was somewhere towards the end of February, when one fine day a mighty sound of hammering arose from the midst of their camp.

"What are they doing now, think ye, Walter?" asked my lady lightly. "Is it possible that they look for so long a siege that they are beginning to build houses for themselves? Truly they are wise, for if my Lord of Salisbury means to stay there until I open my gates to him, he will grow weary of braving these harsh East winds in no better shelter than a tent."

But for once Walter Brand had no answering smile to give her.

"I fear me 'tis a sow that they are making," he said, "and if that be so we had need to look to our arms."

"A sow," repeated the Countess in graver tones. "I have oft heard of such machines, but I never saw one. Thy words hint of danger, Walter. Is a sow then so deadly that our walls cannot resist its onslaught?"

"It is deadly because it brings the enemy nearer us, my lady," answered Walter. "Hitherto our walls have been our shelter; without them we could not stand a moment, for we are outnumbered by the English a score of times over. These sows, as men name them, are great wooden buildings, which can hold at least forty men inside, and with a platform above where about thirty can stand. They be mounted on two great wheels, and can be run close up to the walls, and as they are oft as high as a house, 'twill be an easy matter for the men who stand on the platform to set up ladders and scale our walls, and after that what chance will there be for our poor handful of men? 'Tis not for myself I fear," he went on, "nor yet for the men. We are soldiers and we can face death; but if thou wouldst not fall into the hands of this English Earl, my lady, I would advise that thou, and Marian, and little Mistress Marjory and Mistress Jean, should set out in the boat the first dark night, when it is calm. 'Tis but ten miles to the Bass, and thou couldst aye find shelter there."

Thus spake honest Walter, who was, as I have said, ever timorous where my lady was concerned; but at his words she shook her head.

"And leave the Castle, Walter?" she said. "That will I never do till I open its doors to my own true lord. As for this English Earl and his sows —tush! I care not for them. If they have wood we have rock, my lad, and I warrant 'twill be a right strong sow that will stand upright after a lump of Dunbar rock comes crashing down on its back; so keep up thy courage, and get out the picks and crowbars. If they build sows by day, we can quarry stones by night."

So saying, my lady shook her little white fist, by way of defiance, in the direction of the tents which studded the greensward opposite, while Walter went off to do her bidding, muttering to himself that the famous Randolph himself was not better than she, for she had been born with the courage of Bruce, and the wisdom of Solomon.

So it came about, that, while the English gave over wasting arrows for a time, and turned their attention to the building of two great clumsy wooden structures, we would steal down in a body on dark nights to the little postern that opened on the shore, when the waves were dashing against rocks, and making enough noise to deaden the sound of the picks, and while we women held a lanthorn or two, the men worked with might and main, hewing at the solid rock which stretched out to seaward for a few yards at the foot of the Castle wall. Then, when some huge block was loosened, ropes would be lowered, and with much ado, for our numbers were small, the unwieldy mass would be hoisted up, and placed in position on the top of the Castle, hidden, it is true, behind the battlements, but with the stones in front of it displaced, so that it could be rolled over with ease at a given signal.

We all took turns at the ropes, and our hands were often raw and frayed with the work. 'Twas my lady who suffered most, for her skin was fine, and up till now she had never known what such labour meant.

At last the day came when the English mounted their great white sows on wheels, and filled them with armed men, and loaded the roofs of them with broad-shouldered, strapping fellows, who carried ladders and irons with which to scale our walls. When all was ready the mighty machines began to move forward, pushed by scores of willing arms, while we watched them in silence.

My lady and I were hidden in old Andrew's tower, for no word that Walter Brand could say could persuade her to go down beside Mistress Marjory, and Mistress Jean, and the serving wenches.

Instead of shooting, our archers stood motionless, stationed in groups behind the great boulders of rock, ready for Walter's signal.

On came the sows, until we could look down and see the men they carried, with upturned faces, and hands busy with the ladders they were raising to place against the walls. They were trundled over the narrow strip of land which connected us with the mainland, and stood still at last, close to our very gates.

"Now, lads," shouted Walter, and before a single ladder could be placed, our great blocks of rock went crashing down on them, hurling the top men in all directions, and driving in the wooden roofs on those who were inside.

Woe's me! Although they were our enemies, our hearts melted at the sight. The timbers of the sows cracked and fell in, and we could see nought but a mass of mangled, bleeding wretches. Had it not been that my lady feared treachery, and that she had sworn not to open the gates except to her husband, I ween she would fain have taken us all out to succour them.

As it was, we could only watch and pity, and keep the bairns in the chambers that looked on the sea, so that their young eyes should not gaze on so ghastly a scene.

And when night fell, and there was no light to guide our archers to shoot, though I trust that, in any case, mercy would have kept them from it, the English stole across the causeway, and pulled away the broken beams, and carried off the dead and wounded, and burned what remained of the sows.

After that day we had no more trouble from any attempts to storm the Castle.

But what force cannot do, hunger may. So my Lord of Salisbury, still sitting in front of our gates with his army, in order to prevent help reaching us from land, set about starving us into submission. As yet we had had no need to trouble about food, for, as I have said, we had a store of grain, enough to last for some weeks yet, in the dungeon, and, long ere it was done, we looked for help reaching us by the sea, if it could not reach us by land.

It was soon made plain to us, however, that not only my Lord of Salisbury, but his royal master, King Edward, was determined that the "Key of Scotland" should fall into his hand, for one fine March morning a great fleet of ships came sailing round St. Abb's Head, and took up their station betwixt us and the Bass Rock, and then we were left, without hope of succour, until our stock of provisions should be eaten up, and starvation forced us to give in.

Ah me! but it was weary work, living through the ever-lengthening days of that cold bleak springtime, waiting for the help which never came, which never could come, so it seemed to us, with that army watching us from the land, and that fleet of ships girding us in on the sea.

And all the time our store of food sank lower and lower, and the wenches' faces grew white, and the men pulled their belts tighter round their middles, and poor little Mistress Jean would turn wearily away from the water gruel which was all we had to give her, and moan and cry for the white bread and the milk to which she was accustomed. Mistress Marjory, on the other hand, being five years old, and wise for her years, never complained, though ofttimes she would let the spoon fall into her porringer at suppertime, and, laying her head against my sleeve, would say in a wistful little voice that went to my very heart, "I cannot eat it, Marian; I am not hungry to-night."

As for my lady, she went about in those days in silence, with a stern, set face. It must have seemed to her that when the meal was all gone she must needs give in, for she could not see her children die before her eyes.

But Providence is aye ready to help those who help themselves, and, late one evening, towards the latter end of May, when we had held the castle for five long months, I chanced to be sitting alone in my chamber, when the Countess entered, looking very pale and wan.

"Wrap a plaid round thee, and come to the top of the tower, Marian," she said. "I cannot sleep, and I long for a breath of fresh air. It doth me no good to go up there by day, for I can see nothing but these English soldiers in front, and these English ships behind. But by night it is different. It is dark then, and I forget for a time how closely beset we are, and how few handfuls of meal there are in the girnels.[14] I will tell thee, Marian," and here her voice sank to a whisper, "what as yet only myself and Walter Brand know, that if help doth not come within a week, we must either open our gates, or starve like rats in a hole."

"But a week is aye a week," I said soothingly, for I was frightened at the wildness of her look, "and help may come before it passes."

All the same my heart was heavy within me as I threw a wrap round my head, and followed her up the narrow stone stairs, and out on to the flat roof of the tower.

The footing was bad in the darkness, for although the battlements had been built up again since the day that we destroyed the sows, there were stones and pieces of rock lying about in all directions, and, not being so young and light of foot as I once had been, I stumbled and fell.

"Do not stir till I get a light," cried my lady; "it is dangerous up here in the dark, and a twisted ankle would not mend matters."

She felt her way over to Andrew's watch-tower, and the old man lighted his lanthorn for her, and she came quickly back again, holding it low in case the enemy should see it, and send a few arrows in our direction. By its light I raised myself, and we went across to the northern

[14] Meal-barrels.

turret, which looked straight over to the Bass Rock, and stood there, resting our arms on the wall.

Suddenly a speck of light shone out far ahead in the darkness. It flickered for a second and then disappeared. In a moment or two it appeared again, and then disappeared in the same way. I drew my lady's attention to it.

" 'Tis a light from the Bass," she said in an excited whisper. "Someone is signalling. It can hardly be to the English, for the Rock is held by friends. Is it possible they can have seen our lanthorn? Let us try again. The English loons are likely to be asleep by now; they have had little to disturb their rest for some weeks back, and may well have grown lazy."

Cautiously she raised the lanthorn, and flashed its rays, once, twice, thrice over the waves. It was only for a second, but it was enough. The spark of light appeared three times in answer, and then all was dark again.

"Run and tell Walter," whispered my lady, and her very voice had changed. It was once more full of life and hope. The Bass Rock was but ten miles off, and if there were friends there watching us, and doubtless making plans to help us, was not that enough?

When Walter came we tried our test for the fourth time, and the answer came back as before.

"We must watch the sea, my lady," he said, when we were safely down in the great hall again. "Help will only come that way, and it will come in the dark. Heaven send that the English sailors have not seen what we have, and keep a double watch in consequence."

After that, we hardly slept. Night after night, we strained our eyes through the darkness in the direction of the Bass, and for five nights our watching was in vain.

But on the sixth, a Sunday, just on the stroke of twelve, the silence which had lasted so long was broken by the sound of shouting, and lights sprang up all round us, first on the ships and then on the land.

With anxious hearts we crowded round the loopholes, for we knew that somewhere, out among the lights, brave men were making a dash for our rescue, and we women, who could do nothing else, lifted up our hearts, and prayed that Heaven and the Holy St. Michael would aid their efforts.

Meanwhile, the men manned the walls, ready to shoot if the English ships came within bow-shot, which they were scarce likely to do, as the coast was wild and rocky, and fraught with danger to those who were unacquainted with it.

Presently Walter called for wood to make a fire outside the little postern which opened on the rocks, and we ceased our prayers, and fell to work with a will, with the kitchen-wenches' choppers, on the empty barrels which were piled up in a corner of a cellar. We even drained our last flagon of oil to pour over them, and soon a fire was blazing on the rudely-cut-out landing-stage, and throwing its beams far out over the sea.

And there, dim and shadowy at first, but aye coming nearer and nearer, guided by its light, we saw a boat, not cut in any foreign fashion, but built and rigged near St. Margaret's Hope. It was full of men; we could hear them cheering and shouting in our own good Scots tongue, which fell kindly on our ears, after the soft mincing English which had been thrown at our heads for so many months.

They were safe now, for, as I have said, the ships through which they had slipped dare not follow them too near the coast, in case they ran upon the rocks, and the Castle sheltered them from any arrows which might be sent from the land. It sheltered us too, and we crowded down to the little landing-stage, and watched with breathless interest the boat which was bringing safety and succour to us.

"Bring down the bairns, Marian," said my lady. "Marjory at least is of an age to remember this."

I hastened to do her bidding, and, calling one of the wenches, we ran up and roused the sleeping lambs, telling them stories of the wonderful boat which was coming over the sea, bringing them nice things to eat once more; for, poor babes, the lack of dainty fare had been the hardest part of all the siege for them.

We had hardly got downstairs again, when the boat ran close up to our roughly constructed landing-stage, which was little more than a ledge of rock, and willing hands seized the ropes which were flung out to them.

Then amidst such cheering as I shall never forget, her crew jumped out. Forty men of them there were, strong, stalwart, strapping fellows, looking very different from our own poor lads, who were pinched and thin from long watching, and meagre fare. Their leader was Sir Alexander Ramsay of Dalhousie, one of the bravest of Scottish knights, and most chivalrous of men, who had risked his life, and the lives of his men, in order to bring us help.

"Now Heaven and all the Saints be thanked, we are in time," he cried, as his eyes rested on my lady, who was standing at the head of the steps which led up to the little postern, with one babe in her arms, and the other clinging to her gown, "for dire tales have reached us of pestilence and starvation which were working their will within these walls."

Then he doffed his helmet, and ran up to where she was standing, and I wot there was not a dry eye in the crowd as he knelt and kissed her hand.

"Here greet I one of the bravest ladies in Christendom," he said, "for, by my troth, as long as the Scots' tongue lasts, the story of how thou kept thy lord's castle in his absence will be handed down from father to son."

"Nay, noble sir," she answered, and there was a little catch in her voice as she spoke, "it hath not been so very hard after all. My men have been brave and leal, my walls are thick, and although the wolf hath come very near the door, he hath not as yet entered."

"Nor shall he," said Sir Alexander cheerily, as he picked up Mistress Marjory and kissed her, "for we have brought enough provisions with us to victual your Castle twice over."

And in good sooth they had. It took more than half an hour to unload the boat, and to carry its contents into the great hall. There had been kind hands and thoughtful hearts at the loading of it. There was milk for the bairns, and capons, and eggs. There was meat and ale for the men, and red French wine and white bread for my lady, and bags of grain and meal, and many other things which I scarce remember, but which were right toothsome, I can tell you, after the scanty fare on which we had been living.

And so ended the famous siege of Dunbar Castle, for on the morrow, the English, knowing that now it was hopeless to think of taking it, struck their camp, and by nightfall they were marching southwards, worsted by a woman.

And ere another day had passed, another band of armed men came riding through the woods that lie thickly o'er the valley in which lies the Lamp of Lothian,[15] but this time we knew right well the device which was emblazoned on the banners, and the horses neighed, as horses are wont to do when they scent their own stables, and the riders tossed their caps in the air at the sight of us.

And I trow that if my lady had wished for reward for all the weary months of anxiety which she had passed through, she had it in full measure when at long last she opened the Castle gates, and saw the look on her husband's face, as he took her in his arms, and kissed her, not once, but many times, there, in the courtyard, in the sight of us all.

THE BROWNIE OF BLEDNOCK

There came a strange wight to our town en',
    An' the fient a body did him ken;
He twirled na' lang, but he glided ben,
    Wi' a weary, dreary hum.
His face did glow like the glow o' the West,
    When the drumly cloud had it half o'ercast;
Or the struggling moon when she's sair distrest.
    O, Sirs! it was Aiken-Drum.

Did you ever hear how a Brownie came to our village of Blednock, and was frightened away again by a silly young wife, who thought she was cleverer than anyone else, but who did us the worst turn that she ever did anybody in her life, when she made the queer, funny, useful little man disappear?

Well, it was one November evening, in the gloaming, just when the

THE BROWNIE OF BLEDNOCK. From *Children's Tales from Scottish Ballads,* by Elizabeth W. Grierson. By permission of A. & C. Black Ltd.
[15] The Abbey of Haddington (an old name for it).

milking was done, and before the bairns were put to bed, and everyone
was standing on their doorsteps, having a crack about the bad harvest,
and the turnips, and what chances there were of good prices for the stirks[16]
at the Martinmas Fair, when the queerest humming noise started down by
the river.

It came nearer and nearer, and everyone stopped their clavers[17] and
began to look down the road. And, 'deed, it was no wonder that they stared,
for there, coming up the middle of the highway, was the strangest, most
frightsome-looking creature that human eyes had ever seen.

He looked like a little wee, wee man, and yet he looked like a beast,
for he was covered with hair from head to foot, and he wore no clothing
except a little kilt of green rashes which hung round his waist. His hair was
matted, and his head hung forward on his breast, and he had a long
blue beard, which almost touched the ground.

His legs were twisted, and knocked together as he walked, and his arms
were so long that his hands trailed in the mud.

He seemed to be humming something over and over again, and, as he
came near us we could just make out the words, "Hae ye wark for Aiken-
Drum?"

Eh, but I can tell you the folk were scared. If it had been the Evil
One himself who had come to our quiet little village, I doubt if he would
have caused more stir.[18] The bairns screamed, and hid their faces in their
mothers' gown-tails, while the lassies, idle huzzies that they were, threw
down the pails of milk, which should have been in the milkhouse long ago,
if they had not been so busy gossiping; and the very dogs crept in behind
their masters, whining, and hiding their tails between their legs. The grown
men, who should have known better, and who were not frightened to look
the wee man in the face, laughed and hooted at him.

"Did ye ever see such eyes?" cried one.

"His mouth is so big, he could swallow the moon," said another.

"Hech, sirs, but did ye ever see such a creature?" cried the third.

And still the poor little man went slowly up the street, crying wistfully,
"Hae ye wark for Aiken-Drum? Any wark for Aiken-Drum?"

Some of us tried to speak to him, but our tongues seemed to be tied, and
the words died away on our lips, and we could only stand and watch him
with frightened glances, as if we were bewitched.

Old Grannie Duncan, the oldest, and the kindest woman in the village,
was the first to come to her senses. "He may be a ghost, or a bogle, or a
wraith," she said; "or he may only be a harmless Brownie. It is beyond
me to say; but this I know that if he be an evil spirit, he will not dare to
look on the Holy Book." And with that she ran into her cottage, and

16 Bullocks.
17 Idle talk.
18 Excitement.

brought out the great leather-bound Bible which aye lay on her little table by the window.

She stood on the road, and held it out, right in front of the creature, but he took no more heed of it than if it had been an old song-book, and went slowly on, with his weary cry for work.

"He's just a Brownie," cried Grannie Duncan in triumph, "a simple, kindly Brownie. I've heard tell of such folk before, and many a long day's work will they do for the people who treat them well."

Gathering courage from her words, we all crowded round the wee man, and now that we were close to him, we saw that his hairy face was kind and gentle and his tiny eyes had a merry twinkle in them.

"Save us, and help us, creature!" said an old man reprovingly, "but can ye no speak, and tell us what ye want, and where ye come from?"

For answer the Brownie looked all round him, and gave such a groan, that we scattered and ran in all directions, and it was full five minutes before we could pluck up our courage and go close to him again.

But Grannie Duncan stood her ground, like a brave old woman that she was, and it was to her that the creature spoke.

"I cannot tell thee from whence I come," he said.

" 'Tis a nameless land, and 'tis very different from this land of thine. For there we all learn to serve, while here everyone wishes to be served. And when there is no work for us to do at home, then we sometimes set out to visit thy land, to see if there is any work which we may do there. I must seem strange to human eyes, that I know; but if thou wilt, I will stay in this place awhile. I need not that any should wait on me, for I seek neither wages, nor clothes, nor bedding. All I ask for is the corner of a barn to sleep in, and a cogful of brose set down on the floor at bedtime; and if no one meddles with me, I will be ready to help anyone who needs me. I'll gather your sheep betimes on the hill; I'll take in your harvest by moonlight. I'll sing the bairns to sleep in their cradles, and, though I doubt you'll not believe it, you'll find that the babes will love me. I'll kirn your kirns[19] for you, goodwives, and I'll bake your bread on a busy day; while, as for the men folk, they may find me useful when there is corn to thrash, or untamed colts in the stable, or when the waters are out in flood."

No one quite knew what to say to answer to the creature's strange request. It was an unheard-of-thing for anyone to come and offer their services for nothing, and the men began to whisper among themselves, and to say that it was not canny, and 'twere better to have nothing to do with him.

But up spoke Old Grannie Duncan again. " 'Tis but a Brownie, I tell you," she repeated, "a poor, harmless Brownie, and many a story have I heard in my young days about the work that a Brownie can do, if he be well treated and let alone. Have we not been complaining all summer about

[19] A churn.

bad times, and scant wages, and a lack of workmen to work the work? And now, when a workman comes ready to your hand, ye will have none of him, just because he is not bonnie to look on."

Still the men hesitated, and the silly young wenches screwed their faces, and pulled their mouths. "But, Grannie," cried they, "that is all very well, but if we keep such a creature in our village, no one will come near it, and then what shall we do for sweethearts?"

"Shame on ye," cried Grannie impatiently, "and on all you men for encouraging the silly things in their whimsies. It's time that ye were thinking o' other things than bonnie faces and sweethearts. 'Handsome is that handsome does,' is a good old saying; and what about the corn that stands rotting in the fields, an' it past Hallowe'en already? I've heard that a Brownie can stack a whole ten-acre field in a single night."

That settled the matter. The miller offered the creature the corner of his barn to sleep in, and Grannie promised to boil the cogful of brose, and send her grandchild, wee Jeannie, down with it every evening, and then we all said good-night, and went into our houses, looking over our shoulders as we did so, for fear that the strange little man was following us.

But if we were afraid of him that night, we had a very different song to sing before a week was over. Whatever he was, or whatever he came from, he was the most wonderful worker that men had ever known. And the strange thing was that he did most of it at night. He had the corn safe into the stackyards and the stacks thatched, in the clap of a hand, as the old folk say.

The village became the talk of the countryside, and folk came from all parts to see if they could catch a glimpse of our queer, hairy little visitor; but they were always unsuccessful, for he was never to be seen when one looked for him. One might go into the miller's barn twenty times a day, and twenty times a day find nothing but a heap of straw; and although the cog of brose was aye empty in the morning, no one knew when he came home, or when he supped it.

But wherever there was work to be done, whether it was a sickly bairn to be sung to, or a house to be tidied up; a kirn that would not kirn, or a batch of bread that would not rise; a flock of sheep to be gathered together on a stormy night, or a bundle to be carried home by some weary labourer; Aiken-Drum, as we learned to call him, always got to know of it, and appeared in the nick of time. It looked as if we had all got wishing-caps, for we had just to wish, and the work was done.

Many a time, some poor mother, who had been up with a crying babe all night, would sit down with it in her lap, in front of the fire, in the morning, and fall fast asleep, and when she awoke, she would find that Aiken-Drum had paid her a visit, for the floor would be washed, and the dishes too, and the fire made up, and the kettle put on to boil; but the little man would have slipped away, as if he were frightened of being thanked.

The bairns were the only ones who ever saw him idle, and oh, how they loved him! In the gloaming, or when the school was out, one could see them away down in some corner by the burn[20]—side, crowding round the little dark brown figure, with its kilt of rushes, and one would hear the sound of wondrous low sweet singing, for he knew all the songs that the little ones loved.

So by and by the name of Aiken-Drum came to be a household word amongst us, and although we so seldom saw him near at hand, we loved him like one of our ain folk.

And he might have been here still, had it not been for a silly, senseless young wife who thought she knew better than everyone else, and who took some idle notion into her empty head that it was not right to make the little man work, and give him no wage.

She dinned[21] this into our heads, morning, noon, and night, and she would not believe us when we told her that Aiken-Drum worked for love, and love only.

Poor thing, she could not understand anyone doing that, so she made up her mind that she, at least, would do what was right, and set us all an example.

"She did not mean any harm," she said afterwards, when the miller took her to task for it; but although she might not mean to do any harm, she did plenty, as senseless folk are apt to do when they cannot bear to take other people's advice, for she took a pair of her husband's old, mouldy, worn-out breeches, and laid them down one night beside the cog-ful of brose.

By my faith, if the village folk had not remembered so well what Aiken-Drum had said about wanting no wages, they would have found something better to give him than a pair of worn-out breeks.

Be that as it may, the long and the short of it was, that the dear wee man's feelings were hurt because we would not take his services for nothing, and he vanished in the night, as Brownies are apt to do, so Grannie Duncan says, if anyone tries to pay them, and we have never seen him from that day to this, although the bairns declare that they sometimes hear him singing down by the mill, as they pass it in the gloaming, on their was home from school.

MUCKLE-MOU'ED MEG

"Juden, Juden." It was the Lady Elibank's voice, and it woke her husband, Sir Juden, out of a sound sleep. He had just that day fought a

MUCKLE-MOU'ED MEG. From *Tales from Scottish Ballads*, by Elizabeth W. Grierson. By permission of A. & C. Black, Ltd.
[20] Stream.
[21] Impressed this upon us.

band of raiders and had captured young William Harden, their leader. Harden, who had grown up loving the free roving life of a border raider found the law which forbade raiding difficult. So this day he had taken a band of chosen men, and as an adventure, had ridden over to Sir Juden's to raid his cattle. He had forgotten that Sir Juden was as cunning as a fox so it was not long before Will was captured. It was now morning and Will was safe in the lowest dungeon, awaiting the penalty for such a crime; that of dieing under the great dule tree on the green.

"Juden, Juden," came the voice of Lady Elibank.

"What is it?" he asked drowsily, as he looked across the room to where his worthy spouse, already up and dressed, stood looking out of the narrow casement.

"I was just wondering," she said slowly, "what thou intendest to do with that poor young man?"

"Do," cried Sir Juden, wide awake now, and starting up in astonishment at the question, for his wife was not wont to be so pitiful towards any of his prisoners. "By'r Lady, but there is only one thing that I shall do. Hang the rogue, of course, and that right speedily."

"What," said the Lady of Elibank, and she turned and looked at her angry husband with an expression which seemed to say that at that moment he had taken leave of his senses; "hang the young Knight of Harden, when I have three ill-favoured daughters to marry off my hands! I wonder at ye, Juden! I aye thought ye had a modicum of common sense, and could look a long way in front of ye, but at this moment I am sorely inclined to doubt it. Mark my words, ye'll never again have such a chance as this. For, besides Harden, he is heir to some of the finest lands in Ettrick Forest. Think of our Meg; would ye not like to see the lassie mistress of these? And well I wot ye might, for the youth is a spritely young fellow, though given to adventure, as what brave young man is not? And I trow that he would put up with an ill-featured wife, rather than lose his life on our hanging-tree."

Sir Juden looked at his wife for full three minutes in silence, and then he broke into a loud laugh. "By my soul, thou art right, Margaret," he said. "Thou wert born with the wisdom of Solomon, though men would scarce think it to look at thee." And he began to dress himself, without more ado.

Less than two hours afterwards, the door of the dungeon where young Scott was confined was thrown open with a loud and grating noise, and three men-at-arms appeared, and requested the prisoner, all bound as he was, to follow them.

Willie obeyed without a word. He had dared, and had been defeated, and now he must pay the penalty that the times required, and like a brave man he would pay it uncomplainingly, but I warrant that, as he followed the men up the steep stone steps, his heart was heavy within him, and his thoughts were dwelling on the bonnie braes that lay around Harden, where he had so often played when he was a bairn, and which he knew he would never see again.

But, to his astonishment, instead of being led straight out to the "dule-tree," as he had expected, he was taken into the great hall, and stationed close to one of the narrow windows. A strange sight met his eyes.

The hall was full of armed men, who were looking about them with broad smiles of amusement, while on a dais at the far end of the hall, were seated, in two large armchairs, his captor of the night before, Sir Juden Murray, and a severe-looking lady, in a wondrous head-dress, and a stiff silken gown, whom he took to be his wife.

Between them, blushing and hanging her head as if the ordeal was too much for her, was the plainest-looking maiden he had ever seen in his life. She was thin and ill-thriven-looking, very different from the buxom lassies he was accustomed to see: her eyes were colourless; her nose was long and pointed, and the size of her mouth would alone have proclaimed her to be the worthy couple's eldest daughter, Muckle-Mou'ed Meg.

Near the dais stood her two younger sisters. They were plain-looking girls also, but hardly so plain-looking as Meg, and they were laughing and whispering to one another, as if much amused by what was going on.

Sir Juden cleared his throat and crossed one thin leg slowly over the other, while he looked keenly at his prisoner from under his bushy eyebrows.

"Good morrow, young sir," he said at last; "so you and your friends thought that ye would like a score or two o' the Elibank kye. By whose warrant, may I ask, did ye ride, seeing that in those days peace is declared on the Border, and anyone who breaks it, breaks it at his own risk?"

"I rode at my own peril," answered the young man haughtily, for he did not like to be questioned in this manner, "and it is on mine own head that the blame must fall. Thou knowest that right well, Sir Juden, so it seems to me but waste of words to parley here."

"So thou knowest the fate that thy rash deed brings on thee," said Sir Juden hastily, his temper, never of the sweetest, rising rapidly at the young man's coolness. He would fain have hanged him without more ado, did prudence permit; and it was hard to sit still and bargain with him.

"So thou knowest that I have the right to hang thee, without further words," he continued; "and, by my faith, many a man would do it, too, without delay. But thou art young, William, and young blood must aye be roving, that I would fain remember, and so I offer thee another chance."

Here the Lord of Elibank paused and glanced at his wife, to see if he had said the right thing, for it was she who had arranged the scene beforehand, and had schooled her husband in the part he was to play.

Meanwhile young Harden, happening to meet Meg Murray's eyes, and puzzled by the look, half wistful, half imploring, which he saw there, glanced hastily out of the little casement beside which he was standing, and received a rude shock, in spite of all his courage, when he saw a stronge rope, with a noose at the end of it, dangling from a stout branch of the dule-tree on the green, while a man-at-arms stood kicking the ground idly beside it, apparently waiting till he should be called on to act as executioner.

"So the old rascal is going to hang me after all," he said to himself; "then what, in Our Lady's name, means this strange mummery, and how comes that ill-favoured maiden to look at me as if her life depended on mine?"

At that moment, old Sir Juden, reassured by a nod from Dame Margaret, went on with his speech.

"I will therefore offer thee another chance, I say, and, moreover, I will throw a herd of cattle which thou wert so anxious to steal into the bargain, if thou wilt promise, on thy part, to wed my daughter Meg within the space of four days."

Here the wily old man stopped, and the Lady of Elibank nodded her head again, while, as for young Harden, for the moment he was too astonished to speak.

So this was the meaning of it all. He was to be forced to marry the ugliest maiden in the south of Scotland in order to save his life. The vision of his mother's beauty rose before him, and the contrast between the Flower of Yarrow and Muckle-Mou'ed Meg o' Elibank struck him so sharply that he cried out in anger, "By my troth, but this thing shall never be. So do thy worst, Sir Juden."

"Think well before ye choose," said that knight, more disappointed than he would have cared to own at his prisoner's words, "for there are better things in this world than beauty, young man. Many a beautiful woman hath been but a thorn in her husband's side, and besides that, hast thou not learned in the Good Book—if ever ye find time to read it, which I fear me will be but seldom—that a prudent wife is more to be sought after than a bonnie one? And though my Meg here is mayhap no' sae well-favoured as the lassies over in Borthwick Water, or Teviotdale, I warrant there is not one of them who hath proved such a good daughter, or whose nature is so kind and generous."

Still young Harden hesitated, and glanced from the lady, who, poor thing, had hidden her face in her hands, to the gallows, and from the gallows back again to the lady.

Was ever mortal man in such a plight? Here he was, young, handsome, rich, and little more than four-and-twenty, and he must either lose his life on the green yonder, or marry a damsel whom everyone mocked at for her looks.

"If only I could be alone with her for five minutes," he thought to himself, "to see what she looks like, when there is no one to peep and peer at her. The maiden had not a chance in the midst of this mannerless crowd, and methought her eyes were open and honest, as they looked into mine a little while ago."

At that moment Meg Murray lifted her head once more, and gazed round her like a stag at bay. Poor lassie, it had been bad enough to be jeered at by her father, and flouted and scolded by her mother, because of the unfortunately large mouth with which Providence had endowed her, without being put up for sale, as it were, in the presence of all her father's retainers, and find that the young man to whom she had been offered chose to suffer death rather than have her for a bride.

It was the bitterest moment of all her life, and, had she known it, it was the moment that fixed her destiny.

For young Willie of Harden saw that look, and something in it stirred his pity. Besides, he noticed that her pale face was sweet and confiding, and her gray eyes clear and true.

"Hold," he cried, just as Sir Juden, whose patience was quite exhausted, gave a signal to his men-at-arms to seize the prisoner, and hurry him off to the gallows. "I have changed my mind, and I accept the conditions. But I call all men to witness that I accept not the hand of this noble maiden of necessity, or against my will. I am a Scott, and, had I been minded to, I could have faced death. But I crave the honour of her hand from her father with all humility, and here I vow, before ye all, to do my best to be to her a loyal and a true man."

Loud cheers, and much jesting, followed this speech, and men who would have crowded round the young Knight and made much of him, but he pushed his way in grim silence up the hall to where Meg o' Elibank stood trembling by her delighted parents.

She greeted him with a look which set him thinking of a bird which sees its cage flung open, and I wot that, though he did not know it, at that moment he began to love her.

Be that as it may, his words to Sir Juden were short and gruff. "Sir," he asked, "hast thou a priest in thy company? For, if so, let him come hither and finish what we have begun. I would fain spend this night in my own Tower of Oakwood."

Sir Juden and his lady were not a little taken aback at this sudden demand, for, now that the matter was settled to their satisfaction, they would have liked to have married their eldest daughter with more state and ceremony.

"There's no need of such haste," began Dame Margaret, with a look at her lord, "if your word is given, and the Laird satisfied. The morn, or even the next day might do. The lassie's trousseau must be gathered together, for I would not like it said that a bride went out of Elibank with nothing but the clothes she stood in."

But young Harden interrupted her with small courtesy. "Let her be married now, or not at all," he said, and as the heir of Harden as a prospective son-in-law was very different from the heir of Harden as a prisoner, she feared to say him nay, lest he went back on his word.

So a priest was sent for, and in great haste William Scott of Harden was wedded to Margaret Murray of Elibank, and then they two set off alone, over the hills to the old Tower of Oakwood—he, with high thoughts of anger and revenge in his heart for the trick that had been played him; —she, poor thing, wondering wistfully what the future held in store for her.

The day was cold and wet, and halfway over the Hangingshaw Height he heard a stifled sob behind him, and, looking over his shoulder, he saw his little woebegone bride trying in vain with her numbed fingers to guide her palfrey, which was floundering in a moss-hole, to firmer footing.

The sight would have touched a harder heart than Willie of Harden's, for he was a true son of his mother, and the Flower of Yarrow was aye kind-hearted; and suddenly all his anger vanished.

"God save us, lassie, but there's nothing to cry about," he said, turning his horse and taking her reins from her poor stiff fingers, and, though the words were rough, his voice was strangely gentle. " 'Tis not thy fault that things have fallen out thus, and if I be a trifle angered, in good faith it is not with thee. Come," and, as he spoke, he stooped down and lifted her bodily from her saddle, and swung her up in front of him on his great black horse. "Leave that stupid beast of thine alone; 'twill find its way back to Elibank soon enough, I warrant. We will go over the hill quicker in this fashion, and thou wilt have more shelter from the rain. There is many a good nag on the hills at Harden, and, when she hears of our wedding, I doubt not but that my mother will have one trained for thee."

Poor Meg caught her breath. She did not feel so much afraid of her husband now that she was close to him, and his arm was round her; besides, the shelter from the rain was very pleasant; but still her heart misgave her.

"Thy Lady Mother, she is very beautiful," she faltered, "and doubtless she looked for beauty in her sons' wives."

Then, for ever and a day, all resentment went out of Willie of Harden's heart, and pure love and pity entered into it.

"If her sons' wives are but good women, my mother will be well content," he said, and with that he kissed her.

And I trow that that kiss marked the beginning of Meg Scott's happiness.

For happy she always was. She was aye plain-looking—nothing on earth could alter her features—but with great happiness comes a look of marvellous contentment, which can beautify the most homely face, and she was such a clever housekeeper (no one could salt beef as she could), and so modest and gentle, that her husband grew to love her more and more, and I wot that her face became to him the bonniest and the sweetest face in the whole world.

Sons and daughters were born to them, strapping lads and fair-faced lassies, and, in after years, when old Wat o' Harden died, and Sir William reigned in his stead, in the old house at the head of the glen, he was wont to declare that for prudence, and virtue, and honour, there was no woman on earth to be compared with his own good wife Meg.

WALES

We march round by two and two
The circles of the sacred well,
That lies in the dell.[22]

Wales contributes a happy conclusion to the folk lore of Europe. "The Fairy of the Dell," answers the English question, "What's a Brownie?," and presents witches, devils, and fairies, with the conclusive moral righteousness so characteristic of the European folk tale pattern.

THE FAIRY OF THE DELL

I

In olden times fairies were sent to oppose the evil-doings of witches, and to destroy their power. About three hundred years ago a band of fairies, sixty in number, with their queen, called Queen of the Dell, came to Mona to oppose the evil works of a celebrated witch. The fairies settled by a spring, in a valley. After having blessed the spring, or "well," as they called it, they built a bower just above the spring for the queen, placing a throne therein. Nearby they built a large bower for themselves to live in.

After that, the queen drew three circles, one within the other, on a nice flat grassy place by the well. When they were comfortably settled, the queen sent the fairies about the country to gather tidings of the people. They went from house to house, and everywhere heard great complaints against an old witch; how she had made some blind, others lame, and deformed others by causing a horn to grow out of their foreheads. When they got back to the well and told the queen, she said:

"I must do something for these old people, and though the witch is very powerful, we must break her power." So the next day the queen fairy

THE FAIRY OF THE DELL. From *Welsh Fairy Tales and Other Stories*, by P. H. Emerson.
[22] P. H. Emerson, "The Fairy of the Dell," from *Welsh Fairy Tales and Other Stories*.

sent word to all the bewitched to congregate upon a fixed day at the sacred well, just before noon.

When the day came, several ailing people collected at the well. The queen then placed the patients in pairs in the inner ring, and the sixty fairies in pairs in the middle ring. Each little fairy was three feet and a half high, and carried a small wand in her right hand, and a bunch of fairy flowers—cuckoo's boots, baby's bells, and day's eyes—in her left hand. Then the queen, who was four feet and a half in height, took the outside ring. On her head was a crown of wild flowers, in her right hand she carried a wand, and in her left a posy of fairy flowers. At a signal from the queen they began marching round the rings, singing in chorus:

> We march round by two and two
> The circles of the sacred well
> That lies in the dell.

When they had walked twice round the ring singing, the queen took her seat upon the throne, and calling each patient to her, she touched him with her wand and bade him go down to the sacred well and dip his body into the water three times, promising that all his ills should be cured. As each one came forth from the spring he knelt before the queen, and she blessed him, and told him to hurry home and put on dry clothes. So that all were cured of their ills.

II

Now the old witch who had worked all these evils lived near the well in a cottage. She had first learned witchcraft from a book called The Black Art, which a gentleman farmer had lent her when a girl. She progressed rapidly with her studies, and being eager to learn more, sold herself to the devil, who made compact with her that she should have full power for seven years, after which she was to become his. He gave her a wand that had the magic power of drawing people to her, and she had a ring on the grass by her house just like the fairy's ring. As the seven years were drawing to a close, and her heart was savage against the farmer who first led her into the paths of evil knowledge, she determined to be revenged. One day, soon after the Fairy of the Dell came to live by the spring, she drew the farmer to her with her wand, and, standing in her ring, she lured him into it. When he crossed the line, she said:

> Cursed be he or she
> That crosses my circle to see me,

and, touching him on the head and back, a horn and a tail grew from the spots touched. He went off in a terrible rage, but she only laughed maliciously. Then, as she heard of the Queen of the Dell's good deeds, she repented of her evil deeds, and begged her neighbour to go to the queen fairy and ask if she might come and visit her. The queen consented, and the old witch went down and told her everything—of the book, of the magic wand, of the ring, and of all the wicked deeds she had done.

"O, you have been a bad witch," said the queen, "but I will see what I can do; but you must bring me the book and the wand"; and she told the old witch to come on the following day a little before noon. When the witch came the next day with her wand and book, she found the fairies had built a fire in the middle ring. The queen then took her and stood her by the fire, for she could not trust her on the outer circle.

"Now I must have more power," said the queen to the fairies, and she went and sat on the throne, leaving the witch by the fire in the middle ring. After thinking a little, the queen said, "Now I have it," and coming down from her throne muttering, she began walking round the outer circle, waiting for the hour of one o'clock, when all the fairies got into the middle circle and marched round, singing:

> At the hour of one
> The cock shall crow one,
> Goo! Goo! Goo!
> I am here to tell
> Of the sacred well
> That lies in the dell,
> And will conquer hell.

On the second round, they sang:

> At the hour of two
> The cock crows two,
> Goo! Goo! Goo!
> I am here to tell
> Of the sacred well
> That lies in the dell;
> We will conquer hell.

At the last round, they sang:

> At the hour of three
> The cock crows three,
> Goo! Goo! Goo!
> I am here to tell
> Of the sacred well
> That lies in the dell;
> Now I have conquered hell.

Then the queen cast the book and wand into the fire, and immediately the vale was rent by a thundering noise, and numbers of devils came from everywhere, and encircled the outer ring, but they could not pass the ring.

Then the fairies began walking round and round, singing their song. When they had finished the song they heard a loud screech from the devils that frightened all the fairies except the queen. She was unmoved, and going to the fire, stirred the ashes with her wand, and saw that the book and wand were burnt, and then she walked thrice round the outer ring by herself, when she turned to the devils, and said:

"I command you to be gone from our earthly home, get to your own abode. I take the power of casting you all from here. Begone! begone! begone!"

And all the devils flew up, and there was a mighty clap as of thunder, and the earth trembled, and the sky became overcast, and all the devils burst, and the sky cleared again.

After this the queen put three fairies by the old witch's side, and they constantly dipped their wands in the sacred spring, and touched her head, and she was sorely troubled and converted.

"Bring the mirror," said the queen.

And the fairies brought the mirror and laid it in the middle circle, and they all walked round three times, chanting again the song beginning "At the hour of one." When they had done this the queen stood still, and said:

> Stand and watch to see what you can see.

And as she looked she said:

> The mirror shines unto me
> That the witch we can see
> Has three devils inside of she.

Immediately the witch had a fit, and the three fairies had a hard job to keep the three devils quiet; indeed, they could not do so, and the queen had to go herself with her wand, for fear the devils should burst the witch asunder, and she said, "Come out three evil spirits, out of thee."

And they came gnashing their teeth, and would have killed all the fairies, but the queen said:

"Begone, begone, begone! you evil spirits, to the place of your abode," and suddenly the sky turned bright as fire, for the evil spirits were trying their spleen against the fairies, but the queen said, "Collect, collect, collect, into one fierce ball," and the fiery sky collected into one ball of fire more dazzling than the sun, so that none could look at it except the queen, who wore a black silk mask to protect her eyes. Suddenly the ball burst with a terrific noise, and the earth trembled.

"Enter into your abode, and never come down to our abode on earth any more," said the queen.

And the witch was herself again, and she and the queen fairy were immediately great friends.

6

LATIN AMERICA

Lunes y martes y miércoles—tres
(Monday and Tuesday and Wednesday—three.)
Jueves y viernes y sábado—seis
(Thursday and Friday and Saturday—six)
Y domingo siete![1]

The charm of the Latin American tale is the mixture of old beliefs and customs with newer ones. The stories are of the creation, the concept of animal and man, historical fact turned to fantasy, and religion. All are handled with a light-hearted, humorous touch.

JABUTÍ AND THE FESTIVAL IN HEAVEN

There was once a festival in heaven that was to last for three days; all the animals went, but the second day of the festival had passed, and the turtle still had not arrived because he traveled so slowly. Some of the other animals were already on their way home, while Jabutí was still only halfway there. On the last day the heron offered to carry him on her back. Jabutí accepted and climbed on; but the evil bird kept asking whether Jabutí could still see the ground, and when at last he said he could no longer see the earth below, the heron suddenly dropped him, and the poor fellow went rolling over and over, and as he fell, he cried:

A wretched beast am I;
If this cruel fate should pass me by,
No more feasting in the sky!

And also: "Get out of my way you sticks and stones, or else you will get broken." The sticks and stones drew aside, and down he came and

JABUTÍ AND THE FESTIVAL IN HEAVEN. From *Stories and Storytellers of Brazil*, by C. Malcolm Batchelor. By permission of C. Malcolm Batchelor.
[1] Frank Dobie, "The Hunchback," from *The Tongues of the Monte*.

broke to pieces. But God took pity on Jabutí, and gathering the pieces together made Jabutí as good as new because he had tried so hard to get to Heaven. As good as new—well, not quite, because to this day Jabutí has a back like a patchwork quilt, where his pieces were put together.

JABUTÍ AND THE LEOPARD

There came a time when after tricks and traps had failed, the Leopard found Jabutí asleep on his doorstep where he had been sunning himself.

"Now!" said the Leopard. "I'm going to kill you at last, but to show you how just I am in all matters, I shall let you decide how you are to die."

"Very well!" said Jabutí. "Mention a few things, and I'll choose."

"How would you like it if I dropped you on a rock?"

"That wouldn't do any good, because my shell is so tough!"

(The stupid Leopard had forgotten about the Festival in Heaven.)

"Hmm! How about cooking you in the biggest bonfire that ever was?"

"No good!" said Jabutí. "My shell is too tough!"

"How would it be," asked the Leopard, "if I stamped you so far into the ground that you couldn't budge?"

"No good!" said Jabutí. "Because when the rainy season came, I'd work my way out."

"Well," said the Leopard, growing impatient, "how would it be if I threw you into the river?"

"Oh, no!" cried Jabutí. "Not the river! I'd drown!"

So the Leopard threw Jabutí far out into the river, but Jabutí rose to the surface.

"Ho! Ho!" he shouted. "You didn't know I could swim so well!"

And away he swam, and climbing out on the other side, disappeared into the jungle.

THE LAZY BEE

In a beehive once there was a bee who would not work. Every morning, the moment the sun had warmed the hive, she would come to the

JABUTÍ AND THE LEOPARD. From *Stories and Storytellers of Brazil,* by C. Malcolm Batchelor. By permission of C. Malcolm Batchelor.

THE LAZY BEE. From *South American Jungle Tales,* by Horacio Quiroga. By permission of Methuen & Co. Ltd., Publishers.

door and look out. On making sure that it was a lovely day, she would wash her face and comb her hair with her paws, the way flies do, and then go flitting off, as pleased as could be at the bright weather. So she would go buzzing and buzzing from flower to flower; and then after a time she would go back and see what the other bees were doing in the hive. So it would go all day long.

Meantime the other bees would be working themselves to death trying to fill the hive full of honey; for honey is what they give the little bees to eat as soon as they are born. And these worker bees, very staid, respectable, earnest bees, began to scowl at the conduct of this shirker of a sister they had.

You must know that, at the door of every beehive, there are always a number of bees on watch, to see that no insects but bees get into the hive. These policemen, as a rule, are old bees, with a great deal of experience in life. Their backs are quite bald, because all the hair gets worn off from rubbing against the hive as they walk in and out of the door.

One day when the lazy bee was just dropping in to see what was going on in the hive, these policemen called her to one side:

"Sister," said they, "it is time you did a little work. All of us bees have to work!"

The little bee was quite scared when the policemen spoke to her, but she answered:

"I go flying about all day long, and get very tired!"

"We didn't ask you how tired you got! We want to see how much work you can do! This is Warning Number 1!"

And they let her go on into the hive.

But the lazy little bee did not mend her ways. On the next evening the policemen stopped her again:

"Sister, we didn't see you working today!"

The little bee was expecting something of the kind, and she had been thinking up what she would say all the way home.

"I'll go to work one of these days," she spoke up promptly; and with a cheerful, winsome smile.

"We don't want you to go to work one of these days," they answered gruffly. "We want you to go to work tomorrow morning. This is Warning Number 2!"

And they let her in.

The following night, when the lazy bee came home, she did not wait for the policemen to stop her. She went up to them sorrowfully and said:

"Yes, yes! I remember what I promised. I'm so sorry I wasn't able to work today!"

"We didn't ask how sorry you were, nor what you had promised. What we want from you is work. Today is the nineteenth of April. Tomorrow will be the twentieth of April. See to it that the twentieth of April does not pass without your putting at least one load of honey into the hive. This is Warning Number 3! You may enter!"

And the policeman who had been blocking the door stepped aside to let her in.

The lazy bee woke up with very good intentions the next morning; but the sun was so warm and bright and the flowers were so beautiful! The day passed the same as all the others; except that toward evening the weather changed. The sun went down behind a great bank of clouds and a strong icy wind began to blow.

The lazy little bee started for home as fast as she could, thinking how warm and cozy it would be inside the hive, with all that storm blowing out of doors. But on the porch of the beehive the policemen got in front of her.

"Where are you going, young lady?" said they.

"I am going in to bed. This is where I live!"

"You must be mistaken," said the policemen. "Only busy worker bees live here! Lazy bees are not allowed inside this door!"

"Tomorrow, surely, surely, surely, I am going to work," said the little bee.

"There is no tomorrow for lazy bees," said the policemen; for they were old, wise bees, and knew philosophy. "Away with you!" And they pushed her off the doorstep.

The little bee did not know what to do. She flew around for a time; but soon it began to grow dark; the wind blew colder and colder, and drops of rain began to fall. Quite tired at last, she took hold of a leaf, intending to rest a moment; but she was chilled and numbed by the cold. She could not hang on, and fell a long distance to the ground.

She tried to get to her wings again, but they were too tired to work. So she started crawling over the ground toward the hive. Every stone, every stick she met, she had to climb over with great effort—so many hills and mountains they seemed to such a tiny bee. The raindrops were coming faster when, almost dead with cold and fright and fatigue, she arrived at the door of the hive.

"Oh, oh," she moaned. "I am cold, and it is going to rain! I shall be sure to die out here!" And she crept up to the door.

But the fierce policemen again stopped her from going in.

"Forgive me, sisters," the little bee said. "Please, let me go in!"

"Too late! Too late!" they answered.

"Please, sisters, I am cold!" said the little bee.

"Too late! Too late!" said they.

"Please, sisters, I am cold" said the little bee.

"Sorry! You can't go in!" said they.

"Please, sisters, for one last time! I shall die out here!"

"You won't die, lazy bee! One night will teach you the value of a warm bed earned by honest labor! Away from here!"

And they pushed her off the doorstep again.

By this time it was raining hard. The little bee felt her wings and fur getting wetter and wetter; and she was so cold and sleepy she did not know what to do. She crawled along as fast as she could over the ground, hoping to come to some place where it was dry and not so cold. At last she came to a tree and began to walk up the trunk. Suddenly, just as she had come to the crotch of two branches, she fell! She fell a long, long distance and landed finally on something soft. There was no wind and no rain blowing. On coming to her wits the little bee understood that she had fallen down through a hole inside a hollow tree.

And now the little bee had the fright of her life. Coiled up near her there was a snake, a green snake with a brick-colored back. That hollow tree was the snake's house; and the snake lay there looking at her with eyes that shone even in that darkness. Now, snakes eat bees, and like them. So when this little bee found herself so close to a fearful enemy of her kind, she just closed her eyes and murmured to herself:

"This is the last of me! Oh, how I wish I had worked!"

To her great surprise, however, the snake not only did not eat her, but spoke to her rather softly for such a terrible snake:

"How do you do, little bee? You must be a naughty little bee, to be out so late at night!"

"Yes," she murmured, her heart in her throat. "I have been a naughty bee. I did not work, and they won't let me in to go to my bed!"

"In that case, I shall not be so sorry to eat you!" answered the snake. "Surely there can be no harm at all in depriving the world of a useless little bee like you! I won't have to go out for dinner tonight. I shall eat you right here!"

The little bee was about as scared as a bee can be.

"That is not fair," she said. "It is not just! You have no right to eat me just because you are bigger than I am. Go and ask people if that isn't so! People know what is right and wrong!"

"Ah, ah!" said the snake, lifting his head higher, "so you have a good opinion of men? So you think that the men who steal your honey are more honest than snakes who eat you? You are not only a lazy bee. You are also a silly one!"

"It is not because men are dishonest that they take our honey," said the bee.

"Why is it then?" said the snake.

"It's because they are more intelligent than we are!" That is what the bee said; but the snake just laughed; and then he hissed:

"Well, if you must have it that way, it's because I'm more intelligent than you that I'm going to eat you now! Get ready to be eaten, lazy bee!"

And the snake drew back to strike, and lap up the bee at one gobble.

But the little bee had time to say:

"It's because you're duller than I am that you eat me!"

"Duller than you?" asked the snake, letting his head down again. "How is that, stupid?"

"However it is, it's so!"

"I'll have to be shown!" said the snake. "I will make a bargain with you. We will each do a trick; and the cleverest trick wins. If I win, I'll eat you!"

"And if I win?" asked the little bee.

"If you win," said the snake after some thought, "you may stay in here where it is warm all night. Is it a bargain?"

"It is," said the bee.

The snake considered another moment or so and then began to laugh. He had thought of something a bee could not possibly do. He darted out of a hole in the tree so quickly the bee had scarcely time to wonder what he was up to; and just as quickly he came back with a seed pod from the eucalyptus tree that stood near the beehive and shaded it on days when the sun was hot. Now the seed pods of the eucalyptus tree are just the shape of a top; in fact, the boys and girls in Argentina call them "tops"— trompitos!

"Now you just watch and see what I'm a-going to do," said the snake. "Watch now! Watch! . . ."

The snake wound the thin part of his tail around the top like a string; then, with a jump forward to his full length, he straightened his tail out. The "top" began to spin like mad on the bark floor there at the bottom of the hollow tree; and it spun and spun and spun, dancing, jumping, running off in this direction. And the snake laughed! And he laughed and he laughed! No bee would ever be able to do a thing like that!

Finally the top got tired of spinning and fell over on its side.

"That is very clever!" said the bee, "I could never do that!"

"In that case, I shall have to eat you!" said the snake.

"Not just yet, please," said the bee. "I can't spin a top; but I can do something no one else can do!"

"What is that?" asked the snake.

"I can disappear!" said the bee.

"What do you mean, disappear?" said the snake, with some interest. "Disappear so that I can't see you and without going away from here?"

"Without going away from here!"

"Without hiding in the ground?"

"Without hiding in the ground!"

"I give up!" said the snake. "Disappear! But if you don't do as you say, I eat you, gobble, gobble, just like that!"

Now you must know that while the top was spinning round and round, the little bee had noticed something on the floor of the hollow tree she had not seen before: it was a little shrub, three or four inches high, with leaves about the size of a fifty-cent piece. She now walked over to the stem of this little shrub, taking care, however, not to touch it with her body. Then she said:

"Now it is my turn, Mr. Snake. Won't you be so kind as to turn around, and count 'one,' 'two,' 'three.' At the word 'three,' you can look for me everywhere! I simply won't be around!"

The snake looked the other way and ran off a "onetathree," then turning around with his mouth wide open to have his dinner at last. You see, he counted so fast just to give the bee as little time as possible, under the contract they had made.

But if he opened his mouth wide for his dinner, he held it open in complete surprise. There was no bee to be found anywhere! He looked on the floor. He looked on the sides of the hollow tree. He looked in each nook and cranny. He looked the little shrub all over. Nothing! The bee had simply disappeared!

Now, the snake understood that if his trick of spinning the top with his tail was extraordinary, this trick of the bee was almost miraculous. Where had that good-for-nothing lazybones gone to? Here? No! There? No! Where then? Nowhere! There was no way to find the little bee!

"Well," said the snake at last, "I give up! Where are you?"

A little voice seemed to come from a long way off, but still from the middle of the space inside the hollow tree.

"You won't eat me if I reappear?" it said.

"No, I won't eat you!" said the snake.

"Promise?"

"I promise! But where are you?"

"Here I am," said the bee, coming out on one of the leaves of the little shrub.

It was not such a great mystery after all. That shrub was a Sensitive-plant, a plant that is very common in South America, especially in the North of the Republic of Argentina, where Sensitive-plants grow to quite a good size. The peculiarity of the Sensitive-plant is that it shrivels up its leaves at the slightest contact. The leaves of this shrub were unusually large, as is true of the Sensitive-plants around the city of Misiones. You see, the moment the bee lighted on a leaf, it folded up tight about her, hiding her completely from view. Now, the snake had been living next to that plant all the season long, and had never noticed anything unusual about it. The little bee had paid attention to such things, however; and her knowledge this time saved her life.

The snake was very much ashamed at being bested by such a little bee; and he was not very nice about it either. So much so, in fact, that the bee spent most of the night reminding him of the promise he had made not to eat her.

And it was a long, endless night for the little bee. She sat on the floor in one corner and the snake coiled up in the other corner opposite. Pretty soon it began to rain so hard that the water came pouring in through the hole at the top of the tree and made quite a puddle on the floor. The bee sat there and shivered and shivered; and every so often the snake would raise his head as though to swallow her at one gulp. "You promised! You promised! You promised!" And the snake would lower his head, sheepish-like, because he did not want the bee to think him a dishonest, as well as a stupid snake.

The little bee, who had been used to a warm hive at home and to warm sunlight out of doors, had never dreamed there would be so much cold anywhere as there was in that hollow tree. Nor had there ever been a night so long!

But the moment there was a trace of daylight at the hole in the top of the tree, the bee bade the snake good-by and crawled out. She tried her wings; and this time they worked all right. She flew in a bee-line straight for the door of the hive.

The policemen were standing there and she began to cry. But they simply stepped aside without saying a word, and let her in.

Never before was there such a bee for working from morning till night, day in, day out, gathering pollen and honey from the flowers.

THE PARROT THAT LOST ITS TAIL

In the woods near a farm lived a flock of parrots. Every morning, the parrots went and ate sweet corn in the garden of the farm. Afternoons they spent in the orange orchards eating oranges. They always made a great to-do with their screaming and jawing; but they kept a sentinel posted on one of the tree tops to let them know if the farmer was coming.

Parrots are very much disliked by farmers in countries where parrots grow wild. They bite into an ear of corn and the rest of the ear rots when the next rain comes. Besides, parrots are very good to eat when they are nicely broiled. At least the farmers of South America think so. That is why people hunt them a great deal with shotguns.

One day the hired man on this farm managed to shoot the sentinel of the flock of parrots. The parrot fell from the tree top with a broken wing. But he made a good fight of it on the ground, biting and scratching the man several times before he was made a prisoner. You see, the man noticed that the bird was not badly injured; and he thought he would take it home as a present for the farmer's children.

The farmer's wife put the broken wing in splints and tied a bandage tight around the parrot's body. The bird sat quite still for many days, until he was entirely cured. Meanwhile he had become quite tame. The

THE PARROT THAT LOST ITS TAIL. From *South American Jungle Tales*, by Horacio Quiroga. By permission of Methuen & Co. Ltd., Publishers.

children called him Pedrito; and Pedrito learned to hold out his claw to shake hands; he liked to perch on people's shoulders, and to tweek their ears gently with his bill.

Pedrito did not have to be kept in a cage. He spent the whole day out in the orange and eucalyptus trees in the yard of the farmhouse. He had a great time making sport of the hens when they cackled. The people of the family had tea in the afternoon, and then Pedrito would always come into the dining room and climb up with his claws and beak over the table-cloth to get his bread-and-milk. What Pedrito liked best of all was bread dipped in tea and milk.

The children talked to Pedrito so much, and he had so much to say to them, that finally he could pronounce quite a number of words in the language of people. He could say: "Good day, Pedrito!" and "Nice papa, nice papa"; "papa for Pedrito!" "Papa" is the word for bread-and-milk in South America. And he said many things that he should not have; for parrots, like children, learn naughty words very easily.

On rainy days Pedrito would sit on a chair back and grumble and grumble for hours at a time. When the sun came out again he would begin to fly about screaming at the top of his voice with pleasure.

Pedrito, in short, was a very happy and a very fortunate creature. He was as free as a bird can be. At the same time he had his afternoon tea like rich people.

Now it happened that one week it rained every day and Pedrito sat indoors glum and disconsolate all the time, and saying the most bitter and unhappy things to himself. But at last one morning the sun came out bright and glorious. Pedrito could not contain himself: "Nice day, nice day, Pedrito! Nice papa, nice papa, papa for Pedrito! Your paw, Pedrito!" So he went flitting about the yard, talking gayly to himself, to the hens, to everyone, including the beautiful, splendid sun itself. From a tree top he saw the river in the distance, a silvery, shining thread winding across the plain. And he flew off in that direction, flying, flying, flying, till he was quite tired and had to stop on a tree to rest.

Suddenly, on the ground far under him, Pedrito saw something shining through the trees, two bright green lights, as big as overgrown lightning bugs.

"Wonder what that is?" thought Pedrito to himself. "Nice papa! Papa for Pedrito. Wonder what that is? Good day, Pedrito! Your paw, Pedrito! . . ." And he chattered on, just talking nonsense, and mixing his words up so that you could scarcely have understood him. Meantime he was jumping down from branch to branch to get as close as possible to the two bright gleaming lights. At last he saw that they were the eyes of a jaguar, who was crouching low on the ground and staring up at him intently.

But who could be afraid of anything on a nice day like that? Not

Pedrito, at any rate. "Good day, jaguar!" said he. "Nice papa! Papa for Pedrito! Your paw, Pedrito!"

The jaguar tried to make his voice as gentle as he could; but it was with a growl that he answered: "Good Day, Poll-Parrot!"

"Good day, good day, jaguar! Papa, papa, papa for Pedrito! Nice papa!"

You see, it was getting on toward four o'clock in the afternoon; and all this talk about "papa" was intended to remind the jaguar that it was tea-time. Pedrito had forgotten that jaguars don't serve tea, nor bread-and-milk, as a rule.

"Nice tea, nice papa! Papa for Pedrito! Won't you have tea with me today, jaguar?"

The jaguar began to get angry; for he thought all this chatter was intended to make fun of him. Besides, he was very hungry, and had made up his mind to eat this garrulous bird.

"Nice bird! Nice bird!" he growled. "Please come a little closer! I'm deaf and can't understand what you say."

The jaguar was not deaf. All he wanted was to get the parrot to come down one more branch, where he could reach him with his paws. But Pedrito was thinking how pleased the children in the family would be to see such a sleek jaguar coming in for tea. He hopped down one more branch and began again: "Nice papa! Papa for Pedrito! Come home with me, jaguar!"

"Just a little closer!" said the jaguar. "I can't hear!" And Pedrito edged a little nearer: "Nice papa!"

"Closer still!" growled the jaguar.

And the parrot went down still another branch. But just then the jaguar leaped high in the air—oh, twice, three times his own length, as high as a house perhaps, and barely managed to reach Pedrito with the tips of his claws. He did not succeed in catching the bird but he did tear out every single feather in Pedrito's tail.

"There!" said the jaguar. "Go and get your bread-and-milk! Nice Papa! Nice Papa! Lucky for you I didn't get my paws on you!"

Terrified and smarting from pain, the parrot took to his wings. He could not fly very well, however; for birds without a tail are much like ships without their rudders: they cannot keep to one direction. He made the most alarming zigzags this way and that, to the right, and to the left, and up and down. All the birds who met him thought surely he had gone crazy; and took good care to keep out of his way.

However, he got home again at last, and the people were having tea in the dining room. But the first thing that Pedrito did was to go and look at himself in the mirror. Poor, poor Pedrito! He was the ugliest, most ridiculous bird on earth! Not a feather to his tail! His coat of down all ruffled and bleeding! Shivering with chills of fright all over! How could any self-respecting bird appear in society in such disarray?

Though he would have given almost anything in the world for his usual bread-and-milk that day, he flew off to a hollow eucalyptus tree he knew about, crawled in through a hole, and nestled down in the dark, still shivering with cold and drooping his head and wings in shame.

In the dining room, meantime, everybody was wondering where the parrot was. "Pedrito! Pedrito!" the children came calling to the door. "Pedrito! Papa, Pedrito. Nice papa! Papa for Pedrito!"

But Pedrito did not say a word. Pedrito did not stir. He just sat there in his hole, sullen, gloomy, and disconsolate. The children looked for him everywhere, but he did not appear. Everybody thought he had gotten lost, perhaps, or that some cat had eaten him; and the little ones began to cry.

So the days went by. And every day, at tea-time, the farmer's family remembered Pedrito and how he used to come and have tea with them. Poor Pedrito! Pedrito was dead! No one would ever see Pedrito again!

But Pedrito was not dead at all. He was just a proud bird; and would have been ashamed to let anybody see him without his tail. He waited in his hole till everybody went to bed; then he would come out, get something to eat, and return to his hiding place again. Each morning, just after daylight, and before anybody was up, he would go into the kitchen and look at himself in the mirror, getting more and more bad-tempered meanwhile because his feathers grew so slowly.

Until one afternoon, when the family had gathered in the dining room for tea as usual, who should come into the room but Pedrito! He walked in just as though nothing at all had happened, perched for a moment on a chair back, and then climbed up the tablecloth to get his bread-and-milk. The people just laughed and wept for joy, and clapped their hands especially to see what pretty feathers the bird had. "Pedrito! Why Pedrito! Where in the world have you been? What happened to you? And what pretty, pretty feathers!"

You see, they did not know that they were new feathers; and Pedrito, for his part, said not a word. He was not going to tell them anything about it. He just ate one piece of bread-and-milk after another. "Papa, Pedrito! Nice papa! Papa for Pedrito!" Of course, he said a few other things like that. But otherwise, not a word.

That was why the farmer was very much surprised the next day when Pedrito flew down out of a tree top and alighted on his shoulder, chattering and chattering as though he had something very exciting on his mind. In two minutes, Pedrito told him all about it—how, in his joy at the nice weather, he had flown down to the Parana; how he had invited the jaguar to tea; and how the jaguar had deceived him and left his tail without a feather. "Without a feather, a single blessed feather!" the parrot repeated, in rage at such an indignity. And he ended by asking the farmer to go and shoot that jaguar.

It happened that they needed a new mat for the fireplace in the dining room, and the farmer was very glad to hear there was a jaguar in the neighborhood. He went into the house to get his gun, and then set out with Pedrito toward the river. They agreed that when Pedrito saw the jaguar he would begin to scream to attract the beast's attention. In that way the man could come up and get a good shot with his gun.

And that is just what happened. Pedrito flew up to a tree top and began to talk as noisily as he could, meanwhile looking in all directions to see if the jaguar were about. Soon he heard some branches crackling under the tree on the ground; and peering down he saw the two green lights fixed upon him. "Nice day!" he began. "Nice papa! Papa for Pedrito! Your paw, Pedrito!"

The jaguar was very cross to see that this same parrot had come around again and with prettier feathers than before. "You will not get away this time!" he growled to himself, glaring up at Pedrito more fiercely than before.

"Closer! Closer! I'm deaf! I can't hear what you say!"

And Pedrito, as he had done the other time, came down first one branch and then another, talking all the time at the top of his voice:

"Papa for Pedrito! Nice papa! At the foot of this tree! Your paw, Pedrito! At the foot of this tree!"

The jaguar grew suspicious at these new words, and, rising part way on his hind legs, he growled:

"Who is that you are talking to? Why do you say I am at the foot of the tree!"

"Good day, Pedrito! Papa, papa for Pedrito!" answered the parrot; and he came down one more branch, and still another.

"Closer, closer!" growled the jaguar.

Pedrito could see that the farmer was stealing up very stealthily with his gun. And he was glad of that, for one more branch and he would be almost in the jaguar's claws.

"Papa, papa for Pedrito! Nice papa! Are you almost ready?" he called.

"Closer, closer," growled the jaguar, getting ready to spring.

"Your paw, Pedrito! He's ready to jump! Papa, Pedrito!"

And the jaguar, in fact, leaped into the air. But this time Pedrito was ready for him. He took lightly to his wings and flew up to the tree top far out of reach of the terrible claws. The farmer, meanwhile, had been taking careful aim and just as the jaguar reached the ground, there was a loud report. Nine balls of lead as large as peas entered the heart of the jaguar, who gave one great roar and fell over dead.

Pedrito was chattering about in great glee; because now he could fly around in the forest without fear of being eaten; and his tail feathers would never be torn out again. The farmer, too, was happy; because a jaguar is very hard to find anyway; and the skin of this one made a very beautiful rug indeed.

When they got back home again, everybody learned why Pedrito had been away so long, and how he had hidden in the hollow tree to grow his feathers back again. And the children were very proud that their pet had trapped the jaguar so cleverly.

Thereafter there was a happy life in the farmer's home for a long, long time. But the parrot never forgot what the jaguar had tried to do to him. In the afternoon when tea was being served in the dining room, he would go over to the skin lying in front of the fireplace and invite the jaguar to have bread-and-milk with him: "Papa, nice papa! Papa for Pedrito! Papa for jaguar? Nice papa!"

And when everybody laughed, Pedrito would laugh too.

THE REASON

When the great Bohechio was but a child, he made a wonderful discovery. He had, for his best friend, a dog. The brute, like all of his kind in the lands of the Lucayas, was dumb. The Indians did not think this strange because they did not know that any dog had a voice heard in its bark that tells of joy, or anger, or fear, according as the animal feels. So Bohechio thought nothing of his dog being always silent.

One day the boy went hunting rats among the majagua groves. He wanted strong, fine gut-strings for his new bow, and only the capromy could furnish any fine enough. Although these little animals could be very bold when they were obliged to fight, they were, by nature, timid, and had to watch constantly for enemies. But they could get out of the way quickly, for their ears were sharp in catching the least sound warning them of the coming of any strange thing. Even the light tread of Bohechio's little brown feet was enough to send them scurrying. So the boy could only hope to catch one of these rats if he kept very still for a long time. He could do that, for he had learned the Indian child's first lesson which is to remain motionless as long as is necessary, no matter how tired he may become. Bohechio could trust Guaniquinaje to keep still also, for the little beast, though quick as a flash of lightning in moving, made no noise and could not bark.

At last, by patient waiting, Bohechio and Guaniquinaje caught, a fine, large rat. The dog shook the rat fiercely by the neck until it had ceased to squeal, and was quite dead; then the boy sat down in the shade of a majagua tree to skin and draw it, throwing the carcass to the dog, who, having devoured it, sat on his haunches intently watching his little master. Bohechio could not help glancing at his friend now and then, for the dog's eyes regarded him beseechingly, so that at last Bohechio exclaimed:

"Well, what wouldst thou? Hast not had enough to eat? But there is

THE REASON. From *As Old as the Moon*, by Florence Jackson Stoddard.

still a portion of the meat left. Speak and tell me; I am sure thou couldst talk if thou wouldst but try."

Immediately Guaniquinaje began to talk; he said:

"No one has ever before invited me to speak, and I could not begin first; that would have been bad manners since I am the smallest of the company. Moreover, I am dumb for another reason, my master."

Bohechio was so amazed at hearing the dog speak that he stopped the stretching of his new bow-string to stare at him, and could hardly find voice to ask, "What is the reason?"

"My master," answered the brute, "if I were not dumb you would not have me for your constant friend, for could I talk I should be as important as you, which you would not like, and, besides, you might also have to distrust me lest I should speak two ways, as men often do. However I put my words, you might think I wished to complain, though I might have meant to commend; or you would, perhaps, take for consent what I intended for protest. Vagoniona decreed that the Guaniquinaje should be dumb that man might have always a friend who would not betray him or contradict him."

At that moment the witch Yauna appeared, and Guaniquinaje was so frightened at being found gossiping that he hid his tail between his legs and ran away.

Bohechio, who had never before seen Yauna, stood up with his back against a majagua tree and drew his bow fitted with a tight string.

"If you should shoot me," cried the witch, "you would never know the important thing I have come to do and to tell."

At these words Bohechio lowered his bow and gave ear to the witch, who continued thus:

"I have come to charm the dog so that his ability to talk shall never return; he must not become man's equal, therefore no one shall hear him speak ever again, and man may make him a constant companion, for like the sands of the sea, he shall bear no witness of anything. If you would be a great chief, remember to trust only those who are dumb and to remain dumb yourself about your affairs."

Thus it was that while yet a child Bohechio learned the secret of governing men; it was his great discovery. When he returned to the tribe he said nothing of what had occurred in the forest, and because he knew that secrets are safe only with dumb creatures, he became a great chief when he had grown to be a man. He was the friend of many, but he counted Guaniquinaje his only true friend.

TOA, TOA

When the Father of Men was grieving at losing his friend Huacani, who had been changed into the nightingale because he had tried to discover the unborn souls of human beings, he vented his displeasure, as unreasonable people have often done since then, on innocent folk, and he punished the men who lived in the caves that Huacani had tried to enter. The way in which he punished them was by taking out of the caves all the women and children.

Now the women and children went out with him very willingly, when they were invited, for they were always eager for pleasure and change, and at first they enjoyed themselves. But presently the Father of Men took the women, the babies, and the girls up on a high mountain and left them there, where they couldn't get down alone. The boys he kept with him, making them run about wherever he went. He took them everywhere, telling them they must do as he did if they would become great men. This was unfortunate for the boys; some of them were still very little fellows and their short legs could not get over the ground as fast as their leader was able to do with his great strides.

At last they began to cry. Still striving to run after their great commander, they could not but grieve for their mothers' arms and their mothers' care, nor could they help sobbing or even calling out plaintively, "Toa, toa!" In the Indian language of that land "toa" meant mother. The miserable little boys were weeping and calling for their mothers.

This made the Father of Men angry. He gave the boys a terrible look, but they did not see it; they were so unhappy, their eyes were so full of tears, their poor throats were so dry and achy, and they were so tired roaming all over the world that they could think of nothing but their misery, and heart-brokenly cried, "Toa, toa, toa!"

Just at that moment they came to a river bank, and, on seeing the water, the Father of Men suddenly thought of a way to rid himself of the troublesome, crying children. "In with you," he cried, "all you croakers! into the mud puddles, your proper place, and become frogs that shall be forever grunting and croaking, "Toa, toa."

And into the water tumbled the little boys who, tired with all their leader had expected of them were glad enough to be left to themselves, especially in a place where they might drink their fill. They paddled about in the stream to their hearts' content and never tried to go very far from it. Crouching down always beneath some water-washed stone, their legs gradually doubled up so they could only stretch them out when they took a long leap, and after a time they walked no more but went in great leaps or a hop, skip and jump. By and by they forgot all their life in the cave

TOA, TOA. From *As Old as the Moon,* by Florence Jackson Stoddard.

or in roaming about with the Father of Men. They never learned to talk but they still know, and repeat constantly, the first baby call for their mother and they say, over and over in the same tone and in the soft, long forgotten Indian syllable, "Toa! Toa-a! Toa-a-a-d!"

HATUEY, THE HERO

The long island that is washed by the restless waters of the Atlantic and by the blue waters of the Caribbean Sea and by the warm currents of the Gulf Stream, was known to all the Indians of the Lucayas and of the Antillas. They called it Cuba, the Beautiful Country of the Dead, because it was a lovely and a joyous land where all the people who had not lived there hoped to go some day and to live as happy spirits after they had died. At the same time this island was inhabited by native tribes that were busy and happy over their every-day living, so it was not what we should call a land of the dead by any means.

The rocky shore of the eastern end of this island stood then, as it does now, boldly out in the strip of water that separates it from the neighbouring land where, in the Long Ago, dwelt the brave and warlike men of Haiti. In Cuba the people did not love war; they would not fight if they could help it. When, therefore, the Haitians who had fought the Spaniards desperately after being cruelly treated in return for their hospitality to the strangers, tried to incite the Siboneyes to resist the invaders the simple tribes were hard to persuade.

But there was one Haitian brave who thought the people of Cuba must be saved and he, loving his neighbour as himself, determined to try to rescue the beautiful island.

One dark night there went, across the narrow strait that we call, to-day, the Windward Passage, a frail canoe that sought to hide itself, as night came on, behind the rocks along the shore. It carried three Indian boys and the men who rowed it. With peril to the boat and all in it, a landing was made among the dangerous rocks. The canoe was lifted out of the water and carried away across the open spaces to a tangle of rushes, where it was hidden. Then the larger of the boys called his mates around him.

"Each of us knows well what he is to do, is it not so?" he asked.

The boys nodded gravely.

"You, Mayabonex, what are your orders?"

"To take word to the chief of the Siboneyes that the captain called Velasquez, who has so afflicted the people of Haiti, is about to embark for Cuba."

"And you, Guarocayo?"

HATUEY, THE HERO. From *As Old as the Moon*, by Florence Jackson Stoddard.

"To entreat that Indian who has journeyed toward the setting sun to tell the invaders that in the land of Mexico or of the Aruacos they will find the Gilded One they are ever seeking; so may they lead away those who torment us."

"Have you a word to speak also, Ciguayo?" he asked the smallest boy.

"I bring a message from the good father, Las Casas," said the child; "he bids all to believe that he labours to save them."

"As for me," announced the speaker, who was Manicate, a son of the once mighty chief of that name, "I come to go through the land and whisper to the people to be ready and to be strong, for Hatuey comes to lead them against the stranger. And now each to his work."

The boys raised the necklaces of black beads they wore and made vows upon them; they took off their collars of pearl and shells and swore by them a great promise; again, putting on their ornaments, the badges of their rank, they turned, each a different way, looked a moment about them and, as though they had been shadows, they disappeared, leaving no trace behind them. But through the land these slim shadows moved and everywhere they went the people let them come close and listened to the messages they brought. Already the islanders had heard of the terrible Velasquez and of his band of ruthless followers. Already they knew that the strangers wished to be served with treasure, to gather which, others must be oppressed with toil.

"Why have they not laboured, and searched, and found for themselves, in their own land, what they seek here?" they questioned. "Are they lazy, these white men, that they cannot do as others do?"

Yes, that was what they were. So long had these men of Spain lived by spoil that to work for the thing they would fight for seemed to them preposterous, ignoble; so they were indolent in doing anything but that which made adventure and excitement. In their own land the fields were neglected and devastated, the soil brought no living; so they left their country to ruin and went away, to scatter ruin through other lands which they drained of all possessions. No wonder the Indians trembled at the name of Velasquez, and any who opposed him had a hero's courage.

On a night as dark as that when the boy messengers had come, Hatuey, the Indian chief, reached the shore of Cuba. This savage who had been shocked at the cruelties he had seen the strangers commit, was endowed with as noble a heart as ever beat, for he could risk sacrificing himself in the effort to help others. For this he had come. The Indians of Oriente, the eastern part of the island, came at his call; he gathered an army to oppose the invaders, for, as he told the Siboneyes, the domination of the white men meant the Indian's slavery and death. To the troops who put themselves under him, he said:

"Comrades, we prepare to meet and oppose these strangers who have come to our lands. They call themselves Christians; we do not know what that may mean in their religion, but in ours it would mean, according to

their acts, traitors to justice. You know that, in Haiti, they have taken
from us our lands, our power, our families and our very selves. They
have tormented and killed our fathers and brothers; they have destroyed
our maidens; they have slain this chief here and that one there. Why do
they persecute us, O comrades?"

And the people answered, as with one voice, "Because they are cruel
and evil."

"No," said Hatuey, "it is because they wish us to tear up our land, to
find that which Maonocon has hidden from us, and to deliver it to them
because it is the god they adore. Do you know their god? Behold, I will
show you him they love," and uncovering a small palm basket, a little Indian "haba" he showed them a quantity of gold.

"This," he cried, "is the god that these Christians love tenderly and
serve loyally. It is to satisfy this god that they torment us and persecute
us, destroy our lands and our people and secure to themselves all our
possessions. To find more of this god, they leave Haiti, having taken all
they could and laid waste what served them not, and now they come to
Cuba to do likewise. You they will break and slay with terrible labour
as they have slain my people. But come, let us be before them! Let us make
a feast for this all-powerful god and dance before him our great dance and
then, when the stranger arrives, the spirit of greed shall not be able to
stand against the spirit that fights for us."

The people looked at the glittering metal brought from their mountain
streams and washed, and melted, and hammered into disks and worn in
honour of the Sun whose colour it was. Yes, this was the thing above all
things that the stranger wanted. The words of Hatuey roused them.
Believing as he said, it was, indeed, well to honour this idol of the white
men to appease him if that might be. A great dance was prepared, a great
feast was made; all night they danced, and ate and drank to the Christians'
god of gold. From twilight to dawn they danced until they dropped, one
by one, from fatigue, and slept heavily while the intoxication of the drink
wore off. When they were recovered Hatuey rose again before them and
spoke gravely:

"It is better, you must see after all that has happened in this dance,
that we discard the god of the Christians, that we need not again drink
and dance to him and no longer give him room anywhere, for should we
even swallow this gold and hide it within our bodies, there would the
invaders search for it. We will throw it into the waves that none may
know where to find it."

But they were too wise to drown the treasure by daylight; at night, by
the light of stars only, the gold was lost. Some say it was entrusted to the
four lads who had come bearing the four messages from Haiti; that these
lads, not trusting even their rowers, took their canoe far out in the bay
and dropped into the depths the basket of gold. Nevertheless, the men of
greed discovered that some of the treasure they sought had been sunk in

the sea and when Velasquez landed on the island he came in added fury. He was greeted with an onslaught of the Indians. Led by Hatuey, they fought with desperation, but their valour was useless against the firearms of the fierce white men; they were driven back and back. In the mountains they took refuge and there Hatuey made a mighty resistance.

But prisoners had fallen into the hands of the Spaniards; the brave young Manicate was among them. Not to save his own life would Hatuey yield but when he heard that the enemies were inflicting horrible tortures upon that lad, among other captives who were asked to tell of the chief's camping place, he determined to try but once more for victory and if defeated to yield himself to save others from torment. A last terrible battle was fought; in the mêlée Hatuey was captured. The conquerors gave him a mock trial, condemned him and sentenced him to be burned to death.

They tied this proud and noble Cacique to the iron rod that was planted among the pile of fagots. A priest of the conquerors' camp came and counselled him to be baptized that he might die a Christian, to which Hatuey returned:

"Why should I become a Christian?"

"Because those who die Christians," said the friar, "will go to heaven, where they will be happy forever."

"And will the white men go there?" asked the Indian.

The friar told him that those who had been baptized would surely go.

Then Hatuey cried out in a loud voice, "No, I will be neither baptized nor go to the heaven of those Christians."

When his speech was made known to the Spaniards a fearful shout arose; speedily torches were set to the fagots and the last of the great Caciques perished amid the savage rejoicings of his enemies. Thus he gave his life for the cause of his adopted people and to this day the stranger who loves the land for which the Haitian chief fought and died is called "As Cuban as Hatuey."

THE HUNCHBACK

"Well, then," the old vaquero began, "one time a long time ago, as the old ones say, two hunchbacked men lived in a village in the mountains far, far from other population. One of them was a woodcutter, and he was bright and ready in his mind; he could make *versos* and sing them too. The other was a little stupid, and in his heart he had envy.

"And you have to know, señor, that there is nothing worse in this world than envy. For example, if two individuals go out to dig up a treasure and one of them has envy, the gold, even if the envidioso finds it,

THE HUNCHBACK. From *Tongues of the Monte*, by J. Frank Dobie. By permission of Little, Brown & Company.

will be turned into charcoal or some other matter without value. Did you ever know a rich baker?"

Offhand I could not assert that I ever had actually enjoyed acquaintance with a rich baker.

"There is one explication," the old vaquero went on, looking around him as if to see that the point went home to every man. "While the Most Holy Virgin and San José were journeying with El Niño Dios, they came to the house of a baker. He was baking and the Niñito picked up a bit of dough that had dropped on the floor. La Virgen Mariá took it and composed it into a little bit of loaf and asked the baker permission to cook it in his oven. He was willing. When, after a while, the oven was opened, he saw that the little piece of dough had baked into a loaf larger than his own. He quickly exchanged the two. Because of that envy a baker even if he work day and night will never become rich."

"Bueno, as the relation goes, this second hunchback had envy. But because they both had humps and because they were both ridiculed at times on account of their deformity, even though people did touch their humps and shake hands with them for luck, they were good compañeros. Yes, they were such good companions that they were at the point of licking each other like two friendly oxen.

"One day the woodcutter took his two burros up a mountain a long way off. He cut the wood, loaded it on his little beasts, and started back. He knew, however, that he could not reach home that night. So, late in the afternoon, he camped. The hobbled burros were grazing in a little flat off to one side of him and he was resting against a sharp hill that rose to his back when all of a sudden he heard voices. The country about him was so covered with brush that he could not see any distance, but no one lived in that part of the world. This he knew. He was very curious; also he was cautious. In order to get a view of the ground whence the voices seemed to be coming, he climbed the hill.

"When he reached a good place for the vista, his eyes fell upon a wondrous sight. Down there below him, out in the midst of the brush, was a clearing shaped like a comal. In the center of this basin a huge fire was burning, and there, dancing madly about the fire, a crowd of dwarfs and elves and fairies were singing at the top of their voices:

> Lunes y martes y miércoles—tres.
> (Monday and Tuesday and Wednesday—three.)

These words the little people kept saying over and over. It seemed to be the only line of song they knew. Yet everybody knows that a song has to have more than one line and that the lines must rhyme. Well, after the hunchback had listened to the monotonous chant at least forty times, he stepped out into full view and just as the singing folk came again to "tres," he added in his rich voice:

Jueves y viernes y sábado—seis.
(Thursday and Friday and Saturday—six.)

A great shout of joy came up from the comal. The dwarfs and elves and fairies whirled around more madly and sang even louder and faster than before the rhyming lines:

Lunes y martes y miércoles—tres,
Jueves y viernes y sábado—seis.
Y domingo siete!

"And then they were so happy and so grateful to the hunchback for having completed their song that they rushed up the hill and began dancing around him, all the while singing. But when they saw how deformed he was, they suddenly stopped and said something magical, at the same time softly touching his hump. Behold! In an instant his back was straight and he stood as erect as any soldier that ever saluted. Then quickly they ran with him down the hill and prepared a fine feast. While they ate, the little people continued to leap about and sing their song. It was dark by now and the moon was up. All at once they stopped, each with his finger on his mouth.

" 'Listen!' one said.

"Bum, bum, thump, thump. Sounds like that, low and heavy, were coming from this way and that way.

" 'It is the big devils,' whispered the fairies. 'We must scatter and run. But you,' they said to the woodcutter, 'climb into that cottonwood tree so thick of leaves and you will be safely hidden.'

"Immediately they were gone and the woodcutter skinned up the tree. He settled himself into a fork. Nor was he too soon, for three enormous devils coming from three different directions—the east and the west and the north—met right under the tree. As they began talking, the poor woodcutter up over them was more afraid than he would have been had a pack of lobo wolves been howling at his heels. He dared not move so much as a little finger. He flattened himself against the limb on which he was perched and just listened.

" 'Well,' said the devil from the east to the one from the west, 'what have you been doing all this time since we last met?'

" 'Oh, I have been very busy. I have been over there in the west country called Otilo, and I have made all the people stone blind so that they cannot see a thing, not even the sun. What have you been doing?'

" 'I,' replied the other devil, 'have been working day and night in my kingdom, Soleste, in the east, and I have made every person in it dumb— just as dumb as a stone.'

"Then both these devils turned to the third.

" 'Do not think that I have been idle,' he replied. 'Up there in Borsete, my kingdom to the north, I have made every being so deaf that not a soul can hear it thunder.'

"All three devils clapped their hands and bellowed with laughter and congratulated one another on their accomplishments. The poor woodcutter held in his breath to keep his heart from beating so loud.

" 'Now,' the devil from the east said to his fellow from the west, 'I know you would not want to restore the sight to those blind people in your kingdom. You would not think of doing such a good deed, but just suppose for fun you did. Could you bring back their sight?'

" 'Very easily,' the devil from the west answered. 'As nobody can hear us, I'll tell you what I'd do. I would get up about four o'clock in the morning and, taking some gourds with me, I would go out and collect them full of fresh dew. Of course it is a lot of work to collect a gourd full of dew, but taking a drop off this leaf and a drop off that leaf and half a drop off a blade of grass now and then, a person can finally fill a gourd. Well, after I had collected the dew, I would go in among the blind people and, u≤ing my finger, rub a little on the eyes of each one. Then as soon as the dew evaporated on the grass, every blind person who had his eyes moistened would see as well as a buzzard.'

" 'It's a good thing nobody can hear us telling such secrets,' said the devil from the east. 'Of course I wouldn't think of curing my people of their dumbness, but it could be done.'

" 'Of course you wouldn't do such a deed,' said the devil from the west. 'But, just supposing for fun you take a notion to cure the dumbness, what would you do?'

" 'The cure is as simple as skinning up a tree,' said the devil from the east, gesturing up the cottonwood. 'Over there in my kingdom grows a bush called the cenizo. It has gray leaves, and after a rain it bursts into bloom with thousands and thousands of lavender flowers, so thick that they almost hide the gray.

" 'Well, to cure this dumbness I would wait until the cenizo bloomed. Then I would take some sacks and go out into the hills and I would gather them full of leaves and blossoms mixed. Then I would brew them into a tea. This I would let settle until a wind blew away all the ashes from under the pot. Then I'd carry an olla of the cenizo tea among the people and with a spoon made out of horn ladle it into the mouth of each one. As soon as a person swallowed it, he would immediately say, "Thank you!" After that he could talk as well and as fast as a cañon-full of piñon jays screaming out to the deer that a hunter is coming.'

"Now the devil from the north was questioned.

" 'It takes more knowledge to cure people of deafness than of blindness or dumbness,' he said. 'There is not only just one way to cure them; there is just one place where they can be cured. Up there in my kingdom, beside the capital city, is the Cerro de la Campana. Well it is named Mountain of the Bell, for on its slope next to the city is a round, bare boulder made out of the hardest flint on earth.

" 'Now, if I led a deaf person out close to that rock and then took a hammer and struck the rock, the sound would be so bright and sharp that it would go straight through the deaf one's ear, even if he had a pillow tied around it. Then he would be so acute of hearing that he could hear the beating of a gnat's wings away over on the other side of the cañon.'

" 'Wonderful! Wonderful!' exclaimed the devil from the east and the devil from the west.

" 'Yes, these are wonderful cures,' said the devil from the north, 'but nobody else knows them and we'll never use them. Now let us go south and see what mischief we can do down there. Then we'll separate and visit our kingdoms. A year from tonight we'll come back here and rejoice again over the evil we have caused.'

"Still laughing and congratulating each other, the three devils started southward.

"After he had waited until he knew they were a long way off, the poor woodcutter, who had been flattened up in the tree like a rusty-lizard, managed to limber his legs and arms and climb down. He had certainly heard some wonderful things.

"A bright idea came to him. Here for years he had been working like a slave, earning barely enough with his axe and burros to buy frijoles and corn for tortillas. Now he was the possessor of secrets that not all the doctors on earth knew. He decided that he would be a curandero. He would set out to cure people of blindness and dumbness and deafness.

"So when daylight came, he and his burros traveled straight west. When he came into the country called Otilo, of a truth he found all the people blind. He borrowed some gourds and early in the morning went out to gather dew drop by drop from the leaves of bushes and the blades of grass. Then he took it among the blind, moistening the eyes of each one. When the sun dried the dew on the grass, the people whose eyes had been dampened saw. There was great rejoicing, and the people gave this curer gold and silver and many beautiful things, to say nothing of their blessings. By the time he had brought sight to all the blind, one of his burros had a *carga* of pure riches.

"Then the curandero traveled into the east. It was raining when he got into the kingdom of Soleste. Cenizo plants by the thousands burst into bloom, and hillsides covered with them miles away looked like clouds of lavender. The people in this country were accustomed to weave sacks and mats and ropes out of the fiber of the lechuguilla and palma loca. So the curandero had no trouble finding sacks.

"He filled some of them with the leaves and blossoms of the cenizo. Then he boiled the tea in a big olla. After the wind had blown the ashes all away from this pot and the tea had settled, he began ladling it with a spoon made of horn into the mouths of the dumb. As soon as a person swallowed a mouthful of the tea, he said, 'Thank you!' After that he sang for very joy, all his dumbness gone. The cured ones loaded the curandero's second burro down with wealth.

"He bought a third burro and struck out towards the north. He found the capital city of the kingdom of Borsete, and on the Cerro de la Campana near it, as the devil had described, he found the bare boulder of the hardest flint on earth. He gathered together all the deaf people in the country and led them out to this rock and then struck it with a hammer. Bright and sharp, the sounds penetrated the dullest ears. And when the people found that they could hear, they leaped and laughed, and they gave the curandero still more riches and still more blessings.

"By this time he was as rich as a Potosí, and with all the good he had done and all the blessings he had received, he was very happy. He had been away from home nearly a year. He decided to go back.

"Everybody in the village was amazed at his straight back and at his fortune. He gave gold to all the needy and he told the story of his adventures. The hunchbacked compañero was almost crazy with envy. He wanted to suck the bottle also.

" 'Show me,' he begged, 'the place where the duendes sing and the devils tell their secrets. I want to get rid of my hump and be rich.'

"The curandero's heart, like his hand, was open. 'Prepare yourself,' he said. 'One year ago tomorrow night I heard the devils agree to meet a year thence. I can lead you to the very cottonwood tree under which they will talk.'

"So the two traveled. The curandero showed the hunchback the tree, told him to get up in it and be quiet, and left. About dark the waiting hunchback heard the devils tramping and muttering. They stopped under the tree. There was no laughter from them now.

"Said one, 'All those people I left blind a year ago can see. Their eyes are so good they can see the shadow of a butterfly flying over brown grass. Some stranger came along and rubbed dew on their eyes.'

" 'Thunder and horns!' roared a second devil. 'That same stranger has been in my kingdom to the east. He pulled up hectares of cenizo plants, brewed the tea, and ladled it into the mouth of every dumb man, woman, and child. Everybody there is singing and talking gayly. I had to shut my own ears and leave.'

" 'Devils and more devils!' stormed the third evil one. 'To the north in my kingdom a foreigner found out about that flint boulder that rings like a bell. Actually a devil can't step on thistle-down in the country now without being overheard and chased away. We have been outraged.'

"Then all three devils set in to blaming one another and everybody else because somebody had learned their secrets. They were still quarreling, and the envious companero up in the tree was wondering if they were ever going to say anything profitable, when he heard a medley of glad voices and saw come skipping into the moonlight a bevy of dwarfs and elves and fairies.

"They came right up to the tree and began dancing around the big devils. Perhaps the little ones were happy because so many people in the world had been cured of being blind and deaf and dumb. They had no fear of the devils now, but danced right over their tails, twitched the long hairs growing out of their ears, skipped through the prongs of their pitchforks and teased them in other ways. Then they took up the song they loved best to sing:

> Lunes y martes y miércoles—tres,
> Jueves y viernes y sábado—seis.

"Over and over they sang it, at each repetition faster and louder. The three devils could not get in a word, even to quarrel. After a while the ambitious hunchback became so disgusted at not hearing any secrets that he decided to add to the song, devils or no devils, and at least win a straight back. So at the end of the verse he screeched out:

> Y domingo siete.
> (And Sunday seven.)

"At that the little people instantly vanished and the devils all looked up.
" 'There's that scoundrel who overheard our secrets and used them,' they cried. 'Get him!'
"One of them skinned up the tree and with a jerk tumbled the eavesdropper down. Then they grabbed him and taunted him—

> Y domingo siete,
> Y agui esta su pisiete.

"With that they put a second hump on his back—his pisiete. Then they turned his pockets wrongside out and told him to go home and tend to his own business. True it is that honey was not made for the mouth of a burro."

HOW THE BASILISK OBTAINED HIS CREST

One day the Lord of the Woods called together all the animals that could run and said to them, "Come here, my children; I wish to explain something to you."

HOW THE BASILISK OBTAINED HIS CREST. From *A Treasury of Mexican Folkways,* by Frances Toor. By permission of Crown Publishers.

When all were in his presence, he led them to a savanna and said to them, "I have assembled you to tell you that I wish to see which one of you is capable of winning a race to the big Pich that stands to one side of the road. The winner will receive a prize. I have had a bench placed there for the one who arrives first to sit on."

The Big Fox spoke first in answer to the Lord of the Woods, "My Señor, how can you think it possible that anyone of us can win a race with Big Deer? You surely know that he is much more rapid than we are. Why, he runs like a whirlwind. We shall all remain behind. We haven't sufficient power in our legs to outrun him, not even to arrive at the same time."

The Rabbit added his opinion. "What Big Fox says is true." "Yes, yes," all the others assented in chorus. Even the serpents who run like lightning across the skies, said, "It is true, Our Señor; none of us have the capacity for winning a race with Big Deer in it."

But a young Basilisk slipped down from the branches of a Katsin to the feet of the Lord of the Woods and said to him, "Señor, what is the prize you offer?"

"If you win," he replied, "I shall put a sombrero on your head, so that everybody will know that you have won a race with the Deer."

All the other animals laughed when they saw the poor little Basilisk talking to the Lord of the Woods. "What does he think?" they asked. "He must be insane, that little devil of a Basilisk."

He heard what they said and turned upon them, shouting, "Shut up, you devils! You're afraid of the Deer, but I'm not. I'll show you all what stuff I'm made of. I'm little, yes; that's how you see me. Nevertheless, we shall see if I cannot make myself worthy of a sombrero."

"Look at him, look at him," all the other animals said together.

"Yes, look at him!" exclaimed the Lord of the Woods. "You all shut up! Come, Big Deer, stand here; you next to him, little Basilisk."

The Basilisk obeyed, saying, "Only one thing I ask." "Speak!" he was told. "What I wish is simply this—that you make everyone shut his eyes while we start off."

The Lord of the Woods agreed, "Very well, little Basilisk," and addressing the others, "When I count to three, all of you close your eyes. He who does not obey, shall be punished. Have you all heard?" Then he began, "One, two, three," and the race began.

When the other animals opened their eyes, all they saw was a cloud of dust on the road. Not even the Lord of the Woods was there. He had left by air to arrive first to see who won.

When Big Deer had run some distance, he thought, "Why am I hurrying so? The poor little Basilisk surely must be buried in the dust I stirred up with my claws at the start. Poor little thing!"

When Deer arrived at the Pich, trotting contentedly, the Lord of the Woods received him smilingly. Deer looked at the bench and made a quick movement as if to sit down on it. But before he touched it, the voice of the Basilisk caused him to jump; "Look out, or you will crush me, Big Deer. Go away, for I got here before you did."

Deer, turning around to look at the bench, remained speechless; he only trembled. Then, ashamed of himself, he walked away, thinking, "How did the little Basilisk do it? He must have a devil in his body!"

By this time the other animals had arrived and saw what had happened. The Lord of the Woods approached the little Basilisk and said to him, "Very good! You are an intelligent little fellow. Here's your prize."

Only the Lord of the Woods knew that the little Basilisk was able to seat himself on the bench before Big Deer because he had arrived on the tail of the Deer.

RATONCITO PÉREZ

Once there was an ant. Like other ants she was very hard-working.

One day the ant found a coin, and she said to herself, "What shall I buy? If I buy candy, I will eat it. If I buy a broom, it will wear out."

Finally she decided to buy a dress, some little boots, and a ribbon for her hair. So she did. Then she put on the dress, the little boots, and the ribbon and sat out in front of her house.

Soon a cat went by and said, "My, you are beautiful, little ant! Don't you want to marry me?"

The little ant replied, "How will you speak to me after we are married?"

"I will say mew, mew," answered the cat.

"No, you frighten me," said the little ant.

In a little while a dog went by and said, "My, you are beautiful, little ant! Don't you want to marry me?"

The little ant asked, "How will you speak to me after we are married?"

"I will say bowwow, bowwow," answered the dog.

"No, you frighten me," said the little ant.

A bull came by and said, "My, you are beautiful, little ant! Don't you want to marry me?"

The little ant answered, "How will you speak to me after we are married?"

"I will say moo, moo," answered the bull.

"No, you frighten me," said the little ant.

A lamb came by and said, "My, you are beautiful, little ant! Don't you want to marry me?"

The little ant answered, "How will you speak to me after we are married?"

"I will say baa, baa," said the lamb.

RATONCITO PÉREZ. From *The Healer of Los Olmos,* by Wilson M. Hudson. By permission of The Texas Folklore Society.

"No, you frighten me," said the little ant.

Finally Ratoncito Pérez passed by. Ratoncito Pérez was very clean and well combed.

He said to the little ant, "My, you are beautiful, little ant! Don't you want to marry me?"

The little ant answered, "How will you speak to me after we are married?"

Ratoncito Pérez had a very sweet voice.

"I will say ee, ee, ee."

"I like that! You shall be my husband. Ratoncito Pérez," said the little ant. She was very happy.

The little ant and Ratoncito Pérez lived happily for a long time.

One day when the little ant went out, she told Ratoncito Pérez, "Take care of the soup until I come back."

Ratoncito Pérez peered down into the soup and fell in.

When the little ant returned she found Ratoncito Pérez dead.

All the little animals came and tried to comfort her, but they could not. The little ant would not be comforted. Even to this day she grieves and mourns for the Ratoncito Pérez and his sweet voice.

LEGEND OF THE ALTAR DEL PERDON

Well, Señor, it happened in the time of Don Martin Engriquez de Almanza, the fourth Viceroy—that the Chapter of the Cathedral, desiring to make splendid the Altar del Perdon, offered in competition to all the painters of Mexico a prize for the most beautiful picture of Our Lady of Mercy: which picture was to be placed in the centre of that altar and to be the chief glory of it. And, thereupon, all the painters of Mexico, save only Peyrens, who was a very bad sinner, entered into that competition with a reverent and an eager joy. And then it was, Señor, that Peyrens made plain the wickedness that was in him by his irreverent blasphemies. At a banquet at the Palace a very noble gentleman asked him why he alone of all the painters of Mexico—and he the best of all of them—had not entered into the competition; to which that sinful young man answered with a disdainful and impious lightness that the painting of what were called sacred pictures was but foolishness and vanity, and that he for his part could not be tempted to paint one by all the gold in the world!

Talk of that sort, Señor, as you well may imagine, scalded the ears of all who heard it—and in the quarter where the punishment of such sinning was attended to it made an instant stir. In a moment he found himself lodged behind iron bars in a cell in the Inquisition: that blessed con-strainer to righteousness, for the comforting of the faithful, that then was

LEGEND OF THE ALTAR DEL PERDON. From *Legend of the City of Mexico*, by Thomas A. Janvier. Copyright 1910 by Harper & Brothers. Reprinted by permission.

proving its usefulness by mowing down the weeds of heresy with a very lively zeal.

Being of an incredible hard-heartedness, neither the threats nor the pleadings of the Familiars of the Holy Office could stir Peyrens from the stand that he had taken. Resolutely he refused to recant his blasphemies; equally resolutely he refused to accept his freedom on the condition that he should paint the picture of Our Lady—and he even went so far, when they brought him the materials for the making of that picture, as to tear the canvas to shreds and rags!

And so the days ran on into weeks, and the weeks into months, and nothing changed in that bad matter: save that the Archbishop, saintly man that he was, began to lose his temper; and that the Familiars of the Holy Office lost their tempers entirely—and were for settling accounts with Peyrens by burning his wickedness out of him with heavenly fire.

As it happened, Señor, a great opportunity for such wholesome purifying of him was imminent: because at that time the preparations were being made for the very first auto de fé that ever was celebrated in Mexico, and all the City was on tiptoe of joyful expectation of it. Therefore everybody was looking forward with a most pleased interest to seeing that criminally stiff-necked painter—properly clad in a yellow coat with a red cross on the back and on the front of it—walking with the condemned ones; and then, on the brasero that had been set up in the market-place, to seeing him and his sins together burned to ashes; and then to seeing those sin-tainted ashes carried to the outskirts of the City and scattered pollutingly on the muddy marsh. . . .

On a night, as he lay sleeping on his pallet in his cell in the Inquisition, Peyrens was awakened suddenly he knew not how; and as he wakened he found in his nose a smell so delectable that he thought that he still was asleep and his nose dreaming it: and for him to have that thought was quite reasonable, Señor, because it was the pure fragrance of heaven—to which, of course, human noses are unaccustomed—that filled the room. Then, as he lay on his pallet wondering, a shimmering light began to glow softly in the darkness; and the light constantly grew stronger and stronger until it became a glorious radiance far brighter than any sunlight; and then in the midst of that resplendency—yet the heavenly sparkle of her making the dazzle of it seem like darkness—Our Lady of Mercy herself appeared to him: and he would have died of the glory of her, had it not been for the loving kindness that shone upon him assuringly and comfortingly from her gentle eyes.

Then said to him Our Lady, in a voice sweeter than any earthly music: "Little son, why dost thou not love me?" And Peyrens—his hard heart melted by that gentle look and by that sweet voice, and all of his wickedness cured by that loving kindness—rose from his pallet and knelt before Our Lady, saying with a deep earnestness: "Queen of Heaven, I reverence and I love thee with all the heart of me and with all my soul!" Then, for a time, a serene strange happiness bemazed him dreamfully—and when his bemazement left him the resplendent presence was gone. But with him still remained the heavenly radiance that was brighter than any sunlight, and the heavenly perfume that was sweeter than spikenard and lilies; and while he pondered all these mysteries, awe-bound and wondering, again sounded in his ears that heaven-sweet voice—coming as from a great distance, but with a bell-note clearness—saying to him gently and lovingly: "Paint now thy picture of me, little son!"

Quite possibly, Señor, in the hurry of the moment, Our Lady forgot that Peyrens had no canvas—because in his sinful anger he had destroyed it —on which to paint the picture that she commanded of him; but, for myself I think that she meant to set his wits to work to find the means by which he could obey her command. At any rate, his wits did work so well that even as she spoke he saw his way out of his difficulty; and in an instant—all a-thrill with joyful eagerness to do Our Lady's bidding, and inspired by the splendor of his vision of her—he set himself to painting the portrait of her, just as his own eyes had seen her in her glory, on the oaken door of his cell.

All the night long, Señor—working by the heaven-light that was brighter than any sunlight, and having in his happy nose the heaven-fragrance that uplifted his soul with the sweetness of it—he painted as one who painted in a heaven-sent dream. And when the morning came, and the glimmering daylight took dimly the place of the heaven-light, he had finished there on the door of his cell the most beautiful picture of Our Lady. . . .

As usually is the case with miracles, Señor, the outcome of this one was most satisfactory. The Archbishop and the Chapter of the Cathedral, being brought in haste, instantly felt themselves compelled to adore that miraculous image; and when they had finished adoring it they equally felt themselves compelled to declare that Peyrens by his making of it had earned both his freedom and the prize. Therefore Peyrens was set at liberty and most richly rewarded; and the pictured door was taken from its hinges and, being framed in a great frame of silver, was set upon the Altar del Perdon to be the chief glory of it; and what was best of all—because it made safe the soul of him for all Eternity—the Archbishop formally confined to Peyrens his absolution, through Our Lady's loving kindness, from his bad heresy and from all his other sins. . . .

THE PÁJARO-CÚ—THE LOST BIRD

In the beginning of the world, maybe one thousand, maybe two thousand years ago, the eagle called all the birds together. He was king

THE PÁJARO-CÚ—THE LOST BIRD. From *Tongues of the Monte*, by J. Frank Dobie. By permission of Little, Brown & Company.

over them and they all obeyed him. At the assembly there appeared one totally naked, without one feather to hide its nakedness. Now the king eagle was of the *gente decente*. He was very proud and he and some of the other birds, the official ones, were much offended. He ordered the shameless bird to be put out.

But the dove took pity on the poor naked creature and said that she would give him a feather and that each other bird might give him a feather and thus he could be clothed and saved from being outcast.

"That will be all right," said the eagle, "but someone must act as his sponsor and be responsible for him."

"You are wise, Señor King," the peacock spoke up. "The naked beggar must have a sponsor, for with all the many-colored feathers he is about to receive he will grow offensively vain. I very much doubt the wisdom of this proposal anyway." The truth is that the peacock was jealous of a rival.

During the discussion the owl had said nothing, for the assembly was in daylight, and the owl was sleepy. Now he spoke up and said, "I will act as sponsor." Many of the birds feared the owl and all knew him to be so wise that he could tell when anybody was going to die. As is said yet, "When the owl sings the Indian dies." So the matter was settled and right away the birds began giving the naked one their feathers.

The redbird and the scarlet tanager gave him red feathers, and the robin another shade of red. The bluebird and the jay gave him blue feathers, the parrot and the hummingbird green. The canary gave him yellow, the oriole orange. The blackbird, the crow, and the buzzard gave him black. The mockingbird, the gull, and the pelican gave white. The tall grulla gave him a long mouse-colored feather, and the wren gave him brown. The quail contributed speckled feathers, the guinea silver, and the turkey bronze. Oh, the naked one had feathers of more colors than the rainbow, and he had so many that they were thicker on him than the down on a goose. Now he was clothed in a glory that no other bird on earth ever enjoyed. And he was so vainglorious that he would have absolutely nothing to do with the other birds. He would not even speak to the peacock. That night he left the country.

The next morning the king eagle called again all the birds to give them counsel. The one who had been naked and clothed was not there. Then the eagle was very angry.

"I told you what would happen," the peacock said.

Other birds showed spite also.

"You agreed to act as sponsor," the eagle said to the owl. "Now you are charged to bring in the truant. Go at once."

But the owl went to weeping and said he was too blind to hunt during the day and must wait until night to search.

"You said nothing about this when you agreed to act as sponsor," the king eagle cried out. "I order the hawks to make you prisoner at once."

At that the owl flew into a black cave where nobody could see to follow him.

But the kind-hearted dove felt responsible, for she has a very tender conscience. "I will go hunt for the lost bird," she said. Then she started out to hunt, and the little Aztec doves, and the big white-winged doves, and the plump pigeons and all other members of the dove family went with her, flying here and there through the woods calling, "*Cú, cú, cú.*" The paisano, or roadrunner, undertook to search also, looking close to the ground. He could not say cú, but, as now, he went *cru, cru, cru.* Also he took the owl a lizard to eat. That night the owl searched faithfully, calling *whu, whu, whu* into every dark corner of the woods.

But the *pájaro-cú,* as the lost bird came to be called, could not be found anywhere. Nobody knows where he went to, but he went somewhere, and the owl at night still goes about looking for him and asking *whu, whu, whu,* and by day the paisano with his head and his tail stretched out level with his back runs up and down trails, stopping often to look sharply in this direction and that direction, often rolling out of his mouth as fast as his eyes can wink, *cru, cru, cru,* and all the dove people too, especially in the evening, say softly as they think it is their duty to do, *cú, cú, cú, cú.* But the doves don't expect any answer. It is very strange that a bird with so many bright feathers like the pájaro-cú, cannot be seen, but thus it is. It is thought by many that he went to a foreign land.

JUAN GOES TO HEAVEN

In the city of Monterrey in northern Mexico there is an arroyo which became so deep at the time of the great flood that no man can tell. It is enough to say that the worst rain, or perhaps I should say the heaviest rain (one may not say that any rain is a bad rain), produced the mightest hero of northern Mexico.

Juan Garcia was just a "middle-class Mexican," but he owned the most famous horse in the whole country. This horse could swim.

When the mighty flood was sweeping through Monterrey, sweeping with it chickens, pigs, children, women, and men (most of the men had gone for help) Juan Garcia proved himself a great hero.

Many of the little houses in northern Mexico are built of adobe. Adobe, as you know, is made of mud, mixed perhaps with a little grass. Egyptians when they made their bricks always mixed grass with mud, but there must have been more grass in Egypt than there is in northern Mexico. When the rain fell and the wind blew and the flood descended on Monterrey, these little houses, being built in a country where rain should not fall,

JUAN GOES TO HEAVEN. From *Puro Mexicano,* by J. Frank Dobie. By permission of the Texas Folklore Society.

were melted down much as piloncillo melts when you mash it in hot coffee. The water washed the children and the pigs and the women and the chickens into the arroyo.

Juan Garcia saddled his grey horse and dashed into the mighty flood.

Pigs, being fat, float on top of the water, and, being valuable, should properly be rescued. And Juan Garcia, seeing a fat pig in danger, rescued it and took it safely to his little house high up on the side of the hill. After that, Juan Garcia dashed into the flood and, with the aid of his mighty horse, saved from an unaccustomed death twelve women, three more pigs, and four men.

That was thirty years ago. It is the fact that when one is a hero on one occasion, thereafter his fame will grow, whether he be living or dead; wherefore the fame of Juan Garcia spread mightily. He became the great hero of northern Mexico—the hero who rescued ten, fifteen, even twenty men and women from the mighty Monterrey flood.

It was very bad luck, but Juan Garcia had to die. And after Juan Garcia had gone through many difficulties he finally arrived at the gates of Heaven. I cannot understand why he arrived without his grey horse. But, as a favor to me, picture Juan Garcia at the gates of Heaven without his grey horse. Muy importante he was, and why shouldn't he be important? He knocked as befitted his rank. The assistant of Saint Peter opened the mirilla (the small gate in the big door) and asked the usual questions.

"I am Juan Garcia of Monterrey, the hero of northern Mexico. I dragged twenty people out of the mighty Monterrey flood."

Saint Peter's assistant said, "Juan Garcia, I have never heard of you."

"What?" Juan answered. "I am the hero of the mighty Monterrey flood, and who are you?"

And the gentleman at the gate said, "I am Saint Peter's assistant."

And Juan answered, "Well, neither have I heard of you. Send for Saint Peter himself."

And so, impressed by the great confidence of Juan Garcia in himself, the assistant sent for Saint Peter, who immediately came to the gate.

Thereupon the Angel Gabriel, as I truly believe Saint Peter's assistant to be, said to his master, "Don Pedrito, there is here a person who calls himself the greatest hero of northern Mexico and, according to his statement, he is named Juan Garcia."

"Yes," said Juan Garcia, who was listening, "I am the greatest hero of northern Mexico; I dragged twenty people out of the mighty Monterrey flood; and, as all know, I am entitled to come to Heaven and sit on one of the high places."

Then Saint Peter examined the records and said, "Juan Garcia is really entitled to a seat in the Kingdom of Heaven. Let him enter."

And so Juan Garcia went into the Kingdom of Heaven with Saint Peter on his right hand. Very soon they came to a man all silent with his hand in the breast of his coat, and he occupied a very high place in the hero section. Then Saint Peter said, "Napoleon, this is Juan Garcia."

But Juan Garcia interrupted, "Me! I will introduce myself! Napoleon, I am Juan Garcia of Monterrey, Mexico. I am the great hero of the mighty Monterrey flood. I dashed into the flood and rescued twenty lives."

And Napoleon said, "Juan Garcia, I am glad to welcome you to Heaven and I hope you will be very happy here."

And Juan Garcia next went to Hannibal and introduced himself, saying, "I am Juan Garcia of Monterrey, Mexico. I saved twenty-five men from the mighty Monterrey flood. I, too, am a hero."

And Hannibal said, "Juan Garcia, you are a hero; I hope you will be happy here."

And after Hannibal came Caesar, Julius Caesar, I think it was; and after Juan had introduced himself as the hero of the Monterrey flood, Caesar welcomed him into Heaven. And thereafter Juan Garcia introduced himself and the story of the mighty Monterrey flood to Xerxes and Henry VIII and George Washington and many, many others, even to Pancho Villa. And, my friend, all of these heroes welcomed Juan Garcia and expressed the hope that Juan might be happy on his high seat in Heaven. Thus Juan Garcia came into Heaven as he had come into the praise of northern Mexico.

But, my friend, on one of the highest places Juan Garcia came upon an old man who was all wrapped up in his sarape. Juan patted him on the back and said, "Viejito, I am Juan Garcia of Monterrey, the great hero of the mighty Monterrey flood. I preserved thirty men from the mighty flood."

But el señor del sarape made no response.

Then Juan hit him harder on the back and said, "Viejo, listen! I am Juan Garcia from Monterrey. I am the great hero of the mighty flood, and I have come to Heaven to sit on one of the highest places."

Then, the old one raised his sarape from around his face and said, "Pffffffttt."

And Juan Garcia was terribly shocked. To Saint Peter, who was not very far away, he said, "This hombre is making fun of me. Pancho Villa and Caesar and Hannibal and the other heroes have welcomed me, but this viejo has said only 'Pffffffttt.' "

And so, my friend, Juan Garcia demanded of Saint Peter a complete explanation. And Saint Peter slapped the viejo on the back, and said, "Juan Garcia of Monterrey wishes to introduce himself to you. He is the hero of the mighty Monterrey flood."

And the viejo again lifted his sarape from around his face and again said, "Pffffffttt."[2]

And Saint Peter said to Juan Garcia, "I am sorry, my friend, but this is Noah, and he doesn't give a hang about your Monterrey flood."

---

[2] "Pffffffttt" is a "Bronx Cheer" or a "Razzberry."

7

MIDDLE EAST

And this story was related between the setting of the sun and the rising of the moon, when there was not light to travel by. The story teller was Abed.[1]

ARABIA

Tales from the Arab tribes are flavored with the entertainer's quality. The dominating effort is to bring forth a smile or to arouse the excitement of the adventure that would prove a blessing during the long desert treks. They were originated by the tribesmen during the hot day travels or the night rests on the cold sands.

THE HATTAB (WOODCUTTER) AND THE KHAZNAH (TREASURE)

Related by Haji Abdullah al Fathil in camp on 7th January, 1935.

There was once a poor woodcutter who dwelt in a certain city of Arabia. He had a wife, a pretty grown-up daughter, several small children and a donkey. His other possessions were practically nil. His daily round was to go out of town into the surrounding country in the early morning, dig up dry shrubs by the roots and bring them into the city in the evening for sale.

One day he heard a preacher in the Friday mosque discourse on faith, and among other things heard him say that if only a man had sufficient faith he need do nothing, as all things would come to him.

THE HATTAB (Woodcutter) AND THE KHAZNAH (Treasure), by H. R. P. Dickson. From *The Arab of the Desert*. By permission of George Allen & Unwin Ltd.

[1] Lindsay Drummond, "The Story of Maqdad—He Was the Hero of Hilla," from *Tales from the Arab Tribes*.

After some thought the woodcutter decided to give the ideal trial, and gave out that he intended in future to trust entirely in God and do no more work. "God will surely provide, as I have faith in him," said he, "and I know that he will grant everything needed for my family and my own existence."

In vain did his old wife plead, and in vain his daughter. The wood-cutter was adamant. His only reply was, "God will provide."

On the second day of his idleness his wife begged him to go out and work, for if he sold no wood there was no money in the house and they would all starve. The woodcutter's only reply was, "God will provide."

The wife perforce was obliged to sell some cooking pots to get money to buy food. The third day arrived and the old wife had again to sell some-thing from the house to enable her to buy food. The fourth and fifth day similarly went by, and the furniture in the house got scarcer and scarcer. Nothing, however, would induce the woodcutter to raise a finger to help himself or his family. On the sixth day it so happened two young mer-chants of the town decided to go for a five day's hawking expedition into the desert. They took their falcons, collected a sufficiency of food and prepared to look round for a donkey to carry their supplies and bedding. They heard of the woodcutter and his donkey and decided to hire the latter, seeing that it was doing no work. On their approaching our friend the woodcutter, he readily gave them the donkey, for a silver piece per day. He refused however, to go with the donkey, so the latter was loaded up with food for the chase, and was taken off into the neighboring desert.

The woodcutter thus got five silver pieces for doing nothing, and drew his wife's attention to God's first reward to him for his faith. She, of course, received the silver pieces.

The two young merchants finished their food on the fifth day, and were returning home the following morning. When they drew near to the city and were only about five miles out they decided to make some coffee and then approach the town by afternoon in comfort of mind and body. They accordingly stopped the donkey, unloaded the coffee-making utensils and proceeded to make a fire.

As both were scooping away some sand to make a hearth they suddenly lighted on a large strong wooden box. On opening it they found it was crammed full of gold pieces.

Delighted, the two young men started making plans for getting the box into the town without being noticed by the gate guards. After some dis-cussion they agreed that one should remain and guard the box while the other should go into the town and buy food and bring it out to the other. Then both having dined they would take the donkey into the town after dark and divide the treasure and deposit it in their own houses.

All went well, but when the one buying food in the town had completed his purchase, he said to himself, "It were foolish of me to go shares with my friend in this great treasure, why not keep it all for myself." He accordingly mixed zernik (arsenic) with the food, and took it out of the town to his friend and companion.

Unfortunately the other man was planning how to make away with his friend. His plan was to await his friend's return, help him to load up the heavy box on to the donkey's back and then find some way to shoot him. In this way he also thought to possess all the treasure and take it into the town after dark.

Everything went according to plan. The friend who went into town returned at dusk with the poisoned food, and at once pressed his partner to eat: "You look ill and exhausted," he said. The other agreed to eat, but said, "First help me to load this heavy chest on the donkey's back." This was done. But no sooner did our friend from the town stoop down to untie the kerchief holding the food, when he was shot in the back and fell dead. The murderer, congratulating himself on having got rid of an unwelcome partner, decided to eat his supper and then slowly enter the town as darkness fell. On eating the poisoned food, however, he also fell dead, and the lone donkey, with its box of gold on its back, wondered what would happen next. After waiting a short while and seeing that neither of the men made any move, the donkey, after the manner of its kind, proceeded to the town, passed through the gate unnoticed and returned to his home. There it arrived after dark, and at once began to bump its head on the door, as was its custom. Soon the woodcutter with his wife appeared and seeing the box on their donkey's back, unroped it and opened it. To their great astonishment they found it to be full of golden dinars.

"Quick," said the wife, "let us report the arrival of the gold to the authorities, for it cannot be ours." "Not so," said the woodcutter, "it is a gift of God, the sacred gift, to the man who believed that everything would come to him who had a sufficiency of faith. Behold the reward of my faith. I did nothing. I went not forth to work, and see what God Almighty has sent to my very door. Thanks be to God."

That night the box of gold was secretly buried under the floor of their sleeping apartment, and until the hue and cry over the disappearance of the two young merchants should be over, the woodcutter and his wife decided to lie quiet, only taking out an occasional dinar to make minimum food purchases.

Six months went by, and as no awkward question arose, the couple began to spend more lavishly. They bought a small house and garden (haúta), purchased new fine clothes, and acquired mares, camels, sheep, goats and several slaves and servants.

All seemed to be going well when busy bodies got talking of how the poor woodcutter of the previous year seemed now to have become rich. The story eventually reached the king's ears. He sent for the woodcutter, now a well-dressed and important looking person. "Tell me, my friend," said the king, "how it is that for being one of the poorest of the town's woodcutters last year, you are to-day the lord of a small palace, and owner of horses, camels, slaves in abundance?"

"The answer is simple, my lord," was the reply. "I trusted in God, and he made me rich." "How can that be, my friend?" said the king. "A man does not grow rich by doing nothing, as you are known to have done. You must be lying to me."

"Nay, King, mine is no lie," replied the woodcutter. "What I say is the simple truth, and that I swear by the Almighty One." The king, doubting much in his heart, decided to test the woodcutter, and said, "My friend, I candidly doubt your word and believe you have much wealth hidden away, but you fear to tell me of it. You must be either a very good man beloved indeed of Allah, or a rogue and clever rascal. I propose putting you to the test by asking you two questions. If you answer them correctly you shall be allowed to go your way in peace. But if you fail to reply to the questions then you assuredly are lost, and your property shall be confiscated by the State. My questions are these," he continued:

"(a) What is the hardest thing in the world and at the same time the softest?"

"(b) What is the most terrifying thing in the world?"

The woodcutter returned home very discouraged and related the day's events. His daughter, however, gave her father some answers to the king's questions. He returned the next day and presented himself before the king. His replies to the king's questions were:

"To (a) the answer is, Water, for it is the softest to handle and the hardest to be struck by.

"To (b) the answer is, The sound of the charge of thousands of horsemen, this turns the heart of the bravest man to water."

The king, greatly astonished that such a common and stupid person should answer so well, and suspecting not that someone was behind him, said, "Your answers are right, fellow, but I propose giving you a still further test, for something makes me doubly distrust you now. Go fetch me five buffalos with five white turbans on their heads. Your life will depend on what you do."

Again the disconsolate and despairing woodcutter went home, and again his clever daughter came to his aid. To her father who proposed buying five real buffalos and winding turbans round their horns, she said, "Father, do you not see that the king means not animals in the literal sense, but men?" She advised him to go and wait out side the great mosque on Friday, and after prayers to meet the white-turbaned priests as they came out, and then to ask them the simple question, "Sir, can you tell me what day of the week it is?" From their replies he could discover certainly five fools or "buffalos" among them. Her father did as he was bid. He proceeded to the mosque and as the priests came out accosted them one by one with the words, "Kind friend, can you tell me what day it is?" Most of those questioned answered, "Man, art thou a half wit, that thou askest such a foolish question. Canst not see the world coming out from the Friday prayers?" Nevertheless he found four men who, absent-minded and deep in thought, replied to his question, "Why brother, the day of the week, ahem, yes we don't know. What is it, tell us?" These men he asked to follow him to his house, where meeting his daughter at the entrance he disconsolately told her that he had found four buffalos, but had not been able to find a fifth, and how was he to face the king's anger.

"Thou foolish father," said the girl. "Why, you have succeeded all too well. Go to the king forthwith and take these four men with you, and say you have found the five buffalos with turbans round their heads."

"Did I not say I had only found four men," said her father. "True," she replied, "you have indeed found four men, but tell the king that you are the fifth buffalo. That is the answer for him, and that is the reply that will please him."

The mystified father did as he was told, put a white turban on his own head, took the four men with their clean white turbans to the king, and bowing low said, "My lord the King, behold I have the five buffalos you asked for." The king replied, "I told you to fetch five buffalos with turbans round their heads. You have indeed produced four but where is the fifth?" The woodcutter replied, "Your majesty, I am the fifth."

The king was delighted, and said, "Now I know for a truth that some-one is teaching you the replies that you bring to me—out with it, tell me who it is, and you shall go free and in honour."

Then the woodcutter confessed all, and told the story of his treasure and of his clever daughter. More pleased than ever, the king declared that it was his pleasure to reward such a remarkable daughter by honouring her with his hand, and in due course the marriage was solemnised.

THE STORY OF MAQDAD—HE WAS
THE HERO OF HILLA

And this story was related between the setting of the sun and the rising of the moon, when there was not light to travel by. The storyteller was Abed.

There was or there was not in ancient times a boy living near to Hilla, and only on God is there belief. Now, the name of this boy was Maqdad. He was the son of a great warrior, but his father was slain, in battle, and there was no one to bring money or food to their house. So the boy Maqdad hired himself out to the shepherds and he used to take the

THE STORY OF MAQDAD—HE WAS THE HERO OF HILLA. From *Tales from the Arab Tribes* by Lindsay Drummond. By permission of Ernest Benn Limited.

sheep out in the morning and bring them back at night, and he earned enough to buy a little food for his mother and himself.

One day, when he reached the age of sixteen years, his mother called him, and told him to open a great chest which lay in their house. He opened the chest and found in it a sword of the finest Damascus steel with a hilt of gold, and a shield of leather and iron, studded with gold, a great spear, a dagger wrought in silver, a rich saddle, a mace of the finest teakwood, studded with iron, and all the accoutrements of a warrior.

Then Maqdad's mother said to him: On that wretched day that your father was carried dead into our house I took these weapons from him and from his horse and cleansed them of his blood, and set them in this chest, that one day you might be a mighty warrior in his place. And here is a bag of gold which I took from his body, and I have not spent a single coin from it, though in all these years we have never eaten meat, but only dates and rice and milk and that food which is suitable for the poor. Now take this bag of gold and buy the best horse in the land. Then shall you ride out to the north. For know you that the army of the Shah of the Persians is camped upon the River Tigris, and the Arabs of the great tribes, of Al Fetla, of As Shammar, of Ed Dulaim, are riding against the Persians and are raiding and harrying them that they may be driven from this Arab land.

So Maqdad took the bag of gold and he went to the market in Hilla where there were offered for sale horses of the finest stock and of the finest blood. And there he saw a horse of between two and three years, and its colour was as black as jet and its beauty surpassed the beauty of all horses, and the horse looked at Maqdad with a look of friendship and affection. So Maqdad turned to the merchant and said: What is his price? Now, the merchant looked at Maqdad and saw that he was dressed as a ragged shepherd boy and he laughed and said: O master of wealth, begone from here and do not trouble us further, for we are afraid that you will offer us so much gold that we cannot lift it from the ground, for we are poor and feeble. Please go from here and do not tantalise us further with your wealth. Maqdad was angered at the scorn of the merchant and he said: My wealth is greater than your wealth, and I wager that my purse has more gold than your purse, and the stake shall be my purse against your purse. And the merchant thought: Verily God has deprived this boy of his reason, but let us amuse ourselves and draw a crowd, for it will be good for business. So the merchant called for witnesses and a crowd collected, and the conditions of the wager were cried out.

Then the merchant drew from his pocket a mighty purse and he said to Maqdad: Let us see your money. And Maqdad's heart went cold when he saw the size of the merchant's purse, and he drew out his own purse and it was smaller than the merchant's. And the merchant spread his coins on a carpet and they saw that there were five hundred dinars of gold and a thousand dirhems of silver and two thousand fils of copper. And Maqdad spread out his coins on the carpet and they saw that he had a thousand dinars of gold, and he had not a single coin in silver or in copper. And the witnesses said: The shepherd boy wins the wager.

Maqdad took the purse of the merchant and put the coins of gold and silver with his own gold, but the copper coins he caused to be thrown to the poor. And he turned to the merchant and asked the price of the horse, and a price was agreed on and paid. Then Maqdad asked the merchant for the pedigree of the horse and for his name. The merchant was astonished, and asked: Do you ask the pedigree is written in his legs and his back and his noble head; but Maqdad said: It must also be recorded on paper, and that is what I require. And the merchant handed the pedigree to Maqdad, saying: Verily he is descended from the Prophet's noble mare, the feather coated, and most beautiful of all. His name is Rishan, for he is of that noble breed.

Maqdad took the horse Rishan and mounted him bareback and rode to his home. And his mother brought out the saddle of his father and it fitted the horse Rishan, and she brought out the weapons which she had gleamed in the sun. And she brought him a bag of dates and a bag of cheese and she said: Now shall you ride to the Tigris and to the camp of the tribes, and there shall you enter the guest tent and salute the assembly, and they will bid you to be seated and bring you coffee. Then they will ask your name, for they do not know your face, then shall you reply: I am Maqdad son of Thamir son of Degaither son of Mansur son of Qais son of Hamed the Lame son of Mansur the Father of the Sword. And this name is a known name, and wherever you say it, there shall you be recognized. For your father was a warrior, and your grandfather, and your great-grandfather and all those before him were warriors. Then Maqdad kissed his mother and bid her farewell. And Umm Maqdad wept as she saw her son depart.

Maqdad rode out the road to the north and he rode over the desert which was carpeted with the flowers of spring, and the grace and pace of Rishan was beyond compare. As they went over the desert Maqdad would take his great spear and hurl it in front of him a distance of two hundred paces, and he would put Rishan to a gallop and catch the spear and pluck it from the air before it could touch the ground. In this manner they had travelled many miles when Maqdad saw a gazelle. He put Rishan to a gallop, thinking: Rishan is faster than the gazelle. The gazelle left the track and went off into the desert with Maqdad in pursuit, and Rishan was as fast as the gazelle and drew level with it. But when Maqdad put out his spear to kill it, it turned more sharply than the horse, and in this manner escaped them.

They were now far from the track, and to return to it Maqdad took his course from the wind, and they travelled on and came to awasi which was both wide and deep, and in it further back Maqdad saw a cave. The mouth of this cave was covered by a net, its shape as a spider's web, but each strand was as thick as a man's wrist, and through the meshes of the web it could be seen that in the cave was a boy. He was chained to the wall by an iron band which was around his neck and was in the twelfth year of his life.

Then Maqdad rode down into the awasi; he dismounted and drew his sword, and cried out to the boy: I will release you from this misfortune. The boy answered saying: Return from where you have come, O noble stranger, lest my misfortune become your misfortune, for that web is of magic and evil materials. But Maqdad did not heed the cries of the boy, and he slashed with his sword at the web. But as he cut each strand the severed ends grew and became longer and came out and seized the legs and arms of Maqdad and drew him into the web and he was enveloped and entangled, nor could he move hand or foot.

And the boy called out to him and said: O wretched youth, know you that you are entrapped in the web of Zoro, the giant Magician, and he will return at dusk and take you from the web, then he will ask you your name, and after he will kill you and give your body to me to cook for his supper, for this is his custom. But when he asks your name, say Maqdad, for if your name is Maqdad he will not slay you, rather will he chain you in the manner in which I am chained, and you may escape a dishonourable death to live a miserable life. For Zoro is afraid of none in this world, since it has been revealed to him by his magic book that he will die neither from steel nor from poison, nor have they power over him, but his death will be caused by one named Maqdad, and as for the manner of his death, he knows it not, nor can he discover it. Therefore, if you tell him your name is Maqdad, he will not eat you, being afraid that you may cause him colic or indigestion, resulting in his death. Nor will he slay you, lest your ghost cause him evil, but rather will he chain you here and make you his servant and subject you to his evil, and subject you to his will, that you may do him no harm. My name is Maqdad, therefore he has treated me in this disgraceful manner.

And Maqdad heard the words of the boy and was astonished and he replied: Verily my name is Maqdad. Perhaps I am he who is to cause the death of this tyrant. The boy Maqdad said: But how can this be done? I have caught snakes in this cave, for there are plenty here, and taken their poison and put it in his food, but he laps up the poison like spice. Once when his back was turned, I took the iron spit on which the bodies are cooked and drove it into his heart, even through his body, but he plucked it out and his flesh was as if it had never been pierced, and he caught me and whipped me and thrashed me throughout the night.

The sun set and the world became dark and Maqdad was held in the web in a manner that rendered him powerless. And an evil footstep was heard, and Zoro the Magician was seen to approach. The hearts of the boys were filled with fear, for the body of Zoro was covered in long hair, its colour green, and it gave off an unholy light. As for his height, it was the height of three men, but he carried his back bent like a hunchback.

And Zoro saw Maqdad entangled in the net and he cried out to him and said: Stranger, what is your name? And Maqdad replied and gave his name truly, nor did he lie. And Zoro's face creased with rage. He bared his long fangs, shot out his great arms and freed Maqdad from the web with a magic word. Then he carried Maqdad into the cave, and the web parted to let him through. He fastened around Maqdad's neck a collar of iron, and fastened him to the wall with an iron chain, and Maqdad was powerless in the grip of Zoro. Then Zoro said: O bearer of an accused name, you shall be my servant and you shall be my slave, and should you fail in this I will whip you.

Then Zoro the Magician seated himself at a table and he took from the table a magic book and he set it in front of him and he spoke to it in this fashion: By the power I have over you, O my servant, tell me the truth and answer my questions. And the book answered and replied: I hear and obey you, O my master. And Zoro asked the book: Where shall I find food tomorrow? And the book answered, and its voice was as a woman's voice: In such and such a valley you will find Arabs and you may slay one of them. And Maqdad was amazed to hear the book speak. Then Zoro asked the book and commanded it: In what manner and in what way shall I meet my death? And the book answered: Verily it shall not be through steel and it shall not be through poison, but your death shall be caused by one named Maqdad and he is now here in this cave. But as to the manner of your death, one greater than I, namely, the Angel of Death, controls this matter and it is forbidden to forecast it.

Then Zoro turned on the two boys and his face was the face of one angered with a terrible anger and he demanded of them: Which of you is he who would cause my death? And Maqdad thought: Escape from this situation will be difficult. Now, Maqdad, when he used to take the sheep to the desert to graze, amused himself and practiced at throwing his voice, and in this fashion he could make one sheep talk to another sheep. And he could make any stone or any animal appear to talk to any other stone or animal, yet his lips did not move.

So now Maqdad threw his voice into the chimney, and he answered Zoro and he said: I am he. And Zoro saw that neither of the boys had spoken and the voice came from the chimney and he said in a terrible voice: What is your name? Who are you? How came you here? And Maqdad threw his voice into the chimney and replied: As for my name, it is Maqdad; as for my station, it is that of a warrior. I came here by means, and my mission is to cause your death. And Zoro's fury increased and he commanded: Come out of that chimney. And Maqdad replied: I remain while I wish to remain and I come out when I wish to come out.

Then Zoro went over to the chimney and he thrust in his hand, but the chimney was long and winding. Then Zoro put his head and shoulders into the chimney and he thrust and thrust with his legs and he propelled himself up the chimney. And he thrust in such a manner that he became firmly fixed in that chimney, and he could move neither forward nor back.

The two boys suddenly found themselves free and the younger Maqdad said: We cannot succeed with steel or poison, let us try fire. And they brought wood and piled it under the chimney and they poured on it oil from the lamp and they lit a great fire under Zoro.

Then the book spoke out, and its voice was a woman's voice, and it said: "I speak freely and not by command out of gratitude for you, O noble Maqdad, who have thus far encompassed the destruction of my master Zoro, and you have removed me from his power by placing that fire of yours between me and him. But know, O noble youth, that that fire of yours cannot completely destroy Zoro, and if so much as a hair or fingernail survive from the burning, it will grow during the night into a complete Zoro. But if you place me on the fire I will burn with such a flame that no one evil hair shall survive.

And Maqdad took the book in his hand and said: Lady for such I believe you to be before I destroy you tell me who you are and how you came into this condition. And the book answered and said: My name is Fatima, and I am of Jann and not of the sons of Adam but I sinned against their rules and they imprisoned me in this book and laid upon me the duty of obeying him who might possess it. And I came into the possession of this dog, this Zoro, who is half Jinn and half animal, for his father was a Jinn and his mother was a gorilla, and he has some little skill in magic, but of an evil sort. But place me upon the fire that I may complete the task, and when this book is destroyed, I shall be liberated to return to my race.

And Maqdad placed the book upon the fire and it burnt with an intense blue light, and the body of Zoro was completely consumed. Then the blue light turned into a beautiful girl, who stood before them, and said: Thank you, noble Maqdad, for this deed was a pleasant one and it has been of benefit both to the Jann and to the sons of Adam. I reward you, so command me to do three things before I depart, and you may command me as you desire, and I will obey.

And Maqdad spoke and said: O gentle Lady of the Jann, for the first command, let me and this boy depart in safety from this evil cave. For the second command, let me find my beloved horse, Rishan, outside and unharmed. And as for the third command, I have never spoken with my father nor have I had that instruction in wisdom and in the art of war which it is the duty of a son to acquire from his father. Let me, Lady, have speech with my father.

And the lady of the Jann spoke and said: Wisely chosen, O boy, for had you asked me for a kingdom or for gold I would have given them to you. But princes are less happy than the rest of me, and gold is only a bringer of jealousy, hatred, and evil. And she levelled her finger at the two boys and the fetters fell from them and the evil web at the mouth of the cave collapsed in dust. And she said: You are free to go and Rishan is outside and unharmed.

Leave this cave and mount Rishan and ride in the direction of the north star until the sixth hour of the night. Then shall you see in front of you a fire and a great camp and it will be the camp of your ancestors whom I will bring out from Paradise. For you may not now enter Paradise, since it is written: None shall enter Paradise twice.

Then the two boys went out from the cave, mounted Rishan and they rode out and took their course from the north star.

ISRAEL

You will be left behind as Kunz was left behind to look after the sheep.[2]

Much of the Jewish folklore stems from the legends in their books of civil and religious laws. The scripture was interpreted through the art of storytelling. The stories are therefore religious, philosophical, entertaining, and always point out a moral lesson.

THE STORY OF KUNZ AND HIS SHEPHERD

The proverb runs: "You will be left behind as Kunz was left behind to look after the sheep." And if you ask how Kunz came to be left behind to look after the sheep, I will tell you.

Once upon a time there was a mighty king, who had a counselor called Kunz. Whenever the king needed advice, and the counselors in conference came to a decision, the clever Kunz would go to the king and say: "This is our decision." This fine gentleman always took the credit to himself, pretending that he was responsible for the advice and that the other counselors had to agree with him, for they had neither sense nor understanding. And the good king believed what Kunz told him and considered him as much wiser than the other counselors.

Now the other counselors noticed that the king loved Kunz more than he loved them and they resented it very much, for he was the least important among them. One day they took counsel together how to get the

THE STORY OF KUNZ AND HIS SHEPHERD. From *A Treasury of Jewish Folklore*, by Nathan Ausubel. By permission of Crown Publishers, Inc.

[2] Nathan Ausubel, "The Story of Kunz and His Shepherd," from *A Treasury of Jewish Folklore*.

better of Kunz and humiliate him. So they went to the king and said: "Lord king, we beg of you to forgive us, for we wish to ask you how it is that you think more of Kunz and hold him in higher esteem than the rest of us, although we know that he is the least important among us?" The king replied: "I will tell you how it happens. Whenever you come to a decision on any matter, he reports it to me and says that the idea is his and that you have to acknowledge every time that he is wiser than you and that you have no sense at all. But I do not hold you in disrespect, for you are all good to me." When the counselors heard this, they were very glad and thought: "We will soon bring about his downfall." Then they said to the king: "Be assured that all which Kunz said is a lie, for he has no sense at all. Try every one of us separately and you will see that he cannot give you any advice by himself." The king said: "I will find out very soon," and sent for his beloved counselor Kunz and said to him: "My dear servant, I know that you are loyal and exceedingly wise. Now I have something in my mind that I do not wish to reveal to anyone. Therefore, I want to ask you whether you can find out the truth for me, and if you do, I will reward you liberally." The clever Kunz replied: "My beloved king, ask me and I hope I can give you an answer. Tell me the secret." The king said: "I will ask you three questions. The first is: Where does the sun rise? The second is: How far is the sky from the earth? The third, my dear Kunz, is: What am I thinking?" When Kunz heard these three questions, he said: "Lord king, these are difficult matters, which cannot be answered offhand. They require time. I beg of you, therefore, to give me three days' time, and then I hope to give you the proper answer." The king replied: "My dear Kunz, your request is granted, I will give you three days' time." Kunz went away and thought to himself: "I cannot concentrate my mind very well in the city. I will go for a walk into the country. There I am alone and can reflect better than in the city."

He went out into the country and came upon the shepherd who was tending his flock. Walking along, he talked as it were to himself, saying: "Who can tell me how far the heavens are from the earth? Who can tell me where the sun rises? Who can tell me what the king is thinking?" The shepherd, seeing his master walking about wrapt in thought, said to him: "Sir, pardon me. I see that you are greatly troubled in your mind. If you ask me, I might be able to help you. As the proverb says: 'One can often advise another, though one cannot advise oneself.'" When Kunz heard these words from the shepherd, he thought: "I will tell him. Perhaps after all he may be able to advise me." And he said: "I will tell you why I am so troubled. The king asked me three questions, which I must answer or lose my neck. I have been thinking about them and cannot find the answer." Then the shepherd said: "What are the three questions? Perhaps I may be able to help you in your great trouble." So Kunz thought: "I will tell him, maybe he is a scholar." And he said: "My dear shepherd, these are the three questions which the king asked me. I must tell him where the sun rises, how far the heavens are from the earth, and what the king is thinking." The shepherd thought it was well to know the answers and said to Kunz: "My dear master, give me your fine clothes, and you put on my poor garments and look after the sheep. I will go to the king and he will think that I am you and give me the three questions. Then I shall give him the proper answers and you will be saved from your trouble. Then I shall return here and you will not be in disgrace with your king." Kunz allowed himself to be persuaded, gave the shepherd his good clothes and fine cloak, while he put on the shepherd's rough garments and sat down to look after the sheep, as though he had done it all his life.

When the three days had passed, the shepherd went to the king and said: "Lord king, I have been thinking over the three questions that you asked me." The king said: "Now tell me, where does the sun rise?" The shepherd replied: "The sun rises in the east and sets in the west." The king asked again: "How far are the heavens from the earth?" The shepherd replied: "As far as the earth is from the heavens." Then the king said: "What am I thinking?" The shepherd replied: "My lord king, you are thinking that I am your counselor Kunz, but I am not. I am the shepherd who looks after his flock. My master Kunz was walking in the field one day and saying to himself: 'Who can tell where the sun rises? Who can tell me how far the heavens are from the earth? Who can tell me what the king has in his mind?' He was walking about all the time and talking in such fashion. So I told him he should give me his good clothes and I would give him my rough clothes; he should look after the sheep and I would, with the help of God, guess the answers to these three questions and save him. He allowed himself to be persuaded, and so he is now out in the field, dressed in my rough clothes and tending the sheep, while I am dressed in his beautiful cloak and his best clothes." When the king heard this, he said to the shepherd: "As you succeeded in persuading Kunz, you shall remain my counselor and Kunz can look after the sheep." Hence the proverb: "You will be left behind as Kunz was left behind to look after the sheep." This is what happened to him. May it go better with us.

HUNGER

In the days when King Solomon ruled over Israel there lived in Jerusalem a man who was the richest in all the land. His name was Bavsi.

HUNGER. From *A Treasury of Jewish Folklore,* by Nathan Ausubel; copyright 1948 by Crown Publishers, Inc. By permission of Crown Publishers, Inc.

As great as was his wealth he was wicked and a miser. He oppressed his servants and his slaves and made their days bitter with toil from dawn, as soon as the cock crowed, until late in the night. Because he was stingy he did not give them enough food to eat so that they and their children constantly suffered the pangs of hunger.

Finally, he acquired such an evil reputation throughout the land that the saying became popular: "Stingy as Bavsi." Others even said: "Evil as Bavsi." All manner of stories used to be told about his tightfistedness. It was said, for instance, that he had purposely not married in order not to have to support a wife and children. There was also the story that once his brother paid him a visit and dined with him. Accordingly, on that day Bavsi gave no food to his servants and slaves in order to make up for the expense his brother's dinner caused him.

It happened on one occasion that a great famine raged in the land. The wealthy but upright citizens opened their granaries and distributed food among the poor. But not so Bavsi. He kept his granaries well secured and put additional locks upon the doors. He even reduced the food rations of the people of his household. He became a food profiteer, selling for very high prices. And so his wealth multiplied in those evil times.

Bavsi's conduct aroused scorn among the people and they muttered angrily against him until their indignation finally reached King Solomon. And when the wise King heard what was being said about Bavsi he grew wroth and fell upon a stratagem. He sent a royal chamberlain to him with an invitation that he sup with him. Bavsi was overwhelmed by such an honor from the King and he rejoiced greatly.

"It seems that I have found great favor in the eyes of the King," he thought vaingloriously. "How my enemies will rage over my good fortune!"

All day long Bavsi refrained from eating. He wished to arrive hungry at the King's table so that he might consume more of the royal courses.

Upon Bavsi's arrival at the royal palace a chamberlain conducted him ceremoniously into a separate room and said, "The King will sup with you alone tonight. Therefore, I wish to instruct you in the following rules of conduct when you sit down at table with the King. You must do what I bid you, else the King will grow angry. And woe to you if the King should grow angry!"

"I will do as you bid me," answered Bavsi, a little frightened.

"Remember, first of all," admonished the chamberlain, "you must never ask for anything, neither from the King nor from any of the servants. Secondly, no matter what you may see happen you must not ask any questions nor utter any complaint. And lastly, when the King asks you whether you are enjoying the various courses you must outdo yourself in praising them, even if they should not please you. Promise me, therefore, to remember and obey these rules."

"I promise," swore Bavsi, uneasily.

"Very well then," said the chamberlain. "There is still one hour before supper so I will have you wait in another room until I call you."

The chamberlain then conducted Bavsi into a room. There an open door led into the royal kitchens.

As Bavsi waited patiently he saw through the open door the elaborate preparations being made for the King's and his supper. The aromas of the sizzling roasts and the other courses were wafted to his nostrils. And since he had not eaten all day long, he was very hungry and the smell of the food only teased his appetite. Several times he had to exercise great self-control to keep himself from going into the kitchen so that he might still his hunger. He gritted his teeth and waited for supper.

The time arrived at last. The chamberlain entered and led Bavsi into the royal presence.

"Sit down, my friend," King Solomon said to him affably. "Do not be bashful and eat to your heart's content."

Bavsi seated himself. A servant entered and placed a baked fish on a golden platter before the King. The King commenced to eat and as he ate he exclaimed with rapture, "What a fish! How delicious!"

And when the King had done with the fish the servant then placed a dish of fish before Bavsi.

Overjoyed, Bavsi made an eager move towards the fish before him, but at that very instant another servant snatched it from him and carried it off into the kitchens.

Bavsi was on the verge of saying something about it when he suddenly recalled the instructions the chamberlain had given him, and kept his peace.

A servant then brought for the King a fine broth in a golden bowl. The King drank the broth with relish while Bavsi waited impatiently to be served in turn. When the King had finished his soup the servant, as in the instance of the fish, also brought Bavsi a golden bowl of soup. But no sooner did he make a movement with his hand towards it than another servant quickly snatched it from him. Similarly it happened with the roast and with the other courses.

Bavsi was now beside himself with hunger and indignation. He cast looks of hatred at the servants but he had to remain mute and smiling as he sat facing the King.

To the hungry Bavsi it seemed as if the meal would never come to an end.

"I hope you're enjoying your supper," King Solomon remarked politely.

"I am, indeed, O King! Everything is delicious," the unhappy Bavsi answered.

"I am delighted to hear that," said the King.

"The food has the taste of Paradise in it," cried Bavsi with enthusiasm, recalling further the chamberlain's instructions.

Faint with hunger, the unfortunate guest arose anxious to make his departure. But the King held him back.

"Don't go, my friend!" he said. "Do not part from me so fast. The night is still young. I've commanded my musicians to regale us with fine music."

Reluctantly Bavsi remained.

The musicians entered and played wondrously upon their instruments. But the music only annoyed Bavsi for he could think of nothing but food.

After the musicians had finished, Bavsi once more arose to go.

"Don't go, my friend," said King Solomon. "The hour is too late for you to go home. Sleep this night in the palace."

And Bavsi knew that every word of the King's was a command. So he remained. He did not sleep all night long because of the pangs of hunger. Angrily he began to reflect on the possible meaning of the King's conduct.

"Why did he invite me to a supper which I was not allowed to eat?" he asked himself.

Suddenly it dawned on him that the King had only meant to teach him an object lesson in hunger.

Now, by means of his own experience, he understood the torments of need; he, the wealthy Bavsi, the well-fed one, who had always despised the poor and had laughed at them when they cried that they were hungry.

MIRIAM AND THE SEVEN LITTLE MARTYRS

Miriam, the daughter of Tanhum, and her seven sons were taken into captivity and brought before Caesar in Rome.

To the first son Caesar said, "Bow down before the idol!"

"I will not deny the Holy One, praised be He!" replied the boy. "For He had told us: 'I am the Lord thy God.' "

"Kill him!" commanded Caesar.

And they did as he commanded.

Then they led in the second son.

"Bow down before the idol!" ordered Caesar.

"I will not betray my God!" cried the boy. "For He has written: 'Thou shalt have no other gods before Me.' "

Him, too, Caesar ordered slain.

Next came the turn of the third son.

"Bow down before the idol!" ordered Caesar.

MIRIAM AND THE SEVEN LITTLE MARTYRS. From *A Treasury of Jewish Folklore*, by Nathan Ausubel; copyright 1948 by Crown Publishers, Inc. By permission of Crown Publishers, Inc.

The boy answered, "I will not bow before the idol because God has commanded: 'Thou shalt not bow down thyself to them, nor serve them.' "

And they led him out to die like his brothers.

The same happened with the fourth son. He said, "I will not be faithless to my God who has commanded: 'For thou shalt bow down to no other god; for the Lord, whose name is Jealous, is a jealous God.' "

And him too they led away to die.

When the fifth son came before Caesar he cried out, "Shall I abandon my God who has exhorted us: 'Hear, O Israel, the Lord our God, the Lord is One!' "

He too had to die.

Afterwards they brought the sixth son of Miriam, and Caesar spoke to him in the same manner as he had spoken to his five brothers.

He answered, "I will not turn away from my God, because in His Torah it is written: 'And thou shalt find Him, if thou search after Him with all thy heart and with all thy soul.' "

"Kill him!" cried Caesar.

Finally, they brought the seventh and the youngest son of Miriam.

"Bow down before the idol!" ordered Caesar.

"I will first ask counsel of my mother," the boy answered.

Then he went to his mother and said, "What shall I do, Mother?"

And Miriam replied, "Do you wish to stand without while your brothers rest in the radiance of the Almighty? Heed me then: close your ears to this wicked man and remain true to your dear brothers!"

And so the boy returned to Caesar, and Caesar asked, "Will you obey me now?"

"I will not deny my God," cried the boy, "For it is written: 'The Lord thy God is a merciful God; He will not fail thee, neither destroy thee, nor forget the covenant of thy fathers which He swore unto them.' "

"Take heed of my words!" commanded Caesar. "You are only a child and know not what you do. Do as I bid you and I will spare your life. I will cast my ring, upon which is engraved the image of my idol, upon the floor. You must bend down, therefore, and pick it up, so that everyone will think that you have bowed before my god."

"Woe to you, O wicked King!" replied the boy. "If I fear not to face my Maker, the Ruler of the Universe, how much less should I fear you, who are only a man!"

"Then die!" cried Caesar.

And when Miriam saw how they came to put her youngest to death she was filled with a terrible grief.

"Let me kiss him first!" she pleaded.

Caesar granted her wish and she drew the boy into her arms and kissed and fondled him.

"I swear by your life, O Caesar!" she implored. "Slay me first before you slay my child!"

"That I cannot do," answered Caesar, "for your Torah forbids the killing of a mother with her young."

"You hypocrite!" cried Miriam wrathfully. "Have you followed all the precepts of our Torah that only this precept is left for you to observe?"

And Caesar was enraged and cried out, "Let the child be killed instantly!"

But Miriam would not let go of her boy.

"Be not sad and fear not, my child!" she bade him. "You are now going to Paradise to join your dear brothers who have died before you! And when you see our Father Abraham tell him, 'Thus spoke my mother: You, Abraham, must not be vainglorious because you built an altar on which to sacrifice your son Isaac to the Lord—I raised seven altars for seven sons. You, Abraham, only wished to bring your son as a sacrifice— I sacrificed all my sons. You were only proven—I was bereaved.' "

And, as Miriam spoke thus to her youngest, they killed him in her arms.

She then raised her hands to Heaven and prayed, "My heart exults in the Eternal, because my children remained faithful to Him in death as in life! O you enemies and oppressors of Israel—how vain is your arrogance! Know, that if God punishes us now, it is not because you are mighty, but because it is His Will. O Lord—I implore you—take my soul from me so that I may be united with my dear children! Do not abandon me to the scorn and derision of our enemies, but take me to You!"

And no sooner had she ended her prayer than she sank to the earth and died.

"Fortunate mother!" cried all of Israel when they heard of it. "Now she is joined forever with her children!"

"Poor, unfortunate mother!" wailed the angels. "What a sad fate was her lot!"

And, when the heathen heard of it, they were filled with wonder, and asked, "What sort of God is this Jewish God for whom His worshippers are so eager to lay down their lives?"

THE FIRST TEAR

After Adam and Eve had been banished from the Garden of Eden, God saw that they were penitent and took their fall very much to heart. And as He is a Compassionate Father He said to them gently:

"Unfortunate children! I have punished you for your sin and have driven you out of the Garden of Eden where you were living without care and in great well-being. Now you are about to enter into a world of sor-

THE FIRST TEAR. From *A Treasury of Jewish Folklore,* by Nathan Ausubel; copyright 1948 by Crown Publishers, Inc. By permission of Crown Publishers, Inc.

row and trouble the like of which staggers the imagination. However, I want you to know that My benevolence and My love for you will never end. I know that you will meet with a lot of tribulation in the world and that it will embitter your lives. For that reason I give you out of My heavenly treasure this priceless pearl. Look! It is a tear! And when grief overtakes you and your heart aches so that you are not able to endure it, and great anguish grips your soul, then there will fall from your eyes this tiny tear. Your burden will grow lighter then."

When Adam and Eve heard these words sorrow overcame them. Tears welled up in their eyes, rolled down their cheeks and fell to earth.

And it was these tears of anguish that first moistened the earth. Adam and Eve left them as a precious inheritance to their children. And since then, whenever a human being is in great trouble and his heart aches and his spirit is oppressed then the tears begin to flow from his eyes and lo! the gloom is lifted.

THE PRICE OF ENVY

While a poor woman stood in the market-place selling cheeses, a cat came along and carried off a cheese. A dog saw the pilferer and tried to take the cheese away from him. The cat stood up to the dog. So they pitched into each other. The dog barked and snapped; the cat spat and scratched, but they could bring the battle to no decision.

"Let's go to the fox and have him referee the matter," the cat finally suggested.

"Agreed," said the dog.

So they went to the fox.

The fox listened to their arguments with a judicious air.

"Foolish animals," he chided them, "why carry on like that? If both of you are willing, I'll divide the cheese in two and you'll both be satisfied."

"Agreed," said the cat and the dog.

So the fox took out his knife and cut the cheese in two, but, instead of cutting it lengthwise, he cut it in the width.

"My half is smaller!" protested the dog.

The fox looked judiciously through his spectacles at the dog's share.

"You're right, quite right!" he decided.

So he went and bit off a piece of the cat's share.

"That will make it even!" he said.

When the cat saw what the fox did she began to yowl:

"Just look! My part's smaller now!"

The fox again put on his spectacles and looked judiciously at the cat's share.

"Right you are!" said the fox. "Just a moment, and I'll make it right."

And he went and bit off a piece from the dog's cheese.

This went on so long, with the fox nibbling first at the dog's and then at the cat's share, that he finally ate up the whole cheese before their eyes.

KNOW YOUR ENEMY

A young inexperienced mouse went out to forage for food. Before he started out his wise old granddaddy cautioned him, "Watch out, dear child, for our enemies!"

The young mouse promised faithfully to do so and then dashed out into the barnyard.

The first one he met was a rooster who stretched out his wings and, looking fierce, cried out in a terrible voice, "Cock-a-doodle-do!"

Scared out of his wits, the little mouse scurried back into his hole.

"Grandpa, Grandpa!" he gasped breathlessly. "I've just met a terrible creature with a comb red as blood. When he saw me he threw back his head and screamed at me!"

Grandpa Mouse smiled indulgently and said, "Foolish child! This is no enemy of ours! This was a rooster who crowed. You have nothing to fear from him!"

Taking heart the little mouse went out again and the first one he met was a turkey. He got so frightened when he looked at him that pell-mell he ran back into the mouse-hole.

"Oh, Grandpa!" he cried, trembling with fright. "I just saw a horrible black creature. He had yellow legs, a sharp beak and angry red eyes. When he saw me he shook his head fiercely and cried, 'Gobble, gobble!'"

Grandpa Mouse smiled indulgently.

"Foolish child!" he chided. "He isn't our enemy—he's only a turkey! You will be able to recognize our enemy by the humble way he carries himself. He keeps his head down and has beautiful golden eyes. His fur is smooth and he purrs ever so gently. When you meet him—run for your life!"

KNOW YOUR ENEMY. From *A Treasury of Jewish Folklore,* by Nathan Ausubel; copyright 1948 by Crown Publishers, Inc. By permission of Crown Publishers, Inc.

8
NORTH AMERICA

Soon will thy father Finnur come from Reynir,
Bringing a little playmate for thee, here.[1]

Since the North American folklore represents the many cultures of its inhabitants, it is natural that the variant type of tale be the most commonly found. The German Rumpelstiltskin theme of the Canadian, "Who Built Reynir Church?" is an example. The truly American spirit is found in the Tall Tales of impossible accomplishment, which makes them poor material for dramatization. The American Indian stories do not easily lend themselves to acting out since the plots are too loosely woven or the themes are too adult. The tales included here are the Canadian, the Chinese and Indians of California, the Indians of the middle west, the Negroes of the south, and the folk of the mountain regions and the eastern shoreline.

WHO BUILT REYNIR CHURCH?

A certain farmer once lived at Reynir, in the district of Mýrdal. He was ordered by the bishop to build a good church by his farm-house, but had so much difficulty in getting enough timber before the hay-making season, and then so much trouble in finding proper builders, that he feared he should be unable to finish the work before the winter.

One day as he was walking in his field, a strange man met him, and stopping him, offered him his services in building the church, declaring that he should require the services of no other workman. The farmer asked him what payment he would want for such labour, and the man made the following condition—that the farmer should either find out his

WHO BUILT REYNIR CHURCH? From *Legends of Iceland,* by George E. J. Powell and Eirikur Magnusson.

[1] George E. J. Powell and Eirikur Magnusson, "Who Built Reynir Church?" from *Legends of Iceland.*

name before he had finished the church, or else give him his son, who was then a little boy six years old. The farmer thought these easy terms enough, and laughing in his sleeve, gladly consented to them.

So the strange builder set to work, and worked with a will, by day and by night, speaking but little to anybody, until the church rose beneath his hands as quickly as if by magic, and the farmer plainly saw that it would be finished even before the haymaking was over.

By this time he had rather changed his mind about the payment he had before thought so easy, and was very far from feeling glad that the end of the church-building was so near; for do what he would, ask whom he would, and search the country round as he would, and had done, he could not, for the life of him, find out the name of his quick-handed mason.

One day, he happened to be wandering outside the field, brooding, in deep grief, over what now seemed to be the heavy price he would have to pay to his master-builder, and threw himself down upon a grass-mound; he had scarcely lain there a minute, when he heard some one singing, and listening, he found that the voice was that of a mother lulling her child, and came from inside the mound upon which he had flung himself down. This is what it said:

> Soon will thy father Finnur come from Reynir,
> Bringing a little playmate for thee, here.

And these words were repeated over and over again; but the farmer, who pretty soon guessed what they meant, started up and ran with all speed, to the church, in which he found the builder just nailing the last plank over the altar.

"Well done, friend Finnur!" said he, "how soon you have finished your work!"

No sooner had these words passed his lips than friend Finnur, letting the plank fall from his hand, vanished, and was never seen again.

THE INDIAN CINDERELLA

On the shores of a wide bay on the Atlantic coast there dwelt in old times a great Indian warrior. It was said that he had been one of Glooskap's best helpers and friends, and that he had done for him many wonderful deeds. But that, no man knows. He had, however, a very wonderful and strange power; he could make himself invisible; he could thus mingle unseen with his enemies and listen to their plots. He was known among the people as Strong Wind, the Invisible. He dwelt with his sister in

THE INDIAN CINDERELLA. From *Canadian Wonder Tales*, by Cyrus Macmillan. Reprinted by permission of the Oxford University Press (Canadian Branch), Toronto.

a tent near the sea, and his sister helped him greatly in his work. Many maidens would have been glad to marry him, and he was much sought after because of his mighty deeds; and it was known that Strong Wind would marry the first maiden who could see him as he came home at night. Many made the trial, but it was a long time before one succeeded.

Strong Wind used a clever trick to test the truthfulness of all who sought to win him. Each evening as the day went down, his sister walked on the beach with any girl who wished to make the trial. His sister could always see him, but no one else could see him. And as he came home from work in the twilight, his sister as she saw him drawing near would ask the girl who sought him, "Do you see him?" And each girl would falsely answer "Yes." And his sister would ask, "With what does he draw his sled?" And each girl would answer, "With the hide of a moose," or "With a pole," or "With a great cord." And then his sister would know that they all had lied, for their answers were mere guesses. And many tried and lied and failed, for Strong Wind would not marry any who were untruthful.

There lived in the village a great chief who had three daughters. Their mother had been long dead. One of these was much younger than the others. She was very beautiful and gentle and well beloved by all, and for that reason her older sisters were very jealous of her charms and treated her very cruelly. They clothed her in rags that she might be ugly; and they cut off her long black hair; and they burned her face with coals from the fire that she might be scarred and disfigured. And they lied to their father, telling him that she had done these things herself. But the young girl was patient and kept her gentle heart and went gladly about her work.

Like other girls, the chief's two eldest daughters tried to win Strong Wind. One evening, as the day went down, they walked on the shore with Strong Wind's sister and waited for his coming. Soon he came home from his day's work, drawing his sled. And his sister asked as usual, "Do you see him?" And each one, lying, answered "Yes." And she asked, "Of what is his shoulder strap made?" And each, guessing, said, "Of rawhide." Then they entered the tent where they hoped to see Strong Wind eating his supper; and when he took off his coat and his moccasins they could see them, but more than these they saw nothing. And Strong Wind knew that they had lied, and he kept himself from their sight, and they went home dismayed.

One day the chief's youngest daughter with her rags and her burnt face resolved to seek Strong Wind. She patched her clothes with bits of birch bark from the trees, and put on the few little ornaments she possessed, and went forth to try to see the Invisible One as all the other girls of the village had done before. And her sisters laughed at her and called her "Fool"; and as she passed along the road all the people laughed at her because of her tattered frock and her burnt face, but silently she went her way.

Strong Wind's sister received the little girl kindly, and at twilight she took her to the beach. Soon Strong Wind came home drawing his sled. And his sister asked, "Do you see him?" And the girl answered "No," and his sister wondered greatly because she spoke the truth. And again she asked, "Do you see him now?" And the girl answered, "Yes, and he is very wonderful." And she asked, "With what does he draw his sled?" And the girl answered, "With the Rainbow," and she was much afraid. And she asked further, "Of what is his bowstring?" And the girl answered, "His bowstring is the Milky Way."

Then Strong Wind's sister knew that because the girl had spoken the truth at first her brother had made himself visible to her. And she said, "Truly, you have seen him." And she took her home and bathed her, and all the scars disappeared from her face and body; and her hair grew long and black again like the raven's wing; and she gave her fine clothes to wear and many rich ornaments. Then she bade her take the wife's seat in the tent. Soon Strong Wind entered and sat beside her, and called her his bride. The very next day she became his wife, and ever afterwards she helped him to do great deeds. The girl's two elder sisters were very cross and they wondered greatly at what had taken place. But Strong Wind, who knew of their cruelty, resolved to punish them. Using his great power, he changed them both into aspen trees and rooted them in the earth. And since that day the leaves of aspen have always trembled, and they shiver in fear at the approach of Strong Wind. It matters not how softly he comes, for they are still mindful of his great power and anger because of their lies and their cruelty to their sister long ago.

THE SHROVE TUESDAY VISITOR

In olden times in Canada, Shrove Tuesday, the day before the beginning of Lent, was more strictly observed than it is to-day. The night was always one of great merriment and feasting. Boys and girls of the villages and country places gathered there for the last time before the long period of quiet. They danced until midnight, but the youth or maiden who dared to dance after the hour of twelve was henceforth followed with little luck. This rule was not often broken, for when it was broken the Spirits of Evil always walked the earth and brought disaster to the youthful dancers.

In a remote village on the banks of a great river there dwelt in the seventeenth century a French peasant, a kind and devout old man. He had but one child, a daughter. She was a handsome girl, and naturally enough

THE SHROVE TUESDAY VISITOR. From *Canadian Wonder Tales*, by Cyrus Macmillan. Reprinted by permission of the Oxford University Press (Canadian Branch), Toronto.

she had many suitors among the young men of the place. One of these she prized above all the others, and she had promised to become his wife. On the evening of the Shrove Tuesday before the date set for the wedding, as was the custom, the young people of the village gathered at her home. It was a simple but joyous gathering, the last which the girl could attend before her marriage. Right merrily the dance went on, and all the guests were in high spirits. Soon after eleven o'clock a sleigh drawn by a great coal-black horse stopped at the door. It contained but one man. Without knocking at the door, the new-comer entered. The rooms were crowded, but the rumour soon spread whisperingly around that a new presence had appeared, and the simple villagers strove to get a look at the tall figure in fine clothes. The old man of the house received the stranger kindly and offered him the best he had in his home, for such was the custom in the old days. One thing the gathering particularly noted—the stranger kept his fur cap on his head, and he did not remove his gloves; but as the night was cold this caused but little wonder.

After the silence caused by the stranger's entrance the music swelled, and again the dance went on. The new-comer chose the old man's daughter as his partner. He came to her and said, "My pretty lass, I hope you will dance with me to-night, and more than once, too." "Certainly," replied the girl, well pleased with the honour, and knowing that her friends would envy her. During the remainder of the evening the stranger never left her side, and dance after dance they had together. From a corner of the room the girl's lover watched the pair in silence and anger.

In a small room opening from that in which the dancers were gathered was an old and pious woman seated on a chest at the foot of a bed, praying fervently. She was the girl's aunt. In one hand she held her beads; with the other she beckoned to her niece to come to her.

"It is very wrong of you," she said, "to forsake your lover for this stranger; his manner is not pleasing to me. Each time I utter the name of the Saviour or the Virgin Mary as he passes the door, he turns from me with a look of anger." But the girl paid no heed to her aunt's advice.

At last it was midnight, and Lent had come. The old man gave the signal for the dance to cease. "Let us have one more dance," said the stranger. "Just one more," pleaded the girl; "my last dance before my marriage." And the old man, wishing to please his only child—for he loved her well, —consented, and although it was already Ash Wednesday the dance went on. The stranger again danced with the girl. "You have been mine all the evening," he whispered; "why should you not be mine forever?" But the girl laughed at his question. "I am a strange fellow," said the stranger, "and when I will to do a thing it must be done. Only say yes, and nothing can ever separate us." The girl cast a glance towards her dejected lover in the corner of the room. "I understand," said the stranger. "I am too late; you love him."

"Yes," answered the girl, "I love him, or rather I did love him once," for the girl's head had been turned by the attentions of the stranger.

"That is well," said the stranger; "I will arrange all, and overcome all difficulties. Give me your hand to seal our plight."

She placed her hand in his, but at once she withdrew it with a low cry of pain. She had felt in her flesh the point of some sharp instrument as if the stranger held a knife in his hand. In great terror she fainted and was carried to a couch. At once the dance was stopped and the dancers gathered around her, wondering at the sudden happenings. At the same time two villagers came in and called the old man to the door to see a strange sight without. The deep snow for many yards around the stranger's horse and sleigh had melted in the hour since his arrival, and a large patch of bare ground was now showing. Terror soon spread among the guests; they spoke in whispers of fear, and shrank from the centre of the room to the walls as if eager to escape; but the old man begged them not to leave him. The stranger looked with a cold smile upon the dread of the company. He kept close to the couch where the girl was slowly coming back to life. He took from his pocket a beautiful necklace, and said to her, "Take off the glass beads you wear, and for my sake take this beautiful necklace." But to her glass beads was attached a little cross which she did not want to part with, and she refused to take his gift.

Meanwhile, in the home of the priest, some distance away, there was a strange happening. While he prayed for his flock the old priest had fallen asleep. He saw in his slumber a vision of the old man's home and what was happening there. He started quickly from his sleep and called his servant and told him to harness his horse at once, for not far away a soul was in danger of eternal death. He hurried to the old man's home. When he reached there, the stranger had already unfastened the beads from the girl's neck and was about to place his own necklace upon her and to seize her in his arms. But the old priest was too quick for him. He passed his sacred stole around the girl's neck and drew her towards him, and turning to the stranger he said, "What art thou, Evil One, doing among Christians?" At this remark terror was renewed among the guests; some fell to their knees in prayer; all were weeping, for they knew now that the stranger with the stately presence and the velvet clothes was the Spirit of Evil and Death. And the stranger answered, "I do not know as Christians those who forget their faith by dancing on holy days. This fair girl has chosen to be mine. With the blood that flowed from her hand she sealed the compact which binds her to me forever."

In answer, the old curé struck the stranger hard across the face with his stole, and repeated some Latin words which none of the guests understood. There was a great crash, as if it thundered, and in a moment amid the noise the stranger disappeared; with his horse and sleigh he had vanished as mysteriously and quickly as he had come.

The guests were long in recovering from their fear, and all night they prayed with the curé that their evil deeds might be forgiven. That she might be cleansed from her sins and that her promise to the stranger might be rightly broken, the girl entered a convent to pass the remainder of her life. A few years later she died. And since that day in her little village on the banks of the great river, the Shrove Tuesday dancers have always stopped their dance at midnight; for youths and maidens still keep in mind the strange dancer in the fine clothes who wooed the peasant's only daughter and almost carried her off.

THE GROUNDHOG DANCE

Seven Wolves once caught a groundhog. They said, "Now, we'll kill you and have something to eat."

Groundhog said, "When we find good food, we should rejoice over it, as people do in the green-corn dances. You will kill me, and I cannot help myself. But if you want to dance, I'll sing for you. Now this is a new dance. I will lean up against seven trees in turn. You will dance forward and then go back. At the last turn you may kill me."

Now the Wolves were very hungry, but they wanted to learn the new dance. Groundhog leaned up against a tree and began to sing. He sang,

Ho wi ye a hi

and all the Wolves danced forward. When he shouted "Yu!" they turned and danced back in line.

"That's fine," said Groundhog, after the first dance was over. Then he went to the next tree and began the second song. He sang,

Hi ya yu we,

and the Wolves danced forward. When he shouted "Yu!" they danced back in a straight line.

At each song, Groundhog took another tree, getting closer and closer and closer to his hole under a stump. At the seventh song, Groundhog said, "Now this is the last dance. When I shout 'Yu!' all come after me. The one who gets me may have me."

Then he sang a long time, until the Wolves were at quite a distance in a straight line. Then he shouted "Yu!" and darted for his hole.

At once the Wolves turned and were after him. The foremost Wolf caught his tail and gave it such a jerk he broke it off. That is why Groundhog has such a short tail.

THE GROUNDHOG DANCE. From *Myths and Legends of the Mississippi Valley and the Great Lakes*, by Katharine B. Judson.

THE THREE TESTS

There dwelt in a certain village a woman of remarkable grace and attractiveness. The fame of her beauty drew suitors from far and near, eager to display their prowess and win the love of this imperious creature —for, besides being beautiful, she was extremely hard to please, and set such tests for her lovers as none had ever been able to satisfy.

A certain young man who lived at a considerable distance had heard of her great charms, and made up his mind to woo and win her. The difficulty of the task did not daunt him, and, full of hope, he set out on his mission.

As he travelled he came to a very high hill, and on the summit he saw a man rising and sitting down at short intervals. When the prospective suitor drew nearer he observed that the man was fastening large stones to his ankles. The youth approached him, saying: "Why do you tie these great stones to your ankles?"

"Oh," replied the other, "I wish to chase buffaloes, and yet whenever I do so I go beyond them, so I am tying stones to my ankles that I may not run so fast."

"My friend," said the suitor, "you can run some other time. In the meantime I am without a companion; come with me."

The Swift One agreed, and they walked on their way together. Ere they had gone very far they saw two large lakes. By the side of one of them sat a man, who frequently bowed his head to the water and drank. Surprised that his thirst was not quenched, they said to him: "Why do you sit there drinking of the lake?"

"I can never get enough water. When I have finished this lake I shall start on the other."

"My friend," said the suitor, "do not trouble to drink it just now. Come and join us."

The Thirsty One complied, and the three comrades journeyed on. When they had gone a little farther they noticed a man walking along with his face lifted to the sky. Curious to know why he acted thus, they addressed him.

"Why do you walk with your eyes turned skyward?" said they.

"I have shot an arrow," he said, "and I am waiting for it to reappear."

"Never mind your arrow," said the suitor. "Come with us."

"I will come," said the Skilful Archer.

As the four companions journeyed through a forest they beheld a strange sight. A man was lying with his ear to the ground, and if he lifted his head for a moment he bowed it again, listening intently. The four approached him, saying: "Friend, for what do you listen so earnestly?"

THE THREE TESTS. From *The Myths of the North American Indians*, by Lewis Spence. By permission of J. B. Lippincott Company.

"I am listening," said he, "to the plants growing. This forest is full of plants, and I am listening to their breathing."

"You can listen when the occasion arises," they told him. "Come and join us."

He agreed, and so they travelled to the village where dwelt the beautiful maiden.

When they had reached their destination they were quickly surrounded by the villagers, who displayed no small curiosity as to who their visitors were and what object they had in coming so far. When they heard that one of the strangers desired to marry the village beauty they shook their heads over him. Did he not know the difficulties in the way? Finding that he would not be turned from his purpose, they led him to a huge rock which overshadowed the village, and described the first test he would be required to meet.

"If you wish to win the maiden," they said, "you must first of all push away that great stone. It is keeping the sunlight from us."

"Alas!" said the youth, "it is impossible."

"Not so," said his companion of the swift foot; "nothing could be more easy."

Saying this, he leaned his shoulder against the rock, and with a mighty crash it fell from its place. From the breaking up of it came the rocks and stones that are scattered over all the world.

The second test was of a different nature. The people brought the strangers a large quantity of food and water, and bade them eat and drink. Being very hungry, they succeeded in disposing of the food, but the suitor sorrowfully regarded the great kettles of water.

"Alas!" said he, "who can drink up that?"

"I can," said the Thirsty One, and in a twinkling he had drunk it all.

The people were amazed at the prowess of the visitors. However, they said, "There is still another test," and they brought out a woman who was a very swift runner, so swift that no one had ever outstripped her in a race.

"You must run a race with this woman," said they. "If you win you shall have the hand of the maiden you have come to seek."

Naturally the suitor chose the Swift One for this test. When the runners were started the people hailed them as fairly matched, for they raced together till they were out of sight.

When they reached the turning-point the woman said: "Come, let us rest for a little."

The man agreed, but no sooner had he sat down than he fell asleep. The woman seized her opportunity. Making sure that her rival was sleeping soundly, she set off for the village, running as hard as she could.

Meanwhile the four comrades were anxiously awaiting the return of the competitors, and great was their disappointment when the woman came in sight, while there was yet no sign of their champion.

The man who could hear the plants growing bent his ear to the ground. "He is asleep," said he; "I can hear him snoring."

The Skilful Archer came forward, and as he bit the point off an arrow he said: "I will soon wake him."

He shot an arrow from the bowstring with such a wonderful aim that it wounded the sleeper's nose, and roused him from his slumbers. The runner started to his feet and looked round for the woman. She was gone. Knowing that he had been tricked, the Swift One put all his energy into an effort to overtake her. She was within a few yards of the winning-post when he passed her. It was a narrow margin, but nevertheless the Swift One had gained the race for his comrade.

The youth was then married to the damsel, whom he found to be all that her admirers had claimed, and more.

THE CRY OF THE LOON

Lamplight was friendly and yellow once more in the windows of the Pod, the Podger's cottage at Loon Lake. A young moon silvered the water, and a mild June breeze rustled the leaves of the trees sheltering the porch where the Podgers rested from the labours of opening the cottage and getting settled. Faintly, from far out on the lake, came the lonely, laughing cry of a loon.

"And now," said Pam, "how are we going to turn this summer to account?"

"To what?" said Roger.

"To account. A lot of summer camps nowadays, are turned into drama festivals, or writers' conferences, or musical festivals or folklore festivals, or dance fest—"

"Stop!" said Roger, "I'm weary already. What started you off on all this?"

"Oh, I don't know. I was just thinking. I had a classmate this year who was awfully keen on having a purpose for everything you do. She said the indirection in this world is appalling. She said there must be some sort of purpose back of everything you do, and you should analyze it and see what it is, and change it if it's wrong, and not let any effort go to waste —even the effort to have a good time."

"I've always thought our summers at Loon Lake were very pleasant," said Mrs. Podger defensively. Mr. Podger elevated himself a little from his completely supine position in the porch swing, thrust a pillow or two

THE CRY OF THE LOON. From *The Christian Science Monitor,* by Silence Buch Bellows. By permission of The Christian Science Publishing Society.

under his shoulders, and remarked, "It just happens that I know an old Indian Legend about this place."

"Ah!" said Pam, "Just the thing for a soft summer night. Go ahead, Dad."

Obligingly, Mr. Podger went ahead. "It seems," he said, "that this region was once inhabited by an Indian nation of great bravery, intelligence, and culture. Much of this was due to the old Chief, who was wise beyond the ways of common men. And when he had finished out his days, and his son had become Chief in his stead, the young brave felt the great weight of his responsibilities. His father had taught him how to use mercy and justice in dealing with the tribe. But he had never told his son what to require of his people, that they might best serve their Chief and their nation.

"So, the young man said to himself, 'the ways of nature are ways of wisdom, I will go down to the water's edge, and I will inquire of the things that I see and hear.'

"So he went down to the water's edge, where he saw the sun low in the west; and its rays were warm and kind. So he said, 'Oh, Sun, why do you shine so warmly and kindly?'

"Now the sun shone simply because it was the sun, and had no other reason. But it wished to please the young Chief, so it thought a moment and then it said, 'Oh, Chief, I shine only for the purpose of giving you warmth and light!'

" 'That is a good reason,' said the young Chief, much pleased.

"As the sun sank farther toward the horizon a cool breeze came rustling through the trees. It rippled the waters of the lake, pleasing the young Chief's eye, and it cooled the air around him delightfully. And the Chief said, 'Oh, Breeze, why do you blow so cool and sweet?' Now, the breeze blew because that was its nature, and it has never thought of doing anything else. But, wishing to please and impress the young Chief, it said, 'Oh, Chief, I blow for the express purpose of cooling you after the heat of the day.'

"The Young Chief nodded. 'That is a very good reason,' he said approvingly.

"The sun was gone now, and in a short time the full round moon rose in the east. As the light of the sun faded, and the moon shone brighter and brighter, and cast a silver light over the whole earth. And the young Chief said, 'Oh, Moon, why do you shine so silverly?' Now the moon shone because it was there, and had never given the matter much thought.

"But now, hoping to please the young Chief, it said, 'Oh, Chief, I shine for the sole purpose of giving you light after the sun is gone.'

"The young Chief nodded again. 'That is a good reason,' he said, 'I perceive that you all move with a high and serious purpose.'

"At that moment the young Chief heard a strange call. It was a loon that skimmed over the lake, and came to rest on the moonlit water, calling its wild and lonely cry. And the sound of it pleased the Chief even more than the warmth of the sun, more than the coolness of the breeze, more than the silver of the moon. And he said, 'Oh, Bird, why do you call with such a wild, strange, lonely cry, that speaks to my heart?'

"And the loon said, 'I call with a wild, strange lonely cry because I am the bird that calls with a wild, strange, lonely cry.'

"And the young Chief lifted his face to the silver night, and he said, 'Now, I perceive the real purpose in all things, and I shall lead my people the better for my understanding.'"

A BEAR STORY

Many years ago the Indians were warring among themselves at the village of Hop-pow, near the mouth of the river. A portion of them whipped the others and those who were defeated in the battle moved away from there and went back in the mountains to live, while the victorious warriors also left the village for a few days' stay at a place known as Si-alth.

While the Indians were all away, a bear strayed into one of the Indian houses where he discovered a very large basket filled with beautiful Indian dresses and strings of Indian money and other Indian ornaments. He was very happy when he discovered this basket and began to take the things out and look them over carefully. As he came to the dresses he would try each one on and then dance, but he could not seem to find one that suited his idea of fashion. He kept throwing the dresses aside as he pulled them off. He wanted one that rattled as he danced. At last he found the one he wanted, for when he put it on and danced the shells began to rattle, as there were a great many on the dress. As he danced, to his great delight, and the bells rang like music in his ears, and well satisfied with the dress he pulled it off and put it back in the basket with all the other articles. After he had finished storing them away in the basket he began to tear up the earthen floor, and scatter things all over the house. After doing all the damage he could, he shouldered the large basket and started for the woods, and traveled some distance to a large hollow redwood tree. He decided to stop here and put on the dress with many shells, and began to dance and sing, having a glorious time all by himself as he had no comrades to join in the fun. This is the song he sang while he danced: Ho-wen-ah-a, ho-wen-ah-a, nah-hay, nah-hay. After he had danced for some time, he became exhausted but he managed to keep on dancing, he loved to hear the music of the shells as he danced about.

A BEAR STORY. From *To the American Indian,* by Mrs. Lucy Thompson, Cummins Print Shop, 1916.

After visiting for several days at Si-alth the Indians returned to their homes at Hop-pow. When they reached the village they discovered that everything had been turned topsy-turvey in one of the houses, and that the large basket of Indian dresses was missing. They at once suggested that some of their enemies had returned while they were away and stolen the things, and they all followed in hot pursuit to recover the stolen articles. But they could find no trace of them, and in despair gave up the chase. Some of them made a closer inspection of the house and this time they were sure they saw bear tracks in the soft ground. The Indians now followed the bear tracks closely, which led them to the large redwood tree, and as they approached it they could see that it was hollow and had a large roomy place inside, and glancing in they saw the bear dancing, dressed in one of the dresses. One of the smaller boys became tired watching the bear and asked if he might go up near the tree and the older Indians decided to let him go and asked him to try to get the dresses away from the bear. The boy agreed, and went up until he was afraid to go nearer. The bear's attention was now attracted to the boy, and he saw at once that the Indians had discovered his hiding place, and stopped dancing and left the tree, carrying with him the Indian dresses, determined to take them to his own home, which was in a tree top near by. This tree was hollow up its trunk and in the top of this hollow the bear made his home. He tugged with all his might at the huge basket but it was so large he could not pull it through the hollow to his chest, and when he saw that he could not pull it through it made him mad and he tried to dig the tree up by its roots. He dug so rapidly that he soon found he had dug a cave under the tree, and being fatigued from his strenuous efforts he seized the basket and pulled it after him into the cave. Once in there he thought himself secure from the Indians. As the bear disappeared into the cave with the basket, all the Indians ventured up near the tree and began talking as to what they would do, being very anxious to recover the things as it meant a great loss of riches if they could not recover them again. They finally agreed they would kindle a fire at the mouth of the cave and smoke the bear out of his den, so they gathered up a large pile of wood and dry branches and made a fire. The Indians lined up ready for him when he came out. The owner of the articles was an old man and he took his place near the cave, and with his bow drawn, ready to shoot the bear, but his arrow did not wound the bear fatally, and the bear seized him and crushed him to death. The enraged bear then turned upon the other Indians, but at last he sank to the ground riddled with arrows. They recovered the basket of dresses and returned home in a mournful procession, for one of their members had departed to the spirit land. The bear in his wild revery had also lost his life.

THE PRINCE OF PLENTY

Mahalla, daughter of the Chief of the Sobobas, sat before her tepee playing with her pets, a Coyote kitten and a young Rabbit.

"My daughter," said the Chief, "again I say you must choose a husband. You have scorned the suitors of our tribe. You have driven away the son of the Chief of the Cahuillas. Now I have brought the son of the Chief of the Cocopahs. Him shall you marry."

Mahalla glanced at the young man, but shook her head sadly. "No, Father, my heart goes not out to meet him. I am young. Give me yet a little more time to play with my wild animal friends."

"It is time you should marry," said her Father, and withdrew.

Mahalla arose and sought the tent of the old Medicine Man. She entered and dropped the curtain of deer skin.

The Medicine Man was old, wrinkled and decrepit, yet kind and very wise in the ways of the animals.

"Tonight shall it be, Father?"

"Aye, my daughter. Tonight when the moon is full you shall learn the ways of the Rabbit."

That night, when the village was still, and the people deep in sleep, Mahalla stole from her tepee. Joining the old Medicine Man they went together to the plain. Threading their way among the clumps of sage brush they finally reached an elevation of sand. The odor of the sage was in the air, the grey-green of the foliage was changed to silver by the moonlight. The stars twinkled in an azure dome.

"This, as I have told you before," continued the Medicine Man, "is the call for the Wolf; this for the Puma; this for the Fox." Each he demonstrated with a call made in a low tone for her ear only. "Tonight we will converse with the Rabbit—a modest and kind-hearted animal well worthy of your friendship."

Forming a funnel with his hands before his face the old man gave a peculiar call. Three times he repeated it. Then from the shadows of the mesquite thickets, from the groves of cottonwoods along the river bed, from the fields of sage surrounding them came the Rabbits with long and graceful leaps—Jack Rabbits, Brush Rabbits and Cottontails. As they arrived they flopped their ears in salutation and sat on their haunches.

When the circle was complete the Medicine Man addressed them. "Behold, I have brought you a new friend—the Princess of the Sobobas. She will love you and care for you as I have done. I am an old man, my joints stiffen. The Princess will help you when I am gone." The Rabbits bowed and flopped their ears. "But tell me," continued the Medicine Man, "how fares it this season with the Rabbits?"

THE PRINCE OF PLENTY. From *Legends of Southern California*, by George W. Caldwell.

"Badly, very badly," replied an old grey Jack Rabbit. "See, we are thin and weak. Seeds and berries are scarce this season. We hunt for days to find a small amount."

"That is bad. I am sorry," said the Princess in a sympathetic voice, "tomorrow I will search the hills and plains and wherever I find wild food I will braze a tree that you may see it from a distance. Every day I will search and leave a sign wherever I find the favorite food of Rabbits."

"Mahalla is our friend," the Rabbits agreed. "We will tell the other animals of the good Mahalla."

The next night the Medicine Man introduced the Princess to the Coyotes. They were much in need of wild carrots. Mahalla promised to hunt for them and to leave her sign where they could be found.

On other nights she was made acquainted with the Pumas. They complained of the shortage of roots and berries. Mahalla would help them find fields where the berries grew more plentifully.

Through the teachings of the wise old Medicine Man Mahalla became learned in the language of the wild things. She became the friend of them all. They would come at her call. Their food supplies were marked by signs which they understood and so they were able to live through the lean year in comparative comfort.

Again her Father conversed with her on the subject of her marriage. "You must choose a husband," he said. "Tomorrow you shall meet the Chief of the Yumas, and the Chief of the Hopi. They are great Chiefs and they sue for your hand. Choose between them. Time passes. I grow old. Before I die I would see my daughter's son, who will some day be Chief of the Sobobas. My line must live. Its fate is in your hands."

"Father, I understand. Tomorrow I will choose a husband."

On the next day Mahalla met the Chief of the Hopi. He was small. He was thin. His smile was continuous and vacant. Him, she decided, she could not wed.

She met the Chief of the Yumas. He was big, gross and fat. He was harsh and gruff. He was repellent. Of a certainty she could not wed him.

"How then, will the Princess be suited?" the Father stormed. "One is too fat, another too lean. One is too tall, another too short. One is too old, another too young. Have done with such nonsense. You shall marry. Choose a husband worthy of the daughter of the Chief of the Sobobas."

"Have patience with me, my Father. It is a grievous question. Tomorrow I will choose a mate."

That night Mahalla went into the wilds and called her animal friends around her. When they had gathered she addressed them. "My friends, I have loved you and served you. Your intuition is stronger than mine. Give me your council. Shall I marry the Chief of the Hopi?" A snarl of disapproval went around the circle.

"Shall I marry the Chief of Yuma?" A fiercer snarl of disapproval.

"Will another come—one of whom I have dreamed?" Purrs and bows came from the animals.

The next morning as Mahalla was seated in front of her tepee deeply pondering on the problem of her marriage, she lifted her eyes and beheld a stranger coming down the hill in the pathway to her village. An Eagle feather was in his hair. His robe, rich, but much worn, was of an unknown tribe. His face was eager and alert, his eyes those of a dreamer. When their glances met his face lighted in a smile and he quickened his pace. In Mahalla's eyes came an expression of surprise, then they softened and smiled. Her lips parted in a sigh, and she held out her hands with palms up.

The stranger approached and laid his hands, palms down, upon hers. Long and intently they gazed into each other's eyes.

"At last I have found you," he said, almost in a whisper.

"Long have I waited," she breathed in reply.

"Long have I sought you among all the tribes, but now I am content."

He sat beside her and, hand in hand, they conversed in low voices until the shadows lengthened. Then she arose and went to her Father's tepee.

"I have chosen," she said, "my mate has come."

"Who is he?"

"I know not, Father. I only know that he is my mate—the mate I have waited for."

"Send him to me."

The stranger stood before the Chief. "Who are you? Whence came you? Where go you, and whom do you seek?"

"I am a stranger. I come from afar. I go to all tribes. I seek my mate and happiness, or rather, I have been among many tribes, and I have found my mate. I seek no further. Here I remain. I have found her. She is your daughter, oh great Chief."

"And do you, a stranger, a wanderer, a dreamer, presume to claim as wife the Princess of Soboba who is courted by the great Chieftains?"

"I claim only Mahalla, my mate, by the right of love alone."

"Mahalla is the Princess of Soboba."

"Of that I know nothing. I only know she is my mate, and I am hers. The Great Spirit has so willed it. We know it."

"Nay, bold stranger, it is not so. Begone."

Mahalla, having overheard the stormy interview, hastened to her old friend the Medicine Man and poured out her story with tears. "Shall I leave my Father and my people," she asked, "and flee in the night to a far country?"

The wrinkled old man was silent. With his claw-like fingers he made marks upon a pile of sand. At length he said, "I know not. The Spirits give no sign. The wisdom of Man in such matters is imperfect. You should consult the wild animals. Tonight, at the darkest hour, go you to the counsel place of the animals. Go with love and with faith. Go wearing only your royal breast plates and the Girdle of your Soul. Call all the animals; they love you and will not fail you. They shall decide."

Accordingly, at the darkest hour, Mahalla emerged from her tent and hastened to the desert place where no plant would grow—the counsel place of the animals. She called to the Puma, the Coyote, the Fox, the Rabbit and to all the animals and night birds. She called to the east, the west, the north and the south. They came singly, in pairs and in packs. There was a soft patter of padded feet as they trotted, leaped and loped to the circle. The wings of the Hawk and the Owl made a whirring sound as they circled in the air. The animals sat upon their haunches in a circle around her.

"Hear me, oh, my friends, I love you, and have served you, and will serve you and help you for all time. Give me your aid and counsel now. My mate has called me. My Father opposes. Shall I abandon my people and my Father, and flee to a far country with the mate of my soul—the stranger?"

The animals wagged their heads and counseled together.

"We would see the stranger," said the Fox, and all the animals purred their approval.

"I will bring him," Mahalla replied. "He will surely be waiting near my tepee."

In a short time Mahalla returned hand and hand with the stranger. The animals looked into his face and whispered together. "It is the Prince of Plenty. Happy the tribe that shall hold him." They fawned against his legs and purred their welcome.

"Tell me," said the Princess, "shall we flee together?"

"Too late!" interrupted the Coyote, "the village is aroused. The warriors are pursuing."

All the animals tipped their heads to listen. The angry shouts of men could be heard. Nearer and nearer they came.

"Then we will die together," said the Princess, taking the hand of the stranger. "Death together is better than life without love."

"Hear me, oh friends," said the stranger, "wherever our blood shall mingle together in the sand, that soil shall be sacred to our friends, the wild creatures. Here our blood will fall, and here will spring up the plants that furnish food to the wild creatures only. Plants that shall produce food abundantly so that there shall never be famine again for our friends. You, Puma, and you, Coyote, and you, Rabbit, shall carry the seeds and scatter them on barren spots and on hillsides, and wherever they shall grow that land shall be cursed for Man and sacred to the wild creatures, for nothing that Man can eat will grow with vigor upon it."

The lovers knelt upon the sand, clasped hands and bowed their heads. The warriors were upon them. The heavy war clubs fell and the blood of the lovers mingled in the sand.

With a snarl of rage the Pumas and Coyotes bounded forward. "Go back to your people," they roared. "Go back and tell them you have killed our Princess. Hence-forth the Indian shall know want and famine, but from this ground, consecrated by the blood of the friends of wild animals, shall grow strange new plants to produce food for the wild creatures only. Wherever those plants will grow the soil belongs to us and will produce nothing for Man. The Prince of Plenty has provided for the friends of his mate."

In due time there grew from the blood-moistened ground three plants never known before—the wild buckwheat, the wild barley and the man-zanita. They produced seeds and berries, foods especially suited for wild creatures, but not for Man. The Puma, the Coyote, and the Rabbit carried the seeds to the waste and barren places on the plains and on the rocky hillsides where they grow, to this day, producing abundant food for wild creatures; and to this day there has been bitter warfare between Man, and the Puma and Coyote.

THE RABBIT THAT WOULDN'T HELP DIG A WELL

Once upon a time there was a water famine, and the runs went dry and the creeks went dry and the rivers went dry, and there wasn't any water to be found anywhere, so all the animals in the forest met together to see what could be done about it. The lion and the bear and the wolf and the fox and the giraffe and the monkey and elephant, and even the rabbit,—everybody who lived in the forest was there, and they all tried to think of some plan by which they could get water. At last they decided to dig a well, and everybody said he would help,—all except the rabbit, who always was a lazy little bugger, and he said he wouldn't dig. So the animals all said, "Very well, Mr. Rabbit, if you won't help dig this well, you shan't have one drop of water to drink." But the rabbit just laughed and said, as smart as you please, "Never mind, you dig the well and I'll get a drink all right."

Now the animals all worked very hard, all except the rabbit, and soon they had the well so deep that they struck water and they all got a drink and went away to their homes in the forest. But the very next morning what should they find but the rabbit's footprints in the mud at the mouth of the well, and they knew he had come in the night and stolen some water. So they all began to think how they could keep that lazy little rabbit from getting a drink, and they all talked and talked and talked, and

THE RABBIT THAT WOULDN'T HELP DIG A WELL. From *Journal of American Folk-Lore*, XLVII (1934), 344. By permission of the American Folk-Lore Society.

after a while they decided that someone must watch the well, but no one seemed to want to stay up to do it. Finally, the bear said, "I'll watch the well the first night. You just go to bed, and I'll show old Mr. Rabbit that he won't get any water while I'm around."

So all the animals went away and left him, and the bear sat down by the well. By and by the rabbit came out of the thicket on the hillside and there he saw the old bear guarding the well. At first he didn't know what to do. Then he sat down and began to sing:

> Cha ra ra, will you, will you, can you?
> Cha ra ra, will you, will you, can you?

Presently the old bear lifted up his head and looked around. "Where's all that pretty music coming from?" he said. The rabbit kept on singing:

> Cha ra ra, will you, will you, can you?
> Cha ra ra, will you, will you, can you?

This time the bear got up on his hind feet. The rabbit kept on singing:

> Cha ra ra, will you, will you, can you?
> Cha ra ra, will you, will you, can you?

Then the bear began to dance, and after a while he danced so far away that the rabbit wasn't afraid of him any longer, and so he climbed down into the well and got a drink and ran away into the thicket.

Now when the animals came the next morning and found the rabbit's footprints in the mud, they made all kinds of fun of Old Mr. Bear. They said, "Mr. Bear, you are a fine person to watch a well. Why, even Mr. Rabbit can outwit you." But the bear said, "The rabbit had nothing to do with it. I was sitting here wide-awake, when suddenly the most beautiful music came right down out of the sky. At least I think it came down out of the sky, for when I went to look for it, I could not find it, and it must have been while I was gone that Mr. Rabbit stole the water." "Anyway," said the other animals, "we can't trust you any more. Mr. Monkey, you had better watch the well tonight, and mind you, you'd better be pretty careful or old Mr. Rabbit will fool you." "I'd like to see him do it," said the monkey. "Just let him try." So the animals set the monkey to watch the well.

Presently it grew dark, and all the stars came out; and then the rabbit slipped out of the thicket and peeped over in the direction of the well. There he saw the monkey. Then he sat down on the hillside and began to sing:

> Cha ra ra, will you, will you, can you?
> Cha ra ra, will you, will you, can you?

Then the monkey peered down into the well. "It isn't the water," said he. The rabbit kept on singing:

> Cha ra ra, will you, will you, can you?
> Cha ra ra, will you, will you, can you?

This time the monkey looked into the sky. "It isn't the stars," said he. The rabbit kept on singing.

This time the monkey looked toward the forest. "It must be the leaves," said he. "Anyway, it's too good music to let go to waste." So he began to dance, and after a while he danced so far away the rabbit wasn't afraid, so he climbed down into the well and got a drink and ran off into the thicket.

Well, the next morning, when all the animals came down and found the footprints again, you should have heard them talk to that monkey. They said, "Mr. Monkey, you are no better than Mr. Bear; neither of you is of any account. You can't catch a rabbit." And the monkey said, "It wasn't old Mr. Rabbit's fault at all that I left the well. He had nothing to do with it. All at once the most beautiful music that you ever heard came out of the woods, and I went to see who was making it." But the animals only laughed at him. Then they tried to get someone else to watch the well that night. No one would do it. So they thought and thought and thought about what to do next. Finally the fox spoke up. "I'll tell you what let's do," said he. "Let's make a tar man and set him to watch the well." "Let's do," said all the other animals together. So they worked the whole day long building a tar man and set him to watch the well.

That night the rabbit crept out of the thicket, and there he saw the tar man. So he sat down on the hillside and began to sing:

> Cha ra ra, will you, will you, can you?
> Cha ra ra, will you, will you, can you?

But the man never heard. The rabbit kept on singing:

> Cha ra ra, will you, will you, can you?
> Cha ra ra, will you, will you, can you?

But the tar man never heard a word. The rabbit came a little closer:

> Cha ra ra, will you, will you, can you?
> Cha ra ra, will you, will you, can you?

The tar man never spoke. The rabbit came a little closer yet:

> Cha ra ra, will you, will you, can you?
> Cha ra ra, will you, will you, can you?

The tar man never spoke a word.

The rabbit came up close to the tar man. "Look here," he said, "you get out of my way and let me down into that well." The tar man never moved. "If you don't get out of my way, I'll hit you with my fist," said the rabbit. The tar man never moved a finger. Then the rabbit raised his fist and struck the tar man as hard as he could, and his right fist stuck tight in the tar. "Now you let go of my fist or I'll hit you with my other fist," said the rabbit. The tar man never budged. Then the rabbit struck him with his left fist, and his left fist stuck tight in the tar. "Now you let go of my fists or I'll kick you with my foot," said the rabbit. The tar man never budged an inch. Then the rabbit kicked him with his right foot, and his right foot stuck tight in the tar. "Now you let go of my foot or I'll kick you with my other foot," said the rabbit. The tar man never stirred. Then the rabbit kicked him with his left foot, and his left foot stuck tight in the tar. "Now you let me go or I'll butt you with my head," said the rabbit. and he butted him with his head, and there he was; and there the other animals found him the next morning.

Well, you should have heard those animals laugh. "Oh, ho, Mr. Rabbit," they said, "now we'll see whether you steal any more of our water or not. We're going to lay you across a log and cut your head off." "Oh, please do," said the rabbit. "I've always wanted to have my head cut off. I'd rather die that way than any other way I know." "Then we won't do it," said the other animals. "We are not going to kill you any way you like. We are going to shoot you." "That's better," said the rabbit. "If I had just stopped to think, I'd have asked you to do that in the first place. Please shoot me." "No, we'll not shoot you," said the other animals; and then they had to think and think for a long time.

"I'll tell you what we'll do," said the bear. "We'll put you into a cupboard and let you eat and eat and eat until you are as fat as butter, and then we'll throw you up into the air and let you come down and burst." "Oh, please don't!" said the rabbit. "I never wanted to die that way. Just do anything else, but please don't burst me." "Then that's exactly what we'll do," said all the other animals together.

So they put the rabbit into the cupboard and they fed him pie and cake and sugar, everything that was good; and by and by he got just as fat as butter. And then they took him out on the hillside and the lion took a paw, and the fox took a paw, and the bear took a paw, and the monkey took a paw; and then they swung him back and forth, and back and forth, saying: "One for the money, two for the show, three to make ready, and four to go." And up they tossed him into the air, and he came down and lit on his feet and said:

> Yip, my name's Molly Cotton-tail;
> Catch me if you can.

And off he ran into the thicket.

A DIME FOR THE SACK

Old Boss had all kinds of confidence in John, and said that anything he asked Jesus for he'd send it to him. John had been a favorite around for a while and Boss was going to give him $100 for his holiday. And he called John in and asked him, "John, you go on down and pray the Lord to send you $100 for your holiday, and if he send that, I'll have all kinds of confidence in you." So Boss-man sacked up $99.90 and gave it to two of his little boys. So they saw John going down to the tree that evening and they went along ahead of him and climbed the tree.

John got on his knees and said, "O Lord, I'm praying to you to have a brilliant Christmas, I wants $100." No quicker said than done, the little boys dropped a sack of dough alongside of John. John grabbed the sack and got off his knees and went hopping off to the house and said, "Master I got it, I got it."

So Master said, "You sure, John, you got it?"

"Yes Master, I got it."

"Well now, pour it out on the counter and see how much you got." So John couldn't count but $99.90. "So you can see John, you only got $99.90."

"That okay Boss, he did what he said he did, but he charged me a dime for the sack."

WAITING FOR MARTIN

You see that ghost was named Martin. See it was a hanted house, could no one stay there. And so they put up money to see could they find someone to stay in the house. And so everyone would go to stay in that house couldn't stay there. And so one of the mens went in town, quite natchally was telling about the hanted house. And so the preacher came along. The man said to himself, if anyone could stay in the hanted house, it should be a preacher. So he saw the preacher, and he axed the the preacher, was he afraid of a hanted house. And the preacher says, "Why no, everywhere I go I reads my Bible." So this man takes him on back there to this man what owned this house. So when they got there the

A DIME FOR THE SACK. From *Negro Tales from Pine Bluff*, by Richard Dorson. By permission of Indiana University Press.

WAITING FOR MARTIN. From *Negro Tales from Pine Bluff*, by Richard Dorson. By permission of Indiana University Press.

man told him how much money he had for everyone that stayed in the hanted house. So that night the preacher got his grip and his Bible and went on over to the hanted house. He went on in and he sat down. He opened his Bible, and the preacher began to read. And the verse he was reading was very familiar to everybody. The preacher said, "In those days came John the Baptist preaching in the wilderness of Judey. Repent for the Kingdom of Heaven is at hand." So he read it for a long time. After a while he heard a door squeak. He kept reading his Bible. He read it, "In those days come John the Baptist preaching in the wilderness of Judey."

The spook come on by and just said, "How de do." He kept reading and he never looked up. Way after a while he heard another door open. That spook come on by. The preacher began reading just a little bit faster.

"In those days come John the Baptist preaching in the wilderness of Judey."

After a while he heard another one. This time didn't no door open, but he heard footsteps. He began reading just a little bit faster.

"In those days come John the Baptist preaching in the wilderness of Judey."

This spook got even with him and stopped. He said, "Mister," he said, "will you be here when Martin come?" The preacher kept reading.

"In those days come John the Baptist preaching in the wilderness of Judey."

He's getting scared.

So way after a while the hant touched him again. He said, "Will you be here when Martin comes?"

The preacher kind of looked up slyly and axed, "Who's Martin? Sure I'll be here when he comes." (He's trying to bluff this spook you see.)

Way after while the preacher began to read faster an' faster. This time he heard the turriblest noises of all. This was Martin. Martin dug on up to the preacher he did. This time the preacher put his finger on the Bible.

"In those days come John the Baptist preaching in the wilderness of Judey."

(See he didn't want to look up.)

Martin stood there and listened at him read. After a while Martin shook him. Preacher kept reading. He wouldn't look up. He kept tetching the preacher on the shoulder, and arter a while Martin wouldn't go away, the preacher looked up. And when he looked and saw Martin's face, instead of reading "In those days come John the Baptist," the preacher begin to tremble. And every which way he turn Martin was there. The preacher finally couldn't get out the room. The preacher says, "Oh mama." Way after a while, he was so scared, he hollered, "Oh papa." Martin was chasing the preacher so bad till when he did get a chance he grabbed his Bible and grip and got going. And no one ever saw the preacher again.

(He figgered he'd just take a gait he could hold that was familiar to the spirits.)

HOW MONEY FELL FROM THE SKY

There was once a poor woman who had always hoped that the fact that she was kindhearted would be rewarded with money from the sky. One day, unable to endure her poverty any longer, she began to weep, and wept and wept and wept. Looking up at the sky she moaned aloud, "Oh, sky, if only some money would fall down from above for me."

No sooner had she finished her prayer than silver money actually began to rain down. At first the woman was pleased but as it showed no let up, no pause until she was buried deep beneath heavy silver, she was filled with fear. The heavy silver pressed down upon her, and constrained her so tightly that she prayed wildly, "Take back your money! Take back your money! There is too much of it." Immediately the money was drawn up into the sky until every piece was gone.

When she realized what had happened the woman began weeping as bitterly as before.

A neighbor who had been watching the whole affair came to her and said, "You have said something that has offended the gods in the sky."

"I only said, 'Take your money back, there is too much of it,' " moaned the woman.

"But when the gods bless anyone with good fortune, one should pray silently and thank the gods," the neighbor continued. "One should never say anything aloud, lest one offend the gods."

The weeping woman looked up at the sky knowing she had offended the gods and that never again would they bless her with good fortune. So all she could do was to weep on.

THE OLD BEGGAR

One day a frightfully ugly and dirty old beggar was walking along the street, going from house to house, knocking and calling out, "A pail

HOW MONEY FELL FROM THE SKY. From *Chinese Tales Told in California*, by Jon Lee. Federal Work Projects Administrators, P. Radin.

THE OLD BEGGAR. From *Chinese Tales Told in California*, by Jon Lee. Federal Work Projects Administrators, P. Radin.

of water for my feet! Let someone give me a pail of water to wash my feet!" Nobody paid any attention to the dirty old beggar until he came to a little house belonging to a kind woman.

"What do you wish?" she asked when she answered his knock.

"A pail of water to wash my feet," he told her.

The kind woman filled an old pail with water and took it to the old beggar. "You must be tired, you have evidently travelled a long way," she said.

The old beggar replied as he washed his feet, "You are the first person who has noticed it and answered my request. So remember, put this pail of water under your bed and do not take it out or look at it till morning."

Being superstitious, the kind woman obeyed the old beggar and then forgot all about it. In the morning she went to look at the pail and found it full to overflowing with gold and silver. The kind woman was so astonished that she hurried to her next door neighbor, a greedy old woman, and told her the whole story, giving her some of the money as proof.

The greedy old woman wrung her hands and moaned aloud, "And I chased him away yesterday!"

The next day the same dirty old beggar came along and everybody rushed out to implore him to come and have his feet washed. The greedy old woman fought off the neighbors, dragged the old beggar into her house and forced him to wash his feet in a new pail and to use a fine new towel.

The old beggar went away then, telling her to put the pail under her bed that night. So excited was the old woman that she could not sleep. As soon as the day came she rose and snatched at the pail expecting to see it full of gold and jewels. Instead it was full of snakes, lizards and ants. The old woman was so frightened and disappointed that she fell sick.

The kind neighbor said to her, "It is a lesson to you. Hereafter do not be so greedy and always try to help or be kind to those who are unfortunate."

Although the greedy old woman remained sick she tried to be kind and help all those whom she could. One day a man afflicted with leprosy passed by and said, "You are not looking well, my woman, what is wrong?"

The old woman told him what had happened. He nodded his head and said, "You have changed. You are kind now, not greedy any more. Here is a token from my brother, the dirty old beggar. Take it and you will be well again."

The leper disappeared and the old woman got well and always remained kind.

THE TWIST-MOUTH FAMILY

There was once a father and a mother and several children, and all but one of them had their mouths twisted out of shape. The one whose mouth was not twisted was a son named John.

When John got to be a young man he was sent to college, and on the day he came home for his first vacation the family sat up late in the evening to hear him tell of all he had learned. But finally they prepared to go to bed, and the mother said, "Father, will you blow out the light?"

"Yes, I will," was his reply.

"Well, I wish you would," said she.

"Well, I will," he said.

So he blew, but his mouth was twisted, and he blew this way (the narrator shows how he did it—blowing upward), and he couldn't blow out the light.

Then he said, "Mother, will you blow out the light?"

"Yes, I will," was her reply.

"Well, I wish you would," said he.

"Well, I will," she said.

So she blew, but her mouth was twisted, and she blew this way (blowing downward) and she couldn't blow out the light.

Then she spoke to her daughter and said, "Mary, will you blow out the light?"

"Yes, I will," was Mary's reply.

"Well, I wish you would," said her mother.

"Well, I will," Mary said.

So Mary blew, but her mouth was twisted, and she blew this way (blowing out the right corner of the mouth), and she couldn't blow out the light.

Then Mary spoke to one of her brothers and said, "Dick, will you blow out the light?"

"Yes, I will," was Dick's reply.

"Well, I wish you would," said Mary.

"Well, I will," Dick said.

So Dick blew, but his mouth was twisted, and he blew this way (blowing out of the left corner of the mouth), and he couldn't blow out the light.

Then Dick said, "John, will you blow out the light?"

"Yes, I will," was John's reply.

"Well, I wish you would," said Dick.

"Well, I will," John said.

THE TWIST-MOUTH FAMILY. From *Journal of American Folklore*, October–December, 1905, by Clifton Johnson. By permission of Roger Johnson and American Folklore Society.

So John blew, and his mouth was straight, and he blew this way (blowing straight), and he blew out the light.

The light was out and they were all glad that John had succeeded, and Father said, "What a blessed thing it is to have larnin'!"

SALTING THE PUDDING

I never will forget one time Old Lady Simpson was going to have a woodsawing and thought she'd show off some by having puddin for the crowd. Course, she was bound to have a candy pulling and a goober popping same as usual. The puddin was extry.

Well, that day everything was a-hustle and a-bustle over at Simpson's and here it comes on night and no puddin cooked. The old lady she'd done made her brags all around and she just had to have that puddin. All the gals—they was five of them Simpson gals—was as busy as a bee in a tar barrel, washing and ironing, primping and cleaning up the house like they was looking for a preacher during big meeting. So the old lady she tore out to the kitchen and started chunking things together to make that puddin.

Now, she was give out to be the best puddin maker in the whole settlement. But she was so mixed up that evening she plumb forgot to salt the puddin. Now your reel good puddin don't take but just a tee-nincy pinch of salt, but if it ain't got that, it just ain't puddin.

Old Lady Simpson got the fire going just right in the stove and slammed the puddin in there. Then she rushed around a-dusting the cheers and the organ in the setting room.

About that time it hit her about the salt. Her hands was that filthy-dirty she knowed she couldn't salt the puddin without washing them. So she just went ahead a-dusting and a-scrubbing around, figgering she'd have one of the gals tend to it for her.

"Sue," she says, "will you go salt the puddin? I done got my hands dirty."

"Can't, Maw. I'm greasing my shoes."

"Sairy, how about you?"

"Maw, you know I'm a-trying to git this dress done."

"Berthy, can you salt the puddin?"

"No'm."

"Jenny, go salt the puddin."

"Let Lil do it, Maw. I'm starching and arning to beat the bobtail."

"All right. Lil, you run salt the puddin now, Honey."

SALTING THE PUDDING. From *A Treasury of American Folklore*, by B. A. Botkin. Permission granted by Folklore Society.

"Shan't. I'm a-looking high and low for my hair ribbon. I ain't going do nothing else till I find it."

So the old lady she threw her dust rag across a cheerback and went and washed her hands and salted the puddin.

Just along about the time the old lady got back to her dusting, Lil got to thinking how she had ought to mind her Maw. So she sort of eased into the kitchen there and salted the puddin.

Well, she hadn't no more than got back to s'arching for her hair ribbon when Jenny got to feeling oneasy about being so sassy. So here she come and salted that puddin.

Well, so help me, she hadn't scarcely set back down on the back piazzer and picked up the slipper when she was greasing when here come Sairy and salted that puddin.

Berthy always was the lady of the family. She didn't do nothing much none of the time. She was propped in her room a-reading a novelty when all this come off. But if they was one thing that gal liked better than reading a novelty it was eating puddin. She got to thinking about that puddin and got into a twidget. By and by she got up and she tiptoed to the kitchen. She got there right after Sairy left.

Well, that puddin sure baked pretty and when Old Lady Simpson come a-mincing out with it that night you could just hear everybody sort of bend back and smack their lips.

The preacher had come over to sort of look over the goings on, so naturally he got the first helping. His face just got to shining and he said something about puddin was the best eating going. Then he took a whopping big jawful.

When he bit down to kind of let the flavor soak in, his face looked like somebody had covered up the sun with a blanket.

"Upthem!" he said, and he grabbed for the water gourd.

Well, everybody just set there with their mouths full of teeth and their eyes bugged out. Old Lady Simpson sort of caught on that something was wrong so she up and takes a taste herself. Then she knowed.

"Which one of you gals put salt in this puddin?"

"I done it, Maw!" all five of them says together.

"And I done it, too!" the old lady says. "It sure looks like too many cooks sp'iled the puddin."

And nobody couldn't deny it.

A TRAVELLED NARRATIVE

There is one narrative, formerly common in school-readers, in collections of moral tales for youth, and in the miscellany columns of newspapers, that is thought to have been a favorite with Aristophanes and to
have beguiled the Pharaohs when they had the blues—supposing blues to
have been invented in their time. Every now and again it reappears in the
periodicals and enjoys a new vogue for a couple of months. Many villages
clamor for recognition as the scene of the incident, but as Rutland, Ver-
mont, makes a special appeal, it may as well have happened there as
anywhere.

So let it be in Rutland that the cross-roads store-keeper dwelt who was
burdened by the usual loungers that sat about his shop, talked politics,
squirted tobacco-juice on his stove, and, merely to beguile the time,
nibbled at his dried fish, cheese, crackers, maple sugar, and spruce gum,
consuming in the course of a year a long hundredweight of these commodities. These pickings were made openly and were not looked upon as
thefts any more than are the little pieces of cloth that are taken home
as samples by women who go shopping. Groceries that were not nailed up
—or down—were sort of bait to gather purchasers. The store-keeper did
not mind these abstractions, because he added a penny to a bill now and
then, and so kept even. What he did object to was the sneaking away of
dearer commodities, like white sugar, drugs, tobacco, ammunition, rib-
bons, boots, scented soap, and catechisms.

On a sharp night in December the usual worthies sat about the stove,
telling one another how many different kinds of a great man Andrew
Jackson was and what was the best way to cure mange in dogs. The air
of the shop was close and hot, but those who breathed it believed it pleasanter than the crisp cold outside. Fresh and wholesome air is never so little
prized as where there is most of it. The proprietor, who occupied a rickety
arm-chair and was throwing in his wisdom to make the aggregate im-
pressive, kept his eye roving over his stock, and presently he noticed that
Ichabod Thompson, a shiftless, out-at-elbows fellow, was nibbling more
freely from the cracker-barrel than it was "genteel" to do. He pretended
ignorance of this, and in a little time he saw Ichabod slip a pat of butter
out of a firkin where each pound lay neatly wrapped in cloth, take off his
hat in a pretence of wiping his forehead, drop the butter into that hat, and
put it on again. Ichabod then loitered ostentatiously before the harness
and blanket departments, made a casual inquiry as to current rates for
Dr. Pilgarlic's Providential Pills, went to the stove, spreading his hands for

A TRAVELLED NARRATIVE. From *American Myths and Legends,* by Charles M. Skinner.
By permission of Clara A. Skinner.

a moment of warmth, then, turning up his collar, said he guessed he must be going.

"Oh, don't go yet," said the shop-keeper, kindly. "Sit down a minute while I tell you what happened to Hank Buffum's big sow last week."

Not wishing to come under suspicion by exhibiting anxiety to reach home,—the place to which he never went until all the other places were closed,—Ichabod accepted a seat in the circle. The shop-keeper spun his yarn to a tenuous length. He piled wood into the stove, too, until the iron sides of it glowed cherry-red; the heat became furious, a glistening yellow streak appeared on the suspect's forehead. He wiped it away with his handkerchief. He did not seem at ease. In a few minutes he yawned, laboriously, remarked that he had been up late the night before, and that he must be going home.

"All right," consented the merchant; "but just wait a few minutes till I put up a few ginger-snaps for your missus—some I just got from Boston."

Naturally an offer like that could not be refused. It took an unconscionable time to put up a dozen little cakes, and Ichabod was now sweating butter in good earnest. He accepted the gift thankfully, yet with a certain preoccupation, and as he bent over to tuck his trousers into his boots he showed his hair soaking with grease, his collar limp with it, streaks and spatters down his coat, and spots appearing in his hat. The store-keeper winked at the members of his congress, pointed significantly to the buttertub, then to Ichabod's hat, then laid his finger on his lips. The loungers caught the idea, and when their victim was again ready to start they remembered errands and business for him that kept him for several minutes longer in their company. The butter was now coming down in drops and rills, and the poor scamp was at one moment red with heat and confusion then pale with fear, because thieves fared hardly in that town. On one pretext and another he was detained till the butter was all melted and his clothes, partial ruins, before, were wholly spoiled. He arose with decision at last and said he could not stay another minute. "Well," said the shopkeeper, "we can let you go now. We've had fun enough out of you to pay for the butter you stole. You'll be needing new clothes to-morrow. Give us a call. Good-night."

THE GANDER'S MESSAGE

In the eighteenth century there stood a gambrelled house at Somerset, Massachusetts, where Widow Le Doit lived with her daughter and

THE GANDER'S MESSAGE. From *American Myths and Legends*, by Charles M. Skinner. By permission of Clara A. Skinner.

five stout sons. Biel, the youngest, suffered a fate common to the smallest member of a family in that he was teased and badgered by his brothers so that he often begged his mother's permission to go away and earn his living elsewhere. Above all things he would be a sailor. He was a confirmed roamer, and he wanted more room. In one of his lonely rambles he caught a wild goose that he domesticated and prized until somebody shot her,— he suspected his brothers, but one of her eggs was hatched under a hen and the "cute" little gosling that emerged became a special charge of Biel. A time came at last when the widow yielded to the boy's pleadings and consented that he should go to sea. As a pet, a reminder of home, and possibly as a Thanksgiving dinner in some distant port, the gander kept him company in the ship "L'Ouverture," bound for the western Indies. Three years the ship was gone, for she was to change cargoes and trade in the interests of her owners, so that letters were infrequent, Biel might be in Uruguay, China, or Denmark, or he might be on any of the seas.

On the third Thanksgiving day, when the horn was blown for the great dinner of the year at the old home, a queer call came back: the honk of a goose. Widow Le Doit's eyes filled. She recalled her son's pet gander. Another blast and another call from the meadow. The daughter shuddered a little. "Is the meadow haunted," she asked, "or is something about to happen?"

"Why do you speak of such things, Annie?"

"Because there is only one wild goose in the world that knows our horn and will answer it. Blow once more, mother."

A third blast rang from the horn and echoed against the low hills. A form arose from the grass and the laurel patches in the pasture and flew low toward the house. It alighted before the two women, honked loudly, then flew off again. Annie hid her face on her mother's shoulder. "Biel is dead!" she cried.

The elder woman soothed the younger and tried to laugh at her fears, but the laughter had no ring in it. The two went in, presently, to receive their guests. All seemed dull and oppressed until another call of the wild goose sent a little shudder through the company. It seemed like an omen.

"It is there again!" exclaimed the widow. "I will call it." And stepping to the door she sounded a stronger note than ever on the horn. In a few minutes the wild fowl, as the others thought it, alighted in the yard and pattered up the walk toward the door. Annie sprang upon it and carried it to the table, where it stood stretching its wings and pluming itself, not in the least disturbed by the presence of the company, until, with a sudden rouse, as if it had heard something at a distance that it meant to answer, it stretched forth its neck and uttered a honk that made the roof ring. A step sounded on the door-stone, a brown-faced, sturdy figure dashed in, caught the widow about the waist with one arm, Annie with the other, and smacked them heartily; then gave to each of the brothers such a resounding whack upon his back that he quailed. It was Biel. After a minute of tears, laughter, and handshakings the gander paddled to the edge of the table and cocked up an inquiring eye. "Well, if it isn't our gander!" cried the sailor. "He cut away from the ship two days ago, and I supposed he was a long way ahead of us. Aha! I see; you thought we were wrecked. Not a bit of it. Gold in our pockets and appetites for two. Am I in time for the Thanksgiving dinner?"

CASE OF THE BROTHERS BROWN

Toward the end of the Revolution Captain Ira Brown, having endured his share of the dangers and privations of war, retired to the home of his elder brother, Hezekiah, near Fair Haven, Massachusetts, to rest for a few weeks and forget, so well as he might, the shedding of blood. Hezekiah was a lawyer of no great brilliancy, who lived by egging the farmer and fisher folk of the vicinage into quarrels and suits, that he might be employed as their attorney. At that time the lawyer was paying court to the daughter of a well-to-do merchant, who obviously felt little warmth of interest in him, however, the favored suitor being a young fellow of good family named Seymour. The rivalry for this damsel's hand had established a bitterness between Seymour and the lawyer. On an evil day the captain was taking his daily walk near the shore of Buzzard's Bay when a startled, half-smothered exclamation caused him to look about. A figure dodged out of his sight behind a sand dune. What did that mean? Was somebody preparing to play a joke on him? He climbed the dune and from its top commanded a view of a damp hollow, half filled with bushes. Among these bushes lay the body of Seymour. Crouching at a little distance, with bloody fingers held weakly before his face, was Hezekiah. "What is this?" cried the captain, hurrying to his brother. "You have blood on you. Are you hurt?"

"No—no—I—we met here. He called me a name—you understand? I thought he would fight when I struck him. I struck him again, and—and—

"Hezekiah! You have committed murder!"

"No! No! No! Not that! I didn't mean to hurt him. I thought he would attack me. It was self-defence—self-defence."

"This is dreadful, Hezekiah, to kill an unarmed man."

"I know it. I didn't mean to do it. Save me!"

"Pull yourself together. Take my handkerchief and wipe your hands. Don't shake so. You must get out of this, somehow."

CASE OF THE BROTHERS BROWN. From *American Myths and Legends,* by Charles M. Skinner. By permission of Clara A. Skinner.

"You won't tell. You can't. You're my brother. For our mother's sake, you won't give me up."

"No."

"Swear it. Swear that whatever happens you'll not tell."

"I swear."

"Let me get away. Stay and watch for a minute, and call if you see anyone coming. Or, if anyone does come, decoy him away from here."

And with a face as white as that still face in the shrubbery he peered over the dune's edge, looked about in every direction, and with soft, yet rapid, eager step he went out of sight. Some minutes later the captain took the homeward path. He walked with a firm stride, but his face, too, was pale; his expression was that of astonishment and pain, his fingers locked and shifted behind his back. Two neighbors whom he met, presently, and to whom he hardly gave greeting, had never before seen that mood upon him. That night the captain was arrested and taken to New Bedford jail on a charge of murder. Seymour's body had been found, the captain's bloody handkerchief had been picked up near it, the captain himself had been seen leaving the spot in pallor and agitation. He was a man of arms, quick in quarrel. His motive might appear at the trial.

When the case came before judge and jury, as it did quickly,—for it was not the way in those days to delay trials on quibbles month after month and year after year,—Hezekiah was his brother's defender. Everybody commented on the coolness of the prisoner, on his almost disdainful regard for the lawyer, and everybody noted how his advocate trembled, started, and perspired at various passages in the evidence. The prisoner declined to testify in his own defence, merely pleading innocence. If he were a murderer, the people said, he must have struck his victim for some reason, and probably in a dispute. Of the two brothers the lawyer was the worse case. One might have fancied him to be the accused. The evidence on both sides was quickly taken. The State's attorney made a case against the prisoner, circumstantial, without motive, yet plausible, and the jury found him guilty.

"Have you anything to say why sentence of death should not be passed on you?" asked the judge.

For several seconds the captain looked into his brother's eye. The lawyer quailed, his brow was wet, he could barely stand; it was pitiful to see him.

"I can say nothing," answered the accused.

"I regret the need of condemning one to the gallows who has fought ably for his country; one whose name has borne no stain till now; but I am only the agent of the law, and you are held guilty of the abhorrent crime of murder. You have faced death in other forms. You must now prepare to face it in its most shameful, terrible shape. I sentence you to—"

There was a shriek. It was the lawyer, who, throwing up his hands, fell heavily to the floor.

"It was too much for him. How he feels for his brother!" was whispered in the throng.

A glass of water revived him. His eyes were wild. "I saw him—there—at the door. It was his ghost!" he exclaimed, in hoarse, tense tones. "There! Look! It is he—Seymour! My God! It was I who killed him. My brother is innocent. I am the assassin."

The judge had risen and was looking down in amazement. "Is this true?" he asked, so soon as he could find words.

"He has confessed," replied the captain.

A pallid man with a bandage on his head had been trying for some moments to get through the throng. He raised his hand and caught the eye of the judge. "This man has not told the truth," he said, "though he told what he believed. I am Seymour, hurt, but not a ghost. Let these men go free."

A GIFT FROM ST. NICHOLAS

Among the people leaving old Amsterdam for a home in New Amsterdam before the latter town was much more than come to its majority was Claas Schlaschenschlinger, who practised the profession of cobbler in a little house at the head of New Street and had money enough to entitle him to wear eight pairs of breeches at once, and therefore to cut a wide figure in the society of the new metropolis. He had a pond behind his house, where he kept geese that multiplied to his profit, and he was calmly content with his lot—in fact, with his house and lot—till he fell in love. Nobody is calm or contented after that happens to him. His love would have been a successful enterprise had not the coquettish Anitje, on whom his heart was set, been desired by the burgomaster, Roeloffsen. There were other young women in the colony who might have endured that person's temper, his homeliness, his stinginess, for the sake of the comfortable widowhood promised by his advancing years, because he was the richest man in the town; but Anitje was none of such. She was too good an American already to sell herself for money or position, so she accepted Claas, to the infinite joy of that aspiring artisan. Among his other mean qualities Roeloffsen now developed a revengeful disposition, for, by the time Claas and Anitje were comfortably, and, as they fancied, securely settled, and were occupied in the rearing of an annually increasing family, the burgomaster began a series of expensive and disconcerting improvements,—extending streets through pastures, filling hollows, lowering mounds, bridging rills, and draining puddles. Claas's pond had to go.

A GIFT FROM ST. NICHOLAS. From *American Myths and Legends,* by Charles M. Skinner. By permission of Clara A. Skinner.

The money for his geese tided him over until the next improvement, but the assessment for cutting trees and guttering the street and laying a walk past Claas's house to a marsh, took all the silver he had stored in the old pewter teapot. Worst of all, there arrived from Holland, about this time, to complete his ruin, a blacksmith who filled the soles and heels of New Amsterdam with hobnails, which enabled the wearers to preserve a pair of boots for years, and announced their goings and comings on the plank walks and brick pavements and tavern floors with a clatter like a revolution. So it fell out on Christmas eve of a certain year that Claas, his wife, his six children, and his cat sat before a meagre fire and heard the wind howl and the snow dash against the panes. They digested their supper of bread and cheese and beer with deplorable facility, and bleakly wondered what there would be for breakfast.

Claas sighed forth his sorrow that he had ever left Holland. What could he do to carry him through another week? He might sell the silver clasps on the Bible. Fie! It had been his mother's, and beside—to deface the Good Book! Well, then, what? He sprang up with a laugh, for it had just come to him that on the morning of his departure for America he had found in his best stockings a meerschaum pipe, so beautifully dyed by some faithful smoker that no mere cobbler was fit to use it. Without a question it had been a gift from St. Nicholas, his name-saint. A pipe of such a rich mahogany color was worth the price of a Christmas dinner, and pork and tea for several days beside. He went to the old chest and unburied it from a quantity of gear that had come from the old country with him, took it to the window, and rubbed it carefully on his sleeve. A gust of wind filled the room. Claas cried, "Now, which of you children will do such a thing as not to keep the house shut in weathers like these?" and started to close the door, when he bumped into a little portly stranger who had entered and stood regarding Claas with twinkling eyes.

"Eh? Did somebody call me?" asked the unknown. "Well, seeing that I am in, and have been out there in the cold for hours, I will make free to warm myself at your fire."

The family having made room for him before the excuse for a blaze, the visitor rubbed his glowing cheeks and shining nose and spread his fingers over the ashes. "I must say, Mynheer Schlaschenschlinger," said he, "that you are not very hospitable. You might at least put another couple of logs on the hearth. Humph! 'In need, one learns to know one's friends.'"

"There are more Faderland proverbs than that, also, and one is, 'It is hard combing where there is no hair.'"

"Pooh, pooh! Never talk to me of that. Let me remind you of another: 'Who gives from what he has deserves to live.'"

"Ah, mynheer," answered Claas, with a rueful countenance, "no man has ever been turned from my hearth; but I have nothing left to burn, unless it is my home."

"Aha! Is it so? Been wasting your substance, I see. Well, then, 'Who burns himself behind must sit on the blisters.' There, never mind; I was jesting. 'A good understanding needs only half a word.' " And before Claas could prevent it the stranger had cracked a fine rosewood cane over his knee and tossed it on the embers. Instantly it blazed up merrily, giving as much heat as an armful of hickory logs, so that the cat roused in astonishment at the singeing of her tail and was fain to crawl to a cool corner; and the cane burned for ever so long without going out, making the place seem cheery and home-like once more. Presently the guest began to rub his paunch and look wistfully at the cupboard, glancing aside at the cobbler and his wife, as if wondering how long they would be in taking a hint. Finally he blurted, "I've had no dinner, and I hoped I might be asked to share a bite and sup. This, you know, is Christmas Eve."

Claas winced. "You should be welcome with gladness, if we had some things to eat that we could offer to you."

"Never tell me that you've had your supper. I can eat anything. 'Hunger makes raw beans sweet.' "

"It is hard, what I have to tell. It is that we have no beans."

"Look here, Claas, I don't think you intend to be mean. Never trouble about the beans. A cut from that fowl will do, for it is a fowl I see on that shelf, isn't it? And there is no mistaking that big bread-loaf. And are my eyes dim with the heat, or are those cookies and olyknoeks and mince pies? And never tell me it is water you keep in that bottle."

Claas eyed his friend wearily, yet warily, for he doubted but the little man was daft, while Anitje went to the cupboard to show the visitor how well he was mistaken; that his eyes had turned the flickering shadows and reflections into things that were not there; but she threw up her hands and cried aloud; then ran to Claas with a roast goose on a platter, whereon Claas cried louder, and the offspring cried loudest.

" 'Better a half egg than an empty shell,' as we say in Amsterdam," remarked the ruddy man with a sarcastic wink, and his finger at his nose.

Candles were lighted, and in a minute a brave array of good things smoked on the table, for the wonder of it was that except the wine and schnapps, which were cold and fragrant, they seemed to have come but then from the oven.

"Now, then," said the stranger, beaming, " 'one may not give away his shirt if not sure of his skirt,' as we used to say in Holland, but I think you can spare me a plate of that goose."

So they fell to and feasted themselves in the merriest humor, and the shavers flocked to the knee of the man with the twinkling eyes, who was full of quips and stories, and they pledged one another in glasses of Rhenish—Claas dimly wondering where he had bought those handsome glasses—and in the end the stranger gave Vrouw Anitje a tremendous smack, which only made her blush and Claas to grin, for those greetings were duties and compliments in the simple days. Then Claas showed the pipe he had intended to sell, whereon the stranger cried, "That pipe! I know it. John Calvin used to smoke it. It is a lucky pipe. You must keep it all your days and leave it to your children. Whoop! What's all that?" For at this moment the boys of the neighbourhood, who were allowed on this one night to sit up later than nine o'clock, or had been called by their indulgent parents, greeted their holiday by firing their little cannon.

"Midnight!" exclaimed the twinkling little man. "I must be off. Merry Christmas and happy New Year to you all. Good-night."

And with that the stranger arose and bowed himself into the chimney. Now, whether he stamped among the ashes and sent up such a cloud as to blind them all,—for it is certain their eyes were watery and they fell a-sneezing,—or whether the little gentleman was so very lively he got away through the door before they could say "Jack Robinson,"—which they never did say, there being no such man in the colony—Claas and his wife and children could never agree, Anitje and the girls insisting that he went up the chimney, as if he had been blown away in the draft. In the morning, when the wife swept the hearth before starting a new fire, she heard the chink of silver, and there in the ashes she found a fat purse bearing the words, "A Gift from St. Nicholas."

While she and her husband were marvelling properly upon this an increasing gabble of voices was heard outside, and behold, there was half the town populace staring up at their windows and expressing great astonishment. And with reason, for the house was no longer of wood, but of brick. There was talk of arresting Claas and his family as wizards and dangerous to the well-being of the State, but he told so straight a story, and showed such substantial evidences of his new prosperity, that they made him alderman instead. "The Dutch House," as they called it, was for many years a landmark. When it was torn down, by an alien of British origin, the workmen were slapped about the sconce by unseen hands and had laths and slats vehemently applied to their sitting parts so that the neighbors said St. Nicholas was protecting his own.

APPENDIX

SUGGESTED AGE LEVELS

SIX AND SEVEN YEARS

AFRICA

Who Is King of Birds?	Robert H. Nassau
The Cock	W. H. I. Bleek

ASIA

How Sun, Moon, and Wind Went Out to Dinner	Joseph Jacobs
The Story of the Cat and the Mice	W. F. O'Connor
The Sun and the Cock	W. H. Hudspeth

AUSTRALIA AND THE SOUTHWEST PACIFIC

Wayambeh the Turtle	K. Langloh Parker
Bunnyyarl the Flies and Wurrunnunnah the Bees	K. Langloh Parker
The Story of the Mouse-Deer and other Animals Who Went out Fishing	Edwin H. Gomes
The Magic Cap	Zong In-Sob

EUROPE

England

The Cauld Lad of Hilton	Joseph Jacobs
How Jack Went To Seek His Fortune	Joseph Jacobs
The Story of the Three Little Pigs	Joseph Jacobs

Germany

The Golden Key	The Brothers Grimm
A Riddle Story	The Brothers Grimm

Ireland

The Sprightly Tailor	Joseph Jacobs

Italy

Buchettino	T. F. Crane

Rumania

Why Has the Thistle-Finch Ruffled Feathers?	M. Gaster

Russia

The Cat, the Cock, and the Fox	Norbert Guterman

318

Scandinavia

Ashiepattle and the Troll	P. A. Asbjornsen
Another Haunted Mill	Sir George Dasent
The Cat on the Dovrefell	Sir George Dasent
The Three Billy Goats Gruff	Sir George Dasent

Scotland

The Brownie of Blednock	Elizabeth Grierson

Wales

The Fairy of the Dell	P. H. Emerson

LATIN AMERICA

Jabutí and the Festival in Heaven	C. Malcolm Batchelor
Jabutí and the Leopard	C. Malcolm Batchelor
Toa-Toa	Florence J. Stoddard
How the Basilisk Obtained His Crest	Frances Toor
Ratoncito Pérez	W. M. Hudson

MIDDLE EAST

The Price of Envy	Nathan Ausubel
Know Your Enemy	Nathan Ausubel

NORTH AMERICA

Old Beggar	George E. J. Powell
The Rabbit That Wouldn't Dig a Well	Anonymous

EIGHT AND NINE YEARS

AFRICA

The Partnership of Rabbit and Elephant and What Came of It	Henry M. Stanley
A Tug of War	Robert H. Nassau
Nuts Are Eaten Because of Angangwe	Robert H. Nassau
Who Is King of Birds?	Robert H. Nassau
The Animals Dam	Sanni Metelerkamp
The Cock	W. H. I. Bleek

ASIA

How Sun, Moon, Wind Went out to Dinner	Joseph Jacobs
The Story of the Cat and the Mice	W. F. O'Connor
The Sun and the Cock	W. H. Hudspeth
The Country of the Mice	W. F. O'Connor
A Lesson from Confucius	M. D. Davis and Chow-Leung

AUSTRALIA AND THE SOUTHWEST PACIFIC

The Bank Cat	Altha Westbury
Tim	Altha Westbury
Wayambeh the Turtle	K. Langloh Parker
Weedah the Mocking Bird	K. Langloh Parker
The Story of the Mouse-Deer and other Animals Who Went out Fishing	Edwin H. Gomes

The Magic Cap   Zong In-Sob
The Rat's Bridegroom   Zong In-Sob
Friend Mouse-Deer and the Crocodile   R. C. Winstedt
Daddy-Long-Legs   R. C. Winstedt
The Dancing Crosses   Manuel and Lyd Arguilla
The Mallet of Wealth   Zong In-Sob

EUROPE

Czechoslovakia
   The Twelve Months   M. R. I. A. Baudis
England
   The Cauld Lad of Hilton   Joseph Jacobs
Germany
   The Golden Key   The Brothers Grimm
   The Golden Goose   The Brothers Grimm
   A Riddle Story   The Brothers Grimm
Ireland
   The Sprightly Tailor   Joseph Jacobs
Italy
   Buchettino   T. F. Crane
   Three Great Noodles   W. A. Clouston
   The Value of Salt   R. H. Busk
Rumania
   Why Has the Stork No Tail?   M. Gaster
   Why Has the Thistle-Finch Ruffled Feathers?   M. Gaster
Russia
   Ivashko and the Witch   E. M. S. Hodgetts
   The Cat, the Cock, and the Fox   Norbert Guterman
   A Soldier's Riddle   Norbert Guterman
Scandinavia
   Another Haunted Mill   Sir George Dasent
   The Cat on the Dovrefell   Sir George Dasent
   The Three Aunts   Sir George Dasent
   The Twelve Wild Ducks   Sir George Dasent
Scotland
   The Brownie of Blednock   Elizabeth W. Grierson
Wales
   The Fairy of the Dell   P. H. Emerson

LATIN AMERICA
   Jabutí and the Leopard   C. Malcolm Batchelor
   The Lazy Bee   Horacio Quiroga
   The Parrot That Lost Its Tail   Horacio Quiroga
   The Reason   F. J. Stoddard
   Toa-Toa   F. J. Stoddard
   How The Basilisk Obtained His Crest   Frances Toor
   Ratoncito Pérez   W. M. Hudson
   The Pájaro-Cú, the Lost Bird   J. Frank Dobie

MIDDLE EAST
    Hunger   Nathan Ausubel
    Price of Envy   Nathan Ausubel
    Know Your Enemy   Nathan Ausubel

NORTH AMERICA
    The Indian Cinderella   Cyrus Macmillan
    The Groundhog Dance   Katherine B. Judson
    The Three Tests   Lewis Spence
    The Cry of the Loon   S. B. Bellows
    The Old Beggar   Jon Lee
    A Gift from St. Nicholas   Charles M. Skinner

TEN AND ELEVEN YEARS

AFRICA
    The Story of the Prince Who Insisted on
        Possessing the Moon   Henry M. Stanley
    Nuts Are Eaten Because of Angangwe   Robert H. Nassau
    The Sun   Sanni Metelerkamp
    The Star and the Stars Road   Sanni Metelerkamp
    The Patched Cloak   I. D. duPlessis

ASIA
    The Jackal and the Iguana   F. A. Steel and
                                      R. C. Temple
    Pride Goeth Before a Fall   Joseph Jacobs
    Lo-Sun, the Blind Boy   Norman H. Pitman
    A Lesson from Confucius   M. H. Davis and
                                      Chow-Leung
    Urashimo Taro   Marjory Bruce

AUSTRALIA AND THE SOUTHWEST PACIFIC
    The Bank Cat   Altha Westbury
    Tim   Altha Westbury
    Weedah the Mocking Bird   K. Langloh Parker
    The Magic Cap   Zong In-Sob
    The Rat's Bridegroom   Zong In-Sob
    A Selfish Husband   Zong In-Sob
    Daddy-Long-Legs   R. C. Winstedt
    Rongo and the Lizard-God   K. M. Clark
    The Dancing Crosses   Manuel and Lyd Arguilla
    The Mallet of Wealth   Zong In-Sob
    Mansumandig   M. C. Cole

EUROPE

Czechoslovakia
    A Clever Lass   M. R. I. A. Baudis
    Grandfather's Eyes   Parker Fillmore
    The Twelve Months   M. R. I. A. Baudis

France
  The Stones of Plouvinec   Katherine Pyle
Germany
  The Golden Goose   The Brothers Grimm
Hungary
  The Speaking Grapes, the Smiling Apple, and   W. H. Jones and
    the Tinkling Apricot   L. L. Kropf
Ireland
  Legend of Bottle-Hill   T. Crofton Croker
  Dreaming Tim Jarvis   T. Crofton Croker
  Teigue of the Lee   T. Crofton Croker
  A Legend of Knockmany   Joseph Jacobs
Italy
  Three Great Noodles   W. A. Clouston
  The Happy Couple   R. H. Busk
  The Value of Salt   R. H. Busk
Rumania
  Michaï the Brave and the Executioner   E. C. G. Murray
  Hans' Adventure with the Shadows   Carmen Sylva
  Why Has the Stork No Tail?   M. Gaster
Russia
  The Deserted Mine   Ruth Sawyer
  Ivashko and the Witch   E. M. S. Hodgetts
  A Soldier's Riddle   Norbert Guterman
Scandinavia
  The Lad Who Went to the North Wind   Sir George Dasent
  The Three Aunts   Sir George Dasent
  The Twelve Ducks   Sir George Dasent
Scotland
  Black Agnace of Dunbar   Elizabeth W. Grierson
  Muckle-Mou'ed Meg   Elizabeth W. Grierson

LATIN AMERICA
  The Parrot That Lost Its Tail   Horacio Quiroga
  The Reason   F. J. Stoddard
  The Hunchback   J. Frank Dobie
  Juan Goes to Heaven   J. Frank Dobie

MIDDLE EAST
  The Hattab (Woodcutter) and the Khaznah
    (Treasure)   H. R. P. Dickson
  The Story of Maqdad, He Was the Hero of
    Hilla   Lindsay Drummond
  The Story of Kunz and his Shepherd   Nathan Ausubel
  Hunger   Nathan Ausubel
  Miriam and the Seven Little Martyrs   Nathan Ausubel

NORTH AMERICA

A Bear Story	Lucy Thompson
A Dime for the Sack	Richard Dorson
Waiting for Martin	Richard Dorson
How Money Fell from the Sky	Jon Lee
The Twist-Mouth Family	Clifton Johnson
Salting the Pudding	B. A. Botkin
A Travelled Narrative	Charles M. Skinner
The Gander's Message	Charles M. Skinner
A Gift from St. Nicholas	Charles M. Skinner

TWELVE AND THIRTEEN YEARS

AFRICA

The Prince Who Insisted on Possessing the Moon	Henry M. Stanley
The Search for the Home of the Sun	Henry M. Stanley
The Sun	Sanni Metelerkamp
The Star and the Stars Road	Sanni Metelerkamp
The Patched Cloak	I. D. duPlessis

ASIA

The Four Simple Bráhmans	W. F. Clouston
Lo-Sun the Blind Boy	Norman H. Pitman
Urashimo Taro	Marjory Bruce

AUSTRALIA AND THE SOUTHWEST PACIFIC

A Selfish Husband	Zong In-Sob
Rongo and the Lizard-God	K. M. Clark
The Mallet of Wealth	Zong In-Sob

EUROPE

Czechoslovakia

A Clever Lass	M. R. I. A. Baudis
Grandfather's Eyes	Parker Fillmore

France

The Stones of Plouvinec	Katherine Pyle

Ireland

Legend of Bottle-Hill	T. Crofton Croker
Teigue of the Lee	T. Crofton Croker
A Legend of Knockmany	Joseph Jacobs

Italy

The Happy Couple	R. H. Busk

Rumania

Michaï the Brave and the Executioner	E. C. G. Murray

Russia

The Deserted Mine	Ruth Sawyer

Scotland

Black Agnace of Dunbar	Elizabeth W. Grierson
Muckle-Mou'ed Meg	Elizabeth W. Grierson

LATIN AMERICA

Hatuey, the Hero	J. F. Stoddard
Legend of the Altar Del Perdon	T. A. Janvier

MIDDLE EAST

The Hattab (Woodcutter) and the Khaznah (Treasure)	H. R. P. Dickson
The Story of Maqdad—He Was the Hero of Hilla	Lindsay Drummond
The Story of Kunz and His Shepherd	Nathan Ausubel
Miriam and the Seven Little Martyrs	Nathan Ausubel
The First Tear	Nathan Ausubel

NORTH AMERICA

The Shrove Tuesday Visitor	Cyrus Macmillan
The Prince of Plenty	G. W. Caldwell
A Travelled Narrative	Charles M. Skinner
Case of the Brothers Brown	Charles M. Skinner
The Gander's Message	Charles M. Skinner
The Twist-Mouth Family	Clifton Johnson
A Dime for a Sack	Richard Dorson
Waiting for Martin	Richard Dorson
Salting the Pudding	B. A. Botkin

BIBLIOGRAPHY

These books contain additional information on creative dramatics and story-telling.

Brown, Corrine. *Creative Drama in the Lower School.* New York: Appleton-Century-Crofts, Inc., 1929.

Burger, Isabel B. *Creative Play Acting.* New York: A. S. Barnes and Company, 1950.

Fitzgerald, Burdette S. *Let's Act the Story.* San Francisco: Fearon Publishers, 1957.

Kerman, Gertrude Lerner. *Plays and Creative Ways with Children.* Irvington-on-Hudson, N.Y.: Harvey House, 1960.

Sawyer, Ruth. *The Way of the Storyteller.* New York: The Viking Press, 1953.

Siks, Geraldine Brain. *Creative Dramatics.* New York: Harper & Brothers, 1958.

Siks, Geraldine Brain and Hazel Brain Dunnington. *Children's Theatre and Creative Dramatics.* Seattle: University of Washington Press, 1961.

Slade, Peter. *Child Drama.* London: University of London Press, Ltd., 1954.

Ward, Winifred. *Playmaking with Children,* 2nd ed. New York: Appleton-Century-Crofts, Inc., 1957.

Ward, Winifred. *Stories To Dramatize*. Anchorage, Kentucky: Children's Theatre Press, 1952.

These books contain additional information on the staging of a play for the child audience.

Burger, Isabel B. *Creative Play Acting*. New York: A. S. Barnes and Company, 1950.

Davis, Jed H. and Mary Jane Watkins, with the collaboration of Roger M. Busfield, Jr. *Children's Theatre*. New York: Harper & Brothers, 1960.

Ward, Winifred. *Theatre for Children*, Rev. Ed. Anchorage, Kentucky: The Children's Theatre Press, 1950.

GLOSSARY

ABDULLAH	ab doo lah
ACUSHLA	a coosh la (*a* as in *far*)
AGNACE	agnes
AIKEN DRUM	i kin drum
AI OOM LEEUW	i oom lee wa
ALENKA	a lan ka (*a* as in *far*)
AL FETLA	al feet la (*a* as in *far*)
AL-IOT	al eot
AMBÉ	am (*a* as in *far*) bee
ANANTYA	a (*a* as in *far*) nant (*a* as in *ant*) ya (*a* as in *far*)
ANGANGWE	an gan (*a* as in *far*) way
ANITJE	a (*a* as in *far*) knit ja
ANTILLAS	an (*a* as in *far*) tee llas (*a* as in *far*)
AQUI	ah kee
ARUACOS	a (*a* as in *far*) roo a (*a* as in *far*) cos (*o* as in *cost*)
ASIRVADAM	a (*a* as in *far*) seer va (*a* as in *far*) dam (*a* as in *far*)
ASSAI	a (*a* as in *far*) sigh
AS SHAMMAR	as (*a* as in *far*) sham mar (*a* as in *far*)
ASHIEPATTLE	as (*a* as in *far*) hee pattle
AWASI	a wa (*a* as in *far*) see
BAASJE	baas (*a* as in *far*) ee
BAHANGA	ba han ga (*a* as in *far*)
BAIKAL	by kal (*a* as in *far*)
BAIRN	bairn (*ai* as in *bare*)
BALIEL	bay leel
BALIRA	ba (*a* as in *far*) lee ra (*a* as in *far*)
BALLYDAHIN	ball ee dahn (*a* as in *far*)
BAMANA	ba ma na (*a* as in *far*)
BANDIMBA	ban (*a* as in *far*) deem ba (*a* as in *far*)
BANYAN	ban (*a* as in *an*) yun
BASILISK	baz (*a* as in *man*) i (*i* as in *it*) lisk
BASOKO	ba (*a* as in *far*) so ko (*o* as in *owe*)

BASTIANELO	bas (*a* as in *far*) tee a (*a* as in *far*) nelo
BAVSI	bav (*a* as in *far*) si (*i* as in *it*)
BEEARGAH	bee ar gah (*a* as in *far*)
BERNET	ber (*e* as in *her*) nay
BIEL	bell
BLEDNOCK	bled knock
BOGLE	bo (*o* as in *so*) gul
BOGUN	bo (*o* as *so*) gun
BOHECHIO	bo (*o* as in *so*) e (*e* as in *let*) chee o
BOONDEES	boon dees
BOREEN	bo (*o* as in *so*) reen
BORSETE	bor see tay
BRAHMAN	bra (*a* as in *far*) min
BRAHMANARI	bra (*a* as in *far*) man a (*a* as in *far*) ree
BROER BABIAAN	bru (*u* as in *put*) er ba (*a* as in *far*) bee an
BROSE	bro (*o* as in *so*) uz
BUCHETTINO	butch e (*e* as in *let*) teen o
BUDDHA	bood a (*a* as in *ago*)
BUENO	boo e (*e* as in *let*) nyo
BUNNYYARL	bun yarl
CACIQUE	ka (*a* as in *art*) see kay
CAHUILLA	ka (*a* as in *far*) hoo ya (*a* as in *far*)
CAMPAGNA	kam pa nya (*a* as in *far*)
CAPRONY	kah pro nee
CARRIGROHAN	ka (*a* as in *far*) ree groan
CASSAVA	ka sa va (*a* as in *far*)
CAULD	cold
CENIZO	then ee so
CENTAVOS	sen ta (*a* as in *far*) vos (*o* as in *owe*)
CERRO DE LA CAMPAGNA	therro day lah kam pan a (*a* as in *far*)
CHOULTRY	choul (*ou* as in *loud*) tree
CIGUAYO	the goo a (*a* as in *far*) yo
CLAAS SCHLASCHENSCHLINGER	klass (*a* as in *far*) schlas khen schlinger
COEVAL	ko ev al
COLAH	ko lah
COMAL	ko mahl
COMPANERO	kom (*o* as in *come*) pa (*a* as in *far*) nyay ro
CONFUCIUS	kon foo shus
CORK	kork
CORROBBOREE	ko ro bo (*o* as in *no*) ree
COSPATRICK	kos (*o* as in *toss*) pat rick

COTONAEVITCH	ko to (*o* as in *no*) na (*a* as in *far*) yvitch
CROESUS	kree sus
CUCULLIN	koo koo leen
CULLAMORE	kool a (*a* as in *far*) more
CURRANDERO	koo ran dero
DALHOUSIE	dall hoo see
DAMASCUS	da mas (*a* as in *fat*) kus
DANDAMARYA	dan da mar ya (*a* as in *far*)
DEGAITHER	dee gay ther
DEL PARDON	del per don (*o* as in *tone*)
DHARMAPURI	dar ma (*a* as in *far*) poo ree
DIRHEM	der ham
DOMINGO	do meen go
DON MARTIN	don (*o* as in *on*) mar teen
DON PEDRITO	don (*o* as in *on*) pay dree to (*o* as in *toe*)
DOVREFELL	do (*o* as in *dove*) vre (*e* as in *met*) fell
DUENDAS	doo en das (*a* as in *far*)
DUNGANNON	doon gan non
ED DULAIM	ed do lim
EIFEL	eye fell
ELIE MUROMITCH	a (*a* as in *pay*) lee mo (*o* as in *move*) ro mitch
EL NIÑO DIOS	l nee nyo deos
ENGREQUEZ DE ALMANZA	en gray kez day al (*a* as in *all*) man (*a* as in *far*) za (*a* as in *far*)
ESTÁ	es (*e* as in *let*) ta (*a* as in *far*)
FAN	fan
FATIMA	fa (*a* as in *far*) tee ma (*a* as in *far*)
FIN MCCOUL	feen mk kool
FLORIA	floor ea
FRITZCHEN	fritz ken
GENTE DECENTE	hen tay day then tay
GUANIQUINAJE	goo ahn e (*e* as in *met*) kee na (*a* as in far) he (*e* as in *met*)
GUAROCAYO	goo ar oc yo
HAITIAN	hay tee an
HALVOR	hal (*a* as in *far*) vor
HANNES	hans (*a* as in *far*)
HATTAB	a tab (*a* as in *far*)
HATUEY	a (*a* as in *far*) tway
HEZEKIAH	hez (*e* as in *let*) e (*e* as in *let*) ky ah
HILLA	hé lah (*a* as in *far*)
HOLENA	ho len a (*a* as in *far*)

HOPI	ho (*o* as in *go*) pi
HOPPOW	ho pow
HORANG GAMTE	ho (*o* as in *go*) rang cam (*a* as in *am*) to
HUACANI	wa (*a* as in *far*) can (*a* as in *far*) ee
IMAN	i (*i* as in *sin*) man
INKULA	in ku la
IVAN	ee van (*a* as in *far*)
IVANOVITCH	ee van ovitch
IVASHKO	ee vash (*a* as in *far*) ko
JABUTÉ	ha (*a* as in *far*) boo ta (*a* as in *ale*)
JANN	jan (*a* as in *far*)
JINN	gin
JUAN GARCIA	hwan gar thee a (*a* as in *far*)
JUEVES	hoo a (*a* as in *ate*) ves (*e* as in *let*)
KARATCHAEV	ka ra cha (*a* as in *far*) yif
KAROO	ka (*a* as in *far*) roo
KHAZNAB	kaz nab (*a* as in *far*)
KIEF	kee yef
KNOCKMANY	knock many
KOPJE	kop (*o* as in *cop*) ja
KRANTZE	krantze
KUNZ	kunz (*u* as in *full*)
KUMARA	koo ma ra (*a* as in *far*)
KVASS	kva (*a* as in *far*) zz
LAIRD	la (*a* as in *bare*) rd
LA VIRGEN MARIA	lah verr hen ma (*a* as in *far*) ree ah
LECHUGILLA	lay choo geel lyah
LE DOIT	l' dwa (*a* as in *far*)
LENA	lee na (*a* as in *far*)
LIESCHEN	li (*i* as in *machine*) e (*e* as in *hen*) skhen
L'OUVERTURE	loo ver tyur
LO SUN	low sun
LOTHIAN	low thean
LUCAYAS	loo ka (*a* as in *far*) yos (*o* as in *note*)
LUNES	loo nes
LURE LURE	loor loor
MADELEINE	mad len
MAHALLA	ma hal a (*a* as in *far*)
MAJAGUA	ma ha gwa (*a* as in *far*)
MALAY	may láy
MALLOW	mal low
MANGONELLS	man go nels

MANICATE	mon ee ka (*a* as in *far*) tay
MANSUMMANDIG	man soo mán díg
MAN SUR	man (*a* as in *far*) sor (*o* as in *or*)
MAQDAD	maq dad (*a* as in *far*)
MARTES	már (*a* as in *far*) tez
MARUSA	ma (*a* as in *fate*) rus (*u* as in *us*) a (*a* as in *far*)
MASAMA	ma sa ma (*a* as in *far*)
MATARAU	ma ta (*a* as in *far*) ro (*o* as in *row*)
MAVOURNENE	ma (*a* as in *far*) voor neen
MAYOBONEX	mah yo bo nay
MBOLO	im bo lo
MIAO	mee ow
MICHAÏ	mi (*i* as in *machine*) ky
MIÉRCOLES	me err ko laz (*a* as in *lay*)
MIRRIEH	me re (*e* as in *red*) eh
MORAY	mor ay
MOURNE	mourn
MUGASSA	moo ga sa (*a* as in *far*)
MULLYAN	mool yan (*a* as in *far*)
MUN-GUN	mun gun
MURON	moo rom
MUY	moo ee
MWERA	im wer ah
NGOWA	nn go wah
NGOZO	nn go zoo (*o* as in *go*)
NINITO	ni (*i* as in *it*) nyee to (*o* as in *go*)
NJAGANI	nya ga (*a* as in *far*) nee
NJAGU	nnee ah goo
NJAMBI	nnyam bee
NGUBU	nngoo boo
NYUNNOOS	nyun (*u* as in *use*) noos
NGYANYANI	nn gwah nga nee
OLLA	ol′ lyah
OOLAH	oo lah
OONAGH	oo nagh
OPERENCIAN	o per entz ee en
ORENBURG	or en boorg
ORIENTE	o ree entay
OTILOA	o tee yo
OTOHIMÉ	o to (*o* as in *go*) he me′ (*e* as in *let*)
OUTA WILLEM	o (*o* as in *note*) ta (*a* as in *far*) will lem
PAGODA	pa (*a* as in *far*) go da (*a* as in *far*)

PAISANO	pah sán no
PAJARO-CU	páh hah ro (*o* as in *go*) coo
PEDRITO	pay dree to (*o* as in *go*)
PETYA	pét ya (*a* as in *far*)
PEYRENS	pay renz
PICH	pik
PINON	peen yon
PISIETE	pe (*e* as in *let*) see e (*e* as in *let*) tay
PLOUVINEC	ploo veen ik
POLENTA	po len ta (*a* as in *far*)
POLL	pol (*o* as in *old*)
PORTCULLIS	port cull' is
POTOSÉ	po to (*o* as in *old*) see
QAIS	ghaiz
QUINOA	ki (*ui* as in *kite*) no a (*a* as in *far*)
RAMBÉ	ram (*a* as in *far*) bee'
RATONCITO PÉREZ	rah tone see to pa (*a* as in *may*) reth
RIN GIN	rin gin
ROELOFFSEN	ra (*oe* as in *far*) loff sen
RISHAN	ree shan (*a* as in *far*)
RONGO	ron go
SABODO	sah bo do (*o* as in *owe*)
SAMARADNAM	sam a rad nam (*a* as in *far*)
SAVANNA	sa van nah (*a* as in *far*)
SCRIP	skrip
SCUDI	skoo dee
SEIS	say is
SENOR	say nyor
SEVLE NAILA RTSUA	sev le (*e* as in *every*) nail a (*a* as in *far*) rtsua
SIBONEYES	see bo (*o* as in *go*) nyees
SIETE	see ay tay
SIGNORE	see nyor
SIGNORINO	see nyor eeno
SHROVE	shrov (*o* as in *stove*)
SI-ALTH	si (*i* as in *sigh*) alth
SLOE	slow
SOBOBA	so bo (*o* as in *owe*) ba (*a* as in *far*)
SOLESTE	so less tay
SPRINGBOKKIE	spring bock kee
SU	soo
SUDRA	soo dra (*a* as in *far*)
SURUGA	soo roo ga (*a* as in *far*)

TAO PO	tah o po
TARO	tah ro
TEIGUE	teeg
THAMIR	ta (*a* as in *far*) meer
TIGRIS	ti (*i* as in *like*) gris (*i* as in *it*)
TIMOFEIVITCH	teem o fee yvitch
TOA	toe ah
TRES	traz (*a* as in *ate*)
TROLL	trol (*o* as in *owe*)
TSZE LEE	tchez (*e* as in *let*) lee
TUDURAG-TAG-TAG	too doo rag tag tag
UGANDA	u gan da (*a* as in *far*)
UGULUNGU	u go loon gu
UNZIN	on sin
URASHIMO TARO	u ra (*a* as in *far*) she ma (*a* as in *far*) ta (*a* as in *far*) row
VAIOENÉ	vo neé
VAQUERO	va (*a* as in *far*) care o
VELASQUES	vay las (*a* as in *far*) kez
VIEJITO	vee a (*a* as in *ate*) hee to
VIERNES	vee err nes
VLADIMIR	vlád (*a* as in *glad*) i (*i* as in *it*) mer
WATUSI	wa (*a* as in *far*) too see
WAYAMBEH	wa (*a* as in *far*) yam (*a* as in *am*) beh
WEEDAH	wee dah
WHIT-SUN	whit s'n
WURRUNNUNNAH	woo run nun nah
XANTHINE	zan thin
Y	ee
YANECHEK	ya na (*a* as in *far*) chek
YANGYAK	yang yak (*a* as in *far*)
YEZINKAS	ya (*a* as in *far*) zin kas (*a* as in *far*)
YHI	yee or he
YUMAS	you ma (*a* as in *far*)
ZERNICK	zer nick
ZOLLA	zo lah
ZORRO	zor row

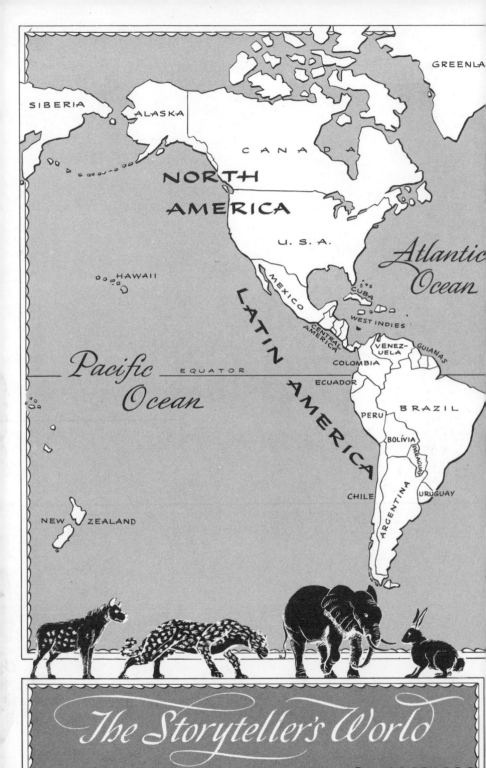

The Storyteller's World